*The Book of
The Thousand Nights
and One Night*

The Book of
the Thousand Nights
and One Night

RENDERED INTO ENGLISH FROM
THE LITERAL AND COMPLETE
FRENCH TRANSLATION OF
DR J. C. MARDRUS
BY POWYS MATHERS

Volume III

LONDON AND NEW YORK

Reprinted ten times
Second edition 1964
Reprinted 1972
First published as a paperback in 1986
by Routledge & Kegan Paul plc

Reprinted 1989, 1993, 1994, 1995 by
Routledge
11 New Fetter Lane, London EC4P 4EE
29 West 35th Street, New York, NY 10001

Printed in Great Britain by
The Guernsey Press Co. Ltd,
Guernsey, Channel Islands

ISBN 0-415-04541-X (vol. III)
ISBN 0-415-04543-6 (set)

Contents of Volume III

CONTENTS OF VOLUME III

The Tale of Abū Kīr and Abū Sīr

SHAHRAZĀD SAID:

IT is related, O auspicious King, that there were once in Alexandria a dyer called Abū Kīr and a barber named Abū Sīr, who had neighbouring shops in the market.

Abū Kīr was a notorious rascal, a detestable liar, and a man of exceedingly ill life. His temples must have been hewn of indestructible granite and his head formed from one of the steps of the synagogue of Jews; otherwise how are we to explain the shameless audacity which he displayed in all his sins? Among countless other pieces of roguery, he used to make most of his clients pay in advance, alleging that he had need of ready money to buy colours . . . and that was the last they saw of the stuffs which they had brought to be dyed. He not only spent the money in pleasant eating and drinking, but also secretly sold the stuffs which had been trusted to him and bought himself amusements of a high order with the proceeds. When the customers came to claim their goods, he would find one pretext or another to make them wait indefinitely. Thus he would say to one: 'As Allāh lives, my master, my wife lay in yesterday and I had to be up and down upon my feet all the time.' Or to another: 'I had guests yesterday and all my time was taken up with them; but if you come back in two days the stuff will be ready for you.' He drew out every piece of business which came his way to such extravagant lengths that at last one of his victims would be bound to cry: 'Come, tell me the truth about my stuffs. Give them back, for I have decided not to have them dyed.' 'Alas, I am in despair!' Abū Kīr would answer, lifting his hands to heaven, swearing every imaginable oath that he would tell the truth, beating his hands together and weeping. 'Dear master,' he would sob, 'as soon as your stuffs were most beautifully dyed, I hung them on the drying cords outside my shop; I turned away for a moment to piss and when I looked again they had disappeared! If you ask me, I think they were stolen by my neighbour, that most dishonest barber.' Then, if the customer were a fine fellow, he would say: 'Allāh will make good the loss!' and go his way; if he were irritable, he would probably swear at the dyer and come to blows with him in the open street. But even so, and in spite of the kādī's authority, no one ever got back his stuffs; because, in the first place, proof was lacking that they had been given and, in the second, there was nothing in the dyer's shop worth seizing. For a long time

Abū Kīr gained a livelihood in this way; but the day came when every merchant and private individual in that quarter had been victimised, and Abū Kīr saw his credit broken beyond repair and his business ruined. He had become so general an object of mistrust that his name had passed into a proverb when anyone wished to speak of bad faith.

When he was reduced to the last straits, Abū Kīr sat down before the shop of his neighbour, the barber Abū Sīr, and complained that starvation stared him in the face. At once the barber, who walked in Allāh's way and who, though poor, was unusually honest, had compassion on Abū Kīr, and said: 'There is a duty from one neighbour to another. Stay with me here; eat, drink, and use the gifts of Allāh until the coming of better days.' With that he took him into his house and supplied all his needs for a very long time.

One day the barber, Abū Sīr, complained to the dyer, Abū Kīr, of the hard times, saying: 'Brother, I am far from being a clumsy barber, I know my business and my hand is light; but, because my shop is poor and I am poor, no one comes to be shaved. Perhaps in the morning at the hammām some porter or fireman gets me to shave his armpits or apply the paste to his groin. Thus I earn a few copper pieces, which hardly feed me and you and the family which hangs about my neck. But Allāh is great and generous!' 'Brother,' answered Abū Kīr, 'you must be very simple to endure hardships so patiently when you have the means to get rich and live largely. Your trade fails and mine is ruined because of the malevolence of our fellow citizens; therefore our best plan is to leave this cruel country and voyage until we find some city where our arts will be appreciated. Travel is a rare thing; how pleasant it is to breathe good air, to forget the crosses of life, to see new lands, fresh cities, to learn to drive a thriving foreign trade in businesses honoured throughout the world, as are yours and mine! Remember that a poet said:

> What's danger, so the feet may roam
> Beyond the town where custom is?
> Better be dead than stay at home,
> A flea with lice for enemies . . .
> Invite your soul to voyages,
> For at the gates of new found lands
> Wait raptures and discoveries
> And gold with laughter in her hands.

Let us shut our shops and set forth together to seek a better fortune.'
He went on to speak so eloquently that Abū Sīr was convinced and
hastened to make his preparations for departure. These consisted in
wrapping his basins, razors, scissors, and iron in an old piece of
patched cloth and saying good-bye to his family. When he returned
to the shop, the dyer said to him: 'Now it only remains to recite the
opening chapters of the Koran, to prove that we are brothers, and to
agree that each shall put his profits into a common fund, to be equally
divided when we return to Alexandria. We should also have an undertaking that whichever of us finds work shall agree to provide for
the other, if he cannot earn for himself.' The barber Abū Sīr sub-
scribed to these conditions, and the two recited the opening chapter
of the Koran to seal their bond.

At this point Shahrazād saw the approach of morning and
discreetly fell silent.

But when the four-hundred-and-eighty-eighth night had come

SHE SAID:

Abū Sīr shut his shop and returned the key to its owner, paying
his rent in full; then the two walked down to the port and embarked,
entirely without provision of food, on board a boat which was about
to sail.

Fate favoured them during the voyage, using the better as its
instrument. Among the passengers and crew, who numbered a hundred and forty souls, there was no other barber than Abū Sīr; so,
when the ship was well started, the barber said to his companion:
'My brother, we need food and drink. I shall go now and offer my
services to the passengers and sailors, in case one should wish to have
his head shaved. If I can earn bread or money or a cup of water, so
much the better for both of us.' 'Go then,' answered the dyer, and
straightway arranged his head more comfortably and went to sleep
upon the deck.

Abū Sīr, throwing a rag over his shoulder as a napkin and taking
in his hand the tools of his trade and an empty cup, began to walk
among the passengers. 'Come and shave my head, O master,' said
one of them and, when the business was done, would have given the
barber money. 'My brother,' said Abū Sīr, 'money is of little good to
me at sea. I would rather have a crust of bread, for my friend and I
have no food.' The man gave him a crust of bread, a piece of cheese,

and a fill of water for the cup. Abū Sīr took these things to the dyer, saying: 'Take this crust and eat it with the cheese. Also here is water.' Abū Kīr ate and drank until there was nothing left, while Abū Sīr renewed his wandering among the passengers who squatted or lay about the ship. He shaved one for two rolls, another for a piece of cheese, another for a cucumber, another for a slice of water-melon, another for a piece of money. By the end of the day he had amassed thirty rolls, thirty half dirhams, much cheese, and a quantity of olives, cucumbers, and excellent botargoes made from the fish roe of Damietta. Also, he had so attracted the sympathy of the passengers that he could have asked anything from them, and had become so popular that his skill reached as far as the ears of the captain. Abū Sīr shaved the captain's head, complaining the while of the miseries of poverty and telling him that he had a travelling-companion to support. The captain, who was an open-handed man and had been, moreover, delighted by the charming manners and great dexterity of this new barber, invited him to come with his friend every evening while the voyage lasted and dine at his own cloth.

The dyer was sleeping when the barber returned, and woke to find great store of rolls, cheese, melons, cucumbers and botargoes piled by his head. 'Where do these come from?' he asked, and Abū Sīr answered: 'From the generosity of Allāh (may His name be exalted!).' At once the dyer threw himself upon all the foods at one and the same time, as if he would have shovelled the lot down into his dear love, his stomach. But the barber said: 'Do not eat these things, my brother, for they may be useful in the future; in the mean-while, the captain has asked both of us to dine with him this very evening.' 'I have the sea-sickness and cannot leave my place,' objected Abū Kīr. 'Go you to dine with the captain and let me peck a little at these simple things.' 'Certainly,' answered the barber and passed the time until dinner in watching his companion eat.

The dyer attacked and bit into the food, as a quarryman splits stones, and swallowed with the noise of an elephant who has fasted for many days and at last takes his fill with gurglings of the throat and belly rumblings. Mouthful came to the help of mouthful, push-ing it through the doors of the throat; gobbet jostled gobbet in the going down; and the dyer's eyes fastened like those of a ghoul upon each handful as it went to the mouth. He breathed and bellowed like a bull which sees its hay or beans.

While this meal was in progress, a sailor came and bade the two

4

men to dinner. 'Will you come with me?' asked Abū Sīr, but Abū
Kīr answered: 'I fear I have not the strength to move. This sea-sickness is the devil.' So the barber went alone and saw the captain sitting
before a cloth on which were spread twenty or more exquisite different coloured dishes. He only waited for the arrival of the barber and
certain other guests before beginning his repast.

At this point Shahrazād saw the approach of morning and
discreetly fell silent.

But when the four-hundred-and-eighty-ninth night had come

SHE SAID:

Seeing the barber alone, the captain asked after his friend, and
Abū Sīr replied that the dyer was sea-sick. 'That will soon pass,' said
the captain, 'sit down by me in the name of Allāh.' He took a large
plate and filled it so liberally with the varied meats that each portion
would have been enough for ten people. When the barber had
finished eating, the captain handed him a second plate, loaded like the
first, saying: 'Take this to your companion.' Abū Sīr did so and
found Abū Kīr still working away with his fangs and crunching with
his jaws like a camel, while enormous hunks followed each other
down into the mighty gulf. 'Did I not tell you not to blunt your
appetite with these simple things?' said Abū Sīr. 'See what admirable
food the captain has sent you! What do you say to these excellent
kabābs of lamb?' 'Give them to me,' growled Abū Kīr, and at once
delved into the plate and fell to eating from both hands with the
greed of a wolf, the swiftness of a lion, the ferocity of a vulture
among pigeons, and the furious stuffing noises of a starved pig. In a
few moments he had licked the plate clean and had handed it back to
Abū Sīr, who returned it to the servant and then, after drinking a
little with the captain, lay down to sleep by the dyer, who snored
through all his vents, drowning the noise of the sea.

Next day and on the following days, Abū Sīr spent his time in
shaving the passengers and sailors, laying by provisions, dining with
the captain, and generously providing for his friend. Abū Kīr contented himself with sleeping, rousing only to eat or pass what he had
eaten. Thus they lived for twenty days and, on the morning of the
twenty-first, the ship came to harbour in an unknown city.

Abū Kīr and Abū Sīr went ashore and, after hiring a small room
in a khān, hastened to furnish it with a new mat and two linen

covers, for which the barber paid. As Abū Kīr still complained of sea-sickness, the barber left him sleeping and carried his instruments into the city, where he exercised his profession at the corners of streets; at first on porters, donkey-boys, scavengers and street sellers; but, later, on well-to-do merchants who were attracted by the rumour of his skill. He returned in the evening and set various foods before his sleeping companion; then he woke the dyer by holding the roast lamb under his nose, and both ate until they were satisfied. Things went on in this way for forty whole days, with Abū Kīr complaining all the time of the remnants of his sea-sickness and Abū Sīr setting rich foods for the joint meal twice a day. The dyer would wolf rolls, cucumbers, fresh onions and kabābs without ever unduly loading that mistress of his, that enormous stomach, but, if ever the barber spoke to him of the unparalleled beauties of the city and invited him to walk in the markets or gardens, he would answer: 'That sea-sickness is still upon me,' and then, having belched and farted in different strains and odours, would fall again into his sleep. And all this time the good and honest barber did not once upbraid his crapulous parasite.

At the end of the forty days, however, the barber fell ill and, being unable any longer to go out to work, begged the doorkeeper of the khān to look after Abū Kīr and buy him such food as he needed. In the course of a few days, Abū Sīr became so much worse that he lost consciousness and lay like one dead. It resulted that Abū Kīr began to feel the pinch of hunger and was obliged to rise from his couch and hunt in the room for something to eat. But, as he never left scraps, he found nothing; without compunction he searched through his companion's clothes and at last found a purse, in which the poor man had hoarded up his gains, copper by copper. Abū Kīr fastened this to his belt and, without giving the barber another thought, walked from the room and fastened the door behind him. As the doorkeeper was for the moment absent, he did not see Abū Kīr go out.

The dyer's first care was to run to a pastry-cook's, where he ate a whole dish of katāif and another of shortbread flakes; these he washed down with a pitcher of musked sherbert and another of sherbert prepared with amber and jujubes.

At this point Shahrazād saw the approach of morning and discreetly fell silent.

But when the four-hundred-and-ninetieth night had come

SHE SAID:

Then he went to the market and bought fine clothes and accoutrements, which he put on before taking a slow walk through the streets and delighting his eyes with the novelties of that unusual city. One thing struck him especially, all the inhabitants, without a single exception, were clothed in uniform colours, either white or blue. There were only white or blue stuffs in the shops, only white or blue perfumes in the flasks of the distillers; the kohl was blue, and the sherbet-sellers sold only white, not red or rose or violet as with us. The greatest of all his surprises came when he looked in through the door of a dyer's shop and saw that the vats held nothing but indigo. Not being able to curb his curiosity, he entered the shop and, drawing a white handkerchief from his pocket, gave it to the dyer, saying: 'O master of the trade, for how much will you dye this handkerchief, and what colour will you give it?' The dyer replied: 'I will do it for twenty dirhams; indigo blue, of course.' 'What,' cried Abū Kir at this outrageous demand, 'twenty dirhams for dyeing a single handkerchief blue? Half a dirham would be the price in my country.' 'In that case,' answered the dyer, 'go and have it dyed in your own country; you will not get it done for less than twenty dirhams in this place.' 'If that is so, I will pay,' said Abū Kir, 'but I want red not blue.' 'What do you mean by red?' asked the man. 'There is no such thing as a red dye.' 'Then dye it green,' said the astonished Abū Kir. 'Green dye? There is no such thing,' answered the dyer. 'Yellow, then,' ventured Abū Kir, but 'I have never heard of a yellow dye!' cried the dyer. So Abū Kir enumerated all the shades of the various dyes which he knew and, when he perceived that the man did not understand a word of what he said, asked if all the other dyers in the city were as ignorant. 'There are forty of us,' answered the man, 'we have formed a close guild, so that no one else in the city may practise our art. The secret is carefully guarded and only handed down from father to son. We have never heard tell of any dye save blue.'

'O master of the trade,' said Abū Kir, 'I also am a dyer; but I dye in an infinity of colours of which you know nothing. Take me into your employ for a small wage and I will teach you the secrets, so that your knowledge will bring you glory among all your guild.' 'We are not allowed to employ strangers,' objected the man. 'What would happen, then,' asked Abū Kīr, 'if I opened a dyer's shop on my own account?' 'That would be impossible!' cried the man of indigo. Abū Kīr said nothing further and left the shop; he sought out a second dyer, then a third, and then a fourth, until he had visited all in the city; but everywhere he met with the same answers and a blank refusal to employ him either as master or apprentice. He then took his complaint to the venerable syndic of the guild, who said: 'I can do nothing. Our custom and traditions forbid us to receive a stranger.'

Abū Kīr's liver swelled with fury; he hurried to the palace and presented himself before the King of that city, saying: 'O King of time, I am a stranger, a dyer by trade, and I can dye in forty different colours . . .'

At this point Shahrazād saw the approach of morning and discreetly fell silent.

But when the four-hundred-and-ninety-first night had come

SHE SAID:

'And yet I have received such and such treatment from the dyers of this city, who know no other colour but blue. I can give the most charming shades of every colour to any fabric: reds of all kinds, as rose and jujube; greens of all kinds, as grass, pistachio, olive and parakeet; blacks of all kinds, as charcoal, pitch and kohl; yellows of all kinds, as citron, orange, lemon and gold. All these colours and more I have at my command, and yet the dyers of this city will have none of me.'

When the King heard this prodigious enumeration of colours whose existence he had never suspected, he trembled with joy and cried: 'As Allāh lives, this is excellent! If you are telling the truth and can rejoice our eyes with all these marvellous colours, banish all care from your heart; for I will myself open a dye-works for you and give you much money with which to start in business. Have no concern for the fellows of the guild; if one of them is so unfortunate as to molest you he shall hang at the door of his own shop.' At once he called the architects of the palace to him, and said to them: 'Go with this admirable master throughout all the city and, when he has found a site to his liking, whether there stand on it a shop, a khān, a house, or a garden, turn out the owner and build upon that place, as quickly as you are able, a great dye-works with forty large vats and forty smaller ones. Follow the instructions of this master dyer in every-thing; be very careful not to think one thought of disobedience to any of his orders.' Then the King gave Abū Kīr a fair robe of honour and a purse of a thousand dīnārs, saying: 'Spend this money on your pleasures until the new works are finished.' He also presented him with two boys to wait upon him, and a marvellous horse, saddled with blue velvet and with housings of blue silk. Finally he placed at his disposal a great and richly-furnished house, served by a suitable multitude of slaves.

Next day Abū Kīr, looking as fine and majestical as some amīr in his dazzling brocade and on his costly horse, rode out, preceded by two architects and the two boys to clear a way for him, and visited all the streets and markets in search of a suitable site for his new works. At last he chose a vast vaulted shop in the middle of the chief market; at once the architects and slaves drove out the owner and began to build in one direction and tear down in another under the orders of Abū Kīr. Still mounted on his horse, he said: 'Do such and such here! do such and such over there!' and, in a very short time, there rose a dye-works unequalled over all the face of the earth.

Then the King called him, and said: 'Now it only remains for you to start work; but that cannot be done without money. Here are five thousand dīnārs of gold to begin with. And remember that I am all impatience to behold the first fruits of your art.' Abū Kīr hid the five thousand dīnārs carefully in his house and, with a few dirhams, bought from a druggist all the necessary colours, which remained unsold in their virgin sacks and were to be had for next to nothing. These he had taken to his new premises, where he carefully prepared and diluted them in the vats.

At this point Shahrazād saw the approach of morning and discreetly fell silent.

But when the four-hundred-and-ninety-second night had come

SHE SAID:

The King sent him five hundred white squares in silk, wool, and linen, which Abū Kīr dyed, some in pure colour, others with mingled, so that not one looked like the other. He hung them out to dry on the lines which had been prepared all along the street outside his shop, and the varied pieces lived under the light and made a gay showing in the sunshine.

All the people of the city were abashed by this novelty; shop-keepers shut their shops to run and see, women and children gave shrill cries of admiration, and one man after another would ask Abū Kīr the names of the colours. 'That is pomegranate red,' he would answer, 'that is oil green, that is citron yellow.' He called over all the colours to a crowd, which showed its limitless admiration with lifted arms and exclamations of delight.

In the middle of this excitement appeared the King, riding through the crowd, preceded by runners who cleared a path for him, and followed by a guard of honour. At sight of the fabrics flaunting their bright colours in the white air, his soul was ravished within him and he stayed motionless for a long time without breathing, showing the whites of his eyes in ecstasy. Even the horses, instead of being frightened by such an unaccustomed spectacle, showed that they were sensible to beautiful colour, and began to dance from side to side as if this flapping glory were the sound of fifes.

Not knowing how else sufficiently to honour his dyer, the King made his wazīr descend from his horse and set Abū Kīr in the saddle; when the stuffs had been wrapped up, he returned to his palace, with the dyer riding on his right, and there loaded his new favourite with gold and privilege. From the dyed fabrics he had robes tailored for himself, his wives, and the chiefs of his palace, while he gave a thousand new squares to Abū Kīr to be dyed in the same fashion. At the end of a certain time, all the amīrs and officers of the city were wearing many-coloured garments, and Abū Kīr, dyer by appointment to the King, had become the richest man in the city. The other dyers, headed by the syndic of their guild, came to excuse themselves before their rival and begged him to employ them as unpaid apprentices; but he sent them away with shame. Before long the streets and markets were crowded by folk wearing fabrics of splendid colours, the work of Abū Kīr, the royal dyer. So much for him.

At this point Shahrazād saw the approach of morning and discreetly fell silent.

But when the four-hundred-and-ninety-third night had come

SHE SAID:

When Abū Sīr, the barber, had been robbed and deserted by the dyer, he lay half dead for three days. At the end of that time the door-keeper of the khān, having seen neither of the lodgers come out, said to himself: 'Perhaps they have slipped away without paying, or perhaps they are dead, or perhaps, again, it is something quite different.' He went to their room and, finding the wooden key turned in the lock of the door, from behind which came a feeble groaning, he entered and found the barber lying, yellow and unrecognisable, upon his mat. 'What ails you, my brother? What has become of your companion?' he asked, and the poor barber answered in a weak whisper: 'Only Allāh knows! I have just come to myself; I do not know how long I have been here. I am very thirsty, my brother; I beg you to take the purse from my belt and buy me something which will strengthen me.' The doorkeeper rummaged the belt throughout all its length and, finding no money, understood that the barber had been robbed by his fellow lodger. 'Take no thought for your sustenance,' he said. 'Allāh will judge each according to his works. From now on I take your cure into my own hands.' He hastened to prepare a good soup, which he poured into a bowl and carried to his patient. He fed him with his own hands, and then wrapped him in a woollen covering so that he sweated. For two months he cared for him, paying all the expenses of his nourishment out of his own pocket, so that at last Allāh performed a complete cure through him, and Abū Sīr was able to rise. He said to the good doorkeeper: 'If ever the Highest gives me the power I shall know how to reward you for your bountiful care of me; and yet, O chosen one, only He is rich enough to give you all that you deserve.' 'Praise Him for your cure, my brother,' answered the old doorkeeper. 'It is because I seek His face that I have acted as I did.' The barber would have kissed his hands, but the saviour protested, and the two parted, calling down, each upon the other, all the blessing of Allāh.

Leaving the khān with his bundle of instruments, the barber wandered through the markets until Fate led him to Abū Kīr's dyeworks, which were surrounded by a crowd who acclaimed the colours of the stuffs hung out to dry. He asked one of the bystanders the meaning of the crowd, and the man answered: 'This is the shop of our lord Abū Kīr, the Sultān's dyer. It is he who has produced these admirable colours by hidden processes and secret art.'

Abū Sīr's heart rejoiced for his old companion and he said to himself: 'Thanks be to Allāh who has opened for him the gate of riches! O Abū Sīr, you were very wrong to think ill of him. If he left you and forgot you, it was from preoccupation in his work. If he borrowed your purse it was to buy colours. Now you will see how cordially he will receive you and repay those services which you did him in his need. How he will rejoice to see you!' Abū Sīr succeeded in worming his way through the crowd until he was at the door of the shop: Looking inside, he saw Abū Kīr stretched lazily on a high couch, supported by a pile of cushions and dressed in a garment fit for kings. Behind him stood four young black slaves and four young white slaves, richly habited; so that he seemed more majestic than a wazīr and taller than a Sultān. Ten workmen were labouring at the vats, taking their orders by signs from the master dyer.

Abū Sīr took a step forward and paused before his comrade. 'I will wait till he lowers his eyes,' he thought, 'and then salute him. Perhaps he will greet me first and throw himself upon my neck and console me.'

At this point Shahrazād saw the approach of morning and discreetly fell silent.

But when the four-hundred-and-ninety-fourth night had come

SHE SAID:

Hardly had their looks crossed and eye met eye than the dyer leapt to his feet, crying: 'Wretched thief, how often have I forbidden you to pause before my shop? Do you want to ruin and disgrace me? Hi, there, you men, seize him!'

The white and black slaves leapt upon the unfortunate barber, threw him to the ground and trampled upon him; the dyer rose and took up a great stick, saying: 'Stretch him on his belly!' When this was done, he beat him a hundred times across the back and then, after he had been turned over, a hundred times across the belly. 'Foul traitor,' he cried, 'if ever I see you before my shop again, I will send you to the King, who will flay and impale you in front of the palace gates! Begone with the curse of Allāh, O pitch-face!' The wretched barber, humbled and in pain, heart-broken by such treachery, dragged himself away weeping, followed by the howls and curses of the crowd.

When he came to his lodging, he stretched himself on his mat and reflected all night, in bitter grief and pain, upon Abū Kīr's evil conduct. In the morning his stripes were a little cooled and he was able to rise. He went out into the street with the intention of taking a bath at the hammām to assuage his scars and wash away the taint of his long illness. He accosted a passer, saying: 'My brother, what is the way to the hammām?' 'The hammām? What is a hammām?' asked the man. Then said Abū Sīr: 'It is a place where one washes and removes the impurities and old skin of the body. It is the most delicious spot in all the world.' 'Go and bathe in the water of the sea,' said the other, 'that is where we take our baths.' 'It is a hammām bath that I wish,' objected Abū Sīr, and the man replied: 'We do not know what you mean by a hammām. When we wish to take a bath, we go to the sea; even the King does so when he needs to wash.'

When Abū Sīr thus learnt that the people of the city knew nothing of hot baths and rubbing, of thorough cleansing and depilation, he went to the King's palace and demanded an audience. After kissing the Sultān's hands and calling down blessings upon him, 'O King of time,' he said, 'I am a stranger, a barber by trade, but I am also skilled in other employments, having had practice in the work of a hammām fireman and a rubber; although, in my country, each of these professions belong to different sorts of men, who keep to them throughout all their lives. To-day I wished to visit the hammām of your city, but none could tell me the way or even understand the word. It is very astonishing that a beautiful city like yours should have no hammām, for a hammām is the chief ornament and centre of delight in any city. In fact, O King of time, the hammām is an earthly paradise.' 'But what is this hammām of which you speak?' asked the astonished King. 'I have never heard of it.' 'O King of time,' answered Abū Sīr, 'a hammām is a building constructed in such and such a fashion, people bathe there in such and such a manner, and experience such and such delights when such and such things are done to them.' Then he expounded in great detail all the qualities, advantages, and pleasures of a hammām, adding: 'But my tongue would become hairy before I could give you an exact idea of the joys of such a place; they must be experienced to be understood. Your city will never be truly perfect until it has a hammām.'

At this point Shahrazād saw the approach of morning and discreetly fell silent.

But when the four-hundred-and-ninety-fifth night had come

SHE SAID:

The King's heart rejoiced, and he cried: 'Be very welcome to my city, O son of excellent parents!' Then he clothed Abū Sīr with his own hands in a splendid robe of honour, saying: 'All that you wish and more shall be given to you; but hasten to build a hammām, for I am impatient to see and enjoy the thing.'

He gave Abū Sīr a magnificent horse, two negroes, two boys, four girls, and a wonderful house. He honoured the barber even more greatly than he had the dyer, and put the best of the palace architects at his disposition, commanding them to build the hammām on whatever site Abū Sīr should choose. The barber went throughout all the city with the architects and, when he had chosen a suitable spot, commanded them to build there. Closely following his instructions, they raised a hammām which had not its equal in the whole world; they ornamented it with interlacing lines, many-coloured marbles, and far-brought curiosities such as ravish the soul. When the building was completed, Abū Sīr constructed within it a vast central basin of transparent alabaster and two others of rare marble. Then he went to the King, saying: 'The hammām is ready; it lacks only plenishing.' The King gave him ten thousand dīnārs, which he hastened to spend on necessary equipment, such as towels of linen and silk, precious essences, perfumes, incense, and the like. As soon as the hammām had been profusely furnished and put in order, Abū Sīr demanded ten vigorous helpers; when the King freely gave him twenty well-built and beautiful boys, he initiated them into the art of rubbing and washing, performing these offices upon them himself and having them practise again and again upon his person, until they were perfect in all the business of the hammām. Lastly he fixed a day for the opening of the place and informed the King of it.

When the day came, Abū Sīr heated the hammām and the water in the basins, burnt incense and perfume in the braziers, and turned on the water of the fountain, which fell so sweetly that beside the tinkling of it all music would have been a discord. The large jet from the central basin was incomparably strange and would have turned aside the spirits of the blest. At length all within the hammām shone so bright and clean that the place surpassed the candours of lily and jasmine.

As soon as the King, with his wazīrs and amīrs, crossed the threshold of the great door, his senses were agreeably amazed; his eyes by the decoration, his nose by the perfumes, and his ears by the voices of the fountain. 'What is this?' he asked in surprise. 'It is a hammām,' answered Abū Sīr, 'but this is only the entrance.' He led the King into the first hall and, causing him to mount the dais, undressed him and wrapped him from head to foot in suave towels. He put wooden bathing clogs upon his feet and introduced him to the second hall, where the Sultān sweated to a marvel. Then, with the help of the boys, he rubbed his limbs with hair gloves, so that all the inner dirt, accumulated by the pores of the skin, came forth in long threads like worms, much to the astonishment of the King. Then Abū Sīr washed him with plenty of water and soap and sent him down into the marble bath, which was filled with rose-scented water. After leaving him immersed for a certain time, he brought him forth and washed his head with rose-water and rare essences. Then he tinted the nails of his hands and feet with henna, which gave them a colour as of dawn. During these processes aloes and aromatic nard burnt about them and soaked them with soft vapour.

The King now felt himself as light as a bird and breathed with all the fans of his heart; his body was so smooth and firm that it gave back a harmonious sound when touched by the hand. His ecstasy knew no bounds when the boys began to rub his limbs with as sweet a rhythm as if he had been a lute. Unnatural strength came to him, so that he felt himself about to roar like a lion. 'As Allāh lives,' he cried, 'I have never felt so robust in all my life! So this is a hammām, O master barber?' 'It is a hammām, O King of time,' answered Abū Sīr. Then said the King: 'By the life of my head, my city was no city until this place was built.' After he had been dried with musk-scented towels, he went up again on to the dais, to drink sherberts confected with sliced snow.

At this point Shahrazād saw the approach of morning and discreetly fell silent.

But when the four-hundred-and-ninety-sixth night had come

SHE SAID:

Then said the King to Abū Sīr: 'What do you consider the worth of such a bath, and what price do you mean to charge?' 'Let the King fix the price!' answered the barber. 'Then,' continued the King, 'I fix the price of such a bath at a thousand dīnārs, no less,' and straightway he gave a thousand dīnārs to Abū Sīr, saying: 'Henceforth you shall charge each visitor to your hammām the same amount.' 'Pardon me, O King of time,' replied the barber, 'not all men are equal, some are rich and some are poor. If I charged each client a thousand dīnārs,

the hammām would soon be shut, for the poor cannot pay so much.'
'What would you wish to charge, then?' said the King, and Abū Sīr
answered: 'I would wish to leave the price to the generosity of my
clients, so that each would pay according to his means and the
measurement of his soul. The poor man would give what he was
able—and, as for the thousand dīnārs, that is a kingly present.' The
amīrs and wazīrs approved his words, and said: 'His idea is just, O
King of time. For you, O beloved, think that all men can do as you
do.' 'Perhaps you are right,' conceded the King. 'In any case, this
man is a stranger and poor, so that it is our duty to reward him
largely for his gift to our city of this bright incomparable hammām.
As you say that you cannot pay a thousand dīnārs for a single bath,
I authorise you to pay a hundred dīnārs on this occasion and each
to add a white slave, a negro and a girl. In the future, as the barber
has so decided, you shall pay according to your means and generosity.' When the wazīrs and amīrs had taken their baths upon that
day, they each paid to Abū Sīr a hundred dīnārs in gold, a white
slave, a negro, and a girl; and, as there were forty of them, the barber
received four thousand dīnārs, forty white boys, forty negroes and
forty girls. Also he was enriched by the King with a thousand
dīnārs, ten white boys, ten young negroes, and ten girls like
moons.

When Abū Sīr had received all this money, and these gifts, he
kissed the earth between the King's hands, saying: 'O auspicious
King, O face of fair destiny, O just and generous one, where am I
going to lodge this army of white boys, negroes and girls?' 'It was
to make you rich that I have had them given to you,' answered the
King, 'for I thought that perhaps you would wish some day to return
to your own country and that you would then be able to leave us
with enough property to render you and yours for ever beyond the
reach of need.' 'O King of time,' replied Abū Sīr, 'such an army of
slaves befits a monarch such as yourself (whom may Allāh bless!),
but I would have no need of them when I sat down with my folk to
eat my simple bread and cheese. Also, how am I going to feed and
clothe all this company, whose sharp young teeth would quickly eat
up all my property and then myself.' 'By my life, that is true!'
laughed the King. 'They are a powerful army and I hardly think you
could sustain them. Will you sell them to me for a hundred dīnārs
each?' When Abū Sīr answered that he would most assuredly do so,
the King called his treasurer and, after paying the barber for the

hundred and fifty slaves, sent all of them back as a present to their former masters. Then said Abū Sīr: 'May Allāh quieten your soul, as you have quietened mine in saving me from the greedy teeth of these young ghouls.' The King laughed again and, after compliments, left the hammām and returned to his palace, followed by the amīrs and wazīrs. Abū Sīr passed that night in his new house, sewing the gold into sacks and carefully hiding each sack when it was filled. He found that the service of his house consisted of twenty negroes, twenty boys and four girls.

At this point Shahrazād saw the approach of morning and discreetly fell silent.

But when the four-hundred-and-ninety-seventh night had come

SHE SAID:

Next morning Abū Sīr had the city criers cry through the streets: 'Creatures of Allāh, come and take a bath at the King's hammām! For three days no price will be asked.' As was to be expected, an enormous crowd thronged the hammām during those days of free bathing. When the fourth morning came, Abū Sīr installed himself in the desk at the entrance of the hammām and took the voluntary contributions of the bathers as they went out. Before evening he had filled a whole chest, by Allāh's grace, and begun to amass that fortune which was destined for him.

Soon the Queen, who heard her husband speak enthusiastically of the baths, determined to try one herself. As soon as Abū Sīr was informed of her intention, he kept the morning for men but reserved the afternoon for women, employing a discreet female to take the money at the desk. When the Queen had experienced the delicious effects of this new bathing, she resolved to come again every Friday afternoon, paying a thousand dīnārs for each visit, which was the same price as paid by the King, who came regularly every Friday morning.

Thus Abū Sīr walked further and further along the road of riches, honour, and glory, remaining all the time the modest and honest fellow he had been. He was always laughing, always affable, always generous to the poor, from whom he would accept no payment. This generosity saved his life, as will be shown in the course of our tale. For the moment it is enough for you to know that a certain sea captain, though he found himself short of money, was allowed by

Abū Sīr to take a full and delightful bath for nothing. When he had been refreshed with sherberts and honourably escorted to the door by the obliging proprietor, he cudgelled his brains for some way of showing his gratitude. You will see that an occasion was not long in coming.

At length Abū Kīr, the dyer, heard tell of this extraordinary hammām; for the whole city spoke of it with admiration, saying: 'It is the paradise of the world.' Resolving to try the joys of it himself, he dressed in his richest clothes and rode out on his gaily-decked mule, with an army of slaves carrying long sticks before and behind him. As soon as he came to the door of the hammām, he smelt the perfume of aloe wood and the scent of nard. He saw a multitude of men going in and out, and the rich and poor waiting their turns together on the benches.

The first person he saw on entering the vestibule was his old companion, Abū Sīr, sitting at the desk, plump, assured and smiling. It was with difficulty that he recognised him, for the hollows of his cheeks were now filled up with benevolent fat and his face shone with pleased prosperity. Though the dyer was disagreeably surprised, he pretended great joy and, with matchless insolence, went up to Abū Sīr and said in a voice of tender reproach: 'Well, well, this is fine behaviour for a friend and a gallant man! You must have known that I had become the King's dyer, one of the richest and most important men in the city, and yet you never came to see me, you never asked yourself: "What has become of my old friend, Abū Kīr?" I have sent my slaves all over the city to hunt for you; but they visited every khān and shop without getting upon your track.' With a sad shaking of the head, Abū Sīr replied: 'O Abū Kīr, have you forgotten the way you treated me when I came to you, the blows and the shame, and the cries of "robber" and "traitor"?' 'What are you saying?' cried Abū Kīr, feigning extreme surprise. 'Were you the man whom I beat?' and when Abū Sīr said that he was, the dyer swore a thousand oaths that he had not recognised him. 'I took you for another,' he explained, 'a robber who had often stolen my fabrics. You were so thin and yellow that it was impossible to recognise you.' He beat his hands together, as if in sincere regret, and exclaimed: 'There is no power or might save in Allāh! How could I have come to make such a mistake? And yet, was not the fault a little with you? For, when you saw me, you did not say that you were Abū Sīr. Also, that day, I was almost beside myself with the cares of business. I beg you, in Allāh's name, my brother, to forgive me and to forget that unfortunate act, for it was written in the Destiny of both.' 'Allāh pardon you, dear companion,' answered Abū Sīr, 'the fault was Fate's and the redress shall be with Allāh.' 'But forgive me freely,' cried the dyer, and Abū Sīr answered: 'May Allāh quit your conscience as I quit it! What can we do against the debts of eternity? Come into the hammām, take off your clothes and have a refreshing bath, with my blessing!'

At this point Shahrazād saw the approach of morning and discreetly fell silent.

But when the four-hundred-and-ninety-eighth night had come

SHE SAID:

'Whence came this fortune to you?' asked Abū Kīr, and Abū Sīr replied: 'He who opened the doors of prosperity to you, opened them to me also.' When he had told his story from the day of his beating, Abū Kīr exclaimed: 'How glad I am to hear that you enjoy the King's favour! I will attempt to increase that favour by telling the King that you have ever been my friend.' Then said the barber: 'What good can come from interfering with the decisions of Fate? Allāh holds all favour or disgrace with His hands. Rather undress at once and taste the joys of water and cleanliness.' He himself led the dyer into the private hall and, with his own hands, rubbed, soaped and worked upon him, without allowing one of his assistants to help. Then he set him on a dais in the cool room and offered him sherberts and refreshments with so much consideration that the ordinary clients were abashed to see the King's dyer receiving that exceptional treatment which was ordinarily reserved for the King himself.

When Abū Kīr was ready to go, he offered Abū Sīr money, but the latter refused to accept it, saying: 'Are you not ashamed to offer it, since I am your friend and there is no cause of difference between us?' 'Be it so,' said Abū Kīr. 'In return for your kindness, let me give you a useful piece of advice. Your hammām is admirable, but lacks in one respect of being altogether marvellous. You have no depilatory paste; when you have finished shaving your clients' heads, you either use the razor or tweezers for the hair on the rest of their bodies. I can give you the prescription of a paste which has no equal. Listen: take yellow arsenic and quick lime, pound them together in a little oil, mix in musk to remove the unpleasant smell, and store in an earthenware pot. I answer for the efficacy of this paste; the King will be delighted when he sees his hairs fall without shock or rubbing, and his skin showing all white and smooth beneath.' When the barber had made a note of this recipe, Abū Kīr left the hammām and hurried to the King's palace.

He bowed low before the King, saying: 'O Sultān of time, I come with a warning.' 'What warning is that?' asked the King, and Abū Kīr cried aloud: 'Praise be to Allāh who has so far saved you from the wicked hands of that enemy to the throne and to the Faith, Abū Sīr of the hammām!' 'What has he been doing?' asked the astonished King. 'Sultān of time,' replied the other, 'if, by evil chance, you enter the hammām again you will be lost beyond recall.' 'How?' asked the King, and Abū Kīr, filling his eyes with feigned terror and sweeping his arms in a great gesture of despair, panted out: 'By poison! He has prepared for you a paste of yellow arsenic and quick lime, which, even though it be only rubbed upon the hairs of the skin, burns like fire. He will suggest the paste to you by saying that it will remove the hairs of your bottom comfortably and without shock. He will apply the paste to the anus of our King and thus kill him by poison through the most painful of all channels. And the reason? The man is a spy, sent by the King of the Christians to slay our master. I have run to warn you, for your benefits are thick upon me.'

The King was thrown into an extreme of terror by these lies; he shivered and his anus contracted as if it already felt the burning poison. 'Carefully keep this thing a secret,' he said. 'I will go at once to the hammām with my grand-wazīr to test the truth of what you tell me.'

As soon as the King and the wazīr arrived, Abū Sīr introduced them into the private room and would have begun to rub and wash the Sultān; but the latter bade him begin with the wazīr. So Abū Sīr made the wazīr, who was a plump old man as hairy as a buck, lie down on the marble, and there rubbed, soaped and washed him with his greatest skill. Then he turned to the King, saying: 'Sultān of time, I have found a drug which acts so marvellously upon hairs that a razor is quite unnecessary.' 'Try it on the lowest hairs of the wazīr,' 'said the King.

At this point Shahrazād saw the approach of morning and discreetly fell silent.

But when the four-hundred-and-ninety-ninth night had come

SHE SAID:

Abū Sīr took a piece of the paste, as big as an almond, from the earthen pot, and spread it on the hair at the base of the wazīr's belly. At once the depilatory effect was so marked that the King was convinced that here was a powerful poison, and turned furiously to the hammām boys, crying: 'Arrest this murderer!' He and the wazīr dressed in haste and returned to the palace, accompanied by their guards who carried the astonished Abū Sīr among them.

The King called the captain of the port and ships, and said to him: 'Take this traitor and fasten him in a sack filled with quick lime; then throw him into the sea beneath the windows of my palace, so that he may die two deaths at once, drowning and burning.' 'I hear and I obey!' answered the captain.

Now this captain of the port and ships was none other than the sailor of whom we have spoken as being beholden to Abū Sīr. He at once sought the prisoner in his dungeon and, taking him on board a small boat, conveyed him to a little island near the city where they could speak freely together. 'I have not forgotten,' said he, 'the courteous kindness which you showed me and I would wish to pay it back. Tell me your trouble with the King and what crime you have committed thus to lose his favour and deserve this horrible death.' 'As Allāh lives, my brother,' answered Abū Sīr, 'I am innocent of all fault and have never done anything to merit such a punishment.' Then said the captain: 'It must be that you have enemies who have blackened your reputation with the King. Every man gains jealous enemies if Destiny too obviously favours him. But fear nothing. You will be safe in this isle, where you may quietly pass your time in fishing until I can contrive to send you back to your own country. Now I go to pretend your death in sight of the King.' When Abū Sīr had kissed his hand, the good sailor took a large sack filled with quick lime and sailed till he came in front of the seaward-looking windows of the palace, where the King was waiting to see his orders carried out. The captain raised his eyes to ask for the signal, and the King, stretching his arm through a window, signed with his finger that the sack should be thrown into the water. Now the King moved his hand so violently that a gold ring, which was more precious to him than his own soul, slipped from his finger and fell into the sea. This ring was a magic one, upon which depended all his power and authority. With it he held in check the people and the army, for he had but to lift his hand and a sudden ray of light, streaming from the ring, would go out against any man and stretch him lifeless on the ground by striking off the head from between his shoulders. Therefore, when the King saw the ring fall into the sea, he would not speak of it and kept his loss a profound secret, lest his power over the people should be gone.

Left alone in the isle, Abū Sīr took the fishing-net which the captain had given him and, in order both to find food and to distract his torturing thoughts, cast it into the sea. When he withdrew it, it was so full of fish, great and small, and of every colour, that he said to himself: 'As Allāh lives, it is a long time since I have eaten any fish. I will give one of these to the two cook-boys of whom the captain spoke, and command them to fry it for me in oil.' You must know that the captain of the port and ships had also the office of supplying the King's kitchen every day with fish. On this particular day, being unable to cast the net himself, he had given the charge to Abū Sīr, and had told him of the cook-boys whose duty it was to come for the catch. After this lucky first cast, Abū chose out the largest and best from among the fish and, drawing his great knife from his belt, thrust it through the still living gills, and lo! when he withdrew the blade, upon its point was a gold ring. Abū Sīr had no idea of the ring's extraordinary powers (as you will have guessed, it was none other than the ring which the King had let fall into the sea) and he therefore slipped it carelessly upon his finger, without thinking overmuch about it.

At this point Shahrazād saw the approach of morning and discreetly fell silent.

But when the five-hundredth night had come

SHE SAID:

When the two cook-boys arrived at the isle, they said to Abū Sīr: 'O fisherman, can you tell us what has become of the captain of the port, who daily gives us the King's fish? We have been looking for him everywhere. In which direction did he go?' 'He went in that direction,' answered Abū Sīr, pointing with his right hand straight towards the youths, and behold! their two heads leapt from their shoulders and their bodies rolled upon the earth.

The beam from the King's ring had killed the two cook-boys.

'Who has done this thing?' cried Abū Sīr when he saw the lads lying dead before him. He looked all about him in the air and on the ground, and then fell into a fit of trembling. He stood there, certain that he was surrounded by invisible and murderous Jinn, until he saw the sea captain coming towards him. The sailor's quick eyes saw the two corpses and the ring shining in the sun, when he was yet far off. In a flash he understood what had happened and cried: 'O my brother, do not move your right hand or I am a dead man!'

Although Abū Sīr wished to run forward and greet his friend, these words perplexed him and he stood rigid until the captain came up and threw his arms about his neck. 'Each has his Destiny about him,' cried the sailor, 'and your fate is stronger than the King's. Tell me how you obtained this ring and in return I will explain its powers.' Abū Sīr told him the tale of the fish, and then the captain explained the deadly quality of the ring, adding: 'Now your life is safe, but the King's is not. You can come back fearlessly to the city and dash the heads from your enemies and from the King himself.' At once he led Abū Sīr on board the little boat and, when they arrived at the city, hastened with him to the palace. The King was holding his dīwān, surrounded by a crowd of wazīrs, amīrs and counsellors; and although he was filled to the nose with rage and care at the loss of his ring, he dared not speak of it or have it searched for in the sea lest his enemies should rejoice. When he saw Abū Sīr, he did not doubt that here was some plot to take his life; therefore he cried: 'Wretch, how have you come out of the sea where you were burned and drowned?' 'Allāh is greater than us all, O King of time,' replied the barber, and he told the King how he had been saved by the captain in return for a free visit to the hammām, how he had found the ring, and how he had unwittingly killed the two cook-boys. 'Now, O King,' he continued, 'I am here to give you back your ring, because your benefits are thick upon me and to prove that I am not a criminal. For a criminal would use the ring to kill his enemies and even the King himself. In return, I beg you to look more closely into the crime of which I was accused and to torture me to death if I am found in any way guilty.' The King took the ring which Abū Sīr handed him and, replacing it on his finger, breathed a deep breath of relief and felt his soul return to his body. He rose and threw his arms about the barber's neck, saying: 'Surely, O man, you are the choice flower of excellent breeding! I pray you, do not blame me too much, but forgive me the harm I did you. As Allāh lives, no other would have returned me my ring.' 'O King of time,' answered Abū Sīr, 'if you would free your conscience, I beg you to tell me what was charged against me.' 'That is unnecessary,' said the King, 'for I am now certain that you were falsely accused; but, as you wish to know, Abū Kīr, the dyer, accused you of plotting with the King of the Christians to murder me with that depilatory paste which you tried upon the lower hairs of my wazīr.'

At this point Shahrazād saw the approach of morning and discreetly fell silent.

But when the five-hundred-and-first night had come

SHE SAID:

'O King of time,' cried Abū Sīr with tears in his eyes, 'I do not know the King of the Christians nor have I ever set foot upon his land. But the truth is this.' He told the King how he and the dyer had sworn to help each other and had sailed from Alexandria together; he told of the tricks and knaveries which Abū Kīr had invented against him, of the beating, and of the prescription for the paste. 'You must know,' he went on, 'that the paste is an excellent thing when put to its proper use and only dangerous when swallowed. In my country the men and women use nothing else, and the hairs fall from their bodies without their knowing it. If the King needs proof of the rest of my story he has but to summon the doorkeeper of the khān and the assistants from the dye-works.' Simply to please Abū Sīr, for he was already convinced, the King sent for the doorkeeper of the khān and the apprentices; and these, when they were questioned, confirmed and even added to the accusations which the barber had made against the dyer.

Then cried the King to his guards: 'Bring me the dyer, bare-headed and bare-footed, with his hands tied behind his back!' The guards hastened first to Abū Kīr's shop and then to his house, where they found him savouring quiet joys and dreaming, without doubt, of his old companion's death. They fell upon him with buffets on the neck, kicks up the bottom, and buttings in the belly; while they trod him under foot, they stripped off all his clothes except his shirt; then they dragged him, with his hands tied behind his back, into the presence of the King. When he saw Abū Sīr seated on the right of the throne, the doorkeeper and the apprentices standing before it, he understood that he was lost and, because of his terror, did that which he did in the very middle of the audience chamber. The King looked at him angrily, saying: 'You cannot deny that you stand in the presence of your old friend, the poor man whom you robbed, stripped, ill-treated, spurned, beat, harried, cursed, accused, and, but for the grace of Allāh, would have killed.' The doorkeeper and the apprentices raised their hands, and cried: 'As Allāh lives, you cannot deny it! We are witnesses before Him and before the King.' Then said the Sultan: 'Whether you confess or deny, you shall receive the full punishment which Fate has decreed for you ... O guards, take him, drag him by the feet through all the city, fasten him in a sack filled with quick lime and throw him into the sea that he may die a double death.' But the barber cried: 'O King of time, I beg you to accept my intercession for this man, for I forgive him.' 'You may forgive his trespasses against you,' answered the King, 'but I do not forgive his trespasses against me ... Guards, take him away!'

The guards dragged Abū Kīr by his feet through all the city, crying his crimes, and then, after fastening him into a sack filled with quick lime, cast him into the sea. Thus he died a double death, being both burnt and drowned. It was his Destiny.

'O Abū Sīr,' said the King to the barber, 'you have but to ask for all you wish and it shall be given you.' 'I only ask the King to send me back to my country,' answered Abū Sīr. 'I can live no longer away from my own folk.' Although the King had wished to make him wazīr in the place of the plump and hairy one, he prepared instead a great ship and filled it with male and female slaves and rich treasures. As he took leave of the barber, he said once more: 'You would not rather become my wazīr?' But, when the barber again refused, the King detained him no longer and allowed the ship to sail towards Alexandria.

Allāh had written a fair voyage for them, so that they arrived safely at Alexandria. When they disembarked, one of the slaves saw a sack which had been cast by the sea upon the beach. Abū Sīr opened this and discovered the body of Abū Kīr, which the currents of God had returned to its own place. The barber had his one-time friend buried upon the shore and raised a monument above him, which became a place of pilgrimage, supported by the dead man's goods. On the door Abū Sīr engraved these lines:

Hold from your lips the bitter gourd of evil
Because that wine leads even to this level.
Upon the water floats the flesh of death,
But quiet pearls eternal lie beneath.
See, the transparent pages of the air
In serene spaces! It is written there:
He who sows good shall gather good from earth,
For every harvest savours of its birth.

Such was the end of Abū Kīr, the dyer, and such the beginning of Abū Sīr, the barber, in a life of happiness and ease. The bay where the dyer was buried is known as the Bay of Abū Kīr unto this day. Glory be to Him who lives in His eternity and brings forth Winter and Summer according to His will!

Then said Shahrazād: 'That, O auspicious King, is all that I know of the tale.' 'By Allāh, it is an edifying story!' cried Shahryār. 'It has roused in me the desire to hear one or two moral anecdotes.' 'Those are the kind of tale which I know best,' answered Shahrazād.

At this point she saw the approach of morning and discreetly fell silent.

But when the five-hundred-and-second night had come Shahrazād said

Moral Anecdotes from the Perfumed Garden

MORAL anecdotes, O auspicious King, are the tales which I know best. I will tell you one or two or three from the Perfumed Garden.' Then said King Shahryār: 'Begin quickly, for a great weariness weighs upon my soul to-night and I doubt whether your head is safe upon your shoulders.' 'Listen, then,' answered Shahrazād with a smile, 'but first I must warn you, O auspicious King, that, though these anecdotes are very moral, they might seem licentious to gross and narrow minds.' 'Do not let that stop you, Shahrazād,' said King Shahryār. 'Only, if you think these moral anecdotes ought not to be heard by this little one, who listens, I do not very well know why, among the carpets at your feet, tell her to depart at once.' But little Dunyazād, fearing to be driven away, threw herself into the arms of her elder sister. Shahrazād kissed her upon the eyes and calmed her against her breast; then she turned to King Shahryār, saying: 'I think that she should be allowed to stay, for "to the pure and clean all things are pure and clean," and there is nothing shameful in speaking of those things which lie below our waists.'

Then she said:

The Three Wishes

I T is related, O auspicious King, that there was once a well-inten-tioned man who had passed all his life in rapt anticipation of that miraculous night, which the Book promises to Believers of burning faith, the Night of Possibility, when a pious man may realise his every wish. On one of the last nights of Ramadān the saint, who had fasted strictly all day, felt himself suddenly visited by divine grace. He called his wife and said to her: 'This evening I feel pure before the Eternal and am persuaded that it is my Night of Possibility. As my wishes will be granted by the Rewarder, I wish to consult with you as to what I should ask, for I have sometimes benefited from your advice.' 'How many wishes will you have?' asked the wife, and, when he told her that he might have three, she continued: 'You know that the perfection of man and his delight are rooted in his manhood; no man may be perfect who is chaste or impotent or a eunuch. It follows that the larger a man's zabb, the greater his manhood and the further he has gone upon the road of perfection. Therefore bow humbly before the face of the Highest and beg for your zabb to grow to magnificence.' Straightway the man bowed himself and, turning his palms towards the sky, prayed: 'O Benefactor, O Generous, enlarge my zabb even to magnificence!'

This wish was no sooner expressed than granted. At once the saint saw his zabb swell and magnify until it looked like a calabash lying between two mighty pumpkins. And the weight of all that was so considerable that he had to sit down again when he would rise, and, when he would lie, get up.

His wife was so terrified by what she saw that she fled away each time that the holy man brought his new treasure to the business. She wept and cried out: 'How can I dare this mighty instrument, whose very jetting would pierce a rock through and through?' At last the poor man said: 'O execrable woman, what am I to do with this thing? The fault is yours.' 'The name of Allāh upon me and around me!' she exclaimed. 'Pray for the Prophet, old empty-eye! As Allāh lives, I have no need of all that; I did not ask for so much. Pray for it to be lessened. That will be your second wish.'

The saint lifted his eyes to heaven, saying: 'O Allāh, I beg you to rid me from these too bountiful goods and deliver me from the trouble of them!' Even as he framed the words, his belly became quite smooth, with no more sign of zabb and eggs than if it had been the belly of a little impubic girl.

Needless to say, this complete disappearance did not satisfy the good man and was even more distasteful to his wife, who began to curse him and accuse him of cheating her. Then the holy man's displeasure knew no bounds, and he cried: 'See what comes of your foolish counsels, O witless woman! I had three wishes and might have chosen great riches in this world or the next. Now two of them have gone for nothing, and I am even in poorer case than I was before. As I have still a third wish, I will ask the Lord to restore that which I had in the beginning.'

His wish was granted and he obtained just such a zabb as he had had before.

The moral of this tale is that a man should be contented with what he has.

Then said Shahrazād:

The Boy and the Rubber

IT is related, O auspicious King, that there was a hammām rubber who was so famous for his skill that he always attended upon the sons of the chief nobles and richest merchants in the city. One day, while he was waiting in the hall for bathers, there entered the son of the wazīr, who was a boy still lacking hair about his body, but with rich plump curves and a most beautiful face. The rubber rejoiced to touch the sweet body of this delicate lad and exclaimed within his soul: 'See how the fat has made silky cushions here! How rich a form, how plump!' He helped his client to lie down upon the warm marble of the hot room and began to knead his body with a special care. When he came to the thighs, he was stupefied to see that this large youth had a zabb scarcely as big as a hazel-nut. He lamented in his spirit and, stopping short, began to beat one hand against the other for despair.

At this point Shahrazād saw the approach of morning and discreetly fell silent.

But when the five-hundred-and-third night had come

SHE SAID:

When the boy saw the rubber so dispirited, he asked him the cause of his grief, and the man replied: 'Alas, my lord, it is for you I weep! I see you afflicted with the greatest ill possible to man: you are young, plump and handsome, and have been blessed by the Creator with all qualities and riches; but you lack the instrument of delight without which a man is not a man and may neither give nor receive. What is life without a zabb and all that a zabb implies?' The wazīr's son lowered his head sadly, as he answered: 'You are right, my uncle. You remind me of the one grief which occupies me when I am alone. If the heritage of my revered father is so little, the fault is mine; for hitherto I have not tried to make it fructify. How can a kid become a powerful he-goat if he keeps away from the kindling females, or a tree grow when it is not watered? Until to-day I have held aloof from women, and no desire has come to wake the sleeping baby in its cradle. Now I think it is time that it came out of its sleep and that the shepherd learnt to lean upon his crook.'

Then said the rubber: 'How can a shepherd lean on a crook no larger than one joint of his little finger?' 'I rely on your generous help, my uncle,' replied the boy. 'Go to the dais where I left my clothes and take from my belt a purse full of gold. If you will procure with that money some girl who can begin my zabb's development, I will make my first experiment to-day.' 'I hear and I obey!' answered the rubber and at once, fetching the purse from the dais, left the hammām.

As he went along, he said to himself: 'This poor boy thinks that a zabb is made of soft toffee and can be pulled out immediately to any length with the fingers. Does he imagine that a cucumber grows in a day or that a banana ripens before it is a banana!' Laughing to himself, he sought out his wife and said to her: 'O mother of my son, I have just been rubbing a very handsome boy at the hammām. He is the wazīr's child; but, although the poor lad has every other perfection, he has a zabb the size of a hazel-nut. When I lamented for his youth, he gave me this purse of gold and asked me to procure a girl who could instantly develop his miserable inheritance. Just as if a zabb could grow to manhood at a single touch! I think it would be as well if this gold stayed in our house; so I suggest that you come back with me and pretend to lend yourself to the experiment. We need fear no results with the poor boy; and there is nothing shameful in the matter. You can pass an hour laughing at him, without fear or danger; while I watch over the two of you and guard you from the curiosity of the other bathers.'

The young wife readily consented to this plan and at once dressed herself in her fairest robes. Even without ornament she could have turned heads and ravished hearts, for she was one of the most beautiful women of her time.

At this point Shahrazād saw the approach of morning and discreetly fell silent.

But when the five-hundred-and-fourth night had come

SHE SAID:

The rubber brought his wife into the presence of the wazīr's son who was waiting, stretched upon the warm marble; he left them alone and placed himself outside to prevent the men who passed from looking round the door.

As soon as the young woman saw the boy she was charmed with his moon-like beauty; and he felt all his desires go out to her. 'What shame,' she said to herself, 'that he has not got what other men have. My husband told the truth: it is scarcely as big as a nut.' Soon, however, the child lying between the boy's thighs stirred in its sleep and, as its smallness was in appearance only, since it was of that kind which retires almost wholly into its father's bosom when at rest, began gradually to throw off its torpor. Suddenly it sprang erect, as great as an ass's or an elephant's, a powerful sight to see. The rubber's wife uttered a cry of admiration and wound her arms about the boy's neck; he mounted her like a triumphant cock and in an hour pierced her once, twice, thrice, and seven times more again, while she struggled and moaned below him in tumultuous happiness.

During this hour the rubber was watching through the wooden trellis of the door and dared not interrupt for fear of a public shame. He kept on calling out in a low voice to his wife, but she did not answer. 'O mother of my son,' he whispered fiercely, 'why do you not go? The day is far spent and the baby waits your breast at home.'

But she, still writhing below her lover, answered with breathless laughter: 'No, as Allāh lives, for I have found a child better worth feeding.' Then said the wazīr's son: 'You may go and give your baby the breast, if you will promise to come back at once.' But she exclaimed: 'I would rather die than deprive this sweet new suckling of its mother even for an hour.'

When the poor rubber heard his wife thus shamelessly refuse to return to him, he was thrown into such despair and rage of jealousy, that he threw himself from the hammām terrace and died in the street below.

The moral of this story is that a wise man does not judge by appearances.

But, continued Shahrazād, I know another which teaches the same lesson even more strongly and proves how dangerous it is to be guided by the seeming of things:

There is White and White

I T is related, O auspicious King, that a certain man fell violently in love with a talented and beautiful girl, and, as she was married to a husband whom she loved and was in all things chaste and virtuous, could find no means by which to seduce her. He patiently made siege for a long time without result and then determined upon a trick which should either conquer or punish her.

It happened that the woman's husband had, as confidential servant, a boy whom he had raised from the cradle and who was entrusted with the guardianship of the house while his master was away. The lover took care to bind this boy to him with ties of friendship, making him such fine presents that soon the lad was entirely devoted and would obey him in all things.

When this point had been reached, the lover said to his friend: 'I should very much like to look over your master's house to-day when he and your mistress are absent.' 'Certainly,' answered the other, and, when the husband had gone to his shop and the wife on a visit to the hammām, he led the lover into the house and showed him all the rooms with their various contents. Then the man, who had already prepared for the trick which he meant to play on the young woman, took advantage of the boy turning his back for a moment to approach the bed in the bedchamber and pour upon the sheet some white of egg from a flask. After that he left the room and went his way.

At this point Shahrazād saw the approach of morning and discreetly fell silent.

But when the five-hundred-and-fifth night had come

SHE SAID:

At sundown the husband shut his shop and, as soon as he reached home, being weary from a long day of buying and selling, went to the bed and would have lain down to rest had he not seen a large stain on the sheet. Being thrown into a great state of distrust, he recoiled, saying to himself: 'Who can have entered my house and done this thing with my wife? This is a man's semen without any doubt.' To make assurance more sure he placed his finger in the liquid, and, after examination, exclaimed: 'It is!' In his fury his first thought was to kill the boy; but he soon abandoned his plan, saying to himself: 'So great a stain could not have come out of so young a boy; he has not yet reached an age when the eggs swell.' He called the lad to him, crying: 'Vile abortion, where is your mistress?' 'She has gone to the hammām,' answered the lad. On this, suspicion became certainty in the mind of the man, for the law of religion compels both man and woman to make complete ablution after they have coupled. 'Run and tell her to return at once!' he cried, and the boy hurried off to the bath.

As soon as his wife returned and entered the bedchamber where her husband waited with rolling eyes, the merchant threw himself upon her without a word, and, seizing her by the hair, flung her to the ground. After administering a rain of kicks and blows, he tied her arms and, drawing a great knife, was about to cut her throat, when she yelled and cried so loudly that all the neighbours of both sexes ran in to help her. Seeing her about to be slain, they pulled the husband away by force and asked why she had merited such punishment. The woman swore that she knew no reason; so the crowd cried to the husband: 'If you have cause of complaint, you may either divorce her or reprimand her gently, but kill her you may not; for she is chaste, and known by us all to be so. We will swear to her chastity before Allāh and before the kādī. She has been our neighbour for a long time and we have never found offence in her.' 'Let me cut the wanton's throat!' answered the merchant. 'If you wish proof of her debauchery, look at this stain which lovers have left in her bed.' The neighbours, men and women alike, approached the bed and, when each had plunged a finger in the mess, all cried: 'It is a man's semen!' But the boy, who had gone forward with the rest, collected some of the liquid which had not been absorbed by the sheet, and put it in a pan which he then held over the fire. When the contents were cooked, he ate a little and distributed the rest to the neighbours, saying: 'Taste this. It is only white of egg.' As soon as they had tasted, they realised that what he had said was true, and even the husband admitted that his wife was innocent and had been unjustly ill-treated. He hastened to make his peace with her and, to seal the truce, gave her a hundred dīnārs and a gold collar.

This short tale proves that there is white and white, and that, in every matter of life, a wise man should differentiate.

When Shahrazād had told these anecdotes to the King, she fell silent. Then said Shahryār: 'In truth, Shahrazād, these tales are infinitely moral. They have so quieted my spirit that I am ready to hear you tell me some altogether extraordinary story.' 'Certainly!' answered Shahrazād. 'My next tale will be as strange as you could wish.'

The Tale of Land Abdallāh and Sea Abdallāh

AND SHAHRAZĀD SAID TO KING SHAHRYĀR:

IT is related—but Allāh sees further!—that there was once a fisherman, called Abdallāh, who had a wife and nine children to support and was very poor, since he had no resource but his net. This net was his shop, his trade, and the door of safety for his house. He would fish every day in the sea and, if he caught anything, would sell it and spend the price on his children, according to the measure which Allāh had meted; but if he caught much, he bought good food for his wife to cook and purchased fruits and the like until all the money was gone; for he would say: 'To-morrow's bread will come to-morrow.' He lived thus from day to day without anticipating Destiny.

A morning came when his wife bore a tenth son (for the other nine children were all sons, thanks to Allāh!) and there was nothing to eat in the house. Then said the woman: 'Dear master, the house has now another dweller and the day's bread is not yet provided. Will you not go out and seek something to sustain us in this painful moment?' 'I am just going out,' he answered. 'I trust in the bounty of Allāh and shall make the first cast of my net in the child's name and see the measure of his future fortune.' 'Trust in Him!' said the wife; and Abdallāh left the house with his net upon his shoulders and walked to the sea shore.

At this point Shahrazād saw the approach of morning and discreetly fell silent.

But when the five-hundred-and-sixth night had come

SHE SAID:

In the infant's name he cast and disposed his net in the water, saying: 'O my God, grant that his life be easy and not difficult, abundant and not spare!' Then, after waiting a moment, he drew in his net and found it full of dung, sand, gravel and weed; but with no sign of the smallest fish. Saddened and astonished, he cried: 'Has Allāh created this child without allowing him any provision? That cannot be, that can never be. He who formed the jaws of man and made his two lips for his mouth did not create in vain. He has taken upon Himself to furnish the needs of these things, for He is the Foreseeing One, the Generous. Let His name be exalted!' He took his net on his back and, moving along the shore, cast it in another place. He waited longer this time and had much greater difficulty in drawing the net to land, for it was very heavy. In it he found an ass, all swollen and stinking with death. The fisherman felt deadly sick and, after quickly freeing his net from the corpse, hurried to another part of the beach. 'There is no power or might save in Allāh!' he said to himself. 'This bad luck comes from my wicked wife. How often have I said to her: "There is nothing more for me in the water and I must earn our food elsewhere. Of a truth, I can do nothing more in this trade; therefore let me practise some other." I have said this till my tongue was hairy with speaking, but she always answered: "Allāh Karīm, Allāh Karīm! His generosity knows no limit, therefore do not despair, O father of my children." Where is all this generosity of Allāh? Is this dead ass the destiny of my last-born child or shall it be bought with gravel or sand?'

For a long time Abdallāh stood still in bitter disappointment, but at last he decided to try one more cast and asked pardon from Allāh for his ill-considered words. 'O Rewarder of all creatures, O Writer of all Destinies, favour my fishing, favour my child, and I promise that one day he shall be a holy man, devoted to the service of Allāh!' Thus prayed the fisherman. 'Grant that I may catch a single fish to carry to my benefactor, the baker! When I would stop before his shop to sniff the scent of the hot bread in the black days of my poverty, he would generously give me enough to satisfy my nine and their mother.' After he had cast his net a third time, Abdallāh gave it many minutes to fill before he began to draw it to land. This he could not do until his hands were all bleeding from the effort; for this time the net was even more heavy. At last he succeeded in drawing it ashore and then, to his stupefaction, he saw a human being, a son of Adam, caught in the meshes of the net. The apparition had a head, face, beard, trunk, and arms like ordinary men, but ended in a fish's tail.

Abdallāh did not doubt for a moment that he was in the presence of some Ifrīt, who, in old time, had been shut in a copper jar for rebellion against our master Sulaimān ibn Dāūd, and cast into the sea. 'It is surely one of those!' he said to himself. 'Because the metal has been rotted by the years and the seas, he has been able to escape from the sealed jar and creep into my net.' Tucking his garment above his knees, the fisherman began to run breathlessly along the beach, with terrified cries of: 'Mercy, mercy, O Ifrīt of Sulaimān!'

'Approach, O fisherman, and do not fly from me!' cried the man in the net. 'I am human as you are, no Marid or Ifrīt, but a human like yourself. Fear nothing, for if you will help me out of this net, I will reward you largely and Allāh will remember it in your favour on the Day of Judgment.' Abdallāh's heart calmed a little at these words; he ceased his flight and began to return very slowly towards the net, advancing one leg and drawing back the other, as the saying is. When he was close, he said to his strange captive: 'You are sure you are no Jinnī?'

At this point Shahrazād saw the approach of morning and discreetly fell silent.

But when the five-hundred-and-seventh night had come

SHE SAID:

'I am not,' answered the man in the net, 'I am a human being who believes in Allāh and His Prophet.' 'Then who threw you into the sea?' asked Abdallāh, and the other replied: 'No one threw me into the sea; I was born there. I am one of the children of the sea, a numerous people who live in the marine depths. We live and have our being in the water, as you upon the earth, and the birds in the air. We all believe in Allāh and His Prophet (upon whom be prayer and peace!) and are well-disposed towards the earth men, since we obey the commandments of Allāh and the precepts of the Book. If I were a Jinnī or evil Ifrīt, would I not have torn your net in pieces instead of having the consideration to ask you to help me, in order that your net, which is your wage-earner and the door of safety for your house, should not be spoiled?' This last argument dissipated any doubts which Abdallāh retained; as he stooped to help the sea man from the net, the latter continued: 'O fisherman, Destiny ruled my capture. I was walking in the water when your net descended about me and caught me in its meshes. I wish to be of service to you and yours. Will you make a pact with me by which each shall swear to be a friend to the other, to give presents and receive them in exchange? For instance, you will come to this place every day and bring me a provision of the fruits of earth: grapes, figs, water-melons, sweet-melons, peaches, plums, pomegranates, bananas, dates and the like. I will receive them from you gladly and, in return, give you on each occasion the fruits of our sea: coral, pearls, chrysolites, aquamarines, emeralds, sapphires, rubies, the precious metals, and all the jewels of the waters. I will fill the same basket you use to bring my fruit. Do you accept?'

Already the fisherman had been ravished with joy at this splendid enumeration; now he stood on one leg, crying: 'As Allāh lives, who would not accept? But first let the Fātihah be between us to seal our pact.' The man from the sea agreed and the two recited the first chapter of the Koran aloud. Then only Abdallāh freed his captive from the net. 'What is your name?' he asked. 'I am called Abdallāh,' answered his new friend. 'If by chance you do not see me when you come in the morning, you have only to call me by that name and I will appear from the water. And what is your name, my brother?' 'I also am called Abdallāh,' replied the fisherman. Then cried the merman: 'You are Land Abdallāh, and I am Sea Abdallāh, so we are twice brothers, by name and friendship. Wait for me a moment, my brother, while I dive and bring you up your first gift from the sea.' With that he leapt from the beach and disappeared below the water.

When a little time passed and he did not appear, Land Abdallāh repented of having freed him. 'How do I know that he will return?' he thought. 'He mocked me, and made these promises to get free. Why did I not keep him prisoner? I could have shown him to the people and made much money. I could have carried him into the houses of the rich, who do not care to go out for their entertainment, and been largely rewarded for my show. Your fish has escaped, O fisherman!'

At this point Shahrazād saw the approach of morning and discreetly fell silent.

But when the five-hundred-and-eighth night had come

SHE SAID:

Even as the fisherman was lamenting, the merman appeared through the surface of the waves, holding something above his head, and climbed on to the beach beside him. His two hands were filled with pearls, coral, emeralds, hyacinths, rubies and other stones, which he handed to his friend, saying: 'Take these, Abdallāh, my brother, and excuse their fewness; for to-day I have no basket to fill. When you bring me one, I will load it to the top with these sea fruits.' The fisher rejoiced at the sight of the shining jewels and, after letting them trickle between his marvelling fingers, hid them in his breast. 'Do not forget our pact,' said the merman. 'Return here every morning before sunrise.' Then he took leave of the fisherman and dived into the sea.

Land Abdallāh returned to the city, drunken with joy, and made his way to the shop of the benevolent baker, who had been good to him in the black days. 'My brother,' he said, 'fortune begins to walk upon our way. I pray you give me an account of what I owe you.' 'Is there need of an account between such friends?' asked the baker. 'If you have a little money to spare, give me what you can; if you have nothing, take as much bread as you need for your family and wait to pay me until prosperity has become your permanent guest.' 'Good friend,' answered the fisherman, 'prosperity has taken up eternal abode with me for the good luck of my latest born and by the munificence of Allāh. Yet all that I can give you is little compared with your kindness when want had me by the throat. Take this as earnest of more to come.' So saying, he pulled so great a handful of jewels from his breast that not half remained. This he stretched out to the baker, saying: 'I beg you to lend me a little money until I have sold my sea gems in the market.' Stupefied by what he saw and received, the baker emptied his till into Abdallāh's hands and insisted on carrying the necessary bread to the fisherman's family himself. 'I am your slave and servant,' he exclaimed and, taking a basket of loaves on his head, walked behind Abdallāh to his house. There he set down the basket and, after kissing his friend's hand, went on his way. Abdallāh gave the loaves to his wife and then went out again and bought lamb, chicken, vegetables and fruit. That evening the woman did mighty cookery and all the family ate abundantly to the health of the new-born, who had brought such fortune on the house.

Abdallāh told his wife all that had happened and handed over to her the rest of the jewels, so that she rejoiced, saying: 'Keep this most fortunate adventure secret; otherwise you will risk grave embarrassment by the folk of the government.' 'I will hide the thing from all except the baker,' answered Abdallāh. 'Although good fortune should be kept secret, I cannot make a mystery of it with the first man who ever befriended me.'

Very early next morning Land Abdallāh returned to the sea bearing a basket full of every kind and colour of fruits. Setting his load down on the sand, he clapped his hands, calling: 'Where are you, Sea Abdallāh?' At once a voice answered from below the waves: 'I am here, Land Abdallāh,' and the merman came up out of the water and climbed ashore. After mutual greetings, the fisherman gave his basket of fruit to the merman, who thanked him heartily and dived back into the sea. A few moments later he reappeared, carrying the basket emptied of its fruit, but heavy with emeralds, aquamarines, and all the splendid harvest of the ocean. When the two had said farewell, the fisherman loaded the basket on his head and made straight for his friend's bakery.

At this point Shahrazād saw the approach of morning and discreetly fell silent.

But when the five-hundred-and-ninth night had come

SHE SAID:

'Peace be upon you, O father of open hands!' he said, and the baker answered: 'And upon you be peace and benediction from Allāh, O face of good omen! I have just sent up to your house a dish of forty cakes which I cooked specially for you. In their preparation I did not spare clarified butter, cinnamon, cardamom, nutmeg, turmeric, artemesia, anise or fennel.' The fisherman plunged his hand into the basket, which shone with a thousand coloured fires, and gave the baker three large handfuls of jewels. When he reached his own house, he chose from the basket the finest specimen of each kind and colour and, wrapping the gems in a piece of cotton, took his way to the market of the jewellers. Entering the shop of the syndic, he showed his marvellous wares, saying: 'Do you wish to buy these?' The syndic looked at him suspiciously and asked if he had any more. When Abdallāh answered that he had a whole basket of them at home, the other said: 'Where is your house?' 'As Allāh lives, I have no house,' answered the fisherman, 'but only a hut of rotten planks at the end of a lane near the fish market.' On hearing this answer the jeweller cried to his lads: 'Arrest this man! He is the robber who was reported to us as having stolen the Queen's jewels!' The assistants beat Abdallāh soundly and all the jewellers flocked together to curse him. Some said: 'He is the man who committed the robbery in Hasan's shop last month,' and others exclaimed: 'That is the wretch who cleaned out so-and-so's place.' Each told a tale of theft by some unknown robber and attributed it to the fisherman; but Abdallāh kept silence and made no sign of denial. He allowed himself, after the beating, to be dragged into the presence of the King by the syndic of the jewellers, who wished to make him confess his crimes in the royal presence and then that he should be hanged at the palace gate.

When all the jewellers had entered the dīwān, the syndic said: 'O King of time, since the Queen's collar disappeared we have done our best to catch the thief and now, with the help of Allāh, we have succeeded. Here is the guilty man and here are the jewels which were found upon him.' Then said the King to the chief eunuch: 'Take these stones and show them to your mistress, begging her to say whether they are those of the collar which she lost.' So the chief eunuch took the splendid gems to the Queen and asked her that question.

The Queen marvelled and replied: 'They are not the same at all. I have found my collar in the chest. These stones are far more beautiful than mine; they cannot have their equal in the world. Run, O Masrūr, and tell the King to buy these stones for another collar, which he can give to our daughter, Prosperity, who has now reached a marriageable age.'

When the King learnt the Queen's answer, he flew into a rage with the syndic of the jewellers for thus apprehending and maltreating an innocent man, and cursed him with all the curses of Ād. 'O King of time,' answered the trembling sheikh, 'we knew that this man was a poor fisherman and therefore, when we saw him with these stones and heard that he had a basket full of them at home, we concluded that such wealth was too great to be got honestly.' At this answer the King's wrath increased and he cried out to the syndic and the rest of the jewellers: 'O vulgar minds, O heretics, O common earthy souls! Do you not know that any fortune, however marvellous and sudden, is possible in the destiny of a true Believer? Wretches, you have the stiff-necked impudence to condemn this poor man without a hearing, without any examination, on the absurd pretext that such wealth is too great for him! You treated him like a thief and dishonoured him among his fellows. Not for a moment did you think of Allāh, Who distributes His favour without the niggardliness common to jewellers. Ignorant fools, do you know, then, the size of the infinite wealth of God, that you dare to judge by your mean and muddy figures what weight may be in the scales of a happy Destiny? Begone out of my sight, O men of misery! I pray that Allāh will ever withhold His blessings from you!' Thus he drove them in shame from before the throne.

At this point Shahrazād saw the approach of morning and discreetly fell silent.

But when the five-hundred-and-tenth night had come

SHE SAID:

The King turned to Abdallāh the fisherman and, before asking him the least question, exclaimed: 'O you who have been poor, may Allāh bless you in the gift which He has bestowed! I give you security. . . . Now do you wish to tell me truly how you came by these jewels, which are so beautiful that no king of the earth has got the like?' 'O King of time,' answered Abdallāh, 'I have at home a fish basket filled with stones like these, a gift from my friend, the Sea Abdallāh.' He told the King the story of his adventure with the merman in all its details, adding: 'I made a pact with him, sealed by a recital of the Fātihah, by which I am bound to bring him every morning at dawn a basket filled with the fruits of the earth and he is bound to fill that basket with the fruits of the sea, which are jewels of great price.'

The King marvelled at Allāh's generosity to His Believers, and said: 'O fisherman, this was written in your Destiny! I have only to tell you that riches demand protection and that a wealthy man ought to have a high rank. As I wish to guard you for all my lifetime, and even after—since I cannot answer for the future and do not know what my successor might do to you through greed and envy—I will marry you to my daughter, Prosperity, a girl already ripe for marriage, and appoint you my wazīr, thus leaguing you directly with the throne before my death.'

The King called his slaves, saying: 'Conduct your master Abdallāh to the hammām,' and the slaves led him to the palace bath. After washing him carefully, they put royal robes upon him and reconducted him to the presence of the King, who straightway named him wazīr. He gave him instruction in his new duties, and Abdallāh thanked him, saying: 'O King, your advice is my rule of conduct and your kindness a shadow in which I take delight.' Then the King sent couriers to the fisherman's house with numerous guards; with men playing upon the fife, the clarinet, the cymbals, the big drum and the flute; and with women expert in dress and ornament: to clothe and deck Abdallāh's wife and the ten sons, to install them in a palanquin carried by ten negroes and to conduct them to the palace amid sounds of music. The woman, with her last-born at her breast, was placed in a rich litter with her nine other children and conducted by the wives of amīrs and nobles to the palace, where the Queen received her with every mark of honour. The King greeted the children and, making them sit turn and turn about upon his knee, caressed them paternally with as much pleasure as if they had been his own sons. In order to show her affection for the wife of the new wazīr, the Queen appointed her to govern all the women of the harīm and made her wazīrah of the apartments.

That same day the King fulfilled his promise by giving his only daughter, Prosperity, to be Abdallāh's second wife. He celebrated the marriage with a great feast for citizens and soldiers, and an illumination of all the streets. At night Abdallāh learnt the delights of young flesh and the difference between the virginity of a little princess and the old used body on which he had rested hitherto.

At dawn next morning the King, who had been awakened before his usual hour by the emotions of the day before, went to his window and saw his new wazīr, the husband of Prosperity, leaving the palace with a basket of fruit on his head. He called out to him: 'What are you doing, my son-in-law? Where are you going?'

At this point Shahrazād saw the approach of morning and discreetly fell silent.

But when the five-hundred-and-eleventh night had come

SHE SAID:

'I am carrying the fruit to my friend, Sea Abdallāh,' answered the wazīr. 'But this is not the hour when men leave the palace,' objected the King, 'and it is hardly fitting that my son-in-law should carry a porter's load on his head.' 'That is true,' replied Abdallāh, 'but I am afraid that I will miss my appointment and appear to the merman as a liar, one whom prosperity has made forgetful of his promise.' Then said the King: 'You are right. Hurry to your friend and Allāh go with you!' Abdallāh took his way through the markets, where the earliest merchants were opening their shops. 'That is Abdallāh, the wazīr,' they said to each other. 'That is the King's son-in-law, who goes down to the sea to exchange those fruits for precious stones.' Some, who did not recognise him, stopped him as he went, saying: 'O fruit-seller, how much for a measure of apricots?' He answered each one very politely: 'They are not for sale. They are already sold,' and thus pleased all. When he came to the shore, he saw Sea Abdallāh rising from the waves. He gave him the fruit and received a new load of brightly-coloured gems. Then he returned to the city and sought the shop of his friend, the baker. He found it closed and waited a little in case the good man had not yet arrived. At last he asked a neighbouring shopkeeper what had become of the baker and, when the man answered: 'I do not know exactly what Allāh has done to him; but I believe that he lies sick in his own house,' hurried to the street in which the baker lived and knocked upon his door. After a few minutes a terrified head appeared at one of the higher windows and soon afterwards the baker, reassured by the sight of the fisherman with his jewels, came down and opened the door. He threw himself weeping into Abdallāh's arms, and said: 'You have not been hanged? I heard that you had been arrested as a thief. Fearing to be taken as your accomplice, I shut up my shop and hid at home. Tell me, my friend, how come you to wear the clothes of a wazīr?' Abdallāh told him the whole story, adding: 'The King has made me his wazīr and married me to his daughter. I have now a harīm, headed by my old wife, the mother of my children . . . I pray you, take this basket; for to-day is the day of your Destiny.' With that he left his friend and returned to the palace with the empty basket.

When the King saw him coming he laughed aloud, saying: 'You see, your friend the merman has played you false.' 'Far otherwise,' answered Abdallāh, 'the jewels with which he filled the basket to-day surpassed those of yesterday in beauty. I have given them all to my friend, the baker, who, in the days when misery had me by the throat, fed me and my children and their mother. He was not un-mindful of me in the days of my poverty and therefore I have re-membered him in the days of prosperity. As Allāh lives, I wish to show that my good fortune has not hardened me against the poor.' The King was edified in the extreme by this reply, and asked the baker's name. 'He is called Abdallāh the baker,' replied the wazīr, 'just as I am called Land Abdallāh, and my friend, the merman, is called Sea Abdallāh.' Then cried the astonished King: 'I am called King Abdallāh. We are all four named the servants of Allāh. And as the servants of Allāh are equal in His sight, being brothers in the Faith, I wish you to go and fetch Abdallāh the baker, that I may make him my second wazīr.'

Land Abdallāh fetched Abdallāh the baker into the presence of the King, who invested him with the proper garments and named him wazīr of his left.

Abdallāh, who had been a fisherman, and was now wazīr on the King's right, fulfilled his new functions to the satisfaction of all, and never forgot to carry the fruits in season to his friend, Sea Abdallāh, in exchange for precious stones and metal. When there were no fresh fruits in the gardens or shops, he would fill the basket with dried raisins, almonds, nuts, pistachios, dried figs, dried apricots, and every kind and colour of dried conserve. Each morning for a whole year he became possessed of a basket full of gems.

One day Land Abdallāh, who had come down to the sea at dawn, according to his custom, sat by his friend's side upon the sand and began to talk about the usages of mermen.

At this point Shahrazād saw the approach of morning and discreetly fell silent.

But when the five-hundred-and-twelfth night had come

SHE SAID:

'Is it beautiful in your country?' he asked. 'It is beautiful,' answered the other. 'If you wish, I will take you with me down into the sea and show you all it contains. You can visit my city and receive the cordial hospitality of my house.' But Land Abdallāh replied: 'My brother, you were created in the water and it is your natural element. That is why you can live beneath the sea without inconvenience. But, before I accept your invitation, please tell me if it would not be fatal for you to live upon the land.' 'It would be fatal,' agreed Sea Abdallāh. 'My body would dry away, the winds of the earth would blow upon me and I should die.' Then said Land Abdallāh: 'It is the same with me. I was created upon the earth and it is my natural element; the airs of it do not inconvenience me, but if I came down into the sea with you, the water would penetrate my body and strangle me, and I should die.' 'Have no fear for that!' cried the merman. 'I will bring you an unguent which, when it is smeared upon your body, will render the water harmless, even if you decide to stay with us for the rest of your life. In this way you can bide with me and explore the sea in every direction, sleeping and waking in the water with no oppression.'

'In that case,' said the wazīr, 'there is nothing to prevent my diving with you. Bring me the unguent and I will try it.' The merman took up the basket of fruits and jumped into the sea. In a few moments he returned, carrying a jar filled with an ointment like cow's grease, coloured yellow gold and having a delicious scent. 'Of what is it made?' asked Land Abdallāh, and his friend replied: 'It is the liver fat of a fish called dandān. Dandān is the greatest of all the fishes in the sea. He can swallow at a single mouthful those things which you on earth call elephants and camels.' 'Then on what does he feed?' cried the old fisherman in a fright. 'He eats lesser fish,' answered the other. 'You know the proverb: The weak are devoured by the strong.' 'That is true,' assented Land Abdallāh, 'but are there many of these dandāns where you live?' 'Thousands and thousands and Allāh knows how many,' answered the other. 'Then, my brother, I pray you to excuse me from making my visit!' cried the wazīr, but the merman reassured him, saying: 'Have no fear; for although dandān is very ferocious, he fears an Adamite because the flesh of man is violent poison to his kind.' 'O Allāh,' exclaimed the wazīr, 'what good would it do me to be a poison for dandān once I was swallowed by dandān?' But, 'You have absolutely nothing to fear from dandān,' said the merman finally. 'When he sees an Adamite, he flees away. Also, he will recognise the smell of his own fat and do you no harm.' Somewhat reassured, Land Abdallāh cried: 'I put my trust in Allāh and in you!' And, after undressing, he dug a hole in the sand and buried his clothes, so that none might steal them while he was gone. Then he smeared himself from head to foot with the unguent, without forgetting the smallest openings. 'I am ready, O brother of the sea,' he said at last.

At this point Shahrazād saw the approach of morning and discreetly fell silent.

But when the five-hundred-and-thirteenth night had come

SHE SAID:

Sea Abdallāh took his companion by the arm and dived with him into the depths of the sea. When they reached the bottom, he bade his friend open his eyes and Land Abdallāh, who felt that he was neither stifled nor crushed by the great weight of water and could breathe even better than on land, after a little hesitation opened them. From that moment he became the guest of the sea.

He saw the water stretching an emerald pavilion above his head, even as on land a pavilion of topaz is spread above the sea. At his feet lay the marine meadows which no eye from earth had violated since the dawn of time. A calm rested upon the mountains and valleys of the deep; a delicate light bathed the infinite transparency of the water; enchantment led the eye down quiet vistas; he saw forests of red coral, of white coral, and of rose coral, with branches motionless in the silence; there were diamond caves held up by pillars of ruby, of chrysolite, of beryl, of gold sapphire, and of topaz; extravagant trees nodded to the whispering water over tracts as great as cities; and shells of a thousand colours and tortured forms shot gay reflections from the silver sand into the crystal above them. In the light about him Land Abdallāh saw fishes like flowers, fishes like fruit, fishes like birds, fishes dressed in red and silver scales and with the shape of lizards, fishes like buffaloes, like cows, like dogs, and even, in some sort, like men. He walked between vast banks of royal jewels, burning with a hundred coloured fires which the water brightened as oil would flames on earth; between banks of gaping oysters holding white pearls, rose pearls, and golden pearls; between hedges of swollen sponge swaying heavily and slowly, stretching like the lines of an army and seeming to delimit and brood over the vast loneliness.

Suddenly Land Abdallāh who, walking always with his arm in his friend's, watched these strange beauties defile past him, saw a long terrace of caves, cut in the flanks of a mountain of emerald. At the doors sat or stood girls, silvered like the moon, with amber coloured hair. They were like the girls of earth, save that instead of buttocks, thighs, and legs, they had slim fish tails. They were the daughters of the sea, and the green caves were their home.

'I suppose these girls are unmarried,' said Land Abdallāh, 'since I see no males among them?' 'They are young virgins,' answered the other, 'who wait at the entrance of their caves for a man to come and choose among them. In other parts of the sea we have cities peopled by male and female; but the girls, when they become marriageable, have to leave the cities for these caves and dwell here until they are chosen.' Soon after making this explanation, he led his friend past a city. 'I see a peopled city,' said Land Abdallāh, 'but I cannot find any shops for buying and selling. Also I am astonished to see that the inhabitants do not cover those parts which ought to be covered.' His friend explained, saying: 'We have no need for buying or selling, for life is easy to us and we can catch the fish, which is our food, on our thresholds with our naked hands. As for the other matter, we see no necessity for covering one part of the body more than another, and, besides, we are differently made down there from the people of earth. Also, if we wished to cover ourselves, we have no stuff.' 'That is so,' assented Land Abdallāh. 'And how is the state of marriage with you?' 'In general there are no marriages with us,' answered the merman, 'for we have no laws to control desire and inclination; when a girl pleases us, we take her; when she ceases to please, we leave her and perhaps she pleases someone else. But you must know that we are not all Mussulmāns; there are many Christians and Jews among us, and it is these who do not admit marriage, for they are very fond of women. We of the Faith live apart in our own city and marry according to the precepts of the Book; our weddings are such as please the Highest and His Prophet (on whom be prayer and peace!) . . . Let us hasten, my brother, for I wish to come quickly to my own city. It would take a thousand years to show you the excellencies of our empire, and you cannot weigh the whole by weighing one of the parts.' Then said Land Abdallāh: 'I am very hungry and I cannot eat raw fish, as you seem to do.' 'How then do you eat fish on earth?' asked the merman, and the other answered: 'We fry or grill them in olive oil or in oil of sesame.' Sea Abdallāh laughed and asked: 'And how are we water dwellers to obtain olive oil or oil of sesame, or light a fire?' 'You are right,' agreed Land Abdallāh. 'I beg you to lead me to your city.'

At this point Shahrazād saw the approach of morning and discreetly fell silent.

But when the five-hundred-and-fourteenth night had come

SHE SAID:

So Sea Abdallāh led him quickly through spaces, where new thing followed new thing before his eyes, and brought him to a smaller city whose houses were caves, little or great according to the number of those who lived in them. The merman stopped before one of these, saying: 'Enter, my brother, for this is my home.' He conducted his friend into the cave and called aloud for his daughter. At once there appeared from behind a shrub of rose coral a girl whose long hair floated in the water; she had fair breasts, an excellent belly, a slim body, and large green eyes under black lashes; but, like all the other people of the sea, she ended with a tail, where one would have expected buttocks and legs. She stopped short on seeing the earth dweller and, after giving him a long glance of curiosity, burst out laughing. 'Father,' she cried, 'who is this Tailless One?' 'This is my friend from the earth,' he answered, 'the man who daily gives me a basket of those fruits which you find so much to your liking. Come to him politely and bid him welcome.' The girl advanced and wished her father's guest welcome and peace, in picked delightful language. As Land Abdallāh was about to answer, the merman's wife came in also, holding her two last babies to her breast, one on each arm; and both the children were crunching large fishes as children on earth crunch cucumbers.

The woman stopped dead on the threshold when she saw Land Abdallāh; setting down the two infants, she laughed with all her

might, crying: 'As Allāh lives, it is a Tailless One! How can anything go without a tail?' She came nearer to the guest and began to
lead her daughter and the two children in an amused examination of
him. They inspected him closely from head to foot and marvelled
especially at his bottom, for never in their lives had they seen a bottom or anything which looked like a bottom. At first they were a
little frightened at this protuberance, but soon grew bold enough to
touch the amusing novelty all over with their fingers. They laughed
again and again, whispering to each other: 'It is a Tailless One!' and
dancing for joy. Soon Land Abdallāh became offended at such casual
manners and said to Sea Abdallāh: 'My brother, did you bring me
here to be laughed at by your wife and children?' 'I ask your pardon
and beg you to excuse me,' answered the merman. 'Pay no attention
to these two women and two children, for their intellects are weak.'
Then, turning to the little ones, he shouted: 'Be quiet!' When they
fell silent through fear of him, Sea Abdallāh smiled at his guest,
saying: 'Do not be too surprised at this behaviour, my brother; for
with us a man without a tail is little worth.'

Even as he was speaking, ten tall and vigorous mermen entered
the house and said to its owner: 'O Abdallāh, the King of the Sea has
heard that you are entertaining a Tailless One from the land. Is that
true?' 'It is quite true,' answered Sea Abdallāh. 'Behold this is he,
my friend and guest, whom I am just going to lead back to the shore
from which he came.' 'You must not do that,' they said. 'The King
has sent us to fetch him, for he wishes to see how he is made. It has
been reported that he has some extraordinary thing behind and some
even more extraordinary thing in front, and the King is very anxious
to see these things and learn their names.'

Sea Abdallāh turned to his guest and said: 'You must excuse me,
my brother; for I cannot help myself. We may not disobey the commands of our King.' 'I am a little afraid of this King,' said Land
Abdallāh. 'Perhaps he will be offended because I have things which
he has not, and therefore kill me.' 'I will be there to protect you and
see that no harm comes to you,' replied the merman, and, somewhat
reassured, the fisherman exclaimed: 'I put my trust in Allāh!' Then
he followed his host into the presence of the King.

When the King saw the landsman he laughed so heartily that he
took a dive off his throne into the water. 'Be welcome, O Tailless
One!' he spluttered at length, and all the high dignitaries laughed
with consuming laughter, pointing out the stranger's behind to each

other and saying: 'As Allāh lives, it is a Tailless One!' 'How is it that you have no tail?' asked the King. 'I do not know, O King,' replied Abdallāh. 'All the men of earth are like me.' 'And what,' asked the King again, 'do you call that thing which you have instead of a tail behind?' Then said Abdallāh: 'Some people call it a bottom and some call it a backside; others speak of it in the plural as buttocks, because it has two parts.' 'Of what use is it?' demanded the King. 'To sit down on when one is tired, that is all,' said Abdallāh, 'but it is a dearly loved ornament in women.' 'And what is the name of that thing in front?' demanded the King again. 'Zabb,' said Abdallāh. 'And what use is a zabb?' continued the King. 'It has many uses,' returned Abdallāh, 'but I cannot explain them, out of regard for the King's majesty. I can say this however: those uses are so necessary that, in our world, nothing is so esteemed in a man as a good weighty zabb, just as a jutting backside is the most excellent thing in women.' The King and his court laughed more than ever at this answer, so that Land Abdallāh, being at a loss, raised his arms to heaven and cried: 'Glory be to Allāh who created the backside to be a glory in one world and a laughing stock in another!' Then, in confusion at so much attention being paid to his lower parts, he did not know what to do with them and said to himself: 'As Allāh lives, I wish either that I were far from here or had something with which to cover myself!'

At this point Shahrazād saw the approach of morning and discreetly fell silent.

But when the five-hundred-and-fifteenth night had come

SHE SAID:

At last the King said: 'O Tailless One, your backside pleases me so much that I am ready to satisfy your least desires. Ask what you will!' 'O King, I wish for two things,' answered Land Abdallāh, 'to return to the earth and to carry back with me many jewels of the sea.' 'You must know, O King,' broke in the merman, 'that my friend has not eaten since he came among us and has no stomach for the flesh of raw fish.' Then said the King: 'Give him as many gems as his soul desires and lead him back by the way he came.'

All the mermen hastened to collect vast empty shells and to fill them with every colour of precious stone. Then they asked the landsman whither they should carry these things and he replied: 'Follow me and my friend, Abdallāh.' With that he took leave of the King and, accompanied by his friend, who bore the fruit basket quite full of jewels, and followed by all the mermen carrying the precious shells, he recrossed the submarine empire and climbed up into the light of earth.

He sat down on the sand, resting and drinking in his native air for a few minutes; then he dug up his clothes and dressed himself, saying farewell to his friend the while and bidding him leave the shells and the basket on the shore until he could send porters to fetch them. As soon as he reached the city, he despatched porters to carry all the treasure to the palace, and himself hastened to the King, his father-in-law.

King Abdallāh received him with great demonstrations of joy, saying: 'We have been very uneasy about your absence.' Land Abdallāh then told him the whole of his maritime adventure from beginning to end; but there is no need to repeat it here. Also, he placed between his hands the basket and the shells of gems.

Though the King marvelled at the tale and the treasure of the sea, he was deeply offended at the lack of manners which the mermen had shown in regard to his son-in-law's behind, and to bottoms in general. 'O Abdallāh,' he said, 'I do not wish you to go down to the sea any more to meet this friend of yours; though no great harm has come to you this time, we cannot say what might happen in the future, for *not every time you drop a cup, will it be worth the taking up*. Also, you are my son-in-law and my wazīr, and it is unsuitable that you should be seen carrying a fish-basket on your head or be an object of derision to more or less tailed and more or less impolite persons. Stay in the palace; for thus you will be at peace and we shall have no more anxiety about you.'

So it was that Land Abdallāh, who did not wish to disobey King Abdallāh in anything, stayed in the palace with his friend Abdallāh the baker and went no more to meet Sea Abdallāh upon the sands. Of Sea Abdallāh we hear no more; but doubtless he was very angry.

All lived in great delight and the practice of every virtue until they were visited by the Destroyer of joy, the Separator of friends. Then they died. But glory be to the Living Who dies not, Who reigns over the Visible and Invisible worlds, Who is Lord of all and watches kindly over His servants, knowing their necessities before they ask and all their acts before they act them!

Shahrazād fell silent and King Shahryār exclaimed: 'O Shahrazād, this tale is indeed extraordinary!' Then said Shahrazād: 'It is indeed, O King. But, although it has had the good fortune to please you, it is in no way more admirable than the Tale of the Yellow Youth.' 'You may tell me that tale,' said Shahryār, and Shahrazād said:

The Tale of the Yellow Youth

Among other stories it is related, O auspicious King, that one night the Khalīfah, Hārūn al-Rashīd, left his palace, accompanied by his wazīr Jafar, his wazīr al-Fazl, Abū Ishāk, his favourite singer, the poet Abū Nuwās, Masrūr the sword-bearer, and Ahmad-the-Moth, his chief of police. They went, each disguised as a merchant, down to the banks of the Tigris and, getting on board a boat, allowed the current to bear them whither it would. For Jafar had told the Khalīfah, who was suffering from sleeplessness and depression of spirit, that there was no better remedy for such weariness than seeing a new thing, hearing a new thing, and visiting a new place.

At length the boat drifted beneath the windows of a house which overlooked the river and they heard from inside a beautiful and mournful voice singing to the lute:

> Wine's red in the cup,
> A bird sings silver on the branches,
> Life must be paid
> So make life pay again.
>
> This boy, my fair friend
> Wine reddens and the white rose blanches,
> Has heavy eyes.
> I kissed a red rose once
>
> On cheeks gay with Spring,
> But, now light downs of youth enfranchise,
> Peaches lie ripe
> Where I thought a rose tree.

On hearing these verses the Khalīfah said: 'That is an excellent voice, O Jafar.' And Jafar answered: 'My Lord, I have never heard so delightful a voice in all my life. But to listen to a voice from behind a wall is only to hear it by half. Would it not be better if we could hear it from behind a curtain only?'

At this point Shahrazād saw the approach of morning and discreetly fell silent.

But when the five-hundred-and-sixteenth night had come

SHE SAID:

Then said the Khalīfah: 'Let us ask hospitality from the master of this house, and perhaps, in that way, we may get to hear the voice more clearly.' They stopped the boat and, stepping out on to the bank, went up to the door of the house, where their knocking was answered by a eunuch, from whom they craved leave to enter. The servant retired and almost immediately the master of the house came to the door himself, saying: 'Welcome, ease and abundance, O my guests! This house belongs to you.' He led them into a cool and lofty hall, the ceiling of which was coloured with designs against a background of gold and dark blue; in the middle of the floor a fountain musically spilled its water into an alabaster basin. Then said the host: 'My masters, I do not know which of you is of the highest rank, therefore I greet you all equally. Deign to seat yourselves in such places as you prefer.' He turned to the end of the hall, where a hundred girls sat on a hundred golden chairs, and, at a sign from his hand, the hundred rose and went out silently, one by one. At a second sign, slaves with girt robes brought large dishes on which were cooked, in every colour, all eatable things which fly in the air, walk on the earth, or swim beneath the seas. Also there were pastries, conserves, and tarts upon which had been written, with pistachios and almonds, verses in praise of the new guests.

When they had eaten and drunken, and were washing their hands, the master of the house said to them: 'Dear guests, if you have honoured me with this visit in order to pleasure me with some command, I pray you speak; for all your desires shall be granted.' 'Indeed, O host,' answered Jafar, 'we entered your house in order to hear more clearly that admirable voice which came to us muffled upon the water.' 'You are very welcome,' said the man and, turning to his slaves, continued: 'Beg your mistress to sing us something.' A few moments after the slaves had departed, a voice of unequalled loveliness rose from behind the curtain at the back of the hall, singing, to a gentle accompaniment of lutes and harps, this song:

Take this cup and drink this wine,
For it is a virgin wine
And the cup is new gold.

A woman who waits
Is the fool of time.

My nights have been many,
To see the brown waters of the Tigris
Under black-veiled stars
Or to watch the moon in the west
Thrusting her silver sword
Into the purple river.

The voice fell silent and the strings echoed the echoes in a whisper, only for a short time. The Khalīfah turned in a marvel of admiration to Abū Ishāk, crying: 'As Allāh lives, I have never heard the like!' Then to the master of the house, he said: 'Surely the woman with the voice is in love and separated from her lover?' 'That is not so,' answered the man. 'She is sad for other reasons. Perhaps, for instance, she is separated from her father and mother, and sings thus when she remembers them.' Then said al-Rashīd: 'It would be indeed astonishing if a separation from parents could rouse such grief.' For the first time he looked closely at his host, as if to read in his face some more likely explanation, and saw that he was being entertained by a young man of great beauty but whose face was the yellow colour of saffron. 'Dear host,' he said in his astonishment, 'we have one more request to make of you, before leaving and going upon our way.' 'Your wish is granted before it is asked,' murmured the yellow youth, and the Khalīfah continued: 'I desire, and those who are with me also desire, to hear whether the saffron colour of your face has been acquired during your life or whether you were born so?'

Then said the yellow youth: 'O guests, the tale of this yellow colour is so strange that, were it written with needles on the corner of an eye, yet would it serve as a lesson for the circumspect. I pray you to give me your best attention.' 'Our best attention is yours,' they answered. 'We are impatient for you to begin.'

At this point Shahrazād saw the approach of morning and discreetly fell silent.

But when the five-hundred-and-seventeenth night had come

SHE SAID:

Then said the yellow youth: You must know, my masters, that I am a native of the lands of Umān, where my father was one of the greatest of the merchants of the sea and owned thirty ships which brought him in an annual income of thirty thousand dīnārs. Being an enlightened man, he had me taught the art of writing and all else which it is necessary to know; also, when his last hour approached, he made me excellent recommendations for my life, to which I listened with respectful attention. Allāh took him into His mercy. May He prolong your lives, O guests of mine!

Some time after my father's death, I sat in my house among my guests (for I was now very rich) and a slave informed me that one of my captains had brought me a basket of early fruit. I had the man in and, accepting his gift of unknown and remarkable fruits, gave him a hundred dīnārs to mark my pleasure. Then, as I was distributing the fruit to my guests, I asked the captain whence it came. No sooner had he answered that he had brought it from Basrah and Baghdād than my guests began to expatiate on the marvels of those two cities, to vaunt the life that is lived there, the suavity of the climate, and the polished benevolence of the citizens. Each capped the other's eulogy until I had no other thought except to visit the places at once. I sold all my goods and properties at a loss, got rid of my men and women slaves, and realised on my ladings and on all my ships with the exception of one. Thus I found myself possessed of a thousand thousand dīnārs, without reckoning the jewels and ingots of gold which I already had by me. I reduced these riches to their smallest compass and, embarking them upon the ship which I had reserved for my own use, set sail for Baghdād.

Allāh had written a fair voyage for me, so that I reached Basrah in good health and with all my riches intact. There I took passage on a smaller boat and went up the Tigris to Baghdād. In that city I discovered that the Karkh quarter was the most fashionable and therefore hired a handsome house there in the Street of Saffron and installed myself with all my belongings. After I had made my ablutions, I put on my finest clothes, rejoicing all the while to be at last in illustrious Baghdād, envy of cities and goal of my desires, and went forth to wander at random through the most frequented streets.

It was a Friday and the people walked as I did in festival garments, breathing the fine air. I let the crowd take me at random and thus came to Karn al-Sirāt, which is the favourite objective of those who stroll in Baghdād. In this place I saw, among tall and beautiful houses, one taller and more beautiful, giving upon the river. On the marble steps sat an old man dressed in white; he had a venerable appearance and was distinguished by a beard which fell to his waist in two equal silver divisions. This old man was surrounded by five boys, quite as beautiful as moons and scented with chosen essences, even as he was.

Being won over by the appearance of the white old man and the beauty of his boys, I asked a passer-by what his name might be. 'That is the sheikh Tāhir ibn al-Alā, friend of youth,' he said. 'Those who enter his house do nothing else but eat, drink, and amuse themselves, according to their fancy, with the boys or girls who dwell there.'

At this point Shahrazād saw the approach of morning and discreetly fell silent.

But when the five-hundred-and-eighteenth night had come

SHE SAID:

Charmed by this description, I cried aloud: 'Glory be to Allāh, who has guided me from my ship to this well-looking old man; for I only came to Baghdād to find such an one!' Then I went up the steps and wished the sheikh peace, saying: 'My master, I wish to ask you something.' He smiled at me, as a father smiles upon his son, and answered: 'What is it you wish?' Then said I: 'I ardently desire to be your guest for to-night.' 'Certainly,' he replied with a still kinder look. 'To-night, my son, I have a new batch of girls; they have just arrived and are of various prices for the evening. Some are ten dīnārs, some are twenty, and others are fifty or even a hundred. It is for you to choose.' 'As Allāh lives,' I replied, 'I think I will make my first experiment with one at ten dīnārs. After that Allāh will see! Here are three hundred dīnārs for one month, since that time is needed for a good trial.' I handed over the three hundred dīnārs, and, when the old man had weighed them in his scales, he called to one of the boys, saying: 'Conduct your master!' The boy took my hand and led me to the hammām of the house, where he gave me an excellent bath and lavished minute attentions upon me. Then he conducted me to a pavilion and rapped upon one of its doors.

At once a kind and laughing girl opened and bade me welcome. 'I leave our guest in your hands,' said the boy and then retired. The girl took the hand which the boy had relinquished and led me into a richly ornamented room, on the threshold of which two little personal girl slaves, as pretty as stars, met us and went before us. I looked closely at their mistress and saw that she was in every way as beautiful as a full moon.

She made me sit by her side and signed to the two little ones, who brought us a broad gold dish on which were arranged roast chicken, baked meats, roast quails, roast pigeons and roast wild-cock. We ate our fill, and never in my life have I tasted such meats or drunk more savoury wines than those which followed, or smelt more lively flowers or eaten of sweeter fruit, suaver jams, or more extraordinary pastry. Later, she gave such tender proof of charm and expert lust that I passed the whole month with her as if it had been a single night.

When the month was finished, the boy came for me and led me first to the hammām and then to the white old man. 'Master,' I said to him, 'I would like one of those at twenty dīnārs.' 'Give me the gold,' he answered; so I fetched the gold from my house and weighed him over six hundred dīnārs, for a trial month with a girl at twenty dīnārs a night. He called another youth to him, saying: 'Conduct your master.' The boy led me first to the hammām, where he attended me with even greater care than I had received the first time, and then to a pavilion which was guarded by four little girl slaves. These, when they saw us, ran to tell their mistress, and presently the door was opened by a young Christian from the land of the Franks, more beautiful and more richly clothed than the girl at ten dīnārs. She took me by the hand with a smile and led me into a room of lavish decoration and surprising dyes.

At this point Shahrazād saw the approach of morning and discreetly fell silent.

But when the five-hundred-and-nineteenth night had come

SHE SAID:

'Welcome to my charming guest!' she said, and then, when she had had me served with food and drink more exquisite than that provided by the other girl, she wished to intoxicate me still more with the beauty of her voice and her skill on instruments of harmony. Therefore she sang to a Persian lute:

O scents rising from the wet earth,
O flowers about Babylon,
Carry a song to my beloved
In that enchanted land
Where her lost kisses starve the world.

I passed a whole month with this daughter of the Franks, and I must admit that I found her infinitely more skilled and gracious in the movements than my first mistress. I am sure that I did not pay at all too high a price for my delights.

After the boy had led me again to the hammām, I hastened to find out the white old man and compliment him on his excellent taste in girls. 'As Allāh lives, O sheikh,' I said, 'I could wish to live in your generous house for ever, for the eyes find joy here and the senses find delight.' The old man was very pleased with my praises and, in return for them, said to me: 'To-night, O guest, is with us a night of unusual festival; only those may join us who are distinguished patrons of the house. We call it the Night of Splendid Vision. You have but to climb up on to the terrace and judge for yourself.'

After thanking the old man, I mounted to the terrace and found it divided down the middle by a vast velvet curtain, behind which there lay on a fair carpet, with moonlight shining upon them, a girl and her lover, close in each other's arms and kissing with their lips. At sight of the girl's unparalleled beauty, I was struck into a daze of marvel and stood there, without breathing or knowing where I was. When at last I could move and knew that I would never have peace until I found out who she was, I went down from the terrace and, running to the girl with whom I had spent the last month, told her what I had seen. Realising my state of excitement, she asked me what need I had to occupy myself with the vision. 'As Allāh lives,' I answered, 'she has stolen reason and faith away from me.' 'So you wish to have her?' she questioned with a smile, and I replied: 'That is the oath of my soul. She is my queen.' Then said the girl: 'That maiden is the daughter of our master, sheikh Tāhir ibn al-Alā, and we are all her slaves. Do you know the cost of a night with her? . . . Five hundred golden dīnārs, and she is a morsel worthy of kings and of that price.' 'By Allāh,' I exclaimed, 'I am ready to spend all my fortune to hold her but for one night.' And that night I did not sleep, for my spirit was troubled concerning the girl.

Next morning I dressed like a king in my richest robes and,

presenting myself before the sheikh Tāhir, said to him: 'I wish that one who is five hundred dīnārs a night.' 'Give me the gold,' he answered; so I weighed him over fifteen thousand dīnārs, the price for a month. He took them and said to one of the boys: 'Conduct your master to your mistress.' The lad led me to an apartment the like of which, for beauty and gold ornament, I had never seen upon the earth. There I beheld that girl lying at ease, with a fan in her hand, and I well-nigh fainted from the emotion of looking at her.

At this point Shahrazād saw the approach of morning and discreetly fell silent.

But when the five-hundred-and-twentieth night had come

SHE SAID:

For she was like the moon at her fourteenth night, and the simple answer she made to my greeting had more of music in it than the cords of a lute. Indeed, indeed, she was beautiful and gracious and wrought exquisitely by the hand of Allāh! I have no doubt that it was of her the poet wrote these lines:

> Lay she naked in the sea
> All the salt would sweetened be.
> Showed she in the sunset West
> Eastward-praying Christian even
> Would look back and think it best
> So to gaze and lose his heaven.
> I saw her gleaming in the night,
> 'O night,' I cried in agitation,
> 'What is this phantom of delight?
> Is it a tender ghost which haunts me,
> Or a heated virgin wants me
> For the joys of copulation?'
> As in answer to this riddle,
> She put down her hands and sighed,
> Clasped the blossom of her middle
> With her fingers, and replied:
> 'Fairest teeth need daily scraping
> With an aromatic twig;
> Chastest parts will sigh for raping
> With a something bold and big.

Mussulmāns, has this not wrung you?
Is there not a zabb among you?'
Here I felt him crack his joint
While the vehemence which swelled him
Lifted up the clothes which held him
To a noticeable point.
So I let him out, but she
Started back in terror:
'I said twig, and here's a tree,
Is there not some error?'

I wished her peace, and with a killing languorous glance she answered: 'Ease, friendship, and generous welcome to my guest!' She made me sit at her side, and maidens with fair breasts served us an initial repast of exquisite fruit, choice preserves, and a royal wine; roses and jasmine were given us, and about us aloes and the wood of scented shrubs burned in gold perfume braziers. At length one of the slaves brought an ivory lute to the girl, who tuned it and sang this song:

Never take wine except from a blithe boy,
For, if you hold him to you while you sup,
His cheeks' reflection strengthens the red joy
And more than roses blossom in the cup.

After these preludes I grew bolder, my hand became braver, my eyes and lips devoured the girl. I found her qualities of knowledge and beauty so extraordinary that I not only passed with her the month for which I had already paid, but continued to weigh out gold to the old white man, her father, month after month, until I had not a single dīnār of those riches which I had brought with me from the land of Umān. When I knew that I would have to separate from her, my tears fell in rivers down my cheeks and night and day were one to me.

At this point Shahrazād saw the approach of morning and discreetly fell silent.

But when the five-hundred-and-twenty-first night had come

SHE SAID:

Seeing me thus, she asked the reason of my tears and I answered: 'Dear mistress, I weep because I have no more money. A poet has said:

> Poverty makes us strangers in our home,
> But money gives us country when we roam.

I weep, light of my eyes, because I fear to lose you.' Then said she:
'When one of the clients of this house is ruined by the house, my
father allows him to remain for three days longer, enjoying the
accustomed pleasures without payment; after that, he requests him
to be gone and show his face no more. But you, my dear, my beloved
one, need have no fear of this fate, for I will find means to keep you
by me as long as you wish to stay. I have my own fortune at my
disposal; even my father does not know how great it is. I will give
you five hundred dīnārs, the price of one night with me, and you
must hand them to my father, agreeing to pay him day by day in
future. Thinking that you still have money, he will accept your
condition; and, when he brings the money to me, as he always does,
I will hand it to you and you can pay for another night. Thus we
shall be together for as long as Allāh wills or until you grow weary
of me.'

For very joy I became as light as a flight of birds; I kissed the girl's
hands and thanked her; for a whole year I remained in this new way,
as happy as a cock among the hens.

At the end of that time, as ill luck would have it, my dear one
grievously slapped one of her slaves in a moment of anger and, out
of revenge, the woman ran and told the whole plot to the old man.

The sheikh Tāhir ibn al-Alā leapt to his feet and came to find me
where I lay without misgiving at the side of my love, playing with
her in gallantry. After attracting my attention, the old man cried:
'When one of my clients is ruined, it is my custom to entertain him
for three days; but you have already enjoyed my hospitality by fraud
for a whole year, eating, drinking, and coupling at your ease . . .
Ho, you slaves, turn this son of a bugger into the street!' The slaves
stripped me and cast me outside the door, with ten small silver pieces
and an old patched cloak for sole resource. The white old man cried
after me: 'Begone, for I do not wish to beat or curse you; but, if you
stay for another hour in our city of Baghdād, the blood of your head
shall answer for it.'

Thus, dear guests, I was exiled from my mistress into a city which
I knew not, though I had dwelt within it for many months. All the
sorrows of the world weighed upon my heart. In my great despair I
cried: 'Behold I, who came across the sea with a thousand thousand

golden dīnārs and the price of my thirty ships, have spent all my
fortune with that calamitous old man and now stand here naked,
heartbroken and humiliated! There is no power or might save in
Allāh, the High, the Glorious!' These gloomy thoughts accompanied me to the banks of the Tigris, where I found a boat about to
go down to Basrah, and arranged with the captain to work my passage as a common sailor.

At this point Shahrazād saw the approach of morning and
discreetly fell silent.

But when the five-hundred-and-twenty-second night had come

SHE SAID:

As soon as I came to Basrah, hunger drove me towards the market
and there I was noticed by a certain seller of spices, who came up to
me and threw his arms about my neck. This man, who had been a
friend of my father, asked how I did, and I told him the whole of my
story from beginning to end. 'As Allāh lives,' he said, 'these are not
the acts of a sane man! But what is past is past. Have you any plans?'
When I answered that I had none, he went on: 'Will you stay with
me and keep my accounts for a daily wage of a silver dīnār, with food
and drink thrown in?' I gratefully accepted, and stayed with him as
a clerk, keeping account of all his incomings and outgoings, until I
had saved a hundred dīnārs. Then I hired a little lodging by the seashore and sat down to wait the arrival of some ship loaded with far-
brought merchandise, that I might buy a profitable lading with my
money and return to sell it at Baghdād, where I hoped to see my love
again.

Fortune brought me such a ship as I expected and, mingling with
the other merchants, I went aboard her. Soon two men came on
deck and, sitting upon chairs, had their merchandise spread out before them. Our eyes were dazzled with pearls, coral, rubies, agates,
hyacinths, and every colour of great gem. One of the men turned to
the landsmen, saying: 'O merchants, there will be no sale to-day, for
we are weary with the sea. I have only shown you these to give you
a taste of our quality.' But the merchants so pressed him to sell that
at last he consented and had the crier cry the jewels piece by piece.
The merchants bid one against the other so excitedly that the first
little bag of jewels reached four hundred dīnārs. At that moment the
owner, who had known me in the old days when my father was the

commercial king of Umān, turned to me and asked me why I did not bid. 'As Allāh lives, my master,' I replied, 'I have only a hundred dīnārs in the world.' To make this confession confused me and tears began to pour from my eyes, so that the owner clapped his hands together, crying: 'O youth of Umān, has all your great fortune gone?' He so pitied me that he turned to the merchants and proclaimed aloud: 'Witness, all of you, that I sell the bag, with all jewels which are in it, to this young man for a hundred dīnārs, though I know well that its contents in gems and precious metals are worth more than a thousand. It is, in fact, a gift from me to him.' The astonished merchants bore witness to the transaction, and the owner handed over to me not only the bag, but also the chair and carpet which he had brought on deck. I thanked him heartily and carried my new possessions to the market of the jewellers.

There I hired a shop and began to buy and sell, making a good daily profit. Among the precious things in the bag I found a little piece of dark red shell which, to judge by the characters graven upon its two faces in the form of ants' legs, seemed to be an amulet made by some master of amulets. It weighed half a pound; but its use and value I was unable to determine. I had it cried many times in the market, but fifteen dirhams was the highest bid. As I was unwilling to let it go at this price and hoped that time might bring me a better bargain, I threw the piece of shell into a corner of my shop, where it remained unobserved for a whole year.

At this point Shahrazād saw the approach of morning and discreetly fell silent.

But when the five-hundred-and-twenty-third night had come

SHE SAID:

One day, as I was sitting in my shop, a stranger entered who wished me peace; then, noticing the piece of shell in spite of the dust which covered it, he cried: 'Praise be to Allāh, at last I have found it!' He carried the thing to his lips and brow, saying to me: 'Do you wish to sell, my master?' 'Certainly,' I replied. 'How much?' said he. 'How much will you offer?' said I. 'Twenty gold dīnārs,' said he. As this appeared to me a large sum, I thought the stranger was having a jest with me, so I coldly bade him be gone upon his way; but he, supposing I found the sum too little, increased it to fifty dīnārs. More and more certain that he was laughing in his sleeve, I not only kept silence but even pretended not to notice that he was there, hoping that he would go away. Then he offered a thousand dīnārs.

When I did not answer, the man smiled at my angry silence and said: 'Why will you not consider my offer?' 'Begone upon your way!' I exclaimed, and on this he increased the price, thousand by thousand, to twenty thousand dīnārs.

Attracted by such strange bargaining, neighbours and passers crowded into the shop and began to lift their voices against me, saying: 'We must not let him ask more for a miserable little piece of shell!' Others exclaimed: 'By Allāh, a hard head and empty eyes! If he will not sell, we will throw him out of the city!'

As I did not know what to think and wished to make an end, I said to the stranger: 'Do you wish to buy or are you having a joke?' 'Do you wish to sell, or are you having a joke?' he retorted. 'To sell,' I said, and he replied: 'My last price is thirty thousand dīnārs; let us conclude the bargain.' Then I turned to the crowd, saying: 'I call upon you to witness this sale. But, first, I insist upon knowing for what purpose the purchaser wishes this piece of shell.' 'First let us make the sale,' the man objected, 'then I will tell you the virtues and uses of the thing.' 'I sell it,' I said, and he exclaimed: 'Allāh is my witness!' Then he produced a sack, bursting with gold, and weighed over to me thirty thousand dīnārs, took the amulet, and placed it in his pocket. 'It is mine, now?' he asked with a deep sigh, and, when I answered that it was indeed his, he in his turn addressed himself to the crowd: 'Be witnesses that he has sold me the amulet and received the agreed price of thirty thousand dīnārs!' When the people began to drift away, he came up to me and said in a tone of ironical pity: 'Poor fellow, if Allāh had given you the sense to hold back in a bargain, you could have made me pay not thirty thousand, not a hundred thousand, but a thousand thousand dīnārs.'

When I heard these words and knew that I had been cheated of a fabulous sum because of my lack of merchant's genius, I felt a great turning and upset within me; some convulsion in my body drew down the blood from my face and sent up in its stead the yellow colour which I have kept ever since, and which so attracted your attention this evening.

It was a long time before I could find words to say: 'Tell me now the use and virtue of this amulet.' The stranger answered:

'The King of India has a beloved daughter, who is more beautiful than any other woman upon the earth; but she is subject to violent headaches. When her father, the King, had made an end of all the resources of medicine, he called together the greatest writers, scientists, and holy men in his kingdom; but none of them could find a cure for the headaches.'

At this point Shahrazād saw the approach of morning and discreetly fell silent.

But when the five-hundred-and-twenty-fourth night had come

SHE SAID:

'Then I, who also was present, said to the King: "My lord, I know a man called Saad Allāh, a Babylonian, who has no equal in all the earth for a knowledge of the remedies which you require. Would you think fit to send for him?" "Fetch him yourself," answered the King, and I went on: "Give me a thousand thousand dīnārs, a morsel of dark red shell, and a valuable present." The King provided me with these things and I at once journeyed from India to Babylon, where I made myself known to the sage Saad Allāh and put the money and the present into his hands. Then I gave him the piece of shell and begged him to prepare me a sovereign amulet against headaches. The Babylonian consulted the stars for seven whole months and then, on an auspicious day, graved mysterious characters on the two faces of the shell, even as you have seen yourself. Without delay I journeyed back to India and gave my treasure to the King.

'He entered his daughter's room and found her chained by four chains to the four corners of the apartment, as had been ordered so that she might not throw herself from the window in the access of her pain. As soon as he placed the amulet on her brow she was utterly cured, and the King, in his joy, loaded me with rich presents and made an intimate friend of me. The princess attached the amulet to a thread round her neck and never allowed it to leave her. But one day, while she was taking her pleasure in a boat with certain companions, one of the girls accidentally broke the thread and the amulet disappeared below the water. Instantly possession entered the princess again, and her head ached so violently that she became mad.

'The King's grief passed the power of words to tell; he called me to him and charged me to bring another amulet from Saad Allāh the Babylonian; but, when I arrived at his city, I learnt that the sage was dead.

'Since then, with ten men to aid me in my search, I have scoured all the countries of the earth to find an amulet made by Saad Allāh the Babylonian. Fate at last led me into your presence and I have bought that which I had never really hoped to find.'

When he had finished his story, the stranger tightened his belt and went away, leaving me as yellow in the face as you see me now.

Without further delay I turned all my possessions into money, sold my shop and, being a rich man again, hastened to Baghdād. As soon as I entered the city, I flew on the wings of love to the palace of the white old man; for, day and night, the thought of his daughter had been with me, and to see her again had been the burning goal of my desire. Absence, I found, had added fuel to the furnace of my soul and lifted my spirit higher into the air of ecstasy.

When I questioned a lad who guarded the door, he bade me lift my head and look. Then I saw that the house had fallen in ruins, that the window from which my mistress used to lean had been torn away, and that desolation reigned darkly over the dwelling. Tears came to my eyes and I said: 'My brother, what has Allāh done to the sheikh Tāhir?' The boy made answer: 'Joy left our dwelling and sorrow came to us when a certain young merchant of Umān, one Abū al-Hasan, went away. He lived for a year with my master's daughter, but at the end of that time all his money was spent and the sheikh cast him from the house. It then appeared that our mistress loved him with great love; for his absence brought upon her a malady which was very near to death. The old man repented when he saw the mortal danger of his daughter; he sent messengers into all lands to find young Abū al-Hasan and promised a hundred thousand dīnārs for success. So far all efforts have been in vain and neither news nor trace have been found. Even to-day the girl is about to render her last sigh.'

At this point Shahrazād saw the approach of morning and discreetly fell silent.

But when the five-hundred-and-twenty-fifth night had come

SHE SAID:

My heart was torn with grief at this recital and I asked the child for news of his master. 'He has fallen into such a state of grief and discouragement,' he answered, 'that he has sold all his girls and boys, and has bitterly repented before the face of Allāh.' Then said I: 'Do you wish me to tell you where Abū al-Hasan may be found?' 'Oh, do so, do so, my brother!' cried the other. 'You will have given back life to a girl, a daughter to her father, a lover to his mistress, and you will have dragged your slave and all the relations of your slave from the most dire poverty.' 'Go and find your master,' I answered, 'demand the promised reward from him and tell him that Abū al-Hasan of Umān waits at the door.'

The little slave ran off, as fast as a mule escaping from the mill, and in the twinkling of an eye returned with the sheikh Tāhir. The old man had changed; his fresh and youthful complexion had disappeared, and in two years he had aged more than twenty. He threw himself weeping upon my neck and kissed me again and again, crying: 'Where have you been, oh, where have you been? My daughter lies at the gate of death because of you. Come in, come in, dear child!' When we had entered the house, the old man first threw himself upon his knees and gave thanks to Allāh for my return, and then counted over a hundred thousand dīnārs to the little slave, who retired, showering benedictions upon my head.

Tāhir entered his daughter's room alone, to break the good news gently to her. 'If you will eat a little, my child,' he said, 'and then take a bath at the hammām, I will show you Abū al-Hasan this very day.' 'O father,' she cried, 'are you telling the truth?' 'I swear by the great glory of Allāh that I am telling the truth,' he answered, and she cried again: 'Praise be to Him! If I may see my lover's face I have no need to eat or drink.' Immediately the old man called out to me to enter, and I entered.

Dear guests, when she saw me, she fell into a swoon which lasted for many minutes; but at length she was able to rise. With mingled tears and laughter we threw ourselves into each other's arms and stayed thus motionless, in a cloud of joy. When at last we could pay attention to that which went on about us, we saw that the kādī and witnesses had already appeared in the hall; our contract was written out immediately, and our marriage celebrated for thirty days and thirty nights with unusual pomp and rejoicing.

Since that time the daughter of the sheikh Tāhir has been my dearly loved wife; it is she whom you heard sing those sad airs by which she pleases to recall the grievous hours of our separation, in order that our present happiness may seem the greater by contrast. Yet how could it seem greater than it is, since we have been blest by the birth of a son as beautiful as his mother? I will now present him to you, O guests.

At this point Shahrazād saw the approach of morning and discreetly fell silent.

But when the five-hundred-and-twenty-sixth night had come

SHE SAID:

So saying, Abū al-Hasan, the yellow youth, left the company for a moment and returned, leading by the hand a ten-year-old boy, as fair as the moon upon her fourteenth night. 'Wish our guests peace,' the father said, and the child did so with exquisite grace. The Khalīfah and his companions were as charmed with the boy's beauty and breeding as with the father's strange tale. When they went their way, they were still marvelling at what they had seen and heard.

Next morning the Khalīfah, Hārūn al-Rashīd, who had been pondering over the tale which had been told him, called Masrūr and bade him assemble in the hall of justice all that year's golden tribute from Baghdād, Basrah, and the people of Khurāsān. Immediately Masrūr heaped up the shining treasure from the three chief provinces of the empire, until there was a hill of gold before the Khalīfah of which Allāh alone could tell the value. Then said al-Rashīd: 'Bring Abū al-Hasan to me.' Masrūr went forth and brought the young man trembling into the King's presence; Abū al-Hasan kissed the earth between al-Rashīd's hands and stood with lowered eyes, not knowing for what crime he had been fetched into the royal presence.

Then said the Khalīfah: 'O Abū al-Hasan, do you know the names of the merchants who were your guests last night?' 'As Allāh lives, I do not, O Commander of the Faithful,' answered the yellow youth. Then al-Rashīd, bidding Masrūr remove a covering which had been thrown over the hill of gold, questioned Abū al-Hasan again, saying: 'Can you tell if there be more gold here, or less gold, than that which you lost by over-hastily selling the shell amulet?' Astonished at finding the Khalīfah familiar with his story, the yellow youth opened wide eyes and murmured: 'O my lord, these riches are infinitely greater.' Then said the Khalīfah: 'Your guests of last night were he who is fifth of the line of Abbās, his wazīrs, and his companions. Also this hill of gold is yours, a present from my hand, to make up for the loss which you sustained by the sale of the talisman.'

When he heard these words, Abū al-Hasan was so moved throughout his being that a new revolution took place inside him

and the yellow colour of his face sank down, to be immediately replaced by such sweet red blood that his previous white and rose were
restored to him and he shone like the moon at her full. The Khalīfah
had a mirror fetched and himself held it before the face of Hasan,
who fell on his knees and gave thanks to the Creator. Then Hārūn
al-Rashīd commanded the gold to be carried to the young man's
dwelling and invited him to become one of his intimate companions.
'There is no God but Allāh!' cried the Khalīfah. 'Glory be to Him
Who changes His creatures and then changes them again, but Himself changes not!'

Such, O auspicious King, is the Tale of the Yellow Youth, continued Shahrazād, but it is not to be compared with the Tale of
Pomegranate-Flower and Badr Basīm. Then cried King Shahryār:
'O Shahrazād, I do not doubt what you say. Hasten to tell me the
tale of Pomegranate-Flower and Badr Basīm, for I do not know it.

The Tale of Pomegranate-Flower and Badr Basīm

AND SHAHRAZĀD SAID:

It is related, O auspicious King, that there was once in the antiquity of years, in days of long ago, a King called Shahrimān who
ruled over the lands of Ajam and lived in Khurāsān. This King had a
hundred concubines who were all barren, so that not one of them
had given him a child, even a daughter. As he sat one day in his
audience chamber among his wazīrs, amīrs and nobles, talking with
them, not of the weary affairs of government but of poetry, science,
history and medicine, and all such things as might make him forget
the grief of his childlessness, his sorrow that the throne which his
fathers had left him should pass to another, a young mamlūk entered,
saying: 'My lord, there is a merchant at the door with a young slave
more beautiful than eye has ever seen.' 'Let them come in!' cried the
King, and the mamlūk hastened to introduce them.

When the girl came in, the King compared her in his soul with
the slim water of a fountain, also, when the merchant moved from
her face a veil of blue silk starred with gold, the hall was lighted as if
by a thousand torches. Her hair fell down her back in seven heavy
braids which touched her anklets, each as the tail which sweeps the

ground from the croup of a noble filly. She was royal and marvelously fine-set; her body surpassed the delicate dancing of the ban tree. Her eyes, which were long and black by nature, shot beams which might have cured the sick and would most certainly have thrown the whole into a disorder. As for that blessing of Allāh, her most desirable bum, it was so vast that the merchant had not been able to find a veil great enough to cover it.

At this point Shahrazād saw the approach of morning and discreetly fell silent.

But when the five-hundred-and-twenty-seventh night had come

SHE SAID:

The King marvelled at all these perfections, and said to the merchant: 'How much, O sheikh?' 'My lord,' answered the other, 'I bought her from her first master for two thousand dīnārs; but since then I have journeyed with her for three years to bring her to this place and in so doing I have spent another three thousand dīnārs. Also I do not wish to sell her, but to give her as a present to Your Majesty.' The King was so charmed with this mode of address that he put a splendid robe of honour upon the merchant and gave him ten thousand dīnārs of gold. The man kissed the King's hand with many expressions of thanks and went his way.

Then said the King to the women of his palace: 'Take her to the hammām and care for her until the last traces of her journey have been washed away; anoint her with nard and other scents; and install her in that pavilion whose windows look out upon the sea.' These things were done.

You must know that the capital of King Shahrimān, which was called the White Town, stood on the sea shore; and it was thus possible for the women of the palace to give the stranger a pavilion overlooking the waters.

The King hastened to her apartment at the first possible moment and was greatly surprised that she did not rise in his honour or pay any attention to him at all. 'She must have been brought up by most mannerless people,' he thought, and looked at her more closely. Then the beauty of her face, which was like the first shy rising of the moon or sun into a tender sky, made him forget her rudeness and he cried: 'Glory be to Allāh, Who has created beauty for the eyes of his servants!' First he sat down by the girl and pressed her tenderly to his breast; then he took her upon his knees and kissed her lips; then he savoured the water of her mouth and found it sweeter than honey. But she said no word and let him do as he would, without either eagerness or resistance. The King had a great feast served in the chamber and carried morsels to her lips with his own fingers, asking her very gently, from time to time, her name and the name of her native land. But she remained silent and did not even lift her head to look at the King; yet her beauty was such that he could not feel anger against her. 'Perhaps she is dumb,' he thought. 'Yet it is impossible that the Creator could make such a body and then deprive it of speech. That imperfection would be unworthy of His hands.' He called the slaves to pour water for her fingers and, while they were presenting the ewer and basin, took occasion to ask them in a whisper whether they had heard the girl talk when they were attending her. 'We can only tell the King,' they answered, 'that, while we were bathing and scenting her, coifing and clothing her, she did not once move her lips in praise or blame. We do not know whether she dislikes us or does not know our language or is dumb; we can only say that we have not seen her move her lips.'

The King was astonished at this news and, supposing that her dumbness might come from some grief, wished to distract her. To this end he assembled all the women and favourite girls of the palace in the pavilion, that she might play with them and amuse herself. Those who could perform upon instruments of music performed upon them, others either sang or danced, or danced and sang together. All were delighted except the girl, who continued motionless in her place, with lowered head, crossed arms, and still unsmiling lips.

Seeing that his plan had not succeeded, the King felt his heart heavy within him and ordered the women to retire. When he was left alone with the girl, he first tried to obtain some answer from her, and then began to undress her.

At this point Shahrazād saw the approach of morning and discreetly fell silent.

But when the five-hundred-and-twenty-eighth night had come

SHE SAID:

He delicately loosed the light veils which covered her and then took off, one after another, the seven robes of different colours which had been put upon her. Lastly he removed her fine chemise and wide drawers with green silk tassels. Her body shone with the purity of virgin silver, so that he loved her with a great love, and, taking her up, pierced her young virginity. When this was done, he rejoiced exceedingly in his heart and said: 'As Allāh lives, is it not a marvel that the many merchants have left this so desirable maiden-head intact!' The King felt so great a yearning towards his new slave that for her sake he left all the other women of the palace, his favourites, and the affairs of his state, and shut himself up with her for a whole year, never tiring of the new joys which he discovered every day. But, during all this time, he did not succeed in drawing from the girl either a word or a nod or a sign of interest.

He did not know how to explain this silence, and at last gave up all hope of ever talking with his love. One day, as he sat beside his fair insensible mistress, his love for her welled up strong within him, and he said: 'Desire of souls, heart of my heart, light of my eyes, do you not know that I love you, that I have left my favourites and my kingdom for your beauty, and that I still rejoice to have done so? Do you not know that I have kept you for my sole treasure out of all the world. Yet more than a year has passed and I have curbed the impatience of my soul and borne with your silence and your cold-ness. If you are really dumb, beloved, I pray you tell me so by signs, that I may finally give up all hope of hearing you speak. But, if you are not dumb, I pray that Allāh will soften your heart, and, of His great goodness, inspire you to break a silence which I have not deserved. And, if this consolation is not to be, may He at least grant that you get with child by me and give me a dear son who may suc-ceed me upon the throne of my fathers. Alas, do you not see that I grow old, lonely and without a child, that I am so broken by grief and years that even now I have no hope of impregnating youthful loins? Alas, alas, if you have the least spark of pity or affection for me, answer me, beloved! Tell me if you are with child or no, that I may die in peace.'

The beautiful slave had listened as ever with lowered eyes and hands clasped about her knees; but now, for the first time since she had entered the palace, she lightly smiled. The King was so moved at this sign of relenting that he thought his palace suddenly lighted by a great fire. He exulted and, feeling sure that she would now con-sent to speak, threw himself at her feet and waited with his arms lifted and his lips half open as if in prayer.

Suddenly the girl raised her head and said with a smile:

At this point Shahrazād saw the approach of morning and discreetly fell silent.

But when the five-hundred-and-twenty-ninth night had come

SHE SAID:

'Great-hearted King, lord, valorous lion, know that Allāh has answered your prayer for I am with child by you. The time of my deliverance is close. I cannot say whether I carry a little boy or a little girl below my heart; but know, also, that if I had not become pregnant by you, I had resolved never to speak a word for the rest of my life.'

When his ears were rejoiced by these unhoped for syllables, the King himself, for very delight, could find no words to say; but his face lighted up and was transfigured, his breast swelled, and he felt himself lifted from the earth by the explosion of his joy. He kissed the girl's hands and head and brow, crying: 'Glory be to Allāh who has granted me the two wishes of my heart, O dear light of my eyes: for I have heard you speak and I have heard you say that you are with child. Glory and praise and thanks to Allāh!'

The King rose and, taking a moment's leave from his mistress, went and sat upon the throne of his kingdom in great delight. He ordered his wazīr to announce the cause of his joy to all the people and to distribute a hundred thousand dīnārs to the poor, to the widows and those who were otherwise in want, as a token of his gratitude to Allāh (may His name be exalted!). These things were done.

The King then returned to his beautiful slave and, sitting beside her, pressed her to his heart, saying: 'O my mistress, queen of my life and soul, now will you tell me why you kept silence, before me and mine, for a whole year and why to-day you made up your mind to speak to me?' 'O King,' answered the girl, 'why would I not keep silence when I came here as a poor stranger with a broken heart and stayed here as a slave, for ever parted from my mother and my brother, and far from the place of my birth?' Then said the King: 'I understand your sorrows and I feel them with you; but how can you speak of being a poor stranger and a slave when you are mistress and queen of this palace and of all I have, and of myself, the King? These are harsh words. If you were sad at being separated from the folk of your house, you had but to tell me and I would have sent to fetch them.'

The beautiful slave made answer: 'O King, I am called Gulnār, which means, in the language of my country, Pomegranate-Flower. I was born in the sea and my father was King of the sea. After he died, a day came when I had occasion of complaint against my mother, whose name is Locust, and my brother, whose name is Sālih. I therefore swore that I would stay no longer in the sea, but would climb on to the land and give myself to the first man who pleased me. One night, when the Queen and my brother had gone to rest early and our palace was plunged in that great silence which obtains below the sea, I slipped from my chamber and, climbing up to the surface of the water, lay down upon the shore of an island in the moonlight. A delicious freshness falling from the stars and the kisses of the land breeze wooed me to sleep; but I awoke suddenly in the grip of a man who, in spite of my struggles, lifted me on his back and carried me to a hut. There he stretched me on my back and would have abused me by force, but I, since he was ugly and evil-smelling, gathered my strength together and hit him so violent a blow in the face that he rolled at my feet. I threw myself upon him and gave him such a thrashing that he no longer wished to keep me, but led me hastily to the market and sold me to the merchant from whom you bought me. My purchaser, who was an excellent and up-right man, refrained from taking my virginity because I was so young; instead, he journeyed with me and led me to you. Such is my story. When I first came into this pavilion, I was resolved not to let myself be touched and had determined, at your first violence, to throw myself through the window into the sea and go to seek my mother and brother. It was through pride that I kept silence all this time. When I saw that you loved me truly and had left all your favourites for my sake, I began to be won over by your kindness and, seeing at length that I was with child by you, began to love you and to put aside all thoughts of escape. For one thing, I would not now have the courage to go back to the sea, where my mother and my brother might die of grief on hearing of my union with an earth dweller and might not believe me when I told them that I had be-come the Queen of Persia and Khurāsān, the wife of the most auspicious of all Kings. That is all I have to say, O Shahrimān. And may Allāh bless you!'

At this point Shahrazād saw the approach of morning and discreetly fell silent.

But when the five-hundred-and-thirtieth night had come

SHE SAID:

After this recital, the King kissed his wife between the eyes, saying: 'Charming Pomegranate-Flower, sea dweller, marvellous princess, light of my eyes, these are strange things you tell me. After this, if you quitted me even for a moment, I would surely die . . . O Pomegranate-Flower, you have told me that you were born in the sea, that your mother Locust and your brother Sālih live in the sea and that your father was King of the sea; but I know nothing of the lives of mermen and have considered all tales about them as old wives' tales. Since you tell me that you are a native of the sea, I now know that such exist and beg you to make me better acquainted with the customs of your race. Tell me, for instance, how a human being can live or move in the water without suffocating or drowning; for that is a most prodigious thing.'

Then said Pomegranate-Flower: 'I will certainly tell you all I know: thanks to the virtue of the names engraven on the seal of Sulaimān ibn Dāūd (prayer and peace be upon him!) we live and walk at the bottom of the sea just as you live and walk on land; we breathe the water as you breathe the air; and the water nourishes our life and does not even wet our garments; it does not prevent us from seeing, or keeping our eyes open; indeed our eyes are so excellent that they can pierce the long vistas of the sea and observe as well by the drowned rays of the sun as by the reflection of the moon and stars in the water. Our kingdom is much larger than all the kingdoms of the earth and is divided into provinces, each of which contains great and populous cities. The peoples differ as on earth in manners and appearance: some are fishes, some are half fishes and half men, having a tail instead of legs and a backside, and others again, like myself, have perfect human form, believe in Allāh and His Prophet, and speak that language which is graven upon the seal of Sulaimān. We live in splendid palaces whose architecture has no equal on the land. Our homes are fashioned of rock crystal, mother-of-pearl, coral, emerald, ruby, gold and silver; but pearls, however great and beautiful, are of little account with us; the hovels of the poor are built of them. Because our bodies are dowered with marvellous agility, we have no need of horses and chariots; though we keep such in our stables for public festivals and far journeys. The chariots are made of mother-of-pearl and gold, with seats of diamond; and our water horses are finer than any king has upon the earth ... But, O King, I do not wish to speak any more just now of the sea countries, for I trust that Allāh will give us a long life together in which to talk at greater length on these interesting matters. For the moment I wish to touch on a more pressing theme, the lying-in of women. Our confinements in the sea are different from yours on land, and, as my own time is near, I am afraid that your midwives will deliver me wrongly. I beg you, therefore, to let me send for my mother Locust, my brother Sālih, and the other folk of my house; so that, after I have been reconciled with them, my cousins and my mother may watch over my confinement and care for our child, the heir to your illustrious throne.'

At this point Shahrazād saw the approach of morning and discreetly fell silent.

But when the five-hundred-and-thirty-first night had come

SHE SAID:

The King marvelled and made answer: 'O Pomegranate-Flower, your wishes are my law and I am the slave of your commands; but tell me, O marvel of nature, how we can possibly let your mother, your brother, and your cousins know in time for your confinement? Even if that is possible, I wish you had told me earlier, for then I could have made the necessary preparations to receive them fittingly.' 'Dear master,' replied the young Queen, 'there is no need of ceremony with my people. Also they will be here in a very few moments. If you wish to see the manner of their arrival, go into the next room and watch both the sea and myself.'

King Shahrimān entered the neighbouring room and took up a position from which he could watch both what Pomegranate-Flower was going to do and anything which might happen upon the sea.

Pomegranate-Flower drew from her bosom two little slips of Comorin aloe wood, placed them in a gold brazier, and set fire to them. When the smoke began to rise, she gave a long shrill whistle and murmured some unknown words of conjuration above the brazier. At once the sea was troubled and opened in the midst; from the division there rose up a very handsome youth with something of the look of Pomegranate-Flower. His cheeks were white and rose; his hair and light moustaches were sea green and, as the poet says, he was more wonderful than the moon, for the moon dwells in but one sign of the sky and the boy owns all the houses of the hearts of men. After him rose a very old woman with white hair, who was none other than Queen Locust, and she was immediately followed by five girls of moon-like beauty, who were the cousins of Pomegranate-Flower and a little resembled her. The youth and the six women walked upon the surface of the sea until they were beneath the windows of the pavilion; then they leapt upwards, as light as foam, and jumped, one after another, through the window, from which Pomegranate-Flower drew back to let them pass.

Prince Sālih and his mother and the cousins threw themselves upon Pomegranate-Flower's neck and kissed her with tears of joy. 'O Gulnār,' they said, 'how could you have the heart to leave us for four years without news of you, to let us weary in ignorance of where you were? The sea grew small before our eyes because of our grief, we had no pleasure in eating or drinking, for our sorrow took savour from the food. We wept and sighed both day and night, so that our faces have grown thin and yellow.' On hearing these reproaches, Pomegranate-Flower kissed the hands of her mother and brother, and embraced her cousins again, saying: 'I was guilty of a great fault against your tenderness when I left you without warning. But who can fight against her Destiny? Let us now rejoice that we have again found each other and give thanks to Allāh.' She made them sit beside her and told them her whole story from beginning to end; but nothing would be gained by repeating it in this place. 'And now,' she said, 'that I am married to this kind and excellent King, now that we love each other, now that I am with child by him, I have sent for you that we may be reconciled and that you may help me in my confinement. I have no confidence in earthly midwives, for they do not understand the women of the sea.' Then said Queen Locust: 'My child, seeing you in an earthly palace we were afraid that you might be unhappy and were ready to persuade you to return with us; for the whole goal of our love is to see you joyful. But, since you tell us you are happy, we have no more to wish. Without doubt it would have been tempting Destiny to marry you with one of our sea princes in its despite.' 'As Allāh lives,' answered Pomegranate-Flower, 'my happiness is now perfect. All delight, honour, and tranquillity is mine and I have come to the end of my desires.'

At this point Shahrazād saw the approach of morning and discreetly fell silent.

But when the five-hundred-and-thirty-second night had come

SHE SAID:

The King heard every word of Pomegranate-Flower and, in his joy, learned to love her a thousand times better than before. His passion became the eternal fruit of his heart and he determined to give new proofs of it in every possible way.

Pomegranate-Flower summoned her slaves with a clap of the hands and bade them set the cloth, while she herself went to the kitchen and superintended the cooking of a feast. When great dishes of roast meats, pastry, and fruit had been assembled, she begged the folk of her house to eat. But for the moment they refused, saying: 'We can do nothing until you have told the King, your husband, that we are here. We have entered his dwelling without leave and he does not know us; therefore it would be great incivility to leave him in ignorance while we enjoyed his hospitality. Go and tell him how happy we will be to see him and to take bread and salt in his presence.'

Pomegranate-Flower sought the King, who was hidden in the next room, and said to him: 'Dear master, you have doubtless heard the praises which I sang of you to my mother, my brother, and the rest, and how I assured them of my happiness in all things, when they would have persuaded me to depart with them.' 'I both saw and heard,' answered the King. 'As Allāh lives, this is an hour of gold for me, now that I am certain of your love.' Then said Pomegranate-Flower: 'Hearing my praises, the folk of my house have become fond of you and I can assure you that they love you dearly. They say that they will not return to their own country until they have seen you and bowed before you and spoken with you as a friend. I beg you come in now, for they greatly desire it, and I wish to see you together in friendship and affection.' With that she led the King into the next room.

He wished the strangers peace most cordially; he kissed the hand of old Locust, embraced Prince Sālih, and begged the company to be seated. Then Prince Sālih expressed in complimentary words the delight of all at seeing Pomegranate-Flower the wife of a great king, and not the plaything of some brutal sultan, who would have deflowered her and then given her to his chamberlain or his cook. He told how greatly they loved Pomegranate-Flower and how, even before she had become a woman, they had wished to marry her to some prince of the sea. 'But Destiny sent her from the waters to the shores,' he added, 'and she has married according to the teaching of her heart.' Then said the King: 'Surely Allāh destined her for me from the beginning! I thank you all for your approval and consent.' After that he made them sit with him about the cloth and talked with them for a long time while they ate. Then he himself led them to their apartments.

Pomegranate-Flower's family stayed in the palace amid special festivity and rejoicing until the queen lay in. At the time appointed she gave birth, between the hands of the old queen and her cousins, to a plump and rosy man-child, who shone with the brightness of the full moon. This infant was carried to Shahrimān, his father, wrapped in magnificent linens, and the King's joy on seeing him was such as neither tongue nor pen can tell. As a thank-offering to Allāh, he gave great alms to the poor, the widows and the orphans; he opened the prisons, and would have freed all his slaves, but they refused to be freed, as they were too happy under such a master. After seven days of unclouded rejoicing, Queen Pomegranate-Flower, with her husband's consent, called the child Badr Basīm or Smile-of-the-Moon.

At this point Shahrazād saw the approach of morning and discreetly fell silent.

But when the five-hundred-and-thirty-third night had come

SHE SAID:

After the naming, Prince Sālih, brother of Pomegranate-Flower and uncle of Badr Basīm, took the little one in his arms and, kissing him in a thousand fashions, carried him up and down the room and lifted him high in the air in his hands. Suddenly he leapt through the window into the sea and disappeared with the child.

King Shahrimān uttered cries of despair and beat himself so violently about the head that he nearly died of it; but Pomegranate-Flower, without the least sign of affliction, reassured him calmly: 'O King of time, do not despair for so small a thing; do not be afraid for your son; for I, who love him even more than you, remain perfectly calm, since I know that my brother would not have done as he has done if it were possible for the little one to suffer or catch cold or even get wet. Although our son is half of your blood he runs no danger in the sea, for he inherits from me the ability to live as easily in the water as on land. I am quite sure that my brother will soon return and the child be none the worse.' Queen Locust and the young aunts confirmed these words; but the King was not utterly reassured until he saw the sea open and Prince Sālih emerge with the baby in his arms. The young man leapt from the sea to the window, and, when he entered the room, it was seen that the child lay as peacefully as if in the breast of its mother, and indeed was smiling like the moon. As the King marvelled and rejoiced once more, Prince Sālih said to him: 'O King, I conceive that you were very frightened when I jumped into the sea with this small one?' 'That was I, O uncle of my son,' answered the King. 'I despaired of ever seeing him again.' Then said Prince Sālih: 'Henceforward you need have no fear, for he is now safe from all the dangers of water, from drowning, from suffocation, even from wetting; for the rest of his life he will be able to leap into the sea and use it as his natural element, since, by means of a certain marine kohl which I have smeared upon his eyelids, and the mystery of the Words of the seal of Sulaimān which I have spoken over him, he has now the same birthright as the children of the sea.'

Prince Sālih handed the child back to his mother, who gave him suck; then he drew a sealed bag from his belt and, opening it, turned out the contents upon the carpet. The King saw, blazing before his eyes, diamonds as great as pigeons' eggs, ingots of emerald half a foot long, strings of mighty pearls, rubies of an unknown red, and the thousand fires of marine gems; so that the room shone with those fantastic lights which are seen in dreams. 'This is a present to excuse my empty hands,' said the Prince. 'When I came, I did not know where my sister was or that a happy destiny had led her to such a king. These gems are trifles to those which I will bring you when I have time.' The King did not know how to thank his brother-in-law for this gift, so he turned to his wife, saying: 'I am confused by your brother's magnificent generosity: each one of these stones is worth my kingdom.' Pomegranate-Flower thanked her brother and said to the King: 'As Allāh lives, these things are not worthy of your rank. We will never know how to pay our debt to you; even if we slaved for you a thousand years we should not be quit of our obligation.'

The King warmly kissed Prince Sālih and insisted that he, his mother, and his cousins should stay for another forty days at the palace, feasting and rejoicing.

At the end of that time Prince Sālih presented himself before the King and kissed the earth between his hands. 'What do you wish, my brother?' asked Shahrimān; and the merman answered: 'O King of time, though we are drowned in your favours, we wish to ask leave to depart, for our souls yearn towards our native sea. Also you must know that too long a stay on earth is bad for our health, since our bodies are habituated to the water.'

At this point Shahrazād saw the approach of morning and discreetly fell silent.

But when the five-hundred-and-thirty-fourth night had come

SHE SAID:

'This is a great grief to me, O Sālih,' said the King. 'And to us,' returned the prince, 'but we will return from time to time to bow before you and to visit Pomegranate-Flower and Badr Basīm.' 'Do so often, in Allāh's name!' exclaimed the King. 'I am indeed sad that I cannot accompany you all into your kingdom; but I have always been very much afraid of the water.' Then the sea dwellers took their leave and, leaping one by one through the window, disappeared below the waters.

Let us follow the fortunes of little Badr Basīm. As his mother did not wish to trust him to nurses, she gave him the breast herself until he was four years old; with the milk he sucked in all the qualities of the sea. Because of this marine nourishment, the little one became stronger and more beautiful every day; the years brought him every advantage; by the time he was fifteen he was the fairest and most muscular prince, the most adroit in bodily exercise, the wisest, and the most learned of his time. Throughout the mighty empire of his father none spoke save of his charm and elegance; for his was the true beauty. The poet did not exaggerate who said of him:

> Young down paints black upon his rose,
> Jade on his apple-flower,
> Grey amber on his sea-born pink.
>
> Until he bids
> His murderers leap on these or those,
> His murderers cower
> Behind his sleepy lids.

> Spent drinkers, if you seek
> A wilder and a sweeter drink,
> Look full upon his shapes
> Until
> Your longing and his shame distil,
> Stronger than grapes,
> A rose wine in his cheek.

> His lovers hold opposing creeds,
> Some say: lace-fine embroidery of night . . .
> I say it is a chaplet of musk beads
> Warm under crimson light.

When the King felt the end of his life draw near, he wished to make sure that his son, whom he loved dearly and in whom he saw so many royal qualities, should mount the throne; therefore he called together the wazīrs and nobles of his kingdom and made them swear obeisance to the worthy prince. Then he came down from his throne in the presence of all and, taking the crown from his head, set it upon the brows of his son and, holding the youth below the arms, caused him to sit upon the vacant seat. After this, to show that he had already transmitted all his power and authority, he kissed the earth between the boy's hands, kissed the hem of his royal robe, and went to stand upon his right hand.

At once the new King, Badr Basīm, with the wazīrs and amīrs upon his left, held the dīwān, promoting the worthy, setting down the false, defending the weak against the strong and the poor against the rich, with so much equity and discernment that his father and the old wazīrs wondered to hear him.

At noon he went with his father to visit his mother, the Queen, wearing the gold crown of his royalty and shining with a splendour as of the moon. Seeing him so fair, his mother wept for joy and, throwing her arms about his neck, kissed him with great tenderness; then she knelt before him and wished him a prosperous reign, long life, and victory over all his enemies.

For a whole year the three lived together in great joy, surrounded by the love of their subjects; at the end of that time old Shahrimān felt his heart leap violently and had hardly time left for embracing his wife and son, and making them his last recommendations. He died in righteous calm and passed into the mercy of Allāh.

At this point Shahrazād saw the approach of morning and discreetly fell silent.

But when the five-hundred-and-thirty-fifth night had come

SHE SAID:

Pomegranate-Flower and Badr Basīm mourned bitterly for a month, without allowing any into their presence, and raised a worthy monument over the tomb of Shahrimān, endowing it with the goods of the dead King, for the benefit of the poor, the widow and the orphan. Queen Locust and the King's uncle, Prince Sālih, and the King's marine cousins, who had already paid many visits before the old man died, came to take part in the public woe and wept that they had not been in time to see his end. All the King's relations mourned together, consoling each other as best they could, until, after many weeks, they a little succeeded in making the young man forget and even persuaded him to occupy himself again in the affairs of his kingdom. Reluctantly he put on new royal robes worked with gold and diamonds and, setting the crown again upon his head, resumed the reins of justice and, for a further year, ruled admirably over his people.

One afternoon Prince Sālih, who had not visited his sister and nephew for some time, came up out of the sea and entered the chamber in which the two were sitting. Pomegranate-Flower embraced him, saying: 'How goes it with you, brother, and with my mother and cousins?' 'Dear sister,' he answered, 'all goes well with them, and their happiness is perfect save that they cannot see you and my nephew more often.' The brother and sister began to talk of one thing and the other, while they ate nuts and pistachios, and soon the prince began speaking in the very highest terms of his nephew Badr Basīm. As he expatiated on the boy's beauty, politeness, strength and wisdom, the young King, who was lying back with his head among the cushions of the couch, pretended to be asleep, as he did not wish to appear to be listening. Thus he heard all which passed between his mother and uncle.

Supposing the boy to be asleep, Prince Sālih began to speak more freely, and said: 'My sister, surely you are forgetting that your son is now seventeen, an age at which it is well to think of marriage? I myself, who know his strength and beauty, and also know that, at his age, there are desires which must be satisfied in one way or another, am afraid that some unpleasant things may happen to him. In my opinion it is necessary to find him an equal match with some princess of the sea.' 'That is also my opinion and chief wish,' answered Pomegranate-Flower. 'I have only one son and it is high time that he also had an heir. I beg you to recall to my memory the various daughters of our country, for I have been away from the sea so long that I do not remember which are beautiful and which are ugly.' Sālih began to enumerate various princesses of the sea, carefully weighing their qualities and showing their advantages and disadvantages; but at the name of each, Pomegranate-Flower would answer: 'No, I do not think that she would do; she has an unfortunate mother, or she has an unfortunate father, or she has a very long-tongued aunt, or her grandmother smells unpleasantly, or she is ambitious, or she has an empty eye.' In this way she found fault with all the princesses. Then said Sālih: 'You are quite right to be difficult in your choice of a bride for the King, since he has no equal either in the sea or upon the land; but I have already given you a list of all the possible princesses. There only remains one of whom I might speak; but I must be quite sure that my nephew is asleep, since there are good reasons why I should not speak of her in his hearing.'

At this point Shahrazād saw the approach of morning and discreetly fell silent.

But when the five-hundred-and-thirty-sixth night had come

SHE SAID:

Pomegranate-Flower went over to her son and felt him and listened to his breathing. The boy had eaten a plate of onions, a food of which he was very fond and which usually plunged him into deep slumber; therefore his mother was the more ready to believe in his pretended sleep and assured her brother that he might speak. Then said Sālih: 'Dear sister, I take this precaution because I wish to tell you of a sea princess whose hand it would be very difficult to obtain, because of her father. Nothing would be gained by my nephew hearing tell of her until the affair is certain; for love enters more often by the ear than by the eye, especially among us of the Faith, whose women wear the veil of decency.' 'You are right,' answered the Queen, 'love is at first a fountain of honey, but changes soon to a vast sea salt with loss. Tell me the name of the princess and her father.' 'Janharah, the Princess Jewel,' answered Sālih, 'daughter of King Samandal, or Salamander, the merman.'

'Ah, now I remember Princess Janharah!' cried Pomegranate-Flower. 'She was only a year old when I left the sea and she was more beautiful than any child of her age. She must have grown into a girl of surpassing loveliness.' 'That is more than true,' said Sālih, 'for her loveliness surpasses all that has yet been seen upon the earth or in the kingdoms of the sea. She is sweet, gentle, appetising, and of a strange charm; I do not think that there could be a complexion to equal hers, or hair, or eyes, or figure; I am sure at least that there will never be such a backside again, heavy, tender, firm and self-possessed, curved deliciously each way. Palm fronds are jealous of its balancing; when the girl turns it, antelopes and gazelles flee away; when she unveils it, the sun is put to shame; if she moves, she falls over; if she leans with it, she slays; if she sits down, the impression of her sitting may never be removed. Do you wonder that with such perfections she is called Janharah?' 'Her mother was inspired by Allāh to give her that name!' exclaimed Pomegranate-Flower. 'I choose her for my son's wife.'

During this conversation Badr Basīm pretended to be asleep, but all the time his soul rejoiced and his heart beat high with hope that he should possess the heavy charms of the Sea King's daughter.

But Sālih continued: 'What shall I say of her father, King Samandal? He is a gross and brutal man, one worthy of all detestation. He has already refused many princes who came as the suitors for his daughter, has broken their bones and cast them with ignominy from his palace. I do not dare to think what welcome he would give to our request. That is why I am doubtful about the matter.' 'The business is a delicate one,' said the Queen. 'We must ponder at length on it, and not shake the tree before the fruit is ripe.' 'Yes, let us each reflect and then speak together again,' agreed Sālih, and with that the conversation ceased, as Badr Basīm pretended to wake up.

The King rose as if he had heard nothing and quietly left the chamber; but already his heart was burning with love and crackled within him as if it had been laid on ardent coals.

At this point Shahrazād saw the approach of morning and discreetly fell silent.

But when the five-hundred-and-thirty-seventh night had come

SHE SAID:

He took care not to say a word of his feelings to his mother and uncle but, retiring early to rest, passed the night in a novel torment of love, revolving in his mind the best way of winning quickly to his desire, and not once closing his eyes in sleep. He rose at dawn and went to wake his uncle, who had passed the night in the palace. 'Uncle,' he said, 'I wish to walk on the sea shore this morning, for my breast is heavy and the breeze will lighten it. I pray you come with me.' Prince Sâlih consented and, leaping to his feet, left the palace with his nephew. For a long time they walked together on the beach without the young King saying a word to his uncle; he was pale and had tears in the corners of his eyes. At length he sat down on a rock and, looking out over the sea, made up this song and sang it:

> Though the flames lick my heart over
> And my soul is red with fever,
> If you gave me choice of water
> Or to see and burn for ever,
> Sure, my burning ghost would wander
> With a memory for lover,
> With the Jewel, with the daughter
> Of the Sea King Salamander.

When Prince Sâlih heard these sad verses, he beat his hands together in despair and cried: 'There is no God but Allâh and Muhammad is the Prophet of Allâh! There is no power or might save in Allâh! My child, I see that you heard my conversation with your mother, and I am sorry for it, since your heart is already engaged, although nothing is yet done about the difficult match.' 'I must have Princess Janharah and no other,' answered Badr Basîm. 'Without her I shall die.' 'Then, my child,' said Sâlih, 'let us go back to tell your mother and ask her leave for both of us to go down into the sea, to visit the kingdom of Samandal.' But the King cried: 'No, I do not wish to ask my mother for a permission which she will certainly not give. She will be afraid for me because King Samandal is rude and brutal; she will tell me that my kingdom cannot remain without a King, and that the enemies of my throne will take advantage of my absence. I know my mother.' Then he began to weep bitterly and added: 'I wish to go with you at once to this Samandal, without telling my mother. We can be back before she notices that I am gone.'

Prince Sālih saw that his nephew was set in his desire, so, being unwilling to add to his sorrow, he drew from his finger a ring carved with the sacred Names and placed it upon the young King's hand, saying: 'This is for your better protection beneath the water. I put my trust in Allāh, whatever may befall . . . Do as I do!' With that he sprang from the rock into the air, and Badr Basīm did the same. They both described a descending curve towards the sea and dived below its waves.

At this point Shahrazād saw the approach of morning and discreetly fell silent.

But when the five-hundred-and-thirty-eighth night had come

SHE SAID:

Sālih wished to show his nephew the place of his own dwelling, so that the old Queen, Locust, and the young Queen's cousins might have the joy of receiving him. Therefore, he led him first into the presence of his grandmother, as she sat among the cousins. When the old woman saw the boy, she sneezed with pleasure, and Badr Basīm went up and kissed her hand. Then his cousins embraced him with shrill cries of joy; and the old woman made him sit at her side and said, kissing him between the eyes: 'O joyous arrival! O day of milk! You light the home, my child! How is your mother, Pomegranate-Flower?' 'She is in excellent health and perfect happiness,' he answered. 'She has sent greeting by me to you and to my cousins.' You will notice that in this he lied, for he had not taken leave of his mother.

While Badr Basīm was being shown the marvels of the palace by his cousins, Prince Sālih told his mother of the love which had entered through the lad's ear at sole mention of the charms of Princess Janharah. 'He has come here with me to ask her hand from her father,' added the Prince.

The old woman became very angry with her son when she heard what had happened, and bitterly reproached him for having been so careless as to speak of Princess Janharah in the King's hearing. 'You know very well that this Samandal is a violent man,' she cried, 'and you know very well that he is arrogant and stupid, that out of greed for his daughter he has refused many princes; and yet you could do no better than to betray us into a position where there is every chance of our being humiliated by a denial and returning with our noses to the ground. In truth, my child, you should not have mentioned so much as the name of the girl in the boy's hearing, even if he had been put to sleep by a drug.' 'That is true,' admitted Sālih, 'but the thing is done now, and he so loves the girl that he swears that he will die if he does not possess her. And is there so much objection? Badr Basīm is at least as beautiful as the princess; he comes of an illustrious line of Kings and is himself the King of a powerful earthly empire. That foolish Samandal is not the only sultān in the world: what difficulties can he make which I cannot counter? He will tell me that his daughter is rich, our boy is richer; that his daughter is beautiful, our boy is more beautiful; that his daughter is well-born, our boy is better born. Believe me, dear mother, in the end I will convince him that he has all to gain and nothing to lose by such a match. I am the cause of this desire on the boy's part; therefore it is only right that I should be the negotiator, even if my bones are broken and I die for it.'

Seeing that there was nothing for it but to let the affair go on, the old Queen sighed and said: 'It would have been better had it never happened; but, since this love was destined, I will let you depart though much against my will. But I shall keep Badr Basīm with me until you return, for I cannot expose him to danger. Go then, and above all be careful of your words, in case some inapt syllable should enrage that brutal King; for there is no end to the impertinence with which he treats the world.'

Prince Sālih filled two large sacks with valuable presents and, loading them upon the backs of slaves, set out over the ocean road which led to the palace of King Samandal.

At this point Shahrazād saw the approach of morning and discreetly fell silent.

But when the five-hundred-and-thirty-ninth night had come

SHE SAID:

As soon as he reached the palace, Prince Sālih begged an audience, and this was granted him. He entered the hall and, finding the Sea King Samandal seated upon a throne of emerald and hyacinth, wished him peace with exquisite politeness and disposed the two sacks at his feet. The King returned peace and begged the prince to be seated, saying: 'Be welcome, Prince Sālih! I have not seen you for a long time and my heart has grieved therefor; tell me quickly for what you have come to ask; since he who gives a present expects a thing equivalent. Speak, and I will see if I cannot do something for you.' Sālih bowed low before the King, saying: 'It is true that I have a desire which can only be satisfied by Allāh and by the magnanimous King whom I see before me, the valiant lion, the generous man, whose glory, magnificence, liberality, politeness, mercy and goodness are known over all the lands and seas, and form a subject of admiring conversation at evening about the camp fires of the caravans.' King Samandal a little abated the terrible frown of his meeting brows, and answered: 'Make your request, O Sālih. It will enter a sympathetic ear and a heart very well disposed towards you. If I can grant it, I will do so without delay; if I cannot, the refusal will imply no ill-feeling. Allāh expects of no soul a content greater than its capacity.' Sālih bowed yet more deeply, saying: 'O King of time, the thing which I wish, you and only you can grant. I would not have dared to come and ask you for anything until I knew that it was within the compass of possibility. The wise have said: *If you would keep a friend, do not ask the impossible*, and I, O King (whom may Allāh preserve for the happiness of all), am neither pretentious nor a fool. Glorious monarch, I come only as an intermediary. I come, magnanimous Sultān, O generous, O greater than the greatest, to ask the hand of your pearl paragon, your priceless gem, your sealed treasure, your daughter, Princess Janharah, in marriage for my nephew, King Badr Basīm, son of King Shahrimān and Queen Pomegranate-Flower, master of White Town, head of all those kingdoms which stretch from the Persian frontier to the extreme bounds of Khurāsān!'

When he heard this, the Sea King Samandal laughed so heartily that he fell over on his backside and continued to kick his legs in the air in a convulsion of merriment. At last he sat up again and looked at Sālih in silence; but only to come out with a sudden: 'Ho, ho!' and fall into a second access of laughter, so loud and strong that it ended in a sounding fart. When he was calmer, he said: 'In truth, O Sālih, I always thought that you were a man of sense, but I see that I was mistaken. For where would be the sense in so preposterous a request?' Without losing countenance, Sālih replied: 'One thing at least is certain: King Badr Basīm, my nephew, is at least as beautiful as your daughter, at least as rich, and at least as well-born; if Princess Janharah is not intended for such a match, for what sort of match, in heaven's name, is she intended? A wise man has said: *For a girl there is but marriage or the tomb.* That is why there are no old maids among us Mussulmāns. I advise you to seize this opportunity of saving your daughter from the grave.' King Samandal's mirth changed to great anger. Leaping to his feet with contracted brows and blood in his eyes, he cried: 'O dog of men, is it for the like of you to speak even the name of my daughter? Are you not a dog and the son of a dog? What is your nephew? What was his father? Dogs and sons of dogs!' Then to his guards he cried: 'Lay hold of this pimp and break his bones!'

The guards rushed upon Sālih and would have seized him; but with the quickness of light he eluded them and fled through the palace door. When he had gained the open, he was astounded to see before him a thousand cavaliers upon sea horses, steel clad from head to foot, and all men of his own house. They had been sent by old Queen Locuṣt who, foreseeing her son's ill reception, had armed these thousand and despatched them after him in all haste.

In a few words the Prince told them what had happened and ended by crying: 'In upon this foolish King!' The warriors leapt from their horses, drew their swords, and rushed, a solid troop, into the throne-room on the heels of Prince Sālih.

At this point Shahrazād saw the approach of morning and discreetly fell silent.

But when the five-hundred-and-fortieth night had come

SHE SAID:

When King Samandal saw this torrent of enemies surging up about him like the shadows of night, he remained quite calm and called to his guards: 'Out upon this stinking buck and all his flock! Swords to their heads!'

Crying their war cries of: 'For Samandal!' 'For Sālih!' the opposing forces shocked together like the waves of a tumultuous sea. The hearts of Sālih's warriors were harder than rock, their turning blades called in the debts of Destiny. The valorous Sālih, the granite heart, the master of sword and lance, drove through necks and breasts, leaping to and fro with a vigour which would have overset mountains. What struggle and blood! What cries cut off by the points of the brown lances! What widowing! Steel crashed and bodies groaned with wounds, until all the lands below the sea re-echoed.

But what are swords against Fate, what shield is there against the writing of Allāh? After an hour the hearts of Samandal's men became even as clay pots, they lay thick in death about the throne. Then Samandal flew into such terrible anger that his remarkable testicles, which usually hung to his knees, were retracted to his navel. Frothing at the mouth, he rushed upon Sālih, who met him with the point of his lance, crying: 'O brutal and faithless, here is the shore of the last sea!' With a sounding blow he knocked him over on the earth and held him down, while his warriors bound him and fastened his arms behind his back. So much for them.

The first noises of the battle so terrified Princess Janharah that she fled away from the palace with one of her servants, a girl called Myrtle, and, passing over the floor of the sea, climbed to the surface of the water. In this way she arrived at a desert island and swarmed to the top of a leafy tree for safety, while Myrtle hid herself in the summit of another.

Destiny willed that much the same should take place at the palace of Queen Locust. The two slaves, who had borne the gifts for Prince Sālih, had run away at the beginning of the fight and hastened back to the Queen with news of the danger. Young Badr Basīm had become most anxious at their tidings, feeling that he was the cause of his uncle's predicament and this ocean war. Being a little frightened of his grandmother, he dared not show his face before her, thinking that she would hold him responsible should any terrible thing happen to Sālih. Therefore he took advantage of the old woman's preoccupation with the messengers to mount to the surface of the sea, meaning to return to his mother in the White Town. Not being certain of his direction, he lost his way and came to the same desert island which harboured Princess Janharah.

He was weary when he reached the beach, and lay down at the foot of a tree. He did not know that this was the tree in which Princess Janharah was hidden, for he did not know that each man's Destiny goes about with him, that it follows more quickly than the wind and that there is no rest for the pursued; he did not know that which had been laid up for him in the gulf of eternity.

He pillowed his head on his arms to sleep and, raising his eyes, saw the face of the princess, taking it to be the moon in the branches. 'Glory be to Allāh who has created the moon to light His evenings!' he cried and then, regarding the portent more carefully, recognised it as a girl's face, fairer than ever any moon had been.

At this point Shahrazād saw the approach of morning and discreetly fell silent.

But when the five-hundred-and-forty-first night had come

SHE SAID:

'As Allāh lives,' he cried, 'I will climb and catch her and ask her name; for she is strangely like the description which my uncle gave of Princess Janharah. Who knows if she be not the same? Perhaps she fled from her father's palace at the beginning of the fight.' He leapt to his feet in great emotion and, standing below the tree, lifted his eyes to the girl and said: 'O supreme goal of all desire, who are you and why are you mounted on a tree in this island?' The Princess leaned forward a little over the fair youth and, smiling at him, said in a voice which sang like water: 'O charming lad, O handsome, I am Princess Janharah, daughter of the Sea King Samandal. I am here because I have fled from my native land and the homes of my native land, and from my father, to escape the sad fate of the vanquished. By this time Prince Sālih will have made a slave of my father and killed all his guards. He will be hunting for me throughout the palace. Alas, alas, O hard exile! O my poor father! Alas, alas!' Large tears fell from her lovely eyes upon the King's face, so that he lifted his arms in love and cried: 'O Princess Janharah, soul of my soul, dream of my sleepless nights, come down, I pray. For I am King Badr Basīm, son of Pomegranate-Flower, a native of the sea. Come down, for your eyes have killed me, your beauty has led me captive.' As if in a trance of joy, the girl answered: 'Praise be to Allāh, O dear master! You are really handsome Badr Basīm, nephew of Sālih and son of Pomegranate-Flower?' 'I am, I am; therefore come down!' he answered, and she continued: 'How foolish was my father to refuse a suitor such as you! What better could he have hoped? Where, in sea or land, could he have found another King so charming and so fair? O my dear, think not too hardly of my father's folly, for I love you with all my heart. If your love is a span, mine is an arm-length. Since I saw you, love has eaten into my liver and I am the victim of your beauty.'

She slipped down the tree into the arms of the young King, who joyfully pressed her against his breast and kissed her everywhere, while she answered caress with caress and movement with movement. At this delightful contact Badr Basīm felt all the birds of the woods singing in his soul. Therefore he cried: 'Queen of my eyes, desirable princess, star who has led me away from my kingdom, my uncle Sālih did not tell me a fourth part of the truth; the other three parts of your beauty were unknown to me. He weighed before me a single carat out of the twenty-four, O all gold.' He went on covering her with kisses of a thousand kinds and then, burning to enjoy the benediction of her bottom, emboldened his hand to touch the tassels of the cords. As if to help him, the girl rose and, suddenly stretching forth her right hand, spat in his face, because she had no water, and cried: 'Creature of earth, leave the form of your humanity and become a great white bird with bill and feet of red!' Immediately the astonished King was changed into a white-feathered bird, with beak and claws of red, and heavy wings incapable of flight.

He stood looking at her with tears in his eyes, but she called her servant Myrtle, saying: 'Take this bird, who is none other than the nephew of my father's greatest enemy, the pimp who has been fighting against my father, and carry him to Dry Island, where he may die of hunger and thirst.'

At this point Shahrazād saw the approach of morning and discreetly fell silent.

But when the five-hundred-and-forty-second night had come

SHE SAID:

You will understand that Princess Janharah had only responded to the young King's passion in order to approach him unsuspected and change him into a bird. This she did to avenge her father and his warriors. When the girl Myrtle had taken up the bird, in spite of its harsh cries and the despairing beat of its wings, she felt pity and could not find it in her heart to carry it to a cruel death on Dry Island. Therefore she said to herself: 'I will take it to some other place, where it will not die but may await its Destiny. Perhaps when her anger is abated my mistress will repent; and then she would be angry at my too swift obedience.' With this possibility in mind, she carried the captive to a green isle, planted with fruit trees and watered by running streams and left it there. . . .

After Prince Sālih had bound King Samandal, he shut him in one of the apartments of the palace, and proclaimed himself ruler in his stead. He hunted all the palace for Princess Janharah, but could not find her. When he was certain that she had disappeared, he returned to his mother, Queen Locust, and told her what had happened, asking at the same time for his nephew. 'I think he is out walking with his cousins,' said the old woman. 'I will send to look for him.' While she was speaking, the cousins entered without the boy. Searchers were sent out into every part and, when they were unsuccessful, all in the palace wept sorely. King Sālih, with a heavy heart, sent a messenger to tell Queen Pomegranate-Flower of the loss.

In an agony of apprehension the young Queen dived into the sea and hurried to her mother's palace, where the old woman, with long preamble, tearful silences, and chorused by the sobbing of the cousins, told the whole story to her daughter. 'Your brother Sālih,' she added, 'who has been proclaimed King in the place of Samandal, has sent searchers in every direction, but we can hear nothing of either Badr Basīm or Princess Janharah.'

The water darkened before Pomegranate-Flower; her heart was filled with the emptiness of desolation; and for many days nothing was heard in that palace below the sea except the loud grief of women.

The grandmother was the first to dry her eyes. 'My daughter,' she said to Pomegranate-Flower, 'do not be too cast down by this misfortune, for there is no reason why your brother should not succeed in finding the lad. If you truly love him and would watch over his interests, you should return to your kingdom to rule in his place and keep his disappearance secret. Allāh will provide.' 'You are right, mother,' answered the Queen. 'I will return. But, oh, I beg you not to slacken your efforts for a moment, not to forget my son! If harm comes to him I will die, for I live my life through him.' 'I promise faithfully,' replied Queen Locust. 'Do not give way to fear, but keep as calm as you are able.' Then Pomegranate-Flower took leave of her mother, her brother and her cousins, and sadly returned to her own kingdom.

At this point Shahrazād saw the approach of morning and discreetly fell silent.

But when the five-hundred-and-forty-third night had come

SHE SAID:

Now let us return to the green island where the relenting Myrtle had left Badr Basīm, changed into a white bird with bill and feet of red.

When the bird saw the girl depart, he wept bitterly and then, being both hungry and thirsty, began to eat the fruits and drink the running water of the island, with mingled grief and astonishment to find himself in feathers. He tried his wings but they could not sustain him in the air, because of the heaviness of his body; so he resigned himself to Destiny, saying: 'How would it advantage me to leave this place since no one would recognise me for what I am?' He stayed sadly in the isle and at evening perched in a tree to sleep. One day, as he waddled about with lowered head, he was seen by a fowler who had rowed to the island to spread his nets. The man was delighted at the magnificent appearance of this quite unknown bird, whose scarlet beak and claws shone so brilliantly against the whiteness of his plumes. With manifold precautions and slow skill he came up behind his quarry and cleverly caught it in his net. Then, rich in this noble game, he returned to the city from which he had come, carrying the bird carefully over his shoulder by the legs.

As he reached home he said to himself: 'I have never seen a bird like this in all the years of my hunting; I will not sell it to an ordinary purchaser, who would not know its value and might kill it for his family to eat; rather I will take it as a present to the King, who will marvel at its beauty and pay me handsomely.' Acting on this thought, he made his way to the palace and there, sure enough, the King was delighted with the bird, because of its scarlet and white colour, and gave the fowler ten gold dīnārs and sent him on his way.

The King had a great cage constructed of gold wire and, shutting the bird within, himself offered it maize and corn; but it would not eat. 'I must try something else,' said the astonished Sultān, and took the bird out of the cage again and set white of chicken, slices of meat, and pleasant fruits before it. At once the bird began to eat with obvious pleasure, giving little cries of satisfaction and ruffling its white plumes. This delighted the King, who cried to one of his slaves: 'Run and tell your mistress that I have bought a prodigious bird, one of the marvels of time; beg her to come and admire it with me and to see the marvellous way in which it eats food which ordinary birds would not touch.' So the slave hastened to tell the Queen, and she came.

But, as soon as she saw the bird, the Queen covered her face with her veil and, retiring indignantly towards the door, would have escaped from the chamber. The King ran after her and held her back by her veil, crying: 'Why do you cover your face, when only I and the eunuchs and your women are present before you?' 'This bird is not a bird, O King,' she answered, 'he is a man, even as you are. He is King Badr Basīm, son of King Shahrimān and Pomegranate-Flower; he was changed into this shape by Princess Janharah, daughter of the Sea King Samandal, because of the victory which his uncle, Sālih, had won over her father.'

'Allāh confound this Princess Janharah and all her works!' cried the bewildered King. 'Tell me the details of the affair, my Queen, in Allāh's name.' Then the Queen, who was the most redoubtable magician of her time, told her husband the whole story. After listening attentively, he turned to the bird, saying: 'Is this true?' and the bird nodded its head, beating its wings.

At this point Shahrazād saw the approach of morning and discreetly fell silent.

But when the five-hundred-and-forty-fourth night had come

SHE SAID:

Then said the King to his wife: 'By my life, and in Allāh's name, my dear, hasten to remove this enchantment; do not let him stay in torment.' So the Queen, after quite covering her face, said to the bird: 'Enter this large cupboard, O Badr Basīm.' The bird at once obeyed by walking into a closet concealed in the wall, the door of which the Queen opened for him. She followed, carrying a cup of water in her hand, and no sooner had she spoken unknown words above it than the water began to boil. At once she sprinkled a few drops on the bird's head, saying: 'By the Magic Names, by the Words of Power, by the Majesty of the Omnipotent Who created the sky and the earth, Who raises the dead, Who gives His destinies to man, I conjure you to leave this present form and to turn back to the shape He made!'

At once the young King trembled, shivered, and returned to his manhood; and immediately the older King, seeing a youth of un-equalled beauty, cried out on the name of Allāh that the lad was well named.

When he was a little recovered from his emotion, Badr Basīm exclaimed: 'There is no God but Allāh and Muhammad is the Prophet of Allāh!' and, going up to the King, kissed his hand and wished him a long life. In his turn the King kissed the lad's head, saying: 'Badr Basīm, I pray you tell me all your story, from your birth until to-day.' So Badr Basīm told his story, without omitting a single detail, and greatly astonished his host with it.

As soon as the recital was over, the King asked the boy what he could do for him, and the other answered: 'O Sultān of time, I would return to my own kingdom; for I have already been long absent from it and I fear that enemies of my throne may be leaguing together to usurp my place. Also my mother must be in great grief and anxiety because of me, and I would not have these prolonged.' Touched by the youth, beauty and filial piety of his suppliant, the King immediately prepared a boat, filling it with his own provisions and tackle, sailors and captain, and sent Badr Basīm on board with a kind farewell.

The youth trusted to his Destiny; but Fate had more adventures yet in store for him. When they were five days out, a furious tempest rose against the ship and broke her upon a rocky coast. Out of all the ship's company only the young King, who as we know was impervious to the seas, managed to save himself alive by swimming to the shore.

When he began to look about him on the beach, he saw a tall city, like a very white dove, brooding over the sea from the top of a mountain. And, down this mountain side, he perceived rushing towards him, with a rapidity of a hurricane, a galloping troop of horses, mules and asses, as many as there were sands upon the beach. This frightened troop halted all about him, and the asses, horses and mules began to make signs at him with their heads, which seemed to signify: 'Return from whence you came.' When he showed that he intended to remain, the horses began to neigh, the mules to breathe heavily, and the asses to bray; but these neighings, breathings and brayings were very sad and full of despair. Some of the animals even began to snuffle and weep; others gently pushed the youth towards the sea with their muzzles; but he would not be driven. Instead of retreating, he advanced towards the city; and all the four-footed beasts accompanied him, some walking in front and some behind in a manner most suggestive of a funeral procession. This impression became all the stronger when Badr Basīm recognised, as it were beneath the noises which they made, a vague chanting such as readers of the Koran utter above the dead.

At this point Shahrazād saw the approach of morning and discreetly fell silent.

But when the five-hundred-and-forty-fifth night had come

SHE SAID:

Not knowing whether he was asleep or awake, sometimes supposing that he was suffering a vision of fatigue, Badr Basīm walked up the hill as a man walks in dreams. Entering the city, he beheld an old man with a white beard, sitting before the door of a druggist's shop. He wished the old man peace, and the latter, charmed by his beauty, rose up to answer his greeting. Then he signed with his hand for the animals to be gone, and they went away slowly, turning their heads from time to time in an intensity of regret.

Badr Basīm told the old man his story in a few words and then asked: 'Venerable uncle, what is this city and what are these strange animals who followed me here lamenting?' 'First come into my shop and sit down,' answered the sheikh. 'When you have eaten, I will tell you all I can.' He led the youth to a dīwān at the back of the shop and brought him food and drink. When he was refreshed, he kissed him between the eyes, saying: 'Give thanks to Allāh, my child, that you met me before seeing the Queen of this place. I did not speak of her before as I did not wish to spoil your appetite . . . This city is called the City of Enchantments; it is ruled over by Queen Almanākh, a sorceress of extraordinary power, a devil in the body of a woman. Her desire never ceases to burn, so that each time a young, strong and handsome stranger comes to this island, she seduces him and makes him mount her an infinity of times, for forty days and nights. By the end of that period he is completely worn out, and she changes him into an animal; in his new form he recovers and adds to his strength and then she transforms herself into a female of his species, a mare or ass perhaps, and is again mounted repeatedly. After that she resumes her human shape and makes new lovers, new victims, of those she can find. There come nights when her desire burns so hotly that she is mounted one after another by every animal on the island. Such is her life.

'I love you with a great love, my child, and would not wish to see you fall into the hands of this unappeased enchantress, who lives only for those things which I have told you. You are more beautiful than any other youth who has come to this island and, therefore, God alone knows what might happen if Queen Almanākh saw you! Those asses, mules and horses, who rushed down the mountain side to meet you, are the other youths who have been changed by the sorceress. Seeing you young and beautiful, they had pity on you and wished to persuade you to go back into the sea; then, as you would not do so, they accompanied you here, singing the rites of funeral over you in their own way.

'Yet, my son, to live with Queen Almanākh would not be an unpleasant thing, were it not for the trick which she plays on her lovers in the end. Now I am a man whom she both fears and respects, because she knows that I am more learned in the arts of sorcery and enchantment than she. But I assure you, my child, that I am a believer in Allāh and his Prophet (upon whom be prayer and peace!) and make no use of my magic to do evil, for evil ever returns against the evil-doer.'

Hardly had the old man finished speaking when a brilliant troop of a thousand girls, dressed in purple and gold, came towards the shop and ranged themselves in two lines in front of the door, to admit the passage of a young woman, more beautiful than them all, mounted upon a diamond-harnessed arab. Queen Almanākh, for it was. she, dismounted outside the shop, with the help of two slaves who held the bridle of her horse, and, entering, saluted the old apothecary with marked respect. Then she seated herself on the dīwān and looked at Badr Basīm with half-closed eyes.

At this point Shahrazād saw the approach of morning and discreetly fell silent.

But when the five-hundred-and-forty-sixth night had come

SHE SAID:

And what a look that was: long and piercing, sweet and shining! Badr Basīm felt himself transfixed as by a javelin or heated sword; but presently the young Queen turned to the sheikh, saying: 'O Abd al-Rahmān, where did you find such a youth?' 'He is my brother's son,' answered the old man. 'He has come to visit me.' Then said she: 'He is very beautiful; would you be willing to lend him to me for one night only? I will simply talk with him; you can have him back intact in the morning.' 'Will you swear not to try your sorcery upon him?' asked Abd al-Rahmān, and she replied: 'I swear it before the Master of Magic and before you, venerable uncle.' With that she gave the old man a thousand gold dīnārs to show her gratitude and, mounting Badr Basīm upon a wonderful horse, rode with him to the palace. Upon the way he looked like a moon riding among stars.

The young King, who was determined to let Destiny have its course, said no word and allowed himself to be taken along, without showing his feelings in any way.

Almanākh the sorceress, who felt her entrails burning for this youth more than they had ever burned before, hastened him into a hall with walls of solid gold, the air of which was refreshed by a fountain falling into a basin of turquois. She threw herself with him upon a large ivory bed and began to caress him in so strange a fashion that all the birds of his being danced and sang. She was not brutal but very delicate; incalculable for number and variety were the assaults of this cock upon that indefatigable hen. 'As Allāh lives,' he said to himself, 'she is infinitely expert. She does not bustle me; she takes her time and gives me mine. I am sure that Princess Janharah cannot be so marvellous; I would wish to stay here all my life without a thought of my kingdom or of Samandal's daughter.'

In fact he stayed forty days and forty nights, passing the time with the young magician in feasting, dancing, singing, kissing, moving, mounting, coupling and the like; so that pleasure was added to joy and joy to pleasure.

From time to time Almanākh would say as a jest: 'O eye of mine, would you rather be with your uncle in his shop?' and he would answer: 'As Allāh lives, my mistress, my uncle is a poor seller of drugs, but you are the elixir of life itself!'

When the evening of the fortieth day had come, Almanākh seemed more agitated than usual by the great number of their couplings. She lay down to sleep; but at midnight Badr Basīm, who pretended to be sleeping at her side, saw her rise from the bed with her face on fire from some emotion. She went to the middle of the hall and, taking a handful of barley from a copper tray, threw it into the water of the fountain. After a few moments the barley germinated, stalks came up out of the water; their ears ripened and turned gold. Then the sorceress gathered the new grains and, after pounding them in a marble mortar, mixed with them certain powders taken from boxes. From this paste she kneaded a cake which she cooked slowly on the hot coals of a stove and, wrapping in a napkin, shut away in a cupboard. Finally she returned to the bed and slept.

In the morning Badr Basīm, who had forgotten old Abd al-Rahmān, called him to mind and decided that it would be as well to inform him of the Queen's actions during the night. He therefore made his way to the shop, where the old man embraced him with effusion and bade him be seated, saying: 'I trust, my son, that you have nothing to complain of in the sorceress Almanākh, although she is an unbeliever.' 'As Allāh lives, good uncle,' answered the boy, 'she has always treated me with great delicacy, in no way forcing me; but last night, seeing her rise from our bed with an inflamed face, I pretended to be asleep and beheld her at a business which frightened me. I have come to consult you about it.' And he told the old man of his mistress's nocturnal practice.

At this point Shahrazād saw the approach of morning and discreetly fell silent.

But when the five-hundred-and-forty-seventh night had come

SHE SAID:

Abd al-Rahmān grew very angry, and cried: 'O wicked and per-jured woman, is this how you keep an oath? Will nothing hold you from your accursed magic? It is time that I drew towards an end with you.' He took from a cupboard a cake similar in every way to that made by the sorceress and, wrapping it in a handkerchief, gave it to Badr Basīm, with these words: 'This cake will make her mischief recoil on her own head; for it is with such cakes that she transforms her lovers after their forty days. You must be careful not to eat a crumb of the one she gives you and must bring it about that she eats some of this. When she has eaten, do and say all she has done and said in trying to magic you; thus you will be able to change her into any animal you please. As soon as she is transformed, get on her back and bring her to me. I will know what to do with her.' The young King thanked the kindly sheikh and returned to the palace.

There he found Almanākh waiting for him in the garden, seated before a loaded cloth, which bore her midnight cake upon a dish in the middle. When she complained of his absence, he answered: 'Dear mistress, I had not seen my uncle for a long time, so I went to visit him. He received me very kindly and gave me food: among other things, there were certain cakes which tasted so delicious that I could not help bringing you one.' So saying, he took the cake out of its wrapping, and the Queen, who did not want to anger him as yet, broke off a morsel and swallowed it. Then she offered her cake to Badr Basīm, who took a piece of it, which he let slip into the opening of his garment while making a feint to swallow it.

At once the sorceress, thinking that he had eaten of the cake, rose swiftly and sprinkled him with a little water from a nearby fountain, crying: 'O weakened youth, become a powerful ass!'

Great was her astonishment when she saw the young man, instead of turning to an ass, rise in his turn and sprinkle her with the water, crying: 'O traitress, become an ass!' Before she could recover from her surprise, Almanākh became an ass; and the prince, leaping upon her back, rode her to the shop of Abd al-Rahmān. He handed over the ass to the old man, while she kicked and struggled in anger.

The sheikh passed a double chain about the beast's neck and fixed it to a ring in the wall. Then he said: 'Now, my child, I must occupy myself in restoring the affairs of our city to order. I will begin by turning back all those poor young men into their original shapes; but before I start on that work, though I am very loath to be separated from you, I am willing to send you back to your kingdom by the shortest road, so that the people there may throw aside their grief.'

The old man put two fingers between his lips and gave a long, loud whistle, which conjured up a mighty four-winged Jinnī. This appearance stood on the point of his toes and asked why he had been summoned. 'O Light,' commanded the sage, 'you will take King Badr Basīm upon your shoulders and carry him carefully to his palace in White Town!' The Jinnī called Light bent down with lowered head and the young King, after kissing the hand of his preserver, mounted upon the Ifrīt's shoulders and held about his neck. The Jinnī rose in the air and flew off as swiftly as a carrier-dove, making a noise with his wings as of a windmill. Tirelessly he journeyed for a day and night, covering a distance of six months, and, coming to White Town, set down his burden upon the terrace of the palace. Then he disappeared.

At this point Shahrazād saw the approach of morning and discreetly fell silent.

But when the five-hundred-and-forty-eighth night had come

SHE SAID:

Badr Basīm, his heart uplifted by the breezes of his native land, hastened to find the room in which his mother now used to weep quietly, hiding the cause of her sorrow for fear of usurpers. He raised the curtain and saw, not only his mother, but also old Queen Locust, King Sālih and the cousins, who had all come to visit Pomegranate-

Flower in her affliction. He entered, wishing them peace, and ran to throw his arms about his mother's neck. She fainted with joy on beholding him, but soon recovered and wept long upon his breast; while the cousins embraced his feet, his grandmother held one of his hands, and his uncle the other. They stood thus for some minutes in so great a joy that none of them could speak; but, when at last they could find words, they mutually told of their adventures and thanked Allāh together for their reunion.

Later, Badr Basīm turned to his mother and grandmother, saying: 'Now only remains that I should marry. I still wish for Princess Janharah; for she is a Jewel indeed.' 'The matter is easy now, my child,' answered Queen Locust, 'for we hold her father prisoner in his palace.' At once she sent for Samandal; but when slaves dragged him in, chained both hand and foot, the young King ordered him to be freed.

Then the youth went up to the sea King and, after begging to be excused if he had been the cause of those first misfortunes, respectfully kissed his hand. 'O King Samandal,' he said, 'it is no longer an intermediary who begs for the honour of alliance with you; it is I, Badr Basīm, King of White Town and of a great empire, asking for the hand of your daughter in marriage. If you do not give her to me, I shall die; but if you consent, I will be your slave and restore your kingdom to you.'

Samandal embraced the youth and answered: 'O Badr Basīm, no one deserves her more, and, as she is a dutiful daughter, she will accept your suit with great pleasure. Now she must be sent for from the isle in which she is hidden.' He called up a messenger from the sea and sent him to find the princess. The merman disappeared and shortly returned with Princess Janharah and the girl Myrtle.

King Samandal embraced his daughter and, after presenting her to Queen Locust and Queen Pomegranate-Flower, pointed with his finger to Badr Basīm, who stood there dumb with admiration. 'My daughter,' he said, 'I have promised you to this great-hearted young King, this valiant lion, this son of Pomegranate-Flower; for he is not only the handsomest youth of his time, but the most charming, the most powerful, the highest in rank and in nobility and, in fact, in everything. I consider that you are made for each other.'

At this point Shahrazād saw the approach of morning and discreetly fell silent.

But when the five-hundred-and-forty-ninth night had come

SHE SAID:

Princess Janharah modestly lowered her eyes at her father's words, and answered: 'Your suggestions, dear father, are my rule of life; your vigilant affection is the shade in which I take my pleasure. Since you desire it, the image of this man shall henceforth be ever before my eyes, his name upon my lips, and his dwelling in my heart.'

When the young King's cousins and the other women heard this answer, they filled the palace with the shrill cries of their pleasure. King Sālih and Pomegranate-Flower sent at once for the kādī and witnesses to write the marriage contract, and the bridal was celebrated with such pomp and magnificence that, in the ceremony of clothing, the garments of the bride were changed nine times. As for the other magnificence of that occasion, the tongue would become hairy in telling of it. So glory be to Allāh, Who unites beauty with beauty and holds back joy only that it may become greater!

When Shahrazād had finished this tale, she fell silent. Then cried little Dunyazād: 'Dear sister, your words are sweet, tender, and savoury! That was an admirable tale.' And King Shahryār said: 'Indeed, Shahrazād, you have taught me many things which I did not know. The tales of Sea Abdallāh and Pomegranate-Flower have delighted me with their descriptions of that kingdom under the water. Do you not know some altogether devilish tale?' Shahrazād smiled and answered: 'O King, I know an altogether devilish tale and will tell it to you at once.'

Ishāk's Winter Evening

AND SHAHRAZĀD SAID:

THE musician, Ishāk of Mosul, al-Rashīd's favourite singer, tells the following tale:

I sat in my house on a winter night, while the winds roared like lions without, and the clouds above spilled noisily over as if they had been great dark waterskins. I warmed my hands at my copper brazier, grieving that, because of the rain, the mud and the darkness, I could neither go forth nor expect the visit of a friend. As my heart grew heavier, I said to my slave: 'Give me some food to pass the time.' While the slave busied himself about my meal, I fell into a dream of the charms of a girl whom I had met at the palace, though I do not know why her memory, of all the memories which have blessed my nights, should have come so obstinately before me. So engrossed was I in my sudden desire that I did not see my slave standing by me with folded arms, waiting my signal to bring in the dishes and set them upon the cloth which he had already laid. Full of my dream I cried aloud: 'Would that young Saïdah were here! Her voice is so pleasant that I should be no more sad.'

I now recall that I said these words in a very loud voice, although my thoughts are usually silent. I was surprised to hear myself, and the slave opened his eyes widely.

Hardly had I spoken my wish when there was an importunate knocking at the door, as if someone were there who would not be kept waiting, and a young voice sighed: 'A lover beats upon the door of light.'

'Someone has lost his way in the dark,' I thought, 'or will the barren tree of my desire bear fruit?' I hastened to open the door myself and, on the threshold, I saw the so desirable Saïdah in a most unusual plight. She was dressed in a short robe of green silk and over her head was thrown a light stuff of gold, which had not saved her from the rain and the water tumbling from the terraces. She must have waded through mud all along the road, for her legs were mired with it. Seeing her so, I exclaimed: 'Dear mistress, why have you run such risks on such a night?' She answered in that dream voice of hers: 'How could I not listen to your messenger? He told me that your desire was great, and I came.'

Although I could not remember giving any order for a message to be carried, and although I knew that my slave could not have gone to the palace while he was standing by me, I did not wish to show my love the strange misgiving of my heart; so I said: 'Praise be to Allāh that He has reunited us, turning the bitterness of desire to honey! Your coming scents the house and calms the heart of its master. My spirit so yearned towards you to-night that I would have gone to you myself if you had not come.'

At this point Shahrazād saw the approach of morning and discreetly fell silent.

But when the five-hundred-and-fiftieth night had come

SHE SAID:

I ordered my slave to bring hot water and essences. When they came, I washed the girl's feet and poured over them a flask of essence of roses. Then I dressed her in a fair green robe and made her sit by me in front of the fruits and drinks. When she had drunk many times, I wished to please her by singing a new song which I had composed; though ordinarily I do not sing until I have been many times supplicated; but she told me that her soul had no desire to hear me. 'Then, dear mistress,' I said, 'be so good as to sing something yourself.' 'Nor that either,' she answered, 'my spirit has no wish for it.' Then said I: 'There can be no joy without singing, eye of my heart.' 'You are right,' she replied, 'but this evening, I know not why, I only wish to hear some man of the people sing, some beggar from the road. Will you not go to the door and see if such an one is passing?' Not wishing to disoblige her and being certain that on such a night there would be no passengers in the street, I opened the door and thrust my head outside. At once, to my great surprise, I saw, leaning on his stick against the opposite wall, an old beggar, who grumbled to himself and said: 'What a noise this storm is making! The wind carries my voice away, so that folk cannot hear me. Pity the poor blind man; for if he sings, no one can hear him, and if he does not sing, he will die of hunger!' With that the old blind man began to tap with his stick on the ground and against the wall, as if searching for his way.

Astonished and delighted by this happy accident, I cried out: 'O uncle, do you know how to sing?' 'I am supposed to know how to sing,' he answered. 'In that case, O sheikh,' I replied, 'will you pass the rest of the night with us and rejoice us with your company?' 'If you wish it,' he said, 'take me by the hand for I am blind of both eyes.' I took him by the hand and led him into the house; then I fastened the door again and whispered to my love: 'Here is a singer who is blind. He can amuse us and yet not see what we are doing. There is no need for you to stand on ceremony or veil your face.'

I made the old man sit before us and invited him to eat. This he did with great delicacy, using the tips of his fingers. When he was satisfied and had washed his hands, I gave him drink and he drank three full cups. Then he asked the name of his host and I answered: 'I am Ishāk, son of Ibrāhīm, of Mosul.' My name did not seem very much to astonish him; he contented himself with answering: 'I have heard tell of you; I am glad to visit your house.' 'I am delighted to receive you,' I answered. 'I have heard that you have a beautiful voice,' he said. 'Let me hear it, please; for a host should give an example to his guest.' At this I began to enjoy myself. I picked up my lute and, playing upon it, sang with all my master's skill. I took great pains with the finale, but when the last notes had died away, the old beggar only smiled with a touch of irony and said: 'O Ishāk, you are not far from being an accomplished singer and tolerable musician.' When I heard this praise, which was rather blame, I grew discouraged and very small in my own eyes; so I threw the lute aside. I made no answer to what the old man said, however, as I did not wish to fall short in hospitality. 'Will no one play or sing?' asked the beggar in a few minutes. 'Is there no one else here?' 'There is a young slave-girl,' I answered. 'Tell her to sing that I may hear,' he said; but I objected: 'Why should she sing when you have already had enough?' 'Let her sing all the same,' said he. My dear love took the lute unwillingly and, after a judicious prelude, sang of her best. The old beggar suddenly interrupted her, saying: 'You have still much to learn.' My girl threw the lute furiously from her and would have risen, had I not fallen at her knees and begged her to remain. To the old blind man, I said: 'As Allāh lives, dear guest, we have done our best and no man can do more. Now it is your turn to show your skill.'

At this point Shahrazād saw the approach of morning and discreetly fell silent.

But when the five-hundred-and-fifty-first night had come

SHE SAID:

He smiled from ear to ear and answered: 'Bring me a lute upon which no hand has ever played.' I opened a chest and took out a new lute, placing it in his hands. He eagerly seized the sharpened goose feather and lightly touched the cords into a harmony. With the first notes I recognised that the blind beggar was infinitely the finest musician of our time; but my emotion and admiration were greater still when I heard him play a small piece in a mode which was altogether unknown to me. And I am not considered a beginner in the art. In a voice of which I have never yet heard the equal, he sang:

She came by the dark roadway of the night,
She knocked, and with her knocked the tempest's spite.
   She cried against the wind about my latch:
'A lover beats upon the door of light.'

When we heard this song, my love and I looked at each other in a stupefied surmise; then she became red with anger and whispered, so that I alone might hear: 'Are you not ashamed to have told the old man all about my visit in those few moments when you were at the door with him? O Ishāk, I did not think that your mouth was so slack that it could not keep a secret for one hour! Such men as you are detestable.' I swore a thousand oaths to her that I had been in no way indiscreet. 'By the tomb of my father Ibrāhīm, I told the old man nothing,' I said, and she believed me. Being quite assured that the beggar could not see her, she let me embrace her at my ease; sometimes I kissed her cheeks, sometimes her lips, sometimes I tickled and sometimes pinched her breasts; sometimes I nibbled her in the most sensitive quarters, so that she laughed and laughed. At length I turned to the old man, saying: 'Will you sing us something else, my master?' 'Why not?' he answered and, taking up the lute again, sang this:

My hands, sure-fingered wandering her dress,
Get drunk upon her wine of nakedness;
   So, while the fuddled fellows fall and sleep,
I bite the white cups for their wantonness.

When I heard this, I did not doubt that the old man was fooling us; so I begged my lover to cover her face. Suddenly the beggar said: 'I wish to go and piss. Where is the place?' I rose and left the room for a moment to fetch a candle with which to light him; but when I returned there was no one in the chamber: the blind man and the girl had disappeared. I hunted the whole house through, but did not find them; yet the doors were firmly locked on the inside, so that they must have gone out through the ceiling or by the earth. I have ever since been persuaded that it was Iblīs himself who pandered for me on that night, and that the girl was unsubstantial, an illusion.

When Shahrazād had finished this tale, she fell silent, and King Shahryār, who had been much impressed by it, cried out: 'Allāh confound the Evil One!' Shahrazād saw that his brows were contracted, so, wishing to calm him, she told the following story:

The Fallāh of Egypt and his White Children

THE amīr Muhammad, governor of Cairo, tells this tale in his book of chronicles:

During my journey in High Egypt I lodged one night in the house of a fallāh, who was headman of his district. He was old and very brown, with a greying beard; but I noticed that his little children were very white with rosy cheeks, light hair, and blue eyes. When our host came to talk with us, after serving us with good cheer, I said to him: 'How is it that you, who are so dark, have fair children, with rose and white skins, with light hair and eyes?' The fallāh drew one of his brats towards him and began to caress the boy's hair as he answered: 'Their mother was a Frank; I bought her as a prisoner of war in the time of Salah al-Dīn the Victorious, after the battle of Hittīn, which freed us for ever from the Christian invaders who would have usurped the royalty of Jerusalem. That was long, long ago, in the days of my youth.' 'I pray you tell us the story, O sheikh,' I said; and he replied: 'Certainly, I will do so; for the tale of my adventure with the Christian maid is very strange.' This is what he told us:

You must know that I am a cultivator of flax; my father and my grandfather sowed flax before me; also, by birth and stock, I am a fallāh of this land. One year I was lucky enough to have a harvest of flax in such perfect condition that it was worth at least five hundred dīnārs. When I offered it in the market and could not find my profit, the buyers said to me: 'Take your flax to Acre in Syria, for you can sell it there to very great advantage.' Acting on their advice, I took all my year's yield to the city of Acre, which at that time was occupied by the Franks, and began at once to do good business. I relinquished half of my flax to the brokers on a six months' credit, and began to sell the rest retail with immense profit.

One day, as I was selling my flax, a young Christian girl came to buy from me with face uncovered and unveiled head, as is the manner of the Franks. White and beautiful she stood before me, and I could admire her fresh fairness at my ease. The more I looked at her face, the deeper love entered into me; so that I took a long time over serving her and, when I had made up her package, let her have it very cheap. As she departed I followed her with longing looks.

At this point Shahrazād saw the approach of morning and discreetly fell silent.

But when the five-hundred-and-fifty-second night had come

SHE SAID:

A few days later she came again to buy and this time I sold even more cheaply, though she did not bargain at all; on this occasion she doubtless perceived that I was in love with her, for, when she came a third time, she was accompanied by an old woman, who stood close by during the sale and was with her on every subsequent visit.

When my heart was quite overthrown by love, I took the old woman aside, saying: 'Do you think a present to you would possibly procure me enjoyment of that girl?' 'I could procure you a meeting and enjoyment,' she answered, 'but only on condition that the thing remained a secret between us three and that you were willing to part with a little money.' 'O helpful aunt,' I exclaimed, 'if my soul and my life were the price I would give them. Money is a little matter.' I then agreed with her for a brokerage of fifty dīnārs and, having paid her, sent her off to sound the feelings of her charge. Soon she returned with a favourable answer, and added: 'Good master, this girl has no place for meetings, for she is a virgin and knows nothing of such things. You must receive her at your house; she will come in the evening and depart in the morning.' This condition I accepted with fervour and hastened to my house where, after having made due preparation of meat, drink, and pastry, I waited as patiently as I could.

Soon the girl arrived, and I led her on to the terrace, for it was summer. We sat side by side and ate and drank together. Now, the house which I occupied looked over the sea; and the terrace was fair under the moonlight and the night was full of stars which showed their reflections in the water. As I looked at these things my spirit changed within me and I thought: 'Are you not ashamed before Allāh, under such a sky and facing such a sea, in a strange land, to rebel against His word and fornicate with a Christian?' I was already lying by the girl's side and she was leaning against me lovingly; but after this revulsion I called upon God to witness that I abstained in all chastity from this daughter of the Franks and, without even having set hand upon her, I turned my back and slept under the benign clarity of the sky.

In the morning the young Frank rose and departed, grieved and silently; while I re-entered my shop and began my selling. Towards noon the girl passed in front of the door, looking very angry, and I suddenly desired her again even to death, for she was a moon of all moons. In my own soul I cried: 'What made you refrain your desire from this woman? You are a lusty fallāh of High Egypt, not an ascetic or a sūfī or a eunuch or a Persian weakling.' Then I ran after the old woman and, taking her apart, said to her: 'I would like another meeting.' 'By Christ,' she answered, 'this time it cannot be managed under a hundred dīnārs.' At once I gave her the hundred dīnārs; and that night the young Frank came to me again. But under the beauty of the naked sky I felt the same unwelcome scruples and, abstaining from the woman in all chastity, drew no more advantage from this interview than from the first. When she saw that this was to be her treatment again, she rose in great anger from my side and went away.

And yet, next morning when she passed my shop, I felt the same desires; my heart beat thickly for love of her and I sought out the old woman. She looked at me angrily and said: 'Tell me, in Christ's name, O Mussulmān, is it thus that virgins are treated in your religion? You will never be able to come near her again, that is, unless you are willing to furnish five hundred dīnārs.' Then the old dame departed.

Trembling with inward flame, I determined to gather in the full value of all my flax and to sacrifice five hundred dīnārs to save my life. I made all my money into a bundle and was about to carry it to the old woman when suddenly . . .

At this point Shahrazād saw the approach of morning and discreetly fell silent.

But when the five-hundred-and-fifty-third night had come

SHE SAID:

. . . I heard a herald crying in the streets: 'Ho, all you Mussulmāns who tarry upon business in our city, learn that our truce with you is ended. You are given a week to put your affairs in order and return to your own country!'

I hastened to sell what flax remained to me, called in my money on that which I had loaned to the brokers, bought merchandise suitable for selling in my own country, and left the city of Acre with a heavy heart. A thousand painful regrets for the Christian girl rode with me upon my way.

I journeyed to Damascus in Syria, where I sold my goods at unusually great profit, owing to the interruption of trade caused by the renewal of war. By Allāh's grace everything prospered between my hands, so that I was able to do a rich wholesale business in Christian prisoners of war. In this way three years passed and, little by little, the bitterness of my sudden separation from the young Frank was sweetened in my heart.

We continued to gain great victories over the Franks, both about Jerusalem and in Syria. After many glorious battles, the Sultān Salah al-Dīn, with Allāh's aid, completely routed the infidels, led their kings and captains captive into Damascus, and took all their cities on the coast. Glory to Allāh!

One day I had occasion to visit the tents of the Sultān's camp in order to show him a very beautiful slave whom I intended to sell. I presented the girl to Salah al-Dīn and, as she pleased him, let him have her for a hundred dīnārs. But the Sultān (may Allāh have him in His mercy!) had only ninety dīnārs with him, for he was using all the money of his treasure for the war. Therefore he turned to one of his guards, saying: 'Take this merchant into the tent where we have collected the girl prisoners of our last engagement and let him choose one of them for the ten dīnārs which I owe him.' Such was the justice of Sultān Salah al-Dīn.

The guard led me into the tent of the captive Franks, and, as I was passing among the girls, I recognised the first who caught my eye as the sweet damsel I had loved at Acre. Since then she had become the wife of a Christian captain in high command. As soon as I saw her, I put my arm about her in sign of possession, saying: 'This is the one I wish.' Then I led her away.

When we came under my tent, I said: 'Damsel, do you recognise me?' She answered that she did not, and I continued: 'I am the friend whom you twice visited in his house at Acre, thanks to my gifts to the old woman, first of fifty, and then of a hundred dīnārs. I abstained from you, in all chastity, and allowed you to depart unhurt and very angry. I was ready to pay five hundred dīnārs for a third meeting, and now the Sultān lets me have you for ten!' She lowered her head for a moment and then, lifting it suddenly, exclaimed: 'That which passed in Acre was a mystery of the Faith of Islām. I raise my fingers and bear witness that there is no God but Allāh and that

Muhammad is the Prophet of Allāh!' Thus she pronounced her act of belief and in that moment was ennobled in the Faith.

'As Allāh lives,' I said to myself, 'I will not penetrate her this time, either, until I have freed her and married her according to the law.' I went immediately to the kādī and, when I had told him of the affair, brought him back to my tent to write our marriage contract.

Then I went into her and she conceived by me, and we dwelt in Damascus.

After we had been together for a few months, an ambassador came from the King of the Franks to Sultān Salah al-Dīn in Damascus, to see to an exchange of prisoners, according to the terms of treaty between the Kings. All the captives, both men and women, were scrupulously returned to the Franks in exchange for our own; but when the ambassador consulted his list, he perceived that there was one woman missing, the wife of a captain in high command. The Sultān sent his guards to find her and, in the end, they reported that she was at my house. The guards were sent back to fetch her, and I changed colour when they came. I went weeping to my wife and told her what had happened, but she rose, saying: 'Lead me to the Sultān, for I know what to say to him.' I conducted her, veiled, into Salah al-Dīn's presence and there I saw the ambassador of the Franks sitting upon his right hand.

At this point Shahrazād saw the approach of morning and discreetly fell silent.

But when the five-hundred-and-fifty-fourth night had come

SHE SAID:

I kissed the earth between the Sultān's hands, crying: 'Here is the woman.' He turned to my wife and asked: 'What have you to say? Do you wish to return to your own land with the ambassador or stay with your husband?' 'I stay with my husband,' she answered. 'I am of his faith and with child by him, the peace of my soul is not among the Christians.' 'You have heard?' said Salah al-Dīn to the ambassador. 'But, if you wish, you may speak to her yourself.' The Frank remonstrated with and admonished my wife, and ended by asking her the same question as the Sultān had asked: 'Will you stay with your present husband, who is a Mussulmān, or return to your former husband, who is a Christian?' 'I will never leave my Egyptian,' she said, 'for my peace is in Islām.' Then the ambassador stamped his foot in rage, and cried: 'Take away that woman!' So I took her by the hand and was about to depart with her, when the ambassador called me back and said: 'An old Christian woman in Acre, your wife's mother, gave me this package for her daughter. She charged me to say that she hopes to see her again in excellent health.' I took the packet from his hands and returned with my wife to the house. There we opened the cloth covering and found in it, not only the clothes which my wife had worn in Acre, but also the fifty dīnārs and the hundred dīnārs, knotted in the same handkerchief and with the same knot as when they had left my hands. Then at last I understood the blessing of my chastity and gave thanks to Allāh.

Soon afterwards I brought my wife to Egypt. She it was, dear guests, who bore me these white children. May Allāh bless them! Since then we have lived happily together, eating our bread as we have baked it. Such is my tale. But Allāh is All-wise.

When Shahrazād had finished this tale, she fell silent, and King Shahryār exclaimed: 'That fallāh was a happy man, O Shahrazād.' Then said Shahrazād: 'Yet, O King, he was not more happy than was Khalīfah the fisherman with the sea apes and the Khalīfah.' 'What is that tale of Khalīfah the fisherman?' asked Shahryār; and Shahrazād answered: 'I will tell it you at once.'

The Tale of Khalīfah the Fisherman

AND SHAHRAZĀD SAID:

IT is related, O auspicious King, that there was once, in the antiquity of time and the passage of the age and of the moment, a fisherman in the city of Baghdād, whose name was Khalīfah. He was so unfortunate and so poor that he had never been able to collect the few copper pieces necessary for marriage; thus he remained a bachelor, though the poorest of his neighbours had wives and children.

One day he took his net upon his back and went down to the water early in the morning, before the other fishermen. He cast ten times without catching anything at all, so he grew angry and sorrowful, and sat down upon the river bank to nurse his despair. Soon he subdued his rebellious thoughts and said: 'May Allāh pardon my revolt! There is no help save in Him! He gives food to His creatures: that which He gives, no one can take away; that which He refuses, no one can provide. Let us take the good days with the bad as they come, and prepare a patient heart against misfortune. Ill-luck is like an abscess which will not burst and depart except under unhurrying care.'

When he had comforted his soul with these words, Khalīfah rose up boldly and pulled back his sleeves. Girding up his robe into his belt, he cast his net into the water as far as his arm might go. After waiting for a minute he took hold of the cord and pulled with might; but the net was so heavy that he had to use all his skill to bring it in without accident. When he had gently hauled it ashore, he opened it, with beating heart, and found in it a large one-eyed and lame ape.

At this point Shahrazād saw the approach of morning and discreetly fell silent.

But when the five-hundred-and-fifty-fifth night had come

SHE SAID:

'There is no power or might save in Allāh!' cried the wretched Khalīfah. 'We belong to Him and we return to Him; yet there is a fatality about this day which I do not understand. I cannot guess what will happen to me before the end of it. But all was written by Allāh!' So saying, he tied the ape to a tree with a piece of cord and, brandishing a whip which he had with him, would have soundly beaten the animal in order to work off his ill-humour, had not the beast, with Allāh's help, moved its tongue and thus eloquently spoken: 'Stay your hand and do not beat me, O Khalīfah. Leave me tied to the tree and cast your net once more, trusting in Allāh. He will give you your bread to-day.'

Hearing these words from a lame and one-eyed ape, Khalīfah lowered his hand and cast his net into the water, letting the cord of it float loose. When he would have drawn it in, he found it heavier than before; but, by tugging gently, he succeeded at last in bringing it to land, only to find in it a second ape. This animal was neither blind nor lame, but instead exceedingly beautiful: it had eyes lengthened with kohl, henna-tinted nails, white pleasantly-separated teeth, and a rosy bottom, quite unlike the raw backsides of other apes. It wore a red and blue coat, most agreeable to the sight, and had gold bracelets on its wrists, gold anklets about its ankles, and gold earrings in its ears. It laughed and winked and clicked its tongue when it saw the fisherman.

'To-day is a day of apes!' cried Khalīfah. 'Praise be to Allāh who has changed all the fishes of the river into monkeys! So this is your beginning, O day of pitch! You are like a book whose contents are known from the first page. This would not have happened if I had ignored the advice of the first ape.' So saying, he ran towards the tree and, cracking his whip three times in the air, cried to his first captive: 'Look, O face of calamity, upon the result of your counsels! Because I opened my day with a sight of your blind eye, I am fated to die of hunger and fatigue.' He brought the whip down sharply over the animal's back and would have raised it a second time, but the beast said: 'Instead of whipping me, O Khalīfah, it would be better for you to go and talk to my companion. This behaviour will advantage you nothing, therefore do as I say. It is for your own good.' Not knowing what to make of this, the fisherman left the one-eyed ape and returned to the second, who laughed heartily on beholding him. 'What are you, pitch-face?' cried Khalīfah, and the fair-eyed monkey answered: 'Do you not know me, Khalīfah?' 'I do not know you, but if you will not answer you shall know my whip,' returned the fisherman. So the ape made haste to say: 'Such language is not suitable, Khalīfah; but if you will talk to me in a different strain and remember what I say, you may grow rich.' Khalīfah threw the whip from him, crying: 'I am ready to listen, O my lord the ape, O King of all the monkeys!' Then said the other: 'I belong to the Jew money-changer, Abū Saada; he is fortunate and successful only through me. Mine is the first face he sees on waking and the last before sleeping at night. That is why he prospers.' Here Khalīfah interrupted: 'Is not the proverb true then in saying: "Unlucky as an ape's face"?' Then he called over his shoulder to the beast by the tree: 'Did you hear that? Seeing your face this morning only brought me weariness and disappointment: you are not like your brother.' 'Leave my brother in peace,' said the handsome ape. 'First prove the truth of my words by fastening me to the cord of your net and casting it into the water. You will see if I am a luck-bringer or no.'

At this point Shahrazād saw the approach of morning and discreetly fell silent.

But when the five-hundred-and-fifty-sixth night had come

SHE SAID:

Khalīfah did as the ape advised and, when he drew in his net, it contained a magnificent fish, as large as a sheep, with eyes like two dīnārs of gold and scales which had the appearance of diamonds. As proud as if he had become master of the whole earth, he showed his prize to the handsome ape. 'You see?' cried the beast. 'Now gather some fresh grass and put it at the bottom of your basket; lay the fish on it and cover it with more grass. Then leave us apes both tied to the tree and carry your basket to Baghdād. If people ask you what you have got, do not answer; but go straight to the changers' market and find out the shop of Abū Saada the Jew, who is syndic of the changers. He will be seated on a dīwān with a cushion at his back and two chests in front of him, one for gold and the other for silver. There will be boys and slaves, servants and assistants all about him. Set your basket down before him, and say: "O Abū Saada, to-day I cast the net in your name and Allāh sent me this fish." When you have delicately removed the grass, he will ask you whether you have shown it to any beside himself. "No, as Allāh lives," you must answer; for then he will take the fish and offer you a dīnār for it. You must refuse. He will offer you two dīnārs; but you must refuse them also. Each time he offers, you must refuse, even if he is willing to give the fish's weight in gold. He will ask what else you want, and you will answer: "By Allāh, I will only sell the fish in exchange for a few words." "What few words are those?" he will ask, and you will reply: "Rise up and say: 'Bear witness, O all who are present in this market, that I consent to exchange my ape for the ape of Khalīfah the fisherman; that I barter my luck for his luck, and my fortune for his fortune.' That is the price of my fish; for I make nothing with gold; I do not know its smell, its taste or its uses." Then, O Khalīfah, if the Jew consents to this bargain, I will become your property; every day I will wish you good morning and every evening I will wish you good night: this will bring you luck and you will earn a hundred dīnārs every day. On the other hand, Abū Saada the Jew will begin his mornings with a sight of this lame and one-eyed brother and will close his evenings with the same. Allāh will afflict him every day with exaction, toil or outrage, so that in a short time he will be ruined and reduced to begging in the streets. Carefully remember what I have said, O Khalīfah, and you shall prosper exceedingly.'

'I gladly accept your advice, O King of all the apes,' answered the fisherman. 'But what shall I do with this one-eyed misfortune? Shall I leave the accursed thing tied to the tree?' 'Loose both of us, that we may return to the water,' answered the ape. 'That will be best.

So Khalīfah untied the ugly and the pleasant ape together, and at once they skipped down the bank into the water and disappeared.

The fisherman washed the fish and placed it in the basket with grass all round. Then he made off towards the city, singing at the top of his voice.

The people in the markets, being used to jest with him, asked what he carried; but he answered with neither word nor look. When he came to the changers' market, he followed the line of shops until he found a great one where he saw the Jew seated majestically upon a dīwān, with servants of every age and colour hurrying to do his work. He looked as if he thought himself the King of Khurāsān; but Khalīfah nevertheless ventured into his presence and stood before him.

At this point Shahrazād saw the approach of morning and discreetly fell silent.

But when the five-hundred-and-fifty-seventh night had come

SHE SAID:

The Jew raised his head, saying: 'A kindly welcome to you, O Khalīfah; tell me now what you wish. If any has sworn at you, hurt, or hustled you, I will willingly go with you to the walī to demand reparation.' But Khalīfah answered: 'By the life of your head, O chief and crown of the Jews, no one has sworn at me, hurt me, or hustled me. This morning I went to the river and cast my net in your name and with your luck, and caught this fish.' With these words he opened the basket and, lifting the fish gently from its bed of grass, held it out with pride to the money-changer. The Jew found the fish admirable, and cried: 'By the Pentateuch and the Ten Commandments I assure you, O fisherman, that I slept last night and the Virgin Mary appeared to me in a dream, saying: "O Abū Saada, tomorrow you shall have a present from me." Doubtless this is the present . . . Now tell me, as you hope to be saved, whether you have offered this fish to any beside myself?' 'As Allāh lives, O chief and crown of the Jews,' answered the fisherman, 'I swear, by the true life of Abū Bakr, that no one else has seen it.' The Jew turned to one of his young slaves, saying: 'Carry this fish to my house and tell my daughter to clean it, to fry one half, to grill the other, and to keep all hot until I return.' Khalīfah also said to the slave: 'O boy, tell your mistress not to burn it. Show her the beautiful colour of the gills.'

When the lad had carried off the fish, the Jew handed a dīnār to Khalīfah, saying: 'Take this for yourself and spend it on your family.' Khalīfah, who had instinctively taken the coin, saw it shining in his palm and, because he did not know its value, cried aloud: 'Glory be to the Lord, Master of Treasures, King of Riches!' He had already taken a few steps away from the dīwān when he remembered the ape's advice and, returning, cast the dīnār down before the Jew. 'Take your gold and give back the poor man's fish,' he said. 'Do you think that you can mock at the destitute in this way?' The Jew thought that the fisherman was having a joke, so he held out three dīnārs with a laugh; but Khalīfah said: 'Enough of this unpleasing jest, in Allāh's name! Do you really think that I would sell my fish for such a trifle?' The Jew then held out five dīnārs, exclaiming: 'Take these for your fish and do not be greedy!' Khalīfah took the five dīnārs in his hand and went away contented. He looked at the gold with marvelling eyes, and cried: 'Glory be to Allāh! There is more in my hand to-day than in all the palace of the Khalīfah!' He had come to the limit of the market before he remembered the ape's words; at once he hastened back to the Jew and disdainfully threw the money at his feet. 'What is the matter with you, Khalīfah, and what do you want? Do you want me to change the gold into silver for you?' But the other answered: 'I do not want your gold or your silver; I want you to give back the poor man's fish.'

The Jew grew angry at this, and called out: 'I give you five dīnārs for a fish that is not worth one, and you are not satisfied! Are you mad? Tell me what you want for the thing?' 'I wish neither silver nor gold,' replied Khalīfah, 'I will sell it cheap in exchange for a few words.' When the Jew heard this mention of a few words, he thought that the fisherman meant the few words of the act of Islamic Faith and wished him to change his religion for the fish. His eyes rose to the top of his head in anger and indignation, his breathing stopped, and he cried, grinding his teeth: 'O nail-paring of the Mussulmāns, do you wish to part me from my faith for a single fish, to make me abjure the law which my fathers followed?' He yelled to his servants: 'O evil day! Fall on this pitch-face and carefully beat his flesh to ribbons! On no account spare him!'

At this point Shahrazād saw the approach of morning and discreetly fell silent.

But when the five-hundred-and-fifty-eighth night had come

SHE SAID:

The servants fell upon Khalīfah with their sticks and beat him till he fell to the bottom of the stairs. 'Let him get up now,' said the Jew; and at once the fisherman jumped to his feet as if he had felt nothing. 'Now will you tell me the price to which you pretend for your fish?' asked Abū Saada. 'I am ready to pay anything in reason, to be done with it; but, in making your demand, remember the unpleasant treatment which you have already undergone.' 'Have no fears for my skin, dear master,' answered Khalīfah with a laugh, 'in the matter of sticks I can stand more strokes than ten donkeys put together. I do not feel them.' The Jew also laughed, and said kindly: 'Come now, tell me what you want; and I swear, by the truth of my faith, that I will give it to you.' 'I have already told it you,' answered the fisherman. 'I ask a few words in exchange for the fish. They have nothing to do with our act of Faith; for, as Allāh lives, if you become a Mussulmān, your conversion would be no advantage to Islām and no loss to the Jews; and, if you remain fixed in your impious error, your infidelity will be no loss to the Mussulmāns and no advantage to the Jews. The few words which I ask are quite different. I wish you to rise up and say: "Bear witness, O all you who are present in this market, that I consent to exchange my ape for the fish of Khalīfah the fisherman; that I barter my luck for his luck, and my fortune for his fortune."'

'That is easy,' said the Jew, and immediately got to his feet and proclaimed the required words. Then he asked the fisherman if there were anything more that he could do and, when the other answered that there was not, bade him be gone in peace. Khalīfah therefore took up his empty basket and his net, and returned to the river bed.

Trusting in the promise of the fair-eyed ape, he cast his net and drew it ashore with difficulty, filled with an abundance of every kind of fish. Immediately there passed a woman balancing a dish upon her head, who bought a fish for a dīnār; then a slave came along who bought a second fish for a dīnār; by the end of the day he had sold his catch for a hundred dīnārs. He triumphantly returned with his gold to the miserable lodging which he rented near the fish market and at once, as night was falling, fell into a great anxiety about his riches. Before lying down on his mat to sleep, he said to himself: 'O Khalī-fah, all in this quarter know that you are a poor man, an unhappy penniless fisherman; but now you have a hundred golden dīnārs, as they are called. Folk will get to know of this; the Khalīfah, Hārūn al-Rashīd, will get to know of this, and one day, when he is short of money, will send by guards to say to me: "I need some money and I hear that you have a hundred dīnārs. I am going to borrow them." I will put on my most pitiful air and weep and answer: "O Prince of Believers, I am a poor man, a nothing: how could I have such a fabulous sum? Whoever told you is a terrible liar; I have never had so much money." Then, to extract my money and to learn its hiding place, he will hand me over to Ahmad-the-Moth, his chief of police, who will strip me naked and beat me until I give up my hundred dīnārs . . . The best way to prevent this loss is not to say anything; and the best way to be able to say nothing is to accustom my flesh to whipping, though, Allāh be praised, it is already passably hard. Now I must make it quite hard, or my native sensibility will weaken me under the blows and make me speak in spite of my soul.'

As soon as he had thought things out in this way, Khalīfah began to put into execution a plan which his mind (being no wiser than the mind of a hashīsh-eater) suggested to him.

At this point Shahrazād saw the approach of morning and discreetly fell silent.

But when the five-hundred-and-fifty-ninth night had come

SHE SAID:

He stripped himself naked and hung a leather cushion, which he had, to a nail in the wall; then, taking up a whip with a hundred-and-eighty lashes, he began to beat, with alternate strokes, his own leathery back and the leather of the cushion. At the same time he uttered loud cries, as if he were already in the presence of the chief of police. 'Ay! Alas, alas!' he cried. 'Ay! a terrible lie! Alas, alas! Ay! Wicked words! Oh, oh! How sensitive a skin! The liars! I am a poor man! Allāh, Allāh! A poor fisherman! I have no money! Ay, ay! None of the vain riches of this world! Yes, I have! No, I have not! Yes, I have! No, I have not!' And he continued his discipline in this way, at first dividing his strokes equally with the cushion, but later forgetting his own turn and giving the cushion two for one and then three and then four and then five for one.

The neighbours heard his cries and lashes sounding through the night and they became anxious. 'What has happened to the poor lad

that he cries in this way?' they asked. 'What are these blows showering upon him? Do you think that robbers have broken in and are
beating him to death?' Then, as the yells and blows became more
sonorous and frequent, they left their houses and ran to Khālifah's
lodging. Finding the door shut, they said: 'The robbers must have
got in by the other side, by the terrace.' So they climbed on to the
neighbouring terrace and from there to the terrace of Khālifah's
house, and let themselves down by the upper opening. They found
him alone and utterly naked, lashing about with his whip, leaping
from side to side on his legs, and protesting his innocence in a continuous babble.

'What is the matter, Khalīfah?' asked the astonished intruders.
'Your cries and blows have set all the quarter in an uproar and are
keeping us awake. We were very frightened.' Instead of answering
their questions, Khalīfah called out: 'What do you all want? Am I
not master of my own flesh? Can I not have a little peace to teach it
blows? How should I know what the future has in store for me?
Depart, good folk, and try the same exercise yourselves; for you are
no more immune from exaction and outrage than myself.' Then,
without paying any attention to his visitors, the fisherman went on
yelling under the blows, which fell heavily upon the cushion.

Seeing him so, the neighbours laughed so heartily that they fell
over on their backsides; then they went their way.

Though in a little while Khalīfah wearied of his pursuit, he would
not close his eyes all night for fear of robbers. Before setting out to
fish on the morrow, he thought again of his hundred dīnārs, and said
to himself: 'If I leave them in my lodging they will surely be stolen;
if I fasten them in my belt some robber will see the bulge and lie in
wait for me and kill me for them. I must do something better than
that.' He thereupon tore his cloak in two and made a bag with the
pieces, afterwards putting the gold in the bag and hanging it about
his neck with a string. Then he took up his net, his basket, and his
stick, and walked down to the river. Arrived at the bank, he cast his
net into the water with the full strength of his arms; but the movement was so sudden and undisciplined that the bag of gold jumped
from his neck and followed the net into the water, where it was
dragged into the depths by the force of the current.

Khalīfah let go his net and, undressing in the twinkling of an eye,
dived after his bag; but he could not find it. He dived again and
again, and, at last, a hundred times; but the bag had disappeared and,

when he walked up the bank to dress, his clothes had disappeared also. He beat his hands together, crying: 'Ah, the vile thieves to steal my clothes! All this but proves the proverb: "A camel-boy never achieves pilgrimage until he has buggered his camel." '

At this point Shahrazād saw the approach of morning and discreetly fell silent.

But when the five-hundred-and-sixtieth night had come

SHE SAID:

Poor Khalīfah wrapped himself in his net, for it was the best covering that remained to him and, taking up his basket and stick, began to stride along the river bank, dancing to right and left, to front and back, panting, reasonless and raging, like a rutting camel or a rebel Ifrīt escaped from his brass prison. So much for Khalīfah the fisherman.

Now we must consider the case of the Khalīfah, Hārūn al-Rashīd; for he is deeply concerned in our tale. There was at that time in Baghdād a man named Ibn al-Kirnās, who was jeweller and man of affairs to the Khalīfah. So important was he in the market that no sale took place in all Baghdād of rich fabrics, jewels, boys or girls, which did not pass through his hands at some point or another. One day this Ibn al-Kirnās was sitting in his shop when the chief broker led up to him a girl such as he had never before seen in that city: there was nothing stored in man's memory to equal the elegance of her slim perfection. Not only was she fair beyond all women, but she knew every science and art which can be known; she was an adept in poetry, singing, and dancing, and could play upon every harmonious instrument. Al-Kirnās bought her, without a moment's hesitation, for five thousand dīnārs and, when he had spent another thousand upon dressing her, took her into the presence of the Khalīfah. She passed the night with al-Rashīd, so that he might be able to prove her talents for himself, and he found her expert in all things. Her name was Heart's-Life and she was brown and fresh of skin.

The Prince of Believers was enchanted with his new slave and, on the morrow, sent ten thousand dīnārs to al-Kirnās. He loved the girl with so violent a passion and his heart lay so completely beneath her feet that he neglected for her the Lady Zubaidah, his cousin, and cast aside all his favourites. He remained with her a whole month, only leaving her chamber for the Friday prayer and hastening back as soon as that was over. Thus it happened that the lords of the kingdom thought his infatuation too grave to be allowed to continue and carried their complaints to Jafar al-Barmakī, the grand-wazīr. Jafar promised to cure the Khalīfah and, for this purpose, waited on him upon the following Friday. He entered the mosque and spoke for a long while with the King concerning the passion of love and all its consequences. 'As Allāh lives, O Jafar,' answered the Khalīfah, 'I count for nothing in this matter. The fault is with my heart; for it stumbled into the nets of love and I cannot release it.' 'Prince of Believers,' continued Jafar, 'the girl Heart's-Life is now in your power, submissive to your orders, a slave among your slaves; and you should know that what the hand possesses the soul does not covet. I wish to show you a way of keeping your heart unwearied of this favourite: leave her from time to time, go hunting or fishing, there are other nets besides those of love. These occupations would be better for you at present than an attention to the affairs of your kingdom; for those would weary you too much.' 'That is an excellent idea, Jafar,' said the Khalīfah. 'Let us go upon some excursion without delay.' As soon as the prayers were over, each mounted his mule outside the mosque and led his escort through the gate of the city, in order to ride over the fields.

They rode hither and thither in the heat of the day and soon left their escorts behind in the distraction of their conversation. It was not long before al-Rashīd felt the pangs of thirst and, looking round to see if there were any dwelling near, saw some object moving far off upon a hillock. 'Can you see what that is, Jafar?' he asked, and the wazīr replied: 'O Commander of the Faithful, I can see some vague thing on that knoll. Doubtless it is a gardener or planter of cucumbers. As there is certain to be water in his neighbourhood, I will ride to fetch you some.' 'My mule is faster than yours,' answered al-Rashīd. 'Wait here for our escorts, while I ride forward myself. I will return as soon as I have drunken.' So saying, the Khalīfah galloped off on his mule more swiftly than the wind of a tempest or water falling from a rock, and, in the twinkling of an eye, had reached the hillock. There he saw a naked man wound with fishing nets and covered with sweat and dust, having red, staring eyes, and a horrible expression. This was Khalīfah the fisherman and he looked like one of those evil Jinn who wander in desert places.

At this point Shahrazād saw the approach of morning and discreetly fell silent.

But when the five-hundred-and-sixty-first night had come

SHE SAID:

Hārūn wished this strange figure peace and Khalīfah answered with a curse and a flaming look. 'Have you a drink of water to give me?' asked the Khalīfah, and Khalīfah answered: 'Are you blind or mad? Do you not see that water flows behind this hill?' Hārūn walked round the knoll and descended to the Tigris where he drank, flat on his belly, and then watered his mule. Returning to Khalīfah, he said: 'What are you doing here, O man, and what is your profession?' 'That question is more foolish than the one about the water,' answered Khalīfah. 'Do you not see the instrument of my trade about my shoulders?' 'Without doubt you are a fisherman,' said the Khalīfah, glancing at the net about his shoulders. 'But what have you done with your cloak, your shirt, and your kilt?' At these words, Khalīfah, who had lost exactly these things, did not doubt that the thief stood before him; therefore he leapt like a beam of light from the top of the hillock and seized the mule by the bridle, saying: 'Give me back my clothes and stop this unseemly joke.' 'As Allāh lives,' answered Hārūn, 'I have not seen your clothes and do not understand what you are saying.' Now, as all the world knows, al-Rashīd had fat swollen cheeks and a very small mouth; so, when Khalīfah looked at him more closely, he supposed him to be a clarinet player, and cried: 'Will you give me back my clothes, you clarinet player, or would you rather dance to my stick and piss your drawers?'

'As Allāh lives, I could not bear the half of a stroke from such a stick,' murmured the Khalīfah, as he looked at the enormous cudgel which the fisherman lifted above his head. Rather than risk a trial, he took off his beautiful satin robe and offered it to Khalīfah, saying: 'O man, take this robe in place of those things which you have lost.' Khalīfah turned the robe about in every direction, and said: 'O clarinet player, my clothes were worth ten times as much as this ugly ornamented garment.' 'That may be so,' answered al-Rashīd, 'but put it on for the time being, until I can find your own for you.' Khalīfah put on the robe and found it too long; therefore he took the knife fastened to the handle of his fish basket and cut off the lower third, which he rolled into a turban. The garment now reached only to his knees, but he preferred it so.

Khalīfah turned to the Khalīfah, saying: 'Allāh upon you, O

clarinet player, tell me how much your playing brings you in every month?' Not daring to vex his questioner, al-Rashīd replied: 'My playing on the clarinet brings me in about ten dīnārs a month.' Then said Khalīfah in a tone of profound commiseration: 'As Allāh lives, I grieve for you, poor man. I can earn ten dīnārs in a single hour, just by casting out my net and pulling it in again; for I have an ape in the water who looks after my interests and drives the fish into my meshes. Would you like to enter my service, chubby cheeks? I will teach you the trade of a fisherman and give you five dīnārs a day as my assistant. Later, if you progress, I will take you into partnership. Also you will benefit by the protection of my stick in case your old master in the clarinet line makes any objection. I will smash him with a single blow.' 'I accept your offer,' answered al-Rashīd, and Khalīfah continued: 'Get down from your mule and fasten him, so that he can carry our fish to the market when they are caught. Now come quickly and take your first lesson.'

Sighing in his soul, the Khalīfah cast despairing eyes about him and came down from the mule. He fastened the beast near by and kilted up such clothes as remained to him, tucking the tails of his shirt in below his belt. Then he took his stand by the fisherman, who said to him: 'Hold this net by the ends, clarinet player, throw it over your arm in such a fashion, and cast it out above the water in such a fashion.' Al-Rashīd plucked up all the courage in his heart and cast the net in the manner directed; in a few moments he tried to draw it back, but it was so heavy that Khalīfah had to help him. As the two brought it slowly to land, Khalīfah cried to his assistant: 'O clarinet of my zabb, if I find the net torn or damaged by stones, I will bugger you. Also I will take your mule.' Happily for Hārūn, the net was intact and filled full with very beautiful fishes; otherwise the Khalīfah would certainly have had to entertain the fisherman's zabb and Allāh alone knows how he would have come out of such an ordeal. For that particular thing was not negligible with Khalīfah. As there was no need to carry out his threat, the fisherman cried: 'O clarinet, you are very ugly and your face is exactly like my bum; but, as Allāh lives, if you pay attention to your new trade, you will become no ordinary fisherman.'

At this point Shahrazād saw the approach of morning and discreetly fell silent.

But when the five-hundred-and-sixty-second night had come

SHE SAID:

'. . . In the meanwhile, mount your mule and ride to the market for two large baskets to hold the surplus of this prodigious catch. I will stay here and look after the fish. Do not bother about anything else, for I have the scales and weights with me, and all other necessities of the retail trade. When we reach the fish market, you will only have to hold the scales and take the money. Be careful not to loiter, or your buttocks and my stick shall cry, "Well met!"' 'I hear and I obey,' answered the Khalīfah and, unfastening his mule, made off at full gallop, laughing as if his heart would break. When Jafar saw him accoutred in so strange a fashion, he lifted his arms to the sky, crying: 'O Commander of the Faithful, without doubt you have found some fair garden on the way and have lain down in it and rolled upon the grass.' The Khalīfah laughed more heartily than ever and the other Barmakids of the escort, who were relations of Jafar, kissed the earth between the King's hands, saying: 'O Prince of Believers, may Allāh drive away your care and establish your joy for ever! Why have you been so long parted from us, when you left only for a mouthful of water?'

Then said the Khalīfah: 'I chanced on a prodigious adventure, the most delightful of my life.' He told them of his meeting with Khalī-fah the fisherman and how he had given his embroidered satin robe to replace the stolen garments. 'By Allāh,' cried Jafar, 'when I saw you depart alone, so richly clad, I had a presentiment that something like this would happen to you. But there is no great harm done, for I can go at once and buy back the robe from the fisherman.' The Khalīfah laughed louder than ever, and answered: 'You should have thought of that earlier, Jafar; the good fellow has already cut away a third of it for a turban . . . But I tell you, Jafar, my one experience of fishing has been enough; I shall not try that form of exercise again. Also I could never hope to equal my first effort; I caught a miraculous abundance, and my master is looking after them and waits for me to return with certain baskets.' 'O Prince of Believers, shall I beat up purchasers for you?' asked Jafar; and Hārūn cried: 'By the pure virtue of my ancestors, I promise a dīnār a fish to all who will run and buy them from my master, Khalīfah.'

Then cried Jafar to the escort: 'Run to the bank and try to obtain fish for the Prince of Believers.' At once all the men of the escort ran in the direction which Jafar indicated and surrounded Khalîfah, as sparrow-hawks surround their prey. They seized on the fish piled before him, quarrelling over each, in spite of the stick with which Khalîfah menaced them. In the end the poor fisherman was overcome by numbers, and cried out: 'After all, these fish are not the fish of Paradise!' By a hearty use of his stick he was able to save the two best fishes from the pillage and, holding one in each hand, he jumped into the water. This he did because he thought that his assailants were brigands or highway cutters. Wading in deep, he lifted his hands, with a fish in each, and cried: 'O Allâh, I pray by the virtue of these heavenly fish, that my assistant, the clarinet player, be not long in coming!'

While he was praying, a negro of the escort, who had been made late by his horse stopping on the road to piss, reached the bank and found the fish all gone. When he spied Khalîfah holding up his fish in the water, he cried to him: 'Come here, O fisherman!' But Khalîfah answered: 'Begone, you zabb-swallower!' These words so annoyed the negro that, lifting his lance, he aimed it at Khalîfah, saying: 'Either you will come here and sell those fish or I will send my lance through your thigh.' 'Do not throw, you rascal,' answered Khalîfah, 'I would rather give you the fish than lose my life.' He waded out of the water and threw the fish down in front of the negro with a gesture of high disdain. After picking them up and wrapping them in a richly embroidered handkerchief, the man felt in his pocket for money. Finding it empty, he said to Khalîfah: 'You have no luck, O fisherman, for I have not a single dirham in my pocket. But if you will come to the palace to-morrow and ask for Sandal, the black eunuch, you will find a generous welcome and a price for your fish which will send you rejoicing upon your way.' Not daring to answer back, Khalîfah cast at the eunuch one glance which said more than a thousand insults or a thousand threats of buggery or a thousand promises to mount his mother or his sister, and made off in the direction of Baghdâd. As he went he beat his hands together and said in a bitter voice of irony: 'Well, to-day, right from the beginning has been the most blessed in all my life. That is evident.' He went past the walls of the city and came to the entrance of the market.

At this point Shahrazâd saw the approach of morning and discreetly fell silent.

But when the five-hundred-and-sixty-third night had come

SHE SAID:

Seeing Khalīfah come carrying his net and stick and basket as usual and yet gowned and turbaned with a robe worth fully a thousand dīnārs, the shopkeepers joined in a procession behind him to see if they could find out the meaning of this thing. As they were passing the shop of the Khalīfah's tailor, the man recognised the robe which he had but lately sent home to the Commander of the Faithful. 'How did you come by that robe, O Khalīfah?' he cried out; but Khalīfah eyed him askance and answered: 'What is that to you, shit-face? . . . Yet, if you must know, it was given to me by my apprentice, to whom I am teaching the trade. If he had not given it to me I would have cut his hand off for robbing me of all my clothes.'

The tailor understood from this answer that the Khalīfah must have met the fisherman on his excursion and played some joke upon him. Therefore he allowed Khalīfah to continue on his way in peace. The fisherman soon came to his own house, where we will find him again to-morrow.

Now it is time to find out what was happening at the palace while the Khalīfah was away. Well, well, I can assure you that some very serious things were happening.

We know that the Khalīfah had only left his palace to take a little air in the fields with Jafar and to forget his overpowering passion for Heart's-Life. The madness which this slave inspired did not torture the Khalīfah only; his cousin and queen, Zubaidah, had not been able to eat, drink, or sleep since the girl had entered the palace, because her soul was filled full to bursting with that jealousy which is common to women. She only waited for an occasion when the Khalīfah should be absent to avenge the continuous affront which she suffered every hour of the day in the eyes of her servants. So, when she heard that her lord had gone out to ride, she prepared a sumptuous feast in her apartments, with drinks of every kind and porcelain plates filled with conserve and pastry. Then she sent, with great ceremony, to invite Heart's-Life, causing the slaves to say to her: 'Our mistress, Zubaidah, daughter of Kāsim, wife of the Khalīfah, invites you to a feast which she is giving in your honour. To-day she has taken medicine and, to obtain the best results from it, it is necessary for her heart to rejoice and her spirit to remain calm.

Knowing of no better rest or greater joy than to see you and hear your wonderful singing, of which the Khalīfah has spoken with such admiration, she begs that you will not refuse her.' Heart's-Life made answer: 'My hearing and obedience are all for Allāh and for the Lady Zubaidah, my mistress.' She rose, not knowing what things the mysterious hands of Destiny held in store for her, and, taking her instruments of music, accompanied the chief eunuch to Zubaidah's apartments.

When she came into the Queen's presence, she kissed the earth many times between her hands and then said in a voice of infinite sweetness: 'Peace be upon the lifted curtain and sublime veil of this harīm, on the descendant of the Prophet, on the heiress to the virtue of the Abbāsids! May Allāh draw out the joy of our mistress even as long as night succeeds to day!' Having made this compliment, she modestly retired among the other women.

Zubaidah, who lay stretched upon a vast dīwān of velvet, lifted slow eyes to the favourite and looked at her fixedly.

At this point Shahrazād saw the approach of morning and discreetly fell silent.

But when the five-hundred-and-sixty-fourth night had come

SHE SAID:

Zubaidah was taken aback by the girl's beauty; for the child had hair of night, cheeks like the red hearts of roses, pomegranates for breasts, shining eyes and languid lids, a bright brow and a face compact of moonlight. The sun rose in the morning from her forehead and the shadows crept at night out of her hair; without her breath there would have been no musk; lacking her, the flowers would never have known their perfume; the moon borrowed from her; branches would not have swayed in the wind without the example of her waist, nor could the stars have shone if they had not learnt their shining from her eyes; bows would never have been stretched in fight to perfect curves, save in imitation of her eyebrows; the coral of the sea had heard of her lips and blushed because of them. When she was angry, her lovers fell dead all along the earth; and when she recovered her temper, their lives came back to them. Her young eye knew more than the oldest sorcerer, for it could magic the two worlds with a single spell. She was the miracle and honour of her time; she was a glory to Him Who fashioned her.

When Zubaidah had detailed these perfections in her own mind, she said: 'Easy and friendly welcome, O Heart's-Life. I pray you sit down and pass our time with the beauty of your art.' 'I hear and I obey,' answered the girl; she sat down and took in her hand a cunningly constructed tambourine. If you had been there you would have remembered these lines of the poet:

> The drum of my breast
> Answers your reckless tambourine;
> Your fingers hurry over—which?
> Be naked, tambourine-player,
> Dance on my heart's floor.

After making this instrument prettily resound, she sang these verses to its accompaniment:

> The birds said to the bird within my breast,
> To the poor wounded song-bird there at rest:
> 'Oh, fly men,
> Callous horde.'
> But I: 'O heart, do what you can for men
> And flirt your feathers like a fan for men,
> For hymen,
> Your reward.'

She sang this song so wonderfully that the birds paused in their flight across the sky, and the palace danced with all its walls. Then she put aside the tambourine and, taking up a rosewood flute, bent her lips and fingers to it. If you had been there you would have remembered these lines of the poet:

> The rosewood flute is dead to-day,
> But when he feels your scarlet lips
> The singing soul of laughter slips
> Into his tube and he is gay.
>
> Blow in my heart, then, and behold
> My seven wounds are seven vents
> And I am young. At all events,
> The rosewood flute is dead and old.

When she had played an air upon the flute, she set it aside and, taking up a skilfully constructed lute, tuned the strings of it. She put it to her bosom, leaning over it with the tenderness of a mother nursing her child; and if you had seen her, you would have recalled the words of the poet:

> Player upon the Persian lute, your hands
> Calm and exalt and follow your commands,
> Even as a doctor, feeling with his skill,
> Makes the hot life-blood hasten or be still.
> Player upon the Persian lute, your fine
> And foreign fingers the sweet cords combine
> Until each hears his native song, and each
> Who does not know, yet understands your speech.

She preluded in fourteen different modes and then sang a song which ravished those who heard it into a paradise of delight.

After this, she rose in her supple grace and danced before Zubaidah; and, after her dance, she executed feats of skill and sleight-of-hand. This she did with such art and with so light a touch that Zubaidah, in spite of her jealousy and desire for vengeance, well-nigh fell in love with her and declared her passion. Even as she checked this feeling, she said in her soul: 'My cousin al-Rashīd is hardly to blame!'

At this point Shahrazād saw the approach of morning and discreetly fell silent.

But when the five-hundred-and-sixty-fifth night had come

SHE SAID:

Zubaidah allowed her hatred to overcome her admiration, and commanded the slaves to serve the feast. Yet her sudden compassion did not altogether desert her and, instead of poisoning her rival as she had intended, she contented herself with having a very strong dose of soporific banj mingled with the pastries which were given to Heart's-Life. As soon as the favourite carried a morsel of one of these to her lips, she fell head over heels and dropped into the blackness of a swoon. Zubaidah feigned great grief at this and ordered the slaves to carry her victim into a secret chamber; then she spread news of the girl's death, saying that she had been stifled by eating too fast, and caused a solemn funeral and mock burial to take place. Lastly she hastened the construction of a sumptuous tomb in the garden of the palace.

When the Khalīfah returned after his adventure with the fisherman, his first care was to ask news of his beloved from the eunuchs; but the eunuchs, whom Zubaidah had threatened with the gallows if they did not obey her, answered mournfully: 'Alas, alas, my lord! May Allāh prolong your days and add to your term the missing years of our mistress, Heart's-Life. O Commander of the Faithful, your absence wrought such despairing grief in her that she could not support the commotion of it, and suddenly death took her. She is now in the peace of our God.'

The Khalīfah began to run through the palace like a madman, stopping his ears and crying aloud for his beloved to all who met him. Those who were in his way threw themselves flat on their bellies or hid behind colonnades. He came swiftly to the garden where the false tomb stood and stretched out his arms over it; leaning his forehead to the marble and weeping bitterly, he cried:

> They say the grave is cold,
>> But I have put all warmth to sleep in you.
> They say the grave is old,
>> But I have given youth to you to keep in you.
> They say the grave is lack,
>> But I have surfeited too soon in you.
> They say the grave is black,
>> But I see rose flowers and a small white moon in you.

For an hour he sobbed out his grief upon the tomb and then shut himself in his own apartments, refusing the consolations of his wife and friends.

As soon as she saw that her ruse had been successful, Zubaidah caused the drugged favourite to be placed in a chest, which had been used for garments, and ordered two of her confidential slaves to carry the box to the market and sell it to the first purchaser, on condition that the lid was not raised. So much for all of them.

When Khalīfah the fisherman woke next morning, his first thought was of the black eunuch who had not paid him for his two fish. 'The best thing I can do,' he said to himself, 'is to go to the palace and ask for that fellow Sandal, that son of a wide-nostrilled bitch. If he does not fulfil his promise, as Allāh lives, I will bugger him.' With that he made his way to the palace. When he got there, he found the place upside down and, at the very door, he saw Sandal, the black eunuch, sitting in the middle of a respectful group of other black eunuchs, talking and gesticulating. As Khalīfah advanced towards these people a young mamlūk would have barred his passage, so he pushed him out of the way, crying: 'Away, you son of a pimp!' Sandal turned his head at this cry and, recognising the fisherman, laughed and told him to draw near. Khalīfah advanced, saying: 'As Allāh lives, I would have recognised you among a thousand, my blond, my little tulip.' The eunuch laughed with all his lungs, and answered kindly: 'Sit down for a little while, O Khalīfah, O master. I will pay you in a moment.' He had just put his hand in his pocket for the money when a cry announced the approach of Jafar, the grand-wazīr, who had just left the Khalīfah.

At this point Shahrazād saw the approach of morning and discreetly fell silent.

But when the five-hundred-and-sixty-sixth night had come

SHE SAID:

The eunuch, slaves, and mamlūks ranged themselves in two lines; and Sandal, receiving a sign from the wazīr, left the fisherman and hurried up to Jafar. The two fell into a long conversation, walking up and down the hall.

But Khalīfah, seeing that the eunuch did not come back to him, thought that this was a trick to escape payment, especially as the eunuch seemed to have forgotten him and took no notice of him at all. He therefore began to fidget and sign to the eunuch to return; then, when the other paid no attention, he cried: 'My lord Tulip, give me my due and let me go.' Sandal was thrown into great confusion by this address, delivered in Jafar's presence, and, instead of answering, began to talk with more and more animation, to distract the wazīr's attention. He might have spared his pains, for Khalīfah came near and cried in a terrible voice and with vast gestures: 'Allāh confound the faithless, you insolent ruffian! Allāh confound the oppressors of the poor!' Then, changing his voice to one of irony, he continued: 'I put myself under your protection, O my lord Hollow-belly. I beg you to pay me what you owe and let me go my way.' This time Jafar heard, but did not understand. Therefore he turned to the confused eunuch, and asked: 'What is the matter with that poor man? Who has been cheating him?' 'My lord, do you not know the man?' said Sandal; but the wazīr replied: 'As Allāh lives, how should I know him since I have never seen him before?' 'But my lord,' went on the unhappy eunuch, 'this is the very fisherman whose fish we brought to the Khalīfah yesterday. I promised him money for his two last fish, and he has come to-day to be paid. I was about to satisfy him when I had to come to you. That is why the impatient lad talks in this way.'

The wazīr Jafar smiled sweetly, and said: 'O chief of the eunuchs, do you speak thus disrespectfully of the master of the Amīr's self? Poor Sandal, what will the Khalīfah say when he learns that you have not honoured Khalīfah the fisherman, his instructor and fellow? ... Do not let him go, for his coming is most fortunate. The Khalīfah mourns in despair for the death of his favourite and I have tried without success all ordinary ways of distracting him, but I think that we can cheer him up with the help of Khalīfah. Keep him here while I go and sound the feelings of the Khalīfah.' 'Do as you judge propitious, my lord,' answered Sandal. 'May Allāh preserve you for ever as the stay, the pillar, the cornerstone of the empire and dynasty! May He shed the shadow of His protection upon you and upon it! May the branch, the trunk, and the root remain unwithered throughout the ages!' So saying, he hastened to join Khalīfah, while Jafar departed to the apartments of al-Rashīd. 'So there you are, hollowbelly!' cried the fisherman and then, when he heard the eunuch order the mamlūks to keep him, he yelled at the top of his voice: 'Keep him? Keep him? There is not much chance of my going before I am paid. I come here for my just due, O tulip of my zabb, and then they imprison me because I am behind with my taxes!' So much for him.

Jafar went gently in and found the Khalīfah bent double, his head between his hands and his breast shaken by sobs. He heard him saying softly:

> Child, who went gathering the flowers of death,
> My heart's not I, I cannot teach my heart;
> It cries when I forget.
> It has not learnt my art
> To forget lips when scented with their breath
> Or the red cup when I am drunken yet.

Jafar bowed low, and said: 'Peace be upon you, O Commander of the Faithful, O Defender of the honour of Allāh, O descendant of the uncle of the Prophet! May the prayer and peace of Allāh be upon him and upon all his seed for ever!'

At this point Shahrazād saw the approach of morning and discreetly fell silent.

But when the five-hundred-and-sixty-seventh night had come

SHE SAID:

The Khalīfah lifted tear-dimmed eyes and a haggard face to Jafar; then he answered: 'The peace and mercy and blessing of Allāh be upon you!' 'Does the Prince of Believers permit his slave to speak or does he forbid?' asked the wazīr; and al-Rashīd asked in his turn: 'Since when has the lord and head of all my wazīrs needed to ask leave to speak?' Then said Jafar: 'My King, when I left you just now I met at the door of the palace, all among the eunuchs, your master and professor, Khalīfah the fisherman. He has much cause of complaint against you. I heard him say: "Glory be to Allāh, I do not understand what has happened. I taught him the art of fishing and he showed no gratitude; also he went to fetch two baskets and never came back. Is that good fellowship or good apprenticeship? Is that how masters of the craft are paid?" I hasten to tell you of this, O Prince of Believers, so that, if you still wish to go into partnership with him, you can do so; and, if you do not, you can tell him that your joint labours are over and that he must look for another companion.'

In spite of the sobs which stifled him, the Khalīfah first smiled and then roared with laughter. Quite suddenly he felt his heart grow lighter, and said: 'By my life, tell me the truth, Jafar. Is the fisherman Khalīfah really in the palace?' 'I swear by your life that he is here in flesh and blood,' answered Jafar. Then said Hārūn: 'As Allāh lives, I must do justice upon him to-day and let him have his due. If Allāh wishes to send him pains and penalties through me, it must be so; if he wishes to send him rank and fortune, it must be so.' So saying, the Khalīfah took a large sheet of paper and, while he was cutting it into little equal pieces, continued: 'You must first write, on twenty of these tickets, sums of money ranging from one dīnār to a thousand dīnārs and the names of the ranks of my kingdom, from the dignity of Khalīfah, amīr, wazīr and chamberlain, down to the most degraded offices of the palace; then on twenty other tickets you must write the names of punishments and tortures, from simple beating up to the gallows and a shameful death.' Jafar thereupon took pen and wrote upon the tickets in his own hand such inscriptions as these: *A thousand dīnārs, to be a chamberlain, amīrship, Khalīfah's dignity, sentence of death, imprisonment, the stick,* and the like. Then he folded all the tickets into the same shape and, casting them into a little gold basin, gave the basin to the Khalīfah, who said: 'I swear by my sacred ancestors, by my royal line which stretches back to Akīl, that I will order Khalīfah the fisherman to draw one of these tickets and reward him according to its writing. Should it be Khalīfah's dignity, I will cheerfully abdicate in his favour; should it be hanging or mutilation or gelding, that also will I cheerfully give him. Let him be brought to me at once!'

Said Jafar to himself: 'There is no power or might save in Allāh! It is quite possible that this poor fellow will draw a bad ticket and thus I shall be unwillingly the cause of his death. The Khalīfah has sworn and nothing will change him. Now I am committed to fetching the unfortunate man. Be it as Allāh wills!' He then went out from the Khalīfah and found the fisherman; but when he would have taken him by the hand and led him in, Khalīfah, who had not ceased to fidget and complain and repent of his coming, thought that he had lost his wits and cried: 'What a fool I was to listen to this ill-omened tulip, this blobber-lipped son of a bitch, this hollow-belly!' But Jafar bade him follow and dragged him along, pressed close by a crowd of slaves and boys, through seven vast vestibules and right to the entrance of the Khalīfah's apartments. 'Be careful, Khalīfah,' he said, 'you are about to enter the presence of the Prince of Believers, the Defender of the Faith.' Drawing aside a large curtain, he pushed the fisherman into the reception hall, where Hārūn al-Rashīd sat throned among his amīrs; but Khalīfah, who did not understand what he saw, was in no way disconcerted. After examining the Khalīfah carefully, he went up to him with a bellow of laughter, and said: 'So there you are, clarinet. Do you think that you behaved well to leave me in the lurch with all the fish, when I had taught you the art and sent you to fetch baskets? I was left defenceless and at the mercy of a flock of eunuchs, who came round me like vultures and stole all the fish. I should have got a hundred dīnārs for them. And I would not be surprised if you were the cause of my being kept here by all these people. . . . Now tell me, clarinet, who has imprisoned you and fastened you to that chair?'

At this point Shahrazād saw the approach of morning and discreetly fell silent.

But when the five hundred-and-sixty-eighth night had come

SHE SAID:

The Khalífah smiled and held out the gold bowl, saying: 'Draw near, Khalífah, and take one of these tickets.' But Khalífah, being unable to contain his mirth, cried out: 'What, has little clarinet given up music and become an astrologer? Yesterday it was fishing. Believe me, clarinet, all this will not take you very far; the more trades, the less profit. Let the astrology business be and either return to your clarinet or let me go on teaching you.' He would have continued in this strain had not Jafar approached him, saying: 'Enough of that! Draw one of these tickets, as the Commander of the Faithful has bidden you.'

He pushed him towards the throne and Khalífah, with a backward blow of his elbow, leaned cursing over the basin and, plunging his hand in heavily, pulled out a handful of the tickets. Jafar bade him put these back and take only one; so the fisherman, elbowing the wazír out of the way again, took a single ticket, saying: 'I shall never again employ a fat-faced clarinet player, or an astrologer for that matter.' So saying, he unfolded the ticket and handed it upside down to the Khalífah: 'Tell me my horoscope, clarinet,' he begged, 'do not hide anything from me!' The Khalífah passed the ticket to Jafar, bidding him read out the writing in a loud voice; so Jafar raised his arms and cried: 'There is no power or might save in Allāh! There is written upon this ticket: *a hundred blows of the stick.*'

'Let justice be done,' said the Khalífah; and, at once, Masrūr seized the protesting fisherman and gave him a hundred heavy blows with the stick; whereat Khalífah, though he did not feel the least pain, yelled lamentably and heaped a thousand curses on the clarinet player. Hārūn laughed immoderately; but Khalífah, leaping to his feet as if nothing had happened, called out: 'Allāh confound your joke, you silly bloat-face; do you think that a stick passes for wit among men of taste?' The soft-hearted Jafar then turned to the Khalífah, saying: 'Let him draw another ticket; perhaps there is a better fate in store for him. You would not wish your old fishing master to depart thirsting from the river of your liberality?' 'You are very imprudent, Jafar,' answered al-Rashíd. 'Kings may not break their word; perhaps the fisherman might come to be hanged if he took a second chance. His death would be at your door.' But Jafar answered: 'By Allāh, death is better than life when a man is so unfortunate!' 'So be it,' agreed Hārūn. 'Let him draw another ticket.' But Khalīfah cried: 'Let Allāh reward your generosity, O clarinet of my bum! Is there no one else in all Baghdād to join you in this game?' 'Take another ticket and Allāh will choose it for you,' said Jafar.

Khalīfah plunged his hand again into the basin and drew out a ticket which Jafar opened and read. 'Well,' said the Khalīfah, 'why do you not announce the reward?' 'O Prince of Believers,' replied the wazīr, 'there is nothing written on this ticket; it is a blank one.' Then said the Khalīfah: 'I was right; there is no fortune waiting for him with us. Tell him to be gone, for I have seen enough of him.' But Jafar ventured to insist that Khalīfah should have a third chance, and al-Rashīd consented to a third but no more. Then said Jafar to the fisherman: 'Poor man, take your third and last ticket.'

At this point Shahrazād saw the approach of morning and discreetly fell silent.

But when the five-hundred-and-sixty-ninth night had come

SHE SAID:

Khalīfah drew again and Jafar, taking the ticket, announced: *one dīnār.* 'Curses upon you, ill-omened clarinet! A dīnār for a hundred strokes!' cried the wrathful fisherman. 'May Allāh give you the like on the Day of Judgment.' The Khalīfah laughed with all his heart, and Jafar, who had succeeded at last in distracting his master from his sorrow, took Khalīfah by the hand and led him from the hall.

As the unfortunate fisherman was leaving the palace, the eunuch Sandal called him, saying: 'Come here, and let us share in the generosity of the Khalīfah.' 'You want to share, do you, pitch-face?' answered Khalīfah. 'Your black hide is welcome to half of my beating; in the meanwhile, until the devil gives it you in hell, you can have the dīnār which your master gave me, that nasty scurvy little clarinet!' So saying he threw the dīnār in the eunuch's face and would have gone out through the door, but Sandal ran after him and pressed a purse of a hundred dīnārs into his hand, saying: 'This is for the fish. Now go in peace.' Khalīfah rejoiced exceedingly; he pressed the purse to his bosom with one hand and picked up the rejected dīnār with the other; then he went on his way, puffed out with glory and delight.

When Allāh has decreed a thing, He brings it to pass, and He had made a decree concerning this Khalīfah. Thus it was that the fisherman, while passing through the slave market, was attracted by a crowd and, urged by curiosity, elbowed his way forward among the rich and poor with considerable vigour. When the people recognised him, they cried to each other: 'Make way for this rich lord, he is going to buy the market! Make way for Khalīfah, the sublime master of buggers!' The fisherman was not in the least dashed by these remarks, for he felt sustained by the dīnārs in his belt. Pushing forward, he saw an old man sitting with a chest in front of him and heard him crying in a loud voice: 'O rich merchants, O noble citizens of our city, who will risk his money at cent per cent and buy this chest with a speculative content? It comes from the harīm of Zubaidah, Queen of the Commander of the Faithful! Allāh will bless the highest bidder!' A general silence answered this appeal, for the merchants feared some trick. At last, with many apologies, one man offered twenty dīnārs, another raised the bid to fifty, and soon the price of the chest stood at a hundred dīnārs. Then cried the auctioneer: 'Going at a hundred dīnārs, a hundred dīnārs, to the last bidder.' But Khalīfah lifted up his voice, and cried: 'A hundred and one!'

At this the merchants, who imagined that he had about as much money as a beaten carpet, began to laugh; but Khalīfah undid his belt, furiously repeating: 'A hundred and one.' 'As Allāh lives, the chest belongs to him,' said the auctioneer. 'I sell it to him only. Take your chest and may Allāh bless the bargain.' So Khalīfah emptied all his money into the man's hand and the chest became his lawful property.

At once all the porters of the market hurled themselves on the chest, fighting as to who should carry it, which did not suit the unfortunate Khalīfah at all, since he had not a penny left to buy an onion. Yet the porters continued to fight, snatching the chest one from the other, until the merchants intervened, and said that Zuraik had got there first. So, in spite of Khalīfah's protestations, they drove away the other porters and lifted the chest on to Zuraik's back, telling him to follow his master. This the porter did.

At this point Shahrazād saw the approach of morning and discreetly fell silent.

But when the five-hundred-and-seventieth night had come

SHE SAID:

As they went along, Khalīfah said to himself: 'I have neither gold, silver, nor copper; I have not the smell of a coin. How am I going to pay this wretched porter? I do not want the fellow; for that matter, I do not want the chest. I have no idea what possessed me to buy it. I suppose it was written in my Destiny. In the meanwhile, I think I know how to deal with the porter; I will make him run up and down and lose his way until he is worn out and refuses of his own accord to go any further. Then I will refuse to pay, and carry the chest myself.'

At once he put his plan into execution: he walked from one street into another and from one square into another, and turned the porter about and about over all the city, from noon till sunset; and at last the man grumbled and asked where the house was. 'As Allāh lives,' answered Khalīfah, 'yesterday I knew very well where it was. To-day I have quite forgotten. We are looking for it.' 'Give me my hire and take the chest,' said the porter, but Khalīfah replied: 'Wait a bit longer, go slowly, give me time to collect my memory and reflect about the position of my house.' A little later, when the porter began grumbling between his teeth again, Khalīfah said to him: 'O Zuraik, I have no money at all with me; my money is all at the house.'

The porter halted, not being able to go any further, and was about to set down his burden when one of Khalīfah's friends passed and tapped him on the shoulder, saying: 'Is that you, Khalīfah? What are you doing so far from your house? What is this man carrying for you?' The fisherman was put quite out of countenance; but Zuraik turned to the passenger, asking: 'O uncle, where is Khalīfah's house?' 'That is a strange question,' answered the man, 'his house is at the other end of Baghdād, in the ruined khān near the fish market.' Then he went laughing upon his way, and Zuraik cried to Khalīfah: 'Get on with you, you cheat.' He made the fisherman walk before him, right to the ruined khān by the fish market, and did not cease to curse and reproach him by the way. 'May Allāh cut off your daily bread, O evil face!' he said. 'How many times have we not already passed your wretched house! Come on now, help me to set the thing down. I would like to see you shut up in it for ever.' Khalīfah helped him down with the chest, and then Zuraik wiped the big drops of sweat from his forehead with the back of his hand, saying: 'Now let us see the greatness of your soul and the generosity of your hand. Hasten to pay me, for I would depart.' 'Certainly, old companion, certainly. Shall I bring you gold or silver?' asked Khalīfah; and the man answered more politely: 'You know, better than I do, what is fitting.'

Khalīfah left the porter at the door and entered his lodging; in a moment he returned with a most terrible whip in his hand: its forty lashes were clouted with sharp nails; one blow of it would have stunned a camel. Whirling the whip above his head, he threw himself upon the porter and beat him so heartily over the back that the poor fellow fled screaming, his hands pawing the air, and disappeared round the corner of the street.

Having thus got rid of the porter (who, we must remember, had insisted on carrying the chest when he was not wanted), Khalīfah began to drag it indoors himself; but he made so much noise that the neighbours gathered together about him and, noticing both the chest and the satin robe, asked him where he had got these things. 'They were given me by an apprentice lad of mine, a clarinet player who calls himself Hārūn al-Rashīd,' answered the fisherman.

At this point Shahrazād saw the approach of morning and discreetly fell silent.

But when the five-hundred-and-seventy-first night had come

SHE SAID:

At these words the neighbours were seized with fear, and said: 'If anyone hears this madman he will be taken up by the police and hanged. Our khān will be destroyed and perhaps we shall be hung at the gate of it, or terribly beaten.' Therefore they bade Khalīfah be silent and, to be sooner quit of him, helped him carry the chest into his lodging and banged the door upon him.

Khalīfah's house was so small that the chest entirely filled it, just as if the former had been made to hold the latter; so Khalīfah was obliged to lie down on the chest to pass the night. While he was thinking over the events of the day, he suddenly asked himself why he should not open the chest and see the contents. He rose and tried to open the lid; but it was securely fastened down. 'Fool that I was to buy a chest that I cannot even open!' he cried, and tried again to break the chains of the lock. At last he determined to wait for the morrow and, stretching himself out again on the lid, was soon snoring loudly.

In an hour he leapt up broad awake, in an access of terror, and struck his head against the ceiling. He had felt something move inside the box! Sleep and judgment fled from his brain at the same moment, and he cried: 'There is a Jinnī inside! Praise be to Allāh that

I could not open the lid! If I had freed him in the dark, what would have happened? This is not one of my lucky days.' Just then the noise in the chest redoubled and he could distinguish a kind of groaning; therefore he searched feverishly for a lamp, with chattering teeth, barking his knuckles against the wall and quite forgetting that he was too poor to own such a thing. 'This is terrible, terrible!' he cried, as he sprang through the door into the street. With fear at his heels he rushed through the night, yelling: 'Help, help! O neighbours, O neighbours, help!' The people of the khān, who were already fast asleep, woke up in considerable emotion and showed themselves, while half-veiled women peered from the doors. They all asked him what had happened, and he replied: 'Give me a lamp, for pity's sake! The Jinn have come to visit me!' At this the neighbours laughed, but one of them gave him a lamp. The light reassured him and he returned to his house; but, as he was leaning over the chest, a voice from within said: 'Where am I? Where am I?' Khalīfah again rushed like a madman into the street, crying: 'Help! Help!' When the neighbours called out to know what was the matter, he shouted: 'Good people, the Jinnī is talking in the box! He is asking where he is.' The neighbours laughed again, and said: 'Tell him he is in hell, you fool. Are we never going to get any sleep? You are a nuisance to the whole quarter. If you are not quiet, we will come down and break your bones.' Despairing of help from his neighbours, Khalīfah determined to go back once more to the house, although he was well-nigh dead from fear. He took up a large stone and, summoning all his courage, broke the lock of the chest and pulled back the lid.

Inside he saw a girl as beautiful as the hūrīs and all shining in the little light with diamonds. She lay languishing with half-closed lids, deeply breathing the air of freedom, and gradually throwing off the vapours of the drug. She lay there, pale and handsome and desirable.

The fisherman, who had never in his life seen even common beauty, knelt before her, saying: 'In Allāh's name, who are you, my mistress?'

At this point Shahrazād saw the approach of morning and discreetly fell silent.

But when the five-hundred-and-seventy-second night had come

SHE SAID:

She opened dark eyes under curved lids, saying: 'Where are Jasmine and Jonquil?' These were the names of her two little slaves, but Khalīfah thought that she was asking for jasmines and jonquils, so he answered: 'Dear mistress, for the moment, I only have a few flowers of dried henna.' Hearing this answer, the girl came completely to her senses and, opening her eyes wide, asked: 'Who are you? And where am I?' This question was made in a voice suaver than sugar, accompanied by a delicious movement of the hands, and Khalīfah, who had somewhere deep within him a most sensitive soul, was moved in the extreme, and answered: 'O mistress, O true beauty, I am Khalīfah the fisherman; and you are in my house.' 'I am not at the palace then?' she asked, and he replied: 'You are not. You are in my house. But that is now a palace. You have become my slave by fair buying and selling in the market, for I paid a hundred and one dīnārs for you with your box thrown in. In fact, I did not know you were inside until you frightened me very much by moving. I think my star is rising into happy spaces, though it used to be so low and dim.' Heart's-Life smiled, and said: 'You bought me without seeing me, O Khalīfah?' 'Without even knowing you were there,' he answered. At once Heart's-Life understood Zubaidah's plot and made the fisherman tell her the whole story of that day. They talked together until the morning, and then the woman said: 'O Khalīfah, have you got nothing to eat? I am very hungry.' 'I have nothing to eat or drink; nothing at all,' he answered. 'For two days food has not passed my lips.' 'Have you money?' she asked, and he said: 'Money? Saving your presence, this cursed chest has run away with my last coin. I am hard aground.' The girl laughed musically at this and begged Khalīfah to go forth and ask food from the neighbours.

The fisherman went out into the morning silence of the khān and began to cry at the top of his voice: 'O neighbours, come to my help! The Jinnī in the box wants something to eat! Give me some food!' The neighbours, who had learnt to dread his voice and also sincerely pitied him because of his poverty, threw down food to him; half of yesterday's loaf from one house, a bit of cheese from another, a cucumber, a radish, and so on. He gathered up these things in the folds of his lifted garment and, returning to the house, gave them to the girl. He prayed her to eat, but she said with a laugh: 'How can

I eat when I have no little jar or pitcher of water? This food would stick in my throat and I should die.' 'Allāh protect you from such a misfortune, O perfection of beauty!' said Khalīfah. 'I will bring you, not a pitcher, but a whole waterskin.' So saying, he ran out again into the courtyard of the khān and bellowed at the top of the compass of his deep chest: 'O neighbours, O good neighbours!' Angry voices cursed him from all sides and asked what he wanted now. 'The Jinnī in the box needs some water,' he answered. Then the neighbours came down, one carrying a cup, one a pitcher, one a pipkin, and one a jar; and he took all these things, bearing one in each hand, one beneath each arm, and balancing one on his head. He returned to Heart's-Life, saying: 'I bring you your desire. Do you wish for anything else?' 'No,' she answered, 'the gifts of Allāh are great enough.' 'Then, dear mistress,' said he, 'speak more of your sweet words to me and tell me the story of your adventure.'

Heart's-Life looked at Khalīfah with a smile, and thus began: 'My story can be told in two words: rival's jealousy. Zubaidah, Queen of the Khalīfah, Hārūn al-Rashīd, imprisoned me in this chest from which your happy Destiny has saved me. I am Heart's-Life, favourite of the Commander of the Faithful. Your fortune is certainly made.' Then said Khalīfah: 'But is this Hārūn al-Rashīd the man I taught how to fish? Is he that scarecrow who sat on a big chair in the palace?' 'You describe him exactly,' she answered, and he continued: 'As Allāh lives, I have never in all my life met such an ugly clarinet player or a greater rascal. First he robbed me, the puff-faced little scoundrel, and then he gave me a dīnār for a hundred strokes with the stick. If ever I meet him again . . .' Here Heart's-Life bade him be silent, saying: 'You must leave this unpleasant form of language behind you in the new situation to which Fate is calling you. You must open the eyes of your soul, you must cultivate politeness and good manners. If you pass the scraper of gallantry over your skin, you will become a polished citizen of high degree, a personage of mark because of his delicacy.'

At this point Shahrazād saw the approach of morning and discreetly fell silent.

But when the five-hundred-and-seventy-third night had come

SHE SAID:

At these words, Khalīfah felt a sudden transformation take place within him: the eyes of his soul opened, his understanding of many things enlarged, and his intelligence refined. All this was for his good. How true it is that fine spirits influence grosser spirits! In a minute of time Khalīfah the fisherman, an insensate and brutal man, was changed by the gentle words of the girl into an exquisite citizen, well-mannered and strangely eloquent.

When Heart's-Life had carefully taught him how to bear himself if he were called again into the presence of the Khalīfah, he exclaimed: 'Be it upon my head and before my eyes! Your counsel, dear mistress, is my rule of conduct, your interest in me is a shade beneath which my soul rejoices. I hear and I obey. May Allāh shower His blessing upon you and satisfy your least desires. Here, between your hands, behold Khalīfah the fisherman, the most devoted of your slaves, the most deferential to your merit. What can I do to serve you?' 'Give me a pen, some ink, and a sheet of paper,' she answered, and immediately Khalīfah borrowed these things politely from the neighbours. Heart's-Life wrote a line to the jeweller, Ibn al-Kirnās, in which she told him what had happened and explained that she was in the house of Khalīfah the fisherman, who had bought her for a hundred and one dīnārs. Then she gave the note to Khalīfah, saying: 'Take this to Ibn al-Kirnās, the Khalīfah's man of affairs; anyone in the jewel market will know his shop. And do not forget what I have taught you of manners and language.' Khalīfah carried the note to his lips and to his forehead, and then hurried to the shop of Ibn al-Kirnās in the jewel market. He bowed with exquisite grace before the jeweller and wished him peace. The jeweller returned his salute with the lips only and hardly glanced at him as he asked his business. Khalīfah stretched forth the note and the jeweller, taking it in the tips of his fingers, laid it unread beside him. He thought that this was some begging demand and therefore bade one of his servants give the man half a dirham; but Khalīfah put aside the coin with great dignity, saying: 'I ask no alms; I only ask you to read this letter.' The jeweller unfolded the paper and read its contents; suddenly he kissed the letter with respect and invited Khalīfah to be seated. 'Where is your house, my brother?' he asked and, when Khalīfah had told him, called his two chief assistants and said to them: 'Accompany my honourable guest to my banker, Moses, that he may receive a thousand dīnārs; then lead him back to me at once.' When Khalīfah returned from receiving his thousand dīnārs from the Jew, he found Ibn al-Kirnās already mounted on a magnificent mule with gay trappings, and surrounded by a hundred slaves very richly dressed. The jeweller pointed out a second and no less perfect mule to Khalīfah and begged him to mount; but he objected, saying: 'As Allāh lives, I have never been upon a mule in my life, dear master. I do not know how to ride.' 'That makes no matter,' said the jeweller, 'you will learn to-day.' Then Khalīfah cried: 'I am afraid that she will throw me and break my ribs; but still, here goes, in the name of Allāh.' With that he leapt nimbly upon the mule's back, but unfortunately he faced the wrong way and took up the tail instead of the bridle. This tickled the mule, who reared and rushed about the street until she unseated her rider. 'I always said that feet were best for walking!' cried Khalīfah, as he picked himself up. But that was the last misfortune of Khalīfah the fisherman. Thenceforth Destiny was to lead him without swerving along a prosperous road.

At this point Shahrazād saw the approach of morning and discreetly fell silent.

But when the five-hundred-and-seventy-fourth night had come

SHE SAID:

The jeweller said to two of his slaves: 'Lead your master to the hammām and see that he has a bath of rare quality; then bring him back to my house, where I shall be waiting.' Then he rode alone to Khalīfah's lodging to bring Heart's-Life also to his house.

The two slaves led Khalīfah to the hammām, which he had never visited in his life, and put him in charge of the most skilful rubber and the best washers. These elicited from his hair and skin pounds and pounds of assorted filth, with lice and bugs of every variety. They cleaned, refreshed, and dried him. Then they dressed him in a sumptuous silk robe which the two slaves had gone out to buy. Thus habited, he was taken to the home of Ibn al-Kirnās, where Heart's-Life had already arrived.

Khalīfah saw the girl seated on a dīwān in the great hall of the house, surrounded by a crowd of slaves and servants eager to wait upon her. Already the porter at the door had risen in his honour and respectfully kissed his hand, already those whom he passed had politely wished him joy of his bath; and he was in a state of considerable astonishment. He pretended to see no change in folk, lest he should seem ill-bred; but answered all with urbane eloquence, so that the sound of his own words surprised and flattered him.

He bowed before Heart's-Life and waited for her to speak the first words; she rose in his honour and, taking him by the hand, made him sit beside her. She gave him a porcelain cup filled with sugared sherbert scented with rose-water, and he both took and drank this delicately. He did not make a noise with his mouth and he drank only a portion of it, instead of draining it all down and plunging in his fingers to lick up the drops, as he would most certainly have done before. He even set the cup down on the tray without breaking it, and gave eloquent expression to the necessary polite phrase: 'May the hospitality of this house endure for ever!' 'And your life also,' answered Heart's-Life, quite delighted with her pupil. After feasting him royally, she said: 'The time has come, O Khalīfah, for you to display all your intelligence. Listen to me and mark well all I say. You must go to the palace of the Khalīfah and, when he has granted you an audience, must say: "O Commander of the Faithful, I have a favour to ask in memory of my teaching with the nets." He will accept in advance and then you must ask him to be your guest tonight. That is all; for he will assuredly come.'

Khalīfah journeyed towards the palace, followed by a numerous retinue of slaves; and, dressed in his robe of thousand dīnār silk, his native beauty shone forth and was revealed. The proverb says: 'Dress an old stick in good clothes and it looks like the bride.' He was seen a long way off by the eunuch Sandal, who ran as fast as his legs could carry him into the throne-hall and said to the Khalīfah: 'O Prince of Believers, I do not know what has happened, but it seems as if Khalīfah the fisherman had become King. He advances in a robe worth more than a thousand dīnārs, the head of a splendid following!' 'Bring him in,' said the Khalīfah.

When Khalīfah was led into the hall where Hārūn al-Rashīd sat in his glory, he bowed as only the greatest amīrs know how to bow, and said: 'Peace be upon you, O Prince of Believers, O Khalīfah of the Master of the Three Worlds, Defender of the people and of our Faith! May Allāh prolong your days, honouring your reign and exalting its dignity; may He sustain your name upon the top pinnacle of greatness!'

The Khalīfah marvelled at this change of heart and fortune. 'Will you tell me where you got this fair robe, O Khalīfah?' he asked. 'From my palace, O Commander of the Faithful,' answered Khalīfah. 'You have a palace, then?' exclaimed Hārūn, and the fisherman replied: 'I have a palace, O Prince of Believers. Yet it will not be truly a palace, unless you light it with your presence to-night. You are my invited guest.' 'Your guest?' said al-Rashīd with a smile. 'Do you mean alone, or does the invitation extend to any who may be with me?' 'It extends to all whom you may desire to bring, my lord,' answered Khalīfah.

At this point Shahrazād saw the approach of morning and discreetly fell silent.

But when the five-hundred-and-seventy-fifth night had come

SHE SAID:

Hārūn signed to Jafar, who went up to Khalīfah, saying: 'We will be your guests to-night, O Khalīfah; the Commander of the Faithful wishes it.' Satisfied with this assurance, the fisherman kissed the earth between the hands of the Khalīfah and, after giving Jafar the address of his new abode, returned to Heart's-Life and told her of the success of his visit.

As for the Khalīfah, he could not understand the matter at all. 'Can you explain to me, O Jafar,' he said, 'how Khalīfah, the boorish laughing-stock of yesterday, can have become, in a single night, a refined and eloquent citizen and a man of riches?' 'Allāh alone knows by what strange roads Destiny will come to its goal,' answered Jafar.

When evening came, the Khalīfah mounted on horseback and rode with Jafar, Masrūr, and one or two others, to Khalīfah's residence. They halted before the door and saw the ground, from the entrance to the reception hall, covered with expensive carpets, and the carpets strewn with the colours of flowers; also they saw Khalīfah stand smiling at the foot of the steps. He held Hārūn's stirrup and wished him welcome with a low bow; then he led him within doors in Allāh's name.

The Khalīfah found himself in a high-ceiled hall, ornamented with a perfection of taste, in the middle of which there was a square throne of ivory and gold upon gold feet. As soon as the Sultān was seated upon this throne, slaves came in bearing enormous dishes of gold and porcelain, and young cupbearers, as fair as fragments of the moon, presented the guests with precious cups, in which were refreshing concoctions, iced with pure musk. Other and more handsome boys entered in little white robes, who served stuffed geese, chickens, roast lambs, and spitted birds of every kind. As soon as these were eaten, young and delightful Christian slaves, elegantly girt in at the waist, lifted the cloths and carried round salvers of drinks and trifling dulcifications. The wines showed red in crystal vases and gushed red from golden jars; as they were poured out by the white hands of the cupbearers, they gave forth an old and pleasant smell. You would have thought of the poet's line:

> Pour that old wine for me
> And for my friend, this child,
> It is a precious wine
> Spilled for a wine-adept,
> I cannot find a name
> For its mild flame
> Except:
> Wine of my friend, this child.

Bewildered by what he saw, the Khalīfah said to Jafar: 'By the life of my head, I do not know which I admire more, the magnificence of our reception or the exquisite, and even noble, manner of our host. These things pass my understanding.' But Jafar answered: 'What we have seen so far is nothing to what He will show, Who says: "Be!" and things are. The aspect of Khalīfah which I most admire is the certainty of his discourse, the wisdom of what he says. That is a sign that his Destiny is a rare one; for, when Allāh gives largely to a man, He dowers him first with wisdom as a sign.'

While Jafar was speaking, Khalīfah returned after a short absence, and said to the Khalīfah: 'Will the Commander of the Faithful permit his slave to bring in a singer and a lute player to charm his hours? There is no woman in all Baghdād more expert in music.' 'The thing is allowed,' answered the Khalīfah; and the fisherman, hastening to the apartments of Heart's-Life, told her that the moment had come.

Heart's-Life, who was already decked and perfumed in readiness, had only to wrap herself in her great izār and cover herself with a light silken veil, Khalīfah took her by the hand and led her into the hall, which sighed with delight at her royal tread.

She kissed the earth between the Khalīfah's hands and sat down near him, without being at all recognised. She tuned her lute and executed a ravishing prelude. Then she sang:

> My life is a feather
> And this is
>   Held up by a breath on a thread;
>   I feed upon hope as on bread,
> O nights in the house of our kisses,
> O nights of our lying together.

Hearing this voice of erewhile and the known beauty of it, the Khalīfah gave a cry and became very pale. As the last words of the song died out on the air, he fell into a swoon.

At this point Shahrazād saw the approach of morning and discreetly fell silent.

But when the five-hundred-and-seventy-sixth night had come

SHE SAID:

Every one crowded round him with sudden cares; but Heart's-Life, using Khalīfah as her mouthpiece, begged all the guests to retire and leave her alone to care for the Khalīfah. When the hall was empty save for the three of them, the girl threw off her izār and veil, and appeared in a dress such as she had worn when the Khalīfah loved her in the palace. She sat down beside al-Rashīd, sprinkling his face with rose-water and fanning him with her fan.

Soon the Khalīfah opened his eyes and, looking up into the face of his beloved, nearly fainted a second time. The girl kissed his hands, smiling and weeping at once, and al-Rashīd cried: 'Is this the Day of Resurrection when the dead rise from their graves, or is it a dream?' 'Commander of the Faithful,' answered Heart's-Life, 'this is neither Resurrection nor a dream. I am your living love; my death was only feigned.' In brief words she told him all that had passed, and added: 'Our present happiness is entirely due to Khalīfah the fisherman.' Al-Rashīd laughed, and then wept and sobbed, and then laughed again. When she had finished speaking, he drew her to him and kissed her long upon the lips, holding her to his breast. For an hour they could not speak, and stayed thus in perfect happiness.

At the end of that hour Khalīfah rose, saying: 'As Allāh lives, O Prince of Believers, I hope it will not be the stick this time.'

The Khalīfah who was now quite recovered, chuckled as he

answered: 'O Khalīfah, nothing that I can do for you will pay my debt. I can only ask you to be my friend and govern one of the provinces of my empire.' 'Can a slave refuse the gifts of his master?' answered Khalīfah, and Hārūn went on: 'Not only are you appointed governor of a province, with a monthly emolument of ten thousand dīnārs, but I desire Heart's-Life to choose for you, from among the noble daughters of our city, a young and suitable wife. For her clothing and dowry I will be responsible. Also remember that I wish to see you every day and have you by my side at feasts, among the first of my intimate friends. You shall have a household worthy of your rank, and anything more which your soul desires.'

Khalīfah kissed the earth between the hands of the Khalīfah. All this promised happiness came to him and many other joys beside. He ceased to be a bachelor and lived for many years with his young wife, whom Heart's-Life chose for him. She was the most beautiful and modest woman of her time. Glory be to Him Who casts down His favours upon His people without taking account of the sum, and distributes joy according to His will!

Then said Shahrazād: 'But do not think for a moment, O auspicious King, that this tale is in any way more admirable and strange than one which I have kept in reserve for the end of this night.' 'I do not doubt what you say, O Shahrazād,' cried King Shahryār. 'Tell me the name of the tale quickly; for it must be indeed wonderful if it surpasses the tale of Khalīfah the Fisherman.' Shahrazād smiled and said: 'O King, my story is called . . .'

The Adventures of Hasan of Basrah

AND SHAHRAZĀD SAID TO KING SHAHRYĀR:

THE marvellous story which I am going to tell you, O auspicious King, has so strange an origin that I must begin with that, if you are to understand how it ever became known to me.

In years and ages long ago there was a King of Persia and Khurāsān called Kindamīr, who was paramount over India, Sind, China, and those peoples who lived in the savage lands beyond the Oxus. He was a man of bravery, a great rider of horses; he could play with the lance, and loved tourneys, hunting and the clash of arms; but, to all other things, he preferred talk with men of intelligence and delicate wit. At his feasts he gave the places of honour near himself to poets and story tellers; and if ever a stranger at the palace told him a new or striking tale, King Kindamīr loaded him with benefits and, after satisfying his least desires, sent him back to his own land with a fine retinue of horsemen and slaves. His own story tellers and poets he treated as equal to wazīrs and amīrs, so that his palace was the favoured home of all who could make verses, construct odes, or cause dead time and vanished things to live in the spoken word.

It is not astonishing that a day came when King Kindamīr had heard all the tales of the Persians, Arabs, and Indians, and had stored them up in his memory, with the fairest passages in the poets and those teachings drawn by the annalists from a study of old-time folk. When he had run through his knowledge and made certain of it, he had nothing more to learn or to hear; therefore his grief and perplexity knew no bounds and he felt that there was nothing to fill his leisure.

He turned to his chief eunuch, saying: 'Bring Abū Alī to me.' This Abū Alī was the King's favourite teller of tales; he was so expert that he could make one story last a whole year, without discontinuing and without a single night wearying the attention of his hearers. But even he had exhausted his store and the resources of his eloquence; for a long time he had been beggared of new tales.

The eunuch fetched Abū Alī into the presence of the King, who said to him: 'Behold, O father of eloquence, you have exhausted your stores of learning, you are beggared of new stories! Yet I have called you into my presence to tell you that you must, in spite of all, find me a wonderful and unknown tale. I thirst for stories of adventure more than ever; so that, if you succeed in charming me with beautiful new words, I will give you great tracts of land in return, with strongholds and palaces and a firmān freeing you from every tax; I will make you my grand-wazīr and seat you on my right; you shall govern according to your whim, with full authority over all the vassals of my throne. Nay, if you desire it, I will bequeath you my throne and, in my lifetime, share all my goods with you. But if your Destiny should be so unfortunate that you cannot satisfy my desire, this my passion which prefers a new tale to all the countries of earth, you may start to-day saying farewell to your family, and tell them that the impaling stake awaits you.'

Abū Alī, the tale teller, felt himself lost, and answered: 'I hear and I obey.' Very yellow in the face, he lowered his despairing head, but, after a little, made bold to say: 'O King of time, your ignorant slave begs one thing more from your generosity before he dies: a year's delay in which to find what you desire. If, when that period is past, the tale is not found and, if found, is not the most beautiful and marvellous that man has heard, I will, without bitterness, experience the stake.' 'A year is very long,' said King Kindamīr to himself, 'no man knows whether he will be alive to-morrow.' Then aloud he added: 'I am so eager for the tale that I grant you a year, on condition that you do not leave your house during that time.' Abū Alī kissed the earth between the King's hands and returned to his home.

He thought for a long time and then called to him his five young mamlūks, who could write and read and were the most learned and faithful of all his servants. To each of these he gave five thousand dīnārs, saying: 'I brought you up, cared for you, and nourished you in my house expressly for a day such as this; now it is for you to help me and save me from the King.' 'Order, O master,' they replied, 'our souls belong to you and we are your ransom!' Then said he: 'Each of you must set out for foreign lands upon the different roads of Allāh; you must hunt all the kingdoms and countries of the earth for wise men, poets, and famous tale tellers; from these you must enquire for the Tale of the Adventures of Hasan of Basrah. If, under Allāh's favour, one of them knows this story, offer him any price to tell or write it for you; for, without that, your master cannot be saved from the stake.' Then he addressed each in turn with particular recommendations; he bade the first visit India and Sind; the second Persia, China, and adjacent lands; the third Khurāsān and its dependencies; the fourth all Maghrib from east to west; and to the fifth, he said: 'And you, O Mubārak, must journey throughout Egypt and Syria.'

At this point Shahrazād saw the approach of morning and discreetly fell silent.

But when the five-hundred-and-seventy-seventh night had come

SHE SAID:

He chose an auspicious day for the departure of the five mamlūks and sent them upon their different ways with an exhortation not to fail him. Yet, at the end of eleven months, the first four returned with very long noses and told their master that, in spite of the most minute researches, in cities and beneath tents, from tale tellers and ordinary poets, they had failed to find track of the story, and that the Adventures of Hasan were quite unknown.

The heart of the old teller, Abū Alī, retracted and the world grew black before his face. 'There is no power or might save in Allāh!' he cried. 'It is written in the Angel's book that the impaling stake awaits me.' And he made his will in expectation of that dark death.

Mubārak, the fifth mamlūk, had traversed all Egypt and the greater part of Syria without finding what he sought; even the famous tellers of Cairo could not help him, though their knowledge of tales passes the imagination. They had never even heard their fathers or grand-fathers, who were in the same trade, speak of the tale; so the young mamlūk journeyed to Damascus, hoping against hope. He was charmed by the climate and gardens of that city, by its waters and magnificence; and he would indeed have enjoyed himself if he had not been preoccupied with his seemingly hopeless mission. As he was walking through the streets on his first evening, in search of some khān wherein to pass the night, he saw, among the markets, a crowd of hawkers, scavengers, donkey-boys, diggers, merchants, water-carriers, and others hastening quickly in one direction. He was about to run with them, out of curiosity, when a young man bumped into him and tripped over the skirts of his robe. Mubārak helped the stranger to rise and, while dusting his back, asked him whither he and the crowd were hastening so fast. 'I can see that you are a stranger,' answered the young man, 'otherwise you would know that we are hurrying for places in the vaulted hall of the sheikh Ishāk, the sublime tale teller of our city, who has the most marvellous stories in the world. He has always a great crowd of hearers, and the last comers cannot get near enough to enjoy the tale at its full; there-fore I beg you to excuse me if I hurry on.' But the young mamlūk took hold of his garment, saying: 'O son of excellent parents, I beg you to take me with you, so that I can find a good place; for I greatly desire to hear the sheikh Ishāk and have come from very far away with no other object.' 'Follow me then and let us run,' cried the youth, and both of them ran towards the hall, jostling peaceable home-going folk to right and left in their great eagerness.

Entering a vast cool hall, Mubārak beheld a venerable old man with a noble face and clear shining brow, raised on a seat in the middle of a silent circle of porters, merchants, nobles, water-carriers, and every condition of folk. He was speaking in a grave voice and taking up the thread of the tale which he had been telling night after night for many months to his faithful auditors. But soon his voice warmed with the prodigious exploits of his warriors; urged by his uncontrollable vehemence, he rose from his seat and ran up and down the hall among his hearers, seeming to brandish his hero's deadly sword and make mincemeat of his enemies. 'So, so, the traitors die; they are damned and fall into the fires of hell! But Allāh help him! He is safe! No, no, he is not! Where are our swords, where are our clubs, that we may fly to succour him? Behold, his foes are down, he comes triumphant from the fight! Glory be to the Master of Valour! And now he walks to the tent where his lover waits for him, her multitudinous beauty makes him forget the perils of the day! Glory be to Allāh who has created woman to pour balm into the heart of the warrior and fire into his loins!'

Old Ishāk brought that evening's instalment to a close with these words; his hearers rose in ecstasy and left the hall, repeating the last few phrases as they went. Marvelling at so admirable an art, Mubārak went up to the sheikh and kissed his hand, saying: 'Master, I am a stranger and wish to ask you something.'

At this point Shahrazād saw the approach of morning and discreetly fell silent.

But when the five-hundred-and-seventy-eighth night had come

SHE SAID:

The old man answered his greeting, and said: 'Speak, for with us there is no such person as a stranger.' Then said the mamlūk: 'I come from very far away to offer you a present from my master, the teller, Abū Alī of Khurāsān, of a thousand golden dīnārs. My master esteems you to be the lord of tellers in this age over the earth, and wishes by his present to witness so!' 'Indeed the fame of Abū Alī of Khurāsān is known to all,' answered Ishāk, 'I accept his gift in a most friendly spirit and would wish to send something back to him by you. Tell me what he likes best, so that my gift may be pleasing.' 'I have succeeded!' said Mubārak to himself; and aloud he answered: 'May Allāh shower His blessings upon you, dear master! ... But Abū Alī has a plenitude of this world's riches and no desire except to adorn his mind with the unknown. He sent me to ask, as a favour from you, for some new story with which to gladden the ears of our King. Nothing would please him so well as to learn from you the Tale of the Adventures of Hasan of Basrah, if by chance it be known to you.' 'Be it upon my head!' exclaimed the sheikh. 'Your wish shall be satisfied; for I am the only teller on the face of the earth who knows that story. Your master, Abū Alī, was right to desire it; for it is one of the most extraordinary tales which have ever been. It was told me long ago by a holy man who is now dead, who had it from another holy man, who also departed into the peace of Allāh. In return for your master's generosity I will not only tell you the tale, but dictate its every detail to you. I only make one condition: that you will swear a certain oath to me when you accept the copy.' 'I am ready to accept all your conditions and peril my soul on their fulfil- ment!' exclaimed the mamlūk; and the old man went on: 'That is well. This is one of those tales which cannot be told to everybody, but only to persons of choice intelligence. Therefore I require you to swear, in your own name and your master's, never to recount a word of it to five kinds of persons: the ignorant, whose gross spirits could not appreciate it; hypocrites, who would be offended by it; schoolmasters, whose feeble and muddy intelligence would not un- derstand it; idiots, for the same reason; and unbelievers, who could not draw from it a profitable moral.' 'I swear this before Allāh and before you, my master!' cried the mamlūk, and at once took the purse of a thousand dīnārs from his belt and gave it to Ishāk. The old man provided him with ink and a reed pen, and saying: 'Write!' began to dictate, word for word, all the Tale of the Adventures of Hasan of Basrah, as the holy man had related it to him. The work went on for seven days and seven nights without a pause, and at the end of that time the mamlūk read over what he had written to the old man, who corrected certain passages and rectified faults of calli- graphy. Then Mubārak joyfully kissed his instructor's hand and, after saying farewell, set out upon the road for Khurāsān. Happiness made him so light and swift that he arrived in half the usual time of the caravans.

Only ten days of the year of grace remained; in ten days the stake would be set up for Abū Alī in front of the palace gate. All hope had died in the heart of the unfortunate teller and he had called his rela- tions and friends about him that they might help him more bravely to sustain the terrible hour. The mamlūk Mubārak burst in upon their lamentations, brandishing the manuscript, and, after kissing his master's hand, gave him the precious sheets. On the first there stood, in large letters, the title: 'The Tale of the Adventures of Hasan of Basrah.'

Abū Alī rose and embraced his mamlūk; he made him sit upon his right hand and, removing his own garments, put them upon Mubā-rak. Among other marks of honour and gratitude, he freed him and presented him with ten horses of a noble race, five mares, ten camels, ten mules, three negroes, and two boys. Then he took the life-giving manuscript and transcribed it afresh in letters of gold upon magnificent paper. He made use of his most excellent calligraphy and put large spaces between the words, so that the reading of the tale should be pleasant and easy. He spent nine whole days upon this work, hardly sparing himself the time to shut an eye or eat a date. And on the tenth day, at the hour fixed for his impaling, he shut the new manuscript in a little gold box and presented himself before the King.

At this point Shahrazād saw the approach of morning and discreetly fell silent.

But when the five-hundred-and-seventy-ninth night had come

SHE SAID:

King Kindamīr called together his wazīrs, amīrs, chamberlains, poets, and learned men. He said to Abū Alī: 'The word of kings cannot be broken; read us now the promised tale and I will not forget that which was agreed between us in the beginning.' Abū Alī drew the marvellous manuscript from its gold box and, unrolling the first leaf, began to read. He unrolled the second leaf, and the third, and went on reading in the midst of universal admiration; the effect of his tale was so great that the King did not wish an end ever to be made to that day's instalment. Teller and hearers ate and drank, and then the reading went on until it was finished.

King Kindamīr, ravished with delight and certain that he would henceforth know no moment of weariness with such a tale at his disposal, rose in honour of Abū Alī and appointed him grand-wazīr upon the spot; he put his own royal mantle on him and gave to him and to his heirs for ever a whole province of his kingdom, with cities, villages and strongholds. He kept him as intimate friend and companion; and also he shut the manuscript and its box in the treasury of stories, from which, whenever weariness knocked at the doors of his spirit, he had it taken out and read to him.

And that, O auspicious King, continued Shahrazād, is the marvellous tale which I am going to tell you; I am able to do so because I have in my possession an exact copy of Kindamīr's manuscript.

It is related—but Allāh is All-wise and All-beneficent—that there was once, in the drift of years long ago, a youth of the city of Basrah who was the most handsome, gracious, and dainty of his time. His name was Hasan, and none had ever been called Beautiful with better cause. His father and mother loved him greatly, for he was the child of their old age, begotten by following the advice of a magician who had made them eat the middle portions of a great snake, according to the prescriptions of our Lord Sulaimān (upon whom be prayer and peace!). At the time appointed, Allāh, the All-hearing, the All-Seeing, permitted that Hasan's father should pass into His peace, and the boy found himself heir to great riches. As he had been badly brought up and spoilt by his parents, he soon wasted his father's savings in feasting and dissipation with young men of his own age; but, when he had nothing left, his mother could not bear to see him sorrow and therefore opened for him a goldsmith's shop in the market with her own portion of the inheritance.

Allāh aiding, Hasan's beauty drew the eyes of all passengers towards his shop, and none crossed the market without stopping at the door to contemplate and marvel at this work of the Creator. The shop became the continuous centre of a crowd of merchants, women, and children, who came together to watch the new youth using his hammer, and admire him at their leisure.

One day, as Hasan sat in his shop and the crowd outside was beginning to diminish, a Persian passed, having a long white beard and a tall white turban. His carriage proclaimed nobility and, in his hand, he carried an old book. After regarding Hasan attentively for some time, he approached, exclaiming loudly: 'As Allāh lives, an excellent goldsmith!' Then he began to scratch his head with a gesture of limitless admiration and so stayed until the rest of the passers had dispersed to the noon prayer. At length he entered the shop and saluted Hasan; the young man returned his greeting and begged him to be seated. The Persian sat down with a tender smile, saying: 'My child, you are a youth of very pleasing appearance. As I have no son, I wish to adopt you and teach you the secrets of my art; it is unique in the world, and thousands upon thousands beg to be instructed in it. Yet now, for the first time, my soul and its love are moved to reveal what I have so carefully hidden, that you may be the depository of my learning after I am dead. I will rear an unpierceable wall between poverty and you, sparing you the fatigue of this trivial trade, which exposes your too charming person to dust and coal and flame.' 'As Allāh lives, O venerable uncle,' answered Hasan, 'I ask nothing better than to be your son and the heir to your skill. When will you begin to initiate me?' 'To-morrow,' replied the Persian, rising to go. He took Hasan's head between his hands and kissed it, and then left the shop without another word.

At this point Shahrazād saw the approach of morning and discreetly fell silent.

But when the five-hundred-and-eightieth night had come

SHE SAID:

In a fever of excitement Hasan shut his shop and ran to tell his mother what had passed. 'What are you telling me, Hasan?' asked the old woman doubtfully. 'How can you believe a Persian heretic?' 'The venerable sage is not a heretic and his turban is of white muslin like those of true Believers,' answered Hasan; but his mother continued: 'Do not make any mistake, my son. These Persians are cheats and libertines; their learning is alchemy, and Allāh alone knows what snares they set in the darkness of their souls for the confounding of their fellow men.' But Hasan laughed, saying: 'Mother, we are poor and have nothing to tempt the cupidity of any. Besides, there is no one in the whole of Basrah with a face and carriage more engaging than this Persian. I have seen in him evident signs of virtue and good will. Instead of criticising him, let us thank Allāh for His compassion.' His mother answered nothing to all this and Hasan's impatient anxiety prevented him from closing an eye all night. Next morning he went very early to the market with his keys, and opened his shop before the arrival of the other merchants. When, in a little while, the Persian entered, he rose in his honour and would have kissed his hands, but the other embraced him instead and asked him if he were married. 'As Allāh lives, I am a bachelor,' answered Hasan, 'though my mother is always urging me to take a wife.' 'That is excellent,' said the Persian. 'If you had been married I could not have introduced you to my secrets. Have you any copper in your shop?' 'I have an old battered brass dish,' answered Hasan, and the sage went on: 'That is what I need. Light your furnace, put the crucible on the fire, and use your bellows. Then cut up the old dish with your scissors.' When Hasan had done these things, the Persian said again: 'Put the brass scraps into the crucible and work at the fire until they melt.' Hasan placed the pieces in the crucible, worked at the fire and blew upon the metal with his air cane until the metal melted. At once the Persian approached the furnace and read unknown incantations over the bubbling metal from his old book; then, raising his voice, he cried: 'Hak! Mak! Bak! Let the virtue of the sun penetrate you, O vile metal! Hak! Mak! Bak! Let the virtue of the gold cleanse you, O vile metal! Hak! Mak! Bak! O brass, be gold!' As he spoke these words, the old man drew from the muslin folds of his turban a small paper packet; opening this, he dropped from it a pinch of saffron-yellow powder into the molten brass. At once the mass hardened and formed an ingot of the most pure gold.

Hasan was amazed; but, at a sign from the Persian, he rubbed one corner of the shining ingot with his testing file, and made sure that he had to do with true gold, of the kind which is most eagerly sought for among jewellers. Again he would have kissed the old man's hands; but the other prevented him, saying: 'Go quickly to the market and sell this gold. Lock away the money which you get for it in your own house and say no word of what you know to anyone.' Hasan hurried to the market and gave the ingot to the crier, who, after determining its weight and quality, sold it for two thousand dīnārs. Hasan took the money and sped on wings of joy to his mother; the old woman was so astonished that she could say nothing; but, when Hasan with a laugh told her it was the fruit of the old man's learning, she lifted terrified hands, and cried: 'There is no God but Allāh! There is no power or might save in Allāh! What did you do with that Persian alchemist, my son?' 'He has begun to instruct me in alchemy,' answered the boy. 'He first showed me how a base metal could be changed into pure gold.' Then, without paying any attention to his mother's forebodings, he took from the kitchen the large brass mortar, in which the woman used to pound garlic and onions and make crushed corn cakes, and ran with it to his shop where the Persian awaited him. He set the mortar down on the floor, began to blow up the fire and, when the Persian asked him what he was doing, answered that he wished to turn his mother's mortar into gold. The sage laughed and exclaimed: 'You are mad to think of showing gold ingots in the market twice in the same day; you would rouse all sorts of suspicions and draw upon our heads the penalties for alchemy.' 'You are right,' answered Hasan, 'but I am very anxious to learn the secret of your art.' The Persian laughed even more heartily than before. 'Again you are mad, Hasan!' he exclaimed. 'Do you think that the art and the secrets of the art can be taught in the open street, or that a lad may serve his apprenticeship in the middle of the market, under the eyes of the police? If you really wish to be seriously instructed, take up all your tools and follow me to my house.' Without a moment's hesitation Hasan took up his tools and followed the Persian.

But, on the road, Hasan recalled what his mother had said about the men of Persia, and, a thousand doubtful thoughts flocking into his head, he halted and began to reflect deeply. The Persian saw him stop and said, with another laugh: 'You certainly are mad, Hasan! If you were as clever as you are delightful, you would never baulk before so fair a Destiny. I wish nothing but your happiness, and you hesitate! . . . Still, my son, as I do not wish you to have the least doubt of my intentions, I will teach you the mysteries of my science in your own house.' 'That will calm my mother's fears,' answered Hasan; and the Persian bade him lead the way.

At this point Shahrazād saw the approach of morning and discreetly fell silent.

But when the five-hundred-and-eighty-first night had come

SHE SAID:

When they arrived, Hasan begged the Persian to wait in the vestibule and ran, like a young stallion leaping in the fields of spring, to tell his mother of their guest. 'Now that he is about to eat food in our house,' he said, 'there will be bread and salt between us and you need have no anxiety.' The mother answered: 'Allāh protect us, my son! The bond of bread and salt is a holy thing with us, but these abominable Persians, fire-worshippers, perverts, perjurers, do not respect it. Calamity still pursues us, my son. . . . You say that, when I have seen him, I will not let him depart from the house; but I swear, by the tomb of your father, that I myself will not stay while this heretic is here. When he has gone, I will wash the tiles of the room and burn incense; I will not touch even you for a whole month for fear of being soiled. Yet, as he is already in our house and we have the gold which he sent us, I will prepare a meal for you two, before I go to take refuge with the neighbours.' While Hasan went back to the Persian, she spread the cloth and, after having made large purchases, prepared a meal on it of roast fowls, cucumbers, ten sorts of pastry and preserves. Then she fled to the neighbours.

Hasan introduced his friend into the dining-room and begged him to be seated, saying: 'There must be the bond of bread and salt between us.' 'Certainly, for that bond is inviolable,' answered the old man. He sat down by Hasan's side and, as the two ate, he said: 'Hasan, my son, I swear by the sacred bond of bread and salt, which is now between us, that if I did not love you very dearly I would not instruct you in those secret matters for which we are met here.' So saying he drew the little packet of yellow powder from his turban and showed it to the youth, adding: 'With a single pinch of this you can transmute ten pounds of brass into gold; for it is quintessential elixir in solid and powdered form; I derived it from the substance of a thousand simples and a thousand ingredients, each more complicated than the last. The enormous labours and fatigues which I first had to undergo I will tell you some day.' He handed the packet to Hasan and, while the boy was eagerly examining it, slipped from his turban a morsel of Cretan banj and mingled it with a pastry. This he offered to Hasan and the latter swallowed it without raising his eyes from the powder; only to fall immediately head over heels in deep unconsciousness.

The Persian uttered a cry of triumph and leapt to his feet, saying: 'Ah, charming Hasan, how many years have I sought you! Now I have you, and you shall not escape my will!' Pulling up his sleeves and fastening his belt, he bent Hasan in two, head to knees, and tied him securely in this position. Then he emptied a chest of the clothing which it contained and put Hasan into it, with all the gold which had resulted from his first alchemical operation. He went out and came back with a porter, who took the chest upon his back and carried it to the seashore. Here a ship awaited him, and the captain, as soon as he was on board, weighed anchor and put out to sea. So much for the Persian ravisher and the chest which contained Hasan.

When the boy's mother found that her son and the chest and the gold had disappeared, when she saw garments strewn about the room and the house door hanging open, she understood that Hasan was lost to her for ever, and that Destiny had run its course. She gave herself up to despair, beating her face and tearing her clothes; she groaned and wept and cried sorrowfully: 'Alas, alas, my child! O life of my heart, alas, alas!' She spent all that night running madly among the neighbours, seeking news of her son, and, when they would have comforted her, she was inconsolable. From that time she continued sitting in grief and tears by a tomb which she caused to be built in the middle of the house. On it was written the name of

Hasan and the date of the day on which he had been ravished away from her love. Also, upon its marble, she engraved these lines, so that she might ceaselessly say them over to herself and weep:

> My son comes to me when the dawn is grey,
> But when I wake for joy he goes away;
>   Though his appearance is but fantasy
> I should be happier if he would stay.

Thus the poor mother lived with her grief.

At this point Shahrazād saw the approach of morning and discreetly fell silent.

But when the five-hundred-and-eighty-second night had come

SHE SAID:

The Persian, who had escaped with the chest on board a ship, was in reality a terrible magician, called Bahrām the Fire-worshipper, because of his alchemical pursuits. Each year he would choose out from amongst the sons of the Mussulmāns some well-made boy, whom he would abduct and use as his perverse and faithless nationality suggested. The Master of Proverbs has said: *He is a dog, the son of a dog, the grandson of a dog; and all his line were always dogs! How then could he be other than a dog, or do other than a dog?* During the voyage he went down every day into the hold and, lifting the lid of the chest, gave Hasan food and drink, feeding him with his own hand and leaving him always in a state of stupor. When the ship came to the end of her voyage, he went ashore with the chest and watched the vessel depart again for the open sea.

Then Bahrām opened the chest, undid Hasan's bonds, and destroyed the effect of the banj by making him breathe at vinegar and casting a powdered counter-banj into his nostrils. Hasan came to himself and looked round; he saw that he was lying upon a beach, the pebbles and sand of which were red, green, white, blue, yellow and black; so that he might be sure that he was not upon his native coast. He rose in astonishment and beheld, seated behind him on a rock, the Persian alchemist; and the old man was looking at him with one closed and one open eye. At once he realised that he had been duped and, calling to mind the unhappy predictions of his mother, resigned himself to the decrees of Destiny. 'I put my trust in Allāh!'

he cried, and walked up to the Persian, who did not move. 'What does this mean, my father?' he asked in a trembling voice. 'Is there not the bond of bread and salt between us?' But Bahrām laughed, saying: 'By Fire and Light, who speaks of bread and salt to Bahrām? I worship the Flame and the Spark, I worship the Sun and the Light of the Sun. I have already raped nine hundred and ninety-nine young Mussulmāns into my power, and you are the thousandth. But, by Light and Fire, you are the fairest of them all! I did not think that you would fall so easily into my toils, O Hasan; but, glory be to the Sun, you are now in my power and shall see how much I love you. First you must abjure your Faith and adore that which I adore.' Hasan's surprise turned to a boundless indignation at these words. 'Sheikh of ill-omen,' he cried, 'what abomination is this?' So the Persian, who had other views for the moment, did not insist on a renunciation that day, but said: 'My proposal was only a test, Hasan, only a test of your Faith; you have come out of it with great credit in the sight of Allāh. My true and single object in bringing you here was to find the needed solitude in which to initiate you. That high and pointed mountain, which looks over the sea, is Cloud Mountain and there I find the necessary elements for my elixir. If you will let yourself be led to its top, I swear by Light and Fire that you will not regret it. If I had wanted to force you, I could have taken you there while you were asleep. When we reach the summit, we will gather the stalks of those plants which grow above the clouds, and I will then teach you further.' Hasan dared not refuse, for there was compulsion in the old man's words; but he wept bitterly and remembered his mother.

'Do not weep, Hasan,' said Bahrām. 'Soon you will see how very useful my advice can be.' Then said Hasan: 'How can we climb that mountain? It is as steep as a wall.' 'Do not let that trouble you,' answered the magician, 'we will go more easily than birds.'

He drew from his robe a little copper drum, which was engraved with talismanic characters and had a cock's skin stretched tightly over it. He beat on this with his fingers, and at once a cloud of dust rose round them, from which came a sound of neighing; in the twinkling of an eye there stood before them a vast black horse with wings, which pawed the ground and jetted flames from its nostrils. The Persian mounted this beast and helped Hasan up behind him; at once the horse beat its wings and rose from the earth. Before the riders had time to open one eye and shut the other, it set them upon the top of Cloud Mountain and disappeared.

The Persian looked at Hasan, with all the evil returned to his eyes, and cried in a shout of laughter: 'Now, Hasan, you really are in my power; for there is no creature here to help you. Prepare to satisfy all my caprices and begin by swearing that there is no power save in Fire, the Father of Light.'

At this point Shahrazād saw the approach of morning and discreetly fell silent.

But when the five-hundred-and-eighty-third night had come

SHE SAID:

But, instead, Hasan recoiled, crying: 'There is no God but Allāh! And Muhammad is the Prophet of Allāh! You, O vile Persian, are an impious infidel and the Master of Power uses me as a sword against you.' With the quickness of light he hurled himself on the sorcerer and, snatching the drum from his hands, pushed him towards the edge of the mountain. Then, thrusting out both his arms, he precipitated the perjured old man into the gulf, so that he turned upon himself in the air and was broken to pieces upon the rocks of the seashore. His evil soul departed and Iblīs gathered his life-breath to fan the fire of hell. Such was the death of Bahrām the Fire-worshipper, magician and alchemist.

Freed from his captor, who would have made him commit every abomination, Hasan first examined the magic drum with its cock's skin; but, being ignorant of how to use it, he would not venture the attempt. Instead, he hung it at his belt and looked about him. He saw that the mountain upon which he stood was so high that it towered over the loftiest clouds, and that its summit was formed of a great plain like a dry sea, far off on which there was a shining flame. 'Where there is fire, there is man,' thought Hasan, and began to walk in the direction of the light, pushing on boldly with no companion save Allāh. As he approached his goal, he made out the shining flame to be the sun beating upon a gold palace with a gold dome, supported upon four high columns of gold.

Being tired with his long walk and all the emotions of the day, he said to himself: 'Whatever king or Ifrīt lives in such a place, I will ask the doorkeeper for a little water and some food; if he is a kindly man he will let me sleep in a corner.' Trusting in his Destiny, he walked up to the great door, which was hewn in a block of emerald, and ventured into the front court.

He had only gone a few paces when he saw two young girls, blossoming in beauty, who sat on a marble bench and played at chess. They were so absorbed in their game that, at first, they did not perceive Hasan's entrance; but soon the younger looked up and saw the beautiful youth standing before them. She rose quickly to her feet, saying: 'Behold, dear sister, here is a handsome young man. He must be one of those luckless youths whom the magician Bahrām brings every year to Cloud Mountain; but how can he have escaped from that devil?' Hasan threw himself at the feet of the younger girl, crying: 'Dear mistress, I am indeed one of those.' Seeing so beautiful a youth lying at her feet, with tear-drops sparkling at the corners of his dark eyes, .the girl was moved even to her bowels and, with a pitying face, exclaimed: 'Bear witness, my sister, that, in your presence and before Allāh, I adopt this young man as my brother; he shall share the pleasure and pain of all my days.' She took Hasan by the hand and helped him to his feet, kissing him as a loving sister might have done; then she led him into the palace and gave him a refreshing bath in the hammām. After that, she dressed him in magnificent garments, throwing away his old and soiled ones, and, finally, with the help of her sister, conducted him to her own room, one going on each side and holding him under the arms. The two girls made their young guest sit between them and kept him company while he ate. When he had finished, the younger said: 'Dearly loved brother, darling brother, whose coming has made the stones of our palace dance for joy, what is your charming name, and what has led you to our door?'

At this point Shahrazād saw the approach of morning and discreetly fell silent.

But when the five-hundred-and-eighty-fourth night had come

SHE SAID:

'Dear sister, and you our elder sister, I am called Hasan,' answered the youth. 'My happy Destiny led me to your palace only after great tribulation.' He told them of his adventures with Bahrām the Fireworshipper, and they exclaimed together indignantly: 'The evil dog! His death was richly deserved and you did well, O brother, to cut him off from the air.'

Then the elder turned to the younger, saying: 'Now, Roseleaf, you must tell your brother our story, so that he shall remember it.' And the delightful Roseleaf said:

Beautiful brother, we are princesses. I am Roseleaf and this is Myrtleberry; we have five other sisters, more beautiful than ourselves, who are hunting at present but will soon return. The eldest of us all is Morning-Star, the second, Evening-Star, the third, Carnelian, the fourth, Emerald, and the fifth, Anemone. We are the daughters of the same father, though not of the same mother; but I, the youngest of all, and Myrtleberry were carried in the same breast. Our father, one of the powerful Kings of the Jinn, is so proud a tyrant that he thinks no one worthy to marry his daughters; he has sworn an oath that none of us shall ever be wed and, to see that this should be kept for ever, he called his wazīrs to him, saying: 'Do you not know of some place which neither man nor Jinnī has ever visited; one suitable as a home for my seven daughters?' 'O King,' answered the wazīrs, 'it is in our thought that women and girls were created by Allāh for no other purpose than to unite their delicate organs with man. The Prophet (upon whom be prayer and peace!) has said: "No woman of Islām shall grow old in virginity." Therefore it would be a great shame upon the head of our King if his daughters did grow old in virginity. And, as Allāh lives, what a sorrow it would be upon their youth!' But our father said: 'I would rather see them dead than married! If you do not at once tell me of the place I seek, your heads shall go to find it.' 'In that case, O King,' answered the wazīrs hastily, 'there is a place in which your daughters can be free from the approach of man: Cloud Mountain, which in old time was inhabited by those Afārīt who rebelled against Sulaimān. They built a gold palace there as a refuge and, since their time, it has been abandoned. Its neighbourhood is favoured with an excellent climate; it abounds in fruit trees and delicious streams cooler than ice and sweeter than honey.' Our father at once sent a formidable escort of Jinn and Marids who, when they had installed us in this palace, returned to his kingdom.

Since we came, we have seen the truth of the wazīrs' words, for this uninhabited country is filled with flowers and rich in forests. It shines with pasturage and orchards; courses of living water flow in it like strings of pearl or bars of silver; the streams push each other out of the way to see the smiling flowers and mirror them; the air is filled with mingled bird song and perfume; ringdoves and turtles chant in the boughs of spring; swans float gloriously upon the lakes, and there are peacocks like young brides, for their garments are encrusted with coral and tinted diamond; the earth is suave with camphor and holds the beauty of Paradise.

Therefore, dear brother, we are not unhappy in such a land, and in our gold palace; we thank Allāh for His favours and only regret that we have no youths to bear us company, no man's delightful face to see on waking, no loving well-intentioned heart to please us. That is why we are so delighted to receive you, Hasan.

When she had told her tale, sweet Roseleaf loaded Hasan with gifts and attentions, as is the custom with brothers and friends, and went on talking to him most affectionately.

Soon the five other princesses came in from their hunting and were pleased beyond measure to find so pleasant a brother waiting for them. They welcomed him warmly and, after the first greeting, asked him to promise to stay with them for a long time. Hasan readily promised, as he could find no reason to urge against the thing.

At this point Shahrazād saw the approach of morning and discreetly fell silent.

But when the five-hundred-and-eighty-fifth night had come

SHE SAID:

He dwelt with them among the marvels of their palace and became the companion of their hunting and walking. His delight and self-congratulation on having such sisters was only equalled by the pride and joy which they took in their miraculous brother. They passed their days in playing together in the gardens and along the streams, and, in the evening, would teach each other: Hasan by describing the customs of his native land and the girls by telling the history of the Jinn. This agreeable life made Hasan daily more beautiful, and he grew as fond of his seven sisters, especially of young Roseleaf, as if they had been all children of the same mother.

One day, as they sat together singing in a thicket, a whirlwind of dust filled the sky and covered the sun before them, a noise like thunder rolled in their direction. The seven princesses said fearfully to Hasan: 'Run and hide yourself in the pavilion!' and Roseleaf, taking him by the hand, hid him in the pavilion of the garden. The dust died down and there appeared a whole army of the Jinn, an escort sent by the King of Jinnistān to bring his daughters to a festival which he was about to give in honour of a neighbouring monarch. When she heard this, Roseleaf ran back to Hasan and kissed him with tears in her eyes, her breast shaken by unhappy sobs. She told him of their departure, and added: 'You, dear brother, can wait our return in the palace; I make you master of it. Here are the keys of all the rooms; but I beg you not to open that door which this key fits.' She pointed out, on the bunch which she gave him, a key ornamented with a single turquoise; and Hasan, holding her close, promised not only to wait for her return, but also not to make use of the forbidden key. The six sisters also found time to come secretly to the pavilion and bid their brother tender farewells, kissing him by turns; then the seven departed with their escort for their father's kingdom.

Hasan lived alone in the palace, a prey to great melancholy, and, as solitude was the only cause of his sorrow, he strove to lessen his regret by visiting the girls' rooms one after the other. His heart beat tenderly when he saw the places which his seven sisters had occupied and the things of beauty which belonged to them. In the course of his visiting he came to the door which might be opened by the forbidden key; but he refrained from opening it and returned the way he had come. Yet, a little later, he thought to himself: 'Why did Roseleaf forbid me to open that door? What can there be behind it so mysterious? But I have sworn not to enter.' As night had fallen and solitude weighed upon him, he lay down to sleep; but the thought of the door so stayed with him and so tortured him that he could not close his eyes. At first he said: 'Shall I open it in spite of all?' and then: 'I will wait for the morning,' but at last, as he still could not sleep: 'I will open the door at once and see what is behind it, even if I die!' He lit a torch and, walking to the forbidden room, placed the key in the lock. The door opened noiselessly, as if of itself, and Hasan entered.

Look about him as he would, he could at first see nothing: no furniture, no mats, no carpet; but at last, in circling the room, he saw a ladder of black wood standing against the wall in one of the corners; and the top of it disappeared through a hole in the ceiling. Hasan set his torch upon the floor and, climbing the ladder, began to adventure through the hole. As his head advanced he found himself in the open air, his eyes level with a terrace which was covered like a garden with plants and flowering shrubs. When he set foot upon it, he beheld, stretching before him under the magic brilliance of the moon, the most beautiful landscape ever seen of human eyes.

At this point Shahrazād saw the approach of morning and discreetly fell silent.

But when the five-hundred-and-eighty-sixth night had come

SHE SAID:

A quiet lake lay sleeping at his feet and all the beauty of the sky was looking down into it; in the ripples by the shore laughed the leaves of dancing laurels, of flowering myrtles, of snow-crowned almond trees, with loops of wisteria. The reflection seemed to echo the night song of the birds; the silken surface of the lake, stretching away between trees, at last bathed the feet of a strangely-builded palace, whose misty domes were lost in the crystal of the sky. The palace joined the lake by a marble and mosaic stair, at the foot of which a royal platform had been built out into the water, with alternating bricks of ruby and emerald, and silver and gold. Upon this platform a veil of green silk, held by four light pillars of rose alabaster, shaded a throne of aloe-wood and gold, climbed by a vine of heavy clusters, whose grapes were pearls. The whole was fenced by a slender trellis, woven of silver and red gold. No king could have realised the harmonious splendour of these things.

As Hasan stood still, for fear of troubling this delightful peace, a flight of great birds came down out of the sky. When they lighted on the border of the lake, he could see that there were ten of them; their white plumage ruffled the grass, as they walked hither and thither upon it. Then, seeming to obey the largest and fairest among them, who had gone slowly up on to the platform and mounted the throne, they slipped out of their feathers with one graceful movement and came forth, as moons from behind a cloud, ten naked laughing girls. They dived into the water, which met each with a sparkle of diamonds, and bathed delightfully, playing together. The fairest swam after the others, caught them, and grasped them in a thousand pretty caresses; she tickled and nibbled them until their laughter echoed all across the lake.

When their bath was over, they came up out of the lake and the fairest sat upon the throne with no other clothing than her hair. As Hasan detailed her beauties he felt his reason depart from him, and said to himself: 'Now I know why Roseleaf forbade me to open that door; my rest has gone for ever.' What marvels did he not behold, for she was the most perfect of the master works of God! She was naked; the balance of her neck and the black fire of her eyes surpassed gazelles, her body the wind-dancing araka; her hair was a winter night, her mouth a rose, sealed with the seal of Sulaimān; her teeth were hailstones in the sun. Her neck was a bar of silver; her belly had its dimples and counter-dimples, her buttocks their valleys and stages; her navel could have held an ounce of black musk; her thighs, though heavy and firm, had the resilience of cushions filled with ostrich down. Between these thighs there lay in its warm nest, like a rabbit without ears, her pretty love tale, with terrace and hollow, hill and vale, and fair regale to banish grief and bale. You would have called it a smooth crystal dome or an inverted silver cup. To such a girl these lines are applicable:

> She comes to me dressed in beauty,
> A tree in roses,
> Her breasts are apples.
> Yet her breasts are more than apples,
> Her flesh than roses;
> For a man may bathe in a bath of roses
> And eat of apples.

She sat, royal and naked, on the throne by the borders of the lake.

At this point Shahrazād saw the approach of morning and discreetly fell silent.

But when the five-hundred-and-eighty-seventh night had come

SHE SAID:

When she had rested from her bath, she bade her companions, who were couched beside her on the platform, to bring her her undergarments; they clothed her only with a gold tissue over the shoulders, a green gauze about her hair, and a brocaded belt; thus she was like a new-made bride, more marvellous than any miracle. Hasan, who watched from behind the terraced trees, could make no movement for very love, though that same love urged him most powerfully to move. 'O princesses, the dawn is near,' said the girl to her companions, 'we must depart, for our land is far and we have rested.' They clothed her in her feathers and, putting on their own, flew off with her, going up like white light into the morning sky.

Hasan followed them with his eyes until they were out of sight and then, as if he had been in a swoon, continued to gaze upon the empty horizon. No human girl had ever thrown his soul into such confusion; tears of desire fell down his cheeks, and he cried: 'Alas, poor Hasan! Your heart is with the daughters of the Jinn, your heart which you thought steeled against the glances of women.' Dreaming with his cheek on his hand, he extemporised these lines:

> She came to tear my heart, and then above
>   The sunrise the white mists have hidden her,
>   (The morning dew received her, dressed in light).
> Who dare pretend that there is sweet in love?
>   If love be sweet, how more than sweet is myrrh.

He sighed in this way until sunrise and then, leaving the platform or the margin of the lake, wandered about it, seeking in the morning air for perfume which should tell him of his heart's desire. He wearied through the day in expectation of the night and, when darkness came, climbed up on to the terrace to wait the return of the birds. But they did not come on that night, or any other night; and Hasan could not eat or drink or sleep. He gave himself up to his passion, growing wan and weak, lying upon the grass and saying: 'Oh, death were better!'

While he was in this woeful state the seven daughters of the King of Jinnistān returned from their father's festival, and the youngest, without even waiting to change her travelling robes, went in search of Hasan. She found him lying pale and changed upon his bed, with half-shut eyes from which tears fell down his cheeks. She gave an unhappy cry at seeing him thus and, throwing herself beside him, held him in her arms and kissed him upon the forehead and eyes. 'Dear brother,' she said, 'my heart breaks to see you as you are. Tell me your grief, that I may find a remedy.' Hasan sobbed and, shaking his head, would say no word; so the girl wept with him, and continued with infinite tenderness: 'Soul of my soul, Hasan, my brother, delight of my eyes! My life has become narrow and flavourless to me seeing the roses vanished from your cheeks and your eyes thus sunken in your head. I conjure you not to hide your pains from a sister who would gladly ransom your life with a thousand of her own.' She covered him with kisses, holding his two hands against her breast, and begged him, upon her knees, so wildly, that at length Hasan with many dolorous sighs and in a faint voice, improvised these lines:

> If you could see the pleasant bands of sleep
>   Eternally defeated by my eyes,
> If you could see the place my heart should keep
>   Emptied, and then invaded by my sights;
> You, with a doctor's skill,
> Might recognise, and fail to cure, my ill.

Then his tears fell abundantly, and he added: 'Ah, sister, what help can you bring to one who suffers for his own fault? I fear that you can do nothing, save let me die alone with my grief.' But Roseleaf cried: 'The name of Allāh be upon you and about you, O Hasan! What are you saying? Surely I shall die if I cannot help you!' Then said Hasan: 'Dear Roseleaf, for ten days I have taken no food, because of such and such things which happened to me.' And he told her his adventure by the lake in all its details.

At this point Shahrazād saw the approach of morning and discreetly fell silent.

But when the five-hundred-and-eighty-eighth night had come

SHE SAID:
Instead of being offended at his disobedience, as she might have been, Roseleaf pitied him with all her heart, and said: 'Calm that spirit which I love, my brother, cool your eyes and dry your tears; for I swear that I am ready to risk dear life itself and my immortal soul to realise your desire upon this unknown girl. In Allāh's name, I swear it! But I counsel you to keep the matter secret from my sisters, for otherwise we might both be lost. If they speak to you of the forbidden door, say that you do not know which it is and, if they grieve to see you brought so low, and question you, answer that you have suffered from their long absence.' 'I will indeed speak in that way,' answered Hasan. 'Your plan is excellent.' He kissed Roseleaf, and felt his heart grow light because he now knew that she was not angry at his disobedience. He even asked for food; so that Roseleaf, after a last kiss, hastened to her sisters, to whom she said, with tears still upon her cheek: 'Alas, poor Hasan is very ill. For ten days food has not entered into him; his stomach was closed by grief for our absence. We left the poor beloved with no one to keep him company; therefore he remembered his mother and his native land, and those memories steeped him in the gall of bitterness.'

The princesses, who had a kindly and sensitive spirit, hastened with food and drink to their brother and did all they could to cheer him with their presence; as a distraction, they described the entertainments and marvels which they had witnessed in their father's palace in Jinnistān. During a whole month they cared most tenderly for him, without succeeding in a perfect cure.

At the end of that time they all went hunting, save Roseleaf, who insisted upon remaining with Hasan. When they had departed, well-pleased that their young sister should have taken upon herself the care of their guest, Roseleaf helped Hasan to rise and, taking him in her arms, assisted him on to the terrace which overlooked the lake. There, pillowing his head upon her breast, she said: 'Now tell me, my lamb, in which of these pavilions by the water did you see her who so greatly moved you?' 'It was in none of the pavilions,' answered Hasan, 'but first on the lake side and then upon the throne of that platform.' Roseleaf became very pale, and cried: 'Oh, sorrow, sorrow! That girl is the daughter of the King of the Jinn, who reigns over the whole vast empire of which my father is but a lieutenant. He lives in a land too far to be reached, environed by a sea which neither man nor Jinnī may cross. He has a guard of warrior girls, sprung from noble parentage, and each of these commands an army of five thousand amazons. You saw the youngest, most beautiful, and bravest of his seven daughters; her name is Splendour. She comes to divert herself in this place at each new moon, bringing with her the daughters of her father's chamberlains. The feather mantles, which carry them through the air like birds, belong to the wardrobe of the Jinn. It is only by means of these garments that we can attain our end; for, if you would become master of her body, you will have to steal her magic cloak. You must wait here in hiding until she comes, and take advantage of the time when she is bathing in the lake to get possession of the plumes. If you take them and nothing more, she shall belong to you. Be very careful not to yield when she begs you to return her mantle; for, if you give it back, you will have destroyed yourself and us and our father with us. Rather seize her by the hair and drag her with you; then she will submit and obey; and what shall happen, shall happen.'

At this point Shahrazād saw the approach of morning and discreetly fell silent.

But when the five-hundred-and-eighty-ninth night had come

SHE SAID:

Hasan was transported with joy; he felt life and strength return to him and, leaping to his feet, took his sister's head in his hands and thankfully kissed her. They both went down again into the palace and passed the time in pleasant talk of this or that with the other princesses.

The night of the next day was new moon, and Hasan went to hide himself behind the platform by the lake. He had not waited long before a beating of wings broke the dark silence of the sky and the birds flew down into the moonlight. They threw aside their feathery cloaks and silken underclothes, and went down into the lake. Splendour, the King's daughter, also dived in the glory of her naked flesh, and she was more beautiful and desirable than the first time. Yet, in spite of the great longing and admiration which held him, Hasan was able to steal unseen to the place where they had left their garments and, taking the plumage of the royal girl, return in safety to his hiding-place.

As soon as Splendour came from bathing she saw, by the disorder of the clothes upon the grass, that some strange hand had been profaning them. Going nearer, she discovered that her own cloak of plumes had been taken; so, with a terrified cry, she began to beat her breast. Ah, how fair she was under the moonlight in her despair! Hearing her cries, her companions ran to her and learnt what had happened. At once each hurried into her own magic garment and, with no care for drying her wet nakedness or putting on her silks, fled away wildly through the air. As swiftly as a frightened deer or doves escaping from a falcon they disappeared beyond sight, leaving their princess, the angry and unhappy Splendour, deserted by the side of the lake.

Although Hasan was trembling with emotion he bounded from his hiding-place towards the naked girl. She fled and he ran after her round the lake, calling upon her by tender names and assuring her that he intended no evil. But she, panting and with arms thrown forward, ran on, giving her hair to the wind, and leapt among the trees like a hind, for fear that her virgin flesh should be surprised. Hasan caught her at last and, winding her hair about his fist, constrained her to follow. She shut her eyes and walked without struggling; so that Hasan, who had turned a deaf ear to her tears and supplications, was able to lead her to his chamber and lock her in. Then he hurried to tell his sister the good news.

Roseleaf went at once into Hasan's chamber and found the forsaken Splendour biting the hands of despair and weeping all her tears. She threw herself at the captive's feet most humbly and said, kissing the earth: 'Peace and the grace and blessing of Allāh be upon you, O Queen! You light our house and perfume it!' 'Is that you, Roseleaf?' asked Splendour. 'Is it thus that you allow the sons of men to treat the daughter of your King? You know my father's might, you know that all the kings of the Jinn bow down before him, you know that he commands legions of Afārīt and Marids, numberless like the sands of the sea; and yet you have dared to receive a man into your dwelling to surprise and betray me! Without you no man could have found the way to the lake where I bathe!'

Then said Roseleaf: 'O princess, O daughter of our King, O most beautiful and admired of women, O lustral one, this boy who surprised your bath has also no equal. In truth, his manners are too exquisite for his intention to have the least harm in it; but, when a thing is written by Destiny, the saying must be fulfilled. And it was the destiny of this beautiful youth which made him become passionately amorous of your beauty. Lovers are excusable, and to be loved as he loves cannot be unpleasing to you. Did not Allāh create women for men? And is not this the most charming boy in all the world? O mistress, if you only knew how ill he has been since he first saw you! He has nearly died for love of you.' She told the princess all the violence of Hasan's heart, and thus ended her appeal: 'Do not forget, dear mistress, that he chose you from among your ten companions as the most beautiful, the most wonderful; and they also were naked and easy to surprise!'

When she heard such discourse, Splendour realised that she would have to renounce all thought of escape, so she gave a resigned sigh.

At this point Shahrazād saw the approach of morning and discreetly fell silent.

But when the five-hundred-and-ninetieth night had come

SHE SAID:

Roseleaf dressed the princess in a magnificent robe and served her with food, making every effort the while to dispel her grief. The fair Splendour was a little consoled, and said: 'I see that it was written in

my Destiny that I should be separated from my father and the land
of my birth. I must submit to the decrees of Fate.' Roseleaf kept her
strenuously in this way of thinking until her tears were dry; then she
ran to Hasan and said to him: 'Go to your beloved at once, for the
moment is propitious. When you enter the chamber, first kiss her
feet and then her hands and then her head. Do not speak until that is
done and, when you venture upon words, let them be eloquent and
very kind.' Trembling with love, Hasan presented himself before the
princess, who looked closely upon him and felt her heart much
softened by his beauty. Nevertheless she lowered her glance, while
Hasan kissed her feet and hands and then between her eyes. 'O queen
of all beauty,' he said, 'O life of life, eyes' joy and garden of the
spirit, O my princess, if you pity me at all, calm your heart and cool
your eyes; for your lot shall be a happy one. Just as my sister is your
servant, so I have no will or wish to be other than your slave. I had
no thought of violating you, but wish to marry you according to the
law of Allāh and His Prophet. I will take you to Baghdād, the city
of my birth, and there buy for you slaves of both sexes and a home
worthy of your magnificence. Ah, if you knew in what delightful
ground rises the City of Peace; how amiable and polished her citizens, how delightful and propitious their address! I have a mother
who is the best woman in the world, and she will love you as a
daughter; she will make you extraordinary dishes, for in all the land
of Irāk there is no better cook.'

Thus spake Hasan to the girl Splendour, daughter of the King of
all the Jinn; but the princess did not answer by word or letter or
sigh. Suddenly there came a knocking at the palace door, and Hasan,
whose business it was to open, excused himself from the princess,
and ran to the entrance, where he found that the six other sisters had
come back from hunting. When they saw his cheeks new-coloured
and his body returned to health, they rejoiced exceedingly; but
Hasan, instead of telling them about Splendour, helped them to carry
their game: the gazelles which they had killed, the foxes, hares,
buffaloes, and other wild beasts. He was very friendly with them,
kissing them on the brow in turn, laughing with them and showing
his pleasure in their coming with an effusion to which they were not
accustomed, since they knew that he kept all his kisses for Roseleaf.
They were agreeably surprised by this change, and the eldest went
so far as to suspect that his transports must have an unknown cause;
she smiled at him slyly, and said with a wink: 'Until to-day, Hasan,

you accepted our caresses without wishing to return them; therefore this demonstration surprises us. Is it that you find us more beautiful in our hunting robes, is it that you have suddenly learned to love us, or is it both?' Hasan lowered his eyes and sighed to break the hardest heart, so that the princesses asked: 'Why do you sigh so heavily, dear brother? Do you wish to return to your mother, your native land? Open your heart to your sisters, Hasan!' But the youth turned to Roseleaf, who had just come up, and, with a blush, begged her to speak for him. Then said Roseleaf: 'It is nothing at all, my sisters. My brother has caught a beautiful bird and wishes you to help him tame it.' 'That is certainly nothing!' cried the sisters. 'Why does Hasan blush for a thing like that?' 'Because Hasan loves the bird. And, ah, with what a love!' she replied; and the sisters exclaimed: 'But, Hasan, how, in Allāh's name, can you show your love for a bird?' As Hasan still looked at the ground and blushed, Roseleaf replied again: 'With the word and the gesture and the act which comes after.' 'It must be a very big bird, then!' said they. 'It is about our size,' said she. 'But hear me further: the human intelligence is very limited. Thus it was that, when we left our poor Hasan alone, he wandered in grief through the palace and his soul was so upset that he mistook the keys and, quite by accident, opened the forbidden door and found the terrace. There such and such a thing befell him.' She told the whole story of Hasan's love, making it appear that he was in no wise to blame, and added: 'In any case our brother is to be excused, for the girl is beautiful. If you but knew how beautiful she is!'

Then said the sisters: 'If she is as beautiful as you say, describe her to us.' 'Describe her!' cried Roseleaf. 'By Allāh, there is none who could do that! Hairs would grow on my tongue before I could give you a faint image of her charms. But I will try if only to prevent you from falling down flat when you see her!

'Glory be to Him Who clothed her in jasmine nakedness! The balance of her neck and the black fire of her eyes surpass gazelles, her body, the wind-dancing araka; her hair is a winter night, her mouth, a rose sealed with the seal of Sulaimān; her teeth are hailstones in the sun. Her neck is a bar of silver; her belly has its dimples and counterdimples; her buttocks their valleys and stages; her navel could hold an ounce of black musk; her thighs, though heavy and firm, have the resilience of cushions filled with ostrich down. Between these thighs there lies in its warm nest, like a little rabbit without ears, her pretty

love tale, with terrace and hollow, hill and vale, and fair regale to
banish grief and bale. You would call it a smooth crystal dome or an
inverted silver cup. To such a girl these lines are applicable:

> She comes to me dressed in beauty,
> A tree in roses;
> Her breasts are apples.
> Yet her breasts are more than apples,
> Her flesh than roses;
> For a man may bathe in a bath of roses
> And eat of apples.

'Such, my sisters, is the eye-glance which I had of princess
Splendour, daughter of the King of the kings of Jinnistān.'

At this point Shahrazād saw the approach of morning and
discreetly fell silent.

But when the five-hundred-and-ninety-first night had come

SHE SAID:

The marvelling sisters cried: 'You are right to be snared by such
beauty, Hasan! In Allāh's name, lead us to her that we may see for
ourselves.' Certain now that they would be on his side, Hasan conducted them to the pavilion where Splendour was and they kissed the
earth between her hands, saying: 'O daughter of our King, your
adventure with this youth is indeed prodigious; but we, who here
bow before you, can predict nothing but happiness; we assure you
that in all your life you will do nought but congratulate yourself on
the possession of our brother, on his delightful manners, his deep
affection, his skill in everything. Consider, too, that he declared his
passion in person, not using a go-between, and asked for nothing
unlawful. If we were not certain that girls need men, we would not
dare to plead so boldly before our princess. Let us marry you to our
brother, and we promise that you will be pleased with him.' They
waited an answer and, when the fair Splendour said neither yes nor
no, Roseleaf went up to her and took one of her hands between her
own. 'Allow me, dear mistress,' she said, and then to Hasan: 'Give
me your hand.' Hasan obeyed and Roseleaf joined the hands of both,
saying: 'With the leave of Allāh and by the law of His Prophet, I
pronounce you man and wife!' And Hasan, in an ecstasy of happiness, improvised these lines:

> You are wet with the water of beauty,
> A half of your flesh is rubies,
> The rest is pearls and amber and black musk;
> Yet you are all gold.
>
> There is none like you
> In Allāh's garden of dead girls,
> So kill me if you wish.

Hearing these verses, the girls cried out together and, turning to Splendour, exclaimed: 'O princess, do you blame us for giving you a youth who can so fairly express himself in verse?' 'Is he a poet, then?' asked Splendour; and they answered: 'Indeed he is. He composes poems with miraculous facility and extemporises odes with thousands of lines, each imbued with the most lively sentiment.' This answer finally won over the bride's heart and she smiled at Hasan under heavy lids; so that he, who had waited for that signal from her eyes, took her in his arms and carried her to his inner chamber. There, with her will, he opened that which there was to open, broke that which there was to break, and unsealed that which was sealed. They sweetly rejoiced together and, in an instant of time, tasted the sum of every joy. Love grew about the heart of Hasan, overtopping all his passions, and every bird of his being broke into song. Now glory be to Allāh, Who joins His Faithful in delight and does not count the gifts He showers upon them! It is You, O Lord, Whom we adore, You upon Whom we cry for aid! Lead us into the narrow way, into the path of those who have experienced the mercy of our God; let us not wander into the road of those who are smitten by the anger of the Lord, those who have gone astray!

For forty days and nights Hasan and Splendour lay together upon the pleasant breast of love, and the seven princesses vied with each other to vary their delights and to make their stay in the palace a thing of wonder. But on the fortieth night Hasan saw his mother in a dream. She upbraided him for forgetfulness and spoke of her eternal tears over the tomb which she had raised in the house at home. He woke sighing and weeping so loud that the seven princesses ran to him and Roseleaf, being more anxious than the others, asked the King's daughter what had happened to her husband. When Splendour answered that she did not know, the youngest princess exclaimed: 'I will find out for myself!' and going up to Hasan asked tenderly: 'What is the matter, my lamb?' Hasan's tears fell more heavily at first; but in the end he sorrowfully told his dream.

At this point Shahrazād saw the approach of morning and discreetly fell silent.

But when the five-hundred-and-ninety-second night had come

SHE SAID:

Then it was Roseleaf's turn to weep and groan, while her sisters said to Hasan: 'We may not keep you here any longer or prevent you from returning to your mother; but we beg you not to forget us and to promise that you will visit us once a year.' His little sister, Roseleaf, threw herself sobbing upon his neck and then swooned for very grief. When she came to herself, she sadly recited verses of farewell and, bowing her head to her knees, refused all consolation. Therefore, while the other sisters made preparations for the journey, Hasan kissed and petted her who loved him most, solemnly swearing to return to her once every year. When all was ready, the girls asked Hasan in what way he wished to return to Basrah. Just as he was about to reply that he did not know, he remembered the magic drum which he had taken from Bahrām, the drum covered with cock's skin. 'Here are the means,' he cried, 'but I do not know how to use them.' Roseleaf dried her tears for a moment and got to her feet, saying: 'Dear brother, I will teach you how to use the drum. This is what you must do.' And, placing the instrument against her thigh, she made the action of beating upon the skin with her fingers. Hasan took the drum, saying: 'I understand,' and beat it in the same way, but very strongly. At once, from every point of the compass, sprang towards them great camels, racing dromedaries, mules, and horses, which came together in a galloping tumult and then ranged themselves in a long line, the camels leading.

The seven princesses chose out the best animals and dismissed the rest; on those which they had chosen they loaded costly presents in bales, with garments and provisions, and placed a magnificent double palanquin on the back of a vast racing dromedary. Then the farewells began, the dolorous farewells! Poor Roseleaf, how sad you were, how multitudinous your tears! Your sister heart broke when Hasan departed with the King's daughter, and you moaned like a dove torn from its mate. Tender Roseleaf, you did not know the full bitterness of the cup, or that your pitiful provision of Hasan's happiness should so soon be the cause of separation. But calm your dear spirit and refresh your eyes, for you shall see him again! Your cheeks, which were roses, seem now pomegranate flowers because of your weeping; therefore do not weep, but calm your dear spirit and refresh your eyes. You will see Hasan again, for that is written in your Destiny.

The caravan set forth amid tearing cries of arewell, and disappeared far off, while Roseleaf fell again into her swoon. It overwent mountains and valleys, plains and deserts, with the swiftness of a bird and, by the leave of Allāh, came without accident to Basrah. As they halted before the door of his house, Hasan heard his mother groaning and lamenting for the absence of her son, and his eyes filled with tears as he knocked upon the door. In a broken voice the poor old woman asked who was there and, trembling in every limb, opened to them. Though her eyes were weak with tears they recognised her son; she uttered a profound sigh and fell fainting. Hasan and his wife so cared for her that she quickly came to herself. Then Hasan threw his arms about her neck, weeping for joy and kissing her tenderly; after the first transports, he said: 'Dear mother, behold my wife, your daughter whom I have brought to serve you!' The old woman looked at Splendour for the first time and her reason fled before the bride's loveliness. 'Whoever you may be, my daughter,' she cried, 'you are very welcome to a house which your face has even now illuminated. . . . What is your wife's name, my son?' When Hasan told her, she exclaimed: 'A name which fits! He was well inspired who called you so, O daughter of benediction!' She took her by the hand and sat down beside her on the old carpet of the house, while Hasan told his story in detail from the moment of his sudden disappearance to the time of his return. His mother marvelled beyond the limits of marvel and did not know how sufficiently to honour the daughter of the King of the kings of Jinnistān.

To begin with, she hastened to the market and bought provisions of exquisite quality; then to the silk market and purchased, from the great merchants, the ten most excellent robes they had. These last she carried to Splendour and put the whole ten upon her at the same time, one above another, to show that nothing was too fine for her merit. Then she kissed her as if she had been her own daughter and went to the kitchen, where she prepared extraordinary meats and unparalleled pastries. In serving her she spared no pains or delicate attentions to make her happy. When the meal was finished, she said to her son: 'I hardly think that the city of Basrah is worthy of your wife; it would be better for us, in every respect, to take up our abode in Baghdād, the City of Peace, under the protecting wing of the Khalīfah Hārūn al-Rashīd. We have suddenly become very rich and I fear that, in Basrah where our poverty is renowned, we will be suspected of having practised alchemy. Let us go as quickly as possible to Baghdād and become known there from the beginning as princes and amīrs from a far country.' 'The idea is a good one,' said Hasan, and at once set about selling the house with its furniture. When this business was accomplished, he took the magic drum and beat upon the skin of it.

At this point Shahrazād saw the approach of morning and discreetly fell silent.

But when the five-hundred-and-ninety-third night had come

SHE SAID:

At once from the hollow air came great dromedaries and ranged themselves in front of the house. Hasan and his mother and his wife took all that was best and lightest of those precious things which they had not turned into money, and set off at a gallop upon the beasts, at such a speed that they had reached the gates of Baghdād, on the banks of the Tigris, before you could have distinguished your right hand from your left. Hasan went forward and purchased through a broker, at the price of a hundred thousand dīnārs, a magnificent palace which had been owned by an important wazīr. There he installed his wife and mother and, after furnishing all the chambers with a luxury which was beyond price, he bought a great train of slaves, both men and women, and a sufficiency of lads and eunuchs. So lavishly did he set up his household that his following was the most remarkable in all the city.

Hasan and Splendour lived delicately in the City of Peace, compassed at every turn by the loving attentions of the old woman, who cudgelled her brains each day to confect some new dish or carry out the novel recipes, so different from those of Basrah, which she learnt from her new neighbours. In Baghdād there are many masterpieces of cooking which may be found in no other place upon the earth. After nine months of happiness and chosen food, Hasan's wife gave easy birth to male twins, more beautiful than young moons. Their names were called Nāsir and Mansūr.

At the end of a year memory came to Hasan of the seven princesses and he recalled his oath. As he had a special longing to see Roseleaf, he first made preparation by purchasing the most beautiful stuffs and desirable trifles in all the land of Irāk, as worthy presents, and then told his mother of his intention. To her he said: 'I have one recommendation above all others to make to you: while I am away, guard the feathery mantle, which belonged to Splendour and which I have hidden in the most secret place of the house, as if it were your life. If my dear wife, by some most unhappy chance, were to see that magic cloak again, her nature, which is the nature of birds, would come back to her and she would fly away from here, even in despite of her own heart. If, dear mother, you let her get sight of it, I shall die of grief or kill myself. . . . Also I beg you to look after her very carefully, for she is delicate and used to petting. Do not scruple to serve her yourself; for servants do not know what is fitting and what is not fitting, what is suitable and what is not suitable; nor can they distinguish the refined thing from the gross. Above all, do not let her set foot outside the house, nor head outside the window, nor mount even upon the terrace of the palace; for I fear the open air for her and the temptations of space. . . . Such are my recommendations, and, if you wish my death, you have but to neglect them.' 'Allāh preserve me from disobeying you, my child!' answered Hasan's mother. 'Pray to the Prophet! Have I become imbecile in my old age that I need such a bushel of advice? Depart with an assured heart, Hasan, and, when you return, you can find out from Splendour herself that all has gone as you wish. . . . But I also have a request to make, my child: let not your absence be longer than is necessary for the journey both ways and a short stay with the princesses.'

Thus Hasan and his mother spoke together, nor did they know the unknown writing in their book of Fate, nor did they know that the fair Splendour had heard their words and laid them up in her memory.

Hasan said farewell to his mother, swearing not to be away longer than need be, and then kissed his wife and the two boys, Nāsir and Mansūr, who were sucking at her breasts.

At this point Shahrazād saw the approach of morning and discreetly fell silent.

But when the five-hundred-and-ninety-fourth night had come

SHE SAID:

Hasan beat upon the cock-skin drum and, after he had bestridden the resultant dromedary, repeated all his recommendations to his mother and kissed her hand. Then he spoke to the kneeling animal, who at once rose upon his four legs and, giving them to the wind, sped rather through the air than over the earth, until he was but a little speck in the distance.

It would be useless to tell of the great joy which Hasan brought to the seven princesses, and specially to Roseleaf, and how they decked the palace with garlands of flowers and lighted it with coloured lights. Let us leave him telling them the news, and more particularly of the birth of Nāsir and Mansūr; let us leave him hunting and playing with his sisters. Be so kind, O honourable and generous hearers, as to return with me to Hasan's palace in Baghdād, where we have left his old mother and his wife. Accord me this favour, O open-handed lords, and you shall see and hear with your admirable eyes and honourable ears that which, in their lives of seeing and hearing upon the earth, they have neither seen nor heard nor suspected. May the blessings and the choice favours of Allāh fall upon you! Now listen carefully, my lords!

O illustrious hearers, for two days after her husband's departure Splendour did not for one moment leave her mother-in-law; but, on the third day, as she kissed the old woman's hand good morning, she said: 'Dear mother, I am greatly desirous of going to the hammām, for I have taken no baths while suckling Nāsir and Mansūr.' 'As Allāh lives, these are unconsidered words, my daughter!' cried Hasan's mother. 'Go to the hammām! Oh, sorrow, sorrow! Do you not know that we are strangers here and have no knowledge of the hammāms in the city? How can we go without your husband first visiting the place, to retain a room for you and to assure himself that all is clean and that cockroaches and blackbeetles will not fall upon you from the dome? But your husband is absent and I know no one who could take his place in so serious a business; I cannot go with you myself, as I am very old and feeble; but this I will do, my dear: I will heat water for you at home and wash your head and give you a delightful bath in our own hammām. I have everything necessary; in fact, the day before yesterday I received a fresh box of scented Aleppo earth and amber and depilatory paste and henna. You can set your heart at rest, all shall be as you desire.' But Splendour answered: 'O my mistress, since when has hammām permission been refused to wives? If you had said these things even to a slave she would not have suffered them; rather than stay in your house she would have demanded to be sold again. Men are fools to think that all women are alike and that a thousand tyrannical precautions are necessary to prevent them from misbehaving. But you ought to know that, when a woman is resolved upon a thing, she will find her way to it in spite of all, and that nothing can interfere with her plans, however impossible or disastrous. Woe upon my youth! I am suspected and they doubt my chastity! Nothing remains but death!' So saying, she burst into tears and called down black calamities upon her own head.

Hasan's mother was touched in the end by these signs of grief, especially as she realised that nothing would turn Splendour from her purpose. Therefore, in spite of her great age and the express instructions of her son, she prepared perfumes and clean linen for the bath, and saying: 'Come, my daughter, you shall have your way, but Allāh protect us from the anger of your husband!' led Splendour from the palace and conducted her to the most famous hammām of Baghdād.

Ah, how much better would it have been if Hasan's mother had been stony-hearted and never visited that hammām! Yet who but the Seer may read the future pages of the Book or know what may chance between two steps upon the road? We, here, are Mussulmāns; we believe and trust in a Supreme Will. We say: 'There is no God but Allāh and Muhammad is the Prophet of Allāh!' Pray to the Prophet, O Believers, O illustrious audience!

When the fair Splendour entered the hammām, the women who lay in the great central hall uttered a chorus of admiring cries and were quite ravished by her beauty.

At this point Shahrazād saw the approach of morning and discreetly fell silent.

But when the five-hundred-and-ninety-fifth night had come

SHE SAID:

They could not take their eyes from her and, if their astonishment was great when the girl stood before them in her veils, what was not their fever of delight when she cast them aside and stepped forth naked! O harp of David enchanting the lion Saul; O lover of Antar the curled warrior, O desert girl, O sweet-thighed virgin Ablah, making the tribes of Arabia shock together for love! O Budūr, daughter of King Ghayyūr, whose eyes set fire to the Jinn; O music of water-courses, O Spring singing of birds, what are you before the nakedness of this fawn? Praise be to Allāh Who created you, O Splendour, and mingled in your body the glory of ruby and musk, the glory of amber and pearls, O all-gold Splendour!

The women left their bathing and their rest to see her better, and followed her about. The fame of her beauty spread from the ham-mām into all the neighbourhood and, in a moment, the halls were so packed by women wishing to gaze upon that marvel that none might move in them. Among these unknown admirers there happened to be a young slave whose name was Tuhfah, belonging to Zubaidah, Queen of Hārūn al-Rashīd. She was more stricken than any by the perfect beauty of this magic moon, and remained with wide eyes in the front rank of those who watched Splendour bathing in the fountain. When the wonderful bath was over and Splendour dressed, the little slave followed her out of the hammām, being drawn almost against her will as by a lodestone, and walked behind the two women until they came to their home. Not being able to enter after them, little Tuhfah had to be content with throwing a rose and a sounding kiss to the object of her admiration; but unhappily the eunuch at the door saw both these things and, being scandalised, rolled his eyes upon her and made shocking remarks. Therefore she returned, sigh-ing, to the Khalīfah's palace and ran to her mistress.

When Lady Zubaidah saw her favourite slave stand pale and troubled before her, she said: 'Where have you come from in such a state, my little one?' 'From the hammām,' answered Tuhfah, and the Queen demanded: 'What did you see in the hammām that you should come back to me with confused senses and languishing eyes?' 'Why should my soul and my eyes not languish, why should my heart not mourn, for her who has stolen away my reason?' cried little Tuhfah; but Zubaidah laughed, saying: 'What are you talking about?' Then cried Tuhfah again: 'What girl or what damsel, what fawn or what gazelle, can equal her?' 'Must I wait all night before you tell me her name, silly Tuhfah?' exclaimed the Queen; and the slave continued: 'I do not know her name; but I swear, by your kindness which is upon my head, that there was, is, and shall be, no creature on the earth to be compared with her. I only know that she lives in a palace on Tigris bank, with one large door facing the city and one the river. They told me at the hammām that she was the wife of a rich merchant, called Hasan of Basrah. O dear mistress, it is not only her beauty which makes me tremble; it is also fear. I think what terrible things might happen if our master, the Khalīfah, heard tell of her. Surely he would have her husband killed and marry my miracle, in in spite of all the laws of righteousness. He would barter the immortality of his soul for something fair but perishable.'

Zubaidah knew that her little slave was usually most wise and measured in her speech; therefore she was the more surprised to hear her, and said: 'Are you sure that you did not dream this marvel?' But Tuhfah answered: 'I swear by my head and by the weight of my obligations to you, dear mistress, that I threw a rose and a kiss after her when she entered her palace. I swear that the sun which shines over Arabia and upon the Turk and lights the people of Persia never brought forth her parallel.' Then cried Zubaidah: 'By the life of the Immaculates, my ancestors, I must test this unique jewel for myself.'

At this point Shahrazād saw the approach of morning and discreetly fell silent.

But when the five-hundred-and-ninety-sixth night had come

SHE SAID:

She called Masrūr, the sword-bearer, and said to him: 'Go at once to that palace which has two doors, one giving on the Tigris and one on the city, and, if you value your head, bring me the girl who lives there.' Masrūr leapt from the presence and, running to Hasan's palace, brushed past the eunuch, who bowed to the earth before him, and came panting to the second floor. The old woman answered his knocking and Masrūr, wishing her peace, entered the vestibule. 'What do you wish?' asked Hasan's mother, and he replied: 'I am Masrūr, the sword-bearer. I am sent by our most gracious lady, Zubaidah, daughter of al-Kāsim, wife of the amīr Hārūn al-Rashīd, sixth in line from al-Abbās, uncle of the Prophet (upon whom be the peace and blessing of Allāh!). I come to fetch the fair girl who lives here into the presence of my mistress.' Hasan's mother trembled in terror, crying: 'O Masrūr, we are strangers here and my son is upon a journey. Before he left he expressly forbade me to allow his wife to leave the house, either with myself or another, and under any pretext however grave. I fear that, if she goes out again, her beauty will bring about some deadly happening and my son will kill himself. O good and pleasant Masrūr, we beg you to have pity on our distress and not to ask us a thing which is beyond our will and power.' 'Do not be afraid, good lady,' answered Masrūr, 'no harm shall come to the girl. My mistress simply wants to see her, to be sure that the reports of her splendid beauty have not been exaggerated. It is not the first time that I have undertaken such a charge and I can assure you that neither your daughter-in-law nor yourself will have reason to regret that you obeyed me. I promise to take her in safety and to bring her back in safety.'

When Hasan's mother saw that all resistance would be useless and even harmful, she left Masrūr where he stood and, hastening to her daughter-in-law, dressed her and little Nāsir and Mansūr in their finest garments. Then, taking the children in her arms, she conducted Splendour into the presence of Masrūr, who led them all from the palace in the following order: first, the sword-bearer himself to clear the way, then the old woman carrying the children, and then Splendour, completely covered by her veils. On arriving at the Khalīfah's palace, the two women were led into the presence of Zubaidah, who sat at ease upon a broad low throne, surrounded by her women and her favourites. Little Tuhfah was in the first rank of the latter.

Handing the two infants to Splendour, Hasan's mother kissed the earth between the throne and made her compliment. Zubaidah stretched forth her hand to be kissed and bade the old woman rise. Then she turned to Splendour, saying: 'O welcome child, there are no men here. Why do you not take off your veils?' At the same time she signed to Tuhfah, who went up to the stranger with a blush and began by touching the fringe of her garment. She carried the fingers which had touched it to her lips and brow, before helping Splendour to throw aside her great veil and lift the little gauze from before her face.

O Splendour, neither the moon which comes out at her full from behind a white cloud, nor the sun in his noon glory, nor the gentle dancing of a branch in the warm Spring, nor the breeze at dusk, nor laughing water, nor all that a man may see and hear and so be driven mad, can ravish like the first glance cast upon you! The rays of your beauty shone into the dark corners of the palace and, for sheer joy, the hearts of your beholders danced like young lambs within their breasts. Sweet folly breathed upon their brows, and the slaves whispered: 'O Splendour!' But we, good hearers, we say: 'Glory be to Him Who made the body of woman to be like the lily of the valley and to give His Faithful a sign and a foretaste of Paradise!'

At this point Shahrazād saw the approach of morning and discreetly fell silent.

But when the five-hundred-and-ninety-seventh night had come

SHE SAID:

When Zubaidah came out a little from her sweet surprise, she rose from her throne and threw her arms about Splendour's neck; she drew her to her breast, kissing her between the eyes. She made her sit by her upon the throne and put round her neck a collar of ten strings of large pearls, which she had carried since her marriage with al-Rashīd. 'O sovereign of enchantments,' she said, 'my little slave made a mistake when she tried to speak of your beauty, for it is for ever beyond the flight of words. But tell me, do you know how to sing, or dance, or play? Surely it must be so; for one like you would excel in everything.' But Splendour answered: 'Indeed, dear mistress, I cannot sing, or dance, or play the lute, I have no excellence in those arts which are common with young women. But I possess one talent which might seem marvellous to you: I can fly in the air like a bird.'

'An enchantment! A miracle!' cried all the women, and Zubaidah said: 'Yet there is nothing astonishing in the matter, O charming one; for you are already more harmonious than a swan and lighter to our seeing than any bird. Yet, if you would carry our souls behind you, I pray you try over one of these wingless flights for us.' 'Indeed, I have wings, lady,' answered Splendour, 'but they are not with me. Yet you have only to ask my husband's mother to bring me my mantle of feathers.'

The Queen turned to the old woman, saying: 'O venerable mother, will you fetch this mantle of feathers, that we may see the charming girl make use of it?' 'Now we are lost!' said the mother-in-law to herself. 'The sight of her mantle will recall her aerial instincts and Allāh alone knows what will happen!' In a trembling voice, she answered: 'My child is troubled by the majesty of your presence and does not know what she is saying. Has anyone ever worn feathers? Such a dress would be only decent for birds.' But Splendour interrupted: 'I swear by your life, O Queen, that my

plumes are shut in a hidden coffer somewhere about our dwelling.'
Zubaidah took a costly bracelet, worth all the treasures of the kings
of the earth, and handed it to the old woman, saying: 'Dear mother,
I conjure you to fetch the mantle. I will look at it just once and then
you can have it back.' But, when the old woman still swore that she
knew nothing of any mantle of feathers, Zubaidah called Masrūr to
her and bade him hunt throughout Hasan's palace until the plumes
were found. Masrūr forced the mother-in-law to give him the keys
and made a thorough search of the palace until he found the feather
mantle in a box hidden below the ground. He brought the garment
to Zubaidah, and the Queen, after surprised examination of the art
with which it was made, handed it to the fair Splendour.

Splendour looked over the cloak, feather by feather, and, when
she had satisfied herself that it was exactly as Hasan had taken it from
her, spread it out and, entering, pulled the two folds across her
breast. She stood in the presence like a large white bird and, to the
great wonder of all, made a trial glide to the end of the hall and back
again, without touching the floor; finally she balanced on her wings
up to the ceiling. She descended as light as a puff of air and, taking
up the two infants, set them one on each of her shoulders. 'I see that
my flying pleases you,' she said, 'I will try to do better.' She sprang
up and lighted upon the sill of the high window. 'Listen to me, for I
am leaving you,' she cried, and Zubaidah called to her sorrowfully:
'Would you leave us, Splendour? Would you cheat us of your
beauty already?' 'Alas, I go,' answered Splendour, 'and that which
goes does not return.' Then to the poor old woman, who had fallen
weeping upon the carpet, she continued mournfully: 'O mother of
Hasan, I grieve to go. I mourn for you and for your son. This separation will tear your hearts and blacken your days, but I can do nothing. The drunkenness of the air is upon me and I must fly. Yet if
your son would find me again, he has but to search for me in the
isles of Wak-Wak. Farewell, O mother of Hasan!' So saying, Splendour flew out into the air and, after poising for a moment on the
palace dome to smooth her plumes, sprang up and disappeared
among the clouds with the two children.

At this point Shahrazād saw the approach of morning and
discreetly fell silent.

But when the five-hundred-and-ninety-eighth night had come

SHE SAID:

Hasan's unfortunate mother lay motionless upon the floor and like to die of grief; Zubaidah leaned over her and, after having brought her to herself a little with the caress of her own hand, said to her: 'Ah, my mother, instead of denying all, why did you not warn us that Splendour might make such use of her enchanted garment? I would not have put it into her power; but how was I to know that your son had married one from among the flying Jinn? Pardon my ignorance, good mother, and do not blame me too greatly.' 'I am the only one to blame,' answered the old woman, 'nor may the slave pardon her Queen. Each carries his Destiny about his neck and that of my son and of myself is to die of grieving.' With these words she went out from the palace, out from among the tears of the women, and dragged herself to her own house. There she sought for the little children and found them not; there she sought for her son's wife and found her not. Then her tears washed her away from life and near to the grave; and she built three tombs in the house, one large and two small, near which she passed her days and nights in moaning. These lines and many others she murmured with a breaking heart:

> My sigh for the lack of the smiles of the children
>   Is an old branch in the rains,
> For my tears were the children and passed with the Spring-time,
>   Yet the old branch remains
> And my tears are the ghosts of the tears of the children
>   And the old branch remains.

So much for her. . . . When Hasan had spent three months with the seven princesses, he decided to leave them in order that his mother and wife should not be disquieted. He therefore beat the cock-skin drum and, when the dromedaries appeared, chose ten and sent away the others. The sisters loaded five with bars of gold and silver, and five with precious stones; then they made Hasan promise to return again at the end of another year, and set about their farewells. They kissed him, one after the other, and each addressed him in some tender poem, while all, balancing with their hips, marked the rhythm of the verses. Hasan answered with this improvisation:

> The gifts of pearl before we parted,
>   Since stirruped feet must ride,
> The gifts of ruby rosy-hearted:
>   These gifts would not abide,
> For my eyes were dim where the pearls had started
>   And the ruby was from my side.

Then Hasan departed on his dromedary, at the head of the convoy, and came without accident to Baghdād the City of Peace.

When he entered his house, he could hardly recognise his mother, for tears, fasting and vigil had changed her so. 'Where is my wife, where are my children?' he asked, as these did not run to greet him; but the old woman could only answer with her sobs. Then Hasan ran like a madman through the rooms until he saw the chest in which he had kept the magic cloak, open and empty. He turned and saw three tombs; he fell all along with his forehead upon the stone of the greatest, and knew no more. In spite of his mother's cares he lay in his swoon from morning until the night; and when at last he came to himself it was only to tear his garments and cover his head with ashes and dust. Suddenly he cast himself upon his sword and would have run it through his heart; but the old woman came between with outstretched arms and took his head upon her breast; also she made him sit down, when for very despair he would have rolled like a snake upon the earth. Little by little she told him all that had passed during his absence and concluded thus: 'So you see, my son, in spite of the magnitude of our misfortune, there is still room for a little hope, since you may find your wife in the islands of Wak-Wak.'

At this point Shahrazād saw the approach of morning and discreetly fell silent.

But when the five-hundred-and-ninety-ninth night had come

SHE SAID:

Hasan felt this sudden hope refresh the fans of his spirit and he rose, saying to his mother: 'I go to the islands of Wak-Wak.' But then he thought: 'Where can they be, these islands whose name is like the crying of a bird of prey? Are they in the seas of India or Sind, in the seas of Persia or China?' In order to find out, he left the house, although life seemed black and aimless to him, and, seeking out the wise men of the Khalīfah's court, asked them, one after another, in what seas those isles might be. But each one answered: 'We do not know. We have never heard tell of them.' So Hasan despaired again and returned to the house with the wind of death playing about his heart. As he relapsed to earth, he said to his mother: 'It is not to the isles of Wak-Wak that I go, but to those isles where the mother of vultures, which is death, has pitched her tent.' For a little he lay weeping into the carpets; but suddenly he sprang to his feet again, saying: 'Allāh has sent me inspiration! I will return to the seven princesses who call me brother and ask them the road to the isles of Wak-Wak.' Without delaying an hour, he mingled his tears with his mother's in farewell and, mounting his dromedary, which he had not yet sent back into the void, arrived in time at the palace of the seven sisters on Cloud Mountain.

The sisters received him with the liveliest joy and kissed him with cries of welcome; but, when it was Roseleaf's turn to embrace her brother, her more loving heart perceived the trouble of his soul, and, without speaking, she wept upon his shoulder. 'Roseleaf, my sister,' said Hasan, 'I suffer most cruelly and have come to seek the sole remedy for my grief. O perfumes of Splendour, the light winds shall never again bring you to refresh my soul!' Then Hasan uttered a great cry and fell down in a swoon.

The frightened princesses ran to him and Roseleaf sprinkled his face with rose-water and her tears. Seven times Hasan tried to rise and seven times fell back again; when at last he could open his eyes, he told his sisters the whole sad story, concluding in this wise: 'I have come to ask you the road to the islands of Wak-Wak; for, when my wife went away, she told my mother that I would find her there.'

Hasan's sisters lowered their heads, as if in a stupor at what they had heard, and looked at each other a long time in silence. At last they cried all together: 'Lift your hand to the vault of heaven, O Hasan; touch the vault of heaven with your hand! That would be easier than to come to the islands of Wak-Wak.' At this answer Hasan's tears fell like a river and wetted his garments, so that the princesses tried to comfort him. Roseleaf tenderly put her arms about his neck and kissed him, saying: 'Refresh your eyes and calm your dear spirit, my brother, and then take hold upon patience; for the Master of Proverbs has said that patience is the key of consolation and that consolation wins at last to the goal. Destiny must run its course and he who has ten years to live shall in no wise die during the ninth year. Dry your tears and be strong; for I will do all in my power to bring you to your wife and children, if it be Allāh's will that you should see them again. Oh, that cursed cloak of feathers! I often thought to beg you to burn it, but each time checked myself for fear of angering you. That which is written is written; now it is for us to try to find a cure for the part of your evil which is curable.' When she had said this, she threw herself at her sisters' feet and prayed them to join with her in finding a way to the islands of Wak-Wak. And the sisters promised with all their heart to help her.

Now the seven princesses had an uncle who specially favoured the eldest of them and came regularly to see her once a year.

At this point Shahrazād saw the approach of morning and discreetly fell silent.

But when the six-hundredth night had come

SHE SAID:

This uncle's name was Abd al-Kaddūs. On his last visit he had given his favourite niece a little bag full of an aromatic substance, bidding her burn a little if she ever needed his help. So, when Rose-leaf begged aid from her sisters, the eldest said to her: 'Run and bring me the bag of scent and the gold brazier.' Roseleaf fetched these things and her sister burnt a pinch of the perfume on the coals of the brazier, thinking upon her uncle as she did so.

The smoke of the brazier gave place to a whirlwind of dust and from this appeared the sheikh Abd al-Kaddūs, mounted upon a snow-white elephant. 'Here I am,' said he, as he dismounted. 'Did I not smell an odour of burning scent? How can I help you, my child?' The eldest princess threw her arms about his neck, as she answered: 'It is more than a year since we saw you, uncle dear. That is why I burnt the perfume.' 'You are the most charming of my nieces,' said the old man, 'I had not forgotten you and was coming to-morrow. But hide nothing from me, for I am sure you wish to ask me something.' 'Allāh guard you and prolong your days!' replied the girl. 'Since you permit it, I will ask you something.' 'I grant it in advance,' said the old man; and at once the princess told the whole story of Hasan, and added: 'I beg you to tell our brother how he may come to the islands of Wak-Wak.'

The sheikh Abd al-Kaddūs lowered his head and put his finger in his mouth; after an hour's deep reflection, he took his finger out of his mouth and raised his head; then, still without speaking, he drew complicated figures in the sand. At last he shook his head, saying: 'Tell your brother that he torments himself uselessly. It is impossible for him to reach the islands of Wak-Wak.' The princesses turned in tears to Hasan, crying: 'Alas, alas!' but Roseleaf took him by the hand and led him up to the old man. 'Dear uncle,' she said, 'let him see proof of what you have told us and give him your sage counsel.' The old man presented his hand to be kissed by Hasan, and addressed him thus: 'My son, you torment yourself uselessly; you could not reach the islands of Wak-Wak even if you had the help of the winged cavalry of the Jinn, of wandering comets, and all turning stars. These islands are inhabited by virgin Amazons, and the father of your wife, King over all the kings of Jinnistān, dwells there in untroubled peace. Between you and his islands are seven vast seas, seven bottomless valleys, and seven topless mountains; they lie on the extreme boundaries of earth and beyond them is nothing. I do not think that you could by any means overcome the obstacles which I have mentioned, and I therefore counsel you to return to your own place or stay here with your charming sisters. Think no more of the islands of Wak-Wak.'

Hasan became as yellow as saffron and fell to the earth with a great cry; the princesses could not refrain their sobs and the youngest, tearing her garments, laid hands upon her own face. When Hasan came to himself, he could but lie weeping, with his head on Roseleaf's knee; therefore the old man pitied him at last and, turning to the princesses, who were wailing lamentably, cried out gruffly to them: 'Be quiet!' The princesses checked the crying in their throats and anxiously waited for their uncle to speak. The sheikh al-Kaddūs laid his hand kindly on Hasan's shoulder, saying: 'Cease from weeping, my son, and pluck up your courage; for, with Allāh's help, I may be able to put a better complexion on this business of yours. Rise up now and follow me.'

At this point Shahrazād saw the approach of morning and discreetly fell silent.

But when the six-hundred-and-first night had come

SHE SAID:

Hasan felt life come back to him; he jumped to his feet and bade a rapid farewell to his sisters, kissing Roseleaf many times. Then he said humbly to the old man: 'I am your slave.'

The sheikh Abd al-Kaddūs took Hasan up behind him on the white elephant and spoke some words into the ear of the mighty beast. At once the elephant lifted its legs to the wind and, as swift as falling hail, as striking thunder, as bright lightning, threw itself through the plains of the air, annihilating all distance under its feet. In three days and three nights they had covered a distance of seven years and there rose before them a blue mountain of blue peaks, in whose midst was a cavern, barred by a blue steel door. When the old man knocked upon this door, a blue negro came out from it, holding a blue sabre and a blue metal shield. The sheikh snatched these arms away with incredible swiftness, and the man drew back to let him pass; the two entered the cavern and the blue negro shut the door behind them.

They walked for a mile along a high vaulted gallery, hewn from blue transparent rock and where the light was blue, and, at the end of it, were faced by two enormous gates of gold. Abd al-Kaddūs opened one of these doors and disappeared through it, bidding Hasan wait for him; at the end of an hour he reappeared, leading a blue horse, saddled and bridled in blue, upon which he mounted Hasan. Then he opened the second gold door, and before their eyes stretched out the blue immensity of space and below their feet a boundless meadowland. 'My son,' said the old man, 'is your mind made up to confront the numberless dangers which await you? Would you not rather return to the seven princesses and let them console you?' But Hasan answered: 'I would rather brave the danger of death a thousand times than suffer the torment of this distance.' Then said the sheikh again: 'My son, have you no mother for whom your absence will be an inexhaustible river of tears? Would you not rather return and console her?' But Hasan answered: 'I will never return to my mother without my wife and children.' Abd al-Kaddūs urged him no more but, instead, handed him a letter, on which was written in blue ink: 'To the very illustrious, to the very glorious sheikh of sheikhs, our master, the Venerable Father-of-Feathers.' Then he said: 'So be it, Hasan! Depart under the protection of Allāh! Take this letter and leave your direction to the horse. He will come to a black mountain of black peaks and set you down before a black cave. When you have dismounted, you must fasten his bridle to the saddle and let him go alone into the cavern. Wait at the door and an old black man will come out to you, dressed in black and black in everything, except for a long white beard which falls to his knees. Kiss his hand and place a corner of his robe over your head; then give him this letter, which is an introduction. He is none other than the Father-of-Feathers, my master and the crown of my head. He alone of all men can help you in your rash endeavour; therefore you must try to win his good graces and must be careful to do everything he says. Allāh be with you!'

When Hasan had taken leave of the sheikh Abd al-Kaddūs, the blue horse neighed and shot into the air like an arrow, while the old man returned to the blue cave.

For ten days Hasan gave the horse its head, and it raced the birds and the tempest without a pause, going on in a straight line over a ten years' distance. It came at last to the foot of a chain of black mountains, stretching from west to east, and halted with a whinny of satisfaction.

At this point Shahrazād saw the approach of morning and discreetly fell silent.

But when the six-hundred-and-second night had come

SHE SAID:

Immediately black horses, as many as rain drops, ran up to them from every side and began to smell at the blue horse and rub themselves against it. Hasan was afraid of their number lest they should wish to bar his path; but the blue horse went on until it came to a black cave among rocks blacker than the wings of night. Hasan dismounted and, after fastening the beast's bridle to the saddle-horn, let it go alone into the cave, while he sat down at the entrance.

He had not waited more than an hour when a venerable old man came out of the cave. He was dressed in black and was himself black, except for a long white beard which fell below his waist. This was the sheikh of sheikhs, the very glorious Alī Father-of-Feathers, son of Queen Bilkīs, wife of Sulaimān (the peace and blessing of Allāh be upon them both!). Hasan knelt before him and kissed his hands and feet. Then, placing his head beneath the skirt of the old man's robe, he handed him the letter from Abd al-Kaddūs. The Father-of-Feathers took the letter without words and returned into the cave. Hasan was beginning to despair when the old man came again, this time robed entirely in white. He signed to Hasan to follow and led him through the cave into a great square hall, paved with diamond, in the four corners of which sat upon carpets four old men dressed in black, each surrounded by an infinite number of manuscripts. A gold perfume brazier burned before each, and about him were seven other sages, his disciples, who wrote upon parchment, or read, or reflected. But when the Father-of-Feathers came in, all these venerable scholars stood up and the four chief sages, leaving their corners, came to sit by him in the middle of the hall. When they had taken their places, the sheikh Alī bade Hasan tell his story to this assembled wisdom.

Hasan at first shed tears in torrents, but at length he was able to overcome his sobbing and tell his tale from the moment of his abduction by Bahrām, the Fire-worshipper, to the time of his meeting with Abd al-Kaddūs, follower of the Father-of-Feathers and uncle of the seven princesses. The wise men listened without interruption; but, when he had finished, cried out together to their master: 'O venerable son of Queen Bilkīs, this young man is worthy of pity; for he suffers both as a husband and as a father. Perhaps we may be able to help him to find his beautiful wife and two fair children.' 'Wise brothers,' answered the sheikh Alī, 'the thing will not be easy. You know how difficult it is for any to reach the islands of Wak-Wak, and how much more difficult the return from them. You know the supreme difficulty, also, of approaching the virgin amazons who guard the King and his daughters in those isles. How then do you expect this Hasan to win to the presence of princess Splendour?' 'You are right, venerable father,' said the scholars, 'but you must remember that this young man has been particularly recommended to us by our brother, the honourable and industrious Abd al-Kaddūs, and that therefore we are in duty bound to favour his projects.'

Hasan threw himself at the old man's feet and covered his head with the skirt of the white garment; then he embraced his knees and besought him to give back his wife and children. Also he kissed the hands of the other old men, who joined in his prayers for succour. At last the Father-of-Feathers said: 'As Allāh lives, never in all my days have I seen a young man so set upon throwing away his life. His rashness blinds him to the enormity of his desire; but I am willing to do all I can to help him.'

The sheikh Alī reflected for an hour, amid the respectful silence of his old disciples, and then said: 'First of all, I will give you something to protect you in case of danger.' He plucked a tuft of hairs from the longest part of his beard and gave them to Hasan, saying:

'If you find yourself in peril, burn one of these hairs and I will come instantly to your aid.'

At this point Shahrazād saw the approach of morning and discreetly fell silent.

But when the six-hundred-and-third night had come

SHE SAID:

The old man raised his head towards the dome of the hall and clapped his hands together as if to summon someone. An Ifrīt came down immediately through the dome and stood before the sheikh, who said to him: 'What is your name, O Ifrīt?' 'I am Dahnash ibn Faktash, your slave, O Father-of-Feathers,' answered the Jinnī. Ali whispered something in the monster's ear and then turned to Hasan, saying: 'Climb on the back of this Ifrīt, my son. He will carry you above the clouds and set you down upon a land of white camphor. There he will leave you, as he is not allowed to proceed further, and you must walk alone across that camphor plain; for, at the end of it, you will be opposite the islands of Wak-Wak. Allāh will then provide!'

Hasan again kissed the wise man's hand, gave thankful farewell to the other scholars, and mounted astride the shoulders of Dahnash, who rose with him through the roof of the cave. After a swift journey through the cloud land, Hasan was set gently down upon a region of white camphor and left by the Ifrīt to continue his journey alone.

And now, O Hasan, O youth of Basrah, O admiration of the markets in that city, breaker of hearts and destroyer of beholders, O you who lived in all happiness among the princesses, raising such tender grief within their souls: now Hasan, urged by your love for Splendour, you have come upon the wings of an Ifrīt to a land of white camphor, where you shall meet with adventures such as no other has encountered upon the earth before!

Hasan walked straight before him across a glittering and scented plain, until he saw far off the appearance of a tent in the camphor desert. As he came near it, he tripped over something concealed in the high grass and, looking down, saw it was a body as white as silver and as great as one of the columns of Irām. Hasan had tripped over a giant and that which he had taken for a tent was the giant's ear, shading his head from the sun. The monster, roused out of his sleep, got to his feet bellowing, and his anger was so great that he swelled his belly with breath until his bottom groaned with the effort: then a remarkable series of farts rolled forth like thunder, so that Hasan was first thrown to the earth and then shot up into the air again, his eyes hanging out from terror. Before he could strike earth the second time, the giant caught him by the neck and held him aloft, like a sparrow in the clutches of a falcon. Then he swung him round and round at the length of his arm, preparing to smash him against the earth.

Hasan struggled with all his might, and cried: 'Who will save me, who will save me? Have pity, O giant!' The giant heard these cries and said: 'As Allāh lives, this little bird does not sing badly. I like its twittering. I will take it to the King.' He lifted Hasan delicately by one leg and strode off through a thick forest until he came to a clearing, where the King of the giants of that land sat upon a rock, surrounded by a bodyguard of fifty monsters fifty cubits high. Hasan's captor approached the King, saying: 'O King, here is a little bird which I caught by the foot and have brought to you because of its delightful singing. It twitters most pleasantly.' Then he gave Hasan little dabs on the nose, and exclaimed: 'Sing, sing, little bird.' Hasan, who did not understand the giant's language, thought that his last hour had come; therefore he began to struggle, crying: 'Who will save me? Who will deliver me?' The King was convulsed with joy and said to the giant: 'As Allāh lives, it is charming! You must take it to my daughter at once. Put it in a cage and hang it near the bed in her room, so that its singing and twittering may delight her.'

At this point Shahrazād saw the approach of morning and discreetly fell silent.

But when the six-hundred-and-fourth night had come

SHE SAID:

The giant put Hasan in a cage, with a large glass for food and a large glass for water, and two perches that he might jump from one to the other and sing: then he carried the cage into the chamber of the giant princess and hung it at her bed's head.

As soon as the King's daughter saw Hasan, she was delighted by his pretty face and form, and began at once to caress and spoil him in a thousand ways, and spoke sweetly in order to tame him. Though Hasan did not understand what she said, when he saw that she did not wish him any harm, he tried by sighs and groans to soften her heart towards him; but the princess took these sounds for harmonious singing, and was delighted. In the end she felt so great an inclination for her pet that she could not bear to be separated from him by night or by day, and felt all her being thrown into a turmoil when he was by. And yet she did not understand how her feelings might be put into action with so small a bird; she spoke to him by signs, but he also did not understand and was far from guessing that anything might happen with this charming but gigantic girl.

One day the princess took Hasan from his cage to clean him and change his garments and, when she had undressed him, made the prodigious discovery that he was not altogether lacking in that thing which distinguished the male giants; though in his case, of course, it seemed to her extremely small. 'By Allāh, I have never seen a bird with a thing like that before!' she said to herself, and began to manipulate and examine Hasan in every way, marvelling at each fresh discovery. As Hasan lay in her hands like a sparrow in the grasp of a fowler, the young giantess noticed that his cucumber was changing to a marrow under her fingers and laughed so heartily that she fell over on her side. 'What an extraordinary bird!' she cried. 'He sings like a bird and yet he pays his compliment to women as politely as if he were a giant!' Feeling that one good turn deserved another, she took him all against her and caressed him in every way as if he had been a man, exciting him with loving gestures until he behaved with her exactly as a sparrow with its mate. From that moment Hasan became the princess's cock in very truth.

Although Hasan was spoiled and petted, and experienced things pleasing enough among the sumptuous charms of the gigantic princess, in spite of the pleasure which he gave her and in spite of the comfort of the cage in which the princess shut him up each time that she had done her business with him, in spite of these and other things, Hasan never for a moment forgot his wife Splendour, daughter of the King of the kings of Jinnistān, or for a moment lost sight of the object of his journey, the islands of Wak-Wak. He would have been very glad to use his magic drum and the tuft of hairs; but his mistress had taken away these precious things when she had changed his clothes; and every time he signed or gestured that he wished them to be returned to him, she thought that he was asking her to couple with him. Thus it was that each time he demanded his drum, he was answered with coupling; and each time he prayed for his tuft of hairs the result was coupling. After a few days he was in such a state that he did not dare to make the least sign of any sort, lest the giantess should terribly misunderstand him.

Hasan grew weak and yellow in his cage until one day the giantess, after a more than usual multiplication of caresses, fell back in an ecstasy while he was still against her, and loosed her hold of him. Immediately Hasan rushed to the chest in which his belongings had been placed and, taking the tuft of hairs, burnt one of them while he called silently upon the Father-of-Feathers.

At this point Shahrazād saw the approach of morning and discreetly fell silent.

But when the six-hundred-and-fifth night had come

SHE SAID:

The palace trembled and the old man came up out of the ground, dressed all in black. 'What do you want, Hasan?' he asked, as the youth clutched at his knees. 'For pity's sake, do not make a noise or you will wake her,' cried Hasan, 'and then I shall have to be her bird again!' The sheikh took him by the hand and, by virtue of his hidden power, led him invisible from the palace. Then he asked what had happened and Hasan told him of his adventures in the camphor land. 'And now,' he concluded, 'if I stay one day longer with that giantess my soul will come out through my nose.' Then said the old man: 'I warned you; and yet this is only the beginning. And I must tell you, if only as a last attempt to persuade you to return, that my hairs will be of no avail in the isle of Wak-Wak and you will have to rely entirely on yourself.' 'And yet I must find my wife,' answered Hasan, 'and I still have this magic drum to help me out of danger.' 'I recognise it!' exclaimed Alī, looking at the drum. 'It used to belong to Bahrām, the Fire-worshipper, one of my old disciples; he was the only one who left the way of Allāh. This drum will also be useless in Wak-Wak; for there all enchantment ceases save that of the King.' Then said Hasan: 'He who is to live ten years will not die during the ninth year. If I am fated to perish in those islands, so be it. Therefore I pray you, O venerable sheikh of sheikhs, to tell me the road which I must follow.' For sole response the Father-of-Feathers took him by the hand, bidding him first shut his eyes and then open them. When Hasan had obeyed both commands, behold! there was no longer any Father-of-Feathers, any palace or camphor land; he stood alone on the shore of an island, whose beach was of many-coloured jewels.

He hardly had time to give one look about him before there came out of the rocks and spray band after band of vast white birds, which flew towards him, shutting out the sun with their wings. He was soon surrounded by a whirlwind of beating feathers and menacing beaks, and heard 'Wak-Wak!' repeated a thousand times by the throats which compassed him. Then he understood that he had come to the forbidden land, and to escape from the birds who would have thrust him back into the sea, ran to take refuge in a little hut, which happily was not far off upon the beach.

As he sat considering his position, the earth groaned and trembled beneath his feet, and, looking forth with bated breath, he saw another cloud, a cloud of dust, sweeping upon him. And out of that cloud lanceheads and helmets and sun-kissed armour dazzled his eyes.

The Amazons! Whither should he fly? On they came and on, as quick as falling hail, as swiftly terrible as lightning, and, in a moment, he was faced by a moving and formidable square of women warriors, mounted on wild gold horses, long-tailed and mighty-limbed, with free tossing heads and movements quicker than the north wind across a stormy sea. Each of the women riders had a sword at her side, a long lance at rest on one arm, and a clutch of terrible weapons in the other; held beneath her thighs, each bore four awfully-headed javelins.

When the warriors saw Hasan standing at the door of the hut, they pulled in their striving horses, and the hoofs of that check sent the stones of the beach high in the air, so that they came down and buried themselves deep in the sand. Both steeds and riders snuffed the tainted wind; the girls' faces showed like moons beneath their helmets, their round heavy buttocks were all of a piece with the tawny rumps of the horses, and their long hair, brown or gold or flame or black, mingled with the mighty tails and manes. Steel head-pieces and emerald breastplates burnt in one flame together beneath the sun.

At this point Shahrazād saw the approach of morning and discreetly fell silent.

But when the six-hundred-and-sixth night had come

SHE SAID:

Out of this square of light an Amazon taller than the rest advanced towards Hasan and halted within a few paces of where he stood. Her face was completely covered by the vizor of her helmet and her great breasts moved beneath a coat of gold mail, more closely knit than a locust's wings. Hasan threw himself in the dust before her and then lifted his head, saying: 'O queen, I am a stranger sent by Fate to this island; I claim the protection of Allāh and of you. Do not repulse me, but rather have pity on an unhappy man who seeks for his wife and children!'

The rider leapt from her horse and dismissed her troop with a wave of the hand; then she approached so that Hasan might kiss her feet and hands and carry the hem of her cloak to his forehead. She looked at him closely and then raised her vizor; Hasan gave a great cry and recoiled in fear, for he saw no delightful amazon, but an old woman of strange ugliness, whose nose was formed like an artichoke, whose eyebrows pointed the wrong way, whose cheeks were wrinkled and falling, whose eyes glanced and cursed at each other, and in each of the nine angles of whose face was a calamity; which things made her look utterly like a pig. Hasan covered his eyes with his garment that he might no longer look upon her face; but the old woman took this as a great sign of respect and was exceedingly moved by it. 'Have no fear, stranger, for I will protect you,' she said. 'I promise you my help in any need; but, first of all, it is essential that no one should see you; therefore, although I am most impatient to hear your story, I will bring you the clothes of an amazon, so that you may be indistinguishable from my virgin warriors.' She left him and returned in a short time with a breastplate, sabre, lance, helmet and the like, in every way similar to those worn by her followers. When Hasan had disguised himself, she led him by the hand to a rock near the sea and sat down beside him, saying: 'Now tell me what has sent you to these islands, which no human before has dared to visit.' After expressions of thanks, Hasan replied: 'Dear mistress, my tale is the tale of a man who has lost his one treasure and wanders through the earth hoping to find it.' Then he told the old amazon the whole story of his adventures. When he had finished, she asked him the names of his wife and children, and he answered: 'In my own land the children were called Nāsir and Mansūr, and my wife Splendour; but I do not know what names they would bear among the Jinn.' So saying, he shed abundant tears.

Pity had sway over the old woman, and she said: 'O Hasan, I swear that a mother could feel no more for a child than I feel for you. As it seems possible that your wife may be one of my Amazons, I will show you all of them naked in the sea to-morrow; I will make them file past you, one by one, so that you may recognise her if she is among the band.'

Thus spake old Mother-of-Lances to Hasan of Basrah, comforting him with hopes that her plan might be successful; for the rest of that day she led him about the island, showing him its marvels and, by evening, she loved him with a great love. 'Be calm, my child,' she said, 'for you are in my heart. Even were you to ask for all my warriors, my young virgins, I would give them to you gladly.' Then said Hasan: 'Dear mistress, I swear by Allāh that I will never leave you until I die.'

Next morning old Mother-of-Lances came down to the sea at the head of her warriors, to the sound of beating drums. Hasan sat on the rock beside the waves and looked, in his disguise, for all the world like some princess.

At this point Shahrazād saw the approach of morning and discreetly fell silent.

But when the six-hundred-and-seventh-night had come

SHE SAID:

At a sign from the old woman the girls came down from their horses and out from their armour, tapered and silvered, a fever of lilies and roses; white and lightly they went down into the sea. The foam fell like flower petals upon their hair, free and wantoning, or built high in towers above their brow; the swelling waves imitated the curves of them; they were like sea-flowers budding above the water.

Hasan looked long at this moonlight of faces, midnight of eyes, these hundred tints of hair, this multitudinous benediction of haunches; but in none could he find the incomparable beauty of Splendour. 'She is not there, good mother,' he said, and the old rider replied: 'Perhaps they are too far off for you to see clearly.' She clapped her hands, and at once all the girls came up out of the sea and fell into line, still wet with water diamonds. Then, one by one, swaying and balancing, they walked past the rock, armed only with the buckler of their hair and the bright sword of their nakedness.

Then, O Hasan, what did you not see? Oh, every colour and every form of little rabbit between the thighs of these kings' daughters! O little rabbits, you were fat and plump and round, and white and domed and big, and vaulted and high and close, and jutting intact, and shut, like thrones, like fishes, and heavy, full-lipped and dumb; you were nests, you had no ears, and you were warm; you were tented and hairless, you were muzzled and deaf; you were little and cuddled, you were split and sensitive, you were dry and delightful; but you were not to be compared with the little rabbit of Splendour.

Hasan let them all pass, and then said to Mother-of-Lances: 'Not one of these girls in any way resembles Splendour.' 'Then, Hasan,' answered the astonished old woman, 'there only remains the seven daughters of our King. Describe your wife to me, that I may recognise her; for, with a good description, I think I can promise to find her.' Then said Hasan: 'To attempt to describe her would be to die frustrated; but I can give you a shadow of her. Her face is white as a happy day and her waist so slight that the sun may cast no shadow by it. Her hair is black and lies upon her shoulders like night on day; her breasts pierce through all silk, her tongue is the tongue of bees; the water of her mouth is as the water of the fountain of Salsabīl, her eyes shine like the streams of Kausar, she is a branch of jasmine; there is a beauty spot on her right cheek and a mother spot below her navel; her mouth is carnelian needing no cup, and her cheeks are the anemones of Numān; her belly is a marble jar and there is fairer workmanship in her backside than in the temple of Irām; her thighs were melted in the mould of perfection, as sweet as the return of friends; between them is the throne of the Khalīfah, the sanctuary of rest and drunkenness, of which the poet wrote this riddle:

> A thing of grace, appealing to the poet,
> And four by five, and six by ten will show it.*

O Splendour, Splendour, because of you I am a darwīsh who has lost his bowl, a pilgrim with a wounded heel, my legs and arms have been cut off!'

While Hasan wept, the old woman reflected for a long time; then

* The riddle: Kaf, which stands for twenty, and sin, which stands for sixty, together spell kus, a low word for the female parts.

she said: 'O Hasan, what evil chance! We are both lost beyond recall; for the girl you have described is surely one of the daughters of our King. You are mad, Hasan! Between the two of you there is a gulf fixed as between earth and sky; your search is a search for death. Listen to me, good Hasan, and do not hazard your soul further upon this enterprise.'

At this point Shahrazād saw the approach of morning and discreetly fell silent.

But when the six-hundred-and-eighth night had come

SHE SAID:

Hasan fell down in a swoon because of the old woman's words and, when he came to himself, wept so bitterly that his garments were wetted as if he had plunged into the sea. 'O aunt of help,' he cried, 'must I then return in despair, having come so far? After your promises, how can I doubt my success without doubting your power? You command all the troops of the Seven Isles, and surely nothing is impossible to you.' 'It is true that I hold supreme power over my amazons,' she answered, 'for that reason, I give you leave to choose any one of them, instead of your wife, if that will turn you from your purpose. You may take her with you to your native city and live with her beyond the vengeance of our King. If you do not consent to this, we are both most certainly lost.' Hasan answered only with fresh tears and sobbing, so that the old woman was discomfited by his grief, and thus continued: 'What, in Allāh's name, do you wish me to do for you? If it were known that I had let you land here, my head would answer for it. If it were known that I had shown you my virgin band all naked, my life would last no longer than the telling.' But Hasan cried: 'I swear that I did not look at the girls save in the way of politeness, nor did I pay particular attention to their nakedness.' 'There you were wrong, Hasan,' answered the old woman, 'for you will never see such a sight again in your whole life. . . . Now, if I cannot tempt you with one of my followers, I am willing to give you so generously of the treasures of this island that you may return to your own place and live extravagantly for the rest of your days.' But Hasan threw himself at the old woman's feet, and cried: 'O my helper, O light of my eyes, my queen, how can I return to my land when I have braved such wearying dangers? How can I leave this isle unsatisfied, when only my thirst for love led me to it? Try to be certain, O lady, that Fate wills me to succeed, since it has let me reach so far!' And Hasan's soul welled up within him and he improvised these lines:

> What could my heart against the eyes
>   Which throw gold cords on kings?
> The rose-fed wind of paradise
> Stayed at your dark hair's garden spice
>   To learn new perfumings,
> And the white stars came down with sighs
> About your slim neck's argencies
>   And danced into a ring.

When the old amazon heard this poem, she realised that it would be cruel to take all hope away from Hasan; therefore she said: 'My son, put by your sadness, for I have now decided to risk all for you. Love has no understanding; I must be its ears and eyes. This is one of the seven islands which makes up Wak-Wak; each is ruled by one of the king's daughters, and it is the eldest, Nūr al-Hudā, who governs here. I will go now and speak to her in your favour; refresh your eyes and calm your dear spirit, for I will soon return.'

When the amazon general came into the princess's presence, she kissed the earth between the hands of Nūr al-Hudā; and the girl, who loved and respected the old woman, rose in her honour and bade her be seated. 'Allāh grant that you bring good tidings!' she said. 'And, if it is a matter of some request, behold, I am ready and favourable.'

At this point Shahrazād saw the approach of morning and discreetly fell silent.

But when the six-hundred-and-ninth night had come

SHE SAID:

Then said Mother-of-Lances: 'O Queen of time, dear daughter, I come to announce a strange happening which may in the end lead to amusement for you. I have found a most beautiful youth weeping bitterly and cast upon our island by the waves. When I asked him his tale, he answered that Fate had sent him to us, seeking his wife, and went on to describe the woman in terms which I must confess reminded me of yourself and your sisters. Also, I must add, that never have I seen, among men or Jinn, so handsome a young man.'

Nūr al-Hudā flew into a great rage, and cried: 'O curse among old women, daughter of a thousand cuckolds, how dared you introduce a man into our island! Offspring of shame, ah, who will give me your blood to drink, your flesh to mash between my teeth?' The old woman trembled like a reed in a tempest, and fell upon her knees, as the princess continued: 'Do you not fear my vengeance and my anger? By my father's head, I do not know why you are not already cut in pieces and made a terrible example for those who will guard our island in the future. . . . Before I do anything, fetch me this rash human who has dared to violate our sacred bounds.' Mother-of-Lances rose in a maze of terror and, as she went forth to look for Hasan, murmured to herself: 'This youth will be the death of me! Why did I not drive him away?' Then, when she came to where she had left Hasan, she cried aloud: 'Rise up, dead youth, for the Queen wishes to speak with you!' 'Into what gulf have I fallen?' thought Hasan, as he followed the old woman into the royal presence.

Nūr al-Hudā sat veiled upon her throne and said no word, while Hasan kissed the earth between her hands and then paid her compliments in verse; but when he had finished, she signed to the old woman to question him. Then said Mother-of-Lances: 'Our mighty Queen returns your greetings and asks you: what is your name, your native land, the name of your wife, and the names of your children?' Hasan, following his Fate, replied: 'Queen of the world, sovereign of time, O peerless of all ages, my poor name is Hasan the unfortunate, and I come from the city of Basrah in Irāk. My wife's name I do not know; my children are called Nāsir and Mansūr.' 'And why did your wife leave you?' asked the Queen through the old woman. 'By Allāh, I do not know,' answered Hasan, 'but it must have been in spite of herself.' 'How, and from where did she depart?' was the next question. 'From Baghdād,' Hasan replied, 'from the very palace of the Khalīfah, Hārūn al-Rashīd, Commander of the Faithful. As for the means: she dressed herself in a cloak of feathers and flew off into the air. She said to my mother: "O mother of Hasan, I grieve to go. I mourn for your son. This separation will tear your hearts and blacken your days, but I can do nothing. The drunkenness of the air is upon me and I must go. Yet, if your son would find me again, he has but to search for me in the isles of Wak-Wak. Farewell, O mother of Hasan!" Thus my wife spake before she flew away, and since then the world has been dark before my eyes.' Then said Nūr al-Hudā with a shake of the head: 'As Allāh lives, if your wife had not wished to see you again, she would never have told your mother her destination; but, on the other hand, if she had loved you truly, she would not have left you.' Hasan swore the solemnest oaths that his wife loved him truly, that she had given him a thousand proofs of her devoted affection, but had been unable to resist the call of the air and the instinct of bird flight. 'I have told you my sad story,' said he, 'I stand before you as a suppliant, praying you to pardon my audacity and to help me find my wife and children. In Allāh's name, O Queen, do not repulse me!'

Nūr al-Hudā reflected for an hour and then raised her head, saying: 'I have tried to find a sufficient punishment for you; but, so far, have not succeeded.'

At this point Shahrazād saw the approach of morning and discreetly fell silent.

But when the six-hundred-and-tenth night had come

SHE SAID:

Then the old woman overcame her fright and cast herself at her mistress's feet, covering her head with the hem of the royal robe, and saying: 'O great Queen, for the sake of the days when I nursed you, do not punish this poor man now that you have heard the trials and perils which he has undergone. Only through the will of Destiny that he should live to old age was he able to come out of those dangers alive. It would be worthy of your sweet nobility to pardon him and not offend the laws of hospitality. Remember that love alone thrust him into his rash enterprise and that much must be pardoned to lovers. Also, O crown of our heads, be sure that I would never have dared to speak to you of this most handsome youth had he not been chief of all men in the invention of verses and the construction of odes. If you do not believe what I say, unveil your face for him and he will celebrate it fittingly.' 'This is in truth the last straw!' answered the Queen with a smile; for in spite of the severity of her attitude, her entrails had been moved within her by the beauty of Hasan and she wished nothing better than to try his skill, in verse and that which so usually follows from it. She feigned to be convinced by her old nurse, and showed all her face, lifting her veil.

Hasan gave a great cry which shook the palace, and fell into a swoon; when Mother-of-Lances solicitously brought him to himself and asked the reason of his indisposition, he said: 'O Allāh, what have I seen! The Queen is either my wife or else is as like her as one half of a bean is like the other.' The Queen laughed so heartily that she fell over on her side; when she could speak, she said: 'This young man is mad! He says that I am his wife! Since when have virgins brought forth without a man or had children by the empty air? . . . Tell me, my dear, in what I resemble your wife; for I can see that you are in some doubt about me.' Then said Hasan: 'O Queen of kings, O shade for great and small, your beauty has made me mad. Your star-defying eyes are those of my wife; the flowers of your cheeks and your breasts' loveliness are hers; you have her lightness; doubtless those things which I may not see are hers also; but between you there is a difference which only my lover's eyes may see and even my lover's tongue cannot express.'

The princess understood that Hasan's heart would never belong to her and, conceiving a violent hatred for him, determined to find out which of her sisters had married against their father's will. 'I will be revenged upon the two of them!' she said to herself; but aloud and to the old woman she said: 'O nurse, go and find my six sisters in their islands and tell them that, since they have not visited me for two years, their absence weighs heavily upon my heart. Invite them to come to me and bring them here yourself; but be very careful not to say a word to any of them of what has happened.'

Ignorant of her mistress's intent, Mother-of-Lances hastened to the islands of the six princesses and easily persuaded the first five to accompany her. But when she came to the seventh island, where the youngest princess lived with her father, the King of the kings of the Jinn, she found it difficult to make her accept. The reason for this reluctance shall now be told. When the youngest princess went to ask her father's leave to visit her eldest sister, the King was perturbed, and answered: 'Dear daughter, favourite of my heart, there is something in my soul which tells me that I will never see you again if you leave the palace. Last night I had a terrifying dream. . . .'

At this point Shahrazād saw the approach of morning and discreetly fell silent.

But when the six-hundred-and-eleventh night had come

SHE SAID:

'Light of my eyes, a dream weighed heavy on my sleep last night. I walked among a hidden treasure and, admiring all, yet fixed my chief delight upon seven shining and precious jewels. The smallest was the most beautiful, the most desirable; therefore I took it in my hand, pressed it against my heart, and carried it out from the place of treasure. As I held it before my eyes in the sunlight, a strange bird, such as I have never seen upon these islands, attacked me, snatched the stone away, and flew into the air with it. This cast me into a stupor of grief and, when I woke, I sent for the interpreters of dreams, telling them what I had seen in my sleep. "O King," they said to me, "the seven jewels were your seven daughters and the smallest is she who shall be ravished away from you by force." I am afraid to let you go with your sisters to visit Nūr al-Hudā, for something terrible may happen on the journey.' Then Splendour (for the youngest princess was Splendour, wife of Hasan) answered her father: 'We must remember, O great King, that Nūr al-Hudā has prepared a festival for me and greatly desires me to go. For two years I have meant to visit her and she would have every reason to resent it if I were to refuse her invitation now. There is no need for you to be afraid, dear father. Do you not recall how, some time ago, I went far off with my companions and you thought me lost; yet I came back in health and safety? This time, I will return at the end of a month. When I left the islands you were perhaps right to be anxious; but what enemy could reach me here? Who could pass over Cloud Mountain, Blue Mountain, Black Mountain, the Seven Valleys, the Seven Seas, and Camphor Land, without finding death a thousand times by the way? Refresh your eyes, lift up your heart, dear father, you need have no fear for me.'

Partly reassured by these arguments, the King gave unwilling consent, on condition that Splendour only stayed for a few days with her sister. After he had given her an escort of a thousand amazons and embraced her tenderly, Splendour first went to kiss her two children in the unsuspected retreat which she had found for them with two faithful slaves, and then followed the old woman and her sisters into Nūr al-Hudā's island.

In order fittingly to receive her sisters, the eldest princess had put on a fair robe of red silk on which were gold birds with emerald beaks and claws; she sat, heavy with jewels, on her audience throne, with Hasan standing before her guarded by girls holding naked swords and pointed lances.

When the old nurse asked for an audience, she was bidden to introduce the eldest of the six visiting princesses. This girl, whose name was King's-Pride, entered the presence clad in a robe of blue silk, and kissed her sister's hand. Nūr al-Hudā rose in her honour and made her sit by her side; then she turned to Hasan, saying: 'Tell me, human, is this your wife?' and Hasan answered: 'By Allāh, she is the rising of the moon, her hair is blacker than charcoal, she smiles and her breasts are proud, she is the work of a cunning silversmith, I would say of her:

> Her veil is torn from the bright blue
> Which all the stars are hasting to,
> Her lips control a hive of bees
> And roses are about her knees,
> The white flakes of the jasmine twine
> Round her twin sweetness carnaline,
> Her waist is a slight reed which stands
> Swayed on a hill of moving sands.

Thus I see her; but between her and my wife there is a difference which my tongue cannot compass.'

Nūr al-Hudā signed to the old woman to introduce the second sister. Talisman, for such was her name, entered, clad in a robe of apricot silk and lo! she was more beautiful than the one who had gone before. Her sister made her sit beside King's-Pride and then asked Hasan if he recognised his wife.

At this point Shahrazād saw the approach of morning and discreetly fell silent.

But when the six-hundred-and-twelfth night had come

SHE SAID:

Then said Hasan: 'O Queen, she ravishes the reason and enchains the heart; she inspires me to this:

> A summer moon on winter's night,
> Were fair, but here's a fairer sight.
>   I said when I saw your falling hair:
> "Night's black fain wing is hiding day."
>   "A cloud, but lo! the moon is there,"
> You, rose child, found to say.

Thus I see her; but between her and my wife there is a difference beyond the compass of my tongue.' The third sister, Evening-Light, was more beautiful than the two who had gone before; she wore a robe of grenade silk. When Hasan was asked of her, he said: 'Queen and crown of my head, this one would rob the sages of their wisdom; my marvel at her has produced these lines:

> You are as slight as a running deer,
> As small as a child with his father's bow,
> Yet you so shine that when you go
> The sun will fly and night appear.

It is so I see her; but between her and my wife, though she seems and walks like her, there is a difference which my tongue cannot tell.' Then the fourth sister, who was named Clear-Sky, entered in a robe of yellow silk covered with pleasant designs. Of her Hasan improvised this song:

> You are the fortunate moon which shone
> On the road I used to take
> Many a glad night for the sake
> Of a once desirous one;
> Yet if now a lover nears,
> Unrecking silver fire,
> Your breasts, two crimson granite spears,
> Are proof against desire.

'This does not paint her fully,' said he, 'it would take a long-breathed ode to do that. Yet I must tell you that she is not my wife.' The fifth sister, the fair White-Dawn, came in with a movement of her hips; she was as supple as a branch, as light as a fawn. When she had sat down and arranged the folds of her gold-worked green silk robe, Hasan made these lines about her:

> Green leaves as fairly shade the red pomegranate flowers
> As you, your light chemise.
> I ask its name which suits your golden cheek,
> You ponder and then speak:
> 'It has no name, for it is my chemise.'
> Yet I will call it murderer of ours,
> A murderous chemise. . . .
> Sure, you are fairer far than these
> Poor compliments and light chemise.

> Your slim legs whisper: 'Stay!'
> When I pass by that way,
> But if I further go
> A sweeter thing does: 'Do!'
> While you say: 'Nay!'

All who were in the presence marvelled at his talent and the Queen herself showed approval, in spite of her resentment. The old amazon took advantage of this lucky turn to say: 'O Queen, did I mislead you when I spoke of this young man's admirable art in constructing verses? Are not his improvisations delicate and discreet? I pray you to forget his boldness and attach him to your person to be your poet on festivals and occasions of solemnity.'

At this point Shahrazād saw the approach of morning and discreetly fell silent.

But when the six-hundred-and-thirteenth night had come

SHE SAID:

But the Queen answered: 'First I will finish this testing. Bring in my youngest sister!' The old woman went out and returned immediately with the princess named World's-Fairing, who was none other than Splendour.

O Splendour, you wore your beauty only, disdaining ornament and lying veils, yet Destiny stalked with you into the hall!

When Hasan saw Splendour, he gave a great cry and fell unconscious to the ground, and, when Splendour heard that cry and recognised her husband, she screamed and swooned all along before the throne.

Nūr al-Hudā no longer concealed her jealousy and anger. 'Seize that human and cast him outside the city!' she cried to her guards; and the guards carried Hasan away and threw him down upon the sea shore. As soon as Splendour came to herself, the Queen called out on her: 'What have you to do with this human, O wanton, O doubly-base? For you married without your father's leave and then you left your husband. Thus you have stained the nobility of your race and the fault must be washed in blood!' Then to her women she cried: 'Bring a ladder and fasten this dead woman to it by the hair; beat her until the blood runs.' After that, she wrote a letter to her father telling him the whole tale of Hasan and Splendour, and de-

scribing the punishment which she was about to inflict. She begged
the King to answer at once with definite instructions for his daughter's final punishment, and intrusted her letter to a swift messenger.

When the King read Nūr al-Hudā's letter, the world darkened
before his eyes, and he sent answer to her that all punishment would
be a feather against that fault and that he left it to her wisdom and
justice to find the form of the death and see it carried out.

While Splendour groaned on the ladder, waiting for her punishment, Hasan came to himself on the sea shore and began to lament
his evil fortune. What might he hope? How might he find help to flee
from that disastrous island? He rose and began to wander hopelessly
about the beach, until these words of the poet came into his mind:

> When you were a thought in the breast of your mother
> My Vision beheld you, My Justice designed;
> Therefore, dream of My Dream, do not seek for another
> While the Thinker remembers the thought of His Mind.

This precept renewed his courage and he walked with better hope
upon the beach, trying to imagine what had happened during his
swoon and why he had been thus cast away. As he pondered, he
came upon two little amazons, twelve years old, violently fighting
each other on the sands, and near the place of their struggle lay a
leather cap with writing and design upon it. He went up to these
children and, while trying to separate them, asked the cause of their
quarrel. When they answered that they were disputing for the cap,
Hasan suggested he should be their arbiter. They consented and he
at once picked up the cap, saying: 'I will throw a stone in the air and
the one who brings it to me shall have the cap.' 'That is an excellent
plan,' said the little amazons.

At this point Shahrazād saw the approach of morning and
discreetly fell silent.

But when the six-hundred-and-fourteenth night had come

SHE SAID:

Hasan picked up a stone and threw it as far as he could; then,
while the little girls were racing for it, he put the cap upon his head
and left it there. Soon the children came back and the one who had
got the stone cried: 'I have won! Where are you, O man?' She came
up to the place where he stood and looked all about without seeing

him; her sister joined her and searched also. 'They are not blind; how is it that they do not see me?' said Hasan to himself, then aloud he cried: 'Here I am!' The little girls looked in the direction of the voice and, seeing no one, began to whimper for fear. Hasan touched them on the shoulder, saying: 'Here I am. Why are you crying, little ones?' At this the girls were terrified and ran away with all their might, screaming as they went as if some evil Ifrīt were after them. 'There can be no further doubt,' said Hasan to himself. 'This is a magic cap, a cap of invisibility. Allāh has sent it to me! Now I can steal back and see my wife.' Dancing for joy, he returned towards the city and, wishing to try the power of the cap on the old amazon, searched through the palace until he found her, chained by a ring to the wall in one of the chambers. To be quite certain that he was really invisible, he went to a shelf on which were ranged a number of porcelain jars and brought the largest of them crashing to the ground. The old woman uttered a cry of terror, thinking she had to do with some malevolent Jinnī sent by Nūr al-Hudā. She began to utter a conjuration, saying: 'O Ifrīt, I order you, by the name graved upon the Seal of Sulaimān, to tell me who you are.' 'I am no Ifrīt, but Hasan of Basrah, whom you protected,' answered Hasan. 'I have come to free you.' So saying, he took off the magic cap and stood before her. 'Woe, woe, for poor Hasan!' cried the old woman. 'The Queen is already sorry that she did not put you to death and has sent slaves in search of you, promising a quintal of gold for you, dead or alive. Do not lose a moment, but flee from this place!' She told Hasan of the punishments which the Queen had in store for Splendour; but Hasan answered: 'Allāh will save her, just as He will save us, from the hands of that cruel princess. This cap is enchanted and, by its help, I can walk where I wish without being seen.' Then cried the old woman: 'Praise be to Allāh, who makes dead bones alive and has sent you this cap for our salvation! Free me quickly and I will show you where your wife is imprisoned.' Hasan cut her bonds and took her by the hand, putting on the cap at the same time. Immediately they both became invisible, and the old woman was able to lead him to a dungeon where Splendour languished, still fastened to the ladder by her hair, and waiting, with what fortitude she might, for death and torture. Hasan heard her murmuring these lines:

> O night of my soul be dark,
> Eyes be rivers, hope be stark;

And hope stir not in your death,
For my eyes that fiery breath
Surely quenched with all their wetting,
Falling down apart . . .
Years on years into my heart
Let eternal worms go fretting,
Yet they will not reach the trace
Of his lost and lovely face.

Although Hasan did not wish to appear over suddenly before his wife, lest the emotion should be too much for her, her deep grief caused him to throw his cap aside and take her in his arms. When she realised that it was he, she swooned against his breast; but Hasan cut her bonds and, with the old woman's help, tenderly brought her to herself. He took her head upon his knees and fanned her with his hand until she opened her eyes, and asked: 'Did you come down from the sky or up through the bosom of the earth? Dear husband, what can we do against Destiny? I beg you to leave my fate to run its course and return instantly by the way you came, for I do not wish to see you also a prey to my sister's savagery.' 'Dearly loved one, light of my eyes,' said Hasan, 'I have come to take you back to Baghdād.' 'You are rash even to madness!' said she. 'Begone, I pray, and do not add to my suffering.' But Hasan reassured her, saying: 'Splendour of my soul, I shall leave the palace only with you and this good old woman. If you would know how, behold this magic cap!'

At this point Shahrazād saw the approach of morning and discreetly fell silent.

But when the six-hundred-and-fifteenth night had come

SHE SAID:

Hasan showed her the working of the cap and told her how Allāh had placed it in his way. Then Splendour wept both for joy and contrition, and said to him: 'All these evils are my fault, since I left our home in Baghdād without your leave. Master and love, spare me your reproaches, for I now know that a wife should put a proper value on her husband. I ask pardon before Allāh and before you. My only excuse is that my soul was filled with a strange longing when I saw my feathers.' 'As Allāh lives, I only am to blame. I left you alone in Baghdād. I ought to have taken you with me,' answered Hasan. 'In future we will depart and return together.' So saying, he put Splendour on his back and took the old woman's hand, so that all three of them became invisible. They left the palace and made haste to the seventh island, where little Nāsir and Mansūr were concealed.

Though Hasan was moved in all his being to see his children safe and sound, he lost no time in an outburst of tenderness. The old woman took the babies astride on her shoulders, while Splendour, thanks to the invisibility of the cap, succeeded in taking three new garments of feathers from the wardrobe of the Jinn. Then all three put on these cloaks of enchanted flight, and left the fatal islands of Wak-Wak for ever.

They flew by short stages and, coming one morning to the City of Peace, alighted on the terrace of Hasan's palace. Descending the stairs, they arrived at the door of the room where Hasan's mother stayed eternally with her grief. The old woman was now very feeble and nearly blind because of her sorrows; yet, when Hasan knocked at the door, she asked courageously: 'Who is there?' 'Dear mother,' answered Hasan, 'Destiny is at the door with joyful news!'

Not knowing whether this was illusion or reality, the old woman ran, as fast as her weakened legs could carry her, and opened the door. She saw Hasan before her with his wife and children and the old amazon standing discreetly behind them. The emotion was too great for her and she fell fainting in their arms. Hasan brought her to herself with the tears which fell from his eyes upon her face, and then pressed her gently to his breast. Splendour showered a thousand kisses upon her, most humbly asking pardon for her fault. Then they presented Mother-of-Lances as their saviour, and Hasan told their marvellous adventures. But it is needless to repeat the story in this place. They glorified Allāh together that He had at last brought them safely into one place.

From that time on they lived delightfully, nor did they miss to go each year, by caravan, thanks to the magic drum, to visit the seven princesses in the green-domed palace upon Cloud Mountain.

It was many long years before the inexorable Destroyer of happiness came in his turn to visit them. Glory and praise be to Him Who reigns over the visible and invisible, the Sole Living, the Eternal, Who knows not death!

When Shahrazād had told this extraordinary tale, little Dunyazād fell upon her neck and kissed her upon the mouth, saying: 'Dear sister, that tale is both miraculous and tasteful. I so loved Roseleaf.

I am very sorry that Hasan did not marry her also!' Then said King Shahryār: 'That tale is indeed astonishing, Shahrazād. It almost made me forget certain unpleasant duties which I have to undertake to-morrow.' But Shahrazād answered: 'O King, that tale is not to be compared with one which I know concerning the Historic Fart.' 'What do you say, Shahrazād?' cried the King. 'What is this historic fart? I have never heard of it.' 'It is a tale which I had intended to tell you to-morrow night, if I were still alive,' answered Shahrazād; so Shahryār said within himself: 'I will not kill her until I have learnt more about this strange matter.'

At this point Shahrazād saw the approach of morning and discreetly fell silent.

But when the four-hundred-and-sixteenth night had come

SHE SAID:

This anecdote comes from The Dīwān of Jovial and Indecent Folk. I will tell it at once.

And Shahrazād said:

THE DIWĀN OF JOVIAL AND INDECENT FOLK

The Historic Fart

IT is related—but Allāh is all-knowing—that there was once in the city of Kaukabān in Yaman, a Badawī of the tribe of the Fadlī, whose name was Abū al-Hasan. At an early age he left nomadic life and had become a polished citizen and rich merchant. He had married in his youth, but Allāh had called his wife into His mercy after a year of marriage; thus it was that Abū al-Hasan's friends were always pressing him to marry again and quoting these words of the poet:

> Rise up and hear the season sing,
> The girls are here for marrying,
> And a glad wife's an almanac
> Whose scented leaves point ever back
> And tell about the Spring.

At length Abū al-Hasan could hold out against these persuasions no longer; so he entered into communication with the old women who negotiate marriages, and became betrothed to a damsel as beautiful as the moon shining on the sea. He gave great feasts to celebrate the wedding and asked not only friends, but also the ulamā, fakīrs, darwīshes, and santons of the city. He opened wide the doors of his house and provided for his guests rice of seven different colours, sherberts, lamb stuffed with nuts, almonds, pistachios and raisins, and a young camel roasted and presented whole. All the guests ate and drank joyfully, and when the bride had been shown seven times, dressed in different and costly robes, she was led round for an eighth circle, so that those eyes might gaze their fill which were not yet satisfied. After that the old women led her into the bridal chamber and, upon a bed as high as a throne, prepared her in every way for the entrance of her lord.

Abū al-Hasan came slowly and with dignified step into the chamber, and sat for a moment on the dīwān to prove, both to himself and to his wife and the women, that he was a man of gravity and good manners. He rose weightily to receive the wishes of the old women and to dismiss them, before going up to the bed where the girl so modestly awaited him; but, ah, horror, his belly was full of heavy meat and drink! He let a fine, terrible, resounding fart! May the Devil be far from us!

Each old woman turned to her neighbour and began speaking in a loud voice, pretending that she had heard nothing; the bride, instead of laughing or mocking, chinked and rattled her bracelets to add to the covering noise. But Abū al-Hasan, more than half-dead with mortification, pleaded a pressing need and ran down into the court. He saddled his mare and, leaping upon her back, fled through the shadows of the night away from his house, his marriage, and his bride. He left the city, he crossed the desert, he came to the sea side and went aboard a boat bound for India. In time he came to the Malabar coast.

There he became acquainted with many men from Yaman, who spoke so well of him to the King of that land that he was appointed captain of the royal guard. He lived in enjoyment of that post for ten years, honoured and respected in the midst of luxury; and whenever the memory of his fart came to him, he banished it from his mind as an unclean thing.

But at the end of those ten years he was seized with a great longing for his native land and pined for his city and his house, and well-nigh died of his exile. One day he could resist the solicitations of his soul no longer; therefore, without even asking leave of the King, he absconded and returned to the land of Hadramaut, and Yaman. He disguised himself as a darwīsh and, journeying on foot towards Kaukabān, came to a hill which overlooked that city. He gazed down upon the terrace of his old house and, with tears in his eyes, exclaimed: 'Pray God that no one recognises me! May He have made them forget!' He came down from the hill and took side-streets that would lead him to his house. As he went he saw an old woman sitting at her door, taking the lice from the head of a little ten-year-old girl. He heard the child saying: 'Mother, I wish to know my age; one of my friends is going to cast my horoscope. Tell me when I was born.' The old woman reflected for a moment, and then said: 'You were born on the night and in the year when Abū al-Hasan let his fart.'

The unhappy Abū al-Hasan turned and fled, giving his legs to the wind. 'Your fart has become a date!' he lamented. 'It will go down the years, as long as there are palm trees.' And he did not cease his flight till he was back in India, where he lived in the bitterness of exile until his death. Allāh pity him!

Then Shahrazād said again:

The Two Jesters

IT is also related, O auspicious King, that there was once in the city of Damascus in Syria a man noted for his droll and indelicate tricks; also there was another in Cairo, not less famous for the same quality. The Damascene jester had often heard tell of his Cairene rival and was the more anxious to meet him since his usual admirers were always saying: 'There can be no doubt that the Egyptian is more spiteful and intelligent, cleverer and more amusing than you. To be with him is much more droll. If you do not believe us, go and see his work in Cairo and you will be forced to acknowledge his superiority.' At last the man said to himself: 'There is nothing for it, I must go to Cairo and see for myself.' He made his luggage and left Damascus for Cairo; and Allāh brought him safe and sound to that city. Immediately he inquired for the dwelling of his rival and paid him a visit; the jester of Cairo received him with a large hospitality and most cordial welcome. The two passed the night in agreeable conversation concerning the affairs of the great world.

Next morning the guest said to his host: 'Dear companion, my sole reason for coming to Cairo was to judge for myself those excellent tricks and passes which I have heard that you play unceasingly upon your city. I would not like to return without instruction. Will you let me have a taste of your quality?' 'Dear friend,' answered the other, 'they have been deceiving you. I am one of those slow fellows who can hardly distinguish his left hand from his right. How could I hope to teach a delicate Damascus spark like you? Still, since my duty as a host requires that I show you the fair things of our city, let us go out for a walk.'

The Cairene led his guest to the mosque of al-Ashar, so that he might tell the people of Damascus of the religious and scientific marvel which he had seen; but on the way he paused at a flower stall and bought a large bunch of aromatic herbs, carnations, roses, sweet basil, jasmine, mint and marjoram. When they entered the court of the mosque they saw many persons satisfying their needs in the line of privies which faced the fountain of ablution; so the Cairo man said to his guest: 'Now tell me, if you wanted to play a trick on this line of squatting persons, how would you set about it?'

At this point Shahrazād saw the approach of morning and discreetly fell silent.

But when the six-hundred-and-eighteenth night had come

SHE SAID:

'The method is obvious,' answered the man from Damascus, 'I would go behind them with a thorny broom and, while I swept, prick all their bums as if by accident.' 'There is something a trifle heavy and gross to my mind about that pleasantry,' said the Cairene. 'Such jokes verge a little towards the indelicate. Now watch me!' He went up to the line of defecators with a friendly smile and offered a spray of flowers to each in turn, saying: 'Allow me, good master.' In confusion and fury, each replied: 'Allāh curse you, you son of a pimp! Where do you think we are, in the dining room?' All the people in the court of the mosque laughed most heartily at the expressions of these people.

Then the man from Damascus turned to his host, and said: 'You have beaten me, O prince of jesters. It is a true proverb which

says: *As fine as an Egyptian; for he can pass through the eye of a
needle!*'

Then Shahrazād said again:

A Woman's Trick

I T is related, O auspicious King, that there was a well-born young
woman in a certain city whose husband was often absent upon
journeys near and far. At length the temptation of the flesh was too
strong for her and, as a balm for her torment, she chose the most
handsome youth of his time. They loved each other with extraordinary devotion and satisfied each other at ease and joyfully,
rising to eat, eating to lie down, and lying down to couple.

One day the youth was solicited by an old white-bearded man, a
double-dealing pervert, a knife for colocasia; but, instead of sub-
mitting, he quarrelled with the sheikh, beat him about the face, and
tore away his evil beard. Therefore the old man complained to the
walī of that city and the walī had the youth seized and thrown into
prison.

When the young woman learnt that her lover was in gaol, she was
both grieved and angry. Delaying only long enough to form a plan,
she put on her most seductive ornaments and, after soliciting an
audience with the walī, entered the hall of requests. As Allāh lives,
she could have obtained all the requests of all the world, showing
herself so supple and so fair. After greeting, she said: 'O our lord
the walī, the youth so-and-so, whom you have put in prison, is my
brother and the sole support of our house. His accuser is a rascally
pervert and the witnesses were false. I come to beg that you will, of
your justice, deliver my brother; if you refuse, our house will fall
in ruins and I shall die of hunger.' At first sight the walī had felt his
heart work powerfully towards the girl; therefore he answered: 'I am
disposed to free your brother. Go now into the harīm of my house
and, when the audiences are over, I will come and talk to you about
the matter.' Understanding what he meant, she said to herself: 'I
swear by Allāh, old dirty beard, that you will not touch me save in
apricot time.' But aloud she answered: 'O our lord the walī, it would
be better if you came to my house where we might talk at greater
ease than in this place; for in a harīm I should be a stranger.' 'And
where is your house?' asked the delighted walī. 'In such and such a

place. I will expect you this evening at sundown,' she answered, and went out from the presence, leaving the walī floundering in a stormy sea.

She next went to the kādī, who was an old man, and said, bowing before him: 'O our master the kādī, I pray you cast the eyes of justice upon my cause; for Allāh will do so to you and more also.' 'Who has oppressed you?' asked the kādī, and she answered: 'A wicked sheikh who has had my brother, the sole prop of my house, imprisoned on false witness. I beg you to intercede for me with the walī that my brother may be released.' When the kādī saw and heard the girl, he fell violently in love with her, and therefore answered: 'I will take up your brother's cause. Go now into the harīm of my house; I will join you when I am at liberty and we can talk together. All will be as you desire.' Low to herself, the girl said: 'Son of a pimp, you shall have me in the time of apricots!' But aloud she said: 'O master, it will be better if I wait for you in my house, where none can disturb us.' 'And where is your house?' he asked. 'In such and such a place,' she answered. 'I will wait for you to-night a little after sunset.' Then she went forth from the kādī and sought the wazīr of the King.

She told the wazīr of the youth's imprisonment and begged him to give an order of release. Then said the wazīr: 'That should not be difficult. In the meanwhile, go into the harīm; I will join you there and we can talk about the matter.' 'By the life of your head, O master,' she answered, 'I am very shy and would not dare to go into your harīm. My own house is better fitted for such a conversation. I will await you there an hour after sunset this evening.' She told him the place of her house and departed for the King's palace.

As soon as she entered the presence, the King marvelled at her beauty, and said to himself: 'By Allāh, here is something to be taken hot and hungry!' Then, aloud and kindly, he asked: 'Who has oppressed you?' 'There can be no oppression,' she answered, 'for our King is just.' Then said the King: 'Allāh alone is just! What can I do for you?' 'Give me an order of release for my brother,' she answered. 'He has been unjustly imprisoned.' 'That is easy,' said the King. 'Go and wait in my harīm, child. Justice shall have its course.' 'In that case, O King,' she ventured, 'I would rather wait in my own house. For such a conversation as ours, the King must know that there are many preparations necessary, baths and the like; those preparations I cannot perfectly make except in my own poor house, which, after to-night, will be a palace.' 'Be it so,' answered the King. When they had agreed about the time of the meeting, the girl left the royal presence and went to find a carpenter.

At this point Shahrazād saw the approach of morning and discreetly fell silent.

But when the six-hundred-and-twentieth night had come

SHE SAID:

To the carpenter she said: 'I wish you to deliver at my house, early this evening, a large cupboard with four shelves, one above the other; each of the shelves must have a separate door with strong locks.' 'By Allāh, good mistress,' answered the carpenter, 'it cannot be done by this evening.' 'But I will pay you anything you like to ask,' she said, and he answered: 'In that case it shall be ready, dear mistress. I ask neither silver nor gold, but only a certain favour which you can well imagine. Come into the back of the shop, where we can talk at ease about the measurements of the cupboard.' But the girl laughed and said: 'My dear carpenter, you have no tact! Do you think that that dirty little place at the back of your shop is suitable for a conversation such as ours? Come round to my house this evening, after you have sent the cupboard, and we will talk about measurements until the morning. . . . Only I have just remembered that I require five shelves and not four. Yes, I need five shelves for all the remarkable merchandise which I wish to lock away.' Then she gave the carpenter her address and returned home.

She took five robes of different colour and shape from a coffer and carefully set them out; she made ready meat and drink, arranged flowers and burnt perfumes. Then she sat down to wait the arrival of her guests.

Towards sunset the carpenter's porter brought the cupboard and, at the girl's order, placed it in the reception hall. The porter had hardly departed and the girl had not had time even to try the locks, before there was a knock at the door. The walī entered, and his hostess, rising in his honour and kissing the earth between his hands, made him be seated and plied him with refreshments. Then she cast eyes a foot long in his direction, together with such burning glances that the walī sat up and trembled with a desire to possess her immediately. But the girl extricated herself from his embrace, saying: 'Surely you lack refinement, my master. Will you not first undress, so that you may be free in your movements?' 'There is no difficulty in that,' cried the wali, as he cast aside his garments and put on a strangely cut robe of yellow silk, and bonnet of the same, which the girl handed to him. This, you must know, is the custom at licentious feasts. Just as the wali, all muffled in his yellow robe and bonnet, prepared to amuse himself, there came a violent knocking at the door. 'Are you expecting some neighbour?' he asked crossly; but she answered in terror: 'By Allāh, I had quite forgotten that my husband is coming back this evening! It is he who is knocking at the door!' 'What will become of me? What must I do?' cried the wali, and she breathlessly replied: 'You must get into this cupboard.' She opened the door of the lowest shelf, saying: 'Get inside.' 'But how?' he asked. 'Squat down,' she said. So the wali got into the cupboard and squatted down, being nearly bent in two. The girl locked the door of the shelf and went to open for her next guest.

This proved to be the kādī. She received him in the same manner; but just as he was preparing to throw himself upon her, strangely dressed in a red robe and bonnet, she said: 'You have not yet written the order for my brother's liberation.' The kādī wrote an order and was handing it to the girl when there came a knocking upon the door. 'That is my husband!' cried the girl in terror, and, after making the kādī climb up into the second shelf of the cupboard, she went and opened for her third guest.

This was the wazīr. He met the same fate as the others; he was swaddled in a green robe and bonnet, and shut into the third shelf of the cupboard, just as the King arrived. The King, in his turn, was rigged out in a blue robe and a blue bonnet, and bundled into the fourth shelf of the cupboard by a violent knocking at the door, just as he was about to do that for which he had come. He was very fat, and to squat in that confined space irked him considerably.

The carpenter entered with famished eyes and would have thrown himself upon the girl at once, had she not said: 'Tell me, carpenter, why you made the fifth shelf so small? I can hardly get anything into it.' 'That is a thoroughly good shelf,' he answered. 'It would hold me and four like me.' 'Try then,' she said, and the carpenter, climbing on stools set one upon the other, managed to worm his way on to the fifth shelf. At once he was locked in.

The girl then took the kādī's order to the guardians of the prison, and they released her lover without question. The two hurried back to the house and, to celebrate their coming together again, coupled long and violently, with plenty of panting and noise. The five in the cupboard heard all that was going on, but did not dare to move. They squatted one above the other and waited eagerly until they should be released.

When the boy and girl had finished their diversions, they got together all the precious things in the house and shut them in portable chests; then they quickly sold the rest, and left the city for another kingdom. So much for them.

Two days later the five in the cupboard were all seized with a simultaneous desire to piss. The carpenter was the first to succumb; and his piss fell upon the King's head. A moment afterwards the King pissed on the wazīr's head, who in his turn pissed on the kādī's head, who in his turn pissed on the walī. All except the King and the carpenter lifted up their voices, and cried: 'O filth!' The kādī recognised the wazīr's voice and the wazīr the voice of the kādī. They called out to each other: 'We are in a nice trap! Happily the King has been spared.' 'Be quiet, for I am here!' cried the King. 'And I have no idea who pissed on my head.' Then the carpenter exclaimed: 'May Allāh in every way exalt the King's majesty! I think I must have done it, for I am on the fifth shelf. Also I made the cupboard!'

At this point the girl's husband returned from his journey; the neighbours, who had not noticed the woman and the youth eloping, watched him as he knocked fruitlessly upon the door. When he asked them why none answered, they could not tell him. With their help he burst in the door and the whole crowd of them entered, only to find the house empty, save for a large cupboard. They heard men's voices proceeding from this cupboard and at once determined that it must be full of the Jinn.

At this point Shahrazād saw the approach of morning and discreetly fell silent.

But when the six-hundred-and-twenty-second night had come

SHE SAID:

Speaking in loud voices, they agreed to set fire to the cupboard and destroy it completely with all which it might contain; but, as they were setting about to do this, the kādī's voice called from inside: 'Do nothing rash, good folk! We are neither Jinn nor burglars, but so-and-so and so-and so.' In a few words he told them of the trick which had been played upon them all; so the neighbours at once broke the locks and delivered, from the five shelves of the cupboard, five men disguised in fancy garments. None of those who beheld the victims come forth could refrain from laughing; but the King, in order to console the bereaved husband, said to him: 'I appoint you my second wazīr.' Such is the story. But Allāh is All-knowing!

When she had made an end, Shahrazād said to King Shahryār: 'You must not think that this is at all to be compared with The Tale of the Sleeper Wakened.' Then, as the King raised his eyebrows at this unknown title, Shahrazād began without delay:

The Tale of the Sleeper Wakened

IT is related, O auspicious King, that there was a young bachelor in Baghdād, during the reign of the Khalīfah Hārūn al-Rashīd, who lived a most strange life and whose name was Abū al-Hasan. His neighbours never saw him invite a man two days running or, by any chance, entertain a citizen of their city. All who came to his house were strangers; and therefore the people of that quarter, who did not understand this peculiarity, called the young man Abū al-Hasan the Eccentric.

It was his custom to post himself every evening at the further end of the city bridge and, when he saw a stranger approach, rich or poor, young or old, to accost him with an urbane smile and beg him to accept the hospitality of his house for his first night in Baghdād. He would lead the stranger home and entertain him royally, keeping him company throughout the night in jovial talk. But on the morrow, he would say: 'Dear guest, I invited you when Allāh was your sole acquaintance in this city; I did so for a reason of my own. But I have sworn never to entertain even a stranger for two days running, though he were the most charming of the sons of men. Thus I am obliged to separate from you and I beg that, if ever you meet me in the streets of Baghdād, you will pretend not to know me; otherwise I shall be obliged to turn from you myself.' After such words as these, Abū al-Hasan would conduct his guest to one of the khāns and, taking leave of him with words of instruction concerning the ways of the city, would never see him again. If, by chance, the two crossed each other's path in the roads or markets, Abū al-Hasan would turn his head, in order that he might not be obliged to salute the other. And for a long time he behaved in this way, entertaining a fresh guest every night.

One evening at sunset, while Abū al-Hasan waited at the end of the bridge, he saw a man coming towards him dressed like a rich merchant of Mosul and followed by a tall dignified slave. This stranger was the Khalīfah Hārūn al-Rashīd in disguise, who was returning from one of his monthly tours of secret examination in and about the city. Abū al-Hasan, who had no suspicion of the stranger's identity, gave him welcome with a gracious bow, and said: 'Blessed be your arrival among us, my master! Do me pleasure by accepting my hospitality for to-night, instead of going to a khān. To-morrow morning you can find a lodging at your leisure.' Then, in order to persuade an acceptance, he told the Khalīfah of his nightly custom, adding: 'Allāh is generous, my master. You will find in my house large hospitality, warm bread, and a clear wine.' The Khalīfah found the adventure so strange and Abū al-Hasan so unusual that he made up his mind to know him better; after a half-hearted refusal for good form's sake, he accepted the invitation in these words: 'Be it upon my head and before my eye! May Allāh increase His benefits about you, good master! I am ready to follow you.' So Abū al-Hasan showed the way and led his new guest to the house, conversing pleasantly the while.

Hasan's mother had made excellent cooking that night; first she served the two with fried cakes stuffed with mince and pine kernels; then with a fat capon islanded among four plump chickens; then with a goose having raisin and nut stuffing; and finally with a pigeon stew. These things looked almost too good to eat until they were tasted.

At this point Shahrazād saw the approach of morning and discreetly fell silent.

But when the six-hundred-and-twenty-fourth night had come

SHE SAID:

The two ate greatly of these things and, all the time, Abū al-Hasan chose the most delicate portions for his guest. After they had washed their hands with basin and ewer, Hasan's mother served dishes with grapes, dates and pears, and almond paste, and pots filled with conserve. The two ate of these and then began to drink.

Abū al-Hasan filled the feast cup with wine and turned to his guest, saying: 'Dear guest, you know that the cock does not drink without calling the hens to drink with him by uttering little cries. Were I to drink of this cup alone, the wine would stick in my throat and I should die. For this one night, I beg you to leave sobriety to malcontents and hunt with me among the wine for joy. For I am glad to-night, since my house has been honoured by such a stranger.' Wishing to make him talk, the Khalīfah began to drink with him and, when the wine had lightened their souls a little, he said to Abū al-Hasan: 'Now that there is bread and salt between us, will you tell me why you behave thus hospitably to strangers, and relate the story of your life; for it must be astonishing?' 'Not astonishing, but certainly instructive, O guest,' replied Abū al-Hasan. 'My name is Abū al-Hasan, and I am the son of a merchant who, on his death, left me a fair inheritance in Baghdād. As I had been brought up very severely during my father's lifetime, I made haste to recapture the lost moments of my youth; but, being a young man of some reflection, I took the precaution of dividing my inheritance into two parts, one of which I realised in gold and the other disposed safely in stocks. I took the cash and spent generously with lads of my own age, whom I entertained as sumptuously as if I had been an amīr. I spared no expense to make our lives delightful and thus at the end of a year, had come down to my last dīnār. Then I turned to my friends, but they had disappeared. I sought them out and begged them to help me in my penury; but they all made excuse and not one of them offered sufficient to keep body and soul together for a single day. So I considered within myself how wise my father had been to raise me strictly. I returned to my own house and there made a resolution which I have kept ever since: I swore, before Allāh, never to be seen in company with my fellow citizens and never to entertain any but strangers. Further, since experience had taught me that a short warm friendship is better than a long one which ends disastrously, I swore never to keep company, even with a stranger, for two days running. Even though he were the most charming of the sons of men! Well I know that the bonds of friendship are cruel bonds, destroying the joys of friendship, so I beg you not to be astonished if I say farewell to you to-morrow morning, after our one night of perfect amity. Also, do not take it ill if I refuse to see you should we ever happen to meet in the streets.'

'There is something marvellous to me about such conduct,' said the Khalīfah. 'I have never known an eccentric who could act so wisely. I admire you very much: it was shrewd of you to keep the second part of your inheritance. Now you are able to enjoy the conversation of a fresh man every day, avoiding all chance of boredom and disagreement. . . . But what you have said concerning our separation on the morrow is very painful to me, as I should have liked to return your hospitality in some way. I beg you to express some wish to me; for I swear, by the sacred Kaabah, that I will satisfy it. Speak freely and do not pitch your demand too low; for Allāh has been good to me in my trade and there is very little which I cannot compass with His help.'

At this point Shahrazād saw the approach of morning and discreetly fell silent.

But when the six-hundred-and-twenty-fifth night had come

SHE SAID:

Abū al-Hasan answered, without any signs of surprise: 'My eye has already been rejoiced with your presence; anything further would be a superfluity. I thank you for your intention; but, since I have neither desire nor ambition, I find it difficult to prefer any request. My state in life suffices me, I do not need to ask help of any.' Then said the Khalīfah: 'In Allāh's name, my master, do not refuse my request. Let your heart prompt you to some desire that I may satisfy it. Otherwise I shall feel humiliated when I say farewell; for a benefit is harder to sustain than an injury, and a man of breeding must return in double measure. Speak, I pray you!'

Seeing that the Khalīfah would not be put off, Abū al-Hasan lowered his head and reflected deeply for a long time; then he raised his eyes, and cried: 'I have found something. But it is the request of a madman; I will not tell it to you lest you should have a wrong idea of me.' 'By the life of my head,' returned the Khalīfah, 'no one can say in advance whether an idea is mad or sane. I am only a merchant, but I have more power than you would think to look at me. Speak, I beg you!' Then said Abū al-Hasan: 'I will speak since you insist; but I swear, by the virtue of the Prophet (upon whom be prayer and peace!), that none but the Khalīfah could realise my wish; for I ardently desire to change places with our master, Hārūn al-Rashīd, Commander of the Faithful, if only for one day.' 'What would you do if you were Khalīfah for one day?' asked Hārūn al-Rashīd, and Abū al-Hasan, after a momentary pause, replied:

'You must know, O stranger, that the city of Baghdād is divided into quarters and that each quarter has a sheikh at its head; unfortunately the sheikh of my quarter is a creature of such horrible ugliness that I doubt not he was born from the coupling of a hyena and a pig. His approach is pestilential; for his mouth is no ordinary mouth, but rather a dirty anus like the hole of a privy; his fish-coloured eyes pop sideways; his scabby lips are like a venereal sore and jet out spittle when he speaks; his ears are sow's ears; his flabby painted cheeks are like an old ape's bottom; the teeth have fallen from his jaws through eating filth; his body is fretted with every foul disease of the earth; as for his anus—well, he has not got one: for he has so long given himself to be a ditch for the tools of donkey-boys, nightmen, and sweepers, that his arsegut has rotted away and is now a cave stuffed with cotton swabs to prevent his tripes from falling out.

'This crapulous creature, with two other foul fellows, sows all the trouble in our quarter; there is no sin that he will not commit, no falsehood that he will not circulate and, because he has a shitty soul, he always exercises his old-womanish spite on clean and honest men. He could not do sufficient harm by the pestilence of his presence if he had not two helpers as gross as he.

'The first is a slave, smooth-faced as a eunuch, with yellow eyes and a voice like the farting of donkeys. This offspring of a dog and a whore pretends to be of noble Arab birth, though he comes, in truth, from the lowest Christian stock. His trade is hanging about among the cooks and eunuchs of the great to filch the secrets of their masters and peddle them through taverns and knocking houses. Nothing comes amiss to him, and if there were a dīnār in a dirty arse, he would lick it gladly.

'The second is a fat jester with fat eyes whose business is to make puns among the markets, where he is well-known for a head as bald as an onion and for so terrible a stammer that you would think he was going to vomit his guts with every word. The merchants do not ask him into their shops because he is so fat that, if he sits on a chair, it flies to matchwood beneath him. This one is more foolish but less disgusting than the other two.

'If I were the Prince of Believers for one day, I would not make myself rich, or my folk rich, but I would free our quarter from these dogs and, after suitable punishment, sweep their bodies into the town ditch. Thus would our quarter know tranquillity and my desire be satisfied.'

At this point Shahrazād saw the approach of morning and discreetly fell silent.

But when the six-hundred-and-twenty-seventh night had come

SHE SAID:

'In truth, O Abū al-Hasan,' said the Khalīfah, 'your wish is that of an upright and good-hearted man, for only one with these qualities would so rail because the evil may flourish with impunity. But I do not imagine that your wish would be so difficult to realise as you think; for the Khalīfah loves a strange adventure as well as any man, and, if he were told, I am sure he would change powers with you for a day and a night.' At this Abū al-Hasan laughed, and answered: 'By Allāh, we have not been talking very seriously! If the Khalīfah were informed, I expect he would shut me up in a mad-house. If your trade should make you known to anyone in the palace, I beg you not to report my vapourings under wine.' 'I take oath not to speak of the matter to a soul,' answered the Khalīfah; but to himself he swore not to let slip this opportunity, which seemed to promise a better jest than any which he had before compassed in any of his disguises. 'It is now my turn to pour the wine, dear host,' he said. 'So far, you have done all the pouring.' He took the bottle and, while filling the cup, cleverly slipped into it a morsel of pure Cretan banj. Then he handed the vessel to Abū al-Hasan, saying: 'May it be wholesome and delicious!' 'Who could refuse the pouring of a guest?' replied Abū al-Hasan. 'But I must warn you that I may not be able to rise in the morning to see you off; therefore I beg you not to forget to shut the door after you.' The Khalīfah promised and Abū al-Hasan drained the cup with a quiet mind. Immediately he fell head over heels so rapidly that the Khalīfah burst out laughing. When he had recovered from his amusement, he called to his slave, saying: 'Take this man upon your back and follow me.' The slave obeyed and, as they were leaving, the Khalīfah added: 'Mark the place of this house so that you can return to it when I bid you.' They went out into the street, but forgot to shut the door.

They entered the palace by the secret wicket and made their way into the Khalīfah's own bedchamber. 'Take off this man's clothes!' said Hārūn. 'Dress him in my night garments and put him into my bed.' As soon as this was done, the Khalīfah sent for all the dignitaries of his palace: his wazīrs, chamberlains, and his eunuchs, together with the women of his harīm; when they had collected, he said to them: 'To-morrow you must all come to this room and particularly obey the orders of this man who lies in my garments upon the bed. Pay him exactly the same respect as you would accord to me and treat him in every way as if he were myself. Give him the title of Prince of Believers and do not refuse the least of his desires. If one of you, even were it my own son, should go against my inclinations in this matter, he would be hanged at the palace gate.'

'To hear is to obey!' they answered and retired in silence, realising that the Khalīfah meant to beguile his weariness in some extraordinary fashion.

Only Jafar and Masrūr remained; to these al-Rashīd said: 'To-morrow you must be the first awake, and come here to take the orders of my substitute. You must not be astonished at anything he may say; and you must pretend to take him for the Khalīfah, whatever he may tell you to the contrary. Give alms to all whom he points out, even if you have to spend all the treasures of my kingdom. Punish, reward, hang, kill, nominate and deprive, exactly as he commands. Nor need you come to consult me first; for I shall be hidden near by to hear and see what passes. Above all, you must be very careful not to let him suspect for a moment that he is a victim of one of my jokes. . . . Let it be as I say. . . . When you wake come and wake me also.'

At this point Shahrazād saw the approach of morning and discreetly fell silent.

But when the six-hundred-and-twenty-eighth night had come

SHE SAID:

Next morning Jafar and Masrūr woke the Khalīfah, who hastened to place himself behind a curtain in the room where Abū al-Hasan was sleeping, so that he might see and hear without being noticed by any. Then Jafar and Masrūr entered the chamber, with all the dignitaries and women and slaves of the palace. They ranged themselves in their usual places in a grave silence, as if it were really the Khalīfah who was about to wake. When all were placed, a slave, who had been instructed beforehand, held a swab of vinegar under Hasan's nose; so that he sneezed once, twice, and thrice, expelling from his nose long filaments which had been collected there by the power of the banj. The slave caught this mucus on a gold plate so that it might not mess the bed, and then wiped Hasan's nose and face with rose-water. Abū al-Hasan came out of his unconsciousness and opened his eyes.

He saw a rare bed, covered with a brocade of scarlet gold starred with pearls; he lifted his eyes and saw a mighty hall with walls and ceiling of satin, with silken hangings, and vases of gold and crystal in all the corners. Then his look travelled downwards and he saw himself surrounded by women and low-bowing slaves of ravishing beauty. Behind them he saw a mass of wazīrs, amīrs, chamberlains, black eunuchs, and musicians; these last had their fingers poised to accompany a circle of singers raised upon a dais. On a stool by his bedside he saw the garments, mantle, and turban of the Khalīfah, and knew them by their colour.

He shut his eyes again; but Jafar went up to him and, after kissing the earth three times, said most respectfully: 'O Prince of Believers, allow your slave to waken you, since it is the time of the morning prayer.'

Abū al-Hasan first rubbed his eyes, from right to left and from left to right; then he pinched his arm, gave a yelp of anguish at the pain, and said: 'I am not dreaming. I am the Khalīfah. . . . And yet I think it must be all that drink which I had with the Mosul merchant and the silly things I said to him.' He turned his face to the wall and would have slept again; so Jafar approached a second time, saying: 'O Commander of the Faithful, allow your slave to be surprised at seeing his lord neglect the morning prayer.' At the same moment he signed to the musicians, who struck up a concert of harp, lute and guitar, with the harmonious singing of the singers. Abū al-Hasan looked in the direction of the sound, and said to himself: 'Did you ever hear the like when you were asleep, O Abū al-Hasan?' And he sat up, doubting his eyes and not knowing what to think. He put his hands where he could see if they were really there, and said: 'Is not this strange? Is not this passing strange? Where are you, O Abū al-Hasan? Where are you, O son of my mother? Are you awake or dreaming? How long have you been Khalīfah? How long have you possessed this palace, this bed, these nobles, these eunuchs, these delightful girls, these musicians, these enchanting singers, and those, and these, and those?' At that moment the music ceased and Masrūr kissed the earth three times before the bed, saying: 'O Commander of the Faithful, allow the least of your slaves to inform you that the hour of morning prayer has passed and that the time has come to go to the dīwan.' Abū al-Hasan was more doubtful than ever, now that he had to do something; so he looked Masrūr between the eyes, and asked angrily: 'Who are you, you? And who am I, I?' 'You are our master, the Prince of Believers, the Khalīfah Hārūn al-Rashīd, fifth of the line of Abbās, descendant of the uncle of the Prophet (upon whom be prayer and peace!),' answered Masrūr most respectfully. 'The slave who dares to address you is the pitiful and rightly-disdained nothing, named Masrūr, who is honoured by the august charge of bearing the sword of our master's will.'

At this point Shahrazād saw the approach of morning and discreetly fell silent.

But when the six-hundred-and-thirtieth night had come

SHE SAID:

'Son of a thousand cuckolds, you lie!' cried Hasan; and Masrūr answered: 'Indeed, my lord, had another than myself been thus addressed by the Khalīfah, he would have died of grief; but your old slave, burdened with years of service and more greatly burdened with your manifold kindness, is sure that the Vicar of the Prophet only speaks thus in order to test him. But let not the proof be carried any further, dear master; if some evil dream has troubled your sleep, let the light of morning drive it from you!'

Abū al-Hasan could contain himself no longer; he fell back on the bed with a shout of laughter and began to wind himself up in the coverings, kicking his legs in the air. Hārūn al-Rashīd, who saw and heard all this from behind the curtain, puffed out his cheeks to prevent himself from laughing.

When Abū al-Hasan had laughed in this strange position for an hour, he sat up again and signed to a little black slave, saying: 'Do you know me? Can you tell me who I am?' The little black slave modestly lowered his eyes, and said: 'You are our master, Hārūn al-Rashīd, Commander of the Faithful, Khalīfah of the Prophet (upon whom be prayer and peace!), Vicar on earth of Him Who reigns in Heaven.' But Hasan cried: 'You are lying, little pitch-face! Son of a thousand pimps, you are not telling the truth!'

Then he turned to one of the young girl slaves, and held out his finger to her, saying: 'Bite this!' The child, knowing the Khalīfah was watching, said to herself: 'Here is a chance to show the Prince of Believers that I can help him in his jests.' Therefore she bit the finger to the bone, so that Abū al-Hasan yelled for the pain of it, and cried: 'Oh, ah, I am not asleep! Ah, oh, I am certainly not asleep!' Then to the same girl, he said: 'Do you know me? Am I what they say?' The slave stretched out her arms, and said: 'The name of Allāh be upon the Khalīfah and about him! My lord, you are the Prince of Believers, Hārūn al-Rashīd, Vicar of Allāh!'

'You are the Vicar of Allāh. Do you hear that, O son of my mother?' cried Hasan, and then to the girl: 'You lie, you drab! Do you think you know who I am better than I do?' At that moment the chief eunuch approached the bed and kissed the earth three times, saying: 'If our master will pardon me, this is the hour when our master usually goes to satisfy his need in the cabinet.' Passing his arm under Abū al-Hasan's armpit, he helped him from the bed and, even as the young man's feet touched the floor, the hall and the palace resounded with the usual salute: 'Allāh's victory to the Khalīfah!'

'Is this not marvellous?' said Hasan to himself. 'Yesterday I was Abū al-Hasan and now it seems that I am Hārūn al-Rashīd. . . . Whoever I am, since this appears to be the time for pissing, let us piss. But I wish I knew if this is the right hour for doing the other thing as well.' He was drawn from these reflections by the chief eunuch presenting him with a pair of gold-embroidered slippers, high-heeled and enriched with pearls, which were reserved specially for the cabinet. Hasan had never seen such things in his life, so he slipped them both into one of his large sleeves, thinking that they were a costly present from someone.

The beholders had so far restrained their mirth but, at this, some turned their heads and others, pretending to kiss the earth, fell in convulsions of laughter on the carpet. Behind his curtain the Khalīfah fell over violently on his side.

Sustaining Abū al-Hasan by the shoulder, the chief eunuch led him to a privy paved with marble and, like all the rest of the palace, richly carpeted. Then he brought him back among the women and nobles in the bedchamber and, passing with him between the two files of them, gave his master into the care of the slaves of the bedchamber. These took off Hasan's night clothes and gave him a basin of rose-water for his ablutions. When he had washed, sniffing eagerly at the perfumed water all the while, they clad him in royal robes, set the crown upon his head, and placed in his hand the gold sceptre of the Khalīfah.

'Am I or am I not Abū al-Hasan?' thought Hasan. But, after a moment's reflection, he shouted in a loud voice so that all might hear him: 'I am not Abū al-Hasan! Who says I am Abū al-Hasan shall be impaled! I am myself, I am Hārūn al-Rashīd!'

'March!' he cried in a tone of assured command, and followed the procession of his subjects to the throne room. With Masrūr's help he mounted the throne amid universal acclamation and, placing the sceptre across his knees, looked about him. He saw his people ranged in good order in front of the hall's forty doors; he saw guards with shining swords, wazīrs, amīrs, nobles and ambassadors; among the silent surge of faces he recognised Jafar, Abū Nuwās, al-Ijlī, al-Rakkāshī, Ibdān, al-Sakar, Umar al-Tartīs, Abū Ishāk and Jadīm.

While his glance swept these faces, Jafar advanced at the head of certain splendidly-clad nobles and, taking a great sheaf of papers from below his mantle, the day's petitions, began to read them aloud. Although Abū al-Hasan knew nothing of such things he showed no embarrassment; he gave judgment in every matter with such tact and justice that the Khalīfah, who was already hidden behind another curtain, marvelled to hear him.

When Jafar had finished his report, Hasan asked for his chief of police; and when Ahmad-the-Moth was pointed out to him, bade him approach. Ahmad came forth from his place with becoming gravity and prostrated himself before the throne. But Hasan bade him rise, and said to him: 'Chief of our police, take ten guards with you and go instantly to such a house in such a street in such a quarter! There you will find a detestable swine, who is the sheikh of that quarter, and, with him, two dogs as evil as himself. Arrest all three and, as a foretaste of what is to come, give them each four hundred strokes on the soles of their feet! . . .'

At this point Shahrazād saw the approach of morning and discreetly fell silent.

But when the six-hundred-and-thirty-second night had come

SHE SAID:

'Dress them in rags and set them on a scabby camel, their faces to its tail; lead them throughout all the quarters of the city and have this cried before them: "Such is the beginning of the punishment for slander, for soiling women, for gossip to the hurt of honest men!" After that you will impale the sheikh through the mouth, as it is by the mouth he sinned and also as he has no anus; then throw his rotten body to the dogs. Take the smooth man with yellow eyes, the baser of the two companions, and drown him in the privy ditch of one Abū al-Hasan, a neighbour. Though the second companion is a jester and very foolish, you shall only punish him in this way: get a skilled carpenter to make a chair which will fly in pieces each time the man sits down on it, and then condemn the jester to keep on sitting down for the rest of his life.'

Ahmad-the-Moth, who had been warned beforehand to carry out any command of Abū al-Hasan, put his hand to his head as a sign that that member would answer for any disobedience and, kissing the earth a second time, left the hall.

The Khalīfah was delighted at seeing Abū al-Hasan acquit himself so gravely in the duties of kingship. He watched while his substitute judged, appointed, dismissed, and saw to the business of the realm with a profound discretion. When Ahmad-the-Moth returned, Hasan asked if his orders had been carried out, and the chief of police, prostrating himself again, gave a paper into his hands. This was none other than the legal process of execution, signed by lawyers and men well-esteemed in the quarter. 'I am satisfied,' said Abū al-Hasan. 'That is the punishment I decree for all slanderers, soilers of women, and those who interfere with the affairs of others.'

Then Hasan signed to his chief treasurer, and said to him: 'Take a bag filled with a thousand golden dīnārs into that quarter from which the chief of police has just returned, and find out the house of one Abū al-Hasan. You will have no difficulty in arriving at the place, for any one will direct you to the house of a man so known and loved. You will enter the house and beg to be allowed to speak to the venerable mother of that man; when you have saluted her with the regard due to her excellence, you will say: "O mother of Abū al-Hasan, our master the Khalīfah sends you this bag of a thousand golden dīnārs. The sum is unworthy of your acceptance, but, for the moment, the treasury is empty and the Khalīfah regrets that he can do no more for you to-day." When you have put the bag into her hands, return and bring me an account of your mission.' The chief treasurer hastened to execute this command.

Abū al-Hasan signed to Jafar that the dīwān was over, and Jafar repeated that sign to the wazīrs, amīrs, chamberlains, and others, who all abased themselves before the throne and went out in order. When Jafar and Masrūr alone remained, they assisted Hasan to rise from the throne and, each supporting him by an arm, led him to the harīm, where the day's feast had been prepared. There women took their places at his side and led him into the eating hall.

Abū al-Hasan heard a ravishing concerted sound of lute and flute, hautbois and clarinet, and the fresh voices of girls singing. 'I can no longer doubt,' he said to himself. 'I am most certainly Hārūn al-Rashīd. I see and hear, smell and walk; I hold the process of those three men's execution, I find honour and respect at every step; therefore I am not dreaming. Therefore I am the Khalīfah.'

At this point Shahrazād saw the approach of morning and discreetly fell silent.

But when the six-hundred-and-thirty-fourth night had come

SHE SAID:

Looking to right and left, he became even more fixed in the certitude of his royalty, for he saw that he was in the middle of a gold hall whose carpeting and hangings were delightfully picked out in all coloured designs. Seven gold lustres, each with seven branches, gave light from the azure ceiling; and, in the middle of the apartment, seven great trays of solid gold, resting upon stools, dulcified the air with the amber and spices of their meats. Beside these trays waited seven girls of incomparable beauty, dressed in robes of varying tint and form, and each held a fan ready to refresh Abū al-Hasan.

Hasan had eaten nothing since the day before; therefore he sat down eagerly before the dishes, while the seven girls fanned the air about him. As he was unused to so much wind when he was eating, he looked at each damsel in turn with a gracious smile, and said: 'I think that one fan will be enough. Tell that negress to fan me, and come and sit down beside me.' He ranged them all in a half circle so that wherever he cast his eyes he might see something delightful, and then began to eat. But soon he saw that the girls did not dare to touch the food out of respect; therefore he pressed them to help themselves without restraint and offered them chosen morsels with his own hands. Then he asked them their names, and they replied: 'We are called Musk, Throat-of-Alabaster, Roseleaf, Pomegranate-Heart, Coral-Lips, Clove and Sugarcane.' 'As Allāh lives,' cried Hasan, 'the names are suitable; nor are musk, alabaster, rose, pomegranate, coral, clove or sugarcane, at all diminished by association with your beauties.' In this way he continued to speak so exquisitely to them during the repast that the Khalīfah congratulated himself more and more on having found this jest.

When the meats were finished, the girls called eunuchs to bring in water, and themselves knelt before Hasan, serving him with a gold basin and perfumed napkins. Then they helped him to rise and accompanied him to a door where the eunuchs pulled aside a large curtain, exposing a second chamber furnished with fruits upon gold plates. After that they intrusted him to the eunuchs and retired.

Abū al-Hasan found this hall more beautiful than the first and, when he sat down, was delighted by a second concert of singing and lute playing. On the gold dishes were ten alternate levels of rare and exquisite fruits, and beside each of the dishes, which were seven, stood a girl with a fan, fairer and more richly-habited than those who had kept him company at meat. Hasan made them sit about him and served them himself with fruit. When he had asked and obtained their names, he paid appropriate compliments, handing a fig to one, a grape to another, a slice of melon to a third, a banana to a fourth. Thus the Khalīfah rejoiced more and more in his quality.

When Hasan had tasted all the fruits, he rose and went into a third hall, more dream-like in its magnificence than either of the other two.

At this point Shahrazād saw the approach of morning and discreetly fell silent.

But when the six-hundred-and-thirty-sixth night had come

SHE SAID:

This was the hall of sweetmeats, where were seven great trays, beneath seven lustres and flanked by seven girls; on each tray were a multitude of crystal vessels and basins of rosy glass, containing every colour and taste of conserve. There were liquid jams and dry, there were leaved cakes, there was every pastry known to man. Amid a fresh outpouring of music, Abū al-Hasan tasted a little of these scented sweets and paid compliments as sweet to the names of the girls who bore him company. Then he was introduced into the hall of drinks, which was more surprising than the other three put together. There were seven gold trays lighted by seven lustres of gold and heaped with a symmetrical arrangement of flagons and rare bottles; hidden musicians played and sang, and the girls beside the dishes were not dressed in heavy robes, as their sisters had been in the other halls, but were simply covered with chemises of light silk. The first girl was brown, the second black, the third white; the fourth was yellow-haired, the fifth was fat, the sixth was lean, and the tresses of the seventh were a bright red. Abū al-Hasan gazed upon them with all the more pleasure since the texture of their garments hid nothing from him; in great delight he bade them sit beside him and pour drink. As each presented the cup he asked her name and, as he drained the wine, took from her a kiss, a bite, or a wandering of fingers in the thigh. He played in this way until the infant began to cry, and then he bade anyone of the seven who cared to take charge of the inconvenient child. All threw themselves upon the nursling at the same time and would have tended it; first one got hold of it and then another, with laughter and excited cries, until the infant suddenly went to sleep again in the bosom of its father.

The Khalīfah silently enjoyed this scene and thanked the lucky destiny which had set him upon the way of so diverting a fellow. But very soon one of the girls, who had received instructions from Jafar, secretly threw a pinch of soporific powder into the cup and presented it to Hasan, saying: 'O Prince of Believers, I pray you drink this cup, for perhaps it will wake the child.' 'Certainly, by Allāh,' answered Hasan laughing, and, after draining the wine, turned to speak with her who had poured it; but his mouth opened in a prodigious yawn and he fell head over heels upon the carpets.

The Khalīfah, who had been waiting for this second sleep, rolled out from behind the curtain, for he could not stand because of his laughter. He ordered slaves to strip Abū al-Hasan of his royal robes and put his own garments upon him. Then he called the slave who had brought Hasan to the palace and ordered him to carry him back to his own house and lay him upon the bed. 'For,' said the Khalīfah to himself, 'if this goes on any longer, either I will die of laughing, or he, poor fellow, will go mad.' The slave took Abū al-Hasan on his back and, carrying him out through the secret door, bore him to his own house. There he disposed him on his bed and departed, taking care, this time, to shut the door.

At this point Shahrazād saw the approach of morning and discreetly fell silent.

But when the six-hundred-and-thirty-seventh night had come

SHE SAID:

Abū al-Hasan lay in a deep sleep until the noon of the following day and did not wake until the effects of the banj were entirely worn off. Before he opened his eyes, he thought: 'On reflection, I prefer Sugarcane, then Coral-Lips; and Pearl-Cluster, the blond, only third, though she did give me that last cup.' Then aloud, he called: 'Come, my girls! Sugarcane, Coral-Lips, Pearl-Cluster, Dawn, Morning-Star, Musk, Throat-of-Alabaster, Pomegranate-Heart, Appleblossom, Roseleaf! Come, my dears, come quickly! Yesterday I was a little tired, but to-day the child is very well indeed.'

He waited for a moment, and then as no one ran to answer his calling, became very angry, and sat up with open eyes . . . He saw that he was in his own poor chamber, and not in that splendid palace from which the day before he had governed all the world; therefore he thought that he was dreaming, and cried: 'Jafar, Jafar, you son of a dog! Masrūr, you pimp, where are you?'

His old mother ran in, in answer to these cries, asking: 'What is the matter, my son? The name of Allāh upon you and about you! What dream have you had, O Abū al-Hasan?' 'Who are you, old woman?' cried her son. 'And who is this Abū al-Hasan?' Then the old woman said: 'As Allāh lives, I am your mother. You are Abū al-Hasan, my dear child. What are these strange words? Why do you appear not to recognise me?' But Hasan cried: 'Begone, O woman of ill-omen! You are speaking to the Commander of the Faithful, Hārūn al-Rashīd! Begone from before the face of Allāh's Vicar upon earth!' The poor mother began to beat herself in the face, exclaiming: 'The name of Allāh be about you, my child! For pity's sake, do not raise your voice in such foolish and dangerous remarks; if the neighbours hear you, we shall be lost. Calm yourself, calm yourself!' But Hasan shouted the more: 'I told you to be gone, execrable old woman! You are mad to mistake me for your son. I am Hārūn al-Rashīd, Prince of Believers, master of the East and West!'

Hasan's mother redoubled the blows upon herself, and moaned: 'Allāh confound the wiles of the Evil One! May His infinite mercy free you from your diabolic possession! How can you be so mad? Do you not see that you are in your own poor chamber, in the house where you have lived from birth with me, your mother? Cast out these dangerous dreams, my child, and drink a little of the water from this cup.'

Abū al-Hasan drank a little of the water, saying to himself: 'It is possible that I am Abū al-Hasan.' He reflected, head in hand, for an hour; and then spoke heavily, as one who comes out of a dream: 'It is possible that I am Abū al-Hasan. I am Abū al-Hasan, this is my room, you are my mother, and I am your son. I am Abū al-Hasan. What sorcery has been at work upon me?'

The old woman wept for joy, thinking that her son was cured, and, after drying her eyes, was about to prepare food for him and question him concerning his dream, when Hasan suddenly bounded out of bed and began to shake her like a madman, crying: 'Vile old woman, if you do not wish me to kill you, tell me at once which of my enemies dethroned me and shut me in this miserable kennel! When I return to my throne, my anger will be terrible! Beware the vengeance of your Khalīfah! I, even I, Hārūn al-Rashīd, will terribly punish those who have done this thing.' He let go of the old woman, and she fell in a heap upon the mat, sobbing as if her heart would break, while Hasan jumped back into bed and held his tumultuous head between his hands.

In a little while the old woman rose up and, because she loved her son, brought him syrup of rose-water and persuaded him to drink it. Then, to change the course of his thoughts, she said: 'I have an interesting thing to tell you, my child, one that will please you very much. Yesterday the chief of police arrested the sheikh of this quarter and his two companions; he gave each four hundred strokes on the soles of his feet and led them backwards on a scabby camel through the hooting and spitting of the whole city. Finally, he impaled the sheikh through the mouth, cast his first companion into the ditch of our privy, and condemned the third to a very complicated punishment, which, I think, consisted in sitting down for ever on a chair which always gave under him.'

At this point Shahrazād saw the approach of morning and discreetly fell silent.

But when the six-hundred-and-thirty-ninth night had come

SHE SAID:

This intelligence, instead of calming Abū al-Hasan, further persuaded him of his royalty. 'Evil hag,' he cried to his mother, 'you prove me right out of your own mouth; for I myself sent Ahmad-the-Moth to punish those three rascals. Do not dare to tell me again that I have been dreaming or that I am possessed by the breath of Satan; rather prostrate yourself before my glory, kiss the earth between my hands, and ask pardon for your ill-considered words.'

His mother no longer doubted that Hasan was mad. 'May Allāh in His pity send down the dew of blessing upon your head!' she cried. 'May He pardon you and give you grace to become a reasonable man once more! For my sake, do not speak the word Khalīfah again and, especially, do not apply it to yourself; for, if the neighbours carry what you say to the walī, he will hang you at the palace gate.' So saying, the woman wept again and beat her breast in despair.

This sight exasperated Abū al-Hasan still further. He seized a stick and fell upon his mother, crying furiously: 'I forbid you to call me Abū al-Hasan! I am Hārun al-Rashīd. If you deny it again, my stick shall prove it to you.' The old woman trembled with fear and indignation, but she did not forget that Hasan was her son; she assumed her kindest voice, and said to him: 'Dear child, I cannot think that your soul has been so snatched from the law of Allāh and His Prophet that you can raise your hand against the mother who bore you nine months in her bosom and fed you with the milk of her tenderness. You are wrong to let your reason confound itself in dreams and to claim a title which belongs only to the Commander of the Faithful, Hārūn al-Rashīd. It is not only dangerous; it is ungrateful. Yesterday the Khalīfah sent his chief treasurer to our house and gave me a bag containing a thousand golden dīnārs, with an assurance that there would be more to come.'

Abū al-Hasan lost any last doubts which he might have entertained, because he remembered that he himself had sent his treasurer with the money. He looked at his mother with great menacing eyes, and cried: 'Will you deny that it was I who sent the gold, will you contend that the treasurer was acting under any orders but mine? Do you still dare to call me your son and say that I am Abū al-Hasan the Eccentric?' Then, as the old woman stopped her ears against these words, the distracted Hasan began to beat her with the stick.

There are limits even to a mother's love; the old woman yelled indignantly for help: 'O neighbours, neighbours! O great calamity! Hasten, O Mussulmāns!' Hasan laid on his stick more furiously, panting: 'Am I, or am I not, Commander of the Faithful?' But, in spite of the blows, the old woman answered: 'You are my son. You are Abū al-Hasan the Eccentric.'

At this point Shahrazād saw the approach of morning and discreetly fell silent.

But when the six-hundred-and-fortieth night had come

SHE SAID:

As they thus struggled, the neighbours rushed into the room, came between mother and son, snatched the stick from Hasan's hand, and indignantly pinioned him. 'Have you gone mad, Abū al-Hasan, that you dare to lift your hand against your poor old mother?' they demanded. 'Have you forgotten the teaching of the Book?' Hasan's eyes sparkled with fury, as he cried: 'Who is Abū al-Hasan? Would you apply that name to me?' The neighbours at once became perplexed, and asked: 'What is that? Are you not Abū al-Hasan the Eccentric? Is this not the mother who brought you up and fed you with the milk of her tenderness?' 'Dogs and sons of dogs, begone from my presence!' answered Hasan. 'I am your master, the Khalīfah Hārūn al-Rashīd, the Prince of Believers!'

Thus the neighbours were assured of Hasan's madness and, not wishing to leave him free in the blindness of his misfortune, they tied him hand and foot, and sent for the porter of the madhouse. In less than an hour the porter came with two strong guards, carrying a bull's hide whip and a great assortment of chains and manacles. Abū al-Hasan struggled violently on seeing them; so the porter gave him two or three cracks over the shoulder with his whip and then loaded him with chains. Without paying attention to his protestations and the title of Khalīfah which he gave himself, the three men carried him to the madhouse, while, all along the way, the people kicked him and struck him with their fists, thinking that he was really mad.

At the madhouse they shut him, like a wild beast, in an iron cage and gave him fifty lashes with the bull's hide as a first step towards his cure. He received the same treatment morning and evening; so that after ten days he changed his skin like a snake. This brought a revolution in his ideas, and he said to himself: 'I am in sorry case! I must be mistaken, since all world treats me as mad; I must have dreamed that I was in the palace; and yet it did not seem like a dream. But, if I try to understand this mystery, I may go mad in very truth.

This is not the only matter which Allāh has made too difficult for man.' While he was thus considering, his mother came weeping to see how he did and lamented very sorely when she saw him brought so low. In a little she mastered her grief and greeted him gently; Abū al-Hasan answered her calmly, saying: 'The blessing and mercy of Allāh be upon you, dear mother.' The old woman rejoiced, and answered: 'The name of Allāh be about you, dear child! Thanks be to Him Who has given you back your reason and restored your wounded mind!' 'I ask pardon from Allāh and from you, my mother,' said Hasan sincerely. 'I do not understand how I came to say all those foolish things and to behave thus insanely towards you. Satan must have possessed me and urged me on; had it been other than myself, he might have gone even further. But all that is finished and I am cured again.' His mother's tears of grief were changed to tears of joy. 'My heart is as light, dear child,' she said, 'as if I had born you again! Blessed be the name of Allāh to all eternity!'

At this point Shahrazād saw the approach of morning and discreetly fell silent.

But when the six-hundred-and-forty-first night had come

SHE SAID:

'You have nothing to reproach yourself with, my son,' she added. 'The fault was with that merchant whom you asked to eat and drink with you and who left the next morning without shutting the door behind him. Every time a door stands open before sunrise, Satan enters that house and takes possession of the minds of those who lie within. Let us thank Allāh that the result was not a great deal worse.' 'You are right, mother,' answered Hasan. 'I was most certainly possessed by Satan. I warned the Mosul merchant to shut the door behind him; but he forgot to do so, and thus brought all our troubles on us. Now that I know the extravagance of my mind has passed, I beg you, O tender mother, to speak to the doorkeeper of this madhouse, that I may be delivered from my cage and daily afflictions.' Hasan's mother went immediately and told the porter that her son had recovered his reason. The man came and, after he had examined and questioned him, receiving sensible answers, knocked off Hasan's fetters and set him free from his cage. Hasan returned slowly to his house on legs which might hardly bear him, and stayed in bed for many days until his strength had come back and the scars of his blows were a little healed. After that he began to weary of his solitude and determined to go at sunset, as of old, to sit at the end of the bridge and invite any stranger whom Fate might send to him.

The evening on which he put his plan into execution was the first of the month, that upon which Hārūn al-Rashīd was accustomed to leave his palace in the disguise of a merchant and, while searching for adventure in the streets of his city, see for himself whether good order reigned within it. Thus it was that Hārūn came to that part of the bridge where Abū al-Hasan sat, and the latter, looking up, saw the Mosul merchant coming towards him, followed as before by a mighty slave.

Either because he considered the merchant the cause of all his troubles or because of his oath never to recognise his former guests, he looked out over the river to avoid a greeting; but the Khalīfah, who had kept himself informed through spies of all which had happened to Hasan, including his sojourn in the madhouse, was by no means inclined to let slip this chance of jesting again with his strange acquaintance. Also Hārūn al-Rashīd, being generous and tender-hearted, was determined to reward Abū al-Hasan in some way or another for the pleasure he had given him. Therefore he went up to Hasan and leaned his head over the other's shoulder, looking into his eyes and saying: 'Greeting, O my friend Abū al-Hasan! My soul desires to embrace you.' But Hasan answered, with his eyes still fixed upon the river: 'I have no greeting for you; walk on; I know you not.' 'What is this, O Hasan,' cried the Khalīfah, 'do you not recognise your guest?' 'As Allāh lives, I do not recognise you,' replied the other. 'Begone upon your way.' But al-Rashīd insisted, saying: 'I recognise you very well. I cannot believe that you can have utterly forgotten me, when only a month has passed since that delightful evening which we spent together at your house.' Then, as Hasan still did not answer and only signed to him to begone, he threw his arm about his neck, and continued: 'This is an ill jest, my brother. I have made up my mind not to leave you until you have taken me a second time to your house and told me why you are angry with me. I see that you have something with which to reproach me.' Then Abū al-Hasan cried indignantly: 'O face of ill-omen, do you expect me to take you to my house again after all the harm which you have done me? Begone, and let me see your back!' The Khalīfah embraced him again, saying: 'O my friend Abū al-Hasan, you are very hard on me! If my visit was really a cause of misfortune to you, be very sure that the fault was unwitting and that I am ready to make all amends. Tell me what happened and I will find some remedy.' So saying, he squatted down beside the unwilling Hasan on the bridge and, hanging his arm brotherly about the other's neck, waited for an answer.

At this point Shahrazād saw the approach of morning and discreetly fell silent.

But when the six-hundred-and-forty-third night had come

SHE SAID:

Abū al-Hasan was a little won over by these caresses, and said: 'I am willing enough to tell you the strange things which happened after that evening of ours and all the misfortunes which followed your failure to shut the door.' Then he told the Khalīfah of those adventures in the palace which he had at first thought real and later considered as an illusion of the devil; he made him acquainted with all his sufferings at the madhouse and with the scandalous reputation which he had now gained among his neighbours. He left out no single detail and put such vehemence and credulity into the recital of his supposed possession by the Evil One, that the Khalīfah could not help laughing aloud. Abū al-Hasan could not understand this laugh, and asked: 'Are you so wanting in sympathy for my misfortunes that you find them amusing, or do you imagine that I am fooling you with some fiction? If you do not believe me, I can settle your doubts with instant proof.' So saying, he drew up his sleeves and bared his shoulders, back and bottom, to show the scars and discolorations left by the bull's hide on his body.

At this sight the Khalīfah became truly sorry for the unfortunate Hasan and, putting aside all thought of raillery, embraced him with real affection, saying: 'My brother, I beg you, in Allāh's name, to take me to your house again, for I am greatly desirous of tasting your delightful hospitality once more. You will see that He will return your generosity a thousandfold to-morrow.' He went on talking so pleasantly and embraced Hasan so affectionately that at last he broke down the latter's resolution never to entertain the same guest twice. But as they went along, Abū al-Hasan said: 'Though I give way to your importunities, it is with considerable regret. I ask you in return to do me one favour: to remember the door when you go out to-morrow morning.' Stifling a laugh internally, the Khalīfah swore that he would shut the door, and kept up a pleasant conversation until they reached the house.

When they had entered and were a little rested, the slave served them with food and afterwards with drink. With their cups in their hands they chatted on of one thing and another, until the drink had begun to move within their reasons. Then the Khalīfah adroitly steered the talk towards love, and asked his host whether he had ever been violently drawn towards women, whether he was married, or whether he had always remained chaste. 'Until recently, my master,' answered Hasan, 'I only loved gay companions, fine meat, old wine, and suave perfumes, and knew nothing in life better than to talk, cup in hand, with my dear friends. But this does not mean that I could not appreciate a woman, especially if she were like one of those extraordinary girls whom Satan showed me during that fantastic dream which made me mad; one of those ever laughing girls, a singer and musician, one skilled in dancing and calming the little child of our inheritance; one who would study our pleasure and consecrate her life to pleasing. If ever I were to meet such a girl again, I would buy her from her father and marry her and love her dearly. But her kind only exists in the Khalīfah's palace or possibly in the abode of his wazīr, Jafar. That is why I prefer the society of passing friends and these old bottles to risking the savour of my whole life on the bad humour and imperfection of some ordinary woman. My present life is calm and, if ever I become poor, I shall at least have the consolation of eating that black bread alone.'

So saying, Abū al-Hasan drained the cup which the Khalīfah handed to him and fell head over heels upon the carpet; for Hārūn al-Rashīd had again mingled powdered Cretan banj with his host's wine. At a sign from his master, the tall slave took Abū al-Hasan upon his back and left the house. The Khalīfah followed him, and shut the door carefully this time, as he had no intention of sending Hasan back to his house. They came to the palace and passed silently in by the secret door which led them to the private apartments of the Khalīfah.

At this point Shahrazād saw the approach of morning and discreetly fell silent.

But when the six-hundred-and-forty-fourth night had come

SHE SAID:

The Khalīfah had Abū al-Hasan dressed in his own night clothes and placed upon the royal bed as before; he gave the same orders and bade Masrūr wake him early, before the hour of prayer. Then he lay down and slept in a neighbouring room.

Next morning at the given hour Masrūr woke the Khalīfah who made his way to the room where Abū al-Hasan lay drugged, and called in to him all the girls whom Hasan had found in the different chambers where he feasted on that other occasion. Also he summoned his musicians and singers and, arranging all in good order, gave them their instructions. Then, while vinegar was being applied to the sleeper's nostrils (a remedy which again brought forth the snot from his nose in a great sneeze) he hid behind his curtain and gave an agreed signal.

At once the singers mingled their delightful voices with the notes of harps and flutes, as sweetly as the angels sing in Paradise. Abū al-Hasan, coming out of his swoon, at first listened a little to the music with closed eyes and then, staring about him, recognised in a flash the bed, the room, the curtains and ornaments, and, above all, the twenty-eight girls whom he had seen, seven by seven, in the delightful halls of his dream. He sat up with starting eyes and rubbed his face with his hands to be sure that he was awake.

At this the concert ceased, even as the Khalīfah had commanded, and a great silence reigned in the chamber. All the women modestly lowered their eyes before the august glances of Abū al-Hasan, who bit his fingers and cried: 'Woe upon you, O Hasan, O son of my mother! To-day the illusion; but to-morrow the bull's hide and the chains, the madhouse and the cage. O infamous merchant of Mosul, may you stifle in the arms of your Master in the deeps of Hell! You have left the door open again. The Evil One has turned my brain over upon itself making me see the same extravagant things. Allāh confound you, O Satan, and all the tools of Satan, and especially all merchants from Mosul! May the city of Mosul fall entirely upon its inhabitants and crush them for ever beneath its ruins!' Then he shut his eyes and opened them again, and shut them and opened them, and cried: 'O unfortunate Hasan, you had better go quietly to sleep again and not wake until the Evil One has left your body. You know what will happen to-morrow if you take any notice of these girls.'

So saying, he cast himself back upon the bed and wound the coverlet about his head; to give himself the illusion that he slept he began to snore like a rutting camel or a herd of drinking buffaloes.

The Khalīfah almost stifled behind his curtain to see and hear these things.

Poor Abū al-Hasan could not sleep; for young Sugarcane, who had been his favourite, sat down on the side of the bed in which he lay grunting, and said gently: 'O Commander of the Faithful, I have to inform your Highness that it is time for the morning prayer.' An angry voice cried in answer, from below the coverlet: 'Allāh's curse upon the Evil One! Satan, begone!' But Sugarcane calmly continued: 'Doubtless the Prince of Believers is suffering from some unpleasant dream. I am not Satan, my lord; I am little Sugarcane. May the Evil One indeed be far from you! I am little Sugarcane, O Commander of the Faithful.'

At this point Shahrazād saw the approach of morning and discreetly fell silent.

But when the six-hundred-and-forty-fifth night had come

SHE SAID:

Abū al-Hasan opened his eyes and threw back the coverlet; he saw little Sugarcane sitting on the side of the bed and the other girls whom he knew standing in three ranks before him: Roseleaf, Throat-of-Alabaster, Pearl-Cluster, Morning-Star, Dawn, Musk, Pomegranate-Heart, Coral-Lips, Clove, and the rest. He rubbed his eyes as if he would drive them into his head, and cried: 'Who are you? Who am I?' They answered in chorus on different notes: 'Glory to our master the Khalīfah Hārūn al-Rashīd, Prince of Believers and King of the whole world!' 'I am not Abū al-Hasan the Eccentric?' demanded the astonished Hasan, and they replied in chorus, as before: 'May the Evil One be far from you! You are not Abū al-Hasan, but the very Father of Beauty! You are our lord and the crown upon our heads!' 'This time I must make certain,' said Hasan; and he bade Sugarcane draw near him. 'Bite my ear, little one,' he said, and Sugarcane sank her white teeth so cruelly into his ear that he yelled terribly: 'I am the Commander of the Faithful! I am Hārūn al-Rashīd!'

At once the instruments struck up a dance tune and the singers broke into a lively song; the girls took hands and lifted quick feet about the bed, singing the song's chorus with such maddening grace that Abū al-Hasan threw the bed coverings one way and the cushions another, cast his nightcap into the air, leaped from the bed, tore off all his clothes and threw himself among the girls, his zabb well forward and his bottom bare; jumping, twisting, contorting and shaking his belly, zabb and bottom, all in a storm of growing laughter. He played the fool so exquisitely that the Khalīfah could no longer contain himself and sent out peal after peal of laughter from behind the curtain, so loud that they subdued the singing and the dancing, and the mirth and the drums, the stringed instruments, the wind instruments, and all the tumult of the dance. Then he was taken with hiccoughs and, falling over on his backside, well-nigh lost consciousness. When he could struggle to his feet, he thrust his head round the curtain, crying: 'Abū al-Hasan, O Abū al-Hasan, have you sworn to kill me?'

The dance stopped suddenly, the girls were frozen in their places, and so great a silence fell that the dropping of a needle would have echoed like thunder. Abū al-Hasan stopped as the others had done and turned his head towards the voice. As soon as his eyes fell upon the Khalīfah, he recognised him as the Mosul merchant and a realisation of the whole truth flashed across his mind like lightning. Though he guessed the riddle of the jest which had been played upon him, he was in no wise abashed; instead, he pretended not to know the Khalīfah and walked towards him, crying: 'So there you are, O merchant of my bum! I will teach you to leave doors open!' The Khalīfah roared with laughter and answered: 'By my sacred ancestors, O Abū al-Hasan, my brother, I swear that I will grant the whole wish of your soul to pay you for your pains! Henceforth you shall be a kinsman to me in my palace.' He clasped Hasan to his breast and embraced him with great delight.

Then the Khalīfah bade the girls clothe Abū al-Hasan in garments from his special wardrobe, choosing the richest and rarest of all. When Hasan was dressed, Hārūn al-Rashīd said to him: 'Now speak: for all that you require shall be given to you.' Abū al-Hasan kissed the earth between the Khalīfah's hands, and answered: 'I beg my generous master to allow me to live ever in the shadow of his majesty.' Hārūn was deeply moved by the delicacy of this request. 'Such disinterested friendship is very dear to me, Hasan,' he replied. 'Not only do I choose you from this moment to be my cup-companion and my brother, but I allow you free entrance and departure about the palace at any hour of the day or night. You need never ask an audience or leave to go. I proclaim also that the apartment of Zubaidah, daughter of my uncle, shall not be forbidden to you as it is to others. When I enter there, you may come to me at any hour.'

At the same time, the Khalīfah assigned to Abū al-Hasan a splendid lodging in the palace and gave him ten thousand golden dīnārs as the first instalment of a pension. Promising to see that he never lacked for anything, he left him and proceeded to the dīwān.

At this point Shahrazād saw the approach of morning and discreetly fell silent.

But when the six-hundred-and-forty-seventh night had come

SHE SAID:

Abū al-Hasan ran without a moment's delay to his mother and told her all that had happened, explaining that it was the Khalīfah himself who had played all these tricks upon him as a jest. 'Allāh be thanked,' said he, 'for all has turned to our advantage.' Promising to come and visit her every day, he returned to the palace, while the noise of his adventure and new position quickly went throughout the city and reached the furthest provinces of the kingdom.

The favour which he enjoyed from the Khalīfah only increased the gaiety and jovial humour of Abū al-Hasan; it did not make him arrogant and unaccommodating. Each day he diverted the Khalīfah and all who were about the palace with the sallies of his wit and the perfection of his pleasantry. Hārūn al-Rashīd could not be parted from him and therefore took him into his own private apartments and into those of Zubaidah: a favour which was not even accorded to Jafar. Zubaidah soon noticed that, on every occasion when Abū al-Hasan accompanied the Khalīfah into her presence, he fixed his eyes steadfastly on one of her women, a girl called Sugarcane, and that the little girl reddened with pleasure beneath these glances. One day she said to her husband: 'O Commander of the Faithful, doubtless you have seen, as I have seen, signs of love between Abū al-Hasan and little Sugarcane. What do you think of a marriage for the two?' 'The thing is possible,' he answered. 'I see nothing against it. I have indeed thought of it for some time; but lately the affairs of my kingdom drove the idea from my head. I am all the more annoyed, as I promised to find Hasan a wife during my second evening at his house. I think Sugarcane will do very well. Now it only remains to question them.'

They called Abū al-Hasan and Sugarcane, and asked them if they wished to be married. Sugarcane contented herself with blushing violently and throwing herself at Zubaidah's feet to kiss her robe as a sign of thanks. But Abū al-Hasan answered: 'O Commander of the Faithful, your slave is drowned deep in the sea of your generosity; but, before he takes into his house this delightful girl with the promising name, he would wish our mistress Zubaidah to ask her one question . . .' 'What question is that?' demanded Zubaidah smiling, and he replied: 'Dear mistress, I would like to know if her tastes are the same as mine. I confess that I only care for gaiety after wine, pleasure in meat, the joy of singing, and the delight of poetry. If Sugarcane loves these things also, if she is sensitive and will never say no to you know what, dear mistress, I will consent to love her with a mighty love. If not, by Allāh, I will remain a bachelor!' Zubaidah turned laughing to Sugarcane and said: 'You have heard all that. What is your reply?' And Sugarcane nodded her head.

The Khalīfah sent at once for the kādī and witnesses, and these wrote out the marriage contract. Feasts of rejoicing were given at the palace for thirty days and nights, and, after that, husband and wife were able to take joy of each other in all tranquillity. They passed their time in eating, drinking and laughter, spending un-counted gold. Dishes for meats and fruits, dishes for pastries and wine-cups, were never empty in their house; each moment of their lives bore the clear imprint of joy. Thus it was that a time came when they had spent all their money on pleasure; and, as the Khalī-fah, owing to the weighty affairs of his kingdom, had forgotten to fix a regular pension for Hasan, they woke one morning without enough money to pay their bills. They were very unhappy, especially as discretion forbade them to ask anything from the Khalīfah or of Zubaidah. They reflected with lowered heads and at last Abū al-Hasan said: 'We have been very wasteful! I do not wish to risk the shame of asking for money, nor do I desire that you should ask it. I have decided on another course, O Sugarcane.' His wife sighed, saying: 'What is your plan? I am ready to help you, for we cannot beg and we cannot change our mode of life.' Then said Abū al-Hasan: 'I knew that you would always help me, dear Sugarcane . . . There is only one way out of our difficulty.' 'Tell me quickly what it is,' said she, and he replied: 'We must die.'

At this point Shahrazād saw the approach of morning and discreetly fell silent.

But when the six-hundred-and-forty-eighth night had come

SHE SAID:

Sugarcane cried out in a fright: 'As Allāh lives, I do not want to die! You will have to carry out that plan without my help.' Abū al-Hasan did not grow angry. 'Daughter of a woman,' he said, 'when I was a bachelor I knew that to live alone was the only life; your lack of sense confirms me in that opinion. If, instead of answering up so quickly, you had taken the trouble to ask for particulars, you would have been highly delighted with the form of death which I propose and still propose. Can you not understand that it is a feigned death and not a real death which will get us gold?' 'How?' asked Sugarcane with a laugh, and he went on: 'Listen carefully to what I say: as soon as I am dead you will wrap me in a winding-sheet and lay me in the prescribed position in the middle of this room, with my turban over my face and my feet turned towards the holy Kaabah in Mecca. Then you will utter piercing screams, howl lustily, shed tears ordinary and tears extraordinary, tear your clothes and pretend to tear your hair. When you are properly tear-swept and dishevelled you will run to Zubaidah and tell her, between sobbings and faintings of every suitable kind, that I am dead; then you will fall to the ground and stay there for an hour, not coming to yourself until they have drowned you with rose-water. I promise that you will see a golden river beginning to flow towards our house.' 'A death like that is very possible,' said Sugarcane. 'I will help you. But how shall I die?' 'Allāh will provide for that,' said he. 'First do exactly as I have told you. Behold, I am dead!' With that he stretched himself out in the middle of the room and died.

Sugarcane undressed him, wound him in a shroud, turned his feet towards Mecca, and put his turban over his face. Then, as she had been bidden, she uttered piercing cries and shed tears ordinary and extraordinary. She tore her clothes, pulled at her hair, and scratched her cheeks. When her locks were all scattered and her face as yellow as saffron, she presented herself before Zubaidah and fell at full length in front of her, with a groan which would have broken the heart of a rock.

Zubaidah, who had already heard the screams and cries of grief from far off, guessed at once that death had had his will of her favourite's husband. Compassionately she cared for the young girl, taking her upon her knees and recalling her to life; but Sugarcane went on groaning and weeping, tearing her hair and beating her breast as she murmured the name of Abū al-Hasan over and over again. At last she was able to tell the Queen in broken words that he had died during the night of indigestion. 'Nothing remains but death for me,' she sobbed, with a final blow upon her breast, 'but may Allāh by so much the more prolong the days of our dear mistress.' Then she fell back again and fainted for very grief.

All the women began to lament about her and to mourn for Abū al-Hasan, who in his life had so pleasantly diverted them. They assured Sugarcane, as she lay there drowned in rose-water even as her husband had prophesied, how greatly they sympathised with her in her dire loss.

Zubaidah wept also for Abū al-Hasan and, after speaking in the usual forms of condolence, called the keeper of her purse and said to her: 'Take ten thousand golden dīnārs from my private chest and carry them to the house of poor Sugarcane, that she may worthily perform her husband's funeral.' The treasurer loaded a bag upon the back of a eunuch and accompanied him to the door of Abū al-Hasan's dwelling.

Zubaidah embraced her favourite with many a sweet word of commiseration and herself led her to the door, saying: 'May Allāh soften the memory of your affliction, O Sugarcane! May He assuage your wounds and lengthen your life by all the lost years of the poor departed!' Sugarcane wetted the hand of her mistress with tears and took her lonely way home.

At this point Shahrazād saw the approach of morning and discreetly fell silent.

But when the six-hundred-and-forty-ninth night had come

SHE SAID:

She entered the room where Abū al-Hasan waited for her, still stretched out stiffly in his winding-sheet, and, after shutting the door, burst into a pleasant peal of lucky laughter. 'Rise up now from among the dead, O father of jest!' she said. 'Come and help me drag in the gold. We shall not starve to-day.' Abū al-Hasan shook off his shroud and, dragging the bag of gold into the middle of the room, began to dance round it on one leg.

Then he congratulated his wife, and added: 'But that is not all. It is your turn now to die and mine to get the gold. We will see if I am as clever with the Khalīfah as you were with Zubaidah. It will be as well for Hārūn al-Rashīd to know that he is not the only one who can play tricks. But I must not stand here chatting. You are dead!'

Abū al-Hasan wrapped his wife in the same shroud and arranged her in the middle of the room, with her feet turned towards Mecca. Bidding her not give a sign of life whatever happened, he set his features in grief, half unrolled his turban, rubbed his eyes with onion until great tears started, and ran with torn clothes and disordered beard into the presence of the Khalīfah. Hārūn al-Rashīd held his dīwān, surrounded by Jafar, Masrūr and other dignitaries. When he saw Abū al-Hasan so changed by affliction from his jovial careless self, he rose from his place in sorry astonishment and ran to him, bidding him tell the reason of his tears. But Abū al-Hasan only re-doubled his sobbing and stood swaying upon his feet, exclaiming from behind his handkerchief: 'O Sugarcane, Sugarcane! O evil day! What am I now?'

The Khalīfah understood that Hasan would tell of the death of his wife, and was moved in the extreme. Tears came to his eyes and he laid his arm about the eccentric's shoulder, saying: 'Allāh have you in His pity, my brother! May He add to your life those days which He has taken from our sweet and charming slave. We gave her to you that she might be a cause of rejoicing and behold, she has led you into the house of grief! Poor Sugarcane!' Hārūn al-Rashīd wept warm tears and wiped his eyes with his handkerchief. Jafar and the other wazīrs wept warm tears and wiped their eyes with their hand-kerchiefs.

Then the Khalīfah called his treasurer and said to him: 'Pay over ten thousand dīnārs to Abū al-Hasan that he may fitly make the funeral of his wife. Have them carried to his dwelling at once.' While the treasurer obeyed, Abū al-Hasan kissed his master's hand in an ecstasy of grief and took leave in a storm of sobs.

But, when he came to the room where Sugarcane lay in her wind-ing-sheet, he cried: 'Did you think that you were the only one who could get a dīnār for every tear? Look at my bag!' He dragged the gold into the middle of the room and, after helping his wife out of her shroud, exclaimed: 'That is not all, my dear. Now we must see to it that our trick does not bring down the wrath of the Khalīfah and Zubaidah upon us. This is what we must do . . .' We will leave him explaining his plan to Sugarcane.

At this point Shahrazād saw the approach of morning and discreetly fell silent.

But when the six-hundred-and-fiftieth night had come

SHE SAID:

The Khalīfah shortened the time of the dīwān and took Masrūr with him to Zubaidah's palace, that they might condole with the Queen on the loss of her favourite. Opening the door of her private apartment, he saw his wife stretched upon her bed surrounded by women who dried her eyes and consoled her. He went up to her, saying: 'O daughter of my uncle, may the years which poor Sugarcane has lost be added to you.' Zubaidah, who had only waited for the coming of the Khalīfah in order to commiserate with him on the death of Abū al-Hasan, was astonished by this remark, and said: 'May the life of Sugarcane be long, O Commander of the Faithful! It would be fitter for me to join in your grief. May you live as much longer than your span as the days of Abū al-Hasan have been shortened. It is true that you see me sorrowing; but it is for the death of your friend and not for the death of my favourite, who, thanks be to Allāh, is in excellent health.'

The Khalīfah, who had the best of reasons for supposing that he knew the truth, could not help smiling. 'By Allāh, O Masrūr,' he said to the chief eunuch, 'what do you think of this? Do you imagine that your mistress, who is usually so wise, has become absent-minded like other women? I suppose that they are all the same. I come to console her and she tries to sadden me by telling me bad news which she knows to be false. Speak to her yourself and tell her what you have seen and heard. Perhaps she will change her tune and not try to fool us any longer.' Said Masrūr to Zubaidah: 'Dear mistress, the Commander of the Faithful is right. Abū al-Hasan has all his health and strength, though he weeps most bitterly for the loss of his wife who died last night from indigestion. I must tell you that Abū al-Hasan has but just now left the dīwān, where he himself announced the death of Sugarcane. He has returned to his own dwelling, enriched by the generosity of our master with ten thousand dīnārs for funeral expenses.' Instead of convincing Zubaidah, these words persuaded her that the Khalīfah was jesting, and she cried: 'This is hardly a day for jokes, O Commander of the Faithful! I know what I am talking about; the keeper of my purse will tell you how much Abū al-Hasan's funeral is costing me. It would be more seemly if we joined in mourning for your friend than made heartless jokes.' The Khalīfah's anger began to rise and he exclaimed: 'What are you saying? By Allāh, I think you must be mad! I tell you that Sugarcane is dead; there is no need to argue about it. I will give you proof.' He sat down on the dīwān and said to Masrūr: 'Go to Abū al-Hasan's dwelling and see for yourself (though there is really no need for proof) which of the two is dead. Then return quickly with the news.' While Masrūr was gone, the Khalīfah said to Zubaidah: 'We will soon see which of us is right; but, as you insist on being obstinate when you are obviously wrong, I am willing to have a bet with you.' 'I accept the bet,' she answered. 'I will wager the dearest thing I have in the world, my Picture Gallery, against anything you like.' 'Then I will bet my Palace of Delights, which is the dearest thing I have,' said Hārūn, 'and allow me to tell you that my Palace of Delights is infinitely more valuable than your Picture Gallery.' 'We need not quarrel about that,' said Zubaidah in a huff. 'If you want to know which is the more valuable you have only to listen to what people say behind your back. Let us bind our wager with the Fātihah.' 'Yes, let the Koran be between us,' agreed the Khalīfah. So they recited the first chapter of the Book together, and then sat in sulky silence, waiting for the return of Masrūr.

At this point Shahrazād saw the approach of morning and discreetly fell silent.

But when the six-hundred-and-fifty-first night had come

SHE SAID:

Abū al-Hasan, who had been on the look out, saw Masrūr from afar off and understood the reason of his visit. Therefore he said to Sugarcane: 'Dear wife, Masrūr is coming straight for our house. He must have been sent on account of an argument which I knew would arise between the Khalīfah and his Queen. Let us first give Hārūn the advantage. Go dead again, my dear, that I may wrap you up.' Sugarcane stretched herself out once more and Hasan arranged her in her former position. Then he sat down beside her with his turban loose and a handkerchief to his eyes. Masrūr entered at that moment and, seeing Sugarcane shrouded in the middle of the room and Hasan plunged in despair beside her, could not contain his emotion, but exclaimed: 'There is no other god than Allāh! I have great grief for you, poor Sugarcane, our sister, O erewhile gentle and delightful! Your Destiny weighs heavy on us all. Swift was your summons of return to Him Who made you! May He take you into the excellence of His compassion!' He embraced Abū al-Hasan and sadly took leave, to return with his news to the Khalīfah; nor was he sorry to prove to Zubaidah that she had been both wrong and opinionated when she contradicted her lord.

He came into the chamber where Zubaidah waited and kissed the earth between her hands, saying: 'Allāh prolong the life of our mistress! The dead woman lies shrouded in the middle of the room, her body is already swollen beneath the winding sheet and smells unpleasantly. And I do not think that poor Abū al-Hasun will long survive his wife.'

The Khalīfah exulted cheerfully at this news; he turned to Zubaidah, who had become yellow in the face, and said: 'O daughter of my uncle, why do you delay to send for a scribe to write the gift of your Picture Gallery in my name?' But Zubaidah began to scold Masrūr and said indignantly to the Khalīfah: 'How can you put faith in the words of this liar and son of a liar? Have I not seen, have not my slaves seen, poor Sugarcane weeping for the death of her husband?' Then she threw her slipper at Masrūr's head, and cried: 'Begone, you son of a dog!' The eunuch, fearing to irritate her further, fled from the presence, bent double and shaking his head.

In anger Zubaidah said to the Khalīfah: 'O Commander of the Faithful, I never thought that you would league with a eunuch to give me pain and make me believe that which is not; yet there can be no doubt that you concerted this report of Masrūr's beforehand. Now, to prove to you that I am right, I will also send someone to see who has lost the bet. If you are right, I will admit that I am mad and that all my women are as mad as I. If, on the other hand, I am proved to be right I demand, over and above our gage, the head of that impertinent black eunuch.' The Khalīfah, who knew by experience the lengths to which his Queen's temper might carry her, gave immediate consent; so Zubaidah called her old confidential nurse to her, and said: 'O nurse, go without delay to the house of Abū al-Hasan, the friend of our master the Khalīfah, and see whether it be himself or his wife who is dead. Then return speedily and report what you have seen.' In spite of her tottering legs, the old nurse set out immediately and hastened towards Hasan's dwelling.

Abū al-Hasan, who was carefully watching the approaches to his house, saw the old woman far off and understood the motive of her coming. 'O Sugarcane,' cried he with a laugh, 'O Sugarcane, I am dead!'

At this point Shahrazād saw the approach of morning and discreetly fell silent.

But when the six-hundred-and-fifty-second night had come

SHE SAID:

As there was no time to lose, he hurried into his shroud and lay down on the ground with his feet pointing towards Mecca. Sugarcane placed his turban over his face and began, with disordered hair, to beat her breasts and utter cries of grief. The old nurse entered and saw these things; sadly she went up to Sugarcane and said: 'May Allāh grant you the years which your man has lost! Alas, alas, O Sugarcane my daughter! Behold you are a widow and a young girl also! What will become of you without Abū al-Hasan, O Sugarcane?' She wept for a space, and then continued: 'Alas, my daughter, I must leave you. It pains me to do so, but I have to hasten to my mistress, Zubaidah, and relieve her anxiety. For that shameless liar, Masrūr, affirmed that you were dead.' 'Would to Allāh that the eunuch had said truth, my mother!' answered Sugarcane with a deep groan. 'I should not be weeping here! Yet it will not be long; for to-morrow morning at latest I also shall be dead from grieving.' She redoubled her tears and lamentations, so that the old nurse embraced her again and was soft and silent in her departure, fearing to disturb the mourner. She hastened to her mistress with news of what she had seen and heard, and, when she had finished speaking, sat down suddenly because she was breathless owing to her great age.

Zubaidah turned haughtily to the Khalīfah and said: 'In the first place we will hang that impertinent eunuch.' In the height of perplexity, Hārūn al-Rashīd sent for Masrūr and would have angrily reproached him for his lies, had Zubaidah given him time. But the Queen, more than ever angered by his presence, cried out to the old nurse: 'Tell this son of a dog what you have just told us!' Though she had not yet recovered her breath, the poor old woman was obliged to repeat her news, and this so angered Masrūr that he cried, unmindful of the presence of the Khalīfah and Zubaidah: 'Toothless old fool, how dare you lie and smirch the whiteness of your hair? Do you think you will make me believe that I did not see poor Sugarcane, dead and wrapped in her winding sheet?' The nurse poked forth her head in suffocated fury, as she answered: 'There is no liar here but you, O black blackman! Yet it is unwise to say that you should be hanged, when you ought to be cut gradually in pieces and made to eat yourself.' 'Be silent, you senile chatterbox!' replied Masrūr. 'Go and tell your story to the girls!' But Zubaidah, outraged by his insolence, burst into a storm of sobs, threw cushions, vases, ewers and stools at his head, spat in his face, and finally cast herself upon the bed, dissolved in bitter tears.

The Khalīfah beat his hands together in great perplexity, and cried: 'As Allāh lives, Masrūr is not the only liar. I am a liar, your nurse is a liar, and you also are a liar!' After an hour's reflection he lifted up his head again, and said: 'We must know the truth; we must go ourselves to the house of Abū al-Hasan.' He begged Zubaidah to accompany him, and set out, followed by Masrūr, the nurse, and a crowd of women, in the direction of Hasan's dwelling.

Although Abū al-Hasan had warned her that such a thing was likely to happen, Sugarcane was afraid when she saw the advance of this host, and said to her husband: 'As Allāh lives, not every time you drop a cup will it be worth the taking up!' But her husband laughed and answered: 'Let us both die, O Sugarcane!' He stretched his wife on the floor, wrapped her in the shroud, wound himself in an odd sheet of silk, and lay down beside her, being careful to place his turban over his face according to the rite. Hardly had his preparations been made when the company entered the chamber.

When the Khalīfah and Zubaidah saw the sad spectacle, they stayed motionless and dumb, until suddenly the Queen, who had been much upset by so many emotions in so short a time, turned pale and fell fainting into the arms of her women. As soon as she came to herself, she shed rivers of tears, crying: 'Alas, alas, for Sugarcane! You could not live after your husband was dead! You have died of grieving!' But the Khalīfah, who was weeping for the death of his friend, exclaimed petulantly: 'It was not Sugarcane who died of grief; it was this poor Abū al-Hasan who was not able to live after his wife was dead. That is self-evident. You think you are right because you can weep and faint.' 'You think you are right because you have a lying slave,' answered Zubaidah.

At this point Shahrazād saw the approach of morning and discreetly fell silent.

But when the six-hundred-and-fifty-third night had come

SHE SAID:

'But where are Abū al-Hasan's servants?' added the Queen. 'Let them be fetched; for they can tell us which died first and which of grieving, seeing they must have shrouded them.' 'You are right,' answered the Khalīfah, 'and, for my part, I promise ten thousand dīnārs to the one who tells me.'

Hardly had he spoken when a voice was heard from below the extemporised shroud, saying: 'Give me the ten thousand dīnārs. I assure our master the Khalīfah that it was I, Abū al-Hasan, who died second and from grief.'

At this speech from the dead, Zubaidah and her women fled towards the door with cries of fear; but the Khalīfah, who understood in a flash the trick which had been played upon him, fell over on his backside in the middle of the room, crying: 'No, no, Abū al-Hasan, it is I who die of laughter!'

When the Khalīfah had finished his guffaw and Zubaidah recovered from her terror, Abū al-Hasan and Sugarcane came out of their shrouds and nerved themselves to tell the whole truth. Hasan threw himself at the Khalīfah's feet and Sugarcane embraced the feet of her mistress. Both humbly asked pardon, and Hasan added: 'When I was a bachelor I despised money, O Commander of the Faithful; but this Sugarcane, whom you so generously gave me, has such an appetite for it that she eats it, sacks and all. She could devour the treasure of our master and the treasurer as well.' Zubaidah and the Khalīfah laughed anew and pardoned the two offenders. Also they counted out the ten thousand dīnārs which Abū al-Hasan had earned by his announcement and a further ten thousand to celebrate that rising from the dead.

This little jest taught the Khalīfah something of his friend's needs; later he ordered his treasurer to pay him a monthly wage equal to that of his wazīr Jafar. More than ever he kept Abū al-Hasan by him as cup-companion and intimate friend. All concerned in this tale lived delightfully until the coming of the Separator, the Destroyer of palaces, the Builder of tombs, the Inexorable, the Inevitable.

When she had made an end of this tale, Shahrazād said to King

Shahryār: 'That is all I know about the Sleeper Wakened; but, if you will allow me, I have a tale which infinitely surpasses this one.' 'Before I give you leave,' answered King Shahryār, 'tell me the title of your story.' 'It is the tale of the Loves of Zain al-Mawāsif,' said Shahrazād, and when Shahryār asked: 'What is the tale?' she smiled and said:

The Loves of Zain al-Mawāsif

IT is related, O auspicious King, that there was once, in years and ages long ago, a handsome youth whose name was Anīs. He was by far the richest, most generous, most delicate, and most delightful young man of his time; and, as he loved all things in the world worthy of love, women, friends, good cheer, poetry, music, perfumes, grass, sparkling water, and walking, he lived ever in the height of happiness.

One afternoon, as he was agreeably sleeping, according to his custom, beneath a locust-tree in his garden, he dreamt that he was playing with four fair birds and a shining white dove. He was taking great joy in smoothing their feathers and embracing them, when a dismal black crow, with menacing beak, pounced on the dove and carried her away, scattering her four gentle companions in confusion. Anīs woke much affected by this dream, and went out in search of someone who might explain it to him; but for long he walked without finding such. He was thinking of returning to his house, when he came to a handsome building near which a woman's voice was singing this song, in accents of most charming melancholy:

> I hear the hearts of lovers sing
> Free in the scents of dawn
> Like birds,
> But my heart does not sing
> Because of a young thing
> Lighter than fawn
> Or branch of birds
> Or scent of dawn.

Anīs felt his soul pierced by the tones of this singing; urged by a desire to know the singer, he went up to the half-opened door and looked inside. He saw a magnificent garden filled as far as the eye could reach with harmonious terraces, flowered arbours and thickets of roses; jasmine, violet and narcissus smiled under the clear sky of Allāh and were sung among by a multitude of birds.

Unable to resist this fair sight, Anīs went through the door and began to walk down the garden, until he saw a white band of playing girls upon a lawn, separated from him by an alley spanned by three arches.

At this point Shahrazād saw the approach of morning and discreetly fell silent.

But when the six-hundred-and-fifty-fifth night had come

SHE SAID:

Coming to the first arch, he saw these words painted upon it in letters of vermillion:

> Our house shall have a narrow door
>   That grief and time may not come in,
>   But friends and laughter, who were thin,
> Shall enter, fatten, leave no more.

On the second arch these words were graved in gold characters:

> May this house rise in air
> As long as birds chant in its garden blooms,
> And friendship scent its rooms
> As long as flowers die of being fair.
> As long as new stars come in spring to browse
> The meadows of the sky,
> As long as fruits on trees are born and die,
> Live all who use this house.

When he came to the third arch, he found that it bore these lines in azure lettering:

> Time and the sun shall move
> Above each gentle chamber
> And luxurious place
> Of this our house;
> But if the shadow of love
> Clamber
> And nibble like a mouse,
> Then time and sun shall leave no trace.

Beyond the third arch he came to the end of the alley and, at the foot of washed marble stairs which led up to the house, he saw a girl of between fourteen and fifteen, leaning among cushions on a velvet carpet, with four damsels to surround and tend her. She was as white as the moon and had slim brows whose curve seemed to have been painted in black musk, her great dark eyes were full of massacre, her coral mouth was as small as a clove, and her chin said perfectly: 'Behold me!' She could have fired hearts of the coldest stone.

Anīs bowed to the earth before her, carried his hand to his heart, his lips, and his forehead, and then murmured: 'Greeting, O queen of purity!' But the girl exclaimed: 'How dared you come into this forbidden place, O most impertinent young man!' 'Dear mistress, the fault was not mine,' he replied. 'The blame is with you and with the garden. Through the half-opened door I saw terraces of jasmine, myrtle and violet, and the garden bowing down with all its flowers before a moon of beauty. My soul could not resist the temptation to join its homage to that of the flowers and the birds.' The girl laughed and asked: 'What is your name?' 'Anīs, your slave,' he answered, and she exclaimed: 'You please me very much, Anīs. Come and sit beside me.'

He sat down and she said: 'I wish for some distraction, Anīs. Can you play chess?' When he answered that he could, she signed to one of her girls, who brought a board of ivory and ebony with gold corners and a set of red and white pieces, the red being carved from rubies and the white from rock crystal. 'Would you like red or white?' she asked, and he replied: 'As Allāh lives, I will take white: for red is the colour of many things and belongs of right to you.' 'That may well be,' she said, as she arranged the men.

The game began; but Anīs paid more attention to his opponent's charms than to the pieces, being ravished by the beauty of hands which seemed paste of almonds and slight fingers as of white camphor. 'How can I play against such fingers?' he cried, but she answered: 'Check to your king, check to your king, Anīs! You will lose!' Then, seeing that he paid little attention to the game, she added: 'Let us have a bet of a hundred dīnārs; that will make you play more seriously.' 'Willingly,' he answered, as he rearranged the men. Zain al-Mawāsif, for such was the child's name, chose that moment to lift the silk veil which covered her hair, so that she shone forth like a column of light. Anīs did not know what he was doing; sometimes he played with the red pieces, sometimes with the white;

he moved wrong continuously and, in the end, lost five games with a hundred dīnārs upon each. 'You are not playing any more carefully,' said Zain al-Mawāsif. 'Let us bet a thousand dīnārs.' But, in spite of this heavier stake, Anīs did not behave any better and lost again. Then said the girl: 'Let us play for all your money against all mine.' Anīs accepted and lost. Finally he played away his shops, houses, gardens and slaves, until nothing remained to him at all.

Zain al-Mawāsif turned to him, saying: 'Anīs, you are a fool! I do not want you to regret having come into my garden and made my acquaintance, therefore I give you back all you have lost. Rise up now, and return upon your way in peace.' But Anīs answered: 'As Allāh lives, my queen, I do not regret having lost. If you asked my life you might have it. But do not for pity's sake make me leave you.' Then said the girl: 'Since you will not take back what you have lost, find the kādī and witnesses and bring them here, so that you make over your possessions to me in due form.' Anīs did as he was bidden; and the kādī, though the pen nearly fell from his old fingers when he saw the beauty of Zain al-Mawāsif, made out the deed of gift and had two witnesses set their seal to it. Then he departed.

At this point Shahrazād saw the approach of morning and discreetly fell silent.

But when the six-hundred-and-fifty-sixth night had come

SHE SAID:

Zain al-Mawāsif turned to Anīs with a laugh, saying: 'Now you may go; for we do not know you.' 'O queen,' said he, 'will you let me go without the satisfaction of desire?' And she answered: 'I am very willing for that satisfaction, Anīs; but I must ask you for something else first. You must bring me four bladders of pure musk, four ounces of grey amber, four thousand pieces of gold brocade, and four harnessed mules.' 'You shall have them,' said he. 'But how?' she asked. 'You have nothing left with which to buy them.' 'Allāh will provide,' said he. 'I have friends who will lend me the money.' 'Then go and get those things,' said she, and Anīs went out to find the friends in whom he trusted.

As soon as he had gone, Zain al-Mawāsif said to Hubūb, one of her maidens: 'Follow him and see what he does. When all his friends have refused to help him and have dismissed him on one pretext or another, go up to him and say: "Good master Anīs, my mistress

wishes to see you instantly." Bring him with you and show him into
the reception hall. After that, what is fated to happen will happen.'
Hubūb bowed low before her mistress and hastened out after Anīs.

Zain al-Mawāsif went indoors and bathed in the hammām. Her
girls tended her as for an extraordinary occasion; they depilated
what there was to depilate, they rubbed what there was to rub, they
perfumed what there was to perfume, they made long what there was
to make long, and they made short what there was to make short.
Then they put a robe worked in fine gold upon her and set a silver
fillet about her head to hold a circle of rich pearls, a circle which
fastened at the back and dropped two knots of rubies upon the virgin
silver of her shoulders. They tressed her heavy black hair, perfumed
with musk and amber, into twenty-four braids which fell to her
heels; and when she stood before them like a new made bride they
fell at her feet, trembling with admiration and crying: 'Allāh preserve
our mistress in her splendour! Allāh guard our mistress from the
glance of envy and from the evil-eye!' While she practised steps of
pretty walking, up and down the chamber, they made a thousand and
then a thousand compliments to her in the sincerity of their souls.

In the meanwhile young Hubūb, who had given her message to
Anīs as soon as she had seen him spurned by all his friends, led him
into the hall where Zain al-Mawāsif waited.

When Anīs saw her in all the brilliance of her fresh beauty, he
stopped as if thunderstruck, and exclaimed: 'Is it she or a bride from
Paradise?' Satisfied with the effect she had produced, Zain al-Mawāsif went up to him with a smile and led him by the hand to a large
low dīwān, upon which she seated herself. After pulling him down
beside her, she signed to her women, who brought in a low wide
table carved from a single mass of silver, on which these gastrono-
mic verses were engraved:

> Cast down your eyes, lift up your souls,
> Dig spoons into the great sauce bowls.
> Eat roast and fried and boiled and grilled,
> Eat jams and jellies, warmed and chilled.
> Eat quails cooked golden to the minute,
> Eat nut-fed lamb with raisins in it.
> Who would the warm stout capon blame,
> Date-coloured with judicious flame,
> Because he could not sing or fly?

(He eats the better.) Nor can I . . .
The golds of man are manifold
But Allāh made this kabāb's gold;
He made this purslane salad sup
The souls of olives from a cup;
He set these twin and ponderous fish
To lie on mint leaves in a dish . . .
I will be silent now and eat
A meal which poets shall repeat
In songs of cooking, sound and sage,
Down all the hungry roads of age.

The women brought perfumed meats; the two young people ate,
and drank wines out of the same cup, sweetening their mouths with
pastries. Then Zain al-Mawāsif leaned over Anīs, saying: 'Since we
have eaten bread and salt together and you have become my guest, I
cannot keep the littlest thing of yours. Whether you like it or not, I
give you back all that I have won from you.' Anīs threw himself in
gratitude at the girl's feet; but she raised him, saying: 'If you really
wish to thank me come with me into my bed. I want to know if you
are really a master of chess, when you set your mind to it.'

At this point Shahrazād saw the approach of morning and
discreetly fell silent.

But when the six-hundred-and-fifty-eighth night had come

SHE SAID:
'I will show you that the white king can beat all the knights,'
answered Anīs, as he took that fair moon in his arms and carried her
to the bedchamber, whose door the girl Hubūb had silently opened
for them. He played a game of chess with the girl, following all the
rules with taste and skill; he played a second and a third and even a
fifteenth game, moving the king so valiantly, never on the defensive,
that the girl owned herself beaten, crying in breathless surprise:
'You have won, O father of lances! Tell your king to rest a little.'
She rose with a smile and hid away the chessmen.

Swimming soul and body in a pleasant sea, they rested for a little
in each other's arms; and then Zain al-Mawāsif said: 'Though you
have valiantly earned this rest, O invincible Anīs, I must confess that
I would like to know if you can make verses as well as you can play

chess. Do you think that you could invent a rhythmic disposition of our meeting and our game, so that we may never forget either?' 'That is easy,' answered Anīs and, sitting upon the scented couch with the girl's little arms about his neck, he improvised this sublime apostrophe:

> The tale of a girl of fourteen
> Met in Paradise:
> Allāh has blown a million white moons
> Into blue infinity,
> But none of them were you.
>
> Light you stood in the garden,
> The slim trees bowed to you,
> The birds would change their note.
>
> 'Your name, O silk?'
> 'What would my name be
> Save Zain al-Mawāsif,
> Gilding perfection?'
>
> 'Here is musk
> And pearls lying in gold
> For a girl of fourteen
> Met in Paradise.'
>
> 'And here am I.'
>
> O belt released,
> O cornflower bright chemise,
> Body of white and diamonds,
> Scent of kisses,
> O thousand scents
> In the corners of my love.
>
> I will tell my drunkenness:
>
> You would say her hair
> Had brought eternal night,
> But for the fire of roses.
>
> I had gone by the swords,
> But her mouth was young wine
> And there bubbled a fountain between her lips.

Allāh set down His two rose cups
On the marble table of her breast,
And in the dimples of her belly
Sprinkled the scents of every dale.

The sweet fort of folly
Lies between two laughing columns,
Bearded and yet a rose . . .

This was the girl of fourteen
I met in Paradise.

Hearing these lines made in her honour, Zain al-Mawāsif laughed and exulted.

At this point Shahrazād saw the approach of morning and discreetly fell silent.

But when the six-hundred-and-fifty-ninth night had come

SHE SAID:

She kissed Anīs, saying: 'O Anīs, you have delighted me! As Allāh lives, I can no longer exist without you!' They passed the rest of that night together, in assaults of kissing and coupling until the morning. And the next day they stayed by each other, resting, eating and drinking in joy, and such was their life for a whole month, a month of transport. At the end of that time young Zain al-Mawāsif, who was married, received a letter from her husband announcing his immediate return. 'May he snap his old bones!' she cried when she read it. 'May such ugliness never return to me! His ill-omened face will break in upon our fair life! What must we do, O Anīs?' 'I am in your hands, O Zain,' he answered. 'Fine trickery is rather the woman's part than the man's.' 'But my husband is a very jealous and violent man,' she retorted. 'It will not be easy to allay his suspicions.' She reflected for an hour, and then said: 'I see no other way, save to introduce you into the house as a perfume-seller and spice-merchant. Therefore study that trade and, above all, be very careful when you are dealing with my husband not to put him out in any way.' Thus they planned together how they should deceive the husband.

When the good man returned from his journey, he saw to his grieved surprise that his wife was quite yellow from head to foot. Not knowing that the child had rubbed herself with saffron, he asked if she were ill, and she replied: 'If I am yellow it is not because I am ill, but because I have been sad and fearful during your absence. For pity's sake do not go away again without taking a companion to defend and care for you; that will ease my mind.' 'I will do so gladly,' he answered. 'By the life of my head, your idea is a good one! Calm yourself now and try to bring back that fine complexion of yours.' With that he kissed her and went down to his shop, for he was a great merchant and a Jew. The girl was a Jewess.

Anīs, who had carefully studied his new trade, was waiting for the husband at the door of his shop; in order to become quickly acquainted with him he offered him perfumes and spices at greatly below the market price. The husband, who had the hardened soul of all Jews, was so satisfied with his bargain and with the young man's delightful manners that he became a regular customer. Indeed, after a few days, he offered him a partnership in his own business, if he should bring sufficient capital. Anīs at once accepted this offer, hoping that it might carry him nearer his beloved, and the two drew up a deed of partnership without delay, sealing it in the presence of two worthy merchants.

The girl's husband invited his partner to eat at his house that night, in order to celebrate their association; he conducted him to his home and, since he was a Jew and Jews are shameless and do not keep their women hidden, made preparation to introduce his wife to Anīs. 'He is a rich and well-bred youth,' he said to her. 'I wish you to come and see him.' But Zain al-Mawāsif, who wished to hide her joy, pretended to be indignant. 'Father of Beards,' she cried, 'how dare you introduce strangers to the inmost places of your house? How can you have the effrontery to show me to him? The name of Allāh be upon me and about me! Must I forget a woman's modesty because you have found a partner? I would rather cut myself in pieces!' 'These are ill-considered words,' grumbled the Jew. 'Since when have we been Mussulmāns, to hide our women? This delicacy is out of place and out of season. We are children of Moses; what have we to do with delicacy?' He spoke thus aloud, but in his soul he said: 'Surely the blessing of Allāh is upon my house, seeing my wife to be so chaste and moderate and wise!' Then he persuaded her to come and entertain his partner.

Anīs and Zain al-Mawāsif were very careful not to show that they knew each other; during the meal the young man kept his eyes modestly lowered, glancing only at the husband and feigning an absolute discretion. 'An excellent young man!' thought the Jew, and he asked Anīs to come again on the next day. Anīs came again and yet again; and each time he behaved himself with tact in everything.

Yet the Jew had already been struck by a strange coincidence. He had a tame bird in the house which he had trained himself; and this bird loved him very dearly.

At this point Shahrazād saw the approach of morning and discreetly fell silent.

But when the six-hundred-and-sixtieth night had come

SHE SAID:

But, during the Jew's absence this bird had transferred his affection to Anīs and become accustomed to perch on his head and shoulders with a thousand pretty caresses; so, when his master returned, he considered him as a stranger and did not wish to recognise him. He kept all his cries of joy and kisses of his beak for young Anīs. 'By Moses and Aaron, the bird has forgotten me!' cried the Jew. 'Such ingratitude makes the illness and sensibility of my wife all the more commendable.' Thus he persuaded himself; but there was another matter which forced itself upon his notice and tortured him with dismal thoughts.

Though his wife was extremely reserved and modest in the presence of his partner, he noticed that she had very extraordinary dreams when she was asleep. She would stretch out her arms, panting for breath; she would sigh and twist herself about, as she called on the name of Anīs and spoke to him as only a passionate lover speaks. The Jew was astonished to behold these things night after night. 'By the Pentateuch,' he cried in his own ear, 'this shows that all women are alike. Even when they are virtuous and continent, like my wife, they must satisfy their evil desires in some way! Far be the Evil One! It is a curse on the world that these creatures should be kneaded from the flames of hell ... I must put this matter to the proof. If my wife withstands the temptation, then her dreams and the conduct of the bird are accidental and of no account.'

Therefore, when it was time for the evening meal the Jew told his wife and partner that he had been invited to the house of the walī on important business, and begged them to wait his return before eating. Then he left them and went out into the garden; but, instead of proceeding to the walī's house, he returned on his tracks and climbed up secretly to the higher storey, whence he could watch the hall from the window of a little room.

He had not long to wait for proofs, kisses and caresses of unbelievable fire; but, as he did not wish to betray his presence, he was forced to witness the lovers' dalliance for a whole hour. After this trying ordeal, he went down into the hall, smiling as if he knew nothing; and, during the meal, he paid more kindly regard than ever to young Anīs, who, for his part, took pains to appear more bashful even than before.

But when the feast was finished and the young man gone, the Jew exclaimed: 'By the horns of Moses, I will burn their hearts with separation!' Then, taking a letter from his bosom, he said aloud: 'I shall have to go on another long journey. This letter comes from my agents in a far country, who require my presence for an important deal.' Zain al-Mawāsif hid her great joy, and said: 'Would you leave me to die in loneliness, dear husband? Tell me at least how long you will be away.' 'Not less than three years and not more than four,' he answered, and she cried in desolation: 'O poor Zain al-Mawāsif! O despair! Can I never keep my husband with me?' Then said the Jew: 'Do not let that distress you; for I have determined to take you with me this time and not expose you to the torment of my absence. Rise up now and call Hubūb, Khutūb, Sukūb, and Rukūb to make your luggage.'

Poor Zain al-Mawāsif became yellow indeed; her eyes filled with tears and she could not speak. Exulting within himself, her husband said to her most kindly: 'What is the matter, Zain?' 'Nothing, my dear,' she answered. 'I am only a little upset by the joyful news.'

Under her husband's eye, she directed the preparations of her women, cudgelling her brains the while for a means of breaking the sad tidings to Anīs. At length she found a moment to trace these lines on the entrance door:

> You are afar from me
> And yet I see the red wound of your heart.
> Jealousy parted us and smiled to see
> Me smile above my smart . . .
> I swear by Allāh it shall not be he,
> Though we must lie apart.

Then she mounted the camel which had been prepared for her and hid herself in the litter, making verses of farewell to the house and garden. The caravan started, with the Jew at its head, Zain al-Mawā-sif in the middle, and her women bringing up the rear. So much for them.

At this point Shahrazād saw the approach of morning and discreetly fell silent.

But when the six-hundred-and-sixty-second night had come

SHE SAID:

Next morning young Anīs was surprised not to see his partner come to the market. He waited for him until the evening and then decided to go to the house for news. When he came to the door, he saw the lines his mistress had written there, and was crushed to earth by the blackness of his grief. As soon as he could do so, he asked tidings of his beloved from the neighbours and learnt that the Jew had taken her away, with her women and much baggage, upon ten camels provisioned for a very long journey.

Anīs began to wander through the solitude of the garden like a man distracted. He improvised these lines:

> This line of trees
> Is the end of her garden,
> Therefore pause and weep;
> Therefore call on the south wind
> That it may blow above this house.
>
> My soul would stay the camel goads.
>
> Come, O cool night,
> Come hither breeze from the desert,
> I know the scent of you now.
>
> But has she bidden you carry back nothing,
> Nothing for my tears?
>
> They roused the camels in the night
> Before the little wind of dawn;
> The camels kneeled,
> They rose, they did not feel you.
>
> Yet I have watered the sand
> Before their feet.

While he was thus reflecting he heard a crow croaking from its nest in a palm tree, and he said again:

> What do you in her garden, crow?
> I can make all the harsh cries for this woe,
> I would have you know.

After this Anīs lay down upon the ground and was overcome by the sleep of sorrow. But his beloved appeared to him in a dream and he was happy with her; they lay in each other's arms. Suddenly he woke and the illusion departed, so that he could only console himself with these lines:

> As bright,
> As soon departed
> As a yellow spark of light
> In the black of night,
> She came in dreams;
> To sleep, to know, to kiss, to love the thing which seems
> Is to wake broken-hearted.

Thus Anīs lamented, living in the shadow of the desolate house, never departing to take food at his own place. So much for him.

When the caravan was a month out from that city, the Jew halted it and had his tents pitched near a town upon the seaside. He stripped his wife of her rich garments and took a long flexible whip to her, saying: 'Vile wanton, this will assoil your filthy flesh. Oh that that young bugger, Anīs, were between my hands!' Then, in spite of her cries and protestations, he lashed her with the full strength of his arm, put an old mantle of pricking hair upon her, and went into the town to find a smith.

At this point Shahrazād saw the approach of morning and discreetly fell silent.

But when the six-hundred-and-sixty-third night had come

SHE SAID:

When he had fetched the smith, he said to him: 'I wish you to shoe this slave's feet and then her hands; she will make a good mount.' The smith looked at the old man in astonishment, and said: 'As Allāh lives, this is the first time I have ever been called upon to shoe a human! What has she done to deserve such a punishment?' Then said the Jew: 'By the Pentateuch, this is a usual punishment among us Jews when our slaves misbehave themselves!' But the smith, who was quite captivated by Zain al-Mawāsif's beauty, looked at the Jew in disgust and spat in his face; then, instead of touching the girl, he improvised these lines:

> O filthy mule, I'd hammer in
> A thousand nails beneath your skin
> Rather than torture these fair feet
> For which gold anklets were more meet;
> If a poor smith can judge of things,
> You should have nails, and she have wings.

Then the smith ran to the walī of the town and told him what he had seen, dwelling on the marvellous beauty of Zain al-Mawāsif and the horrible cruelty of the Jew. The walī ordered his guards to go to the camp at once and bring the fair slave, the Jew, and the other women into his presence.

At the end of an hour the guards introduced the old Jew, Zain al-Mawāsif, Hubūb, Khutūb, Sukūb and Rukūb, into the audience hall where the walī, dazzled by Zain's beauty, said to her: 'What is your name, my child?' 'Your slave's name is Zain al-Mawāsif, O master,' she answered, moving her hips. 'And who is this very ugly man?' demanded the walī. 'It is a Jew,' she answered again. 'He took me away from my father and mother, violated me, and has tried, by continuous ill-treatment, to make me abjure Islām, the sacred Faith of my fathers. He tortures me every day to break down my resistance; see, here are evidences of his continual beating.' She modestly uncovered her upper arms and showed her stripes to the walī, adding: 'Dear master, the honourable smith will testify to the barbaric treatment which this Jew intended for me. My women will confirm his words. As for me, I am a Mussulmān, a Believer, and I bear witness that there is no God but Allāh, and that Muhammad is the Prophet of Allāh!'

The walī turned to Hubūb, Sukūb, Khutūb and Rukūb, saying: 'Is this true?' and they answered: 'It is true.' Then the walī flashed his eyes upon the Jew, and cried: 'Woe, woe upon you, enemy of Allāh! Why did you take this child from her father and mother, her house and land? Why did you torture her? Why did you try to make her renounce our holy Faith? Why did you try to lead her into the horrible errors of your vile belief?' 'Dear master, I swear by the

lives of Jacob, Moses and Aaron, that this girl is my wedded wife,'
replied the Jew; but the walī cried: 'Beat him with sticks!' The
guards threw the old man to earth and gave him a hundred blows on
the soles of his feet, a hundred upon his back, and a hundred over his
buttocks. As he still continued to affirm that Zain al-Mawāsif was his
wife, the walī cried again: 'Cut off his hands and feet, since he will
not confess!'

Hearing this terrible sentence, the Jew exclaimed: 'By the holy
horns of Moses, since I can save myself in no other way, I confess
that this woman is not my wife and that I stole her from her father's
house.' 'He confesses,' cried the walī. 'Let him be thrown into prison
and stay there all his life! Thus shall all misbelieving Jews be
punished!' The guards dragged the Jew to prison, and doubtless he
died there, alone with his ugliness and unbelief. May Allāh have no
mercy upon him! May He cast that recreant soul into the lowest fires
of hell! We are Believers! We testify that there is no God but Allāh,
and that Muhammad is the Prophet of Allāh!

Zain al-Mawāsif kissed the walī's hand and, returning to the camp
with her four women, ordered the camel-boys to strike the tents and
start the caravan for the land of her beloved.

They travelled without incident and, on the evening of the third
day, came to a Christian monastery, holding forty monks and a
patriarch. This patriarch, whose name was Danīs, sat taking the air
outside the door and saw the beautiful girl pass upon her camel; he
felt his old dead flesh become alive; his feet shivered, his back
shivered, his heart shivered, and his head shivered. He rose from his
seat and, bowing to the earth before Zain al-Mawāsif's litter, invited
her to dismount and rest her company. He strongly urged her to
stop that night at the monastery, alleging, as an excuse, that the
roads were infested at night by brigands. Not wishing to refuse any
offer of hospitality, even though it were from a Christian and a
monk, Zain al-Mawāsif came down from her camel and entered the
monastery with her companions.

At this point Shahrazād saw the approach of morning and
discreetly fell silent.

But when the six-hundred-and-sixty-fifth night had come

SHE SAID:

The patriarch Danīs had been put on fire by love for the delights of Zain al-Mawāsif, therefore he set himself to resolve the hard question of how he should declare his passion. At length it occurred to him to send the most eloquent of the forty monks to plead his cause; but, when the monk found himself in the presence of this moon of beauty, he felt his tongue tie itself into a thousand knots, while his belly finger spoke eloquently beneath his robe and surged up like the trunk of an elephant. Zain al-Mawāsif laughed with all her heart at this, and so did Hubūb, Khutūb, Sukūb and Rukūb; but when the monk continued to stand there speechless, with his affair so high, the girl signed to her followers, who rose and pushed him out of the room.

When Danīs saw his monk return with a woebegone expression, he said to himself: 'Doubtless he was not eloquent enough.' So he sent a second monk. But, when the second monk stood before Zain al-Mawāsif, the same things happened to him as to the first. He was dismissed and returned, with hanging head, to the patriarch, who sent a third monk, a fourth, a fifth, and finally all the forty, one after another. Each time, however, the ambassador returned with no good news, having been unable to speak his message except by signs from his inheritance. Then Danīs remembered the proverb: 'A man should scratch with his own nails and walk on his own feet,' and determined to see to the matter himself.

With grave and measured steps he entered Zain al-Mawāsif's apartment; but her delightful presence reduced him also to a swollen silence. Amid a storm of mocking laughter, he left the room, with his nose hanging to his feet.

When he had gone, Zain al-Mawāsif rose and said to her women: 'We must slip away from this monastery as quickly as possible, lest these horrible monks and their stinking elder should violently soil us in the night.' Favoured by the darkness, the five glided out from the building and urged their camels upon the road to their own country. So much for them.

When the patriarch and his forty monks rose in the morning and found that Zain al-Mawāsif had disappeared, their tripes twisted in great despair. They met together in the church where it was their custom to bray like asses together; but, instead of singing their usual anthems and saying their ordinary prayers, they improvised in this way:

The first monk sang:

> O Lord, who made the passion of her fire
> And tipped her arrows with a sharp desire,
>> Give her sweet body back to us, O Lord,
> O Lord, who tipped her arrows with desire.

The second monk answered:

> O Lord, who gave her eyes to make me whole
> And with her beauty wearied out my soul,
>> Give me to tire her body out, O Lord,
> O Lord, who let her weary out my soul.

Then the third monk sang:

> O Lord, who made her lips as honey sweet
> Yet sharper than the sickle in the wheat,
>> Grant me to be the honey to her steel,
> O Lord, who made her to mow down the wheat;
>> O Lord, make me the carpet of her heel,
> Who made the dream above her visiting feet.

The fourth monk replied:

> O Lord, who let the silver of her star
> Come down upon the dark in which we are,
>> Grant us a quiet tongue concerning this,
> O Lord, who silvered over her cymar.

The fifth monk sobbed and sang:

> O Lord, who cast the fullness of her hips
> And made her spittle more than raisin drips,
>> Favour the onyx tears I weep for her,
> O Lord, who made her as the raisin drips.

The sixth monk continued:

> O Lord, who made her roses on a stem
> With golden starlight shining on to them,
>> Grant that those roses pierce me to the heart,
> O Lord, who made the starlight smile on them.

Then the seventh monk intoned:

> O Lord, who let her madden in our ways
> And lost her there, my kneeling spirit prays
>   That she come back to madden us again,
> O Lord, to dance and madden in our ways.

The rest of the monks sang also in the same vein and then the patriarch controlled the sobbing tremors of his voice and also sang:

> O Lord, my soul is full of heaviness,
> Because she paused and stabbed our happiness,
>   Grant that she heal the wounds she made in joy,
> O Lord, who stabbed the heart of happiness.

> O Lord, who sent her as a silver mole
> To fret my heart and tear into my soul,
>   May she return to ravage them again,
> O Lord, who made the body and the soul.

When they had finished these songs, they threw themselves face down upon the flagstones of their church and wept. They determined to make an image of the fugitive and set it upon the altar of their unbelief; but death surprised them before they could accomplish this, making a term to their torment and sending them down into the graves which they had digged for themselves inside the monastery.

At this point Shahrazād saw the approach of morning and discreetly fell silent.

But when the six-hundred-and-sixty-sixth night had come

SHE SAID:

The vigilance of Allāh had decreed a safe passage for the caravan. And when Zain al-Mawāsif had entered her dwelling in her native land, had put all in order, and had perfumed her bed with precious amber, she sent Hubūb to tell Anīs of her return.

Anīs, who had passed all his days and nights in weeping, was stretched out in sad sleep upon his couch, dreaming that his loved one had returned. As he had faith in the truth of dreams, he rose and went towards her house; he passed through the garden door and at once felt all the air scented with the musk of her near presence. As if his feet were winged, he flew to the chamber where Zain al-Mawāsif waited for him, and the two fell into each other's arms. For a long time they stayed thus, showering upon each other passionate tokens of their love, and then, that they might not swoon for happiness, they drank from a cup of refreshing drink made with lemon, sugar, and water of flowers. After this they regaled each other with the stories of their absence, breaking off every now and then to kiss. Allāh alone knows the number and violence of their loves that night. Next morning they sent young Hubūb for the kādī and witnesses, who wrote out their marriage contract. They lived together in perfect joy until the Reaper of lads and girls came to them. But glory be to Him Who scatters beauty and pleasure according to His justice! And prayer and peace be upon Muhammad, Lord of Messengers, who has made a Paradise for his Believers!

When Shahrazād had made an end of this story, little Dunyazād cried: 'Dear sister, your words are full of savour and sweetness, of purity and excellence!' Then said Shahrazād: 'All that is nothing to what I would tell the King, if he would let me, concerning the Lazy Youth.' 'I give you permission to speak,' said King Shahryār. 'Your words have satisfied me, and also I do not know the Tale of the Lazy Youth.' So Shahrazād said:

The Tale of the Lazy Youth

IT is related, among many other matters, that one day, while Hārūn al-Rashīd sat upon his throne, a young eunuch entered, holding in his hands a red gold crown, encrusted with pearls, rubies, and inestimable jewels. The child kissed the earth between the hands of the Khalīfah, saying: 'O Commander of the Faithful, our mistress Zubaidah sends me with greetings to tell you that this marvellous crown, which is well-known to you, still lacks a large gem for its top, and that no one has been able to find a jewel sufficiently beautiful to fill the empty place. She has had search made among the merchants and has gone through her own treasures, but the crown still lacks its chief ornament. She therefore begs you to institute an enquiry yourself, that her desire may be satisfied.'

The Khalīfah turned towards his wazīrs, amīrs, chamberlains and lieutenants, saying: 'I command you all to find a stone large enough and fair enough to satisfy my Queen.'

They went carefully through the stores of jewels belonging to their wives and found nothing suitable; therefore they reported their unsuccess to the Khalīfah. Hārūn al-Rashīd became sad and said to them: 'How is it that I, who am King of the kings of earth, cannot obtain so much as a wretched stone when I desire it? Woe upon you all! Go and enquire among the merchants.' They enquired among the merchants, and these answered with one voice: 'Hunt no further, for our lord the Khalīfah will only find that jewel in the hands of a certain young man of Basrah, whose name is Abū Muhammad Lazybones.' So they informed the Khalīfah, saying: 'Our lord the Khalīfah will only find that jewel in the hands of a certain young man of Basrah, whose name is Abū Muhammad Lazybones.'

The Khalīfah ordered his wazīr Jafar to command the amīr of Basrah that Abū Muhammad Lazybones be sent to him in Baghdād without delay.

At this point Shahrazād saw the approach of morning and discreetly fell silent.

But when the six-hundred-and-sixty-seventh night had come

SHE SAID:

Jafar therefore wrote a letter and bade Masrūr, the sword-bearer, carry it to the amīr al-Zubaidī, governor of Basrah.

As soon as the amīr al-Zubaidī received these orders from the Khalīfah, he gave all honourable welcome to the envoy and provided him with guards to conduct him to the palace of Abū Muhammad. When Masrūr arrived at that place, and was received at the door by a troop of richly apparelled slaves, he said to them: 'Tell your master that the Commander of the Faithful requires his presence in Baghdād.'

The slaves retired, and in a few moments young Abū Muhammad himself appeared upon the threshold and bowed even to the earth. 'Obedience to the Prince of Believers!' he said. 'I beg my honourable guests to enter my house for a moment.' 'We cannot delay here,' answered Masrūr. 'The Commander of the Faithful eagerly waits your coming.' Then said Abū Muhammad: 'Yet it is necessary to give me time to prepare for the journey. Come in and rest.' Masrūr and his companions made a few difficulties for form's sake and then followed the young man.

From the vestibule inwards, they saw magnificent blue velvet curtains wrought with fine gold, precious marbles, and carved woods; they saw astonishing jeweller's work upon the walls and ceilings, and on every tapestry. Their host led them to a hammām, shining with cleanness and scented like the heart of a rosetree, a bath more splendid than any in the Khalīfah's palace. After they had bathed, slaves clad them in sumptuous robes of green brocade, sewed with subjects in pearl and gold, and, after wishing them the wishes of the bath, handed them sherberts and sweet cakes. Then five lads entered, each as fair as the angel Hārūt, and presented the guests with purses of five thousand dīnārs, as a gift of welcome. The first slaves then led Masrūr and his following into the guest hall, where Abū Muhammad awaited them on a silk dīwān, leaning his arms upon cushions heavy with pearls. He rose in their honour and made them sit beside him, pressing such admirable meat and drink upon them as has not been found upon the cloths of emperors.

At length the young man rose, saying: 'I am the slave of the Commander of the Faithful! My preparations are complete and we may depart for Baghdād.' He went forth with his guests and, while they were mounting their horses, the slaves helped him into the saddle of a white mule like virgin silver, whose harness shone with the fires of gold and winked with precious stones. Masrūr and young Abū Muhammad rode at the head of the escort and, coming after a pleasant journey into the City of Peace, entered the Khalīfah's palace.

When he was introduced into the presence, the youth most modestly kissed the earth three times before the throne and, when Hārūn invited him to be seated, sat most respectfully. 'O Commander of the Faithful,' he said, 'though your slave has not been told, he knows very well why you require his presence. Therefore, instead of bringing a single jewel, he has thought it his humble duty to carry a large assortment with him. If our master, the Khalīfah, will allow it, I shall open the coffers of my loyal present.' 'I see nothing against that,' said the Khalīfah.

Abū Muhammad had two chests brought into the hall and drew from the first, among other marvels ravishing to the eye, three gold trees with gold branches, whose leaves were emerald and aquamarine, whose fruits were rubies for pomegranates, pearls for apples, and topaz in place of oranges.

At this point Shahrazād saw the approach of morning and discreetly fell silent.

But when the six-hundred-and-sixty-eighth night had come

SHE SAID:

While the Khalifah marvelled at the beauty of these trees, Abū Muhammad took from the second coffer a pavilion of silk and gold, encrusted with hyacinths and emeralds, rubies and sapphires. The central pole was of Indian aloe wood and all the outside folds of the pavilion were picked out in coloured jewels; the inside was ornamented in marvellous dexterity with the graceful leaping of beasts and the flight of birds; and these beasts and birds were of gold, of chrysolite and garnet, of emerald and fabulous metals.

When young Abū Muhammad had taken these various parts of the pavilion from the coffer, he set them down at haphazard upon the carpet and, standing motionless before them, lifted and lowered his eyebrows. At once the pavilion rose of itself in the middle of the hall, as prompt and orderly as if twenty expert slaves had had the raising of it. The three trees came and planted themselves at its entrance, protecting it with their brilliant shade.

Abū Muhammad looked a second time at the pavilion and gave a whistle that was almost a sigh; immediately the jewelled birds began to sing and the gold beasts answered them with sweet harmony. Then Abū Muhammad whistled again and all was silence.

The Khalifah and those who were with him did not know whether they slept or waked; but Abū Muhammad kissed the earth again between Hārūn's hands, saying: 'O Prince of Believers, do not think that I have brought these little gifts, which seem not displeasing to you, with any interested motive; they are simply part of the homage which we all owe to our master. They are nothing in comparison to those which I would bring later, if I were allowed.'

When the Khalifah had a little recovered from his astonishment, he said: 'Young man, can you tell me how these things have come to you, a simple subject among my subjects? You are known as Abū Muhammad Lazybones, and I am aware that your father was but a common cupper at the hammām, who left you no inheritance. How then, in so short a time and while you are still so young, have you reached to this eminence of riches and distinction?' 'I will tell you my tale, O Commander of the Faithful,' answered Abū Muhammad, 'for it is so strange and filled with such marvellous prodigies that, were it written with needles in the corner of an eye, yet would it serve as a rich lesson to the circumspect.' Al-Rashīd's imagination

was fired by this preliminary and he begged the young man to speak.
So Abū Muhammad Lazybones began:

Know then, O Commander of the Faithful (whom may Allāh
bless!), that I am, as you say, Abū Muhammad Lazybones, the son of
a poor bath cupper, who died without leaving anything to my
mother and myself. Those who told you this of me spoke the truth;
but they did not tell you how I earned my name . . . From infancy
I was the slackest and laziest boy on the earth. Indeed, so great was
my laziness that, if I was lying on the ground and the sun beat with
all his fires on my bare head at noon, I had not the energy to move
into the shade and would rather let myself be roasted like a colocasia
than move an arm or leg. Thus my skull became proof against any
sort of blow, and, if you were now to command Masrūr to split my
head, you would see his blade fly to pieces in the attempt.

I was fifteen when my father died (Allāh have him in mercy!) but
I was little better than two years old, for I would neither work nor
move, and my poor mother had to go out to service in order to feed
me. I passed my days lying on my side, without the strength to drive
away the flies which made their homes upon my face.

At this point Shahrazād saw the approach of morning and
discreetly fell silent.

But when the six-hundred-and-sixty-ninth night had come

SHE SAID:

One day, by a rare chance, when my mother had finished a
month's work with those for whom she laboured, she came to me
with five pieces of silver in her hand. 'My child,' she said, 'I have just
heard that our neighbour Muzaffar is setting out for China. Now you
know, my son, that this good old man does not disdain the poor or
drive them away; therefore take these five dirhams and come with
me to him. You must give him the money and beg him to buy you
goods in China, which, under Allāh, may give you a great profit in
Basrah. Here is a chance for us to become rich, and he who refuses
the bread of Allāh is an Unbeliever.' When I heard my mother speak
in this way, I became lazier than ever and lay back upon myself as if
I were dead. In vain my mother begged me, conjured me, in the
name of Allāh and by the tomb of my father. I pretended to snore.
'By your poor father's excellence,' she said at last, 'I swear that, if
you will not obey me and come with me to the sheikh, I shall no

longer give you food or drink but let you die of want.' I understood from her tone that she would be as good as her word, therefore I let out a sulky grunt which signified: 'Help me to sit up.' She took me by the arm and helped me to sit up; then I began to cry for very weariness and sighed: 'Give me my slippers.' She brought them, and I said: 'Put them on for me.' She put them on my feet, and I said: 'Help me to get up.' She lifted me and I exclaimed with a groan: 'Hold me up while I walk.' She came behind and supported me, pushing me gently forward, and I began to walk very slowly, pausing at each step to get my breath and lolling my head upon my shoulders. At last I came like this to the sea shore and found old Muzaffar making ready to sail. He was surrounded by friends, who hailed my arrival with stupefaction, crying: 'This is the first time we have ever seen Abū Muhammad Lazybones walking abroad. This is the first time he has come out of his house.'

I went up to the sheikh, saying: 'O uncle, are you not the sheikh Muzaffar?' 'At your service, O Abū Muhammad,' he replied, 'O son of my old friend, the dead cupper, whom may Allāh ever harbour in his pity!' I held out the five silver pieces and said: 'O sheikh, I pray you take these five dirhams and buy goods for me in China. Perhaps thus, through your great kindness, we may make a profit.' The sheikh Muzaffar took the money and knotted it under his belt in the name of Allāh. Then he took leave of my mother and me, and went on board with other merchants who were accompanying him to that far land.

Allāh had willed that the sheikh Muzaffar should arrive safely at the port of his desire. He and his friends bought, sold, and trafficked according to their will, and then re-embarked on the same ship which they had chartered at Basrah.

When they had sailed ten days, Muzaffar rose suddenly from his place and beat his hands together in despair, crying: 'About ship! We must return to China!' 'But why, O Muzaffar?' asked his astonished friends, and he answered: 'Because I have forgotten to spend the five dirhams of Abū Muhammad Lazybones.' 'But, by Allāh, dear master,' objected the other merchants, 'surely you would not condemn us to infinite danger and loss of time for so small a matter?' 'We must return to China,' he said. 'His father was my friend and I gave my word.' 'Let not that trouble you,' said they, 'for rather than put the ship about, we will each give you five gold dīnārs as interest upon the five dirhams. You can present the boy with all that gold when we arrive.' Muzaffar accepted this offer, and each of the merchants straightway handed him five dīnārs to be kept for me.

The ship went on her way and put in to provision at a certain isle, where Muzaffar and his friends disembarked to take the air and walk upon the shore. As the old man was returning to the ship, he saw an ape-seller with a string of twenty apes. Among these beasts there was one which looked very miserable, a small, bald, shivering, tear-stained object. And, whenever their master was not looking, the other apes would leap upon the wretched one, biting and scratching him, and pissing on his head. Muzaffar's kindly heart had pity on the unfortunate creature and he asked its price. 'I will sell it for five dirhams, to get rid of it,' answered the owner, and the sheikh exclaimed: 'That is just the sum which Abū Muhammad gave me. I will buy the ape for him and he can earn his bread by showing it in the markets.' He paid my five dirhams to the ape-seller and had the wretched monkey taken on board by one of the sailors. Then he re-embarked and waited to set sail.

As he and his companions were making their final preparations, they saw the fishers of that island diving to the bottom of the sea and bringing up shells filled with pearls. The monkey saw this also.

At this point Shahrazād saw the approach of morning and discreetly fell silent.

But when the six-hundred-and-seventieth night had come

SHE SAID:

He leapt over the ship's side into the water and came up, after a certain time, holding in his hands, and even in his mouth, shells filled with pearls of marvellous size and beauty. He climbed on board and laid his spoil at Muzaffar's feet. Then he went on signing with his paw, as if to say: 'Fasten something round my neck.' The sheikh tied a bag round his neck and the ape dived again into the water. Soon he emerged with the sack full of shells containing finer and richer pearls than before. He plunged many times and on each occasion brought remarkable riches to the merchant.

Muzaffar and his friends cried out in stupefaction: 'There is no power or might save in Allāh! This ape knows secret things which are hidden from us! And all this is for Muhammad Lazybones, son of the cupper!' Soon after, they left the island of pearls and came before favouring winds to Basrah.

As soon as he disembarked, the sheikh Muzaffar came to knock at our door and, when my mother asked who was there, begged her to open, saying that he had returned from China. 'Rise up, Lazybones!' cried my mother. 'Muzaffar has returned from China. Open the door and welcome him. Ask him what he has brought you, for perhaps Allāh means to satisfy our necessity through him.' 'Help me to get up,' I said, and she did so. I shuffled myself somehow to the door, catching my feet in the skirts of my robe at each step.

When I opened the door, Muzaffar entered, followed by his slaves. 'Greeting and benediction upon him whose five dirhams brought luck to our voyage!' he cried. 'Behold your profit, my son!' The slaves set down the sacks of pearls in our hall, while the old man gave over the gold to me and put the ape's cord in my hand. 'This has all come from your five dirhams,' he said. 'Do not ill-treat the ape, my son, for he is an ape of benediction.' So saying, the good old man departed.

As soon as we were alone, O Commander of the Faithful, I turned to my mother, saying: 'This proves which of us two was right, my mother. You used to make my life a burden every day by bidding me rise up and work; and I would always answer that He Who created me would feed me.' 'You were right, dear child,' my mother answered. 'Each man carries his Destiny about his neck and may in no wise escape it.' Then she helped me to count the pearls and to sort them according to their size and excellence. . . . After that, I put aside my laziness and went every day to the jewellers' market to sell my pearls. So great was my profit that I was able to buy land and houses, shops and gardens, palaces and slaves, women and boys.

The ape followed me everywhere, eating of my food, drinking of my cup, and never taking his eyes from me. One day, as we sat in my palace, he signed to me that he wished writing materials. I brought him pen, ink, and paper; he placed the paper on his left hand in the manner of scribes, plunged the pen into the ink, and wrote: 'O Abū Muhammad, find a white cock and bring it to me in the garden.' I at once procured a white cock and, running with it into the garden, saw the ape waiting for me, with a snake between his paws. He took the cock and set it on the snake, so that the two fought together, and the cock conquered the snake and killed it. Then, as is not the manner of cocks, it ate the snake.

The ape took hold of the cock, tore out all its feathers and planted them one after another in the garden. Then he killed the bird and watered the feathers with its blood. Finally he cleaned the cock's gizzard and set it in the middle of the garden.

At this point Shahrazād saw the approach of morning and discreetly fell silent.

But when the six-hundred-and-seventy-first night had come

LITTLE DUNYAZĀD said: 'For pity's sake, dear sister, tell us what Abū Muhammad's ape did when he had planted the feathers in the garden and watered them with the cock's blood?' 'Certainly,' answered Shahrazād, and continued:

Then the ape stood before each of the feathers in turn, clicking his jaws and making little cries which I could not understand. Finally he squatted before me, gathering himself for a spring, and then leapt so high into the air that he disappeared for ever from my sight. At that moment all the cock feathers in my garden grew into gold trees with leaves of emerald and aquamarine, and bearing rubies and pearls and topaz in place of fruit. Also the cock's gizzard became this marvellous pavilion, which I make so bold as to offer to the Khalīfah, together with three of the trees.

As each stone of my new treasure was worth a ransom, I asked the sheriff of Basrah, the descendant of our Prophet, for the hand of his daughter in marriage; and he granted my request, after he had seen my palace and garden. I live with my wife now in all health and happiness. I attribute my good fortune to my youthful confidence in the boundless generosity of Allāh; for those who believe in Him shall lack nothing.

When the Khalīfah Hārūn al-Rashīd had heard this tale, he marvelled and cried: 'The favours of Allāh are infinite, my son.' He kept Abū Muhammad with him to dictate his story to the palace scribes, and only allowed him to leave Baghdād when he had loaded him with gifts and honours, whose magnificence fully equalled those which he had himself received. And yet Allāh is more generous and more powerful!

When Shahrazād paused, King Shahryār said to her: 'The moral of your story is an excellent one.' 'It is, O auspicious King,' answered Shahrazād. 'Yet the tale is not to be compared with one which I have in reserve to tell you.' And she said . . .

The Tale of Young Nūr and
the Warrior Girl

IT is related, O auspicious King, that there was once, in the antiquity of time and the passage of the age and of the moment, an Egyptian merchant adventurer, whose name was Crown. He had passed his early life in voyaging on land and sea, among isles and through deserts, by shores known and unknown; and, in so doing, had affronted dangers and fatigues whose recital would have blanched the hair of little children. But, at the time of this tale, he had done with travel and lived happy and respected in his palace, seated upon his dīwān, his brow girt with a turban of immaculate white muslin. He lacked nothing; for the rooms of his palace, his harīm, his chests and presses were filled with sumptuous garments, with silks of Hims and Baalbakk stuffs, with Damascene swords and with Baghdād brocades, Mosul gauze and Moorish mantles, and all the embroideries of India, in such profusion that no king of earth has known the like. Also he had many black and white slaves, Turkish mamlūks, concubines, eunuchs, blood horses and mules, Bactrian camels and racing dromedaries, Greek and Syrian boys, small Circassian girls, little Abyssinian eunuchs, and women from all lands. There is no doubt that he was the most honoured merchant of his time.

But incomparably his richest and fairest possession was his fourteen-year-old son, who far surpassed the beauty of the moon upon her fourteenth night. Neither the cool of springtime, the dancing branches of the ban, the rose in her bud, nor light shining through alabaster, could equal this boy, or his walking, or the tints upon his cheeks, or the stainless white of his body. Inspired by the child's beauty, a poet sang:

> Boys' crimson lips:
> 'But all your singing is insane,
> You must not sing of us again.'
> So I obey and sit and sing
> Of trees, of girls, of everything,
> Inanely and in vain:
>
> Till beauty takes me by the throat,
> Lifting the theme, changing the note,

> And I make maddest music for
> Your flash of eyes declaring war,
> The black musk spirt on white by your
>   Boy's crimson lips.

Another sang of him:

> I came to a battle, a torment of red,
> And asked of the dying:
> 'Ah, what is the prize?'
> Then one died sighing:
> 'A fair boy's eyes,'
> And 'Eyes' the smile of a dead man said.

A third sang:

> When he came to see me and found me ill
>   'Oh, when did this happen?' the sweet boy cried,
> 'About the time when I heard on the sill
>   Your footstep,' I replied.

Another said:

> Moons with their pale flame,
> And gazelles came.
> 'Bow down, gazelles, before this fawn,
> And moons, before this dawn!'

Yet another said:

> Save by his forehead and his hair
>   We tell not day and night apart;
> Who then of his dark mole would dare
>   To say it mars the rose's art?
> Or could the red anemone be fair
>   Without her heart?

Another wrote of him also:

> Beauty's waters were made clear
> When his eyes lay mirrored there;
> So, fierce archers everywhere,
>   Let us sing, let us be glad
>   For eyes and arrows of my lad.

His dim white lawns and tissues hide
The silver dawn of his backside,
As mists before a moon may ride;
    Let us sing, let us be glad
    For lawns and silvers of my lad.

All swift, all black his eyes' attack,
The mole upon his cheek is black,
But blacker still my tears of lack;
    Let us sing, let us be glad
    For this thrice darkness of my lad.

Young moon and silver rush's limb,
His face and brow are bright and slim,
My body, too, is thin for him;
    Let us sing, let us be glad
    For the white slightness of my lad.

His eyes drank blood and were not red,
The smile upon his lips was bread,
He looked away and I lay dead . . .
    Let us sing, let us be glad
    For the turned eye smile of my lad.

And out of a thousand poets who sang of him, there was one who made this song:

By arched bows that guard his eyes,
By their dark sweet treacheries,
By the white sword of his form
And his black hair's scented storm,
By the laughing eyes which keep
Fires to burn the rose of sleep,
By curled scorpions of small hair
With bright stings to stab despair,
By the lily and the vine,
By the honey and the wine,
Buttocks of this boy of mine;
By the skin of apricot,
Silver feet which he has got;
By the sun which rises pale,
By the moon, his finger-nail,

> By star and spring, for he is both,
> I swear that I have loved this oath!

One day, while this admirable youth was sitting in his father's shop, some boy friends came to talk to him and proposed that he should visit with them a garden which belonged to one of their number. 'You shall see for yourself how beautiful it is, O Nūr,' they said.

At this point Shahrazād saw the approach of morning and discreetly fell silent.

But when the six-hundred-and-seventy-second night had come

SHE SAID:

'I shall be very glad to come,' answered Nūr, 'but first I must get leave from my father.' He went to ask permission, and the merchant not only accorded it but gave his son a purse full of gold that he might not be a charge on his companions.

Nūr and the other boys mounted their mules and their donkeys, and came at length to a garden which held all things to sweeten the mouth and delight the eye. They entered by a vaulted gate which might have been the gate of Paradise; for it was made with marble of alternate colour and shaded by climbing vines heavy with clusters of red and black grapes, and white and gold grapes. A poet has said:

> Grapes big with wine, are you more sweet
> Black-coated like the crow
> Yet twinkling in the sombre vine
> As henna-painted fingers shine
> When China queens sit all a-row
> With folded saffron feet,
>
> Or pressed to drunken honey in the vats?

As they entered they saw these lines written in fair azure lettering above the gate:

> Would you have gardens, come to me . . .
> The breeze, the perfumed vagabond,
> False to all else, is true to me
> And he shall heal your misery.
> The flowers give coloured robes to me
> And laugh with all their petalled sleeves,
> And they shall heal your misery.

The wet sky gives an alms to me,
Gaudily bending down my trees;
My fruit shall heal your misery.
The Seven Stars drop gifts to me
Of watered gold and cloudy pearl,
And Zephyr fans the gold for me;
My night shall heal your misery.
The loves of dawn are swift with me.
To lie upon my eager streams
And kiss the sleeping flowers for me . . .
Shall I not heal your misery?

They saw the keeper of the garden sitting in the shade beneath a trellis of climbing grapes, and he was as fair as Ridwān who guards the treasures of Paradise. He rose in their honour with cordial greeting and, after helping them to alight, offered himself to be their guide to the beauties of the garden. Following him, they could admire the watercourses moving like snakes among the flowers and quitting them only with regret. They could admire the plants heavy with their scents, the trees weary beneath their fruit, the singing birds, the spice shrubs and the flower thickets of that enchanted place. Above all things and beyond all words, the rare fruit trees rejoiced them. These have been sung by every poet; here are a few out of a thousand of their songs:

POMEGRANATES

Polished delicates are we,
   Ruby mines in silver earth,
Maidens' blood of high degree
   Curdled into drops of worth,
Breasts of women when they see
   Man is near, and stand them forth.

APPLES

Musky-sweet apples smile yellow and red,
One cheek for living love, one cheek for dead,
   One yellow and dead,
   One living and red;
Musky-sweet apples smile yellow and red.

APRICOTS

Who doubts you sweet
With savoury almond-stones,
Apricots?
When you were young
You had star-flowers,
Now you are little suns
Ripe in the leaves.

FIGS

Figs white, O black, O welcome to my plate,
    White girls of Greece, hot Ethiopian girls,
Though pampered feeders not appreciate,
    So sure of my desire, experienced figs . . .

Wrinkled and young and knowing on high boughs,
    Balanced in every wind and yet rose soft,
More than the blown flower camomile allows
    You wear a wavering scent, honey and sun.

PEARS

Half acid to a lover's taste,
Flirting hips on a black waist,
Little Ionian,
Little Aleppo,
Little yellow and green girls.

PEACHES

We think we fell in a proud virgin's blood,
    Therefore we fend our velvet with a mesh
        Against the airs:
    Eat through our scarlet skin to soft wet flesh,
To sweet gold flesh, but guard lest in full flood
        You meet the heart of poison unawares.

ALMONDS

'As in their sea green shell the pearls,
In triple green we hide, shy girls;

We care to pass the green of youth
In hauberks bitter and uncouth,
Until the waking comes and we
Wanton white hearts from out our tree.'

Small white ones, many in a hand,
Your green down, as I understand,
Is the smooth boyhood of my friend,
And your long halves from end to end
His pretty eyes, O pearls in jade,
Sweet, white, unfaithful, unafraid.

JUJUBE-PLUMS

They hang in showers
From ropes of flowers,
    They're gold bells in a tone,
They make the spice
Of Paradise
    And stand beside the throne;
The law was written in their wood
And from the roots of their abode
    The four great streams are sown.

ORANGES

The breeze on the hill
Laughs with the orange trees,
Smiling in flower-mist.
Oranges,
Women who deck young bodies
With gold robes
For holiday;
Fire-balls holding snow,
Red snow which cannot melt.

May I not think of my dear lad,
His golden granulated moon?

CITRONS

Heavy with perfume braziers of green gold
Hung in their leaves,

The branches of the citron bend.
Wavering to end
The pain which grieves,
Or eddying to invoke
Joy with their fold and fold
Of spiced green golden smoke.

LEMONS

Snow that takes on saffron,
   Silver turning gold
      Are lemons.
Moons which waver into suns,
   Chrysolite bells and manifold
      Are lemons, lemons.
Camphor ripening to corn light,
   Breasts that else could not be told
      Are lemons, lemons, lemons.

BANANAS

Heavy bars of gold, or swaying
   Or slow ripened in our presses,
Flasks of scent, with widows praying,
   Widows dreaming of caresses;

Buttered flesh like paste of cooking,
   Yellows of so bold a shape
Little girls cannot help looking,
   Hardly help surmise a rape.

DATES

We grow to the sound of the wind
Playing his flutes in our hair,

Palm tree daughters,
Brown flesh Badāwī,
Fed with light
By our gold father;

We are loved of the free-tented,
The sons of space, the hall-forgetters,

> The wide-handed, the bright-sworded
> Masters of horses.

> Who has rested in the shade of our palms
> Shall hear us murmur ever above his sleep.

These are some out of countless poems which have been made about fruits. But it would take more than a lifetime to say all the songs which have been made about the flowers of that garden, the jasmine and the jacinth, the waterlily and the myrtle, the carnation, the narcissus, and every red and white of roses.

Soon the keeper of the garden led the boys along alleys to a pavilion which sat throned among green grass. He invited them to enter for rest and made them sit on brocaded cushions about a basin of water, praying young Nūr to take the middle place.

At this point Shahrazād saw the approach of morning and discreetly fell silent.

But when the six-hundred-and-seventy-third night had come

SHE SAID:
He offered the boy a fan of ostrich feathers upon which these lines were painted:

> My white untiring wing
> Fans scented air
> For a young thing,
> To make his sighs
> Surmise
> Of Paradise,
> Before he's there.

When the lads had taken off their mantles and turbans, they began to chat together and could not keep their eyes off their fair comrade. The keeper of the garden served them himself with a luxurious repast of chicken, goose, quails, pigeons, partridges, stuffed lamb, and baskets of fruit from the branches. As they were washing their hands with a musk soap and drying them on napkins of gold-embroidered silk, the keeper entered with a great handful of roses and said to his guests: 'Before you touch the drinks, I wish you to dispose your souls to pleasure with the colour and scent of these flowers. But, dear friends, I will not give you roses save for a song about roses.'

The boy who owned the garden took the flowers and, plunging his head among them, breathed there for a long while; then he signed for silence and improvised these lines:

> You hide your crimson blushets in green sleeves,
> Balmed hearts of all slight crystal, riders in rose
> Who lead the coloured armies of the flowers;
>
> Sweeter you open shameless to the breeze
> Than kissed wine on child mouths.
>
>   Your rainbow blood
> Riotously compares you with gold dawn,
> With cups of purple wine, with garnet fruit
> On emerald branches, O silver-quivered
> Desirous roses; and you chain your loves
> With different-tinted coquetry of robes
> So that they do not tire. . . .

When they heard this admirable praise of the rose, the boys could not contain their enthusiasm, but repeated, swaying their heads in chorus: *With different tinted coquetry of robes.* He who had sung opened the basket of roses and covered his guests with them; then he filled a great cup with wine and sent it about. At his turn, young Nūr felt a certain embarrassment, because he had never drunken wine; his palate was as virgin to fermented drink as was his body to the touch of women. He was still a maiden and his parents had not yet given him a concubine, as is the custom of nobles with pubic sons, to give them knowledge and experience. His comrades knew of Nūr's virginity and had not overlooked it when they arranged the pleasure party.

Seeing that he hesitated before the cup as before a forbidden thing, his friends so laughed that Nūr, in pique, raised the vessel to his lips and drained it to the last drop. The other boys gave a cry of triumph and the garden's owner approached Nūr with another cup, saying: 'You are very right not to abstain longer from the precious drops of drunkenness. They are the mothers of virtue, the balms of misery, the sovereign cure of body and soul alike. Charming friend, all here are your servants and slaves; therefore I pray you take this cup and drink this wine which is only less exciting than your eyes.' Nūr could not refuse and emptied the second cup.

Soon the grape ran hot in young Nūr's mind and at once one of his fellows cried to their host: 'All this is good, O generous friend, but our joy will not be complete without singing and the sound of women's lips. The poet has said:

> Let the small cup and the deep cup go round;
> Old friends, begin!
> Take little cups from little hands
> Whose camphor tips are fairylands,
> But wait to suck the mighty in,
> For the lute's sound.'

The young host answered with a smile and, leaving the hall for a moment, returned leading in by the hand a girl dressed all in blue silk.

At this point Shahrazād saw the approach of morning and discreetly fell silent.

But when the six-hundred-and-seventy-fourth night had come

SHE SAID:

She was a slight Egyptian admirably waisted, straight as the letter alif and with Babylonian eyes; her hair was darkness, but her white was the white of silver in the mine or of a peeled almond. She shone so in her sombre robe that you would have taken her for a Summer moon on a Winter night. How then would she not have breasts of white ivory, a harmonious belly, a glory of thighs, and buttocks like cushions? Would there not be a thing rose-balmed in front of them, like a small scent bag folded in a larger? Surely it was of her the poet sang:

> You are that hind which led the lions in
> Made tame by your black bow,
> Egyptian girl.

> Your tented dim silk hair has fallen low
> And you are couched therein,
> Egyptian girl.

> Crystal grows grey, and the blue airs begin
> To hide their shame in snow,
> Egyptian girl;

You hide your roses with your hand, but, lo!
We see the hand, we sin,
Egyptian girl.

Then the young master of the garden said to the girl: 'Pleasant queen of stars, we caused you to come into our garden solely to please young Nūr, our guest and friend, who honours us with his visit for the first time.'

The young Egyptian sat down by Nūr's side with a strange glance of the eyes; then she drew a bag of green satin from beneath her veil and took out of it thirty-two little pieces of wood. These she joined together, two and two, as man to woman and as woman to man, until she had formed an Indian lute of exquisite design. She raised her sleeves, uncovering her wrists and arms, pressed the lute like a baby to her breast, and touched it with her finger-nails. At this touch the lute shivered and moaned, suddenly remembering its life and destiny: it recalled the earth of its planting, the waters of its refreshment, the places where its stem had silently grown, the birds of its hospitality, the woodcutters, the clever craftsman, the varnisher, the ship which had carried it, and all the fair hands between which it had passed. These memories made it sing and it seemed to answer thus to the questioning fingers:

I was a green branch of nightingales,
And, while they taught me music in gold nights,
I dared not stir my leaves.
Now, a fragile lute which grieves
Beneath the touch of tiny nails,
Now, clasped by slim delights
And lying on young breasts,
Remembering my nightingales,
I bring a woodland bliss
To lovers' feasts
And spill wine's ecstasy where no wine is.

After this prelude of the lute speaking by itself to the soul, the pretty Egyptian ceased playing for a moment; then, fixing her eyes upon young Nūr, she touched the strings again and sang . . .

At this point Shahrazād saw the approach of morning and discreetly fell silent.

But when the six-hundred-and-seventy-fifth night had come

SHE SAID:

> The night is witch-blown glass of blue,
> Out of a green mystery the nightingale
> Invites us:
>
> The breathing of the naked night
> Into the silver horn of the moon
> Invites us;
>
> Suspicious age is sleeping;
>
> Here are myrtles and gold flowers,
> The rose's jars are spilled
> And wine and stars;
>
> The cup is full to-night.

Drunken with these lines and wine and love, young Nūr threw hot glances on the slave, who answered with a smile. He leaned over her desirously and she pressed the points of her breasts against him, kissing him between the eyes, and leaving all to his hands. Giving way to his trouble, Nūr crushed his lips to her mouth and breathed her like a rose; but she, warned by the glances of the other boys, slipped from his grasp, took up her lute again, and sang:

> I, who so often sang of wine and rose,
> Suddenly found them when I kissed your mouth,
> O light, O fair repose,
> O balm, O South!

When he heard this burning declaration, Nūr was lifted up by love and improvised in his turn:

> You walk as proudly as a pirate ship
> Walks on the sea, you have a falcon's eyes,
> Your hair is a black youth sold with white girls,
> Your words are scarlet dyes,
> You wear your silver beauty as a belt
> Which will not slip
> For any speech,
> You will not melt
> For gold

> Or for my soul
> Or for my sleep
> Or for my eyes,
> O roses set too high for man to reach.

When the young man who was their host saw Nūr's state, he judged the time had come for the delightful Egyptian to initiate him into the joys of love; so he signed to the other boys and they retired from the hall one by one.

As soon as the girl saw that she was alone with the handsome Nūr, she rose up and stripped off her ornaments and her clothes until she was naked except for her hair. Then she sat on the boy's knees and kissed his eyes, saying: 'Eye of my soul, a gift is ever proportioned to the generosity of the giver. For your beauty and because you please me, I give you all I have. Take my lips, take my tongue, take my breasts, take my belly, and all else.' Nūr accepted this miraculous present and gave a still more marvellous one in return; so that, when they had finished, the girl, who was both charmed and surprised by his skilful generosity, asked him why his comrades had told her that he was a virgin. 'But I was,' he answered. Then said she: 'It is astonishing that you should be so expert at the first attempt!' And he retorted, laughing: 'There is fire in the youngest flint.'

Thus, among roses and laughter and multiple delights, young Nūr learnt love, in the arms of an Egyptian as bright as a bird's eye and whiter than an almond.

At this point Shahrazād saw the approach of morning and discreetly fell silent.

But when the six-hundred-and-seventy-sixth night had come

SHE SAID:

Surely such initiation was written in his Destiny; for, without it, how could we understand certain more marvellous matters which he was to meet on the road of his happy life?

When their loving was over, Nūr perceived that the stars were beginning to shine and that the breath of God was bringing up the evening breeze; therefore he said: 'By your leave' to the girl, and left her in spite of her supplications. He mounted his mule and returned as quickly as he might to the house where his father and mother were anxiously waiting him.

As soon as he had crossed the threshold his mother ran to take him in her arms, and said: 'Why have you been so long away from home, my dear?' Then, as Nūr opened his mouth to answer and she smelt the wine upon his breath, she exclaimed: 'Unhappy Nūr! What have you done? If your father smells this, there will be great trouble.' Now Nūr had held up against his drink while he was in the Egyptian's arms, but the cold night air had unmanned him, so that he staggered from left to right like a drunken man. When his mother saw this, she hastened him to bed and covered him up warmly. Soon the merchant Crown entered the bed-chamber. He was a faithful observer of Allāh's law, which forbids fermented drink to His Believers. Seeing his son worn and pale, he asked his wife what the matter was, and she replied: 'The fresh air gave him a violent headache when he was walking in the garden with his friends at your suggestion.' Annoyed by this reproach and uneasy concerning his son, the merchant leaned over Nūr to find out how he did; but, when he smelt the boy's breath, he shook him roughly by the arm, and cried: 'You have broken the law of Allāh and His Prophet, vile boy! And now you dare to enter your father's house without purifying your mouth!'

As he went on harshly scolding him, young Nūr raised his hand, without knowing what he did, and hit his father so violently in the right eye that the old man fell to the ground. The merchant got to his feet and solemnly swore by the third divorce that he would banish his son on the morrow, after having cut off his right hand.

As soon as her husband left the room, Nūr's mother tore her garments in despair, for she knew that there was no retreat from such an oath. She stayed all night weeping by the bedside of her drunken son and succeeded, at length, in dissipating the fumes of wine by making him sweat and piss excessively. He came to himself with no memory of what had passed; so the poor woman told him of his terrible action and his father's more terrible oath. 'Alas, regrets are useless now,' she said. 'There is only one thing for you to do until the affair has blown over: you must flee from the house before dawn. Take this purse of eleven hundred dīnārs and depart for the city of Alexandria. When the money is spent, send for more and give me news of yourself.' With that she wept again and kissed her son.

At first Nūr also wept for shame; then he fastened the purse to his belt, took leave of his mother, and crept unnoticed from the house.

He found a boat, which took him down the Nile and landed him safely at Alexandria.

Nūr found Alexandria a marvel among cities: a place of sweet climate and delightful inhabitants, with fruit and flower gardens, broad streets and magnificent markets. He took pleasure in wandering through the various quarters of the city and visiting the markets one by one. While he passed among the sellers of flowers and fruit, he saw a Persian riding upon a mule, with a girl seated behind him who was all fruits and flowers together, and had a waist of five hands' span.

At this point Shahrazād saw the approach of morning and discreetly fell silent.

But when the six-hundred-and-seventy-seventh night had come

SHE SAID:

She was as white as a nut, as a bleak in the fountain, as a jerboa in the desert. Her face shone like the sun, and her great dark Babylonian eyes looked out from below the guard of stretched bows. The light tissue which covered her hinted at unimagined splendours: at cheeks smoother than satin and planted with roses, at teeth which were ranges of pearl, at straight forthcoming breasts, at thighs like the tail of a fat-tailed Syrian sheep, holding a treasure in their topmost snows and carrying a backside moulded from paste of pearl, roses and jasmine. Glory be to Him Who made her!

When Nūr saw this child, who so surpassed his brown Egyptian garden girl, he followed the fortunate mule which carried her and walked behind until the rider dismounted in the slave market.

The Persian helped the girl to the ground, and led her by the hand to the public crier, that she might be put up for sale. The crier made way for her through the crowd and set her upon an ivory seat inlaid with gold. Then he let his eye travel over the purchasers, and thus addressed them: 'Merchants, buyers, masters of money, citizens and men of the desert, O generous bidders near and far, I pray you open the auction! No blame to the first bidder! Examine and then speak, for Allāh alone knows all! Bid, gentlemen, bid, I pray you!'

At this invitation the syndic of all the merchants of that city, an old man against whom none dared bid, walked slowly round the seat and, having minutely examined the slave, exclaimed: 'Nine hundred and twenty-five dīnārs!'

'Nine hundred and twenty-five dīnārs I am bid!' cried the auctioneer. 'This generous gentleman has bid nine hundred and twenty-five dīnārs for a pearl of price!' Then, as none dared raise the bid, he turned to the girl, saying: 'O queen of moons, are you willing to belong to this venerable syndic?' From beneath her veils the girl answered: 'Are you mad or has something gone wrong with your tongue that you make me such an offer?' 'Why do you say that, O queen of all fair girls?' asked the astonished crier; and the child, showing the little pearls of her mouth in a smile, went on: 'Are you not ashamed, before Allāh and upon your beard, to sell maidens of my quality to sapless and decrepit old men? I dare swear this dotard's unfortunate wife has used much language in her day about his impotence. Why, it was of this very syndic that the poet wrote:

> Such a zabb as I have for my own!
> > It must have been made out of wax,
> For the more it is fingered, the smaller it's grown.
> > Yes, excitement's the way to relax
> > > Such a zabb,
> > The best way to make it relax.

> When there's no one to see or to heed
> > He ramps and is wanting to fight,
> But he falls fast asleep in the moment of need,
> > Is there nothing on earth to set right
> > > Such a zabb,
> > Is there nothing to make him go right?

> He spends when I'm wanting to keep,
> > When I'm wanton he closes his hand,
> He sleeps when I wake, and he wakes when I sleep,
> > Is there anywhere else in the land
> > > Such a zabb,
> > In the length and the breadth of the land?

When the crowd heard the maiden's disrespectful quotation, they were extremely shocked, and the crier said: 'You have blackened my face before these merchants, my mistress! How can you say such things of our syndic, a man most wise and respectable, a sage even?' 'If he is a sage, so much the better,' she answered. 'The lesson may not be lost on him. Anyway, sages without zabbs are no use; they ought to run away and hide.'

At this point Shahrazād saw the approach of morning and discreetly fell silent.

But when the six-hundred-and-seventy-eighth night had come

SHE SAID:

In order that the girl should not say anything more about the old syndic, the crier called out again at the top of his voice: 'Gentlemen and generous merchants, the auction is open! I offer this daughter of kings to the highest bidder!' Another merchant who had not witnessed the syndic's discomforture, was charmed by the slave's beauty, and cried: 'I bid nine hundred and fifty dīnārs!' But the girl burst out laughing and said to the man, who had come near to examine her: 'Oh sheikh, have you a good strong chopper at home?' 'I have, dear mistress,' he replied, 'but what of it?' Then said she: 'Because, before there is anything further between us, you should cut off the greater part of that artichoke which you call a nose. Here is a little poem which you ought to know, as it applies to you especially:

> His nose, a tower of ruddled skin,
>   Has two great doorways fringed with hair,
> By which the race of man might enter in
>   And all the world be bare.'

When the large-nosed merchant heard this, he was so angry that he gave a terrific sneeze and, seizing the crier by the collar, began to pummel him in the neck, saying: 'Vile fellow, have you brought this impudent chit to curse at us and laugh at us?' The crier turned in his grief to the girl, and exclaimed: 'As Allāh lives, I have never had such a day as this in all the time of my profession! Can you not hold your tongue and let me earn my money?' Then, to cover the difficulty again, he continued with the auction.

Thus it happened that a third merchant with a very long beard wished to buy the slave; but, when he would have opened his mouth, she broke into a laugh. 'O crier, look,' she said, 'the order of nature is changed in this man; for, although he is a fat-tailed sheep, he carries his tail on the end of his chin! You must not dream of selling me to a man with so long a beard; for intelligence goes in inverse ratio to the length of hair upon the face.'

The crier despaired at this and would no longer carry on the sale.

He took the girl by the hand and gave her back to the Persian, saying: 'She is unsaleable. May Allāh open another door of purchase to you.' 'Allāh is the most generous!' said the Persian to the girl, without showing any sign of annoyance. 'Come, my child, we will find a suitable purchaser somewhere else.' He led her away with one hand and the mule with the other, and, as they went along, the girl shot the black steel-tipped arrows of her eyes among the crowd.

Then for the first time, O marvellous child, you saw young Nūr, and felt the teeth of love biting your heart. You stopped suddenly and said to your master: 'Sell me to him. He is the one I wish.' The Persian turned and saw a youth decked with the beauty of boyhood and elegantly clothed in a plum-coloured mantle. Then he said to the girl: 'This young man was among the crowd and he did not bid. How can I offer you to him against his will? Such conduct would lower your price.' 'I see no difficulty,' she answered. 'I do not wish to belong to anybody except this youth; no other shall possess me.' With that she walked boldly up to Nūr and, giving him a glance charged with temptation, said: 'Why did you not bid? Am I not beautiful?' 'O queen,' Nūr replied, 'is there beauty like yours in the whole world?' 'Why did you not want me, then, when I was put up for sale?' she asked. 'I do not think you like me.' 'Allāh bless you, dear mistress!' cried Nūr. 'If I had been in my own country I would have bought you with all my riches, but here I am a stranger and have nothing save a thousand dīnārs.' 'Offer that and you shall never regret it,' answered the girl. So Nūr undid his belt and weighed over a thousand dīnārs to the Persian in the presence of the kādī and witnesses. To confirm the act of sale, the girl declared: 'I consent to be sold to this delightful youth for a thousand dīnārs.' 'As Allāh lives, they were made for each other!' cried the crowd, and the Persian said: 'May she be a cause of blessing to you, my son! Rejoice together in your youth, for you both deserve this happiness.'

At this point Shahrazād saw the approach of morning and discreetly fell silent.

But when the six-hundred-and-seventy-ninth night had come

SHE SAID:

Young Nūr went to the great khān of the city, followed by the girl with swaying hips, and hastened to hire a room. He excused its meanness to the slave, saying: 'If I were in Cairo I would lodge you in a worthy palace; but I am a stranger here and have nothing for our needs save the trifle which I have paid for this room.' 'Do not be uneasy on that account,' she answered with a smile. 'Take this ring and sell it in the market. Then buy all that is necessary for a feast, with the best food and drink, with fruits and flowers and perfumes.' She handed him a ruby ring of great value and Nūr hurried forth, to return in a short time with the necessary provisions. Kilting his robe, he spread the cloth and carefully prepared the meal. Then he sat down beside the smiling girl, and the two ate and drank without stint. When they were satisfied and the wine had begun its charming business, young Nūr, who was a little intimidated by the bright eyes of his slave and wished to find out more about her before giving way to the tumult of his desires, kissed her hand and said: 'Sweetheart, will you not tell me your name and the country of your birth?' 'I was about to tell you of my own accord, dear Nūr,' she said, and after a moment's pause continued:

'My name is Miriam and I am the only daughter of a powerful Christian King who reigns in Constantine. When I was little, I received the best possible education from skilful masters. I learnt to ply the needle and the bobbin, to embroider silks, to weave carpets and girdles, to work in gold upon stuffs of silver, and in silver upon stuffs of gold. All that might polish the wit or enhance the beauty of woman I learnt speedily, and grew up in my father's palace hidden from the eyes of men. The women, who looked at me with tender eyes, said that I was the marvel of time. Many kings and princes asked for my hand in marriage; but my father rejected all their suits, as he could not bear to be separated from his only daughter, whom he preferred to his life and to all his sons.

'A time came when I fell ill and vowed that, if I recovered, I would go on pilgrimage to a very holy monastery. I was cured, and, in accordance with my vow, set sail with one of my maids of honour. Hardly had we lost sight of land when our ship was attacked and taken by Mussulmān pirates. I was led a slave into Egypt and sold to that Persian merchant whom you saw to-day. Happily he was impotent. Happily also my master suffered a long and dangerous illness while I was in his house and I nursed him with great care and attention. When he recovered, he wished to repay my kindness and begged me to make some request. I at once asked him to sell me, but only to such purchaser as I should choose myself. The generous Persian promised, and took me to the market, where, eye of my heart,

Fate so fixed my choice on you that I could not even see the decrepit oldsters who desired me.'

When she had told him this, the young Christian looked at Nūr out of eyes flaming with the gold of temptation, and said: 'How could I have belonged to another?' With rapid movements she cast aside her garments and came out naked from them. Blessed be the womb that bore her! Then might Nūr understand the gift which had been made to him: a princess soft and white like lawn, distilling a faint amber from every part, as rose distils rose from its sweet nature. He pressed her in his arms and found, in her secret deep, an untouched pearl, rejoicing and inflaming him. He passed his hand over her legs and over her neck and set it to wander through the ways of her hair, while he dropped kisses on her cheek, as many as there are pebbles in the sounding sea. He sweetened his lips with her lips and made his palms resound on the tender resilience of her backside. She let him see an aptitude and amplitude of gifts more than human; for, in her own person, she combined Greek lust with the amorous science of the Egyptian girl, the movements of Araby with the heat of Ethiopia, the shocked candour of Christian women with the deep knowledge of Indian girls, the experience of Circassians with the passion of Nubians, the coquetry of Yaman with the muscular violence of a High Egyptian wench, the narrowness of China with the ardour of Hijāz, and the vigour of Irāk with a more than Persian delicacy. Foldings gave place only to refoldings, kisses to further kisses, and couplings to recouplings, until they fell asleep in each other's arms, a little overcome by the wine of joy. Glory be to Allāh, Who has made the fairest sight in all His world of two lovers lying in bed after delight, hands holding hands, and hearts beating together!

At this point Shahrazād saw the approach of morning and discreetly fell silent.

But when the seven-hundredth night had come

SHE SAID:

When they woke next morning, they began their game again with greater intensity, fuller heat and multiplicity, longer repetitions, wider variations, deeper experience, and riper strength; so that the Christian princess marvelled to see such virtues as the Faithful have, and cried aloud: 'Indeed, my dear, a religion which inspires its holders to such valiance and virtue must be the best, the most human, and the only true of all religions.' She wished to ennoble herself in Islām at once and therefore asked her lover: 'Eye of my heart, what must I do to be ennobled in the Faith? I would become a Mussulmān even as you are; for the peace of my soul is not among the Christians, who make a virtue of horrible continence and honour the emasculate priesthood. They are perverts who know not life, and are unhappy because they are never warmed by any sun. My soul would stay here, where it can flower with all its roses and sing with all its birds. Tell me how I can become a Mussulmān.' Delighted that his great virtue should have converted the princess, Nūr answered her: 'Dear mistress, our religion is simple and has no exterior complications. Sooner or later all infidels will see the excellence of our belief and flock to us of themselves as from darkness to light, as from the incomprehensible to the easy, as from the impossible to the natural. If you wish to wash away the filth of your Christianity, O princess of benediction, you have but to pronounce these few words: "There is no God but Allāh and Muhammad is the Prophet of Allāh!" Even as you make that confession you will become a Believer and a Mussulmān.' Immediately Princess Miriam, daughter of the Christian King, raised her finger and said in a loud voice: 'I pronounce and bear witness that there is no God but Allāh and that Muhammad is the Prophet of Allāh.' Even as she spoke she became ennobled in Islām. Glory be to Him, Who, by such simple means, opens the eyes of the blind and the ears of the deaf, loosens the tongue of the dumb, and lightens the perverted heart! Glory be to the Master of Virtue, the Giver, the sole Good! Amen.

As soon as this important act had been accomplished by the grace of Allāh, the two rose from the bed of their delight, and, after going to the privy, made their ablutions and prayed their prayers. Then they ate, drank, and talked pleasantly with each other, so that Nūr marvelled more and more at the wisdom and knowledge of the princess.

When the time of prayer came in the afternoon, Nūr betook himself to the mosque and Miriam went to walk by Pompey's Pillar. So much for them.

When the Christian King of Constantine learnt that his daughter had been captured by Mussulmān pirates, he despaired well-nigh to the grave and sent noble riders in every direction to buy or take her back, by will or force. But all his messengers returned after a certain time and brought him no news. Therefore the King summoned his chief of police, a little old man, blind of the right eye and lame of the left leg. This official was a very devil among spies; he could unravel a spider's web without breaking the threads, steal a sleeper's teeth without waking him, coax the mouthful from a famished Badawī, and bugger a negro three separate times before the man could turn round. The King ordered this invaluable servant to go through every Mussulmān country, and not to return without the princess. In case of success, he offered him honours and prerogatives without number, and, in case of unsuccess, the impaling stake. The blind and lame old man set out instantly in disguise, and fruitlessly visited the cities of friend and foe until he came to Alexandria.

On the day of which we tell, he had gone with his slaves for a pleasure party to Pompey's Pillar, and Fate led him to meet Princess Miriam as she was taking the air. He trembled with joy and, kneeling before her, would have kissed her hand; but she, who had now learnt the decent virtues of Islām, slapped his ugly face, crying: 'Evil dog, what are you doing upon faithful ground? Do you think that you have any power over me?'

At this point Shahrazād saw the approach of morning and discreetly fell silent.

But when the seven-hundred-and-first night had come

SHE SAID:

'I am not to blame in this matter, O princess,' answered the man. 'I must take you with me to your father, for otherwise the impaling stake awaits me. Your father is dying of despair and your mother never leaves weeping and imagining what may have come to you among these piercers.' 'I have found the peace of my soul here, and only here,' replied the princess. 'I will never leave this blessed land, and, if you do not return at once to my father, I myself will have you impaled on Pompey's Pillar.'

The lame Christian understood that he would never get the princess to follow him of her own free will, so, with a polite 'Excuse me, dear mistress,' he signed to his slaves to seize her. The men bound and gagged her, in spite of the fierce resistance of her nails, and under cover of night carried her on board a ship which was about to set sail for Constantine. So much for the one-eyed wazīr and the Princess Miriam.

Young Nūr could not understand his slave's delay in returning, so he left the khān and wandered among deserted streets to find her. When he came at last to the port, certain watermen told him that a ship had just set sail, carrying a girl who answered in every respect to the description which he gave of Miriam.

Nūr wept aloud, crying: 'Miriam, Miriam, Miriam!' until an old man, touched by his beauty and despair, benevolently asked him the reason of his grief. When Nūr had told him his misfortune, the old man said: 'Do not abandon hope, my child. The ship which has just left is bound for Constantine and we also are bound for that port to-night, my crew of a hundred Mussulmāns and I, their captain. If you sail with me you may recapture the object of your desire.' Nūr kissed the sailor's hand and followed him on board the ship, which immediately set her sails and made for the open sea.

Allāh had written a safe voyage for them and, after fifty-one days, they reached Constantine; but no sooner had they set foot ashore than they were all seized by Christian soldiers and cast into prison by order of the King who wished to avenge his daughter's abduction on all foreign merchants and sailors.

For you must know that Princess Miriam had been returned to Constantine early on that same morning, that the streets had been decorated in honour of her coming, and that all the people had gone forth to meet her. The King and Queen had ridden to the port, followed by all the nobles and dignitaries of the palace; and the Queen, after tenderly embracing her daughter, had anxiously asked her, before all else, whether she was still a virgin or whether, to the misfortune and shame of her house, she had lost that seal which there is no replacing. The princess burst out laughing before all that noble company, and cried: 'That is a silly question, dear mother! Do you think that one can remain a virgin among the Mussulmāns? Do you not know that the Book of our Faith has set it down that no woman shall grow old a maid in Islām?'

At this point Shahrazād saw the approach of morning and discreetly fell silent.

But when the seven-hundred-and-second night had come

SHE SAID:

The Queen had only asked this question publicly in order that the news that her daughter was still a maid might spread quickly and authoritatively among the people; therefore, when she heard Miriam's loud and unexpected answer, she turned bright yellow and fell fainting into the arms of her women, who were all extremely moved by the magnitude of this scandal. Furious at what had happened and raging especially at the freedom with which his daughter had spoken of it, the King felt his gall bladder like to burst in the deeps of his liver, so he hastened the princess to the palace amid general consternation, amid abashed nobles, and amid ancient matrons fuming sourly at the news. He convened a council of state and asked his wazīrs and the patriarchs of the church for their advice. These considered together, and then answered: 'O King, there is only one way to wash the princess from the stain of Islām, and that is to bathe her in the blood of Mussulmāns. You must take a hundred infidels out of the prisons, neither more nor less, and cut off their heads. The blood which flows from their necks must be collected and the princess must bathe in it, as in a second baptism.'

The King ordered the hundred Mussulmāns who had been cast into prison to be brought before him; and among their number came young Nūr. The captain's head was cut off first, and the heads of his crew followed the same way: each time the blood jetting from their trunks was caught in a large basin. Nūr's turn came at last; his eyes were blindfolded, he was placed on the bloody carpet, and the executioner was actually brandishing his sword above the boy's head when an old woman approached the King, saying: 'O King of time, the hundred heads are cut and the basin is full of blood. It were better to spare this young Mussulmān and give him to the service of the church.' 'By Jesus, you are right!' cried the King. 'The hundred heads are there and the basin is full. Take this one and use him for the service of the church.' The old woman, who was the church's chief guardian, thanked the King and, while he and his wazīrs went to see about the strange baptism of the princess, led young Nūr with all speed to the church.

Delighting in the boy's beauty, the old woman made him undress and, giving him a long black robe, a priest's tall bonnet, a large black veil to go over the bonnet, a stole and a broad belt, dressed him in these herself, so that he might know the proper way to wear them. Then she gave him careful instructions in his duty and, for seven days, supervised and encouraged his toil, while he lamented with all his faithful heart the low necessity of such a service.

On the evening of the seventh day, the old woman said to him:

'My son, soon Princess Miriam, who has been purified by a baptism of blood, will come to church to pass all night in praying God for forgiveness. I tell you this in order that you will be able to do her bidding when I am asleep or call me in case she faints in the excess of her contrition. Do you understand?' And Nūr answered, with shining eyes: 'I understand.'

A short while afterwards, Princess Miriam came to the door of the church, dressed in black from head to feet and having her face covered with a black veil. She bowed low before Nūr, thinking him a priest, and then, walking slowly up the aisle, went into a gloomy oratory. Not wishing to disturb the royal devotion, the old woman retired to her bedchamber, leaving Nūr to watch the door.

At this point Shahrazād saw the approach of morning and discreetly fell silent.

But when the seven-hundred-and-third night had come

SHE SAID:

As soon as Nūr heard the old woman snoring like an ogress, he slipped into the church and made his way towards the oratory, which was lit by a little lamp burning before the images. (May the fire of hell destroy them!) He went quietly into the oratory and said in a trembling voice: 'Miriam, I am Nūr.' At first the princess thought she was dreaming, but, after a moment's hesitation, threw herself into her lover's arms. They stayed kissing and not speaking for a long while; then they told each other what had happened since they separated, and gave thanks to Allāh because they had been reunited.

To celebrate that moment, the princess threw off all the mourning garments which her mother had made her wear in memory of her lost virginity. Nūr also cast aside his priestly raiment and, naked, took the naked girl upon his knees. They began a series of extra-ordinary loves, such as that place of lost souls had never witnessed. All night they gave themselves to every diverse passion, proving their violent love again and yet again. Nūr felt his strength come back to him and, in that moment, could have butchered a thousand priests and patriarchs, one after the other. May Allāh exterminate the Infidel and give strength to His true Believers.

Towards dawn the bells of the church began to call the wicked to prayer; so Miriam put on her sorry garments again, with many re-gretful tears, and Nūr redressed himself in the robes of impiety.

(May Allāh, Who sees all, excuse that necessary act!) When they had kissed a last time, the princess said: 'I suppose, dear Nūr, that you have learnt the places and surroundings of this church during the last seven days?' 'I have, dear mistress,' answered Nūr, and she continued: 'Listen carefully, for I have made a plan which will enable us to flee for ever from this land. To-morrow, at the setting in of night, open that door of the church which overlooks the sea, and make your way down to the shore. There you will find a little ship with a crew of ten, and a captain who will take your hand as soon as he sees you. Be very careful to wait until he names your name; above all, do nothing precipitate. Have no fear for me, for I shall find a way to join you, and Allāh will deliver us both out of this cruel people's hands. One other thing, dear Nūr: you can play an excellent trick on the patriarchs by stealing all which is of great account and little weight in the church's treasure, and emptying the chest where they keep the gold which rewards their imposture.' Having repeated her instructions word for word, Miriam left the church and with downcast eyes re-entered the palace, where her mother was waiting to preach to her concerning repentance and chastity. May the Faithful be for ever preserved from chastity, that impure thing; may they never have to repent for ought save harm done to a fellow creature! Amen.

When night began to fall and the old woman to snore, Nūr laid hands on all the precious treasures of that church and stored in his priest's belt all the gold and silver which he found in the patriarchs' coffer. Laden with these righteous spoils, he hastened to the little harbour by the sea, where he found a small vessel whose captain took his hand and spoke to him by name. The man gladly helped him on board with his precious burden, and then gave the signal for departure.

But instead of obeying their captain's order to cast off the ropes from the stakes on shore, the sailors began to murmur. One of them lifted his voice, and said: 'O captain, you know very well that we have received quite different orders from the King. He intends to send his wazīr aboard to-morrow to go on a scouting cruise after certain Mussulmān pirates, who are said to have threatened to capture the Princess Miriam.' Furious at this resistance, the captain cried: 'Do you dare to disobey me?' and with one blow of his sword cut off the speaker's head. The blood-red sabre shone in the night like a torch; but this prompt action did not cow the rest of the men, who continued to murmur. Then, in a flash, they met the same fate as their comrade, dropping their heads one after another upon the deck. The captain pushed their bodies overboard with his foot.

At this point Shahrazād saw the approach of morning and discreetly fell silent.

But when the seven-hundred-and-fourth night had come

SHE SAID:

The captain turned to Nūr, and cried in a voice which brooked no gainsaying: 'Let us be off! Cast off the ropes and set the sails, while I mind the tiller.' As Nūr had no arms with which to defend himself or cut his way to shore, he obeyed as well as his lack of experience permitted; soon the little ship, guided by the captain's firm hand upon the bar, made for the open sea with all sails set and ran before a favourable wind for Alexandria.

As they went, poor Nūr lamented secretly, not daring to complain openly before the sparkling eyes and enormous beard of the captain. 'Alas, alas, that this should have fallen upon my head when I thought that I had finished with my troubles! Each thing is worse than that which went before,' he said to himself. 'If only I understood all this! What will come to me with this bloodthirsty man? Surely I shall not escape alive!' All through the night, as he looked after the sails and tackle, he gave himself up to these desolating thoughts; but at morning, when they were in sight of a town where they might take on new hands, the captain rose of a sudden, as if in great agitation, and cast his turban at his feet. Then, before Nūr's incredulous eyes, he burst out laughing and snatched away his beard and moustaches. In his place on deck there stood a girl as fair as the moon rising over the sea.

Nūr recognised Princess Miriam and cast himself at her feet in admiration and great joy; he confessed how terribly he had feared the captain for his beheading capacity, and Miriam laughed consumedly at his terror. When they had kissed, they returned to their duty of working the ship into harbour. They engaged a sufficiency of sailors and put out to sea again, but the princess, owing to her marvellous knowledge of navigation and ocean ways, continued to give orders during every day. She lay with her beloved each night beneath the naked sky and tasted all delights of him in the sea-fresh air. May Allāh guard them and increase His favour towards them!

Their voyage was favourable and they sighted Pompey's Pillar without mishap. When the ship had come into port and the crew had disembarked, Nūr said to Miriam: 'Now we have come to safety, to a Mussulmān land. Wait here for me a moment while I buy you those things necessary for a decent entry into the city. You have no robe or veil or slippers.' 'Do not be long,' cried Miriam as Nūr disembarked. So much for them.

On the morning after their departure, the Christian King was informed that Miriam had disappeared after her midnight vigil in the church of the patriarchs, that the new worker at the church was also not to be found, that a little ship had put off from the shore, and that the headless bodies of ten sailors had been found on the sand. The King reflected for an hour, with a boiling rage in his belly, and then said: 'If my ship has gone and my daughter has gone, doubtless they have gone together.' He called to him the captain of the port and the one-eyed chief of police. 'You have heard the news,' said he. 'My daughter has returned to the land of the Mussulmāns to find her piercers. If you do not bring her back alive or dead, nothing will save you from the impaling stake. Get you gone!'

The lame old one-eyed wazīr and the captain of the port armed a vessel in all haste and set immediate sail for Alexandria, where they arrived at the same moment as the fugitives. They recognised the little ship lying at anchor and Princess Miriam seated on a pile of cordage upon the bridge. At once they sent a boatload of armed men over the side, who took possession of the princess's boat and, after setting fire to it, gagged the girl and carried her back to their own vessel. Without a moment's delay, they put out again to open sea and, arriving at Constantine, handed the princess back to the King her father.

At this point Shahrazād saw the approach of morning and discreetly fell silent.

But when the seven-hundred-and-fifth night had come

SHE SAID:

When the King met his daughter's eyes, he leaned furiously forward on his throne, shaking his fist at her and crying: 'Woe, woe upon you, you wanton harlot! Surely you have abjured the faith of your fathers and set your heart upon those who took away your seal! Hardly will your death wash out this taint upon our faith and on our name! Make ready to be hanged at the church door.' 'You know my frankness, father,' answered the princess calmly. 'Tell me, then, what crime I have committed in returning to a land where the sun heats all things with his rays and the men are solid men and virtuous? Would it not rather have been a crime if I had stayed here among the priests and eunuchs?' The King answered her not at all, but cried to the executioners: 'Take this vile daughter from before my face and see that she is very long in dying.'

As the executioners were laying hold on the girl, the one-eyed wazīr limped up to the throne and, after kissing the earth between the King's hands, said to him: 'O King of time, allow your slave to make one prayer to you before the princess dies.' 'Speak, faithful old wazīr! Speak, old prop of Christ!' answered the King, and the wazīr continued: 'For a long time your most unworthy slave has felt himself moved towards the charms of our princess. Therefore he begs you not to put her to death but to reward him with her hand in marriage for all his accumulated proofs of devotion to the throne and to the Cross. He is so ugly that the marriage will be sufficient punishment for any faults which the princess has committed. Also, he takes it upon himself to keep her closely guarded in his palace, safe from all possibility of flight.'

'I see no objection,' said the King, 'but, poor old friend, what will you do with this hell-brand? Are you not afraid of horny consequences? By Christ, I would put my finger in my mouth and reflect a long time before doing anything so rash.' 'I have no illusions, sire,' replied the wazīr. 'I know the difficulty of the situation, but I also know very well how to keep my wife away from her excesses.' The King laughed so heartily at this that he shook the throne. 'O halting father,' he cried, 'I can only say that I hope you will soon have two great elephant tusks upon your brow. . . . But remember this: if you allow my daughter to escape and add but one more to her heinous catalogue of offences, your head shall answer for it. Only on that condition do I give my consent.' But the old wazīr accepted the condition and kissed the King's feet.

Then the priests, the monks, and the patriarchs, with all the dignitaries of Christendom, were informed of the marriage; and great feasts were given in the palace. When the ceremonies were over, the disgusting old man made his way into the princess's bedchamber. Surely Allāh will not allow ugliness to touch such splendour! May that stinking pig breathe out his soul before he soils such purity! We will find these two again.

When Nūr returned with a veil, a robe and a pair of citron-yellow leather slippers, he saw a great crowd coming and going about the harbour, and, learning from them that a Christian ship had carried off a girl and set fire to a little vessel lying by the quay, changed colour and fell into a swoon. When he came to himself, he told his sad adventure to the bystanders, who all reproached his conduct bitterly, saying: 'You have got what you deserved! Why did you leave her alone? What need was there to buy a veil or new citron-yellow leather slippers? Could she not have come ashore as she was? Could she not have covered her face with a bit of sail-cloth? As Allāh lives, you have got what you deserved!' While they were thus speaking, the old man who owned the khān where Nūr and the princess had lodged, came up to the group and recognised his young friend. When he had asked and been told the cause of Nūr's grief, he said: 'The veil was superfluous, the new robe was superfluous, and the yellow slippers were superfluous; but to talk about them now smacks infinitely more of superfluity. Come with me, my son. You are young and should be enjoying yourself instead of weeping and despairing for a woman. The race of pretty girls has not yet quite died out in our country; we will be able to find you some expert and desirable Egyptian who will make you forget all about your Christian princess.'

At this point Shahrazād saw the approach of morning and discreetly fell silent.

But when the seven-hundred-and-sixth night had come

SHE SAID:

'Nothing will make me forget my loss, good uncle,' answered Nūr sadly. 'Nothing will console my grief.' 'Then what will you do?' asked the sheikh. 'The ship has gone and your tears avail you nothing.' 'I will return to the city of the Christian King and bear away my mistress by force,' replied the youth. Then said the old man: 'My child, do not listen to these rash suggestions of your soul. Though you succeeded in bringing her away once, avoid a second attempt, and do not forget the proverb: *Not every time you drop a cup will it be worth the taking up.*' 'I thank you for your prudent counsels, my uncle,' answered Nūr, 'but nothing can frighten me; I will get back my love even at the price of dear life itself.' Then, as Fate provided him with a ship ready to set sail for Christian lands, young Nūr embarked in haste.

The old owner of the khān had good reason for his warnings, because the Christian King had sworn, by Jesus and the impious books, to exterminate the race of Mussulmāns on land and sea and, for that purpose, had armed a hundred warships to scour the waters, ravage the coasts, and carry ruin, bloodshed and death into all parts. As soon, therefore, as Nūr's ship came into the sea of the isles, it was taken by one of these warships and towed into Constantine harbour. This happened on the first day of the feast given for the marriage of the one-eyed wazīr with the Princess Miriam. The better to celebrate the wedding and to glut his vengeance, the King ordered all the Mussulmān prisoners to be impaled immediately.

This cruel order was carried out, and, one by one, the Believers were impaled in front of the palace where the marriage was in progress. When none remained to suffer save Nūr, the King looked at him carefully, and said: 'I do not know how it is, but, by Christ, I think this is the same young man whom I spared before to work in the church! He escaped once; how, then, has he returned? . . . Ho, ho! Let him be impaled twice!' At that moment the lame wazīr prostrated himself before the King, saying: 'Sovereign of time, I have sworn an oath to immolate three young Mussulmāns before the door of my house to bring good fortune to my marriage. I pray you let me choose three out of the last shipload.' 'I did not know that you had sworn that oath,' answered the King. 'You might have had thirty instead of three. But now only this one remains; take him in the meanwhile.' The wazīr led Nūr away, meaning to water the threshold of his palace with his blood, but, when he came to reflect that his vow would not be accomplished unless he immolated three youths together, he had him thrown, fasting and in chains, into the stable of his palace until such time as he should procure two more victims.

Now there were, in the wazīr's stable, twin horses of surpassing beauty and noblest Arab breed, whose pedigrees were fastened in little bags round their necks by chains of turquoise and gold. One, called Sābik, was white as a dove; the other, known as Lāhik, was blacker than a crow. These two horses were famous in Christian and Mussulmān lands; they were the envy of kings; but one of them had a white blemish on his eye, which the wisest veterinaries had not been able to cure. The wazīr himself, who was deeply learned in medicine, had tried to remove the mark, but had only succeeded in increasing its density.

When Nūr was thrown into the stable, he saw the blemish on the horse's eye and began to smile. The wazīr noticed this smile and asked the reason of it. 'I smiled at that blemish,' answered Nūr. So the wazīr said: 'I have heard that the men of your race know more about horses and their cure than we. Was it that knowledge which made you smile?' Nūr was extremely skilful in the veterinary art, therefore he replied: 'You are right; there is no one in Christendom who could cure that horse; but I could easily do so. What will you give me to-morrow if the animal is then as bright-eyed as a gazelle?' 'I will give you life and liberty,' answered the wazīr. 'I will name you chief of my stables and horse-doctor to the palace.' 'Undo my bonds, then,' said Nūr. The wazīr undid the bonds, and at once the young man called for suet, wax, lime and garlic; with these he mixed concentrated juice of onions and made a plaster which he applied to the ailing eye. Then he lay down upon a pallet in the stable and left the cure to Allāh.

At this point Shahrazād saw the approach of morning and discreetly fell silent.

But when the seven-hundred-and-seventh night had come

SHE SAID:

Next morning the wazīr limped into the stable and lifted the plaster. His joy and astonishment knew no bounds when he saw his horse's eye made bright again like the light of morning. He put his own mantle upon Nūr and appointed him chief of his stable and first horse-doctor of the palace, assigning him a room above the stalls, separated from his own apartment by a courtyard only. Then he returned to the feasting, without a thought that no man escapes his Destiny or that there are blows in the sleeve of Fate which shall sound down the ages.

That was the seventh day of the festivities; upon that night the hideous old man was due to take possession of his bride. (Cursed be the Far One!) The princess knelt at her window, hearing the last tumult of cries sent up in her honour and sadly dreaming of her beloved, the strong and handsome Egyptian lad who had plucked her flower. Memory brought a great wave of sadness to bathe her soul. 'That foul old man shall never touch me!' she said. 'I will kill myself! I will throw myself into the sea!' As she spoke thus bitterly, she heard a boy's voice below her window, singing Arab songs of separation. It was Nūr. Having finished his work upon the two horses, he had mounted to his chamber and now leaned from his window dreaming of his mistress. This was the song he sang:

> In every cruel region
>   I have sought dead felicity,
> A ghost has led me on;
>   Alas, alas for me!
>
> Crazed by my imagining
>   I think I see
> You in each pretty thing;
>   Alas, alas for me!
>
> Now I think that I hear lutes
>   Distantly, plaintively
> Answer the sighs of flutes;
>   Alas for you and me!

When Princess Miriam heard the faithful heart of her lover singing, she was moved almost outside herself with joy; but, being wise and self-controlled, she dismissed her servants without letting them see anything of her trouble. Then she took paper and pen, and wrote:

'In the name of Allāh, the Merciful, the Compassionate! And after! The peace and blessing of Allāh be upon you, O Nūr!

'Your slave Miriam salutes you; your slave Miriam burns for you! Read and carry out what I shall write.

'Nightfall is the time of lovers; therefore at nightfall take the two horses, Sābik and Lāhik, and lead them outside the city by the Sultān's Gate. I will find means to join you there. If any ask what you are doing, say that you exercise the horses.'

She fastened this letter inside a silk handkerchief and waved it out of the window until she saw Nūr come near. Then she let the handkerchief fall. Nūr picked it up and opened it. He carried the paper to his lips and forehead, after he had read it, to show that he had understood. When night, eagerly expected, had fallen at last, he saddled the two noble horses and, passing from that city without remark, held them outside the Sultān's Gate and waited for the bride.

When Princess Miriam saw her disgusting and one-eyed husband enter her room, she shivered with repulsion; but, as she had a plan to carry through, she controlled herself and, rising in his honour, begged him to be seated by her side. 'You are the pearl of the East and West, my queen,' said the lame old man. 'It is at your feet that I should be.' 'A truce to compliments,' answered the princess. 'Where is the supper? I am hungry and we should eat before all things.'

The old man called his slaves, who instantly set before them great dishes, covered with every delicacy which in the air may be, or swim in sea, or walk the earth in its degree, or grow on any tree. They ate together, and the princess constrained herself to hand her husband morsels, so that he was ravished by her attention, and flattered himself on the unhoped success of his marriage. Suddenly he fell head over heels, unconscious; for Miriam had privily thrown into his cup a pinch of Moroccan banj, capable of stretching an elephant full-length. Allāh does not allow ugliness to soil His beauty.

At this point Shahrazād saw the approach of morning and discreetly fell silent.

But when the seven-hundred-and-eighth night had come

SHE SAID:

As soon as Princess Miriam saw the wazīr rolling at her feet like a swollen pig, she filled two bags with his gems and gold, girt on a sword which had been tempered in the blood of lions, and, covering her face with a great veil, slipped down from the window by means of a cord and arrived in the courtyard unperceived. She hurried out of the city, without being questioned, and, when she saw Nūr holding the horses, ran towards him. She leapt on Lāhik's back, crying: 'Mount Sābik and follow me!' Nūr jumped on the back of the second horse and set off at full gallop after the retreating princess. They rode like that all night until the dawn.

Not until she judged that there was sufficient distance between them and possible pursuit, did Miriam allow the horses to draw breath. They had come to a place refreshed by green meadows, by fruit trees, wild flowers and silver water; as the dawn breeze wooed them to quiet pleasure, the two sat down peacefully side by side and told each other of their separation. When they had drunk of the stream and eaten fruit, they washed and lay down in each other's arms, refreshed, ready, and loving. In one assault they made up for all the loss of abstinence and then went to sleep in the silent air of morning.

At noon they were wakened by the shaking of the earth under ten thousand hoofs. They opened their eyes and saw a whirlwind of dust

hurrying towards them, from which came flashes as of cloudy lightning. Soon they heard the jingling of swords; for a whole army had
come in search of them.

That morning the Christian King had risen early to have news of
his daughter, for he had misgivings concerning her marriage with
one whose marrow had so long since been melted. When he found
her husband unconscious on the floor and no sign of the princess, he
dropped vinegar into the old man's nose and then cried out on him
in a terrible voice: 'O wretch, where is your wife?' 'Oh King, I do
not know,' answered the poor wazīr, as he came to himself. So the
King split the one-eyed head with a single blow of his sword and the
blade came out shining through the jawbone. May Allāh keep that
old man's unbelieving soul for ever on the lowest beach of hell!

Even as the wazīr fell dead, trembling grooms came to inform the
King of the disappearance of Sābik and Lāhik with their new guardian. The King at once understood that his daughter had fled with the
horses, and ordered his three chief nobles to set themselves each at
the head of a band of three thousand men, and take up the pursuit.
He himself collected a troop of patriarchs and put himself at the head
of the combined army.

Seeing this great host approach, Miriam leapt into the saddle and
cried to Nūr: 'Stay behind, I beg you, for I wish to fight with them
alone, though they are as numerous as sand upon the seashore.'
Whirling her sword aloft, she improvised these lines:

> The day of my strength, of my riding
> > Alone;
> Blue single steel, flashing, dividing
> > Alone!

> My hour of breaking terrible towers
> > Alone;
> My hour of black wild riding hours
> > Alone! See me alone!

So singing, she rode out in the face of her father's army.

At this point Shahrazād saw the approach of morning and
discreetly fell silent.

But when the seven-hundred-and-ninth night had come

SHE SAID:

The King rolled his eyes, as if they had seen quicksilver, when he saw her coming. 'By the faith of Christ,' he cried, 'she is mad! She is going to attack us!' He halted his troops and went forward alone to meet her, calling: 'O perverse daughter, do you dare come up against me and all the army of Christendom? Did you renounce all shame when you renounced your God? If you do not sue for my mercy you are most certain of death.' 'What is past cannot be called back,' answered Miriam. 'That is a mystery of Islām. I believe that there is One God, even Allāh, and that Muhammad is the Prophet of Allāh! Though I drink a bitter cup, I will never leave my Egyptian lover!' She made her horse caracole in front of the Christian arms, and sang this song, while she slashed the air with her sparkling sword:

> I call sweet pasture for my blade
> Because he never bade retreat,
> > Retreat, retreat, retreat;
> > Ride if you dare!
>
> I call your heads to the red sand,
> Your hearts to vultures and to crows,
> > To crows, to crows, to crows;
> > Ride if you dare!
>
> I call my sword a cup-bearer
> Because he pours a cheer of myrrh,
> > Of myrrh, of myrrh, of myrrh;
> > Ride if you dare!
>
> I call for my grief's bitter bath,
> My feet tread out a path of blood
> > Like myrrh! The crows retreat;
> > Ride if you dare!

Thus she sang, and then flattered her horse with her hand, whispering in his ear: 'This is your day of race, your day of nobility, O Lāhik!' The son of the sand heard and shivered; he threw himself forward like the North wind, jetting fire from his nostrils. With a terrible roar Princess Miriam charged the left wing of the Christians and, even as her horse went by, mowed off the heads of nineteen riders with her sword. Then she galloped back to the middle of the line, and defied the Christians with loud cries.

Seeing the havoc which she had made, the King called the first of his noble troop-leaders, a mighty warrior as quick as fire, whose name was Bartaut. He was the chief prop of that throne and the first noble of them all, because of his strength and bravery; the essence of his being was knighthood. He advanced towards the King upon a fine powerful horse of famous race; he was armoured in a coat of gold mail as close-knit as the wings of the locust. He carried a sharp destroying sword, a lance like a ship's mast, which could have overcome a mountain in one shock, four keen javelins, and a terrible mace quilled with spikes of steel. Thus weaponed and coated he had the appearance of a tower.

'You see the carnage wrought by this unnatural girl, O Bartaut?' said the King. 'It is for you to conquer and bring her to me, living or dead.' He had his knight blessed by patriarchs covered in motley clothes and lifting crosses above their heads. They read the Gospel over him and called down the blessing of their idols upon him. But we invoke the strength and majesty of Allāh!

When he had kissed the standard of the Cross, Bartaut spurred into the plain, blaring like an elephant and horribly cursing our Faith. May he be damned eternally! On her side, the princess roared like a lioness fighting for her cubs and bore down, bellowing, upon her foe. The two shocked together, mountains moving, furiously head to head and yelling like devils. Anon they separated and feinted; then they came together again in a storm of blows, given and guarded marvellously. Often they were hidden by the dust of their riding; the heat of their approaches was so great that the stones beneath them flamed like coals. This first engagement continued for an hour with equal skill and courage on both sides.

But a time came when Bartaut, who was the first to lose his breath, wished to make an end; therefore he transferred his mace to his left hand and, with his right, hurled one of his javelins at the princess. He growled like thunder as he let it speed. The bright swift flight of that javelin blinded the eyes of men; but the princess turned it aside with the flat of her sword, so that it hissed harmlessly into the sand far off from where they fought.

'Kill, kill!' cried Bartaut, as he hurled his second javelin; but the princess turned that aside also, and the third and the fourth. Mad with humiliation, the Christian knight took his mace back into his right hand and, with a roar like twenty lions, hurled it mightily at his foe. The enormous mass boomed heavily through the air and would have most assuredly broken Miriam to pieces, had she not caught it as it flew, and held it. Glory be to Allāh Who made such a girl! She brandished the mace in her turn, so that the eyes of all the army were dazzled by her strength, and then galloped upon Bartaut, snarling as a she-wolf snarls, her breath hissing like horned vipers. 'A lesson in the use of the mace!' she cried.

At this point Shahrazād saw the approach of morning and discreetly fell silent.

But when the seven-hundred-and-tenth night had come

SHE SAID:

When Bartaut saw her bearing down upon him, earth and sky slipped away from before his eyes, together with all the courage of his heart; he turned his horse and fled, keeping his shield behind him as a protection. But the heroic princess followed hard and, whirling the mace about her head, threw it with all her might. It crashed upon his shield, heavier than bolt from arbalist, and, breaking out four of the knight's ribs, pitched him from the saddle. He rolled in blood upon the dust, tearing at the desert with his nails; but his death was painless, for Azrāïl came to him in that last hour and bore his soul away to compt before Him from Whom no secrets are hid.

Princess Miriam galloped towards the dead man and, leaning low from her horse's back, picked up the fallen enormous lance, and wheeled again. When she had retreated a few paces, she thrust the mighty weapon deep into the earth and, checking Lāhik in face of her father's army, leaned her back against the spear-shaft; then she stayed immobile with lifted head. She was made one body with the horse and with the lance, unbreakable as a mountain, immovable as Fate.

When the Christian King saw Bartaut's end, he beat his face for grief and then called upon Bartūs, the leader of his second troop, an intrepid fighter at hand to hand. 'O Bartūs,' he said, 'go forth and avenge your brother-in-arms!' So Bartūs bowed before him, and galloped his horse against the princess.

She did not move; her horse stood steady as a bridge. She met the scorpion sting of the knight's lance as he rode her down; and the warriors craned forward to see the terrible marvels of that fight.

Shrouded in dust, the foes laid on stupendous blows which groaned in the air before they fell; they raged together in a mist of terrifying taunts. 'By Christ, there is need of all my strength!' panted Bartūs. And, brandishing a murderous pike, he hurled it at Miriam, crying: 'That, that!'

He did not know that Miriam was the incomparable heroine of East and West, the warrior girl of land and sand, the valley and mountain soldier of all time.

She saw the movement and interpreted it; even as the pike brushed her breast, she seized its shaft and cast it back; it passed through her foe's belly and shattered the column of his spine. He fell as a tower falls, and the jangle of his arms sounded all across the plain. His soul hurried to meet the soul of his comrade among the anger of a Mighty Judge.

At this point Shahrazād saw the approach of morning and discreetly fell silent.

But when the seven-hundred-and-eleventh night had come

SHE SAID

Princess Miriam made Lāhik prance about the opposing army, as she cried: 'Where are the slaves? Where are the knights? Where are the heroes? Where is my one-eyed husband? Are you all frightened of a woman, O Christians?'

In mortification and despair the King called his third troop-leader, an illustrious lover of boys called Fasyān the Farter. 'O Fasyān, O bugger of all time,' he said, 'it is for you to go up against this wanton and avenge the deaths of your companions.' Fasyān bowed low in assent, and then galloped out towards the girl, trailing behind him such a thunder of prodigious farts that the sails of a ship might have been filled by them and the hair of little children turned to white.

Miriam came to meet him on Lāhik, swifter than driving hail; the two crashed together, warring hills, and the knight aimed a terrible blow at the princess. She avoided it with ease and broke the lance of her foe in two; then as Fasyān was carried past, she lunged backwards with the heel of her own lance and broke his impious backbone. With a shrill cry she wheeled her horse upon the dying man and, through his open mouth, pegged his head mightily to the earth with her bright weapon.

Seeing their three champions thus slaughtered one after another, the Christian hosts stood in dumb surprise, until they felt the breeze of panic pass above their heads, with a doubt of the humanity of such a girl. Then they turned tail and, giving their chargers to the wind, sought safety in flight. Miriam devoured the distance behind them, cutting off groups of straggling knights, flailing with her sword, filling a thousand cups with death, casting a thousand swimmers into the sea of Destiny. Her heart rejoiced, so that it seemed bigger than the world; some she killed and some she wounded and all she strewed wide upon the earth. The Christian King fled in the middle of his warriors, surrounded by frightened priests and patriarchs, lifting his arms on high, as you may see a shepherd driven in the middle of his flock before a storm. Nor did the princess cease her following and slaughter until the sun veiled his face with a pale mantle.

Then, and then only, Mirian checked her victorious course and returned to her beloved. Nūr had been disquieted for her. He took her in his arms that night and made her forget the fatigues and dangers by which she had saved them in a sweet succession of caresses. Next morning they discussed in what place it would be most pleasant for them to live and, having decided on Damascus, set out for that delightful city. So much for them.

The Christian King returned to his palace in Constantine, with his nose hanging to the ground and the sack of his stomach turned about for the death of Bartaut, Bartūs and Fasyān; he called a council of state and described the shame which had been brought upon him. 'She is the child of a thousand filthy horns,' he said. 'I do not know where she has gone, but we may be sure that it is to some Mussulmān land, for she says that the men of those places are vigorous and untiring. The harlot is a brand straight from Hell; she does not find Christians sufficiently membered for her desire. O Patriarchs, I ask your advice in this distressing matter.' The patriarchs, monks, and nobles reflected for an hour, and then answered: 'O King of time, after all that has happened it only remains for you to send a letter and gifts to the Khalīfah al-Rashīd, who is master of those lands which will receive the fugitive. You must write in your own hand, with every kind of promise and oath of friendship, to persuade him to arrest the lovers and send them back, under escort, to our city. That will not bind us to anything with that chief of Unbelievers; for, when the prisoners are returned to us, we can massacre their escort and forget our promises. It is our custom to forget our promises when they have been made to Unbelievers, to Muhammadans.' Thus spake the patriarchs and counsellors of Christendom: may they be damned in this life and the next, for their little faith and monstrous crimes!

At this point Shahrazād saw the approach of morning and discreetly fell silent.

But when the seven-hundred-and-twelfth night had come

SHE SAID:

The soul of the King of Constantine was as base as any of the souls which counselled him; therefore he did not hesitate to put this treacherous plan into execution. He did not know that perfidy turns sooner or later back to the perfidious, and that the eye of Allāh watches over the Faithful to guard them from their stinking foes.

He took a reed and paper, and wrote a letter in Greek characters to Hārūn al-Rashīd, in which, after repeated phrases of admiration and friendship, he said:

'O powerful amīr of the Mussulmāns, our brothers, I have an unnatural daughter, called Miriam, who has been seduced by a young Egyptian of Cairo and borne away from me and taken into the lands which you most gloriously rule. O powerful amīr of the Mussulmāns, our brothers, I beg you to make inquisition until they are found and then to send them back to me under sure escort.

'In return, I will load that escort with honours and do all that I can to be agreeable to you. Among other things, I promise, as a fruit of my gratitude, to have a mosque built in my capital by any architects whom you shall care to choose. I will send you unimaginable riches, such as the memory of man cannot parallel: girls like hūrīs, beardless boys like moons, treasures that the fires of time shall never touch, pearls, coloured jewels, horses, mares and foals, camels with their young, and an array of mules loaded with the fairest products of our clime. Also, if that be not enough, I will draw close the confines of my kingdom to make your frontiers greater. I seal these promises with my seal, I, Cæsar, King of those who bow before the Cross.'

When he had sealed this letter, the King gave it to the new wazīr by whom he had replaced his old one-eyed servitor, and said to him: 'If you obtain audience of this Hārūn fellow, address him thus: "O very powerful Khalīfah, I come to claim our princess; she is the object of my mission. If you hearken favourably to our request, you can count upon my master to send you gifts of great price." ' To make his messenger still more zealous, he promised, in case of success, to load him with prerogatives and give him the princess for his wife. Then he dismissed him with a final recommendation to place the letter in the Khalīfah's own hands.

After a long journey, the ambassador arrived in Baghdād, where he rested for three days. Then, having enquired his way to the palace. he solicited an audience and was led into the dīwān. There he threw himself before the Khalīfah and kissed the earth three times between his hands, before giving the letter to him. Hārūn al-Rashīd unsealed the letter and, after reading it, showed himself favourable to the request which it contained, though he knew that it proceeded from a King who knew not Allāh. He wrote commands to the governors of all his provinces, insisting that the two fugitives should be found and sent at once to his court, and promising the direst punishment in cases of disobedience. Messengers, on horseback and on racing dromedaries, carried these orders to the walīs of each province, and, in the meanwhile, the Khalīfah entertained the Christian ambassador and his suite within the palace.

When the princess had routed the army of her father with her single sword and had pastured the vultures with the three knights who had dared to come against her, she set out with Nūr for Syria and came without accident to the gates of Damascus. Since, however, they had journeyed by short stages, stopping at each fair place to give themselves up to love, they arrived at Damascus some days after the Khalīfah's riders had brought the order for their arrest to that city. Being quite ignorant of what awaited them, they fearlessly gave their names to the police spies and were immediately arrested by the walī's guards. These guards made them turn their horses' heads, before they had set foot in the city, and galloped them, by ten days of forced marches, across the desert to Baghdād. When they arrived, worn by fatigue, they were led between soldiers into the dīwān.

At this point Shahrazād saw the approach of morning and discreetly fell silent.

But when the seven-hundred-and-thirteenth night had come

SHE SAID:

As soon as they knew themselves in the august presence of the Khalīfah, they prostrated themselves before him and kissed the earth. The chamberlain on duty cried: 'O Commander of the Faithful, these are Princess Miriam, daughter of the Christian King, and Nūr, her ravisher, son of the merchant Crown of Cairo. They were both arrested at the gate of Damascus by the walī of that city.' The Khalīfah looked at Miriam and was delighted by her. 'Are you Miriam, daughter of the Christian King?' he asked, and she replied: 'I am Princess Miriam, slave to one man only, to the Prince of Believers, the Protector of the Faith, the descendant of the Lord of Messengers.' Pleased with this reply, the Khalīfah turned to Nūr and was charmed by him also. 'Are you young Nūr, son of the merchant Crown of Cairo?' he asked, and the youth answered: 'I am Nūr, slave to the Commander of the Faithful, the prop of empire, the warrior of the Faith.' Then said the Khalīfah: 'How did you dare to ravish this Christian princess, in defiance of the law?' So Nūr asked leave to speak, and told the Khalīfah the whole of his adventure in its smallest details. But nothing would be gained by repeating it in this place.

Then al-Rashīd turned to Princess Miriam, saying: 'Your father has sent this ambassador with a letter of his own writing in which he assures me of his gratitude and of his intention to build a mosque in Constantine, if I send you back to his dominion. What have you to say?' Miriam threw back her head and answered in a voice both proud and sweet: 'O Commander of the Faithful, you are Allāh's representative on earth; you are the stay of the law of the Prophet (upon whom be prayer and peace!). I am now a Mussulmān, believing in the unity of Allāh; I make my profession in your presence and say: There is no God but Allāh and Muhammad is the Prophet of Allāh. How then, O Prince of Believers, can you send me back to those infidels, who set up equals to Allāh, who believe in the divinity of Jesus the son of man, who adore idols, and revere the Cross? They even render superstitious worship to many who have died and passed into the burning anger of our God. If you were to give me up to these Christians I would accuse you in the Day of Judgment, before Allāh and before His Prophet, your cousin (upon whom be prayer and peace!). For in that day the grandeurs of this world shall be as nothing.'

The Khalīfah exulted in his soul when he heard Miriam's profession, and answered with tears in his eyes: 'My daughter, I pray that Allāh will never put it in my heart to deliver a Mussulmān who believes in Him into the hands of infidels! May He guard you and spread His blessing and mercy about you, and increase the conviction of your faith within you! For your bravery you may ask me what you will. I swear to refuse you nothing, even to the half of my kingdom. Refresh your eyes, O Miriam, lift up your heart and banish every care. . . . Would it please you to be married to this young man, son of our servant Crown, the Cairene merchant?' 'Why would it not please me, O Prince of Believers?' answered Miriam. 'Has he not bought me? Has he not plucked that within me which there was to pluck? Has he not risked his life again and again for my sake? Has he not given peace to my soul by his revelation of the Faith?'

At once the Khalīfah summoned the kādī and witnesses, and had a contract of marriage drawn up for the two lovers. Then he called the Christian ambassador to him, saying: 'You have seen with your eyes and heard with your ears that I cannot agree to the request of your master. The Princess Miriam is a Mussulmān and belongs to us. I will not commit an action for which I could not account to Allāh and His Prophet on the Last Day. It is written in the Book of Allāh: "Power shall never be given to the Infidel over the Believer." Return to your master and tell him what you have seen and heard.'

At this point Shahrazād saw the approach of morning and discreetly fell silent.

But when the seven-hundred-and-fourteenth night had come

SHE SAID:
When the ambassador realised that the Khalīfah would not give up the Christian King's daughter, he dared, through spite and pride, to lose his temper. 'By Christ,' he cried, 'were she twenty times a Mussulmān, she must go back to her father. If not, he will lay waste your kingdom and cover your land, from the Euphrates to Yaman, with ravaging troops.'

'How?' cried the Khalīfah. 'Does this Christian dog dare to threaten us? Let his head be cut off and set up at the entrance to the city! Let his body be crucified as an example to all ambassadors!' But Princess Miriam exclaimed: 'O Commander of the Faithful, do not soil the glory of your sword with this dog's blood! I will punish him myself!' With that she snatched the Christian ambassador's sword from its scabbard and, cutting off his head with a single stroke, cast it from the window. She spurned the body with her foot and signed to the slaves to drag it out.

Marvelling at her promptness, the Khalīfah put his own mantle upon her and dressed Nūr in a robe of honour. He loaded them with rich presents and, when they expressed the desire, gave them a magnificent escort to Cairo and letters of recommendation both to the walī of Egypt and to the ulamā. Thus Nūr and Princess Miriam returned to the old folk in Egypt, and the merchant Crown became very proud when he saw his son come back thus royally married. He pardoned Nūr for his previous conduct and, in his honour, gave a feast to all the notables of Cairo, who vied with each other in finding splendid gifts for the young couple.

For long years Nūr and Miriam lived together in delight, stinting themselves in nothing, eating well, drinking well, and coupling heavy, dry, and long. They were honoured in the midst of tranquillity until the Destroyer came to them, the Separator of friends, Who overturns all palaces and towers, and gluts the hunger of the tomb. Glory be to the Only Living, Who knows not death, Who holds in His hands the keys of the Visible and Invisible! Amen.

When King Shahryār had heard this tale, he half rose and cried: 'O Shahrazād, these heroic deeds have altogether delighted me!' Then he sank back among the cushions, saying: 'I think after that you can have no more stories to tell me. I will reflect now concerning my duty to your head.' 'There is no time to be lost,' said Shahrazād to herself, when she saw the King's eyebrows bending together; so aloud she cried: 'This heroic tale is indeed admirable; but it is nothing to certain others which I would tell you, if you would give me leave.' 'What are you saying, Shahrazād?' asked the King. 'What tales can these be, for you to imagine them more admirable than the last?' 'The King shall judge for himself,' replied Shahrazād with a smile. 'For the moment, to pass the rest of our watch this night, I will only tell you a short and easy anecdote. It is taken from the Recitals of Generosity and Conduct.'

At once she began:

THE RECITALS OF GENEROSITY AND CONDUCT

Salāh al-Dīn and His Wazīr

IT is related, O auspicious King, that the wazīr of the victorious Salāh al-Dīn had a young Christian boy among the number of his favourite slaves, who was so beautiful and tender that the eyes of all men loved him. One day, as the wazīr was walking with this child, he was seen by Salāh al-Dīn and commanded to approach. The Sultān, casting a delighted glance upon the boy, asked the wazīr whence he came. 'From Allāh, my lord,' answered the wazīr a little uncomfortably. As Salāh al-Dīn went on his way, he smiled and said: 'Now, O our wazīr, you have found a way to control us by the beauty of a star and prison us in the enchantment of a moon.'

This made the wazīr reflect, and he said to himself: 'I cannot keep this child now that the Sultān has remarked him.' So he prepared a rich present and called the Christian lad to him, saying: 'O youth, I swear by Allāh that I would never consent to be separated from you were it not necessary.' Then he gave the boy the present, and added: 'You will carry this to the Sultān, and be yourself part of the present, for I give you up to our master.' Lastly he gave him a note to hand to Salāh al-Dīn, on which were written these lines:

> I had a soul once, even I,
> My lord,
> But now unstarred and earthy it.
> Here is a white moon for your sky,
> My lord,
> Because your sky is worthy it.

This gift pleased Salāh al-Dīn intensely, and, as he was greathearted by nature, he recompensed the wazīr for his sacrifice by loading him with riches and favour, and making him feel on all occasions that the two were friends.

At this point Shahrazād saw the approach of morning and discreetly fell silent.

But when the seven-hundred-and-fifteenth night had come

SHE SAID:

It happened that the wazīr soon afterwards acquired a most delightful and accomplished girl for his harīm, and, from the moment she came, she drew his heart towards her. But, before he would allow himself to place his affection with her as he had placed it with the boy, he said to himself: 'It is possible that the fame of this new pearl of mine will reach the Sultān's ears. It will be better for me to send her to him as a gift before I grow to love her. The sacrifice will be less and the loss not so cruel.' He called the girl to him and gave her a richer present than before, telling her to carry this to the Sultān and to say that she herself was part of the gift. He also gave her, for Salāh al-Dīn, these lines traced on a piece of paper:

> Dear lord, there was a silver moon,
> And a gold sun came after soon
> > Into the royal sky;
> Now they will dance, a moon and sun,
> In pretty constellation
> > To please a royal eye.

For this the wazīr's credit redoubled with Salāh al-Dīn, who lost no opportunity of showing his gratitude. Thus it was that the wazīr soon had hosts of envious enemies, who tried to damage his credit in order to bring about his fall. With statements and hints they attempted to make Salāh al-Dīn believe that the wazīr still had a great inclination towards the Christian boy and that, when the fresh breeze of the North brought memories of their old-time walks, he would desire the boy and call to him with all his soul. They let it be understood that he bitterly repented his gift, biting his nails and tearing at his teeth in spite. Instead of listening to these unworthy reports, Salāh al-Dīn, who had confidence in his wazīr, cried angrily to the calumniators: 'Let these cursed tongues be still or the heads which hold them shall answer for it!' Then, as he was also just, he added: 'Nevertheless, I will put your lies to the proof, so that your barbs may return against you.' He called the boy, and learning that he could write, said to him: 'Take paper and pen, and write to my dictation.' The boy therefore wrote, as if coming from himself, the following letter to the wazīr:

'Old master of my love, you must know from your own feeling

how great is my tenderness for you, how sweet the memory of our delights. I am sad in this palace, for nothing here can make me forget your goodness, and the majesty of the Sultān prevents me from tasting his favours. I pray you find some way of taking me back; for the Sultān has never been alone with me and you will find me as I was.'

The Sultān sent a little slave, who gave the letter to the wazīr, saying: 'The Christian lad, who was once yours, gave me this letter for you.' The wazīr took the letter, looked at it for a moment, and then, without unsealing it, wrote on the back:

> I, who am wise, will not be setting
>   My body whole
> In lion's teeth, or lifting the red coal
>   Of cast regretting,
> Nay, my soul given, I'll not bear the fretting
>   Which was that soul.

The Sultān exulted when he had read this answer, and took care to recite it before the fallen faces of those envious others. He called the wazīr to him and, after renewed assurance of friendship, asked him: 'O father of wisdom, can you tell us how you come to have such control over yourself?' Then said the wazīr: 'I never let my passions come even to the threshold of my will.'

But Allāh knows all!

Then Shahrazād said: 'Now, O auspicious King, that I have told you how a wise man's will may conquer his passion, I wish to tell you a story of passion itself.' And she continued:

The Lovers' Tomb

ABDALLĀH, son of al-Kaisī, tells this story in his writings.

He says:

I went one year on pilgrimage to the holy House of Allāh and, when I had accomplished my rites, returned to pay a second visit to the tomb of the Prophet (upon whom be the prayer and blessing of Allāh!). As I sat one night in a garden not far off from the tomb, I heard a voice singing sweetly in the silence, and gave all the attention of my charmed ears to its song:

> I am a nightingale singing of tears,
>> She is a dove who will not sing or say;
> I am a lost black way,
>> She shines and disappears;
> I am a night of fever years,
>> She is the day.

Then came silence, and I was looking about me for this passionate singer when I saw him coming towards me, a youth of heart-ravishing beauty whose face was bathed with tears. I could not help crying: 'By Allāh, a most beautiful young man!' and stretching out my arms to him. He looked at me, and asked: 'Who are you, and what do you want?' Bowing before his beauty, I answered: 'What would one want of you save to look at you and give thanks to Allāh? I am your slave, Abdallāh ibn Maamar al-Kaisī, whose soul desires to know her lord. Your song has troubled me and the sight of you has carried me away. I would sacrifice my life for you!' The youth looked at me—oh, but his eyes were dark!—and bade me sit beside him. I came closer, my spirit trembling within me, and he said: 'Since your heart is concerned with me, I will tell you what has happened. I am Utbah, son of al-Hubāb, son of al-Mundhir, son of al-Jumāh al-Ansārī. Yesterday, as I made my devotions in the mosque of my tribe, many beautiful women came in, swaying with their hips, and guarding, as it were, a young girl whose every charm exceeded theirs, though they were altogether murderous in beauty. This moon came up to me without being noticed in the crowd, and said: "Long, O Utbah, have I sought this opportunity to speak with you. Would you be married to one who loves you and desires you as a husband?" Before I could answer she disappeared and slipped away among her companions, who took her with them outside the mosque and were lost in the crowd of pilgrims. Since then I have not been able to find her in spite of all my searchings; but my soul and my heart are with her and, even were I among the delights of Paradise, I would know no pleasure without seeing her again.'

At this point Shahrazād saw the approach of morning and discreetly fell silent.

But when the seven-hundred-and-seventeenth night had come

SHE SAID:

His downy cheeks glowed red as he spoke and my love glowed redder still; therefore I said to him: 'O Utbah, O my cousin, put your hope in Allāh and pray to Him to pardon your transgressions! I am ready to help you, with all my power and means, to find the girl; for my own soul is drawn towards the charm of you, and I would gladly do even more to see your eyes rest upon me with content.' So saying I pressed him to me and kissed him as brother kisses brother, all night I calmed the trouble of his sweet soul, and those moments were delicious but unsatisfied.

Next morning I took him to the mosque and made him enter before me. We waited until noon, at which hour the women had come before; but, to our grave disappointment, though the women came they had not the girl among them. Seeing my friend's despair I begged him to wait until I had questioned the other damsels. I went up to them and learned that the girl was a virgin of noble birth, one Raiyā, daughter of al-Ghitrīf, chief of the Banū Sulaim. 'O women of good omen,' said I, 'why has she not come with you to-day?' 'How could she have come?' they answered. 'Her father, who has given his protection to pilgrims across the desert from Irāk to Mecca, returned yesterday with the riders of his tribe to the Euphrates, and took his daughter with him.' I thanked the women for their news and returned to Utbah. 'The tidings are not the best that I could wish,' I said, and told him that Raiyā had returned to her tribe with her father. 'But, O Utbah, O my cousin,' I added, 'do not be downhearted, for Allāh has given me riches beyond counting and I am ready to spend them all to pleasure you. From this moment, I make your cause my own. Follow me, if you please.' So he rose and followed me to the mosque of al-Ansārīs, which was his own mosque.

We waited until the congregation was full, and then I addressed the people in these words: 'O Ansarite Believers here together, what is your considered opinion of Utbah and Utbah's father?' They answered with one voice: 'He is of a noble family and a noble tribe among the Arabs.' So I continued: 'Know, then, that Utbah, son of al-Hubāb, is consumed by a violent passion. I have come to beg for your help in bringing about his happiness.' 'We shall be glad,' said they, and I went on: 'In that case you must come with me to the tents of the Banū Sulaim, to the abode of their chief al-Ghitrīf, and ask the hand of his daughter for your cousin.' Utbah and I and all that gallant assembly mounted our horses and rode without drawing rein until we reached the tents of the riders of al-Ghitrif, where they had pitched them six days' journey across the desert.

When al-Ghitrif saw us coming, he came to the door of his tent to meet us; we greeted him and said: 'O father of Arabs, we come to beg hospitality.' 'Be welcome beneath our tents, O noble guests!' he answered, and gave his slaves the necessary orders for our reception. The slaves spread mats and carpets in our honour, and sheep and camels were killed to make us a feast.

At this point Shahrazād saw the approach of morning and discreetly fell silent.

But when the seven-hundred-and-eighteenth night had come

SHE SAID:

But when the moment came for sitting down to that feast, we refused; and I addressed the sheikh al-Ghitrif in the name of all: 'By the holy bond of bread and salt and by the faith of Arabs, we will not touch your meat until you have granted what we ask.' 'And what do you ask?' said al-Ghitrif. 'We have come,' I answered, 'to solicit the hand of your noble daughter, Raiyā, for that brave, good, victorious and illustrious young man, Utbah, son of al-Hubāb al-Ansāri, son of al-Mundhir, son of al-Jumāh.' The face and eyes of Raiyā's father changed, but he answered calmly: 'O brother Arabs, there is but one who can answer the demand of the illustrious Utbah; it is for her to speak. I will go to her now.' So saying he rose from among us, very yellow in the face, with an anger burning him which gave the lie to his words.

When he found his daughter in her tent, she was frightened by his expression, and asked: 'Why are you so angry, my father?' He sat down silently beside her and then, as we heard afterwards, said to her: 'I have given hospitality to al-Ansāris who have come to ask your hand in marriage for one of them.' 'Al-Ansāris are one of the noblest families of the Arabs,' she answered. 'Your hospitality was fitting. Which of them wishes to marry me?' 'Utbah, son of Hubāb,' he answered, and she exclaimed: 'He is a known young man and worthy to mingle his blood with ours.' But al-Ghitrif cried out in a fury: 'What are you talking about? Have you had anything to do with him? I have sworn to my brother to give you to his son; none but my nephew shall enter the direct line of my nobility.' 'Then what will you answer al-Ansārīs?' said she. 'They are very noble Arabs and exceedingly punctilious on all matters of honour and precedence. If you refuse me to them you will draw down their vengeance on you and all our tribe. They will think that you despise them, and never pardon you.' 'That is true,' agreed her father, 'but I will wrap up my refusal by asking an exorbitant dowry. The proverb says: "It is easy not to marry a daughter if you ask enough for her."'

He left the girl and returned to us, saying: 'Dear guests, the daughter of our tribe makes no objection to the marriage, but she demands a dowry worthy of herself. Could any of you pay the price of this incomparable girl?' 'I can!' cried Utbah; so al-Ghitrīf continued: 'Very well, then, my daughter demands a thousand bracelets of red gold, five thousand golden dīnārs of Hajar coinage, a necklace of five thousand pearls, a thousand squares of Indian silk, a dozen pairs of yellow leather boots, ten sacks of Irāk dates, a thousand head of cattle, a mare of the tribe, five chests of musk, five flasks of rose essence, and five coffers of ambergris. Do you consent?' 'I consent, O father of the Arabs,' answered Utbah. 'Nay, I will increase the list.'

I returned to Madīnah with my friend, and we succeeded, after some difficulty, in gathering together all the things which had been demanded for the dowry. I spent my money freely and with more pleasure than if I had been buying for myself. We returned to the tents of the Banū Sulaim and gave the things to al-Ghitrīf, so that the sheikh was obliged to receive as guests all al-Ansārīs who flocked together to make their compliments on the marriage of his daughter. The feasting went on for forty days and, during that time, numerous sheep and camels were killed and every variety of meat was kept simmering in large cauldrons, so that none might go hungry.

After the forty days we prepared a sumptuous palanquin on the back of two camels in file and placed the new bride within it; then we joyfully set out, followed by a whole caravan of camels bearing presents. My dear friend Utbah exulted to think the day would soon come when he should be alone with his beloved; he never left her for a moment during our travels, except to come down out of the palanquin for a few minutes and delight me with his grateful conversation.

At this point Shahrazād saw the approach of morning and discreetly fell silent.

But when the seven-hundred-and-nineteenth night had come

SHE SAID:

I rejoiced and said in my soul: 'O Abdallāh, you are Utbah's friend for ever! By denying yourself, you have touched his heart; surely one day your sacrifice will be more than rewarded. One day you will know his love in its most desirable and exquisite form.'

When we had only one day's march left us before Madinah, we halted at night in a little oasis. Peace was there and the moon laughed down upon our joyful company; twelve palm trees stood slim above our heads and answered the song of the night wind with the rustle of their girlish leaves. Even as those who made the world of old, we rejoiced in the quiet hour, the cool water, the green sappy grass, and all the sweetness of the air. But, alas, even were a man winged he could not escape from Destiny. My friend Utbah was due to drink his cup to the lees, and at one draught. We were roused from our sleep by a terrible attack of armed riders, who fell upon us with cries of hate. These were men of the tribe of Banū Sulaim, sent by al-Ghitrīf to carry back his daughter. He had not dared to violate the laws of hospitality under his own tents, but had waited, according to desert custom, to attack us after we had moved away. He counted without the valour of Utbah and our warriors. We met their assault with great valour and, after killing many of them, put the rest to flight. Yet Utbah, my friend, took a lance-thrust in the battle and, when he had dragged himself to camp, fell dead in my arms.

Young Raiyā gave a great cry and fell across the body of her lover; she mourned all night, and in the morning we found her dead of a broken heart. May Allāh take the two of them into His mercy! We dug a grave in the sand and buried them side by side; then we returned in deep grief to Madinah. I finished what I had to finish in that place and returned to my own country.

Seven years later, desire came to me to go on pilgrimage once more and my soul yearned to visit the tomb of Utbah and Raiyā. When I came to the grave, I found it shaded by a fair tree of an unknown kind, which al-Ansārīs had piously planted. I sat down weeping upon a stone in the shadow of the tree, and said to those who were with me: 'My friends, tell me the name of that tree which weeps with me over the grave of Utbah and Raiyā?' And they answered: 'It is the Tree of Lovers.' Dear Utbah, would that I rested with you in the peace of God beneath the shadow of that tree!

Such is the tale of the Lovers' Tomb, O auspicious King, said Shahrazād, and then, as she saw King Shahryār saddened by her story, she hastened to tell him of the marriage and divorce of Hind.

The Divorce of Hind

I T is related that young Hind, daughter of al-Numān, was the most beautiful child of her time; she had borrowed her eyes, together with her slimness and lightness, from the gazelles of Allāh. The fame of her reached the ears of al-Hajjāj, governor of Irāk, and he asked for her in marriage. Her father would only let her go for a dowry of two hundred thousand silver dirhams to be paid before marriage, and a further two hundred thousand to be paid in case of divorce. Al-Hajjāj accepted these conditions and took Hind to his house.

Now the governor of Irāk, to his great grief, was quite impotent. He had reached the world with an ingrowing zabb and obstructed anus, and, being thus deformed, had refused to draw the breath of life, until the devil appeared to his mother in human form and advised her to rear him on the blood of two black goats, a black buck, and a black snake. The mother followed this prescription and the child lived; but deformity and impotence, which are the gifts of Satan and not of Allāh, stayed with him always.

For a long time after he had taken her to his house, al-Hajjāj did not dare to approach Hind except by day; nor would he touch her in spite of his great desire to do so. Hind soon understood the reason for this conduct and lamented her case before her women.

One day al-Hajjāj came to feast his eyes upon her beauty as was his custom; she stood with her back turned to the door, looking at herself in a little mirror, and singing:

> Oh, take away this purple dress
> And robe me in my camel's-hair;
> For I of flaming Arab blood
> Am mated to a gelded mule.
> The flutes are in the wilderness,
> The black tents of my tribe are there;
> Oh, save me from the multitude,
> O desert death, be merciful.

When al-Hajjāj heard Hind compare him with a mule, he left the chamber, a prey to sharp disappointment, without his wife having noticed either his arrival or departure. He sent for the kādī, Abdallāh ibn Tāhir, to divorce him, and Abdallāh appeared before Hind, saying: 'O daughter of al-Numān, al-Hajjāj Abū Muhammad sends you these two hundred thousand dirhams and has charged me to carry out the formalities of divorce in his name.' Then cried Hind: 'Thanks, O thanks to Allāh! My vow is lifted and I am free to return to my father's house! O son of Tāhir, you could have announced no better news than my liberation from this importunate dog. Keep the two hundred thousand dirhams as a reward for your most auspicious tidings.'

At this point Shahrazād saw the approach of morning and discreetly fell silent.

But when the seven-hundred-and-twentieth night had come

SHE SAID:

Soon afterwards, the Khalīfah Abd al-Malik ibn Marwān heard tell of Hind's incomparable beauty and wit, and sent to woo her for his wife. She answered him by a letter in which, after praise to Allāh and respectful greeting, she said: 'O Commander of the Faithful, a dog has dirtied the platter by sniffing at it with his nose.' The Khalīfah read this letter with shouts of laughter, and sent the following reply: 'O Hind, if the dog has dirtied the platter, we will wash it seven times and then purify it by the use to which we put it.'

Hind saw that the Khalīfah still desired her in spite of the difficulty, so she accepted him on one condition. This condition she wrote in a letter, as follows: 'O Commander of the Faithful, I will only set out on my journey to come to you if al-Hajjāj walks barefoot beside my camel and leads it all the way.'

The Khalīfah laughed even more and sent an order to al-Hajjāj that he should lead Hind's camel by the bridle. The governor of Irāk dared not disobey this unpleasant order, so he went bare-footed to Hind's dwelling and took hold of her camel by the bridle. Hind mounted into her litter and all along the road made delightful game of her camel-boy. She said to her nurse: 'Nurse, open the curtains of the palanquin a little.' The nurse put aside the curtains, and Hind threw a golden dīnār down into the mud. Then she leant out and cried to him who had been her husband: 'O chancellor, please will you pick up that silver piece?' Al-Hajjāj picked up the coin and returned it to Hind, saying: 'It is a gold dīnār, not a silver piece.' Hind laughed and replied: 'Glory be to Allāh, Who can change silver into gold in spite of the mud into which it has fallen!' Hajjāj recognised another humiliation in these words and became red with angry shame; but he lowered his head and stifled his resentment, for Hind was now the bride of the Khalīfah.

When she had made an end of this little tale, Shahrazād fell silent, and King Shahryār said: 'These anecdotes are very pleasant, Shahrazād. Now I should like to hear some altogether marvellous story. If you do not know one, tell me so at once.' But Shahrazād cried: 'Was there ever a more marvellous tale than the one I have in mind to tell you now? Is it permitted?' 'It is permitted,' answered Shahryār.

The Strange Tale of the Mirror of Virgins

AND SHAHRAZĀD SAID TO KING SHAHRYĀR:

It is related, O auspicious and high-minded King, that there was once, in the antiquity of time and the passage of the age and of the moment, a Sultān in the city of Basrah, whose name was Zain. He was an admirable youth, delightful to look upon, generous and valiant, noble and powerful; but, in spite of those gifts which set him above his time, he was a reckless prodigal and expert dissipater of gold, who, by large gifts to his greedy young favourites, by expenses on women of every hue and size, and by continual purchase of new virgins at exorbitant prices, had at last exhausted even the immense treasures laid up by his warlike ancestors. One day his wazīr kissed the earth between his hands, announcing that the chests of gold were empty and that there was not wherewithal to pay for the refreshment of the morrow; then, fearing that the stake would be his portion for such unwelcome news, he retired as quickly as he might.

When the young Sultān learnt that all his riches were consumed, he repented that he had not set aside a portion for the black days of Destiny. He grew very sad, and said to himself: 'Nothing remains to you, O Zain, except secret flight. You must leave the favourites whom you love, your girl mistresses, your women, your affairs of state; you must abandon the throne of your fathers to whomsoever comes to take it. It is better to be a beggar upon the road of Allāh than a penniless and disrespected King. The proverb says: *The grave is a finer place than poverty.*' Revolving such thoughts as these, he waited for nightfall to disguise himself and slip from the palace. He was about to take up a staff and depart upon his way, when Allāh the All-seer, the All-hearer, brought back into his mind the last recommendation of his father. Before dying, the old King had said to him: 'Above all do not forget, my son, that, should Fate turn against you on any day, you will find a treasure in my Hall of Manuscripts which will enable you to make head against all misfortune.'

Zain had forgotten these words, but now he remembered them and ran to the Hall of Manuscripts. He opened the door and entered, trembling with joy; but the more he looked and moved and examined, the more he overturned papers and registers, and muddled the annals of the reign, the less did he find gold or the smell of gold, silver or the smell of silver, or anything which looked at all like a precious stone. His breast could not contain his despair when he found nothing; he began to crumple and hurl the records of his ancestors in all directions and was stamping them under his feet in rage when he suddenly felt an object of hard metal beneath them. He drew this forth and, finding it to be a heavy casket of red copper, hastened to open it. Inside was nothing but a small piece of parchment, sealed with his father's seal. Though Zain felt very disappointed, he opened the message and read these words: 'Take a pickaxe, my son, and go to such and such a part of the palace; dig in the earth and trust in Allāh.'

Then said Zain: 'It seems that I am to be a labourer and not a beggar. Yet it is my father's will and I must not disobey.' He went down into the garden and, taking a pickaxe from against the wall of the gardener's house, carried it to the place mentioned in the message, a cellar which stretched below the palace.

At this point Shahrazād saw the approach of morning and discreetly fell silent.

But when the seven-hundred-and-twenty-first night had come

LITTLE DUNYAZĀD rose from her carpet, crying: 'Your words are very sweet and fresh and savoury, dear sister.' Shahrazād kissed the little one between the eyes and answered: 'They are nothing to those which I would give you to hear to-night, if our wise and exquisitely-mannered King permitted it.' 'I permit it,' said Shahyrār, and Shahrazād thus continued:

Zain took a lighted torch into the cellar and, by its illumination, began to tap the flooring with the handle of his pickaxe. When he discovered a place which gave back a hollow sound, he started to dig strongly and removed several of the paving stones without finding the least sign of treasure. Therefore he leaned against the wall and said to himself: 'Since when has a King had to follow his Destiny into the bowels of the earth, instead of calmly and unlaboriously waiting for it?' Nevertheless, when he had recovered his breath, he continued rather hopelessly to remove the squares, until he came at length upon a heavy slab of white stone hidden beneath them. He lifted this and found under it a trap door fastened down by steel locks. He broke the locks with his pickaxe and opened the door.

He found himself at the top of a magnificent white marble stairway which descended into a vast square hall, built of white Chinese porcelain and crystal. The ceilings and the columns of this hall were of sky-blue lazulite. When he came down into it, he saw that it contained four tables of nacre, upon each of which stood ten great urns, alternate porphyry and alabaster. 'I wonder what those jars contain,' said he. 'Probably my dead father filled them with old wine. If so it should, by now, be supremely excellent to drink.' He mounted on one of the tables and lifted its lid from an urn. O surprise! O joy! O dance! It was filled to the brim with gold dust. Zain plunged in his hand without being able to reach the bottom of the jar, and brought it out gilded and rippling as if with sunlight. He lifted the lid from a second urn and found it crammed with dīnārs of gold and golden sequins. He examined each of the remaining forty urns and found that those of alabaster were all filled with gold dust, and that their porphyry sisters were heavy with dīnārs and gold sequins.

Zain trembled, expanded, blossomed with delight; he sang for joy and thrust the torch into a niche of the crystal wall; he pulled one of the alabaster urns towards him and let the gold dust run down over his head, over his shoulders, over his belly; he bathed with greater delight than he had ever known in the most delicate hammām. 'Sultān Zain, Sultān Zain,' he cried, 'do you remember that you were about to take a beggar's staff and wander upon the roads of Allāh? Lo, this golden blessing has descended on your head because you trusted in the Giver's generosity and did not hoard His gifts! Refresh your eyes, calm your dear soul; fearlessly spend this second treasure and trust in Him!' As he was speaking he had tilted the contents of all the alabaster urns on to the porcelain floor; next, from the urns of porphyry, he poured tinkling showers of dīnārs and sequins upon the heap of bright dust, until the urns were exhausted and the harmonious crystal walls had ceased their echo. Finally he plunged like a lover into this gold heap, while the torchlight splashed all the polished hall of white and blue with yellow stars and flames from the bosom of that cold golden fire.

When the young Sultān had bathed in this gold and thus forgotten the misery which had threatened him, he rose, shining like a gold boy, and examined every detail of the hall with the utmost curiosity. He marvelled most that his father had been able to hollow out and build the place so secretly that none had heard of it. At last his eyes noticed in a small corner, tucked away between two slim crystal columns, a little coffer, like, but much smaller than, the one he had found in the Hall of Manuscripts.

At this point Shahrazād saw the approach of morning and discreetly fell silent.

But when the seven-hundred-and-twenty-second night had come

SHE SAID:

He opened it and found a jewelled key wrought in gold. 'Perhaps this key opens the locks which I broke,' said he, 'but, if that be so, how were they locked from the outside? This must be the key to something else.' He examined all the walls very carefully and soon found, in one of the china panels, a keyhole, into which he inserted the key. He tried it and it turned. A door opened and led him into a second and more marvellous hall. It was made entirely of green earthenware with a gold gloss, so that he seemed to be in the hollow heart of a sea emerald. There was no decoration in this chamber, but, in the middle, under the dome, six girls stood silent on pedestals of solid gold and shone from themselves as if they had been made of moonlight. Zain went towards them in his surprise, to see them better and to greet them; but he found that they were not living and had each been carved out of a single diamond.

'Where in Allāh's Name can my father have got such things?' cried Zain. He examined the girls more closely and saw that they ringed a seventh pedestal on which was no diamond girl, but a piece of silk which bore this message in coloured threads:

My son, these diamond girls cost me many pains to get; but, though they are beautiful, you must not think that they are the most beautiful. There is a seventh girl, infinitely brighter and fairer, who is worth more than a thousand of the others. If you wish to see that seventh and place her upon the waiting pedestal, a labour of love from which my death prevented me, you must go to the city of Cairo. There you will easily find an old faithful slave of mine, called Mubārak. Tell him what has happened and he will lead you to the place of the incomparable seventh girl. You will acquire her and rejoice your eyes for ever. The blessings of Allāh be upon you, O Zain!

When he read these words, the young Sultān said to himself: 'I will go to Cairo without delay, for the seventh girl must be wonderful indeed if she is worth a thousand of the others.' He left the underground hall and, returning with a basket, carried some of the dīnārs and gold sequins to his own apartment. He worked late into the night, journeying to and fro unseen, until a goodly pile of the gold lay ready to his hand. Then he locked the door of the vault and retired to bed.

Next morning he called his wazīrs, amīrs, and the nobles of his kingdom, and told them that he intended to go into Egypt for a change of air. He appointed his grand-wazīr, the old man who had feared the stake for his unwelcome news, to govern the kingdom during his absence. Then he departed without ceremony, attended only by a small band of chosen slaves, and, by Allāh's grace, arrived without adventure at the city of Cairo.

He could find no one of the name of Mubārak save the syndic of the markets, a very rich merchant who lived generously in a palace, the gates of which were ever open to the poor. Sultān Zain had himself conducted to this palace, where he was greeted by many slaves and eunuchs. These led him across a vast courtyard into a magnificent hall, where Mubārak waited upon a silken couch. As Zain approached, the old man rose in his honour and begged him to be seated, saying: 'Dear master, blessing has come into my house!' He spoke in friendly fashion to his guest on this and that, without being so rude as to ask his name or the reason of his coming. 'O my host,' said Zain, 'I have come from Basrah seeking one Mubārak, a faithful slave of the dead King, my father. I am called Zain; I am the present Sultān of Basrah.'

At this point Shahrazād saw the approach of morning and discreetly fell silent.

But when the seven-hundred-and-twenty-third night had come

SHE SAID:

Mubārak rose from his couch and threw himself at Zain's feet, crying: 'Praise be to Allāh Who has brought master and slave together! Speak and I shall hear! I was your dead father's slave. The man who has a son does not die. O son of my master, this palace is your palace, and I am yours.' Zain raised Mubārak and told him the whole story of his adventure. But nothing would be gained by repeating it in this place. 'So you see,' he added, 'I have come to Egypt that you may help me to find the seventh diamond girl.' 'I am ready in all loyalty,' answered Mubārak, 'I am still a slave; my life and my goods belong to you. But before we set out in search of this diamond girl, my lord, it would be better for you to repose after your journey and allow a feast to be given in your honour.' 'You say that you are a slave,' objected Zain, 'but you are free, because I make you so. You say that I had better rest, but I am not tired. Let us set out at once.' Seeing that the Sultān's mind was made up, Mubārak kissed the ground before him a second time, in sign of thanks for his freedom, and then rose, saying: 'Have you reflected on the dangers which we may encounter, my lord? The diamond girl is in the palace of the Old Man of the Three Isles; and the Three Isles are forbidden to all who do not know the right conjuration. I am one of the few who may enter, but the undertaking is dangerous.' 'I am ready for all danger in this quest,' answered the Prince. 'My breast is puffed with courage; I will seek the Old Man of the Three Isles.'

Mubārak ordered his slaves to make preparation, and the two departed after ablution and prayer; for many days and nights they rode across plains and deserts, and over meadowland filled only by grass and the presence of God. Their eyes met ceaseless novelty upon the way and their surroundings were more strange as they advanced. They came at last to a prairie of inviting freshness, where Mubārak turned to the slaves, saying: 'You will wait here, guarding the horses and the food, until we return.' Then he begged Zain to follow him, and said: 'My lord, there is no might or help save in Allāh! We are now on the threshold of those forbidden lands which hold your diamond girl. We must go on alone and without hesitation. We must be strong.' After walking for a long time, they came to the foot of a high mountain which barred all the horizon with its bulk.

'What power will take us over this mountain, Mubārak? Who will give us wings to reach its top?' asked the Prince, and Mubārak replied: 'We have no need of climbing or of wings.' He took from his pocket an old book in which unknown characters were traced backwards, looking like the feet of ants; from this he read verses in a strange tongue before the mountain, waving his head from side to side the while. As soon as he had finished, the mountain rolled back on both sides, splitting in the middle and leaving a passage broad enough for one man. Mubārak entered this first and went forward resolutely, leading the Prince by the hand. After an hour of terrible journey they came to the other end of the split, and, as soon as they had gone out from it, the mountain came together again. So perfect was the join that it left no crack for the point of a needle.

They found themselves on the borders of a lake as great as the sea; and far off upon it were three green islands. The shore on which the two adventurers stood was gay with flowers and trees which bent over to smile into the water; birds made melody among scented shrubs, and the heart was uplifted by that place.

Mubārak sat down and said to Zain: 'My lord, those islands are our destination.' 'But how can we reach them?' asked Zain. 'Take no thought for that,' the other answered. 'They are as fair as the gardens of Allāh and soon a boat will come to take us to them. Only, my lord, I must beg you to make no sign of astonishment at whatever you may see. Above all, be very careful not to start back, even if the boatman takes some unexpected shape. Finally, if you say a word after we have gone on board, the boat will carry us both beneath the waves.' 'I will keep my tongue between my teeth,' answered Zain earnestly. 'I will imprison any surprise within my soul.'

At this point Shahrazād saw the approach of morning and discreetly fell silent.

But when the seven-hundred-and-twenty-fourth night had come

SHE SAID:

As they were speaking, a boat appeared so close to them upon the lake that they did not know whether it had come up out of the bosom of the water or floated down from the sky above. It was made all of red sandalwood; its cordage was of silk, and it had a mast of fine amber. The sailor in charge wore the body of a man, but his head was an elephant's head, with two great ears falling and dragging on the ground like Hagar's train. The boat stopped five yards from the shore, and the elephant-headed boatman lifted each of the companions in his trunk and set them, light as feathers, in his vessel. Then he plunged his trunk into the water and, using it as oar and rudder both, put off from the shore. He raised his great ears and gave them to the wind above his head, so that they bellied out as if they had been sails. He kept turning them to catch the breeze and sent the vessel forward across the lake like a large bird. When they had come close to one of the islands, he took his two passengers again in his trunk and, after setting them gently upon the sand, put out and disappeared.

Mubārak took the Prince by the hand again and led him into the interior of the island, following a path paved with jewels of every colour. They walked forward until they came to a magnificent palace built up of emeralds, surrounded by a moat, whose outer bank was planted at intervals with trees so tall that they shaded the whole building. Access to a great door of solid gold was given by a tortoiseshell bridge, six fathoms long and three broad.

Not daring to cross this bridge, Mubārak halted and said to the Prince: 'We can go no further. If we wish to see the Old Man of the Three Isles we must make a magic conjuration.' He drew four bands of yellow silk from beneath his robe and, keeping two himself, gave two to the Prince. When he had fastened one band round his waist and placed one on his back, he bade Zain do the like. Then, drawing two light silk prayer-rugs from the same receptacle, he spread them out on the ground and sprinkled grains of musk and amber upon them, while he muttered incantations. Finally he seated himself cross-legged on one of the rugs and, when the Prince had occupied the other, said to him: 'I will now call upon the Old Man of the Three Isles. God grant that he be not angry when he comes! For I must confess I am not at all sure how he will receive us. If he be not pleased by our coming he is capable of appearing as a horrible monster; if, on the other hand, he is glad of our visit he will assume the form of a very charming old man. In whatever shape he arrives, you must rise in his honour, without leaving your rug, and greet him most respectfully. Then you must say: "O powerful master, O King of kings, behold we have entered into the majesty of your jurisdiction and passed through the door of your protection. I am your slave, Zain, Sultān of Basrah, son of that King whom the Angel of Death has carried into the peace of our Lord. I come to solicit of your power and generosity the same favours which you accorded to your servant, my father." Then, if he asks you what you wish, you will answer: "My lord, I wish the seventh diamond girl." ' 'I will remember,' answered Zain.

Mubārak began to make conjuration, fumigation, recitation, adjuration, and incantation, until the sun was covered by a shield of black cloud, from which sprang a red tongue of lightning, followed by a clap of thunder. A furious wind blew towards them and in it they heard a terrible crying; the earth trembled as it will tremble upon the last day when Isrāfīl shall shake it apart.

Zain was very frightened by these things, though he would not let his terror show. 'It is a bad sign,' he said to himself; but Mubārak read his thought and smiled, saying: 'On the contrary, the omens are excellent; all goes well, by Allāh's grace.'

At this point Shahrazād saw the approach of morning and discreetly fell silent.

But when the seven-hundred-and-twenty-fifth night had come

SHE SAID:

Even as he spoke, the Old Man of the Three Isles appeared before them in venerable human form, but so beautiful that he might only be surpassed by Him to Whom all beauty and all power belong. He went up to Zain, smiling as a father smiles upon his son; and the Prince rose in his honour upon the rug and bowed to the earth before him. He made those compliments and greetings which Mubārak had advised and then explained the object of his coming to the isle.

The old man smiled even more pleasantly, and then said: 'I loved your father very greatly. Each time he came to visit me I gave him a diamond girl and had her carried to Basrah myself, lest the camel-boys should damage her. But you must not think that I have any less friendship for you, O Zain. It was without solicitation that I promised your father to protect you and persuaded him to write those two messages which you found. I am very ready to give you the seventh diamond girl, who is worth a thousand of the others, but I ask for something in exchange.' 'As Allāh lives, my lord, all that is mine is yours,' answered Zain, 'and I include myself in saying all that is mine.' 'But what I ask is not an easy thing, my child,' returned the old man with a smile. 'I do not think that you will ever be able to find it. . . . I require you to bring me a girl of fifteen who is at once beautiful and a virgin.' 'If that is all you wish, my lord,' cried Zain, 'the thing is easy. There is nothing commoner in our land than beautiful virgins of fifteen.'

At this the old man laughed so heartily that he fell over on his backside; when he had a little recovered from his mirth, he said: 'Are they so easily found?' 'I can bring you ten such,' answered Zain. 'I have already had hundreds of such girls in my palace and much enjoyed depriving them of their quality.' The old man laughed again and then said with a most pitying glance: 'My child, what I demand is so rare that no one has been able to satisfy me yet. If you thought that the girls you had were virgins, you were the more mistaken. Women have a thousand ways of creating belief in a maidenhead which is not there; they have fooled the greatest tumblers of all time. As I see that you know nothing about such things, I will furnish you with a certain means of testing a girl's state, without her knowledge, without touching her, without undressing her. This is important, as the virgin I want must never have been handled by a male or shown those parts of herself to the eye of man.'

'By Allāh, he is mad!' said Zain to himself. 'If it is as difficult to tell a maiden as he pretends, how can it be done without seeing or touching?' He reflected for quite a while, and then cried: 'I see it now! I will be able to tell them by their smell.' 'Virginity has no smell,' answered the old man smiling. 'By looking them straight in the eye, then,' cried Zain again. 'An eye has no virginity,' said the old man. 'How then am I to tell, my lord?' asked Zain, and the other answered: 'That is just what I have promised to show you.'

He then disappeared from their eyes and returned in a moment carrying a mirror in his hands. 'O Zain,' said he, 'I ought to tell you that it is impossible for a simple man to know whether a woman is pierced or a virgin; that is a knowledge belonging only to Allāh or His Elect. As I cannot pass on my skill in this matter, I give you a mirror, which is a surer judge than any human. When you find a girl of fifteen, whose beauty is perfect and whom you either suppose or have been told to be a virgin, look in this mirror and you will see her naked image. Have no fear of gazing upon it, for only a direct glance from man destroys virginity. If the girl be not a virgin, her history will appear to you great and yawning like a gulf, and the mirror become stained as with fog. But if Allāh has kept the child's maidenhead, the thing will seem no larger than a peeled almond, and the mirror remain pure and untarnished.'

At this point Shahrazād saw the approach of morning and discreetly fell silent.

But when the seven-hundred-and-twenty-sixth night had come

SHE SAID:

The old man gave the magic mirror to Zain, adding: 'I hope that Destiny will allow you to find the fifteen-year-old girl whom I require. Do not forget that she must be entirely beautiful; for virginity means nothing without beauty. Also, take great care of the mirror, for its loss would bring misfortune upon you.' Zain reassured the Old Man of the Three Isles and, after taking leave of him, accompanied Mubārak to the lake. The man with the elephant's head conveyed them across the water in his boat; the mountain opened to let them pass; they found the slaves in charge of their horses, and returned without adventure to Cairo.

Prince Zain consented to rest for some days in Mubārak's palace from the fatigues and emotions of their quest. 'Surely the Old Man of the Isles is very simple,' he thought, 'to give that diamond girl in exchange for a human virgin. Does he imagine that there are no maidens left on earth?' When he was rested, he called Mubārak to him and said: 'Let us rise up now and go to Baghdād and Basrah, where little virgins are as many as locusts. We will choose the fairest of them all and exchange her for the diamond girl.' 'Why go so far, my lord?' answered Mubārak. 'Are we not in Cairo, the city of cities, the dwelling of wit, the preferred meeting place of the world's beauty? Take no further thought for the search; I myself will undertake it.' 'How?' asked the Prince, and the other continued: 'I know a crafty old woman who is very expert in the matter of little virgins; she will find us what we want. I will bid her bring together all the fifteen-year-olds in Egypt and make a first choice of them, so that our task may be easier. I will promise her a generous commission and, whether the parents consent or no, she will leave no child untried in all Egypt. We will only have to choose the fairest Egyptian from her choice; if she is common we will buy her, if she is of noble family we will ask her hand in marriage and you can wed her in name alone. Then we will go to Damascus, Baghdād and Basrah, and, after testing the virginity of our candidates in the mirror, either purchase or marry those who most strike us with their beauty. When we have collected all that is fairest from each city, we can make a final choice

with the assurance of having found the greatest marvel of our time.'
'Your plan is excellent!' exclaimed Zain. 'Your wisdom is only
equalled by your eloquence.'

Mubārak sought out the unparalleled old bawd of whom he had
spoken—she could have taught subtlety to the Devil—and, after
giving her a large commission in advance, told her his requirement.
'The girl is destined to wed my master's son,' he said, 'therefore you
need have no fear for your reward.' 'Calm your heart and refresh
your eyes, dear master,' answered the old woman, 'I will consecrate
my life to the finding. Also I have several fifteen-year-old virgins on
my lists, all of incomparable beauty and noble birth. When I bring
them before you one by one, I warrant you will find it hard to choose
out the most excellent moon in that array.'

Thus spake the old woman in her ignorance of the mirror, and set
out confidently to haunt the roads and avenues of her experience. She
lost no time in bringing a first choice of fifteen-year-old girls to
Mubārak's palace, and led them in one by one, covered in veils and
modestly casting down their eyes, to the hall where Zain and Mubārak sat with the mirror. If you had seen all those lowered eyes,
candid faces, and little shy figures, you could not have doubted the
purity of any; but none of these things deceived the mirror. Zain
looked in the glass each time that a girl passed before him, and her
reflection appeared naked to his eyes. Every part of her body was
visible; each detail of her little history was thrown into relief as if it
had been presented to him in a casket of diaphanous crystal.

As each girl passed, poor Zain was far from finding a tiny object
like a peeled almond; it astounded him to think into what gulfs his
unaided judgment might have thrown the unfortunate Old Man of
the Isles. As he did not wish to bring shame on any by discovering
that which Allāh had hidden, he never told the old woman the cause
of his dissatisfaction, but contented himself with wiping the fog off
the mirror. Spurred by the hope of gain and not in the least discouraged by her first failure, the old woman brought a second choice,
a third and a fourth and a fifth; but the result was always the same.
Multitudes and multitudes of Egyptian intimacies you saw, O Zain,
of Coptish intimacies, of Nubian, Abyssinian, and Sudanese; of
Moroccan intimacies, of Arab and Badawī; intimacies of girls in
every way beautiful and delightful; but never one that looked at all
like a peeled almond!

After this disappointment the Prince and Mubārak journeyed into

Syria and hired a magnificent palace in the fairest quarter of Damascus. Mubārak entered into negotiation with all the old women whose business was with marriage and the like; and these old women, on their part, entered into negotiation with every kind of little girl, tall and short, Mussulmān, Jew, and Christian. Knowing nothing of the magic mirror, they confidently brought their candidates into the hall where Zain waited; but, for all their modest mien, unsullied looks, quick blushing cheeks, and fifteen years, the Syrians were no more successful than the Egyptians. The old women were obliged to retire one after the other, trailing their noses to the ground.

'It is extraordinary,' thought Zain, and to Mubārak he said: 'This does not seem to be the country for our purpose. Let us try elsewhere. I cannot rest for thinking of the diamond girl and I will in no wise give up my search.' 'I do not think that anything will be gained by going elsewhere than Irāk,' answered Mubārak. 'There, surely, we shall find what we require. Let us prepare the caravan and depart for Baghdād, the City of Peace.'

At this point Shahrazād saw the approach of morning and discreetly fell silent.

But when the seven-hundred-and-twenty-eighth night had come

SHE SAID:

Allāh had decreed that Mubārak and the Prince should arrive safely in Baghdād, without meeting robbers on the way. As in Damascus, their first care was to hire a palace; the one which they chose stood upon the Tigris and had a garden like the Khalīfah's Garden of Delights. They collected a large train of slaves and kept up a daily display of hospitality to all and sundry, ever distributing the broken meats among the poor. Now there was in that quarter a certain Imām named Abū Bakr who was a vile and common man, hating the rich simply because he was poor. Misery hardens a base heart, just as it ennobles a lofty heart. When he saw an abundance of Allāh's gifts blessing the cloth of the new comers, he took them in aversion. One day, he went to the mosque for afternoon prayer and stood among the assembled people, crying: 'O Believers, it is my duty to inform you that we have two strangers in our quarter, who ostentatiously spend great sums of money every day, simply to offend the eyes of the poor. We do not know these strangers; we do not know for certain that they are robbers who have come to spend in Baghdād the vast sums which they have stolen from the widow and orphan of their own country. But I adjure you, in the name of Allāh and by the merits of our lord Muhammad (upon whom be prayer and peace!), to be on your guard against them and not to accept any of their false hospitality. For I am sure that, if our master the Khalīfah learnt that there were such men in our quarter, he would hold us responsible for their ill-doing and chastise us because we sent him no warning. I wash my hands of the matter; I will have nothing to do with the strangers or with those who accept their bounty.' 'You are right, O Abū Bakr!' replied the congregation with one voice. 'We will send a complaint to the Khalīfah and he shall enquire into their antecedents.' Then the people came out of the mosque, and the Imām returned to his own house to meditate a means of harming the two strangers.

Mubārak soon learned what had happened at the mosque and began to dread the threats of Abū Bakr, believing that, if the news became noised abroad, it would frighten away the old women. Therefore he put five hundred golden dīnārs into a bag and went to the Imām's house. Abū Bakr opened to his knocking and crossly asked him what he wished. 'O Abū Bakr, O our master the Imām,' answered the visitor, 'I am Mubārak, your slave. I come to you from the amīr Zain, who has heard of your great learning, piety, and vast influence in the city; he wishes me to present his homage and say that he places himself entirely at your service. As a mark of good will, he sends this purse of five hundred dīnārs, as one loyally making a gift to his sovereign, and wishes to be excused for the smallness of the present when compared with the worth of the receiver. But, if Allāh wishes, he will be able in the future to prove in some more substantial way the force of his obligation. He feels that he is lost in the boundless desert of your benevolence.'

When Abū Bakr saw the purse and had made sure of the contents, his eyes became very soft, and he answered: 'Dear Lord, I humbly implore pardon from the amīr, your master, for any unconsidered language which I may have used about him. I repent most bitterly if I have at all been lacking in respect for him. Dear friend, I pray you to be my mouthpiece to speak to him of my contrition, my readiness to serve in anything. To-day I shall repair in public my quite accidental fault, and thus, I trust, earn a little of the amīr's regard.' Then said Mubārak: 'I praise Allāh for that He has filled your heart with good intent towards us, O Abū Bakr, our master! I beg you not to forget to honour our threshold with a visit, after the prayer, and ennoble the minds of us with your society. We know well, the amīr Zain and I, that blessing will accompany your holy feet into our poor dwelling.' So saying, he kissed the Imām's hand and returned to the palace.

Abū Bakr went again to the mosque and cried among the Faithful: 'O all Believers, O my brothers, there is none, however noble, who has no enemy; envy fastens like an asp to the feet of those whom Allāh has blessed. I stand before you to-day in order to free my conscience and to assure you that the strangers, about whom I spoke yesterday with so little knowledge of my subject, are both, by a singular chance, endowed with a great nobility, exquisite tact, every virtue, and inestimable qualities of soul. The enquiries I have made have proved to me that one of them is an amīr of exceedingly high rank, whose presence is an honour to our quarter. I call upon you to reverence these two strangers when you meet them, and to accord them the great respect which is their due. The peace of Allāh be upon you!'

Thus Abū Bakr destroyed the effects of his first speech, and then hastened to change into a new robe, whose skirts trailed upon the ground and whose sleeves fell nobly to his knees. Thus adorned, he made his way to Zain's palace and entered the reception hall.

At this point Shahrazād saw the approach of morning and discreetly fell silent.

But when the seven-hundred-and-twenty-ninth night had come

SHE SAID:

He bowed to the earth before the Prince, who answered his greeting with great cordiality and bade him be seated beside him upon the dīwān. Food and drink were served and Mubārak joined in the eating and drinking. All three talked together like old friends. Delighted by the Prince's geniality, the Imām said: 'O my lord Zain, do you think of lighting our city with a long visit?' Now, in spite of his youth, the Prince was shrewd and quick to seize an advantage, so he replied: 'My intention is to remain in Baghdād until my object is accomplished.' 'And what is your noble object?' asked Abū Bakr. 'Your slave would be delighted to help you in any way, for he is quite devoted to your interests.' Then said Prince Zain: 'My object is marriage, O venerable sheikh. I want to find a girl of fifteen at once entirely beautiful and quite a virgin. Her beauty must be without its equal among the youth of her time and her maidenhead past cavil, both within and without. I came to Baghdād to find such a one, after having searched in Egypt and Syria without success.' 'Such things are rare and very difficult to find,' said the Imām. 'If Allāh had not set me in your path, your stay would have been endless and the old women would have spent their time in vain. But I know exactly where such a pearl may be found; I will tell you, if you will allow me.'

Zain and Mubārak both smiled at this. 'O holy Imām,' said the former, 'are you sure of the virginity of the girl you mention? And if so, how are you sure? If you have seen that thing in the girl, she is no longer a virgin in my sense; for true virginity resides as much in keeping the seal invisible as in keeping it unbroken.' 'Indeed, I have not seen it myself,' answered the Imām, 'but I will cut off my right hand if it be not as I say. Also, my lord, how can you or any man be certain before the marriage night?' 'That is easy,' said Zain, 'I have but to look at her for one moment, dressed and veiled.' Out of respect for his host the Imām did not wish to laugh, but he answered: 'Our master must be more than ordinarily skilled in the science of reading faces, if he can determine the virginity of a strange girl by regarding her through her veil.' 'Yet it is as I say,' retorted Zain. 'If it be possible, let me see the girl; I will reward your services at their just value.' 'I hear and I obey!' replied the Imām and at once set out upon his quest.

Abū Bakr had told the truth when he said that he knew of a girl who would meet the Prince's requirement. She was the daughter of the chief of the Imāms of Baghdād; her father had brought her up far from the eyes of men, in simple seclusion as the Book commands. She had blossomed like a flower in his home, having never looked upon ugliness. She was white and elegant, she had come without flaw from the mould of beauty; her eyes were black, her little hands and feet were fragments of the moon. She had all the grace of a circle on one side and of a straight line on the other; but that which lay between her columns, having never been seen, cannot be described. Perhaps the mirror, by Allāh's aid, may be able to tell us of it in the future.

Abū Bakr made his way to the house of his chief and, after the usual greetings, made him a long speech, sprinkled with texts, on the advisability of marrying little girls as soon as they were ripe. He explained the whole situation, and thus concluded: 'This amīr is noble, rich, and generous, ready to pay any dowry. He makes only one condition: that he shall first look upon the child for a moment when she is dressed and veiled and covered with the izār.' The girl's father reflected for an hour, and then said: 'I see no objection.' He called his wife, and said to her: 'O mother of Latīfah, rise up now and take our daughter and walk with her behind Abū Bakr, our good son; for he will lead you to a palace where Fate awaits the child.'

At this point Shahrazād saw the approach of morning and discreetly fell silent.

But when the seven-hundred-and-thirtieth night had come

SHE SAID:

The wife of the sheikh of the Imāms veiled herself and sought her daughter, saying: 'O Latīfah, your father wishes you to see the streets for the first time to-day.' When she had combed and dressed the child, she went out with her and followed ten paces behind Abū Bakr to the palace, where Zain and Mubārak waited in the reception hall. O Latīfah, you went in with wide dark eyes, astonished above their little veil. You had never seen a man, save your venerable father, and you did not lower your eyes, for you knew not false modesty or false shame, or any of those false things by which girls learn to take the hearts of men. You were shy, but you looked straight forth with your black eyes, so that Zain's reason fled from him. He had never seen even the shadow of your beauty among the women of his palace or among the girls of Egypt and Syria. The reflection of you showed naked in the mirror and he could see, nestled like a little white dove between your thighs, a miracle sealed with the unbroken seal of Sulaimān (upon whom be prayer and peace!). He looked and rejoiced, O Latīfah, for it had in every way the appearance of a peeled almond. Glory be to Allāh, Who keeps the keys of every treasure for His Faithful!

As soon as Prince Zain knew that he had found the girl he needed, he sent Mubārak to enter into negotiations for immediate marriage. Mubārak and Abū Bakr interviewed the child's father and, after formally obtaining his consent, led him to the Prince's palace. Kādī and witnesses were sent for, a marriage contract was written out, and the wedding was celebrated with unusual pomp, with feasting and rich gifts to the poor of that quarter. As the other guests were departing, the Prince kept Abū Bakr and said to him: 'To-night we leave for a far country. Here are ten thousand golden dīnārs, a preliminary reward for your services. When I return to Basrah, I will be able to show my gratitude in some better way. Perhaps you would care to become my chamberlain.' After giving his hand to the Imām to kiss, he commanded his folk to set out. The girl was placed in a camel litter; Mubārak went first, Zain brought up the rear, and the whole caravan started for the Three Isles.

Their destination was very far from Baghdād and the journey took long months to accomplish. Every day the Prince felt himself drawn more and more by the charms of the little virgin who was his wife. He loved her with all his heart for her natural sweetness, and tasted true passion for the first time. He thought bitterly of the day when he should hand her over to the Old Man of the Three Isles, and would certainly have carried the girl to Basrah if he had not sworn to do otherwise.

At length they entered the forbidden country and came to the isle by the same miraculous stages as before. After greetings and compliments, Zain gave back the mirror and presented the veiled girl to the old man. The latter took the mirror but did not use it, for his eyes were mirrors as he looked upon the child. After a long glance he threw his arms round Zain's neck, and kissed him with effusion, crying: 'I am indeed satisfied with your diligence; this damsel is all that I required. Her beauty is the one perfection of beauty upon earth, her virginity is above reproach, she is sealed as with the seal of our master Sulaimān (upon whom be prayer and peace!). Return now to your own place and, when you enter the green earthenware hall, you will find the seventh diamond girl standing among the six others, outdoing them a thousandfold with her brightness. Now tell this child that you are leaving her and that all bonds are broken between you.'

When Latīfah heard this, she sighed and wept, for she had grown to love the handsome Prince. And Zain wept also, as he explained the contract which he had made with the Old Man of the Isles. 'You are divorced,' he said, and went sobbing from that place, while Latīfah swooned despairingly.

Zain and Mubārak returned to Basrah, and, throughout the journey, the younger man bitterly reproached himself for having deceived his bride. He would not be comforted, and stood desolate amid the great rejoicings which broke out in Basrah at his coming. He withdrew from the feasting and, in spite of Mubārak's insistence, even refused to go down into the green underground hall and look at the seventh diamond girl. Mubārak was now wazīr. He went on beseeching his master until at last he consented to visit the statues. Zain crossed the porcelain and crystal hall, whose floor flamed yellow with the rest of the gold, and entered the gallery of green earthenware.

At this point Shahrazād saw the approach of morning and discreetly fell silent.

But when the seven-hundred-and-thirty-first night had come

SHE SAID:

He saw the six diamond girls standing in their places; but, on the seventh pedestal, there stood a naked smiling child, brighter than any diamond. For joy and stupefaction he could not speak, but Latīfah said: 'It is indeed I. Alas, alas, I fear that you were expecting something more precious.' 'As Allāh lives,' cried Zain, 'I came down here with a broken heart. My father was right when he said that the seventh was worth a thousand of the rest.'

As he spoke, there was a clap of thunder and the earth about them shook. The Old Man of the Isles appeared with a pleasant smile upon his face. He took Zain's hand and placed it in Latīfah's, saying: 'Since your birth, my son, you have been under my protection. I had therefore to think out some way of assuring your perfect happiness. At last I found this means and this treasure; a little virgin girl is more than diamonds; unsullied beauty and youth is all the wealth and medicine of the soul.' The old man kissed Zain and disappeared.

Latīfah and her King loved each other with a great love through years of delicate and chosen life, until the Separator came. Glory be to the Sole Living Who knows not death!

Shahrazād fell silent and King Shahryār exclaimed: 'That was a strange and delightful tale, Shahrazād!' Shahrazād smiled as she replied: 'O King, that mirror is not to be compared with the Wonderful Lamp.' 'What wonderful lamp is that?' asked the King, and Shahrazād answered: 'It is Alā al-Dīn's Lamp. I am just about to tell you of it.' Then she said:

The Tale of Alā al-Dīn and
the Wonderful Lamp

IT is related, O auspicious King, that there was once—but Allāh knows all—in the antiquity of time and the passage of the age and of the moment, a poor tailor in a certain city of China. I do not for the present remember the name of that city. This man had a son, called Alā al-Dīn, who was backward in booklearning and, from his earliest years, a most disappointing little rascal. When the child was ten, his father wished to have him taught some honourable trade; but, as he could not afford to pay for instruction, he had to be content with taking him into his own shop to learn the business of a tailor. The wayward lad, who was accustomed to wander about playing with his companions, could not constrain himself to stay in the shop for one whole day. Instead of attending to the work, he took every advantage of his father's absence or attention with a client to slip out and play in the streets and gardens with young urchins of his own inclination. His conduct continued to be so idle and disobedient that his father soon ceased from checking him, and let him go his own disastrous way. The poor man was stricken down by illness in the midst of his grief, but even his death did not turn Alā al-Dīn from his dissolute courses.

Seeing that her husband was dead and her son good for nothing, Alā al-Dīn's mother sold the shop with all which it contained, and, when the little money she gained from this sale had been expended, spun wool and cotton, day and night, to win food for herself and her child.

Now that he no longer had a father to fear, Alā al-Dīn gave himself up without restraint to his vagabonding tendency; he spent all his days away from home and only returned for meals. But, in spite of this, his mother fed him with her toil and wept as she worked. By the time Alā al-Dīn was fifteen he was as handsome and well-built as you could wish; he had two black magnificent eyes and a skin of jasmine.

One day, as he was playing with his friends in the square near the entrance to the market, a darwīsh, who was a Moor, stopped and gazed attentively at the children. Soon his look became fixed on Alā al-Dīn to the exclusion of the others, and he watched him with an unwinking fire in his eyes. This darwīsh, who came from the far interior of Morocco, was a powerful magician, deeply learned in astrology and the reading of faces. He could move high mountains against each other by his sorcery. As he looked long at Alā al-Dīn, he said to himself: 'This is the lad I need; this is the lad for whom I have searched, for whom I left Morocco.'

At this point Shahrazād saw the approach of morning and discreetly fell silent.

But when the seven-hundred-and-thirty-second night had come

SHE SAID:

Without losing sight of Alā al-Dīn, he drew one of the other boys aside and asked him several questions concerning Alā al-Dīn's father and mother, and what his name and position in life might be. Then, fortified by the answers which he had received, he went up to Alā al-Dīn with a smile, and led him into a corner, where he said: 'My child, are you not Alā al-Dīn, the tailor's son?' 'I am Alā al-Dīn,' answered the boy, 'but my father has been dead for a long time.' At these words, the darwīsh took the boy in his arms, and kissed him long on both cheeks, weeping tumultuously the while. 'Why do you weep, my lord?' asked the astonished Alā al-Dīn. 'Did you, by chance, know my dead father?' 'My child,' answered the Moor in a sad and broken voice, 'why should I, who am your uncle, not weep, when I suddenly hear of the death of my poor brother? Sweet nephew, I left my native land and confronted all the perils of a long journey, solely to see your father once again. And now, alas, you tell me he is dead.' He paused for a moment, as if suffocated by his emotion, and then continued: 'Dear brother's son, my blood called to yours when I saw you; it singled you out among all your little friends. When I parted from my brother, you were not yet born, he was not yet married; and yet I recognised you. That consoles me a little for his loss. Yet woe, woe to my head! Where are you now, dear brother, whom I longed to kiss? Alas, alas, who may boast that he has outstripped the feet of Destiny, or turned aside the prescription of our God!' He embraced Alā al-Dīn again, and thus went on: 'I give praise to Allāh, my son, that I have met you. You shall be my consolation, and take your father's place within my heart; he who leaves a son does not die.'

The Moor took ten gold dīnārs from his belt and gave them to Alā al-Dīn, asking at the same time where his mother lived. Delighted by the gift and smiles of the old man, Alā al-Dīn took him by the hand and, leading him to one side of the square, pointed out the street in which his mother's lodging stood. Then said the Moor: 'Give those ten dīnārs to my brother's wife, with every cordial and respectful greeting. Tell her that your uncle has voyaged to this place after a long absence and that he hopes to visit her to-morrow morning. Say he is very anxious to greet her, to visit his brother's tomb, and to see those places in which the departed passed his life.'

Alā al-Dīn kissed the old man's hand and ran joyfully to his mother's house, arriving there an hour before the meal for the first time in his life. 'Mother,' he cried, 'my uncle has voyaged to this city after a long absence and sends you his greetings.' 'Are you making fun of me, my child?' asked his astonished mother. 'What uncle is this? Since when have you had a living uncle?' 'A living uncle?' retorted Alā al-Dīn. 'This man is my father's brother. He took me to his breast, kissed me with many tears, and himself bade me announce his coming.' Then said his mother: 'My child, I know very well that you had an uncle, but he has been dead for many years; I do not know since when you have had another.' The woman looked at her son strangely and, seeing him occupied with some other interest, forbore to speak further about his uncle that day. Alā al-Dīn, for his part, said nothing of the money which the Moor had given him.

Next morning Alā al-Dīn left the house early; and the Moor found him in the same place, and with the same companions, as on the day before. The old man approached the lad and, taking him by the hand, embraced him tenderly; then he gave him two dīnārs, saying: 'Hand these to your mother and say that your uncle will feed with you this evening. She will be able to buy excellent food with this money. . . . Now show me the way to your house once more.' 'Upon my head and eyes, dear uncle,' answered Alā al-Dīn, and again he pointed out the road which led to his mother's house. The Moor then left him and he ran to his mother, holding out the two dīnārs, and crying: 'My uncle is coming to eat with us this evening!'

At this point Shahrazād saw the approach of morning and discreetly fell silent.

But when the seven-hundred-and-thirty-third night had come

SHE SAID:

When she saw the two dīnārs, Alā al-Dīn's mother said to herself: 'Perhaps I did not know all my husband's brothers.' She hastened to the market where she bought the materials for an excellent supper, but when she would prepare them, she had to borrow cooking-pots and the like from her neighbours, because she had sold all her own. She spent her day in the kitchen and, towards evening, said to Alā al-Dīn: 'The meal is ready, but perhaps your uncle does not know the way to our house. Go out and wait for him in the street.' As Alā al-Dīn was about to obey, there came a knock at the door; he ran to open and found the Moor standing outside with a porter, who carried a load of fruits, pastries, and refreshing drinks upon his head. Alā al-Dīn led them both inside and, after the porter had set down his load and been dismissed with payment, brought the darwīsh into his mother's presence. The old man bowed, and said brokenly: 'The peace of Allāh upon you, O wife of my brother!' Then, while the woman answered his greeting, he wept silently. 'Where used the dead man to sit?' he asked and, when the place was shown to him, cast himself upon the ground, kissing and sighing: 'Alas, alas, I am very distressed for you, vein of my eye, my brother!' Then he wept and lamented, with a face so wrung and such a heaving of his entrails that he seemed like to faint, and quite persuaded Alā al-Dīn's mother that he was really the brother of her husband. She lifted him from the ground, saying: 'My brother, you will kill yourself with weeping!' She went on sweetly consoling him until he was well enough to drink a little water and sit down to meat.

When they were all seated round the cloth, the Moor spoke as follows:

'Wife of my dear brother, you must not be surprised at thus seeing me for the first time, or blame me that I never made myself known to you when my brother was alive. Thirty years ago I left this country, and since then I have wandered through Ind and Sind, and in Arabia, and in Egypt, where I abode in the magnificent city of Cairo, the miracle of the world. At last I set out for the further parts of Morocco, where I have lived for twenty years.

'But one day, as I sat in my house, I began to think of my native land and my brother. Desire came to me to see the flesh of my flesh, so that I wept for my life's exile. At length my longing grew so great that I determined to set out for the dear land which saw my head come forth when I was born. I said to myself: "O man, many years have slipped away since you left your native city and the home of your only brother. Before death comes to you, rise up and seek your kind; for none may reckon without the calamities of Fate, the accidents and revolutions of time. Would it not be great misery to die before you had set eyes on your dear brother, especially as he may be in poverty while Allāh has blessed you with riches? It is possible for you to do two meritorious things at one time, to visit a brother and to succour him."

'Therefore I rose and prepared for my journey. When I had made Friday's prayer and spoken the Fātihah of the Koran, I mounted my horse and left home. After great peril and fatigue by the way, Allāh brought me to my city. I wandered about the streets and quarters, hunting for my brother's house, and Allāh led me to a sight of this child, playing among his companions in the square. Hardly had I seen him, O wife of my dear brother, when I felt my heart blossom because of him. Blood called to blood, and I recognised my nephew. Then I forgot my weariness and well-nigh swooned for joy.'

At this point Shahrazād saw the approach of morning and discreetly fell silent.

But when the seven-hundred-and-thirty-fourth night had come

SHE SAID:

'But alas, his first news told me that my brother had passed into the high mercy of Allāh. Do you wonder that I nearly fell down for grief? But perhaps the boy has told you how he consoled me by his resemblance to the dead, and by bringing to my mind the proverb: *He does not die who leaves a son.*'

When the Moor had finished speaking, he saw Alā al-Dīn's mother weeping bitterly because of the memories of her husband which his recital had invoked; to change the dark current of her thoughts, he turned to Alā al-Dīn, and asked: 'What trade have you learnt, my son? By what labour do you help your mother and gain a living for your little household?'

Alā al-Dīn hung his head in shame, and his mother answered for him: 'Did you say trade, O brother of my husband? A trade for Alā al-Dīn? As Allāh lives, he knows nothing at all, nor have I ever seen a more contrary child! All day he runs about with the little scamps and vagabonds of the quarter. My sorrow, his father died through disappointment in him, and now I myself am failing fast. My eyes are so worn by waking and weeping that I can hardly see to spin wool to buy us bread. O brother of my husband, I swear that he never comes home except for meals. Sometimes I am tempted to shut the door against him, that he may be obliged to work for his living; but my mother's heart has not the strength to do so. Age comes, and I am getting very old; my shoulders can hardly bear the burdens as they used to do. My fingers can scarcely turn the spindle now. I think that life will soon betray me, even as Alā al-Dīn has betrayed me.'

The old woman wept, and the Moor said sternly to Alā al-Dīn: 'I did not know these things, my nephew. Why do you walk as a wastrel in a staggering path? Are you not ashamed, Alā al-Dīn? Such conduct does not suit a fine young man like yourself, well-born and dowered with excellent brains. It dishonours you to let your poor mother work, when you are old enough to carve out a position for yourself and keep the two. Thanks to the goodness of Allāh, there are a multitude of men in our city who could teach you every trade under the sun. You have but to choose, and I will take it upon myself to pay the necessary fees. Then, when you are a man, you will have a trade to protect you from all the assaults of Destiny. If you do not wish to be a tailor, let me know what other occupation would suit you, and I will see that you are instructed in it.'

Instead of answering, Alā al-Dīn continued to look at the floor in silence, as if to signify that he still preferred his idle life; so the Moor, understanding his repugnance to labour with his hands, tried to catch him in another way. 'Do not let my insistence and suggestion offend you, or give you pain, dear nephew,' said he. 'If trades seem unpleasant to you and you yet wish to become an honest man and worthy citizen, I am ready to open a fine shop for you in the great market and install you there. I will stock the place with costly stuffs and silk brocades, so that you may soon be on terms of equality with the great merchants. You shall become accustomed to buying and selling, taking and giving, and your reputation in the city shall be such that it will do no hurt to the memory of your dead father. What do you say to that, Alā al-Dīn?'

When Alā al-Dīn understood that he had the chance of becoming a great merchant, dressed in fine clothes, with a silk turban and a beautiful belt of many colours, he rejoiced exceedingly and smiled at the Moor, leaning his head to one side, as if to say: 'Most certainly I accept.'

At this point Shahrazād saw the approach of morning and discreetly fell silent.

But when the seven-hundred-and-thirty-fifth night had come

SHE SAID:

Understanding that his proposal was accepted, the Moor went on: 'Now that you are willing to become a person of importance, a dignified merchant with a shop of his own, try to show yourself worthy of these things. Be a man, my nephew! To-morrow, if Allāh wills, I will take you to the market and begin all by buying you a fair new robe, such as rich merchants wear, and the things which go with it. After that, we can look for an auspiciously situated shop.'

Seeing this generosity and hearing these exhortations, Alā al-Dīn's mother blessed the goodness of God in sending her a relation to save her from want and set Alā al-Dīn's feet in the way of right behaviour. She served the meal with a light heart, as if twenty years had dropped from her shoulders, and, while they ate and drank, the three chatted of Alā al-Dīn's future. The Moor began to initiate the boy into aspects of the life and behaviour of merchants, and easily succeeded in rousing his interest. Then, as he saw that half the night was spent, he took leave of Alā al-Dīn's mother and kissed Alā al-Dīn. Before he left, he promised to return on the morrow, so that Alā al-Dīn could not shut his joyful eyes all night for thinking of the delightful life which opened out before him.

Early next morning there was a knock at the door and, when the old woman went to open it, she found the Moor standing outside, faithful to his promise of the day before. He refused her invitation to enter and, when Alā al-Dīn, who was already up and dressed, ran to wish his uncle good day and kiss his hands, he bade farewell to the woman and led the lad to the market. He entered the shop of the greatest merchant there, and asked for the costliest robe which the man had suitable to Alā al-Dīn's figure. The merchant showed them many delightful dresses and the Moor bade Alā al-Dīn choose which of them he would. Skipping for joy, the youth picked out a robe of striped and shining silk, a white turban decorated with gold, a Kashmir belt, and boots of bright red leather. The Moor paid for all without haggling, and then handed the package to Alā al-Dīn, saying: 'Now we will go to the hammām, since before putting on new clothes a bath is both necessary and auspicious.' He conducted Alā al-Dīn into the private hall of the hammām and, after washing him with his own hands, took a bath himself. Then he called for refreshments, and the two drank together and were content. At length Alā al-Dīn put on his robe of striped and shining silk, placed the fair turban upon his head, girt himself with the Indian belt, and put the red boots upon his feet. So dressed, he was more beautiful than the moon and held himself like a king's son. Glorying in his transformation, he kissed his uncle's hand and thanked him for the gifts. 'That is only a beginning,' said the Moor, as he embraced him. They left the hammām together and visited the shops of the merchants in the principal markets. In these places the Moor pointed out rare stuffs and costly ornaments to Alā al-Dīn, teaching him the names of everything, in order to prepare him for the time when he should buy and sell. He took him to visit the remarkable buildings of the city, the chief mosques, and the great khāns where the caravans put up. Then, after an inspection of the Sultān's palace and its garden, he led him to the khān where he himself lodged and presented him as his nephew to the other merchants with whom he was acquainted. He invited them all to a feast in the boy's honour and regaled them with the choicest meats, keeping Alā al-Dīn by him at the cloth until the evening.

At nightfall he led Alā al-Dīn back to his house, and the boy's mother, poor woman, rejoiced in her heart when she saw her son so magnificently habited. She blessed her brother-in-law a thousand times, saying: 'O brother of my husband, even if I try all my life I shall never be able to thank you enough for your kindness.' 'There is no merit in what I do, no merit at all,' answered the Moor. 'Alā al-Dīn is my son and I must try to be a father to him, in place of the dead. Have no more care for him, but lift up your heart and rejoice.' Alā al-Dīn's mother held her arms on high, and cried: 'I pray to Allāh, by the honour of the old and the later saints, to guard you and lengthen your life for us, my brother, that you may be, as it were, a wing to shade this fatherless boy! And I pray that he, for his part, will be ever obedient to your commands and do nothing of which you disapprove.' 'Have no fear,' replied the Moor. 'Alā al-Dīn has become a man of sense; he is a good boy and of a good family. I am confident that he will be a worthy descendant of his father and bring great joy to your declining years . . . As to-morrow will be Friday and all the markets will be shut, I shall not be able to open the shop as I promised; but I shall do so without fail on the day after. To-morrow I will continue Alā al-Dīn's course of instruction by taking him to visit the gardens beyond the city, where the rich merchants walk together. I wish him to become accustomed to the sight of wealth and breeding; for, until to-day, he has companioned only with children.' The old man took leave of the woman, kissed Alā al-Dīn, and retired.

At this point Shahrazād saw the approach of morning and discreetly fell silent.

But when the seven-hundred-and-thirty-sixth night had come

SHE SAID:

Alā al-Dīn lay awake all night pondering his good fortune, and rose with the first light to walk up and down the house in his new clothes, tripping, from time to time, in the unaccustomed skirts. When his impatience told him that the Moor was late, he went to the door and there saw him approaching. He ran forward, like a young stallion, and kissed the old man's hands. The Moor embraced him very kindly and led him away. They walked together, talking of many things, until they had passed the gates of the city and come to the notable houses and handsome garden-girt palaces which lie beyond. Alā al-Dīn had never seen these before, and was more and more delighted as each fresh one appeared. They went past the buildings into the open country and drew nearer the goal the Moor had set himself. Before they had gone quite far enough, however, Alā al-Dīn began to get weary and said: 'See, my uncle, we have passed all the gardens and have nothing before us except that mountain. I am tired and hungry; may we not rest a little?' The old man drew a cloth filled with fruits and cakes from his girdle, and handed it to Alā al-Dīn, saying: 'These will appease your hunger and thirst, my son; but we must walk a little further to reach the marvellous place I have in mind to show you. It has not its equal in the world. Be resolute for a little longer, Alā al-Dīn, for you are a man now.' He continued to encourage him with advice for the future, until they came to the foot of the mountain, at the end of a deserted valley filled only with the presence of God.

This place was the Moor's goal; to reach that valley he had left Morocco and come to China.

'Here we are, my son,' he said, with a smile, to the weary boy, as he sat down beside him on a rock and tenderly put his arm about his neck. 'Rest a little. I am going to show you something which the eyes of man have never seen before. Here and now you shall behold a garden more beautiful than all the gardens of the earth. When you have seen it, you will thank me and forget your weariness. More, you will bless the day when first you met me.' He allowed the boy to rest for a short while, round-eyed with astonishment to think that he should see a garden in that place of fallen rocks and withered shrubs. Then he said: 'Rise up now, Alā al-Dīn, and collect the dryest twigs and fragments of wood which you can find among these shrubs. Bring them to me, and you shall see the sight for which I led you hither.' Alā al-Dīn went among the bushes, and collected a heap of dried twigs and brushwood, which he carried to the old man. 'That is excellent,' said the Moor. 'Now retire a few paces and keep behind me.' When Alā al-Dīn had placed himself some distance behind his uncle's back, the Moor took a tinder-box from his belt and set fire to the wood; as soon as it crackled and blazed, he opened a tortoise-shell box and threw a pinch of incense from it into the flame. A thick smoke immediately rose, which he waved from side to side with his hand, muttering spells in an unknown tongue. Soon the mountain trembled, the rocks were troubled, and the earth gaped, leaving a hole ten cubits across. At the bottom of this hole appeared a horizontal marble slab, five cubits square, in the middle of which there was a copper ring.

Alā al-Dīn gave a frightened cry when he saw these things, and, taking the skirts of his robe in his teeth, turned his back and fled precipitately. But the Moor was upon him in a single bound, his eyes blazing with anger. Taking the terrified boy by the ear with one hand, he gave him a heavy slap across the face with the other, so that Alā al-Dīn turned giddy and sank to the ground.

The Moor treated him thus harshly in order to have dominion over him once and for all, since, without his aid, he could never reach the object which he had in mind. He now lifted him kindly from the earth, and said sweetly: 'I only struck you in order to make a man of you, Alā al-Dīn. I am your uncle, your father's brother, and you must obey me. Now listen carefully and do not miss a word of what I say. You have seen the earth opened by my spells and fumigation, but I was only working for your advantage. Below that marble slab is a treasure written in your name and only to be opened in your presence. It will make you richer than all the kings of the earth. As a proof that it is yours, let me tell you that no one in the world except yourself could lift that slab. In spite of my great power, nay, were my power a thousand times greater than it is, I could not touch that copper ring, or lift the marble. Nor might I descend a single stair of those which lie beneath. Only you can undertake the opening of this treasure. Do as I bid you, and we will divide the mighty riches equally between us.'

At this point Shahrazād saw the approach of morning and discreetly fell silent.

But when the seven-hundred-and-thirty-eighth night had come

SHE SAID:

Poor Alā al-Dīn had quite forgotten his weariness and the buffet which he had received. 'Tell me what to do and I will obey,' he cried; so the Moor kissed him many times on the cheek, and continued: 'You are dearer than a son to me, Alā al-Dīn. I have no other relation; you are my heir and my posterity. For your sake I undertook my far journey; if I was a little short with you, it was only to chide you for turning your back upon your marvellous Destiny . . . First come down with me into the hole, take hold of the ring, and lift up the slab.' So saying, he jumped first into the hole and helped Alā al-Dīn down beside him. 'I am only a boy,' protested Alā al-Dīn, 'how can I lift so heavy a slab? If you help me I may be able to do it, but not otherwise.' 'Ah, no, no,' answered the Moor. 'If I set hand to it you could do nothing, and your name would be for ever taken from that treasure. Try by yourself and you will find that you can lift the marble as easily as a feather. As you take hold of the ring, say over your name and your father's name and your grandfather's name. That is all you have to do.'

Alā al-Dīn took hold of the ring and tugged at it, saying: 'I am Alā al-Dīn, son of Mustafā, the tailor, son of the tailor, Ali.' The slab moved easily under his hand; he set it on one side and looked down into a cave, where twelve marble steps led to a double door of red copper studded with boltheads of the same. Then said the Moor: 'Go down into the cave, my son, and enter by the copper door, which will open of itself at your coming. You will then find yourself in a monstrous cavern, divided into three communicating halls. In the first hall you will see four mighty bronze jars filled with liquid gold; in the second, four silver jars filled with gold dust; and in the third, four gold jars filled with coined gold pieces. Pass these things by and hold your robe close in about your waist lest it touch any of the jars; for, if it do so, you will instantly be changed to a block of black stone. At the end of the third hall you will find another door, in all respects like this, which will lead you into a magnificent garden of heavy-fruited trees. Do not linger in that place either. Walk straight across and you will come to a columned staircase with thirty steps, climbing up to a terrace. Now pay even stricter attention. When you are on the terrace, you will see a niche facing you between columns and, in that niche, upon a pedestal of bronze, a little copper lamp. The lamp will be burning, but you must extinguish it and, after pouring its oil upon the ground, hide it quickly in your bosom. Do not fear for your robe; for that oil is not ordinary oil and will leave no trace . . . Then you must return to me by the way you have gone; though you may pause in the garden and eat some of the fruits, if you have a mind to them. When you come back to me with the lamp, we shall be rich and glorious for ever, my child.'

The Moor then drew a ring from his finger and put it on Alā al-Dīn's thumb, saying: 'This will guard you from all danger and preserve you from every evil. Be bold, fill full your breast with courage, for you are no longer a child. Nothing but good will come of this; we shall be rich and honoured for the rest of our lives when we have the lamp . . . Only be very careful to lift your robe high and hold it close in against you; otherwise you and the treasure will be lost together.'

Then he embraced Alā al-Dīn, giving him many little friendly taps upon the cheek. 'Depart in safety, my dear child,' he said.

Alā al-Dīn felt his heart puffed up with courage. He ran down the marble steps and, lifting his robe to his belt, went through the copper doors which swung aside to let him pass. Without forgetting a single one of his uncle's recommendations, he walked through the three halls, giving the jars a wide berth, hurried across the garden, climbed the thirty columned stairs and, reaching the terrace, walked over to the niche which showed opposite to him.

At this point Shahrazād saw the approach of morning and discreetly fell silent.

But when the seven-hundred-and-thirty-ninth night had come

SHE SAID:

He saw a lighted lamp standing on a bronze pedestal, took it in his hand, and emptied the oil upon the terrace. Then, seeing that the outside was also dry, he hid it in the bosom of his robe and went down from the terrace into the garden.

He stood on the last step to look at the garden and gazed for the first time upon its trees. He saw that they bent beneath the weight of fruits unusual in form, size, and colour. Each branch of each tree bore fruits of different tints; some white and transparent like crystal, some with the troubled white of camphor, and some a blank white as of virgin wax. Some fruit was red like grains of pomegranate, and some blood-orange red; there were light green and dark green fruit; there were blue and violet and yellow, with an infinite variety of other colours. Alā al-Dīn did not know that the white fruits were diamonds, pearls, nacre and moon-stones; that the red were rubies, carbuncles, hyacinths, corals and carnelian; that the green were emeralds, beryls, jade, prase and aquamarine; that the blue were sapphires, lapis, turquoise and lazulite; that the violet were amethyst, jaspers and sardonyx; that the yellow were topaz, amber and agate; and that those of unknown colours were opal, aventurine, chryso-lite, cymophane, hematite, tourmaline, peridot, jet and chrysoprase. The sun scattered his rays through these jewels on to the garden, and the trees burnt as with magic fire.

Delighted with their aspect, Alā al-Dīn went up to one of the trees and plucked some of its fruit to eat; but he found them uneat-able and only in form like the oranges, figs, bananas, grapes, melons, apples, and excellent fruits of China. When he found that they were not for his taste, he supposed them to be made of coloured glass, and, though bitterly disappointed, set about plucking some as presents for his mother and young comrades. He selected many of each colour and went on stuffing them into his belt and pockets and inside his robe, until he looked like an ass loaded on both sides. Staggering a little under this burden, he carefully lifted his robe in at the waist and made his way safely through the three halls, without in any way touching their jars.

As soon as he had gone out by the copper door and stood upon the first step of the stair, the Moor said impatiently: 'Where is the lamp?' 'I have it here in my bosom,' answered Alā al-Dīn. 'Take it out and give it me!' cried the Moor; but the boy replied: 'How can I give it you now, when it is all loaded away among the glass marbles with which I have stuffed my clothes? Let me come up, help me out of the hole, and I will set the marbles in a safe place, so that they can-not roll down the steps and break. After that I will be able to reach the lamp and give it you. I am very sure I want to be rid of the thing, for it has slipped round to my back and is bruising me.' The Moor raged at this delay, thinking that Alā al-Dīn wished to keep the lamp for himself. So he cried out in a terrifying devil's voice: 'Son of a dog, give me the lamp or die!' Alā al-Dīn, who did not understand this change of front and was terrified lest he should receive another slap, turned his back and prudently retreated into the cave, to wait for his uncle to become calmer.

The Moor stamped and tore his beard, for the cave was forbidden to him by magic, and he could not follow Alā al-Dīn. 'You shall be punished as you deserve, vile boy!' he cried, as he ran to the still smouldering fire and threw incense upon it to an accompaniment of spells. The marble slab rose of itself and returned to its place; the earth trembled and shut again over the cave, leaving Alā al-Dīn entombed beneath.

As has been told you, this Moor was a redoubtable magician from the interior of Morocco. He was no uncle, no relation at all, of Alā al-Dīn; but an African, born and bred in that hotbed of evil sorcerers.

At this point Shahrazād saw the approach of morning and discreetly fell silent.

But when the seven-hundred-and-fortieth night had come

SHE SAID:

From his earliest youth he had avidly studied sorcery and spells, geomancy and alchemy, astrology, fumigation, and enchantment; so that, after thirty years of wizardry, he had learnt the existence of a magic lamp in some unknown place, powerful enough to raise its owner above the kings and powers of the world. Having penetrated the secret so far, he redoubled his labours and, by a last supreme experiment in geomancy, learnt that the lamp was to be found in a cavern near the city of Kolo-Ka-Tse in China. He had started immediately and arrived, after a laborious journey, at that far place which we have already visited. His first labour was to discover the exact site of the cave; when he had done so, he sat down at his divining table and learnt that the treasure and the lamp had been written, by the powers of earth, in the name of Alā al-Dīn, son of Mustafā. That is why he had sought out the boy and used his wiles to gain his friendship and lead him to the valley. He had been eager to obtain the lamp at once, so that he might keep it for himself and imprison Alā al-Dīn for ever in the cave; but, as we have seen, Alā al-Dīn had retreated into the cave and been shut there without the lamp having changed hands.

As soon as he had left the boy to perish of hunger and thirst, the Moor departed; probably for Africa. It is certain that we will hear of him again.

When Alā al-Dīn re-entered the cave, he felt the earth tremble and feared that the roof would fall in upon his head. He ran to the entrance, but discovered that the marble slab had returned to its place and was immovable against his pressure. He became very frightened and began calling loudly to his uncle for help, promising to give him the lamp immediately. It was only when there was no answer to his cries that he began to doubt if the Moor was altogether as he had given himself out. Considering that no real uncle would call his nephew a son of a dog, he gave up all hope of escape from that side and made his way through the halls towards the garden; but the door into the garden was shut fast against him. He ran back to the mouth of the cave and cast himself weeping on the steps below the slab. He was buried alive with all that useless gold! He sobbed and sighed as he thought, for the first time in his life, of his mother's goodness and the ingratitude with which he had repaid it. Death seemed to him the more bitter since he could not first delight his mother by some change in his behaviour, which would show her that he understood her excellence. As he grieved, he began to twist his arms and rub his hands together in despair, crying: 'There is no power or might save in Allāh!' The working together of his hands caused him to rub the ring which the Moor had given him as a protection. The terrible old man did not know that this ring would save the boy's life, or he would have torn it from him by force or wiled it away from him. All magicians are like this Moor: in spite of their evil power, they have not the prevision of ordinary men in simple matters. In their pride and self-confidence, they never appeal to the Master of all men; their minds are obscured by a smoke thicker than their fumigations, their eyes are veiled as with a kerchief; they totter among shadows.

At this point Shahrazād saw the approach of morning and discreetly fell silent.

But when the seven-hundred-and-forty-first night had come

SHE SAID:

As soon as Alā al-Dīn had unwittingly rubbed the ring upon his finger, he saw a great black Ifrīt rise from the earth before him, with red flaming eyes, who said in a voice of thunder: '*I am master of earth and wave; but slave of the ring and the wearer's slave. What will you have, master, what will you have?*' Alā al-Dīn was terrified and would certainly have fallen into a swoon in any other place or circumstance; but, as he sat with death and hunger in the cave, this terrible apparition seemed a door of safety. He lifted up his heart, and answered: 'Master of earth and air and wave, please let me out of this cave.'

Hardly had he spoken when the earth opened above his head and he found himself standing in the open air, near the spot where the Moor had lighted his fire. The Ifrīt had disappeared.

Trembling with joyful relief, Alā al-Dīn gave thanks to God for his deliverance from the Moor. When he looked about him and saw the city in the midst of its gardens in the distance, he hastened towards it, without once looking back. He reached home worn out and breathless, at midnight, to find his mother weeping with anxiety for his late return. She opened to him and took him in her arms as he fainted across the threshold.

When he came to himself, his mother gave him a little rose-water to drink, and asked what had happened. 'Mother, I am so hungry,' answered Alā al-Dīn. 'Give me something to eat.' His mother brought him all the food which there was in the house and he began to eat it so eagerly that she cried: 'Do not hurry, my son, do not hurry. You will crack your throat! I can wait for the story until you have finished. Eat more slowly, eat more slowly. Though Allāh knows I was anxious enough. But take smaller mouthfuls, my child, take smaller mouthfuls!' As soon as he had made the platter clean, Alā al-Dīn took the waterjar and emptied all its contents down his throat. Then, with a sigh of contentment, he said: 'Now I can tell you my adventures with the wicked old man who said he was my uncle. He made me see death within two inches of my eyes! For all his tenderness, he was no uncle of mine. He was a Moor, a sorcerer, a liar, a cheat, a twister, a dog, a devil of all devils. Listen, mother, to what he did . . . O mother, I am glad to be rid of him!' Then he took several long breaths and told his mother the whole story. But there is nothing to be gained by repeating it in this place. When he had finished, he undid his belt and let the marvellous provision of transparent fruit fall upon the mattress, and the lamp tumbled out also.

'To think that I risked my life for these silly things!' he said, and then, as he turned over the glinting jewels: 'I am not a child, to play with coloured marbles!'

His mother, while listening to the tale of his misfortunes, had kept up a running fire of such curses upon the Moor as a mother's anger may find in its extremity. Thus she was already calm and able to take her son to her bosom, saying: 'Let us thank Allāh that he has withdrawn you safe and sound from the hands of that wizard! He would have killed my child for a copper lamp, not worth half a dirham! I was a fool. I might have known from his bleared eyes that he was an Unbeliever and no kin of your poor father.' She went on soothing Alā al-Dīn until he fell into a sound sleep with his head upon her knees; then she carefully lowered him on to the mattress and lay down to sleep beside him.

At this point Shahrazād saw the approach of morning and discreetly fell silent.

But when the seven-hundred-and-forty-second night had come

SHE SAID:

When they woke next morning, they kissed again with great love and Alā al-Dīn assured his mother that he now saw the errors of his youth. 'I will work for you like a man,' he said, 'I will go and seek employment this very day. But first I must have something to eat.' 'Alas, my son,' answered his mother, 'I gave you all the food we had in the house last night. Wait for a little and I will sell some of my spinning for bread and meat.' 'Leave your spinning for the time, dear mother,' said Alā al-Dīn. 'If you take that old lamp to the market you will surely get enough for it to feed us during the day.' 'You are right, my son,' agreed his mother. 'Also to-morrow I will take out the glass marbles and sell them in the negro's quarter, for black men will give the best price for them.'

Alā al-Dīn's mother took the lamp and was just about to leave the house with it, when she noticed that it was very dirty. 'If I polish it,' she said, 'I will get a better price.' She went to the kitchen and, mixing a little ash in water, began to clean the lamp. But the moment she rubbed the surface, an Ifrīt of terrifying appearance surged out of the thin air towards her, his vast black head scraping against the ceiling. He bowed before her and said in a voice deafeningly loud: '*I am master of earth and air and wave, but slave of the lamp, and the bearer's slave. What will you have, mistress, what will you have?*'

Alā al-Dīn's mother, who was not used to such appearances, stood rooted to the floor with knotted tongue and open mouth. Then, from sheer terror, she fell forward in a swoon.

Alā al-Dīn had been standing near his mother in the kitchen; now, seeing that the apparition was not so monstrously ugly as the one he had seen in the cave, he took the lamp from the old woman's limp hand and held it firmly, saying: 'O slave of the lamp, I am hungry. I bid you bring me an excellent repast.' The Jinnī vanished and reappeared in a moment, bearing on his head a great tray of massive silver which held twelve gold dishes of scented and hot-tasting meats, six warm loaves as white as snow but gilded about their sides, and two large flasks of old clear excellent wine. In his hands he carried a stool of ebony inlaid with mother-of-pearl and silver, and two silver cups. He arranged the contents of the tray upon the stool, and discreetly disappeared.

Seeing that his mother still lay in her swoon, Alā al-Dīn sprinkled rose-water over her face. This, combined with the fine smells steaming up from the dishes, soon brought the poor woman to herself. When he had helped her to her feet, Alā al-Dīn said: 'You need not be frightened, mother. Come and eat, for Allāh has sent us that which is well worth eating. For pity's sake, do not let everything get cold!'

When she saw this wonderful meal spread out before her, Alā al-Dīn's mother forgot the cause of her fainting, and cried: 'May Allāh prolong the life of our noble Sultān! Surely he has heard of our poverty and sent one of his cooks to us with this tray!' 'Dear mother,' answered Alā al-Dīn, 'this is no time for supposition or question. Start eating before everything gets cold!'

They fell to with great delight and were so tickled by the marvellous quality of the meats and wines that they joined the evening meal to the morning meal, without once rising from the cloth. When at last they could take no more, the old woman set aside the rest of the food for the morrow and locked the costly dishes in the kitchen cupboard. Then she returned to Alā al-Dīn, who told her how the slave of the lamp had provided the repast.

This news threw the woman into a violent agitation, and she cried: 'My child, I conjure you, by the milk which you suck, to throw away that lamp and take off that ring; for they are the gifts of devils. I would die if I saw such an Ifrīt again! I feel the food rising up in my throat to stifle me! The Prophet (upon whom be prayer and peace!) commanded us to have no dealings with the powers of earth and air.' 'I would obey you in anything,' answered Alā al-Dīn, 'but I cannot throw away the lamp or the ring. The ring saved my life in the cave and the lamp must be equally precious, since it could bring us our food and also entice that evil Moor to journey from his far country. But I will hide the lamp, if you like, so that you need never set eyes on it.' 'Do as seems good to you, my son,' answered his mother. 'I for one will have nothing more to do with the slave of the ring or the slave of the lamp. Never mention them in my hearing, in case the speaking of their name should cause them to appear.'

At this point Shahrazād saw the approach of morning and discreetly fell silent.

But when the seven-hundred-and-forty-third night had come

SHE SAID:

Though the two had finished the rest of the food early on the following day, Alā al-Dīn did not wish to have recourse to the lamp again so soon, for fear of frightening his mother. Instead he took one of the gold plates and, hiding it under his robe, carried it forth to a certain Jew who was craftier than the devil. The Jew examined the plate, scratched it a little with his finger nail, and said in a voice entirely devoid of interest: 'How much do you want for it?' 'You know its value better than I do,' answered Alā al-Dīn, who had no knowledge at all of precious metals. 'I am willing to rely on the good faith of your estimate.' At once the Jew, who was satisfied that the dish was of pure gold, took a single dīnār from the drawer in the wall and gave this coin, which represented, perhaps, a thousandth part of the dish's value, to Alā al-Dīn. 'Take it, my son, take it,' he said. 'By Moses and Aaron, I would never have given such a great sum to another; but I hope to persuade you to deal with me in the future.' Alā al-Dīn clutched the dīnār and ran off in the highest feather, so that the Jew bitterly regretted that he had not given less. Had there been a chance of his overtaking the boy's young feet, he would certainly have gone after him and tried to drive a better bargain.

Alā al-Dīn got change by buying bread from a baker, and ran to give the bread and money to his mother. 'Go and buy us food, dear mother,' he cried, 'for I am not clever enough.' His mother bought food, and on that day they ate and were content.

After that, it became Alā al-Dīn's custom, when the money ran out, to go to the market and sell another gold plate to the Jew. The poor old man was obliged to give him a dīnār each time, as he had so rashly paid that price on the first occasion, and feared that the boy would go elsewhere. When the twelve dishes were gone, Alā al-Dīn wished to sell the large silver tray and, as it was too heavy to carry, brought the old merchant to see it. 'I can give you two dīnārs for that,' said the Jew, and the boy was so delighted that he threw in the two silver cups as a make-weight.

Thus Alā al-Dīn and his mother were able to live for several days longer. The boy, who had quite renounced his old companions, spent all his time in the markets, talking seriously to merchants and persons of distinction, and learning many useful things from their conversation.

When the two dīnārs were exhausted, Alā al-Dīn warned his mother so that she might leave the house, and then rubbed the lamp again upon that part of it which still shone from the old woman's application of water and ashes. The Jinnī appeared and said, quite gently because the lamp had been rubbed gently: '*I am master of earth and air and wave, but slave of the lamp and the bearer's slave. What will you have, master, what will you have?*' 'Slave of the lamp, I am hungry,' said Alā al-Dīn. 'I wish exactly the same meal as you brought the first time.' The Jinnī disappeared and returned in the twinkling of an eye with all things as before.

Soon the old woman returned to the house and was again astonished by the tempting sight and savour of the dishes. In spite of her wholesome fear of wizardry, she sat down with her son and ate until she had had enough. Even after that, the two continued at the cloth, being pricked on by the quality of the food, until they had lengthened out the morning meal into the evening meal, and night had fallen.

At this point Shahrazād saw the approach of morning and discreetly fell silent.

But when the seven-hundred-and-forty-fourth night had come

SHE SAID:

As soon as the remnants of this repast were finished, Alā al-Dīn took one of the gold dishes to the market, meaning to sell it to the

Jew; but, while he was passing the shop of a venerable Mussulmān goldsmith, renowned throughout the city for his fair dealing, the sheikh called him by name and invited him to enter. 'My son,' said the old man, when the boy was seated, 'I have often observed you pass in the market, hiding something under your robe. Then following you with my eyes, I have seen you enter the shop of my neighbour the Jew, and come out from it without your hidden burden. Now I feel that I ought to tell you a thing which your few years could not have told you; that Jews are the sworn enemies of the Faithful and consider it lawful to rob them on every occasion; also that this Jew is the most dishonest and detestable of all, filled beyond his kind with hatred of those who believe in Allāh. If you have something to sell, show it to me first and I swear, by the truth of our God, that I will assess its value justly, so that you may know what you are about when you sell it. Show me what is under your robe, and Allāh curse all Jews!'

Alā al-Dīn did not hesitate to show his gold dish to the jeweller, and the sheikh after casting an eye over it, asked: 'How many of these have you sold to the Jew, and what did he give you for each?' 'I have sold him twelve at a dīnār each,' answered Alā al-Dīn. The venerable goldsmith flew into a righteous rage, and cried: 'Ah, the cursed Jew, son of a dog, grandson of Satan!' Then he weighed the dish in his scales, and went on more calmly: 'This dish is made of the finest gold and is worth two hundred dīnārs. One way and another, the Jew has robbed you of more in a day than his tribe could take from us in a week; for we are on our guard against them now. Unfortunately we cannot have the Jew impaled, for lack of witnesses; but in the future you will know how you stand . . . If you wish it, I will give you two hundred dīnārs at once for your dish; but if you would rather have it valued by any other merchant, I will pay something over his highest offer.' As he had no reason to doubt the goldsmith's probity, Alā al-Dīn took the two hundred dīnārs. And, later, he sold the other eleven dishes at the same honest price.

Though Alā al-Dīn and his mother became rich in this way, they did not abuse the blessings of Allāh, but continued to live modestly, giving their surplus to the poor and needy. Also Alā al-Dīn continued his instruction in refinement, by assiduously frequenting the great merchants and men of high quality who met in the markets. Soon he had learnt good manners and was able to mix on terms of equality with goldsmiths and jewellers. At their shops he soon perceived that the fruits which he had brought back from the garden and had supposed to be coloured glass marbles, were in reality gems beyond the price and imagination of kings. As he was now much wiser than before, he spoke of this discovery to no one, not even to his mother; but collected the jewel fruit from the cushions and corners of the couch, and hid them in a locked box which he bought especially. The wisdom of this conduct was soon to be proved in most glorious fashion.

At this point Shahrazād saw the approach of morning and discreetly fell silent.

But when the seven-hundred-and-forty-fifth night had come

SHE SAID:

One day, when he was talking with certain merchant friends outside a shop, two of the Sultān's heralds passed, clearing their way with long sticks, and crying: 'Merchants and citizens, let it be known that our great-hearted master, the King of time, the lord of minutes and of centuries, bids you shut your shops and hide immediately behind the closed doors of your houses. The pearl of all pearls, the gentle, the marvellous Badr al-budūr, youngest of the moons of God, daughter of our Sultān's glory, will pass through the streets to bathe at the hammām. May her bath be delicious! If any dare to disregard this order and peep through doors or windows, he shall have his choice of the sword, the stake, or the scaffold. This notice is hereby given to all who wish to keep the blood within their necks.'

On hearing this proclamation Alā al-Dīn was seized with an irresistible desire to see the Princess Badr al-budūr, for the greatness of her beauty was common talk among the people. So, instead of returning home as all the rest of the citizens had made haste to do, he ran to the hammām and hid himself behind the great door, in such a position that he might look through the crack of it and see the Sultān's daughter passing to the bath.

He had only been in place for a few minutes when a crowd of eunuchs appeared, making way for the princess's train. Alā al-Dīn saw her among her women, a little moon outshining a host of stars; but, when she came to the threshold, she unveiled her face and he was dazzled with unimagined sunlight. She was fifteen, neither more nor less; when you had seen her, you found the letter alif crooked in your reading, the young branch of the ban a clumsy thing, a crescent

moon of no account after her brow. The lids hiding her black eyes
were two rose leaves, her nose was as faultless as a king's sword, her
neck was as soft as a dove's, her small chin smiled; surely she had
been washed to that whiteness in the fountain Salsabíl. A poet said
of her:

> You have decked your hair with a wing torn from night
>> To make the brow white,
> You have enchanted your eyes with black kohl
>> To trouble the soul,
> And have made spells on your cheek with a burnt rose
>> To shatter repose.

The blood sang twice as quickly through Alä al-Dín's head; he
learnt beauty for the first time, and knew suddenly that all women
were not old and ugly like his mother. This fair discovery struck
him to stone behind the door, and it was many minutes after the
princess had passed into the hammäm before he had strength to slip
from his hiding-place and totter to his house, suffering the great
change of love. 'Who could have thought such beauty?' he murmured to himself. 'Glory be to Him Who made and painted her with
perfection!' His head was buzzing with such considerations when he
entered his mother's presence, and fell motionless before her upon
the díwän.

His mother anxiously questioned his appearance, but he would
not answer; she brought him meats, but he would not eat. 'What is
the matter, my child?' she asked. 'Are you ill? Have you any pain?'
'Let me alone,' he answered after a long silence. Then, as she insisted,
he ate a little of the food in silence, keeping his eyes upon the cloth;
and, greatly to his mother's anxiety, he remained in that state of
dream and pale languor until the morning.

When day dawned, his mother questioned him again with tears in
her eyes, saying: 'In the name of Alläh which is upon you, my son,
tell me what is the matter and do not torture me any longer by your
silence. If you have taken any ill, I will go for the doctor . . . There
is a very famous Arab physician in our city now; the Sultän sent for
him especially. The miracles of his learning are upon every tongue.
Shall I not fetch him for you?'

At this point Shahrazäd saw the approach of morning and
discreetly fell silent.

But when the seven-hundred-and-forty-sixth night had come

SHE SAID:

Alā al-Dīn lifted his head and answered sadly: 'I am not ill. I am quite well. Only I thought that all women were like you. Yesterday I found out that this is not so.' 'What are you talking about, Alā al-Dīn?' asked his mother, and he continued: 'I know what I am talking about. I have seen Princess Badr al-budūr going into the hammām. I have learnt the meaning of beauty, and now I am good for nothing. I shall know no rest, my wits will not return to me, until I have won her in marriage from the King, her father.'

Alā al-Dīn's mother thought that he had gone mad, and cried: 'The name of Allāh be about you, my child! Think of your lowly station, and calm yourself!' 'I am not mad and I shall not calm myself,' answered Alā al-Dīn. 'Nothing will make me give up the fair Badr al-budūr. The more you talk, the more determined I shall be to ask her from her father.' 'Do not say such things!' cried the old woman. 'If the neighbours hear you and report your words to the Sultān, you are lost. Even if you have taken this fatal resolution, who will you get to carry your petition?' 'To whom could I give such a delicate commission except to you, dear mother?' he replied. 'I have every confidence in you and feel sure that you will carry the business to a successful conclusion.' 'I will do nothing of the kind!' she exclaimed. 'I am not mad; I have not forgotten that you are the son of one of the poorest tailors in this city and that I myself, your mother, come of a scarcely better line. This princess will be given only to some son of powerful kings.' Alā al-Dīn reflected for a moment and then answered: 'I have considered these difficulties for many hours, but they have not changed my determination. If you really love me as a son, I beg you to do as I ask. If you will not, my death shall follow as a matter of course and you will lose me. For the last time, dearest mother, remember that I am your son.'

The old woman burst into tears, and sobbed: 'I am your mother, sweet son, you are the very stone of my heart's fruit. I have wished for nothing in the world but to see you married before my death. If you wish to marry, I will go at once and find some woman who is your equal. . . . But even then, I will not know what to answer when they ask me of your trade and profit, of your inheritance and property . . . So how, if I am certain of rebuff among lowly folks, could I ask the King of China for his only daughter? Reflect for a moment and you will see that the thing is impossible. I know that our Sultān is great-hearted and never sends one of his subjects away empty-handed or without justice done; I know that he generously rewards the least merit which is brought to his notice; but what have you done to merit the smallest of his favours? What gift have you, how-ever humble, to lay at his feet with your petition?' 'You have touched the marrow of the matter!' exclaimed Alā al-Dīn. 'If a rich gift can get me what I wish, I can carry off the prize from any man on earth. Those coloured fruits which I brought you from the hid-den garden, esteeming them to be valueless glass marbles, are pre-cious stones of such rarity that no king on earth has ever seen the like. If you wish to judge the matter for yourself, with the eyes of your inexperience, bring me a large china dish from the kitchen and I will show you.'

At this point Shahrazād saw the approach of morning and discreetly fell silent.

But when the seven-hundred-and-forty-seventh night had come

SHE SAID:

In a bustle of astonishment Alā al-Dīn's mother ran to the kitchen and brought a large clean white dish to her son. Alā al-Dīn had al-ready taken the magic fruits from their hiding-place; now he ranged them with infinite skill upon the dish, grouping and contrasting them in form, size, and colour, until the old woman's eyes were dazzled, and she cried out: 'O beautiful, beautiful!' Then she shut her eyes against these brilliant fires. 'I admit that your present will be accepted,' she said. 'The difficulty is not in that. It is in myself, your messenger. I could never sustain the presence of the King's majesty; I should either stand before him tongue-tied or else swoon to the ground in my confusion. Even supposing that I were so insane as to carry your message, how could I couch your request? What would happen? Either they would think me mad and I should be thrust from the presence, or else the King would be thrown into a violent rage and punish the two of us most terribly. Again, if neither of these things happened and the Sultān was pleased to accept your present, he would ask me who you are, who was your father, what you do, how much you make, and the like; and I would have to say that you have no trade and that your father was the poorest tailor in all the city.' 'Do not worry about that,' answered Alā al-Dīn. 'The Sultān

will never ask you such questions, when he sees my gems of marvel
spread out, like fruit, upon a dish. Do not exercise your mind over
difficulties which will never come, but go about my business with an
assured heart; for you must remember that I have a lamp which is
more than all the trade and profit in the world.'

He went on speaking to his mother with such warm assurance
that she was at length convinced, and made ready for her interview
by putting on the most beautiful garments which she possessed.
When she had tied the dish of gems into a shawl, she left the house
and made her way to the palace. She pressed into the audience hall
behind a crowd of suitors and took her place among the front rank,
in an attitude which betokened humility even amid the humble bearing of that silent crowd. When the King entered, followed by his
wazīrs, amīrs and guards, the chief scribe stood before the throne
and called to the petitioners one by one. Each cause was judged upon
its merits, there and then, so that some went away exulting, and
others cast down; but the greater part were not called for lack of
time. Among these last was Alā al-Dīn's mother, because she had
not the courage to speak or thrust herself forward.

When the sitting was over and the King had retired there was
nothing left for the poor old woman except to take her way sadly
back to her own house, where Alā al-Dīn waited impatiently at the
door. As soon as he saw his mother returning with the dish, he
feared the worst and, dragging her into the house, stood before her,
looking very yellow in the face, and questioned her with his eyes.
The woman told him all that had passed. 'You must excuse your
mother this time, my son,' she said. 'I am not used to palaces, and
the sight of the King so troubled me that I could neither speak nor
thrust myself forward. But to-morrow, if Allāh wills, I shall be
braver.' Though he was grieved at the delay, Alā al-Dīn rejoiced
that the worst had not happened, and consoled himself with hope
throughout the night. Next morning his mother went again to the
palace, carrying the dish in a shawl and telling herself, as she walked,
that she had quite conquered her timidity.

At this point Shahrazād saw the approach of morning and
discreetly fell silent.

But when the seven-hundred-and-forty-eighth night had come

SHE SAID:

She entered the dīwān and placed herself in the front rank before the throne, but again terror held her down and she could do nothing to draw attention to herself. The sitting ended and she returned sorrowfully to tell Alā al-Dīn of her unsuccess and promise that things would go better on the morrow. Alā al-Dīn was obliged to lay in a new stock of patience. He lectured his mother on her lack of resolution, but his words had little effect, for the poor woman went to the dīwān on the six following days, always taking the dish with her, and always too bashful to press her suit. She would certainly have gone on in this way for a hundred days, until Alā al-Dīn was dead of despair, had not the King himself noticed her at length and been filled with curiosity about her. At the dīwān's end on the tenth day, he turned to his grand-wazīr, saying: 'That old woman, who holds something done up in a shawl, has been here regularly for many days and yet has asked for nothing. What does she want?' Though the grand-wazīr knew nothing of Alā al-Dīn's mother, he would not be at a loss for an answer, and therefore replied: 'She is one of the many old women who come to the dīwān upon some foolishness; probably someone has sold her some rotten barley, or a neighbour has used bad language, or her husband has beaten her.' But the King would not be put off in this way. 'I wish to question her,' he said. 'Bring her before me.' The wazīr placed his hand to his brow in sign of assent and led the old woman trembling to the foot of the throne, where she fell rather than prostrated herself, and kissed the earth as she had seen the other suitors do. She stayed thus abased until the wazīr touched her on the shoulder and helped her to rise. Then said the King: 'I have seen you come to the dīwān for many days and stand here asking nothing. Tell me what you desire and I will have justice done.' Encouraged by this kindness, Alā al-Dīn's mother answered: 'May Allāh pour His blessings upon the head of our master the Sultān! Before making her plea, O King of time, your slave begs for the promise of security, in case her words seem strange or offensive to the royal ears.' The great-hearted Sultān promised security and ordered the hall to be cleared so that the woman might speak freely. When none but the grand-wazīr remained, he said kindly: 'You may speak, for the hand of Allāh is upon you, O woman.' Then Alā al-Dīn's mother, who had quite recovered her fortitude, spoke up, saying: 'I ask pardon beforehand for the strange audacity of my request.' This roused the Sultān's curiosity, and he hastened to reply: 'Speak quickly and with a quiet mind, my woman; for I pardon all that you say and ask.'

Alā al-Dīn's mother again prostrated herself before the throne and again called down the blessings and favours of Allāh upon the King. Then, without reservation, she told all that had happened to Alā al-Dīn since the criers had gone about the streets, bidding the citizens keep their houses while the Princess Badr al-budūr went processioning to her bath. When she had painted a picture of Alā al-Dīn's love despair, she fell into a confused silence for a moment, and then said in a low voice: 'It only remains for me to entreat you, O King of time, not to blame me for my son's madness, or punish me because my mother's heart could refuse him nothing.'

The King had listened carefully but, when the old woman had made an end, he laughed benevolently, instead of flying into a temper, and said: 'Now tell me what you have hidden in that shawl.'

At this point Shahrazād saw the approach of morning and discreetly fell silent.

But when the seven-hundred-and-forty-ninth night had come

SHE SAID:

Alā al-Dīn's mother undid the shawl and silently presented the plate of jewel fruit to the King; the whole dīwān was lighted up as if by coloured torches, and the Sultān fell back on his throne, hiding his eyes. Then he took the dish in his hands and fingered the marvellous stones one by one for a long time. At last he turned to his wazīr, crying: 'By the life of my head, here is beauty indeed. These fruits are the most delightful of all time! Have you ever seen, nay, have you ever heard that anyone dreamed of the like?' 'I do not think that anyone has dreamed of the like, O King of time,' answered the wazīr. 'These stones are, each of their kind, without a parallel; a single one of the smallest is worth all my master's treasure.' 'Then do you not think that this young Alā al-Dīn, who sends them to me, is worthier of my daughter's hand,' asked the King, 'than any king's son in the world?'

The wazīr changed colour at this question, which he neither expected nor desired, for he had an ardent son to whom the King had promised Badr al-budūr. After a perplexed silence, he answered sadly: 'You are right, O King of time. But perhaps your Highness forgets that the princess is promised to my son. I ask you, as a favour, to allow me a delay of three months in which to find a fairer and more costly dowry for my son than this young stranger's gift.'

The King, who was an expert in gems, knew that no one might find him a present equal to the marvels which he had just received; but, as he did not wish to grieve his wazīr unduly, he answered kindly enough: 'I grant you that delay; but, if you cannot find a dowry equal to or excelling these bright fruits which Alā al-Dīn sends me, I can do no more for your son, even in memory of your good and loyal service.'

Then he spoke affably to Alā al-Dīn's mother: 'You may return joyfully and in peace to your son and tell him that his request is granted. Tell him that my daughter is already betrothed to him, but that the marriage cannot take place for three months, as fitting garments and furnishing could not be procured in a less time.'

Alā al-Dīn's mother lifted her arms to heaven, praying for the King's long life, and then flew on the wings of joy back to her house. Alā al-Dīn saw her face lighted with happiness, and asked: 'O mother, am I to live or die?' The old woman sat down wearily on a couch and lifted her veil, as she answered: 'I have good news for my Alā al-Dīn. The King's daughter is betrothed to you already. Your gift has been well received, but your marriage cannot take place for three months. That delay, I am sure, was granted at the secret solicitation of the grand-wazīr, a most calamitous old man, who doubtless has his reasons. But I trust in Allāh that nothing but good will come, and that your wild dreams will be made true, my dearest son . . . Allāh confound that wazīr and even him with the lowest of the people, for my heart misgives me concerning his whisperings in the King's ear. If it had not been for him, I am sure our good King, who was so transported by the jewels you sent him, would have allowed the marriage to take place to-day, or to-morrow at the latest.'

Without pausing for breath, she gave Alā al-Dīn a full account of what had happened at the dīwān, and cried when she had finished: 'May Allāh guard the life of our glorious King and preserve my son for the joys which wait upon his Destiny!'

At this point Shahrazād saw the approach of morning and discreetly fell silent.

But when the seven-hundred-and-fiftieth night had come

SHE SAID:

Alā al-Dīn luxuriated in his contentment and cried out: 'Glory be to Allāh, Who has covered our house with His blessing and given a princess of most royal blood into our line!' He kissed his mother's hand with many thanks for her kindness, but the old woman took him to her heart and embraced him tenderly, pouring forth wishes for his prosperity and with them mingling tears that her husband, the tailor, could not be there to view the proud destiny of their wilful son.

From that time they impatiently counted the hours which separated them from the joyful ending of the three months' delay, and occupied themselves in feasting and giving alms to the poor, so that the Rewarder of all men might see that they were worthy of His generosity.

Two months had passed in this way when Alā al-Dīn's mother, who went out every morning to the market to buy necessaries for the marriage, noticed, as she walked along laden with a thousand packages both great and small, that the shops were decorated and hung with leaves, lanterns, and coloured flags which stretched across the way; that the streets were packed with palace dignitaries, clad in ceremonious brocades and riding upon noble horses; and that the shopkeepers and people rich and poor alike were bustling about with cries and demonstrations of unusual joy. She asked the oil-merchant with whom she dealt what festival this might be, which caused such commotion of joy among the people; and the man answered in a shocked voice: 'Surely you are jesting! Anyone would think you were a stranger in our city, not to know that this is the bridal day of Princess Badr al-budūr and the grand-wazīr's son. She will soon be coming out of the hammām; these splendid gold riders are the guards of her escort.'

Alā al-Dīn's mother waited to hear no more; forgetting the rest of her purchases, she fled through the markets and arrived at her own house breathless with sorrow and indignation. She sank upon the couch and, when Alā al-Dīn ran to her, gasped out: 'Destiny has turned an evil page for you, my son! All is lost. Your promised happiness has withered away!' 'What terrible thing has happened?' cried Alā al-Dīn in a fright, and she continued: 'Alas, alas, the Sultān has forgotten his oath. To-day he marries Badr al-budūr to the son of that pitch-faced old man, the grand-wazīr, whom I so much sus-

pected. All the city is decorated for this evening.' Fever leaped into
Alā al-Dīn's brain and he stood shaking for a moment, as if he would
have fallen dead; then he remembered the wonderful lamp and
gained control of himself. He turned to his mother and said calmly:
'I do not think the wazīr's son will taste those sweets to-night ... Do
not trouble any more about the matter; rise up and prepare food ...
With Allāh's help I shall see what is to be done.'

Alā al-Dīn's mother prepared a meal which her son ate heartily.
Afterwards Alā al-Dīn shut himself in his own room, begging her
not to disturb him, and, after locking the door, took the magic lamp
from its hiding place. As soon as he rubbed it in the required spot,
the Ifrīt of the lamp appeared before him, crying: '*I am master of
earth and air and wave, but slave of the lamp, and the bearer's slave.
What will you have, master, what will you have?*' 'Listen carefully, O
slave of the lamp,' answered Alā al-Dīn, 'for now it is no question of
bringing me meat and drink, but a matter of much greater importance. The Sultān received a present of jewels from me, and promised
me the hand of his marvellous daughter, Badr al-budūr, in marriage.
He insisted on a delay of three months and, during that time, has
forgotten his oath. He is marrying the girl to his wazīr's son, without
even returning me my present. This I cannot allow, and I have called
upon you to help me to prevent it.' 'Speak, O Alā al-Dīn, my
master,' said the Ifrīt. 'There is no need for you to give me these
long explanations. Command and I shall obey.' 'Very well, then,'
answered Alā al-Dīn. 'This evening, when the newly married couple
are put to bed, and before they have had time even to touch each
other, you must carry the bed here to me. I will look after the rest.'
'I hear and I obey!' replied the Ifrīt, as he carried his hand to his
forehead and disappeared.

At this point Shahrazād saw the approach of morning and
discreetly fell silent.

But when the seven-hundred-and-fifty-first night had come

SHE SAID:

Alā al-Dīn went out to his mother and sat talking with her as
calmly as if nothing had ever threatened his marriage. When evening
came and the old woman went to bed, he returned to his chamber and
locked himself in to await the coming of the Ifrīt. So much for him.

When the feasts and ceremonies, the receptions and rejoicings had finished in the palace, the bridegroom was led into the marriage-chamber by the chief eunuch, who speedily retired, shutting the door behind him. The young man undressed and, lifting the curtains, lay down in bed to await his bride. Soon she was led in by her mother and the women of her train, who undressed her, clad her in a simple silk chemise, and took down her hair. Then they placed her in bed as if by force, while she tried, or seemed to try, to fight against them and escape. As soon as she was couched beside the wazīr's son, the women retired with many wishes for a worthy consummation, and the mother went last, shutting the door with that heavy sigh which is customary upon such occasions.

As soon as the two were alone together, even before they could have given each other the least caress, they felt their bed lifted into the air; in the twinkling of an eye they were haled out of the palace and set down in a place which they did not know. But we know that it was Alā al-Dīn's chamber. As they lay motionless for fright, the slave of the lamp prostrated himself before Alā al-Dīn, saying: 'I have done your bidding, my master. Tell me what more you require.' 'Take this young pimp and shut him in the privy for the night,' said Alā al-Dīn. 'To-morrow morning return for orders.' The slave of the lamp roughly lifted the wazīr's son from the bed and, carrying him to the privy, thrust his head into the hole of it; then he breathed upon him a cold and stinking breath which stiffened him like wood in that position.

When Alā al-Dīn found himself alone with the Princess Badr al-budūr, he did not dream for a moment of abusing her situation, though he loved her with a great love. Instead, he bowed before her with his hand upon his heart, and said passionately: 'O Princess, you are safer here than in your father's palace. I have only carried you to this unknown place in order that you need not submit to the vile caresses of the wazīr's idiot son. Though you were promised to me in marriage, I shall not even touch you until you have become my lawful wife.'

The princess, who knew nothing of her father's promise to Alā al-Dīn, wept and did not answer; so the boy, to calm her and prove that his intentions were not evil, laid himself fully dressed by her side upon the bed and placed a naked sword between them. Then he turned his back and slept as calmly as if he were alone in his bachelor's bed, with Badr al-budūr, for whom he longed, a thousand miles away.

Her trouble and fright prevented the princess from shutting an eye all night; she lay a prey to tumultuous thoughts until the morning. Though it must be admitted that she had less to complain of than her husband, with his head in the hole of the privy and his body petrified by the Ifrīt's breath, it is equally true that neither could look upon their wedding night as altogether satisfactory.

At this point Shahrazād saw the approach of morning and discreetly fell silent.

But when the seven-hundred-and-fifty-second night had come

SHE SAID:

Next morning, the slave of the lamp presented himself before Alā al-Dīn without being summoned. As the youth was not awake, the Ifrīt called to him and thus greatly terrified the princess who could see no one there. Alā al-Dīn rose from the bed and, going apart with the slave of the lamp so that Badr al-budūr might not hear what he said, bade him to bring the wazīr's son from the privy, replace him in the bed, and return the bride and groom to the spot from which he had taken them in the Sultān's palace. 'Above all,' he said, 'watch over them and prevent any attempt at a caress.' The Jinnī withdrew the shivering young man from the privy and placed him at the princess's side; then he transported them to the marriage-chamber in the King's palace, so quickly that they could not see who or what had lifted them. Perhaps this was as well, as one sight of the slave of the lamp might have frightened them to death.

Hardly had the bridal bed been set down in its proper place, when the King and Queen entered to ask after and congratulate the young pair upon their marriage night, and to be the first to wish them a long life together. Moved by the occasion, they came up to the bed and kissed their daughter tenderly between the eyes, saying: 'May your union be blessed, child of our heart! May you see the fruit of this night stretching far down the years in beauty, glory and nobility! How has the night been? How has your husband behaved?' Then they fell silent, waiting for an answer; but lo, instead of the fresh and smiling face which they had hoped to see, tear-stained cheeks were turned towards them, and instead of the joyful answer, they heard sobbing.

They went round to the husband's place and would have questioned him, but he had slipped from the room the moment they had entered it, to wash away the vile matters with which his face was slubbered. Supposing that he had gone to the hammām to take that bath which is usual after the consummation of a marriage, they turned again to their daughter and asked anxiously for the cause of her distress. As she continued silent, they supposed that it was the shame of a first night which held her so, and that her tears were the tears of circumstance; therefore they stood quietly by to give her time to collect herself. But as the moments passed and her tears showed no signs of abating, the Queen said tartly: 'Are you going to answer, my girl? Enough of these airs! I was once a bride myself; but I had better manners than to behave like a flustered hen. Surely you owe your father and myself a little respect?' Finding herself deserted on all sides, the princess felt that she must speak; so she answered with a heavy sigh: 'Allāh pardon me if I have been lacking in respect, but I am sad and troubled and confused by what happened in the night.' Then she told all which had passed, as it had seemed to her: that she had felt the bed move beneath her as soon as she lay by her husband's side; that it had been transported from the marriage-chamber to some room in an unknown house; that her husband had been taken away from her and replaced by a handsome youth who had slept by her all night, with a sword between them, and made no offer to caress her; that her husband had been returned to her in the morning, that the bed had been carried back to the palace, and that the bridegroom had slipped away to wash off a whole collection of horrible matters which smeared his face. 'Even as he left me,' she said, 'I saw you two come in to wish me happiness. Woe, woe, for death only remains to me!' She hid her face in the pillows and sobbed as if her heart would break.

The Sultān and his wife looked at each other with the whites of their eyes; their faces fell into casts of despair, for they supposed that the taking of her virginity had sent their daughter mad. Not wishing to disturb her further, the Queen bent over her and said coaxingly:

At this point Shahrazād saw the approach of morning and discreetly fell silent.

But when the seven-hundred-and-fifty-third night had come

SHE SAID:

'Dear child, a first night is always like that; but do not tell anyone, for these things are not usually spoken and people might suppose that you had gone mad. Get up now and think no more about it; also wear a smile, if you can, for I do not wish your sorrowful looks to spoil the forty days of festival which are taking place throughout all our kingdom. Think no more about it, and you will soon forget what has happened.'

The Queen called her women to make Badr al-budūr's toilet, and went out with her astonished husband to find her son-in-law. She met the wretched young man coming from the bath, and began to question him; but he hid the whole matter, fearing to be made a laughing-stock, and answered: 'Why should you question me so strangely? Nothing out of the ordinary has happened.' This reply confirmed the Queen in her belief that the princess was suffering from some nightmare or shock to the brain; so she said: 'Glory be to Allāh that all has passed off without undue pain! I beg you to be very gentle with your wife, my son, for she is delicate.'

Then she left him and returned to direct the day's revels from her own apartment.

Alā al-Dīn made a good guess as to what had happened at the palace, and passed the day in enjoyment of the excellent trick which he had played upon the wazīr's son. But, towards evening, as he felt that it would be injudicious to allow his rival any respite, he rubbed the lamp, and said to the Jinnī: 'Go to the Sultān's palace, O slave of the lamp, and, as soon as the bride and bridegroom are in bed, bring them to me as before.' The slave of the lamp disappeared and returned almost immediately with the bed, which he set down in Alā al-Dīn's chamber. Then he took away the wazīr's son and fixed him again with his head in the privy. Alā al-Dīn took the empty place beside the princess, placing a naked sword between them, and, turning to the wall, slept calmly till dawn. On the morrow the Ifrīt brought back the husband and returned the bed to the palace.

The King, who was more anxious than before for news of his daughter, came alone to the marriage-chamber, fearing to bring the Queen with him lest she should give rein to her bad temper. As soon as the wazīr's son heard his step approaching, he leaped from the bed and hurried from the room to cleanse himself at the hammām. The Sultān came up to his daughter and tenderly embraced her, saying: 'I am sure you have not had that terrible nightmare again, my dear. Tell your father how you passed the night.' Instead of answering, the princess burst into tears and hid her face in her hands, that she might not see the astonished anger of the King. Her father gave her time to calm herself and then, as she went on sobbing, drew his sword and cried terribly: 'I swear that I will cut off your head if you do not tell me the truth at once!'

This second terror overcame the first in the mind of poor Badr al-budūr, and she answered in a broken voice: 'Have pity, dearest father, and do not be angry with me; for, now that mother is not here, you will be able to listen to me. When you have heard me, I am sure you will be sorry, and guard me from the terrible death which seems to wait for me. If I have the same experience again to-night, you will find me lifeless on the bed to-morrow. Therefore have pity, and give me a compassionate hearing.'

At this point Shahrazād saw the approach of morning and discreetly fell silent.

But when the seven-hundred-and-fifty-fourth night had come

SHE SAID:

Being relieved of his wife's presence and having a kindly heart, the King soothed and consoled his daughter. When her tears were dry, he said: 'Now tell your father exactly what happened to put you in such a fright.' The princess laid her head upon his breast and told him the whole terrible history. 'And now, dearest father,' she concluded, 'you had better question the wazīr's son, if you wish to confirm what I have said.'

The Sultān felt his eyes fill with tears because of the love which he bore his daughter. In his perplexity, he cried: 'Alas, my child, it was my fault for marrying you to a young wretch who cannot take care of you. I only wished your happiness, my dear; how could I tell that you would be frightened to death? Now I will call that young fool and his father, and strictly demand an explanation. Whatever they say, you need have no further anxiety, for I promise on my life that these things shall not happen again.' He left his daughter in charge of her women and returned to his apartments, raging with bitter anger.

He summoned his grand-wazīr, and cried at him in a terrible voice: 'Where is that little pimp, your son? What has he told you about these last two nights?' 'I cannot guess the reason of your concern, O King of time,' answered the wazīr. 'My son has told me nothing that would explain your rage. With your permission, I will go and question him.' The wazīr ran from the presence, bent double with mortification, and soon found his son in the hammām, washing off the foul substances which covered him. 'You dog,' he cried, 'why have you not given me the truth? If you do not tell me what has happened during these last two nights, this day shall be your last.' The young man hung his head, and answered: 'Alas, my father, shame prevented me from telling you of the vile treatment to which I have been subjected; for I could not defend myself nor form a guess as to the author of my woes.' Then he told his father the whole story in all its details. But it would be useless to repeat it in this place. 'I would rather be dead than live such a life,' he groaned. 'Before your face, my father, I swear the oath of triple divorcement. I beg you to seek out the King and persuade him to declare that my marriage with his daughter, Badr al-budūr, is null and void. That is the only way by which I can get any peace; I would much rather sleep in a bachelor's bed than pass my nights with my head in the privy.' The wazīr was greatly cast down by his son's words; for his highest ambition had always been to marry the lad into the royal family. Yet he was convinced by what he had heard, and exclaimed: 'I agree that it is impossible for you to put up with such treatment. But think how much you will lose by this divorce! Would it not be better to have patience for one more night, if I promise to have armed guards set all about the marriage-chamber?' 'You can do as you like about the guards,' answered his son, 'but I am never going to set foot in that ill-omened room again.'

So the wazīr returned to the King and stood before him with lowered head. 'What have you to tell me?' asked the Sultān. 'That what our princess has said is true in every particular,' answered the wazīr, 'but the fault was not with my son. One thing is certain, Badr al-budūr must not be exposed to these terrors because of my poor boy; therefore I beg that you will allow them to be divorced.' 'You are right,' answered the King. 'They are divorced. Had the bridegroom been other than your son, I would have divorced them with my sword.' The King gave orders that the public rejoicing should cease throughout China, and proclaimed by heralds that his daughter was divorced from the son of the grand-wazīr, that the marriage had never been consummated and that the princess remained a maiden pearl, in all things pure and unpierced. Out of respect for his wazīr, he named the unfortunate bridegroom governor of a far province and despatched him to his post on that same day.

At this point Shahrazād saw the approach of morning and discreetly fell silent.

But when the seven-hundred-and-fifty-fifth night had come

SHE SAID:

When Alā al-Dīn learnt, with all the rest of the citizens, that Badr al-budūr had been divorced while yet a virgin, and that her wretched husband had been banished, he cried out for very joy: 'Blessed be the wonderful lamp! This is far the best thing which could have happened. The divorce has taken place without the Jinnī having had to destroy that young fool utterly.' He prided himself that his vengeance had matured without the King, or the wazīr, or even his mother, knowing that he had any part in the business, and set himself to wait in all tranquillity for the rest of the three months to pass. When the last day came he sent his mother, dressed in her richest garments, to remind the Sultān of his promise.

As soon as Alā al-Dīn's mother entered the dīwān, the Sultān recognised her and turned to the wazīr, saying: 'There is Alā al-Dīn's mother. You will remember that she brought us a dish full of miraculous jewels three months ago; I am sure that she now comes to demand that I fulfil my promise and marry my daughter to her son. I give great thanks to Allāh that He reminded me of my oath, when I would have broken it and given Badr al-budūr to another.' The wazīr, who still bitterly resented his humiliation, answered with some cunning: 'It is true, dear master, that kings must never go back upon their word; but, also, it is the duty of every father to know something of his son-in-law. The King has made no enquiries concerning Alā al-Dīn, but I have. He is the son of a poor tailor who died in the direst poverty. How can the son of such a man be rich?' 'Riches come from Allāh,' replied the King. 'That is true,' agreed the wazīr, 'but we have no assurance that this Alā al-Dīn is as wealthy as he would have us suppose. I suggest that the King should demand such a dowry from him as only a King's son could pay. Then, if the sum is brought, my lord may know that he has not given his daughter to one unworthy of her.' 'Your tongue is gifted with a wise eloquence, dear wazīr,' said the King. 'Lead the old woman forward.' The wazīr signed to the captain of the guard, who conducted Alā al-Dīn's mother to the foot of the throne.

After she had kissed the earth three times between his hands, the Sultān said: 'Be it known to our dear aunt that we have not forgotten our promise; but nothing has so far been said concerning the dowry for our daughter; our aunt must remember that she is a very worthy princess . . . Tell your son that the marriage will take place when he has sent me the following treasure for my daughter: forty vast dishes of solid gold filled to the brims with those same varied jewel fruits which you brought me before on a porcelain dish; these dishes must be carried to the palace by forty girl slaves, each as beautiful as the moon, guarded by forty negro slaves, handsome and young and strong; they must come to me magnificently dressed and lay the jewels at my feet. That is all I require, good aunt. Nor do I feel justified in asking more, when I remember the present which your son has already sent me.'

Terrified by this demand, Alā al-Dīn's mother prostrated herself before the throne and silently retired. When she reached home, she said to Alā al-Dīn: 'Indeed, my son, I was right when I counselled you to give up all thought of Princess Badr al-budūr.' Then, with many sighs, she told Alā al-Dīn of her reception by the King and the dowry which he demanded. 'I knew you were mad,' she said. 'I will grant you the gold dishes and the jewels, for I believe that you would be foolhardy enough to go back to the cave and strip the magic trees; but the forty girl slaves and the forty young negroes, what will you do for them? You would never have been asked so much, my son, if it had not been for that rascally wazīr. I saw him whispering into the King's ear as I went in. If you do not renounce your project, Alā al-Dīn, you will be lost beyond recall.' 'When I saw you come in, looking so worried, I thought that you brought bad news,' answered Alā al-Dīn with a smile. 'Now I see that you were but worrying about trifles, as you always do. The King's demand is nothing compared with my power to heap riches upon him. Calm your dear spirit and refresh your eyes; leave the King to me, and go and prepare a meal, for I am very hungry.'

At this point Shahrazād saw the approach of morning and discreetly fell silent.

But when the seven-hundred-and-fifty-sixth night had come

SHE SAID:

As soon as his mother had gone out to buy food in the market, Alā al-Dīn shut himself up in his own chamber and rubbed the lamp. The Jinnī appeared and bowed before him, saying: '*I am master of earth and air and wave, but slave of the lamp and the bearer's slave. What will you have, master, what will you have?*' Then said Alā al-Dīn: 'O Ifrīt, the Sultān will give me his daughter, the marvellous Badr al-budūr, if I send him forty dishes of solid gold, filled to the brim with jewel fruit like those which I plucked from the trees in that garden where I found your lamp. The dishes must be borne by forty girl slaves, each as fair as the moon, and guarded by forty handsome young negroes, strong, well-built, and magnificently dressed. These things I ask of you in my turn. I command you by virtue of the lamp to bring them to me.'

The slave of the lamp departed and returned immediately with the eighty slaves, whom he ranged along the outside wall of the house. Each of the forty women carried on her head a vast basin of solid gold, filled to the brim with pearls, diamonds, rubies, emeralds, turquoise, and a thousand other kinds of gem, all like the fruit of trees in shape, colour and size. These jewel fruits were even more marvellous than those which had been given to the Sultān upon the porcelain dish; also, each of the basins which held them was covered by a silk gauze worked with gold flowers. As soon as the Jinnī had arranged this wonderful procession, he bowed before Alā al-Dīn and was dismissed.

At that moment Alā al-Dīn's mother came back from the market, laden with provisions, and, seeing so many and such strange folk about her door, feared that the Sultān had sent to chastise Alā al-Dīn for his insolence. But her son reassured her, even before she had time to take off her veil. 'Do not take off your veil, dear mother,' he said, 'for I wish you to go forth again at once, to lead these slaves to the palace. As you see, the forty women are carrying my dowry. I beg you to accompany the train as spokeswoman, even before you get the dinner.'

Alā al-Dīn's mother led forth the eighty slaves, one behind the other, in groups of two; each girl was immediately preceded by one of the young negroes, and each group was separated by an interval of ten feet. When the last group had set out, the old woman brought up the rear, while her son closed the door and retired to wait calmly on the event.

As soon as the first group reached the open street, the citizens began to crowd about them; by the time the procession was complete, the roads were blocked by an excited concourse, full of rumour and exclamation. All the markets emptied their folk to run after and admire so strange and magnificent a spectacle. Each several group was an exquisite marvel in itself; for to each there went the white beauty of a girl, the black beauty of a magnificent negro, grave cadenced walking, the fire of the gold basin, the flames of the man's belt, the sparks from off brocade. Not one who saw these things doubted that some fabulous prince had come to their city.

The train came at last to the palace, and the guards so marvelled at the first couple that they fell back in admiration and left a clear lane for their passage. The captain of the guard, on seeing the first negro, thought that he must be the King of the negroes in person, coming to visit the Sultān; therefore he prostrated himself and would have kissed the skirt of the slave's robe. But the first negro smiled and said, as he had been instructed by the Ifrīt: 'We are but the slaves of him who shall come when the time is ripe.' So saying, he crossed the threshold followed by the first girl, and then, at the same intervals, by the rest of those harmonious pairs. The eighty slaves crossed the first courtyard and drew up in exquisite order in the second, which gave upon the great reception hall of the palace.

The Sultān, sitting upon his throne and governing the affairs of his kingdom, saw this black and white procession filling the courtyard with its splendour; therefore he dismissed the dīwān and ordered the newcomers to be admitted. The slaves entered gravely, two by two, and slowly ranged themselves in the form of a wide crescent before the throne. The girls, helped by their black guards, set down their gold basins upon the carpets before them; then the whole eighty prostrated themselves and kissed the earth between the King's hands. With one movement they rose and with one movement drew the gauze coverings from their loads. Then they stood impassively with their arms crossed over their breasts, in an attitude of the deepest respect.

Then, and only then, Alā al-Dīn's mother advanced to the centre of the glittering crescent and, after prostrating herself, said to the dumbfounded King: 'O Sultān of time, your slave, my son Alā al-Dīn, has sent me with the dowry for your noble daughter. He has charged me to say that you have gravely undervalued the princess in your demand; but he hopes that you will excuse the meagreness of this tribute and remember that it is, if you will allow it to be so, but the first wave of a rich and shining sea.'

The King, who lay back with open mouth and wide eyes, staring first at the basins, then at the jewel fruits in the basins, then at the delightful slaves who had carried the basins, and then at the young negroes who had accompanied the girls who had carried the basins, could hardly pay attention to what Alā al-Dīn's mother was saying. He sat for an hour of time, dumbly debating the relative excellence of the girls, who might have been taken for summer moons, and the black youths, who had the appearance of being each a king. At last, feeling too abashed to speak directly to the old woman, he turned to his wazīr, exclaiming: 'What shall be said of our riches before these things, or of our palace before this magnificence? What can we say of a man who is able to send us such things in less time than it took us to ask for them? How can the merits of my daughter stand against this profusion of beauty?' In spite of his bitter resentment, the wazīr could not help crying: 'As Allāh lives, all this is marvellous enough. Yet I would not say that it is worth that treasure which is Badr al-budūr.' 'Nay, all this out-values her exceedingly,' answered the King. 'At least you cannot say that I have taken a step in the dark in marrying her to a man as rich, generous, and noble as my son, the lord Alā al-Dīn.' He turned to the other wazīrs, amīrs and notables who surrounded the throne and questioned them with his eyes; and they all bowed low to the earth three times, to show that they agreed with what the King had said.

At this point Shahrazād saw the approach of morning and discreetly fell silent.

But when the seven-hundred-and-fifty-eighth night had come

SHE SAID:

The King hesitated no longer, but instead of pausing to enquire what Alā al-Dīn's other qualifications as a husband might be, turned to the old woman, saying: 'O venerable mother of Alā al-Dīn, I beg you to inform your son that, from this moment, he is one of my royal house and line, and that I wait impatiently to embrace him as my son and to marry him by the Book to my daughter, Badr al-budūr.'

Alā al-Dīn's mother ran more swiftly than the wind, until she found her son at home and told him what had passed. Alā al-Dīn was overjoyed at the news, after his so long waiting, but he did not wish to show how drunk he was with rapture. Quite calmly he answered: 'All this happiness comes from Allāh and from your blessing upon me, dear mother, and from your tireless zeal in my cause.' He kissed her hands with many murmurs of thanks, and then begged leave to retire to his chamber to prepare for the coming visit.

As soon as he was alone, he rubbed the lamp and said to the Jinnī who came and bowed before him: 'O slave of the lamp, I wish to take a bath and, after the bath, I wish a robe more magnificent than the greatest king of earth has set aside for the greatest occasions; it must be so beautiful that experts will judge that it cost at least a thousand thousand dīnārs. That is all for the moment.'

The slave of the lamp bended his back completely, saying: 'O master of the lamp, mount upon my shoulders.' Alā al-Dīn mounted, letting his legs hang over the broad breast; and the Ifrīt, whose contact made the youth also invisible, rose in the air and carried him to such a hammām as the kings and rulers of the earth have never seen. It was made all of jade and transparent alabaster, with pools of rose carnelian and white coral. The ornamentation was a cunning pattern of large emeralds; the eyes and every other organ of sense rejoiced together in this place, for each thing, alone and in the general harmony, was perfection. The air was of a delicate freshness, cool where that was suitable and of a balanced heat where such was fitting. No bather troubled the peace of those white vaults; but when the slave of the lamp had set Alā al-Dīn upon the dais in the entrance hall, a young Ifrīt of immortal beauty, like but infinitely more engaging than a girl, appeared before the boy and helped him to undress. Then he threw a perfumed towel about Alā al-Dīn's shoulders, raised him tenderly, and led him to the fairest of the halls of that bath, one which was paved with a close-set pattern of jewels. Then other young Afārīt, as handsome and ensnaring, received him from the hands of their companion and, after reclining him comfortably upon a marble bench, began to rub him and wash him with scented water of different flowers. They kneaded his limbs with admirable art and then laved them again with musk-scented rose-water. Their skilled care gave his skin the fresh tint of a rose petal, compact of white and vermilion; and he felt so light that he was tempted to fly like a bird. The first youth came for him again and led him back to the dais, where he refreshed him with a sherbert of musk and snow and summer flowers. When he had drunk, Alā al-Dīn found the slave of the lamp standing before him with a robe which it would be impossible for me to describe. Helped by his attendant's pleasant hands, he put this magnificence upon him and became like the dream of some great king's son. As soon as he was dressed the Ifrīt lifted him and carried him back to the chamber of his house.

'And now do you know what more I want?' asked Alā al-Dīn. 'I do not know, O master of the lamp,' replied the Ifrīt. 'But command and I shall obey.' Then said Alā al-Dīn: 'I desire that you bring me a horse of pure breed who has no brother in all the world for beauty, no, not even in the stables of kings. His harnessing must be worth at least a thousand thousand golden dīnārs. At the same time you will bring forty-eight graceful slaves, richly, cleanly and elegantly clad, of which twenty-four, in two files of twelve, shall clear the way before my horse, and the other twenty-four, in two files of twelve, bring up the rear. Also, be careful to select twelve girls of incomparable and moonlike beauty, each the pet example of her race, to serve my mother. Each must bring a different-coloured robe with her, worthy the wearing of a king's daughter. Lastly, you must hang about the neck of each of the forty-eight slaves a bag containing five thousand dīnārs of gold, so that I may have money when it pleases me. That is all that I wish for to-day.'

At this point Shahrazād saw the approach of morning and discreetly fell silent.

But when the seven-hundred-and-fifty-ninth night had come

SHE SAID:

Hardly had Alā al-Dīn finished speaking when the Jinnī disappeared and returned with the horse, the forty-eight young slaves, the twelve girls, the forty-eight bags of gold, and the twelve robes of different stuff and colour. All these things were finer in their quality even than Alā al-Dīn had required. He dismissed the Ifrīt, saying: 'I will call you when I have need.' Then he kissed his mother's hands in leave-taking and gave her into the care of the twelve girls, bidding them serve her in everything and teach her the correct usage of the robes which they had brought.

Alā al-Dīn mounted his horse and left the courtyard; although it was the first time he had been in the saddle he rode with such accomplishment that chosen cavaliers might have envied him. Two files of twelve slaves opened the way for him, four slaves at his sides held up the cords from the housing of his horse, and the rest followed after.

A mighty crowd, greater than that which had greeted the jewel slaves, ran together from the markets and flocked in windows and upon terraces to see Alā al-Dīn's train go by, for there was no more room in the streets. At their master's order, the forty-eight slaves threw handfuls of gold among the crowd to right and left, so that great cheers rang through the city for the generosity and surpassing beauty of this rider and his slaves. Alā al-Dīn on horseback was a handsome sight to see; the natural garden of his face had been rendered more excellent by the virtues of the lamp; and, as he rode, the diamond feather in his turban streamed back like light itself. In an uproar of acclamation Alā al-Dīn came to the palace; but the rumour of his approach had gone before him, and the royalty of China was prepared to do him honour.

The King himself waited at the top of the stair which led down to the second courtyard and, as soon as Alā al-Dīn had dismounted with the aid of the grand-wazīr, he walked down three of the stairs to do him reverence. Alā al-Dīn climbed to meet him and would have prostrated himself; but the Sultān, who marvelled at the richness of the boy's dress and the nobility of his bearing, received him in his arms and embraced him as if he had been his own son. Then the air shook with the concerted joy of the amīrs, wazīrs and guards, and with the sound of trumpets, clarinets, hautboys and drums. With one arm passed about Alā al-Dīn's neck, the King led him into the vast reception hall and, after making him sit beside him on the bed of the throne, embraced him a second time. 'As Allāh lives, my son,' he said, 'I grieve that my Destiny has not made us acquainted before to-day, and am sorry that I delayed your marriage with your slave, Badr al-budūr, for these three months.' Alā al-Dīn answered with such charming suitability that the Sultān's love for him increased, and he continued: 'There is no king on the earth who would not wish you for a son-in-law, Alā al-Dīn.' Then he spoke affectionately with the youth, wondering at the wit and eloquence of his replies, while a magnificent feast was prepared before them. When all was ready, they ate alone in the throne room, served by the grand-wazīr, whose nose trailed almost to the ground for spite, and by amīrs and other high dignitaries of the court.

As soon as they were satisfied, the King, who was more than ever mindful of his promise, called the kādī and witnesses, and bade them write out a marriage contract for Alā al-Dīn and the Princess Badr al-budūr. The kādī obeyed, with all due observance to the forms of the sacred Book, and, when he had finished, the Sultān embraced Alā al-Dīn for the third time, saying: 'My son, do you wish to enter the marriage-chamber to-night, and consummate your vows?' 'O King of time,' answered Alā al-Dīn, 'if I were not to listen to the great love which I have for my wife, I would go into her this very night.

But as I wish the consummation to be made in a palace worthy of my love and belonging to her alone, allow me to put off the full realisation of my delight until I have built for her the palace of my dreams. For this purpose, I pray that you will allow me to take possession of the vast square opposite your own palace, so that my wife may not be too far separated from her father, and I myself may be near enough to serve you in everything. I can promise that the building will be set about without delay.' 'My son, it is hardly necessary for you to ask permission,' answered the King. 'Take all the ground that you require in front of my palace, and hasten on the work of construction, for I wish to see another generation of my posterity before I die.' Alā al-Dīn reassured the King with a smile and, after embracing him tenderly in farewell, returned to his own house, accompanied as before, amid the loud wishes of the people.

After telling his mother what had passed, he retired to his own chamber and rubbed the lamp once more.

At this point Shahrazād saw the approach of morning and discreetly fell silent.

But when the seven-hundred-and-sixtieth night had come

SHE SAID:

When the Ifrīt appeared, Alā al-Dīn said to him: 'First, O slave of the lamp, I have to praise the zeal which you have shown in my service. Now I have a more difficult task to set you: I wish you to build me, with the least possible delay, a palace worthy of my bride, on the open ground in front of the Sultān's dwelling. I leave to your good taste and proven knowledge the details of its ornament and the choice of such precious material as jade, porphyry, alabaster, agate, lazuli, jasper, marble and granite. But I insist upon one particular: in the middle of the palace you must raise me a vast crystal dome supported by columns of alternate gold and silver, and pierced by ninety-nine windows, crusted and set about with diamonds, rubies and emeralds. The ninety-ninth window you must leave unornamented, though perfect in construction. Do not forget to lay out a fair garden with fountains and watercourses, and to give great breadth to the courtyards. Also, I require you to construct a secret underground chamber and fill it with a rich treasure in gold coin. I leave such things as the kitchens, the stables, and the provision of slaves, to your good sense and liberal mind. When all is ready, come and tell me.' 'I hear and I obey,' answered the Jinnī, as he carried his hand to his brow and disappeared.

At the morrow's dawn the Ifrīt came to Alā al-Dīn's bed, saying: 'Master of the lamp, your will has been done. I pray you, come and approve the fruit of it.' Alā al-Dīn agreed, and the Ifrīt carried him off and showed him a palace, standing opposite the King's and infinitely more noble, set in a fine garden and approached by two broad marble walks. After pointing out the admirable architecture of the whole, the slave of the lamp took his master to examine the interior in detail; and Alā al-Dīn found that his orders had been carried out with unimaginable splendour and a luxury even beyond the power of his wishing. He inspected the vast secret treasure-house below the earth, crammed with sacks of golden dīnārs; he saw the kitchens, offices, store houses and stables, and found them vast, clean, and pleasing to him. He admired the horses and mares, feeding from silver mangers, or being dressed by expert grooms. He reviewed the slaves and eunuchs according to their rank and then, turning to the Ifrīt, who was invisible to all else, sincerely congratulated him on his marvellous preparation. 'You have only forgotten one thing,' he said, 'a carpet from this palace to the other, so that my wife may pass across without wearying her feet.' 'You are right,' answered the slave of the lamp, 'but the thing is already done.' And lo, a cloud-soft carpet of velvet stretched between the two palaces, glowing with every tint of meadow and garden!

'Now all is perfect,' cried Alā al-Dīn, 'and you may take me back to my house.' The Ifrīt lifted him and took him back to his house, just as the folk of the Sultān's palace began to open the doors and set about their occupations of the day.

As they came forth, the slaves and porters fell back aghast to find the mighty ground in front of the palace blocked by a structure even more imposing, and to see a cloud-soft velvet carpet stretching before them and entering the garden opposite, where the blossoms and leaves and grasses of its texture vied with the natural lawns and flowerbeds on either hand. Their eyes followed beyond the carpet and saw the palace blazing with jewels, its crystal dome appearing above the roofs like the rising of the sun. They reported these things to the grand-wazīr, who carried news of them to the King, saying: 'Sultān of time, there can be no doubt that our Lady Badr al-budūr's husband is a skilled magician.' 'Your insinuation surprises me, O wazīr,' replied the King. 'You should know that a man who can make such presents must be rich and powerful enough to have a palace constructed in a single night by natural means. Surely you are blinded by jealousy?'

Realising that the King loved Alā al-Dīn too much to be influenced against him, the wazīr became prudently silent. So much for him.

At this point Shahrazād saw the approach of morning and discreetly fell silent.

But when the seven-hundred-and-sixty-first night had come

SHE SAID:

As soon as Alā al-Dīn reached his home, he bade one of his mother's twelve slaves waken the old woman, and commanded the whole delightful band to dress her in one of the magnificent robes which they had brought. When she was dressed, he told her that the time had come for her to conduct the bride from the King's palace to his own, and gave her instructions as to her behaviour at such a time. Alā al-Dīn's mother set out with her twelve girls, and Alā al-Dīn himself followed soon after on horseback with his train. The two troops separated when they came between the palaces, Alā al-Dīn turning into his new abode and his mother entering the Sultān's gateway.

The King received Alā al-Dīn's mother with every mark of respect, and ordered his chief eunuch to take her to Badr al-budūr in the harīm. The princess rose in her honour and embraced her; then, begging her to be seated, she had her served with sweet cakes and preserves, and bade the slaves continue with her own toilet. Just as her women had finished decking the new bride with the fairest of the jewels which her lord had sent, the Sultān entered the harīm. As the two were now related, he was able to see the face of Alā al-Dīn's mother unveiled for the first time. He easily perceived, from the delicate lines of her face, that she had been very beautiful in youth; even now, when she was dressed and tended so carefully, she had an air of greater nobility than many of the princesses and amīrs' wives about the court. He complimented her gracefully upon her appearance, and so touched the heart of the tailor's widow that her eyes filled with happy tears.

The three talked together pleasantly, learning each other more and more, until the Queen came in and, after greeting Alā al-Dīn's mother with sufficient politeness, sat among them, without paying any attention to the conversation. She disapproved of the marriage of her daughter to an unknown young man, and took sides with the grand-wazīr; but, because of her husband, she dared not openly betray her feelings.

When the time came for the princess to leave for her new home, she embraced her father and mother very tenderly, mingling most proper tears with a thousand kisses. Alā al-Dīn's mother led her out, preceded by ten eunuchs in their state dresses and followed by a hundred girls as pleasantly habited as dragonflies. Four hundred slaves, alternate black and white, were drawn up in two rows from one palace to the other; they held golden torches in which burned large candles of amber and white camphor. The princess passed slowly between these living walls, treading the velvet meadows of the carpet, while musicians played sweet welcome from the garden alleys and palace terraces; far away the happy shouting of the people added a note of good augury to this concerted music. Alā al-Dīn came smiling to meet his bride, and she, on seeing her bright handsome, was pleased to be led into the feast-hall under the glowing windows of the dome. The three sat down to a meal prepared on gold plate by the slave of the lamp; and Alā al-Dīn had his place between the two women. They ate and drank to the sound of songs from invisible singers in the air, boy and girl Afārīt chanting in chorus, and Badr al-budūr said to herself: 'I did not know that there were such marvels anywhere.' She would stop eating and drinking to listen and to look, nor was there need for Alā al-Dīn and his mother to ply her with food and wine for she had eaten and drunk deep of miracles.

That was such a day as was not seen in the times of Iskandar and of Sulaimān.

At this point Shahrazād saw the approach of morning and discreetly fell silent.

But when the seven-hundred-and-sixty-second night had come

SHE SAID:

When night came, the platters were taken away and a troop of four hundred dancers came into the hall. These were the daughters of Marids and Afārīt, having the movement of birds and being dressed like flowers; to an airy music they danced those dances which the maidens use in Paradise. Then Alā al-Dīn took his wife by the hand and led her, with cadenced steps, to the marriage-chamber. The girl slaves, led by Alā al-Dīn's mother, followed in good order. They undressed Badr al-budūr, and she was like a narcissus slipping from the green shawl of its youth. They left the chamber, and Alā al-Dīn was joined to Badr al-budūr, the King's daughter. That was such a night as was not seen in the times of Iskandar and of Sulaimān.

At dawn, after the dark hours of delight, Alā al-Dīn left the princess's arms and, dressing himself magnificently, mounted a superb horse from the stables, in order to visit the Sultān. The King rejoiced at his coming and, after kissing him, asked for news of Badr al-budūr. Alā al-Dīn made the expected answer, and added: 'I have hastened to you thus early, O King of time, to beg that you will light my palace with your presence and partake with us of the first meal after our coming together. I trust that you will bring the grand-wazīr and your amīrs to do us honour.' The Sultān accepted immediately and left the palace with Alā al-Dīn, followed by his grand-wazīr and the amīrs.

With every step towards his daughter's dwelling, the Sultān's admiration grew greater, his cries of astonishment more shrill. What then shall be said of his marvelling eyes when he saw the interior of that sumptuous building? But, above every other harmony and magnificence, he preferred the hall of the crystal dome, with its airy columns springing to meet the jewelled fires of the high windows. He counted the number of the windows and found that there were ninety-nine, neither more nor less; also he saw the last window was unfinished and lacked ornament. 'This is the most remarkable palace of its time upon earth,' he said. 'I can find no word for my admiration . . . But I wish to know why that window has not been finished; for it mars the perfection of the whole.' 'O King of time,' answered Alā al-Dīn with a smile, 'do not think that this window is forgotten, or that I have let it appear as it does through economy or negligence. I wished, if I may make so bold, to leave it to our lord the Sultān to finish that work, so that the glory of his name and reign might, as it were, be worked into one of the stones of his daughter's dwelling, and thus consecrate it as worthy of her for all time.' The King was flattered by this attention, and thanked Alā al-Dīn for the delicacy of his thought. He sent his guards at once to collect the cleverest craftsmen in jewelry and those who had the largest stock of gems, to complete the incrustation of the window. While waiting for them to come, he went to see his daughter and asked news of her

first night; the pleased smile with which she answered was sufficient
to set all his fears at rest. He embraced Alā al-Dīn again and congratulated him in suitable terms. Then he accompanied the wedded
pair to a meal at which he found the meats beyond question perfect
to the taste, and the silverware altogether admirable.

At this point Shahrazād saw the approach of morning and
discreetly fell silent.

But when the seven-hundred-and-sixty-third night had come

SHE SAID:

Soon the jewellers and goldsmiths were led in by the guards and
conducted to the gallery below the dome, where the King climbed
up to interview them. He showed them the unfinished window, saying: 'I require you to finish the necessary work upon this window,
incrusting your patterns in pearls and every colour of precious
stone.' The jewellers and goldsmiths bowed before him and then
closely examined the decoration of the other windows, exchanging
astonished glances from time to time as they did so. After they had
consulted together, they prostrated themselves before the Sultān,
saying: 'O King of time, we have not in all our shops enough gems
to decorate one hundredth part of this window.' 'I will furnish you
with what is necessary,' answered the King, and he had the jewel
fruit of Alā al-Dīn's dowry brought to them. 'Use what you need
and give me back the rest,' he said. The jewellers took measurements
and made calculations, checking and checking their results. Then
they said humbly: 'O King of time, these jewel fruits will not
be enough to ornament one tenth of the window.' So the King
called to his guards: 'Go to the houses of my wazīrs, amīrs and
rich notables; collect all the precious stones which they have
and bring them to me.' The guards hurried forth to execute this
order.

While waiting for their return, Alā al-Dīn, who observed signs
of uneasiness in the King and was mightily pleased by them, wished
to distract him with some music. He signed to one of his attendant
Afārīt, who led in a troop of singing girls so fair that each might have
said to the moon: 'Begone, that I may take your place!' and with
such pure voices that each might have said to the nightingale: 'Be
silent, and hear me sing!' Their choruses relieved the King's em-
barassment for a time.

But as soon as the guards came back and handed over to the jewellers all the gems which they had spoiled from the richest houses in the capital, the King said to the craftsmen: 'And now?' 'As Allāh lives, dear master,' they anwered, 'we are still very short of the account. We need at least eight times as much material as we have here; also, however fast we worked, it would take us three months of unremitting toil to decorate the window.'

The King felt his nose nigh brush his feet for bitter shame, and Alā al-Dīn, satisfied that he had sufficiently proved his power, said to the jewellers: 'Take back your stocks of precious stones, and go your way,' then to the guards: 'Return those jewels to their owners,' and lastly to the King: 'Sultān of time, it would not be becoming of me to receive back that which I have given. I trust that you will allow me to return the jewel fruits and take upon myself the ornamentation of this window. As I cannot bear to be watched while I work, I pray you to wait for me with my wife Badr al-budūr.' So the King betook himself to the chamber of the princess.

Alā al-Dīn drew the magic lamp from a nacre cabinet and with it summoned the Ifrīt. 'Slave of the lamp,' he said, when the Jinnī appeared, 'I wish you to make the ninety-ninth window exactly like its fellows.' The slave of the lamp withdrew and immediately there sounded a multitudinous and invisible hammering and filing about the window; in less time than it takes a thirsty man to drink a cup of water, the ninety-ninth window glittered with intricate jewel work and might not be recognised from its fellows.

At Alā al-Dīn's entreaty the Sultān came up to the gallery; but he supposed at first that he had mistaken one side of it for the other. It was not until he had circled the dome several times that he realised that the work had been completed. As soon as he was convinced of the truth, he kissed Alā al-Dīn between the eyes, saying: 'The more I know of you, my son, the more I love you.'

At this point Shahrazād saw the approach of morning and discreetly fell silent.

But when the seven-hundred-and-sixty-fourth night had come

SHE SAID:

The King called his grand-wazīr and pointed out the marvel of the window to him. 'What do you think now, O wazīr?' he asked in a voice of irony, and the wazīr, though he was surer than ever that

Alā al-Dīn was a sorcerer, a heretic, and an alchemical philosopher, thought it prudent to answer: 'Allāh alone is great!'

From that time, the Sultān spent the evening of each day with Alā al-Dīn and Badr al-budūr, finding new marvels in the palace on every visit. Alā al-Dīn did not let himself be puffed up or softened by this new life; instead, he devoted those hours when he was not with his wife to improving the condition of those about him and finding objects for his generosity among the poor of the city. He did not forget the poverty of his childhood, and every time he rode abroad his slaves were ordered to scatter gold dīnārs among the crowd. Twice a day the broken food from the palace was distributed among the destitute, and sufficed to feed five thousand. Alā al-Dīn's generosity and modesty drew the hearts of the city to him, so that there was none, high or low, who did not mention this new bene-factor in his prayers. He put the seal upon his popularity by winning a great victory against certain tribes which had revolted from the Sultān. In this engagement he showed a warlike quality and reckless courage, which made Badr al-budūr love him more ardently than ever. She never grew weary of congratulating herself that she had found the one man worthy to be her husband. For many years Alā al-Dīn's existence was an unbroken harmony of happiness, in the love of his wife and mother, in the love of the people, and in the admiring love of his father-in-law. So much for Alā al-Dīn.

Now we will turn to the Moorish magician, who had been the un-willing and unconscious first cause of Alā al-Dīn's happiness. When he had left the boy to die of hunger and thirst in the cave, he re-turned to his own land in the interior of far Morocco and spent his days in mourning over the useless pains which he had taken to secure the lamp. He brooded over the fatality which had snatched from his lips a morsel which he had confected with so much care, and not an hour passed without his cursing the day when he had met Alā al-Dīn. On one occasion, when the bitterness of his gall rose even to his lips, he felt that he must become acquainted with all the details of Alā al-Dīn's death. So he took his table of divinatory sand from a mystical cupboard and, seating himself before it on a square mat within a red circle, flattened the sand, marked the male and female points, set out the mothers and children of that art, and mur-mured geomantic spells above them. 'Let me behold, O sand, let me behold,' he cried. 'Where is the magic lamp? How did Alā al-Dīn die?' He shook the sand according to the canons of sorcery, so that the figures grew and the horoscope was formed. He looked upon these things and learnt that Alā al-Dīn was alive, that he was master of the lamp, that he lived in honoured splendour, married to the Princess Badr al-budūr, daughter of the King of China, and that he was known to all the frontiers of the world as Alā al-Dīn the Great Amīr. As soon as his evil operations had given him these unexpected tidings, the sorcerer foamed at the mouth and spat into the air and upon the ground, crying: 'O son of bastards and bitches, I spit in your face! Black dog, foul gallows-bird, I piss upon your head!'

At this point Shahrazād saw the approach of morning and discreetly fell silent.

But when the seven-hundred-and-sixty-fifth night had come

SHE SAID:

For an hour the Moor spat in the air and upon the earth, for an hour he trampled his imagination of Alā al-Dīn beneath his feet, swearing terrible oaths and screaming out insults, until he felt a little calmer. Then he swore to be revenged upon Alā al-Dīn because he had gained the lamp. He set out immediately for China, and, as his rage lent him wings, he made no pauses in his journey, but meditated the means of his vengeance as he was borne along. Soon he arrived in the capital city of China. He alighted at a khān where he secured a lodging, and started next morning to explore the public places of the city. Wherever he went he heard tell of nothing but the amīr Alā al-Dīn, the beauty of the amīr Alā al-Dīn, the generosity of the amīr Alā al-Dīn, and the magnificence of the amīr Alā al-Dīn. 'By light and fire,' he muttered to himself, 'they will soon be calling out for the death of the amīr Alā al-Dīn.' When he came to Alā al-Dīn's palace and saw what a noble thing that was, he cried: 'So the tailor's son lives here, the little lad who had no bread! Alā al-Dīn, Alā al-Dīn, you shall soon see that my Destiny cries in the top of yours; your mother shall spin again, and with my own hands I shall dig the ditch where she shall come to weep.' By entering into conversation with the shopkeeper he found that Alā al-Dīn had gone upon a hunting expedition which had already lasted several days. 'This is the beginning of his fall,' he thought. 'I can work more freely while he is away. But first I must know whether he has taken the lamp with him or left it at the palace.' For this purpose he returned to his room in the khān and questioned his geomantic table. The horoscope told him that Alā al-Dīn had left the lamp in the palace.

Drunken with joy, he made his way to the market of the copper-smiths, and entered the shop of one who sold copper lamps. 'I need twelve new polished copper lamps,' he said, and, when the merchant produced a dozen shining lamps, he paid the price without bargaining and placed his purchases in a basket, which he had already procured.

Then he wandered through the streets towards Alā al-Dīn's palace, crying: 'New lamps! New lamps! New lamps for old!' Seeing his large turban and hearing his unaccustomed cry, all the little street boys left their games and ran after him, hooting and chanting: 'Mad! He is mad!' But the Moor took no notice and easily drowned the sound of their yelling with: 'New lamps! New lamps! New lamps for old!' Followed by the shouting and jostling boys, he came to the place in front of the palace and began to walk up and down, up and down, crying his cry louder and louder as time went on. At last Badr al-budūr, who happened to be in the hall of the ninety-nine windows, heard this unaccustomed clamour and opened one of the jewelled lattices.

She saw the excited squealing crowd of urchins, and heard distinctly the strange offer of the Moor. So she laughed and her women laughed with her. But one of them said to her: 'Dear mistress, when I was tidying our master's chamber yesterday, I saw an old copper lamp standing on a stool. May I show it to the old Moor and see if he will in truth exchange it for a new one?' Now this old lamp was none other than the magic lamp, which Alā al-Dīn had forgotten to shut up in its nacre cabinet before he went away. Who can war against the decrees of Destiny? Princess Badr al-budūr knew nothing of this lamp or of its marvellous powers, so she answered: 'Certainly. Give the lamp to a eunuch and tell him to try to exchange it for a new one. If he succeeds, we will be able to laugh at that old fool.'

The girl went to Alā al-Dīn's chamber, took the lamp, and gave it to a eunuch, who left the palace and showed it to the Moor, saying: 'My mistress would exchange this lamp for a new one.'

When the magician saw the lamp, he recognised it at once and began to tremble. 'What is the matter?' asked the eunuch. 'Is the lamp too old for you?' But the Moor had already fought down his agitation; he snatched the lamp, with the swiftness of the vulture pouncing upon a dove, and hid it in his bosom. Then he held out his basket to the eunuch, saying: 'Take your choice.' The eunuch picked out a fire-new and highly-polished lamp, and carried it quickly to Badr al-budūr, with peals of laughter at the folly of the Moorish merchant. So much for the eunuch and Alā al-Dīn's lamp.

At this point Shahrazād saw the approach of morning and discreetly fell silent.

But when the seven-hundred-and-sixty-sixth night had come

SHE SAID:

The magician hurled his basket of lamps at the hooting mob of boys and ran away from the palace, dodging down a thousand by-streets of the city until he had thrown off all possible pursuit. When he came to a deserted place, he drew the lamp from his bosom and rubbed it. The slave of the lamp appeared, and cried: '*I am master of earth and air and wave, but the slave of the lamp and the bearer's slave. What will you have, master, what will you have?*' For the Ifrīt had to obey the owner of the lamp, even though he were vowed to wickedness and perdition as was this Moor.

'Slave of the lamp,' said the Moor, 'I order you to snatch up the palace which you built for Alā al-Dīn, and to transport it, with all its contents, to my country at the back of Morocco, and there set it down among its gardens. You will carry me also.' Then said the slave of the lamp: 'Shut one eye and open one eye and you will find yourself in Alā al-Dīn's palace in your own land.' In a flash the thing was done, and the Moor found himself in Alā al-Dīn's palace in the wild parts of Morocco. So much for him.

Next morning the Sultān left his palace to visit Badr al-budūr, according to his custom; but there was no palace, only a large waste space, cut by the empty ditches of the foundations. At first he rubbed his eyes, thinking that he had gone mad, and then the beams of the rising sun and the limpid morning air persuaded him that he was seeing the truth. To make quite sure, he climbed to the highest storey of his own palace and looked out of a window; but there was no palace, only a waste space over which, had it not been for the ditches, riders might have galloped their horses.

The unhappy father wept and plucked at his beard, though he did not then know the full extent of his loss. While he moaned upon a couch, his grand-wazīr came to him to announce that the dīwān was assembled. 'Come here,' said the King and, when the wazīr had approached, cried out angrily: 'What has become of my daughter's palace?' 'Allāh have the King in His keeping!' answered the wazīr. 'I do not understand what he would say.' 'Then you know nothing?' asked the King sadly. 'I know nothing, nothing at all,' answered the wazīr. 'That is because you have not looked out towards Alā al-Dīn's palace,' said the King. 'I walked in its gardens yesterday at evening,' ventured the wazīr, 'but I saw nothing unusual, except that the great door was shut because the amīr was from home.' The King led the wazīr to the window and made him look forth. 'Far be the Evil One!' cried the old man. 'The palace has disappeared! Now will you admit, my lord, that the whole thing was the work of a most skilful sorcery?' The King lowered his head and reflected for an hour, then raised his head and exclaimed terribly: 'Where is that wretch, that adventurer, that sorcerer, that impostor? Where is that son of a thousand dogs, who calls himself Alā al-Dīn?' The wazīr's heart swelled with triumph as he answered: 'He is still hunting, but has promised to return to-day before the noon prayer. Shall I go forth to meet him and ask him what has happened to his palace?' 'By Allāh, you shall do nothing of the sort!' shouted the King. 'Let him be dragged before me in chains, for the robber and liar that he is!'

At this point Shahrazād saw the approach of morning and discreetly fell silent.

But when the seven-hundred-and-sixty-seventh night had come

SHE SAID:

The wazīr passed on this order to the captain of the guard, who rode out of the city with a hundred followers, and met Alā al-Dīn at a distance of five parasangs from the gate. He surrounded him with guards, and said: 'O amīr Alā al-Dīn, O our master, we pray you to excuse us; but we are the slaves of the Sultān, and he has ordered us to drag you before him in chains. We cannot disobey him, but we are also heavily in debt to your bounty, and ask again to be excused.'

For a moment Alā al-Dīn was dumb with surprise and consternation, but soon he answered: 'Good folk, do you know why the Sultān acts in this way, when I am innocent of any crime against him or the State?' 'As Allāh lives, we do not know,' answered the captain of the guard; so Alā al-Dīn got down from his horse, exclaiming: 'Carry out your orders; for the King's command is binding upon any loyal subject.' The guards regretfully wound a heavy chain about his arms and neck and waist, and made him follow them on foot while they rode back to the city.

As soon as they came to the outlying walls, the citizens, seeing Alā al-Dīn treated in this way, supposed that the King would have him beheaded for some unknown cause; therefore, as he was dearly loved by all for his affable generosity, they closed in behind him, arming themselves with swords, bludgeons, sticks and stones. This threatening escort had grown to thousands upon thousands by the time the prisoner had been led to the back of the palace. And there was such hooting and menace of rude weapons that the guards were hardly able to take their captive into the palace without being torn to pieces. After Alā al-Dīn disappeared from their sight, the people continued to howl outside the gates, demanding that their amīr be returned to them.

The Sultān's rage was so great that he did not even ask for an explanation when Alā al-Dīn appeared before him; instead, he cried out to his executioner: 'Cut off this vile impostor's head at once!' The executioner led Alā al-Dīn out on to a terrace above the mob and made him kneel upon the red leather of death; then he bandaged his eyes, took off the chain, and said: 'Make your peace with Allāh!' But, even as the man flashed his sword three times about his head, the crowd below, with an angry bellowing, began to climb the walls and force the doors. In an extreme of terror, the King cried to the executioner: 'Do not strike the blow!' and to the captain of his guard: 'Tell the people that I give them back this wretch's life.' This announcement was made from the terrace and calmed the tumult of the mob, so that they left the doors and descended from the walls.

Alā al-Dīn's eyes had been ostentatiously unbandaged to convince his following; now he rose from the bloody mat and said with tears: 'O King of time, I beg you tell me what I have done to earn so great a disgrace?' 'What have you done?' answered the King furiously. 'You pretend not to know? Then follow me.' He led him to the other side of the palace, which overlooked the site of Alā al-Dīn's vanished dwelling, and bade him look through a window. Alā al-Dīn looked and saw no palace and no garden, no sign, save the ditches, that garden or palace had ever been. The world grew dark before his eyes and he could not speak. 'O vile impostor,' cried the King, 'where is my daughter, the stone of my heart's fruit, my only child?' Alā al-Dīn uttered a despairing sigh, and answered: 'O King of time, I do not know.' Then said the Sultān: 'Listen well. I do not ask you to bring back your evil palace, but if you do not return my daughter to me at once, your head shall answer for it.' Alā al-Dīn reflected for an hour with lowered eyes, and then replied: 'O King of time, none may escape his Destiny. If it is my fate to be beheaded for a crime which I have not committed, nothing can save me. But I have a right to ask a delay of forty days in which to hunt for my beloved; for she has gone through no fault of mine and also I swear, by our sacred Faith and by the merits of our lord Muhammad (on whom be prayer and peace!), without my knowledge.' 'I grant you that delay,' said the King, 'but after it has passed nothing can save you from my wrath. If you do not return my daughter, I will find means to fetch you back from the uttermost parts of the earth to a terrible punishment.' Alā al-Dīn left the presence with bowed head, and the dignitaries who saw him passing across the palace could not recognise him, for he was so changed by grief. He wandered through the waiting crowd, asking with haggard eyes: 'Where is my palace? Where is my wife?' and the people said to each other: 'Poor Alā al-Dīn, the Sultān's cruelty has driven him mad!' Finding himself an object of compassion, Alā al-Dīn hastily left the city at haphazard and fled through the open country.

At this point Shahrazād saw the approach of morning and discreetly fell silent.

But when the seven-hundred-and-sixty-eighth night had come

SHE SAID:

He came at last to a great river, and as he looked into its obscure depths, he thought: 'It is useless to seek Badr al-budūr, for I know nothing of her fate. It were better to drown all thought in the waves of this river.' But then he remembered that he was a Mussulmān and, lifting up his heart, bore witness to the unity of Allāh and the mission of His Prophet. This act of faith and subjection comforted him, and, instead of casting himself into the water, he knelt down to make his ablution for the evening prayer. Squatting on the bank, he took up water in the hollows of his hands and began to work the fingers together. This movement caused him to rub the ring which the Moor had given him for protection in the cave. As he knelt, the Ifrīt of the ring bowed down before him, saying: '*I am master of earth and air and wave, but slave of the ring and the wearer's slave. What will you have, master, what will you have?'* Alā al-Dīn recognised the apparition by its hideous aspect and terrifying voice; he sprang to his feet and cried delightedly: 'May Allāh bless you, O slave of the ring, O friend in need and deed! I pray you to bring me back my palace and my wife.' 'Master of the ring, that cannot be,' answered the Ifrīt. 'I am only the slave of the ring and may not undo the work of the slave of the lamp.' 'In that case, O slave of the ring,' exclaimed Alā al-Dīn in his perplexity, 'since you may not meddle with a business that seems not to concern you, since you may not bring the palace back to me, I order you, by the virtue of the ring you serve, to carry me to the palace and set me down beneath the windows of my wife, Badr al-budūr.' As he finished speaking, he found himself set down gently beneath the windows of the princess in his own magnificent garden, far in the wilds of Morocco. The sight of his palace tranquillised his soul and caused him to draw easy breath; hope came back to his heart and joy came with her. Just as a man who has given a sheep's head to be cooked cannot lie down and sleep until he has seen it come perfect from the oven, so Alā al-Dīn could not rest, though he was worn by grief and wandering. He thanked Allāh for the fortunate turn which his adventure had taken and then stood up in full view of the windows.

Since she had been snatched away with the palace, the princess had been tortured both by grief for her husband and by fear of the magician's wooing; therefore she neither ate nor drank, and ever rose before dawn from the couch on which she had not slept. On that evening, when Alā al-Dīn rubbed the ring, a certain slave, guided by the hand of Destiny, had opened one of the windows in the crystal hall and, as she looked forth, was saying: 'Dear mistress, come and see how lovely the trees look in the airs of evening.' Suddenly she uttered a great cry: 'My master, my master! There is my master, Alā al-Dīn, under the windows!'

At this point Shahrazād saw the approach of morning and discreetly fell silent.

But when the seven-hundred-and-sixty-ninth night had come

SHE SAID:

Badr al-budūr rushed to the window, and the parted lovers recognised each other. 'Come, come quickly, my dear one,' cried Badr al-budūr, who was the first to recover herself. 'You need have no fear, the magician is away.' The slave ran down and opened a secret door, by which Alā al-Dīn gained access to his wife's chamber. Laughing and crying, as if joy had made them drunk, they fell into each other's arms. It was not for some minutes, when they were seated more calmly side by side, that Alā al-Dīn said: 'Before all else, Badr al-budūr, tell me what has become of that copper lamp which I left on a stool in my chamber before I went off to hunt.' 'Dearest, that lamp was the cause of all our misery,' cried the princess, 'but it was not entirely my fault that it should have been so.' She told Alā al-Dīn of the exchange of lamps, and added: 'After he brought me here, the wicked Moor told me of the lamp's virtue; he said that, by its means, he had carried our palace into Morocco.' 'What does he want of you?' asked Alā al-Dīn, without the least reproach. 'He comes to me each day and tries to seduce me to his will,' replied Badr al-budūr. 'To conquer my repulsion, he always insists that you have been beheaded by the King as an impostor, and that you are only the son of a miserable tailor called Mustafā; he claims that you owe all your honour and fortune to his own kindness. On each occasion I have received him with silence and turned head, so that he has retired with drooping nose. But I am always afraid that he will use violence. I thank Allāh that He has sent you to me!' 'Now tell me where he keeps the lamp,' said Alā al-Dīn. 'He never leaves it in the palace,' answered Badr al-budūr. 'He carries it in his bosom wherever he goes. Once he drew it forth to taunt me with it.' 'That is well, that is very well!' exclaimed Alā al-Dīn. 'His punishment shall be our salvation. Now leave me alone for a moment in this room.'

As soon as Badr al-budūr departed, Alā al-Dīn rubbed the ring on his finger, and said to the Ifrīt who appeared in answer to his summons: 'Slave of the ring, are you learned in the matter of soporific powders?' 'I understand them better than anything else,' answered the Ifrīt. 'Then bring me an ounce of Cretan banj,' commanded Alā al-Dīn, 'and let it be strong enough to kill an elephant.' The Ifrīt vanished and returned in a moment with a tube, which he handed to Alā al-Dīn, saying: 'Here is Cretan banj of the finest quality.' Alā al-Dīn dismissed the Jinnī and called to Badr al-budūr. 'Dear love,' he said, when she came in, 'we can get the better of that vile sorcerer, if you will do exactly what I say. Now listen carefully, for time presses and he may arrive at any moment.' He gave her minute instructions, and handed her the tube of banj; then he hid himself in a large cupboard and waited for the coming of the Moor.

Badr al-budūr did not like the part which had been assigned to her, but she rose and allowed her women to comb and coif her hair in the fashion which most suited the perfect pride of her face. Then she dressed herself in her fairest robe, girt herself in a gold belt blazing with diamonds, and hung a collar of equal pearls about her neck. When she had clasped heavily-jewelled bangles about her wrists and ankles, and had been perfumed with seven sorts of scent, she looked like some hūrī chosen to be Queen of Paradise. She regarded herself tenderly in the mirror, while her women crowded round with cries of admiration, and then posed herself amorously among her cushions.

At this point Shahrazād saw the approach of morning and discreetly fell silent.

But when the seven-hundred-and-seventieth night had come

SHE SAID:

The Moor came at his usual hour; the princess rose in his honour for the first time and with a smile begged him to be seated beside her. The magician was delighted at being so well received and, because of the light from those lovely eyes, dared only sit upon the edge of the dīwān. 'You must not be astonished, dear master, because I am changed to-day,' said the princess with a languishing glance. 'My nature is opposed to sadness and now has conquered my grief. I have reflected on my husband's death and realise that the decree of Destiny must run its course. My tears cannot recall him, and therefore I have put aside my tears . . . But I have not offered you any refreshment.' She rose in her flowerlike beauty and moved over to a broad stool, loaded with wines and sherbets. With her back to the Moor, she cast a pinch of the banj into a gold cup of honour which was already filled with wine, and bade one of her slaves carry it to the magician. 'This is less than the smile of your eyes, O princess,' said the Moor, as he took the cup and drank it off. Before he could lower the gold from his lips, he fell head over heels upon the carpet at the girl's feet.

Hearing the fall, Alā al-Dīn uttered a cry of triumph and, leaping from the cupboard, ran towards the motionless body of his enemy. Opening the top of the old man's robe with trembling fingers, he drew forth the lamp. 'Leave me again, Badr al-budūr,' he said, 'for it is time that we draw towards an end.' When his wife had retired, he rubbed the lamp and, as soon as the Ifrīt appeared, bade him return the palace to China, gently and without shock. Two very slight tremblings followed, one of the uplifting and one of the setting down, and lo, the palace was back in its old place in face of the Sultān's dwelling!

Alā al-Dīn found Badr al-budūr and kissed her upon the lips, saying: 'We have come home, my love; but it is night and we cannot see your father until the morrow. Let us rejoice together alone, as we have done before.' As neither had eaten for many hours, they sat down together in the hall of ninety-nine windows and were served with a repast of succulent meats and clear wines. Then they passed the rest of the night in the unimaginable joy of each other's arms, until the morning.

At dawn the Sultān rose to weep for his daughter in that place where her dwelling had been; when he took his first sad look and saw Alā al-Dīn's palace shining in its gardens under the morning sun, he started back with a cry and rubbed his eyes, for he supposed that he beheld a mirage, or some unsubstantial picture of his grieving brain. But the towers and terraces remained solid and unshaken; so the King began to run, forgetting all his dignity, shouting for joy and hustling the guards and porters out of his way. In spite of his great age, he leapt up the alabaster stairs of Alā al-Dīn's palace and threw himself into the hall where Alā al-Dīn and Badr al-budūr waited his coming with smiles. They rose in his honour and ran towards him; he caught his daughter in his arms and the two mingled their tears of gratitude together.

At this point Shahrazād saw the approach of morning and discreetly fell silent.

But when the seven-hundred-and-seventy-first night had come

SHE SAID:

'But you look happy and in good health, my child!' exclaimed the old King, when he could get his breath. 'Yet you must have known great grief and fright at being separated from your father? I should have expected to find you quite yellow. Tell me everything which has happened and hide nothing, my dear.' 'My colour has come back to me,' answered Badr al-budūr, 'because I have found my father and my husband once again. But, believe me, I have wept and fasted and feared, far from this place, in the power of a Moorish magician, who wished to enjoy my body. Yet was it all my own fault, for giving away something which was not mine.' She told the King the whole story of the flight of the palace and showed him the motionless body of the sorcerer lying behind a curtain. 'That, O King of time,' cried Alā al-Dīn, 'is the cause of all our woe and my disgrace. But Allāh shall punish him!'

The Sultān became convinced of Alā al-Dīn's innocence and kissed him tenderly, taking him to his bosom. 'Dear son,' he said, 'you must not blame me too much for my harshness, since my justification was my great love for Badr al-budūr, which you, of all people, should appreciate. A father's heart is full of tenderness, and I would rather lose my kingdom than one hair from my daughter's little head.' 'You had every excuse, my father,' answered Alā al-Dīn. 'You supposed that you had lost your daughter through my fault, and, to a certain extent, it was so. I ought to have foreseen the magician's vile design and been on my guard against it. You will never know the full extent of his perfidy until I have leisure to tell you the whole story of my life.' The Sultān kissed Alā al-Dīn again and answered: 'Certainly, at some future time, you must find occasion to tell me all; but it is more important now to get rid of that evil body at our feet.' Alā al-Dīn ordered his young slaves to take out the body of the Moor and burn it on a bed of dung in the city square, and to cast the ashes into the public cesspool. These things were done in sight of the whole city, whose people rejoiced at this well-merited punishment and at Alā al-Dīn's restoration in the graces of the King.

The Sultān announced by heralds, with a sound of pipes and drums, that he freed all who had been cast into prison as a sign of public rejoicing; he gave large alms to the poor, and had both palaces, as well as the whole city, lighted with coloured fires at night. Thus Alā al-Dīn escaped death a second time, thanks to the grace which was in him. And you will see that same grace save him a third time, if you listen further to my tale.

Some months after Alā al-Dīn's return—months during which he and his wife had lived in perfect happiness under the tender and vigilant eye of Alā al-Dīn's mother, who had now become a great lady, but without arrogance—his wife entered the crystal hall from which he was looking out upon the garden, and said sadly to him: 'Dear master, though Allāh has showered His favours upon us, He has denied me the consolation of a child. We have been married a long time and I have felt no life stirring within me. I beg you therefore to let me call to the palace an aged female saint named Fatmah, who has just arrived in our city and is said to cure sterility by the laying on of hands.'

At this point Shahrazād saw the approach of morning and discreetly fell silent.

But when the seven-hundred-and-seventy-second night had come

SHE SAID:

Alā al-Dīn at once gave his permission and sent four eunuchs to fetch the old saint to the palace. They soon returned leading the holy dame, her face muffled in a thick veil and a triple chaplet of mighty beads swinging over her bosom. She walked by the aid of a large stick, for her body was broken by age and virtuous practices. The princess ran to meet her and asked for her blessing, kissing her withered hand the while. In a low deep voice the old woman called down the blessings of Allāh and made a long prayer for the continued prosperity of her hostess. Badr al-budūr begged her to be seated in the place of honour on the couch, and said: 'O saint of God, I thank you for your prayers. As I know that He will refuse you nothing, I hope, through your intervention, to satisfy the dearest want of my soul.' Then Badr al-budūr blushed and continued in a smaller voice: 'Saint of God, I desire that He of His mercy will grant me a child. Tell me what I must do to merit that favour, for I am ready to accomplish anything to earn a gift which would be sweeter than life itself. If you are successful in your prayers, I will give you all which you may desire, not for yourself, since you are beyond all earthly needs, but for the poor in whom you take most virtuous delight.'

As Badr al-budūr spoke her wish, the saint's eyes, which had been lowered till then, opened and shone with a dire light. Her face seemed on fire within and her whole body shook from jubilation; she looked at the princess without speaking a word and then, stretching out her hands, laid them upon the suppliant's head and seemed to mutter a silent prayer. 'My daughter, my dear mistress,' she said at last, 'the saints of Allāh have shown me the way by which you may lure the fecundity of nature to your body; but I think you will find that way impossible.' Badr al-budūr threw herself at the old woman's feet, clasping her knees and crying: 'Tell me the means, my mother, for nothing is impossible to Alā al-Dīn, my dear husband. Speak, or I shall die here at your feet.' The saint lifted her finger and spoke: 'If you would bear a child, you must hang in the crystal dome of this hall an egg taken from the bird Rūkh, who lives on the highest peak of Caucasus. If you look long at this egg for many days, your interior nature will undergo modification and the dead shall live. That is all I have to say, my daughter.' 'I know nothing of the Rūkh, my mother, and I have never seen her eggs,' cried Badr al-budūr, 'but I am quite sure that Alā al-Dīn can instantly procure me one of these prolific marvels, even from the highest nest upon Mount Caucasus.' She would have kept the saint, but the latter said to her: 'I must now depart to relieve the misfortunes of others and griefs greater than your own. But to-morrow, if Allāh wills, I shall return most eagerly for news of you.' Then, in spite of the princess's gratitude which would have loaded her with jewels, she departed in all haste.

Soon after she had gone, Alā al-Dīn returned and came to kiss his wife, as he always did even after the shortest absence; finding her preoccupied and anxious, he asked her the cause in some alarm.

At this point Shahrazād saw the approach of morning and discreetly fell silent.

But when the seven-hundred-and-seventy-third night had come

SHE SAID:

Badr al-budūr answered breathlessly: 'I shall die if you do not quickly get me a Rūkh's egg from the highest peak of Mount Caucasus.' Alā al-Dīn laughed as he answered: 'Dearest, if it only requires that to keep you alive, I think that you need have no anxiety. But tell me what you will do with the egg when you have got it.' 'The holy old woman has prescribed that I shall look long upon it, as a cure for my sterility,' replied Badr al-budūr. 'I wish to hang it in the middle of the crystal dome in the hall of windows.' 'You shall have the thing at once, my dear, I promise you that,' said Alā al-Dīn.

Leaving his wife, he retired to his own chamber and drew forth the magic lamp which he now kept ever in his bosom. When the Ifrīt appeared in answer to his rubbing, Alā al-Dīn addressed him in friendly fashion: 'O excellent Ifrīt, O obliging slave of the lamp, I wish you to bring me at once an egg of the gigantic Rūkh, who lives on the highest peak of Caucasus, that I may hang it in my crystal dome.'

As these words left Alā al-Dīn's lips, the Ifrīt twisted his whole body in a horrible fashion, his eyes blazed and he yelled so terribly in Alā al-Dīn's face that the palace shook to its foundations and the amīr himself was driven like a stone from a sling against the opposite wall. 'Miserable human,' cried the Jinnī in a thunderous voice, 'what is this that you dare to ask? O vile and most ungrateful master, have you the effrontery to demand this thing, after all that I have done for you? You would have me bring you the offspring of my supreme master, the most holy Rūkh, to hang in your miserable crystal dome? Mad fool, do you not know that I and the lamp and all who serve the lamp are the great Rūkh's slaves, vowed in obedience to the Father of Eggs? It is well for you that you are safeguarded by the lamp and carry that ring of security upon your finger; otherwise I would grind you to powder beneath your palace!' In shocked surprise, Alā al-Dīn answered: 'O Ifrīt of the lamp, as Allāh lives, this demand does not come from me; it comes, through my wife Badr al-budūr, from a most holy saint, a true mother of fecundity, whose cure of the barren is the surprise of time.' The Ifrīt suddenly grew calm and resumed his ordinary voice. 'I did not know that,' he said. 'So matters stand thus: the crime is not yours but that vile creature's! O Alā al-Dīn, you are lucky that the suggestion was not yours; for it would have led infallibly to the destruction of yourself and of your wife and of your palace. That was your holy old woman's object; she is no more a holy old woman than I am, but a man disguised, the brother of the Moorish sorcerer. He resembles your dead enemy as one half of a bean is like the other. True is the proverb which says: *The younger dog is fouler than his elder, for the race of dogs ever declines.* Your new foe is more adept in magic and deeper in crime than his elder brother; when he learnt through geomancy that his brother had been destroyed by you and burnt by order of the Sultān, he vowed vengeance and came hither from Morocco, in the garb of an old holy woman. He succeeded in gaining introduction to the palace and then suggested the terrible crime against my supreme master. But now that I have put you on your guard, you should be able to cope with his wiles. The blessing of Allāh be upon you!' So saying, the Ifrīt disappeared.

Inwardly raging, Alā al-Dīn returned to his wife in the hall of windows, and said to her: 'O Badr al-budūr, light of my eyes, before

I can obtain that egg for you, I must hear the old woman describe the remedy with my own ears. Therefore recall her and, while I hide behind the curtain, make her repeat her suggestion, on the pretext that you have forgotten exactly how it ran.' 'Be it upon my head and before my eyes!' answered Badr al-budūr, and she sent in haste for the old woman.

At this point Shahrazād saw the approach of morning and discreetly fell silent.

But when the seven-hundred-and-seventy-fourth night had come

SHE SAID:

Soon the pretended saint, still muffled in her veil, entered beneath the crystal vault and approached Badr al-budūr, but Alā al-Dīn bounded upon her from his hiding place, sword in hand, and before she could say: 'Bim!' severed her head from her body with one blow.

'O what a woeful crime, Alā al-Dīn!' cried Badr al-budūr in terror; but her husband smiled and, lifting up the severed head by its topknot, showed it to the princess. To her horror and amazement she saw that it was shaved like a man's, save for the topknot, and that the face was covered with extravagant hair. In order not to keep her in suspense, Alā al-Dīn at once told his wife the truth concerning this Fatmah, who was neither saint nor woman. 'O Badr al-budūr,' he cried at length, 'let us give thanks to Allāh Who has delivered us from our enemies for ever!' They threw themselves into each other's arms, murmuring their gratitude to the Merciful for all His favours.

After that, they lived happily for many years in company with Alā al-Dīn's mother, that good old woman, and the aged Sultān, who was Badr al-budūr's father, and had many children, each as beautiful as the moon. When the Sultān died, Alā al-Dīn inherited the throne of China, and nothing marred their contentment until they, in their turn, were visited by the Destroyer of delights and Separator of friends.

The Parable of True Learning

'THAT, O auspicious King, is all I know concerning Alā al-Dīn and the Wonderful Lamp. But Allāh knows all!' 'The story is admirable, Shahrazād,' answered King Shahryār, 'but I admit that it astonished me by its discretion.' Then said Shahrazād: 'In that case, O King, allow me to tell you the tale of Kamar and the expert Halīmah.' 'Do so, Shahrazād,' cried the King; but she smiled as she replied: 'But, even before that, I wish to tell you a precept, which our fathers have handed down concerning The True Learning, that it may teach you the admirable virtue of patience and fortify you to wait, without anger against your slave, the happy fulfilment of that Destiny which Allāh means to your race through me.' 'Let me hear this precept without delay,' said Shahryār, 'and also tell me what destiny Allāh can mean to my race through you, when I have no posterity.' 'O King,' murmured Shahrazād, 'allow your slave to keep a still tongue yet awhile concerning the mystery of those twenty silent nights in which your benevolence allowed her to repose because she was ill and during which the splendour of your destiny was revealed to her.' Then, without another hint, Shahrazād, the wazīr's daughter, said:

It is related that a handsome and studious young man once lived in a certain city, where every branch of knowledge was freely taught. He had a great desire to be for ever learning something fresh, that his life might lack no happiness. One day a travelling merchant told him that there existed, in a far country, a sage who was the holiest man of Islām and who, though wiser than the sum of all others at that time, practised the simple trade of a blacksmith, as his father and grandfather had done before him. Straightway the young man took his sandals, his foodbag and his stick, and journeyed towards that far country, hoping that he might learn a little of the blacksmith's wisdom. After forty days and forty nights of danger and fatigue, he came to the city which he sought, and was directed to the smith's shop. He kissed the hem of the saint's robe and then stood before him in silence. 'What do you desire, my son?' asked the smith, who was an old man with a benign face. 'Learning,' answered the youth. Without a word the smith put the cord of the bellows into his hand and bade him pull it. The new disciple pulled the cord of the bellows until sunset. On the morrow he did the same thing; for weeks, for months, and finally for a whole year, he worked the bellows, without receiving a word from the master or the many disciples who were engaged in various kinds of the like hard and simple toil. Five years passed before the young man dared to open his lips, and say: 'Master!' The smith paused in his work and the other disciples ceased their occupations to look on anxiously. The master turned to the young man in the silence of the forge, and asked: 'What do you wish?' 'Learning,' answered the youth, and the smith said, as he turned back to the fire: 'Pull the cord.' Another five years passed, during which the disciple pulled the cord of the bellows from morning to night, without rest and without having a word addressed to him. When any of the disciples needed guidance, he was allowed to write his question on paper and hand it to the master when he entered the forge in the morning. The smith, who never read these writings, sometimes threw them into the fire and sometimes placed them in the folds of his turban. By throwing the question into the fire he showed that it was not worth an answer; but, if he placed it in his turban, the disciple would find an answer in the evening, written in gold characters upon the wall of his cell.

When the ten years were over, the old smith approached the young man and touched him on the shoulder; then the youth left hold of the cord for the first time in ten years, and a great joy descended upon him. 'My son,' said the master, 'you may now return to your own country, knowing that you carry the whole learning of the world about with you. You have acquired patience.'

He gave his disciple the kiss of peace, and the young man returned to his own country, as one inspired with light, one who sees clearly.

'That is an admirable parable!' cried King Shahryār. 'It inclines me to thought.' He reflected for a minute, and then added: 'Now, O Shahrazād, tell me the tale of Kamar and the expert Halīmah.' But Shahrazād said: 'Let me postpone that story yet again, O King, for to-night I do not feel inclined to it; I would rather begin the purest, freshest, pleasantest tale of all I know.' 'Certainly, Shahrazād,' said the King, 'my spirit is also turned towards such things to-night. Also, by waiting for the other tale, I shall learn to profit by your parable.' So Shahrazād said:

Farizād of the Rose's Smile

IT is related, O auspicious King, that there was once, in the days of long ago, a King of Persia named Khusrau Shāh—but Allāh knows all—whom the Giver had dowered with power, beauty and youth, and above all with so just a heart that, during his reign, the tiger and the kid walked side by side and drank together from the same stream. This King delighted to see for himself what passed in his capital city and used to walk about at night, disguised as a foreign merchant, accompanied by his wazīr or some other dignitary of the palace.

One night, as he wandered through the poorest quarter of the city and was passing the mouth of a little court, he heard young voices talking from the end of it. Entering with his companion, he perceived that the voices came from a very small and humble house; so he placed his eye to a crack in the door and looked within. He saw three young girls chatting together, seated about the light upon a mat which bore the remnants of their evening meal. These girls, who were as like as sisters, were entirely beautiful; but the youngest was visibly fairer than the other two.

The eldest said: 'As we are talking of wishes, my wish is to marry the Sultān's pastrycook. You know how I love pastries and especially those admirably delicate and delicious leaved cakes which are called Sultān Cakes. Only the King's pastrycook can make them. I am sure, dear sisters, that you would be whole-heartedly jealous of me when you saw how a diet of fine pastry could round out my white curves and delicately calm the colour of my cheeks.'

The second said: 'I am not so ambitious; I would be content to marry the Sultān's cook. How I should love to do so! I could satisfy all my repressed desires for those rich and extraordinary meats which are only served at the palace; especially those baked stuffed cucumbers, which trouble my heart when I only see them carried on the heads of porters during the King's feast days! How I would eat! And if my husband allowed me, I would bring you some of those cucumbers from time to time, but I fear that he would not allow me.'

The two sisters who had already expressed their wishes turned to the third who kept silence, and asked jestingly: 'What is your wish, little one? Why do you lower your eyes and not speak? Do not be anxious, for, when we are married, we promise to arrange a wedding

439

for you with one of the royal grooms, so that you may be ever near us. Is that your wish?'

The youngest blushed, and answered in a voice as pleasant as running water: 'O my sisters!' As she spoke no more, the other two laughed and goaded at her until she decided to tell all and said, without raising her eyes: 'My wish is to marry our master, the Sultān. I would give him fair posterity. Our sons should be worthy of their father, and our daughter would be a smile of the sky, and I should love her; her hair would be silver and gold; her tears, if she wept, would be falling pearls; her laughter, if she laughed, would be gold coins; and if she smiled, her smiles would be buds of rose glowing upon her lips.'

Khusrau Shāh and his wazīr saw and heard these things, but at this point they retired, fearing to be discovered. The Sultān felt a desire to satisfy these three wishes growing among the laughter of his heart, so he bade his companion mark down the house, that he might fetch the three girls on the morrow into the royal presence. Next morning the wazīr executed this order and brought the three sisters before the throne.

At a sign from the King's head, the three came nearer trembling, and the Sultān smiled good-naturedly upon them, as he said: 'Peace be with you, O young girls! To-day is the day of your Destiny, when the wishes of your heart shall be accomplished. And I know what those wishes are, O young girls, for nothing is hidden from the kings of the world. O eldest, you shall marry our pastrycook to-day, and you, O second sister, shall marry our cook.' Then the King paused and turned to the third sister, whose heart beat so violently that she was like to sink to the carpet. He raised her up and made her sit on the bed of the throne. 'You are my Queen,' he said, 'and this palace is your palace.'

The three weddings took place that day, the Queen's in unprecedented splendour and that of the other girls with the ordinary usages which befitted their husbands' rank. Thus spite and jealousy entered the hearts of the two older sisters, and even so soon they began to plot the downfall of their youngest. Yet they were careful not to let their feelings show, and accepted with feigned gratitude the marks of affection and unusual liberties of intimacy which their sister heaped upon them in spite of their low degree. Far from being satisfied with the realisation of their wishes, they were tortured with hate and envy for the good fortune of the Queen.

After nine months, Allāh allowed the Queen to give birth to a princely boy, as fair as the crescent of the new moon. Because she requested it, her two sisters were her midwives; but, instead of being touched by her favour and the beauty of the child, they found in this birth an occasion to break the heart of their sister. While the mother was still in her pains, they took the child and set it aside in a basket of osiers substituting for it a little dead dog, which they showed to the women of the palace as the fruit of the Queen's labour. Khusrau Shāh saw the world darken before his eyes when he heard this thing, and he shut himself away, refusing all care for the kingdom. But the Queen's grief was greater, her soul was humbled and her heart was racked by grief.

The two aunts set the basket of the newborn child afloat on the running water of a canal which washed the foot of the palace; but Destiny had decreed that the Sultān's chief gardener should see the basket floating by, as he walked on the side of the canal. Guiding it ashore with a spade, he looked within and saw the handsome infant. You may be sure that his astonishment was as great as that of Pharaoh's daughter when she found Moses among the reeds.

This chief gardener had been married for many years and, though he and his wife ardently desired children, none had been vouchedsafe by the Almighty. Therefore the two had lived sadly in the isolation of the barren. Thus it was that, when the gardener discovered the perfect child, he took it up in the basket and ran joyfully to his own house at the further end of the King's gardens. 'Peace be upon you, O daughter of my uncle!' he cried in a broken voice to his wife. 'See what the Generous has sent us upon a blessed day! This child, who is the child of Destiny, shall be our child also.' He told his wife of the manner in which Allāh had answered their constant prayers, and she took the child and loved it. Glory be to Allāh Who has planted the seed of motherhood in the breasts of barren women, as He has given to lonely hens the instinct to cover pebbles when they have no eggs!

At this point Shahrazād saw the approach of morning and discreetly fell silent.

But when the seven-hundred-and-seventy-fifth night had come

SHE SAID:

In the following year the bereaved queen again gave birth to a son, and he was fairer if possible than the first; but the hatred of the two sisters was not abated and they played the same pitiless trick upon their sister, setting adrift the second baby on the canal and showing a young cat to the palace as the fruit of the Queen's labour. Consternation took hold of every heart, and the Sultān's shame was so great that he might have given himself up to fury, if the virtues of humility and justice had not been so deeply implanted in his soul. The Queen was drowned in bitterness and her heart wept.

Allāh, Who watches over little children, caused the basket of the second son to swim into the chief gardener's view, so that he was saved from the water and taken up and adopted as his brother had been.

And, that all might be fulfilled, He quickened the Queen a third time, and she gave birth to a princess; but the jealousy of the two elder sisters had increased with time, and they were determined to compass the Queen's final destruction by abandoning the little girl in the same way. However she was saved by the large-hearted gardener, even as her two brothers had been, and cared for and nourished and loved by the same foster parents.

This time the two sisters produced a little blind mouse as the new offspring, and the Sultān, in spite of his sense of justice, could contain his fury no longer. 'Allāh has cursed my race because of this woman!' he cried. 'I have taken a monster to be the mother of my children. Only death can assoil my dwelling from such a taint!' He pronounced sentence of death against his Queen and bade his executioner be present; but when he saw her dear form, which he had loved, standing before him drowned in tears, he felt great pity and, turning aside his head, bade the woman be shut for the rest of her days in a closet in the depths of the palace. There she stayed with her tears, a prey to all the sorrows of the world.

But her two sisters knew the great joy of a satisfied hatred, and were able to stuff themselves without bitterness with the dishes of their husbands' confecting.

The days and the years pass as swiftly over the heads of the innocent as over the heads of the guilty, bearing at an equal rate a Destiny to all. The gardener's three adopted children grew to so exquisite a youth that the eyes of all were startled at beholding them. The eldest was called Farīd, the second Farūz, and the third Farizād.

Farizād was a smile of the sky, her hair was silver and gold; her tears, when she wept, were falling pearls; her laughter, when she laughed, was gold coins; and, when she smiled, her smiles were buds of rose glowing upon her lips. Her father, her mother and her brothers, when they called her by name: 'Farizād!' could not help adding: 'Rose-Smile.' But more often they called her simply Rose-Smile. Folk marvelled at her beauty, wisdom and sweetness, and at her strength when she rode out to hunt with her brothers, or shot with the bow in their company, or hurled the javelin; they marvelled at the elegance of her manners, her knowledge of poetry and occult science, and the splendour of her hair, which was silver and gold. Her mother's friends wept with emotion to look upon her.

While his adopted children had grown up about him, the King's gardener had passed, amid their loving respect and cheered by their great beauty, into the confines of extreme old age. But his wife went before him into the mercy of Allāh, and this death was so great a grief to the small family that the gardener resolved to stay no more in that house, where the dead woman had been the serene source of all their happiness. He threw himself at the Sultān's feet and begged to be relieved of that office which he had borne for so many years, and the King regretfully gave him leave to depart. But he would not let him go, until he had given him a magnificent dwelling near the city, with great policies of arable land, woods and fields, and having—in the midst of a perfect garden, laid out by the old man himself, and a vast park stretching between high walls, peopled with coloured birds and beasts, wild and tame—a palace richly furnished after the old man's heart.

The good old gardener lived pleasantly for some time in this retreat, surrounded by the affectionate care of the three children, and then passed into the peace of our Lord. He was wept as a real father has seldom been wept; moreover, he carried with him, beneath that stone which is never lifted, the little which he knew concerning the birth of Farīd, Farūz, and Farizād.

The brothers lived with their sister in this domain of natural beauty, and had no other dream or ambition; for they had been taught with wisdom and simplicity.

The two boys would often go hunting in far woods and fields, while Farizād of the Rose's Smile preferred to wander in the gardens.

One day, as she was about to visit them, her slave informed her that an old woman was at the gate, marked with every sign of benediction, who solicited permission to repose for an hour or two in the shade of the wonderful trees. Farizād, whose heart was as compassionate as her body and soul were beautiful, received the old woman in person and fed her from a porcelain dish of fruit, pastry, and both dry and wet conserve. Then she led her through the gardens; for she had learnt that it is always profitable to listen to the words of those to whom years have brought experience.

Rose-Smile sustained the tottering feet of her guest through the alleys and at last sat down beside her in the shade of the most handsome tree which the garden held. After edifying talk of this and that, she asked the old woman what she thought of the domain, and if it pleased her.

The old woman reflected for an hour, and then answered: 'Dear mistress, I have spent a long life wandering over the length and breadth of Allāh's world, and I have never rested in a more delightful spot; but, just because you are unparalleled upon earth as the sun is unparalleled in heaven, I cannot help wishing that this fair garden, which holds you, held also the three incomparable things which it lacks at present.' Farizād of the Rose's Smile was astonished that her garden should lack three incomparable things, and said to the old woman: 'I pray you tell me what those things are, good mother.' 'I will tell you,' replied her guest, 'to reward you for the loving hospitality which you have given to an old and unknown woman.' She was silent for a moment, and then said:

'Dear mistress, if the first of these things were in your garden all the birds would flock together to regard it, and would sing in chorus; for the nightingales, chaffinches, larks, warblers, goldfinches and doves, together with all the infinite races of the birds, would recognise its supremacy. It is Bulbul al-Hazar, the Talking Bird.

'If the second of these incomparable things were in your garden, the light wind would leave singing among the trees to hear it, and the lutes and harps of your home would break their cords; for the light wind singing among the trees and the lutes and the harps of your home would recognise its supremacy. It is the Singing Tree, and neither the light wind in the trees nor lutes and harps can make so musical a harmony as the thousand invisible mouths which are its leaves.

'Dear mistress, if the third incomparable thing were in your garden, the waters of your garden would cease to run murmuring, to look upon it. For the waters of land and sea, with runlets and waves, with proud rivers marching through cities and tiny brooks babbling among flowerbeds, would recognise its supremacy. It is the Gold Water. A single drop, let fall in an empty basin, will swell and jet up a birth of golden sprays, rising and falling and never overflowing. With that water, which is all gold and has the transparency of the topaz, Bulbul al-Hazar, the Talking Bird, quenches his thirst, and by that water, gold and topaz cool, the thousand mouths of the singing leaves of the tree are slaked.

'O my mistress, O princess, if these three marvellous things were in your garden, your beauty would be exalted, O child of shining hair.'

At this point Shahrazād saw the approach of morning and discreetly fell silent.

But when the seven-hundred-and-seventy-sixth night had come

SHE SAID:

'All this is admirable, visage of blessing, my mother,' cried Farizād of the Rose's Smile, 'but you have not told me where these three incomparable things are to be found.' The old woman answered, as she rose to depart: 'Dear mistress, these three marvels, which are worthy of your eyes alone, lie in a place near the frontiers of India, and the road to them leads behind this palace. If you ever send anyone to look for them, tell him to follow the road for twenty days and on the twentieth day to say to the first man whom he meets: "Where are the Talking Bird, the Singing Tree, and the Gold Water?" The stranger will answer with the necessary directions. Now may Allāh reward the generosity of your soul with all things which have been created for beauty! His blessing be upon you, O blessed!'

Murmuring further benedictions, the old woman wrapped her draperies about her, and retired. When she had gone, Farizād came out of the dream which her words occasioned and would have run after her to ask more precise directions; then, seeing that it was too late, she repeated over and over again the few instructions which she had obtained, so that she might not forget them. Though she tried not to think of the three marvels, she felt an irresistible desire rising in her soul to possess them, or see them at the least. She walked in the alleys of her garden and visited the familiar nooks of it; but all was without charm for her and full of weariness. She found importunate the voices of the birds who gave her greeting as she wandered.

Farizād became sad and wept among the alleys; her tears as they fell left a trail of pearls behind her on the sand of the paths.

Soon Farīd and Farūz returned from hunting and, not finding their sister Farizād under the jasmine bower where she usually waited their return, were grieved at her negligence and went to look for her. Almost at once they found the pearls of her tears lying upon the sand of the alleys, and said to each other: 'Our sister is sad. What can have troubled her soul to make her weep?' They followed the trail of pearls and presently found her crying in a thicket. They ran towards her and kissed her; they petted her, saying: 'Little Farizād, where are the roses of your joy and the gold of your gaiety? Answer us, O sister.' Farizād smiled faintly, because she loved them, and a very little rose was born crimson upon her lips. 'O my brothers,' she said and then fell silent, because she was ashamed of her first desire. 'What is this unknown trouble, O Rose-Smile?' they asked. 'Trust in our love and tell us of your grief.' So Farizād decided to tell, and said: 'I do not love my garden.' Then she wept, and the pearls fell from her eyes upon the grass. 'I do not love my garden any more,' she said again, as they waited in anxious silence. 'There is no Talking Bird, no Singing Tree, and no Gold Water in it.'

Swayed by the intensity of her desire, Farizād told her brothers excitedly of the good old woman's visit and of the excellence of the Talking Bird, the Singing Tree, and the Gold Water. Her brothers were astonished, and said to her: 'Calm your eyes and refresh your dear soul, my sister; even were these things upon the inaccessible peak of Kāf, we would bring them to you. Tell us where they are to be found, so that our search may be easier.' Blushing again because she had expressed her first desire, Farizād told them what the old woman had said of the way. 'That is all I know of it,' she added; but they cried together: 'We will set forth at once, dear sister.' Yet she entreated them in alarm: 'No, no, do not go, my brothers.' Then said Farīd, the eldest: 'Your desire is upon our head and before our eyes, O Farizād. But it is for the elder to fulfil it. My horse is still saddled and will carry me to the frontiers of India without flagging.' Then, to his brother Farūz, he continued: 'You must stay here to watch over our sister; she must not be left alone in the house.' He leapt into the saddle and bent down to kiss his brother and sister. 'Dismount, dear brother!' cried Farizād. 'Give up this journey, for it may be full of danger. Rather than suffer your absence, I wish never to see the Talking Bird, the Singing Tree, and the Gold Water.' But Farīd kissed her again, saying: 'Little sister, have no fear for me; my absence will not be long and I am sure that Allāh means me no harm by the way. See, I give you this knife, whose hilt is crusted with the pearls of the first tears you ever shed. It will keep you informed of my condition. Examine the blade from time to time; as long as it stays clean and bright, you will know that I am well and fortunate; but if it shows dull or rusty, I shall have met with some accident or been thrown into captivity; if it becomes spotted with blood you may be certain that I have ceased to live. Should that last happen, I beg the two of you to call down the compassion of Allāh upon me.' He handed the knife to his sister and galloped off, without waiting for a reply, along the road which led to India.

He rode for twenty days and twenty nights, through solitudes filled only with green grass and the presence of God, and on the twentieth day came to a meadowland at the foot of a mountain. In this meadowland there was a tree and beneath the tree a very old man was seated. His face was hidden entirely by the long hair of his head, by the unkempt tufts of his eyebrows, and by a prodigious beard, as white as new-carded wool. His arms and legs were very thin, and his hands and feet were tipped with nails of extraordinary length. With his left hand he told a chaplet of beads, while he held his right immovable at the height of his brow with the index finger raised, to attest the unity of Allāh. There can be no doubt that he was an old ascetic who had left the world for unknown years and years.

As this was the first stranger whom Farīd had encountered on the twentieth day, he dismounted and advanced towards him, saying: 'Greeting, O holy man!' The sheikh answered his greeting, but his voice was so muffled by the thick moustache and beard that Farīd could not recognise the words he said.

'I must make him hear,' said Farīd to himself, for he had but halted to enquire his way. Taking a pair of scissors from his haversack, he said: 'Venerable uncle, allow me to give you some few attentions which your ceaseless preoccupation in saintly thought has prevented you from accomplishing yourself.' As the old man said neither yes nor no, the prince set himself to cut and trim the mighty beard, the moustaches, brows, and hair, and finally the nails, until the snipping and paring had shorn away twenty years at least. Then, as barbers do, he said: 'May it be a refreshment and delight!'

When the old man felt himself lightened from all this encumbrance, he was extremely satisfied, and said to the traveller, with a benign smile and in a voice as clear as a child's: 'May Allah shower His blessings upon you, my son, for the courteous attention which you have paid to a very old man. And I, myself, O traveller of good omen, am ready to help you with my counsels and experience.' 'I have come from far off, to find the Talking Bird, the Singing Tree, and the Gold Water,' answered Farīd. 'Can you tell me in what place I must look for them?'

The old man suddenly ceased to tell his beads, but he did not answer; so Farīd asked again: 'Why do you not speak, good uncle? I do not wish to allow my horse to grow cold, if you do not know.' 'I know the place, my son, and the road which leads to it,' replied the old man at length, 'but the favour which you have done me is so great that I cannot make up my mind to expose you to the terrible dangers of such an enterprise. Turn back, my son, and ride to your own place; for many and many a young man has passed this way before you and not one has ever returned.' 'Only show me the way,' said Farīd proudly, 'and do not trouble yourself about the rest; for Allah has given me a strong arm.' 'How will a strong arm defend you against the Invisible,' demanded the old man slowly, 'especially when Those of the Invisible are numbered in thousands upon thousands?' 'There is no power or might save in Allah, O sheikh!' exclaimed Farīd. 'My Destiny is about my neck; if I turn from it, it will follow me. Only tell me what I must do, and I will be eternally obliged.'

When the Old Man of the Tree saw that he could not dissuade this young adventurer, he put his hand in a bag which hung about his waist and drew from it a ball of red granite. This he handed to Farīd saying . . .

At this point Shahrazād saw the approach of morning and discreetly fell silent.

But when the seven-hundred-and-seventy-seventh night had come

SHE SAID:

'Mount your horse and throw this ball in front of you; it will roll ahead and guide you. When it stops, dismount and fasten your horse's bridle to the ball; then the animal will wait your return, without moving from that place. Climb on foot up that mountain whose summit we can see from here. You will behold great black stones on every side and you will hear voices which are not of the torrents, not of the winds in the abysses, for they belong to Those of the Invisible. They will shout terrible words at you, enough to freeze the blood of man, but you must not listen; for, if you look behind you while they call from near and far, you will be changed to a black stone like the others. If you can resist their calling and come to the top of the mountain, you will find a cage there with the Talking Bird inside it. You must say: "Greeting, O Bulbul al-Hazar! Where is the Singing Tree? Where is the Gold Water?" And the Talking Bird will answer. And Allāh have you in His keeping!'

The old man sighed and fell silent; as he spoke no more, Farīd leapt into the saddle and threw the ball in front of him with all his force. The round red granite rolled and rolled and rolled before, and Farīd's horse, which was as a stream of light among other horses, could hardly follow it through the briars it broke, the hollows it leapt, and the little hills it overcame. It did not slacken its pace until it came among the first rocks of the mountain; but there it stopped suddenly. Prince Farīd dismounted, and twisted the bridle of his horse about the granite ball; at once the creature grew still upon its four legs, as if it had been nailed to the ground.

At first Farīd heard nothing as he began to climb the mountain, and only saw about him as he went masses of black basalt shaped like human bodies. Though he did not know it, these were the bodies of the young lords who had gone before him into that desolate place. Suddenly a cry rose among the rocks, such as he had never heard before, and two other cries followed it, to right and left, which could not have issued from a man's throat. Nor were they the howlings of savage winds among the rocks, nor the moaning waters of the torrent, nor the sound of cataracts hurling themselves into a measureless abyss; for they were the voices of Those of the Invisible. Some said: 'What do you want? What do you want?' Some said: 'Stop him. Kill him! Stop him. Kill him!' Some said: 'Throw him down! Throw him down!' And some said: 'He is charming! He is charming! Come to us! Come to us!' and seemed to laugh.

Prince Farīd went on climbing bravely, without turning his head; but soon the voices became so numerous and terrible, sometimes bellowing and touching his face with their breath, sometimes far off and far behind, sometimes so menacing, and sometimes so seductive, that at last the poor boy trembled in spite of himself and, forgetting the advice of the Old Man of the Tree, turned his head in the direction of a more frightful cry which breathed upon his face. At once the voices rose to a single laughing yell of triumph and then fell awfully silent, as Prince Farīd changed where he stood into a block of black basalt.

And his horse, also, was turned to a formless black rock at the foot of the mountain, and the ball of red granite rolled back towards the Old Man's Tree.

When Princess Farizād made her examination of the knife on that day, she turned pale and trembled, because the bright blade had become dull and rusted. Farūz ran up to help her and she lapsed into his arms, crying: 'Farīd, Farīd, where are you? Why did I let you go? I am unhappy. O wicked Farizād, I will never love you more!' She sobbed as if her heart would break, and Prince Farūz, though he was no less afflicted, set himself to console her. 'What has happened was fated to happen,' he said. 'Now I will set out to find our brother, and also bring you back the three things which you desire.' 'Do not go for my silly wishes,' begged Farizād. 'If misfortune befell you also, I should die.' But her tears could not turn the second brother from his resolution. He mounted his horse and, after kissing his sister farewell, gave her a chaplet of pearls made from the second tears which she had wept as a child. 'If ever these pearls seem to be stuck together and will not run through your fingers,' said he, 'you may know that I have met the same fate as my brother.' Farizād embraced him sadly, sighing: 'God grant that does not happen, dearest! May He send you both back to me in safety.' So Prince Farūz took the road which led to India.

On the twentieth day of his riding, he found the Old Man of the Tree sitting, as Farīd had seen him, with the index finger of his right hand held on a level with his brow. After greeting, the sheikh informed the prince of his brother's passing and made every effort of eloquence to turn him back. Then, seeing that he could not shake his resolve, he gave him the ball of red granite, which led him to the foot of the fatal mountain.

As Prince Farūz climbed courageously, the voices rose about his steps; but he would not listen to them. Menaces, curses, and flattering calls had no effect on him; but a sudden desolate cry of 'Brother, dear brother, do not pass me!' made him turn his head, and he was at once turned into black basalt.

Farizād ceased not day and night from telling the pearls and when, on the twentieth day, they no longer obeyed her fingers but seemed stuck together, she cried: 'O poor devoted brothers, lost through my caprice, I come, I come!' She fought down her sorrow and would waste no moment in lamentation; she disguised herself as a man and set out on horseback upon the same road, armed from head to heel.

On the twentieth day, she came upon the Old Man sitting under his Tree beside the road, and saluted him respectfully. 'Saintly father,' she said, 'have you seen two young and handsome lords pass by, seeking the Talking Bird, the Singing Tree, and the Gold Water?' 'Sweet mistress Farizād of the Rose's Smile,' answered the old man, 'I both saw them and gave them direction, but I fear that Those of the Invisible have caught them, as they have caught so many others.' Hearing the old man call her by her name, Farizād stood in perplexed silence, while the saint continued: 'Mistress of splendour, those who spoke to you of the three incomparable things, so often sought upon this road by lords and princes, told you the truth; but they did not say that terrible danger hedges the undertaking with impossibility.' He told the princess all that she risked in going after her brothers; but she replied: 'O holy man, my soul is troubled within me, for it is a soul easily frightened; but I cannot turn back when the safety of my brothers is concerned. Hearken to a loving sister's prayer, and show me a way to deliver them.' 'O Farizād, O King's daughter, here is the granite ball which will lead you upon your brothers' tracks,' said the sheikh after a pause, 'but you will never free them until you have gained possession of the three marvels. Yet, as you do not risk your immortal soul from any desire to vanquish the impossible, but only from love of your brothers, the impossible shall become your slave. No human may resist the calling of the Invisible, but the sons of men may use guile against their strength, and come off victorious.'

So saying, the Old Man of the Tree handed the red granite ball to Farizād and then took a wisp of cotton from his belt, crying: 'This light wisp of cotton shall conquer the Invisible! Lean down the glory of your head, O Farizād.' She bent the silver and gold glory of her head, and the old man cried again: 'May the daughter of men conquer the armies of the Invisible with a wisp of cotton!' Then, dividing the cotton into two parts, he put one into each of Farizād's ears, and signed to her to depart.

Farizād followed the ball, as her brothers had done, and began hardily to climb the mountain. The voices rose about her feet among the rocks of black basalt in a terrible howling, but she heard only a vague humming and, being unable to distinguish any words, felt no fright at all. Though her feet were only used to the fine sands of her garden alleys, she went on unwearying and came at last to the top of the mountain. There, in a flat space, she saw a gold cage standing on a gold pedestal, holding the Talking Bird bright within it.

She ran forward and placed her hand upon the cage, crying: 'I have you, bird! You shall never escape me!' At the same time she pulled the wisps of cotton from her ears and threw them far from her, for already the voices of the Invisible were still, and a silence slept upon the mountain.

At this point Shahrazād saw the approach of morning and discreetly fell silent.

But when the seven-hundred-and-seventy-eighth night had come

SHE SAID:

The voice of the Talking Bird rose in the breast of that silence, singing clear:

> Farizād,
> Rose's Smile,
> Farizād,
> Rose's shape,
> Why should I,
> Farizād,
> Farizād,
> Seek escape?
>
> For I know,
> Rose's smile,
> Better far,
> Farizād,
> Farizād,
> Than you know,
> Farizād,
> Who you are.
>
> To the grave,
> Farizād,
> Farizād,

I am slave,
Rose's smile,
Farizād,
To the grave.

Thus sang the Talking Bird, O lutes! Farizād forgot her weariness and said to the miracle: 'O Bulbul al-Hazar, O marvel of the air, if you are my slave, prove it to me!'

Bulbul sang this answer:

Farizād,
You to say,
Farizād,
You to say
And for me,
Farizād,
To obey.

Then Farizād asked where she might find the Singing Tree, and Bulbul bade her turn to the opposite slope of the mountain. There she saw a tree so great that it might have shaded a whole army, and wondered exceedingly how she should be able to unroot it and carry it away. Seeing her perplexity, Bulbul sang again that it was enough to break off the least branch of that tree and to plant it in her garden. So Farizād walked towards the Tree and listened to the singing of its leaves. Then she understood that she was in the presence of the second marvel, for neither light winds in Persian gardens, nor Indian lutes, nor Syrian harps had ever made music to be compared with the concerted singing of the thousand invisible mouths, which were the leaves of that melodious tree.

When Farizād had sufficiently recovered from her ecstasy to pluck a small branch, she returned to Bulbul and asked him where she might find the Gold Water. The Talking Bird bade her turn towards the West and look behind a blue rock which she would then see. So she turned her steps to the West and beheld a mass of tender turquoise, and a slim stream of liquid gold gushed from its azure wall upon the further side; but though the jet was gold, it was as cool and translucent as a water of topaz. With the splendid water Farizād filled a crystal urn which stood in a niche of the blue rock, and returned to Bulbul, carrying both her prizes.

Thus Farizād of the Rose's Smile gained possession of the three incomparable things.

'O most beautiful, I have yet one more prayer to make,' she said. 'The goal of my setting forth has not yet been attained.' The Bird invited her to say on, and she murmured in a trembling voice: 'My brothers, O Bulbul, my brothers!'

For a moment Bulbul was terrified, for he had been used so long to serving Those of the Invisible; but soon he called to mind that the princess had conquered, and sang in answer:

> With the fountain, fountain, fountain,
> Fountain water, fountain tinkle,
> In the urn, the urn of crystal,
> Farizād, Farizād,
> Rise, O rose, oh, rise and sprinkle
> All the black stones of the mountain,
> With the fountain, with the fountain,
> Farizād, Farizād.

Farizād took the crystal urn in one hand and, holding the gold cage and the singing branch in the other, began to retrace her steps down the mountain. As she passed any black basalt rock, she would sprinkle it with water and it would take on life and change into a man. Soon her brothers were restored to her by this means and ran to embrace her, while all the other noble youths, wakened from their stony sleep, hastened to kiss her hand and declare themselves her slaves. The whole troop reached the bottom of the mountain in safety and, when Farizād had restored their horses with the gold water, rode off in the direction of the Old Man's Tree.

But the Old Man was not in the meadowland, and his tree had disappeared. Farizād questioned Bulbul concerning this, and he answered in a voice which had become suddenly serious: 'Why do you wish to see the old man, Farizād? He gave a daughter of men the teaching of a cotton wisp, so that she overcame the importunate voices of evil, and now, as a master retires before his work, he has gone to his own place. His wisdom remains with you and the evils which afflict the human race may not take hold of you, because you have learnt not to lend the attention of your soul to outside happenings. Outside happenings only exist because the attention of the soul is lent to them. You have learnt serenity, which is the mother of happiness.'

So spake the Talking Bird in the place where the Old Man's Tree had stood, and all who heard marvelled at the depth and beauty of his language.

At first the troop kept together upon the road, forming an escort about Farizād, but soon the lords and princes branched off, one after the other, to go to their homes, and, on the evening of the twentieth day, Farīd, Farūz, and Farizād arrived alone and without accident at their palace.

When they had dismounted, Farizād hung the gold cage under the jasmine arbour and, as soon as Bulbul sounded the first note of his voice, all the birds of the garden flocked together to regard him, and sang his praise in chorus. For the nightingales, chaffinches, larks, warblers, goldfinches and doves, together with all the infinite races of the birds, recognised his supremacy. In voices high and low they sang responses among the leaves to his solitary couplets, and acclaimed each skilful trill of his in the language of their kind.

And Farizād went to the fountain basin of alabaster, in whose depths she had been used to behold the silver and gold splendour of her hair, and let fall into it one drop of water from the crystal urn. The gold bead swelled and jetted up a birth of golden sprays, rising and falling and never overflowing, and filling the sun-flecked air with the cool of a sea cave.

And with her own hands Farizād planted the Singing Branch, so that it took root and grew in a few moments to as great and fair a tree as the one from which it came. It sang with all its leaves and neither light winds in Persian gardens nor Indian lutes nor Syrian harps had ever made such music; to hear the thousand invisible mouths which were its leaves, the waters of the garden ceased to run murmuring, the birds fell silent, and the wandering breeze among the roses hushed the silken sighing of its dress.

The days of monotonous happiness began again: Farizād resumed her walks among the alleys, staying for long hours to talk with the Talking Bird, to listen to the Singing Tree, and to delight her eyes with the Gold Water; while Farīd and Farūz returned to their hunting and riding in the neighbouring woods.

At this point Shahrazād saw the approach of morning and discreetly fell silent.

But when the seven-hundred-and-seventy-ninth night had come

SHE SAID:

One day, as the two brothers rode out hunting, they saw the Sultān approaching by the same narrow wood path in which they went, so they hastened to dismount and prostrate themselves. The King, who was surprised to see two richly-dressed and unknown cavaliers so near his city, bade them rise that he might behold their faces. They rose and stood before him with an air of nobility which admirably suited their respectful mien; the King was struck by their beauty, and looked them up and down for a long while, then, as his heart was drawn towards them, he asked them where they dwelt. 'O King of time,' they answered, 'we are the sons of your old slave, the chief gardener, who is now dead. We dwell not far from here, in the house which you gave him.' The Sultān rejoiced to make the acquaintance of his faithful servant's children; but he was astonished that they had not presented themselves at the palace, and said so. 'O King of time,' they answered, 'pray forgive us our absence from before your generous face; but we have a young sister, who was our father's latest trust to us, and we watch over her with so much love that it has never occurred to us to leave her.' Touched by this answer, the Sultān exclaimed: 'I never thought that I had in my kingdom two youths so charmingly accomplished and so free from ambition. I will, if I may, visit your dwelling and rejoice my sight further with such a prodigy.' Immediately Farūz led him forward, and Farīd rode ahead to inform his sister of the King's coming.

Farizād heard the news with a certain dismay, as she was unused to receiving guests; in her perplexity she consulted her friend Bulbul, the Talking Bird. 'O Bulbul,' she said, 'the King is about to honour our house with a visit, and we must entertain him. Teach us how to behave, that he may go upon his way content.' 'Dear mistress,' answered Bulbul, 'it will be useless for you to get the cook to prepare multitudinous dishes for the King. To-day a single one will serve him, a dish of cucumber stuffed with pearls.' Farizād thought that the Bird's tongue had betrayed him; so she cried with a laugh: 'O Bird, Bird, what are you thinking of? Cucumber stuffed with pearls, indeed! There never was such a dish. If the King honours our cloth, he will want to eat, not to swallow pearls. You meant to say: cucumbers stuffed with rice.' But the Talking Bird answered angrily: 'Not at all! Not at all! Not at all! Stuffed with pearls, with pearls, with pearls! Not with rice, not with rice, not with rice!'

So Farizād, who had every confidence in her miraculous pet, bade the old cook prepare a dish of cucumbers stuffed with pearls, of which there were naturally great store in the house.

Soon Farūz led the Sultān into the garden, where Farīd greeted him and helped him to dismount. Farizād of the Rose's Smile, veiled for the first time in her life, on Bulbul's advice, came to kiss his hand. The King wept, for her sweet grace and the jasmine purity which exhaled from her reminded him that he was growing old without a daughter. As he blessed her, he said: 'He who leaves posterity does not die! O father of these fair children, may Allāh grant you a place upon His right hand in Paradise!' Then, glancing again at the bowing Farizād, he continued: 'But now, I beg you, O scented stem, O daughter of my servant, lead me to some delightful thicket, where we may be shaded from the heat.' So the trembling Farizād led him towards the depths of the garden, followed by her two brothers.

The first marvel which struck the eyes of Khusrau Shāh was the spray of Gold Water. He paused for a moment before it, and cried: 'Marvellous gold rain, cooling the eyes!' As he would have examined it more closely, he heard the music of the Singing Tree and lent a ravished ear to it for many silent minutes. 'Music of dreams!' he cried. But as he would have walked nearer to the tree, its singing ceased and a great silence fell upon the garden. The voice of the Talking Bird rose small and sweet and clear from the breast of that silence: 'Welcome, King. Welcome, King. Welcome, Khusrau Shāh! Welcome, welcome!' Then, as the last note ceased, all the birds of the garden answered in their own tongue: 'Welcome, welcome, welcome!'

Khusrau Shāh felt his heart made tender by astonishment, and he cried: 'O house of peace! Would I might cast aside my power and live with the children of my old slave for ever!' The brothers and sister pointed out the beauties of the Singing Tree and the Talking Bird to him, and Farizād said: 'The getting of these marvels is a tale which I shall tell our lord the King when he is rested.'

The Sultān reposed under the jasmine arbour and there the cucumbers stuffed with pearls were served before him on a gold dish.

The King was extremely fond of stuffed cucumbers and rejoiced when he saw them; but when he found that they were filled with pearls instead of rice or nuts, he exclaimed: 'Surely this is a novel way of cooking cucumbers?' Farizād was on the point of dropping the dish and fleeing in confusion, when the Talking Bird called the Sultān gravely by name, and said to him: 'O Khusrau Shāh, O Khusrau Shāh, since when has a Queen of Persia given birth to animals? If you could believe that impossibility, O King of time, this impossibility should mean nothing to you. Dear master, do you not remember the words which were spoken in a humble dwelling one evening twenty years ago? If you have forgotten, Farizād's slave will repeat them to you.'

Imitating the sweet speech of a young girl, the Bird went on: 'My wish is to marry our master, the Sultān. I would give him fair posterity. Our sons should be worthy of their father and our daughter would be a smile of the sky, and I should love her; her hair would be silver and gold; her tears, if she wept, would be falling pearls, her laughter, if she laughed, would be gold coins; and, if she smiled, her smiles would be buds of rose glowing upon her lips.'

The Sultān hid his face in his hands and sobbed; for his old grief was even greater in the recalling than in the happening. Far thoughts flowed from their place in the deeps of his soul into his heart and tore it savagely.

But Bulbul raised his voice again and this time gaily, saying: 'Unveil before your father, Farizād!'

Farizād lifted her veils and her hair fell down with them, so that the Sultān saw it and stretched out his arms with a happy cry. 'Behold your daughter, O King!' sang Bulbul. 'Surely her hair is silver and gold, and there are pearls of joy upon her lids and a young rose coming to blossom at her mouth!'

The King then looked upon the two brothers and recognised himself in them. 'Behold your sons, O King!' sang out the voice of Bulbul. While Khusrau Shāh stayed still for very happiness, with his arms about his children, the Talking Bird told him the whole story of their birth from beginning to end. But nothing would be gained by repeating it in this place. As the tale went on, the Sultān and his children mingled their tears and kisses together. Glory be to Allāh, the Great, the Unfathomable, Who blesses His people with reunion!

'My sweet ones,' cried Khusrau Shāh, when they had all a little recovered from the emotion of their meeting, 'let us ride in all haste to tell your mother.' But we shall not try to describe the poor woman's joy when she saw, after her lonely years, the love and splendour of her children. Let us rather give thanks to Allāh for that infinite justice which struck the two jealous sisters dead from rage upon that happy day, and gave years and long delights to Khusrau Shāh and to his Queen, and to the princes and to Farizād, until they were visited by the Separator of friends, the Destroyer. Glory be to Him Who, seated among eternity, knows no change!

That is the marvellous Tale of Farizād of the Rose's Smile. But Allāh knows all!

When Shahrazād made an end of this story, little Dunyazād cried: 'Dear sister, your words are sweet and delightful, fresh and savoury! I found the story charming.' 'So did I,' agreed King Shahryār. Then Dunyazād whispered to Shahrazād: 'I think I see a tear in the King's left eye, and a second tear in his right eye.' Shahrazād cast a quick look at the King, and said with a smile, as she embraced the little one: 'I trust the King will be as pleased by the tale of Kamar and the expert Halīmah.' 'I have never heard that tale, Shahrazād,' answered Shahryār, 'and you know how eagerly I have waited for it.' But Shahrazād exclaimed: 'If Allāh wills, and the great King allow, I shall begin it to-morrow.' So Shahryār, who remembered the parable of true learning, said to himself: 'I must be patient until to-morrow.'

At this point Shahrazād saw the approach of morning and discreetly fell silent.

But when the seven-hundred-and-eightieth night had come

LITTLE DUNYAZĀD cried: 'O Shahrazād, in Allāh's name begin the Tale of Kamar and the expert Halīmah!' So Shahrazād said:

The Tale of Kamar and the Expert Halīmah

IT is related that there was once in the antiquity of time—but Allāh knows all!—a worthy merchant called Abd al-Rahmān whom the Giver had favoured with one son and one daughter. The daughter's name was Morning-Star, because of her perfect beauty, and, since the boy was altogether like the young moon, they called him Kamar. When they grew up from babyhood, the merchant, who saw that Allāh had dowered them with dangerous charm, feared the evil-eye of envy and all the wiles of corruption; so he kept the two shut up in his house until they were fourteen, and never allowed them to see anyone, except the old slave who ministered to their wants. But a day came when the merchant, contrary to his custom, seemed in a jovial and bending humour; so his wife said to him: 'O father of Kamar, our son has become a man and can do as men do. Tell me now, is he a girl or is he a boy?' 'A boy, surely,' cried the astonished Abd al-Rahmān. 'In that case,' retorted his wife, 'why do you keep him shut up from the eyes of the creation like a girl, instead of taking him to the market and seating him beside you in the shop? Why do you not introduce him to the world and let people know that you have a son to succeed you? I pray to Allāh that your life may be long, but, when you have to die, no one will know of the existence of your heir if you keep him imprisoned in this way. It will be all very well for him to say: "I am the son of Abd al-Rahmān." Folk will quite justly answer: "We never heard that Abd al-Rahmān had a son or anything like a son." Then, woe upon our house, the government will seize your goods and cheat the boy of his inheritance. . . . And with Morning-Star it is the same! I wish to make her known to our relations; for that might lead to a suit in marriage and we could re-joice again in her wedding as we rejoiced in our own. This world is made of life and death, O father of Kamar, and we may not know the day of Destiny.'

The merchant Abd al-Rahmān reflected for an hour, and then answered: 'Oh daughter of my uncle, it is true that no man may escape the Destiny which hangs about his neck; but I only hid the children for fear of the evil-eye; surely you cannot reproach me for my prudence?' 'Far be all Evil!' exclaimed his wife. 'Pray for the Prophet, O sheikh!' So he cried: 'The blessing of Allāh be upon Him and His!' and she continued: 'Now put your trust in Allāh, for He can safeguard our children from all ill-omen. Here is the turban of white Mosul silk which I made for Kamar; I sewed a roll of holy verses in a silver tube among its folds; therefore you need have no fear. Take Kamar with you to-day, show him the market and intro-duce him to his father's shop.' Without waiting for a reply, she went to fetch young Kamar, whom she had advised to dress in his best, and led him into the presence of his father. Abd al-Rahmān rejoiced to see him, and said: 'The name of Allāh be upon you and about you, O Kamar!' Then, being overpersuaded by his wife, he took the boy by the hand and led him forth.

At this point Shahrazād saw the approach of morning and discreetly fell silent.

But when the seven-hundred-and-eighty-first night had come

SHE SAID:

But no sooner had they left the threshold and ventured into the street than they were surrounded by a crowd of passengers, who halted in trouble of spirit, snared by the sweet damnation of Kamar's looks. Yet the streets were as nothing to the market; on their entrance, all who walked there immediately ceased from walking and surged about the two. Some kissed Kamar's hands, others saluted his father, and yet others cried: 'O Allāh, the sun has risen twice this morning! The little crescent moon of Ramadān has come again! Here is the new moon in the market!' A babel of admiration and good wishes rose about father and son, and, although Abd al-Rahmān in confusion and anger pushed and expostulated, the citizens continued to stand in close rank, feasting their eyes on beauty and calling down the blessing of Allāh upon that day. Doubtless they excused themselves with these words of the poet:

> Who beauty loveth and created hath
> With the same breath which bade us fear Thy wrath,
>   Lover and Lord, we pray Thee to remove
> Either restraint or beauty from our path.

The merchant's perplexity knew no bounds when he found his son the centre of a packed mob of men and women, all gazing at him with shining eyes. Under his breath he heaped on his wife all those curses which he would have liked to have applied more loudly to these vulgar admirers. As none of his entreaties had any effect, he finally pushed roughly through the people and, gaining the shelter of his shop, seated Kamar so far back that passers could only see him from a distance. At once the shop became the one centre of interest in the market, and hour by hour the jostling of great and small grew heavier about it; for those who had seen wished to see again and those who had not seen most ardently desired to see.

When the spectators were at their thickest, a darwīsh with an ecstatic eye came towards the shop and, seeing Kamar sitting beside his father, halted with a profound sigh, and said these lines in a broken voice:

I saw the thin branch of the ban
Where shines the moon of Ramadān
  In sickle saffron glow.
'What is your name?' 'Lūlū,' said he,
'Lūlū, a pearl.' Then I: 'Lī? Lī?
Lī? Lī? O pearl, are you for me?'
  He: 'Lā! lā!, Lā! lā!, no!'

Then the old darwīsh came up to the counter, stroking his long white beard, his great age making a way for him among the crowd. He looked at the boy with tear-filled eyes and offered him a branch of sweet basil; finally he sat down quite close to him upon the front bench of the shop. If you had seen his emotion, you might have applied these words of the poet to him:

Where, Ramadān's gold moon to fasters,
There is a slight fair boy, my masters,
You may be sure to see draw near
A sheikh, snow-bearded and severe,
Who has so studied lore of love,
Below, behind, about, above,
With licit and with illicit,
That he could take degrees in it.
Between the lasses and the lads
He's lost his pleasant body pads,
A toothpick in a shroud is he,
But oh, a Moor for buggery!
They say his interest in woman
Is rather casual, though human;
But I can tell you, for a fact,
He holds his own in either act.
With bearded and with breasted youth
He seeks the principles of truth,
And in young concave, young convex
Holds fair the balance of his sex . . .
(With this proviso, certainly,
That he's a Moor for buggery.)

Seeing the ecstasy of this darwīsh, the people drew their own conclusions, saying: 'As Allāh lives, all darwīshes are alike! They are all knives for colocassia, making no difference between male and female.' And others cried: 'Far be the Evil One! He burns for the pretty boy! Allāh confound such darwīshes!'

The merchant Abd al-Rahmān thought that the best way out of these difficulties would be to return home earlier than usual. In the hope of persuading the darwīsh to depart, he drew some money from his belt and held it towards him, saying: 'Take to-day's chance, O darwīsh!' Then he turned to his son, and exclaimed: 'My child, I trust that Allāh will punish your mother according to her deserts, for she has given us a hard day!' Finally, as the darwīsh did not move or make any motion to take the money, he said to him: 'Rise up now, uncle, for I wish to shut the shop.' He got to his feet as he spoke and began to close the two leaves of the door, so that the darwīsh was obliged to rise from the bench, to which he had seemed nailed, and go out into the street; yet he never took his eyes from young Kamar. Also, when the merchant and his son had shut the shop and battled their way through the crowd, he followed them out of the market and came behind them to their house, his stick beating a rhythm to their footsteps. Seeing his tenacity, and not daring to curse him, both because of the bystanders and because of his respect for religion, the merchant turned round, and asked: 'What do you want, O darwīsh?' 'O my master,' the man replied, 'I greatly desire to be your guest to-night; and remember that he who invites a stranger invites God.' Kamar's father exclaimed as heartily as he could: 'Welcome to the guest of Allāh! Enter my poor house, O darwīsh!' But below his breath he said: 'I know what he is after; if he has evil intentions towards my son and should be so unlucky as to try anything, I will kill him and bury him in the garden and spit upon his grave! But first I suppose I must give him something to eat, for he is my guest met upon the road of Allāh.' He led the old man into his house and bade the negress take him food and drink and water for his ablutions. The darwīsh invoked the name of Allāh as he washed and, placing himself for prayer, recited all the Chapter of the Cow, followed it with the Chapter of the Table, and finished with the Chapter of Immunity. Then, and not till then, he invoked the Name a second time and ate with discretion and dignity.

As soon as Abd al-Rahmān learnt from the negress that the darwīsh had finished his repast, he determined to test the old man's intention; so he called his son, saying: 'O Kamar, go to our guest and ask him if his need is satisfied; talk with him a little, for the words of those who walk over the length and breadth of the world are pleasant to hear, and the tales they tell are profitable. Sit quite near him, and if he takes your hand do not snatch it away; those who teach often prefer to have some direct contact with their pupils, as a surer means of transmitting knowledge. In all things show him the respect due to a guest and to an old man.' Then he sent his son into the darwīsh and hastened to post himself at a window in the upper storey, through which he could see and hear all that went on in the hall.

As soon as the lovely youth appeared on the threshold, the holy old man was so moved that tears jetted from his eyes and he sighed as a mother sighs who has lost and found her child. Kamar went up to him and, in a voice which would have turned the bitterness of myrrh to honey, asked if he lacked for aught and had taken sufficient of Allāh's blessing. Then, with a graceful movement, he sat down quite close to him and, as he sat, unintentionally exposed a thigh whiter and smoother than almond curds. Well-inspired was the poet who sang:

> All men shall rise on Resurrection Day
> Up to the sky,
> Or when the pearl and almond you display,
> Sweet, of your thigh.

But instead of allowing himself any kind of liberty with the charming youth, the old man retired a few paces from him and sat down again in an attitude of assured decency and self-respect. He went on looking at him in silence and shedding tears, so that Kamar was surprised and asked if he had offended him, or if the hospitality of the house had been insufficient. For sole response the darwīsh recited, with great elegance and dignity, these musical lines:

> The horses of beauty have drawn up my heart,
> For beauty is perfection, to a spot
> High in the hills, where longing has no part
> And flesh is not.

Kamar's father saw and heard these things in great astonishment. 'I offended against Allāh,' said he, 'when I suspected this wise darwīsh of perverse intentions. May He confound the Tempter who lures us to have evil thoughts about our brothers!' He hastened down to the hall and greeted his guest most benevolently, saying: 'I conjure you, in Allāh's name, my brother, to tell me the reason of your tears and sighs when you beheld my son; for surely such an effect must have a cause.' 'You are right, O father of hospitality,' answered the darwīsh. So the merchant said again: 'Then will you not tell me that cause?' 'Good master,' replied the old man, 'why should you force me to open a closed wound and turn the knife of memory within?' 'I do not force you,' exclaimed Abd al-Rahmān, 'but I beg you to satisfy my curiosity. Has not a host the right to do so?'

At this point Shahrazād saw the approach of morning and discreetly fell silent.

But when the seven-hundred-and-eighty-second night had come

SHE SAID:

Then said the old man:

I am a poor darwīsh who wanders for ever over Allāh's world, marvelling at the work of His hand by day and night.

One Friday morning my fate led me to the city of Basrah, where I saw the markets, shops and stalls open and filled with merchandise, loaded with food and drink and all which may be bought and sold; but no trace among any of them, or coming and going before any of them, of merchant or purchaser, woman or little girl, or dog or cat or children playing. In all the streets was but loneliness, silence, and the presence of God. I was astonished, and said within my soul: 'Where can these people have gone so swiftly, leaving their goods exposed on every stall?' Then, as I was tortured by hunger, I made my way to the best furnished tray of a pastrycook and ate my fill. After that, I helped myself from the stall of a seller of roast meat and devoured two or three, or it may have been four, skewers of fat lamb, with one or two chicken hot from the oven, and a few light warm rolls such as my tongue and nose had never savoured in all my pilgrimage. Giving thanks to Allāh, I next went up into the shop of a sherbert-seller and drank one or two goblets of sherbert perfumed with nard and benzoin. I took only enough to remove the edge from my thirst, for my throat had long been unused to the drinks of rich citizens. Then I thanked the Beneficent once more that He has allowed to His Believers on this earth a foretaste of the fountain Salsabīl.

As soon as I had stilled the cravings of my body, I began to ponder again on the strange appearance of that city. It seemed to me that the streets could only have been abandoned a few minutes before my coming, and I was beginning to fear the echoes of my own footsteps in that solitude, when I heard the sound of approaching music. In the trouble of my mind I took this as a final proof that the city was bewitched. Certain that the music proceeded from evil spirits, I fled into a grain shop and hid myself at the back of it, behind a sack of beans; but as I am curious by nature—Allāh pardon it in me!—I placed myself in such a position that I could see all which happened in the street, without myself being seen. I had hardly made myself comfortable when I saw a shining band, which may not have been of spirits, but was certainly of Paradisal hūrīs. Forty girls with unveiled faces, painted by moonlight, advanced in two ranks, with a movement of the feet which in itself was singing. Lute players and dancers went before, lighter and whiter than the doves of summer, so that I could not but suppose that they were presences from many-columned Irām, or from the gardens of Allāh.

The last had just passed the shop where I lay hidden, when a mare with a starry front came into my view, her bridle held by two young negresses, and a woman riding upon her so dressed in beauty and youth that I lost my breath and well-nigh fainted behind my sack of beans. Her clothes were sewn with jewels, her neck and wrists and ankles were banded with them, and her hair powdered with the colour of them. Upon her right hand walked a slave, bearing a naked sword whose hilt was carved out of a single emerald. The mare marched on in majesty, like a queen proud of the crown upon her head. This vision of youth passed, leaving the dagger of passion in my heart, my soul in chains, and my eyes ready to remember and say to all other beauty: 'You are ugliness.'

As soon as the sound of the music had faded from my ears, I came out from behind the sack and left the shop; immediately I saw the markets take on life and the merchants and purchasers appear as if by magic and go about their business. I determined to ask one of them the meaning of what I had seen and the name of the woman who rode upon the starry-fronted mare; but the first man I questioned turned yellow in the face and, pulling up his draperies, ran away from me, as if the hour of his Destiny pursued him. I stopped a second merchant and asked the same question; but he looked in the opposite direction, as if he had not heard me, and passed by. I accosted many more; but they all remained silent and avoided me as if I had come up out of a cesspool or were brandishing a terrible sword. Then I determined that my last resort was the barber; for I knew that those who exercise that profession have ever an itching tongue and a word lying near the end of it. Therefore I entered a barber's shop and, giving him all my money, asked him the question. The man rolled his eyes in terror and then answered: 'If you would keep your head upon your neck, good uncle, you must not speak of what you have seen. Also I advise you to leave the city without delay. I can say no more; for the matter is a mystery which tortures all Basrah. Men die like locusts here, if they are not hidden before that procession comes. The slave who walks with a naked sword ruthlessly decapitates any head she sees. That is all I can say.'

As soon as the barber had finished shaving my head, I left that city, finding no peace until I had gone out from the shadow of its walls. I travelled over field and desert until at last I came to this place. Day and night, eating and drinking and sleeping, I could think of nothing but that snatch of beauty seen at unawares. When I passed your shop to-day and beheld your son, his beauty reminded me of the marvel of Basrah; for he is as like her as if the two were twins. It was that resemblance which caused my tears, my sighs, and my emotion. Surely I must be mad.

When the darwīsh had finished his tale, he looked at young Kamar and shed fresh tears. Then he said, sobbing: 'Now in Allāh's name, show His servant the door which leads from your house and let him depart upon the road of his Destiny. I pray one prayer for you: that He Who has created two perfect creatures in your son and in the girl of Basrah, may crown His work by bringing about their union.'

So saying he rose, in spite of the merchant's entreaties that he should stay, and went out sighing into the street. So much for him.

Young Kamar could not close his eyes all night for thinking of the girl who had appeared in the old man's story. At dawn he went into his mother's room and woke her, saying: 'Make me a bundle of clothes and provisions, for I must set out on the road to the city of Basrah, where my Destiny awaits me.' His mother lamented and called her husband, to whom she repeated this unexpected determination. Abd al-Rahmān tried to reason his son away from his purpose; but Kamar would only answer: 'If I do not go to Basrah immediately, I shall surely die.' So the merchant and his wife were compelled to acquiesce with sighs of foreboding, and you may be sure that Kamar's father put all the blame upon his wife. 'O Abd al-Rahmān,' he muttered to himself, 'this is the end of all your careful prudence! There is no power or might save in Allāh! That which is written must come to pass; none may fight against the decrees of Destiny!' Meanwhile Kamar's mother, doubly grieving at her husband's anger and her son's loss, was constrained to prepare for the boy's departure. She gave him a little bag into which she had fastened forty large jewels of the first water, rubies, diamonds and emeralds. 'Guard this carefully, my son,' she said, 'for it will be of use if you should come to lack money.' The merchant gave his son ninety thousand gold dīnārs, and the two old people, with many tears, embraced him in farewell. Abd al-Rahmān gave him into the care of the master of a caravan which was setting out for Irāk, and Kamar left the city of his birth in its company. Later, by the blessing of Allāh, he arrived without accident at Basrah.

At this point Shahrazād saw the approach of morning and discreetly fell silent.

But when the seven-hundred-and-eighty-third night had come

SHE SAID:

It was on a Friday morning that he came into the city, and he was thus able to control the truth of the darwīsh's tale; for the markets were empty, the streets deserted, and the shops lay open with all their goods, but with no sign of buyer and seller. As he was hungry, he ate and drank his fill and then, on hearing distant music, hid himself as the darwīsh had done. He saw the girl pass with her forty maidens and, at the first glimpse of her unveiled face, swooned in the corner where he had concealed himself.

When he came to himself, he found the market thronged and folk bustling about their business as if nothing had happened. Still dreaming of the woman's face, he bought magnificent garments from the chief merchants and took a long and detailed bath at the nearest hammām. He came out shining like a young king, and searched out the shop of the barber who had shaved the darwīsh's head. He entered it with courteous greeting, and said to the proprietor: 'O father of light hands, I wish to talk to you in private. I beg you to shut your shop and take this purse to pay you for the loss of custom.' The barber took the purse of dīnārs which Kamar handed to him and, after weighing it with a quick gesture of the hand, thrust it into his belt. When the two were alone together, the boy said again: 'O father of light hands, I am a stranger in this city and wish to learn why the markets were deserted this Friday morning.' Quite won over by the fine air and open-handed generosity of his questioner, the barber answered: 'That is a secret which I have never tried to penetrate, though I am very careful to shut myself away on Friday mornings; but, as the matter seems to touch you deeply, I will do for you what I would not do for my own brother. I will make you acquainted with my wife, who sells perfume among all the harîms of Basrah and knows everything which passes in the city. As you are obviously impatient, I will go at once to my wife and put your case before her. Wait here until I return.'

The barber hurried home and gave his wife the purse, telling her of Kamar's enquiry. At once the shrewd and kind-hearted woman cried: 'May he be welcome to our city! I am ready to serve him with my head and eyes. Bring him to me at once.' So the barber returned to his shop and led Kamar to his own home, where the woman set him in the seat of honour upon the couch, and greeted him: 'Let this be a home of liberty to our charming guest! The house is your house and we, the masters of it, are your slaves! It is for you to command and for us to obey.' Then she served him with sweet refreshments on a copper tray and made him take a spoonful of every kind, saying, as he swallowed each: 'May it be a delight and a comfort to the heart of our gracious guest!'

As soon as he had tasted all, Kamar placed a large handful of gold pieces on the knees of the barber's wife, saying: 'Excuse the poverty of this gift; I swear by Allâh that you will find me more generous in the future. Now, good mother, I pray you tell me all you know concerning the object of my anxiety.' So the barber's wife said:

My son, light of my eye and crown of my head, one day the Sultân of Basrah received as a gift from the Sultân of India a pearl so beautiful that it must have been born from the glance of a sunbeam on the sea. It was both white and gold, according to the way the light struck it, and there was a movement in its breast as of a fire burning below milk. The King looked at it for a whole day and then determined to carry it on a silk ribbon round his neck, so that he might behold it always. As it was virgin and imperforate, he called the jewellers of Basrah to him, saying: 'I wish you to pierce this sovereign pearl. He who can do it without harm may ask the wish of his heart and it shall be granted. He who has the misfortune to be clumsy and to spoil my pearl shall die the most terrible of deaths; for I will behead him after having practised upon him those tortures which are worthy of his sacrilegious ineptitude. What have you to say to this, my jewellers?'

The jewellers became afraid, and answered as with one voice: 'O King of time, to pierce a pearl like that is a most delicate undertaking. To operate on an ordinary pearl requires fingers picked from a hundred thousand, and the greatest of us must expect some few accidents before we succeed. We beg that you do not put us to a trial of which we are altogether unworthy; for we can tell the King where he may find the skill which we lack. Surely the sheikh of our guild can pierce this pearl.' 'Who is your sheikh?' demanded the King, and they replied: 'He is Ubaid, the master jeweller. He has more skill than the rest of us put together. He has an eye in the end of each finger and each of those eyes is of a superhuman sensibility.' 'Bring him to me!' cried the King.

The jewellers departed and returned with their sheikh, Ubaid, who kissed the earth between the King's hands and waited for an order. The Sultān told him what was required and mentioned the rewards and penalties attaching to success or failure. The jeweller Ubaid took the marvellous pearl and examined it for an hour; then he cried: 'I deserve to die if I cannot drill this pearl of marvel!' With the King's permission, he squatted down, there and then, and placed the pearl securely between his two heels; then, fetching certain fine tools out of his belt, he began to use them with a supreme lightness of touch and the careless dexterity of a child playing with a top. In less time than it would have taken another man to blow an egg, he had drilled the pearl, without in the least roughening it or chipping it, so that the two ends of the hole were equal and symmetrical. He wiped it on his sleeve and returned it to the King, who trembled for joy and satisfaction. At once the Sultān threaded the pearl upon a silk cord and, as it hung like a little sun about his neck, looked down at it on every side with a glow of great content.

Then he turned to the jeweller, saying: 'Now for your wish, O master craftsman!' Ubaid reflected for an hour, and then replied: 'Allāh prolong the life of our King! But the slave whose crippled hands have had the notable honour of touching our master's pearl, possesses a young wife without whose advice he dare do nothing; for he is an old man and, after the fashion of old men, he has to spoil his wife in order not to be distasteful to her. I beg you, O King of time, to allow me to consult my wife, for perhaps she may have some better wish to suggest than any which I could imagine for myself.

Allāh has not only given her youth and charm, but also a sound judgment and rich imagination.' 'Go quickly, O Ubaid,' answered the King, 'for I shall have no rest until I have fulfilled my promise.' So the jeweller hastened to his wife and told her all. As soon as she heard that the Sultān would satisfy her husband's any wish, the girl exclaimed: 'Glory be to Allāh, my day has come before its time! For I have a wish already formed, a strange and delightful wish. Thanks to Allāh's goodness and your wisdom in affairs, we are rich and out of reach of want for ever. Therefore we have no need to ask money, and my wish can be satisfied without the King expending a single dirham of his treasure. I desire, only and simply, leave to ride through the city every Friday morning with a train like that of a princess, and that the markets and streets be cleared before me and that no one dare to show himself or look upon me under pain of death. Surely that is a small reward for the piercing of a pearl.'

'Allāh Karīm!' cried the astonished jeweller. 'Who may boast that he understands what passes in the brains of women?' But then, as he loved his wife and was too old and ugly to risk her discontent, he said: 'O daughter of my uncle, your wish is upon my head and before my eyes. But consider this: if the merchants leave all their goods without guard and go to hide themselves as you pass by, the dogs and cats will raid their counters and the loss will be upon our conscience.' 'That is no difficulty,' said his wife. 'An order must be given for all dogs and cats to be shut away on Fridays. I wish especially for the shops to remain open while my train goes through the city. But all the citizens, great and small, must hide themselves behind the closed doors of the mosques and none put forth his head without losing it.'

The jeweller Ubaid went in confusion to the King and told him of his wife's wish. 'I see no reason against it,' said the King, and straightway gave order, through his heralds, that the citizens should leave their shops open on every Friday morning, two hours before the prayer, and hide themselves in the mosques. They were warned that, if they showed their heads in the street, they should lose them; and were advised to shut away all dogs and cats, donkeys and camels, which might harm the goods left unguarded upon the stalls. Since that time, the jeweller's wife has gone in procession every Friday morning, two hours before the noon prayer, and no man or dog or cat has dared to show himself in the street. It was she whom you saw this morning, my lord Kamar, going about in glory with her forty girls and attended by the young slave with the naked sword.

The barber's wife fell silent and looked at Kamar with a smile; then she added: 'But I see, dear master and face of sweetness, that the tale alone is not enough for you, that you will not be content unless you see the old jeweller's wife again.' 'Such is my desire, good mother,' answered Kamar. 'It was to see her that I left my country and a weeping father and mother in my house.' 'Then tell me what valuables you have, my son,' requested the woman. 'Mother,' the boy replied, 'I have jewels of four grades: the first are worth five hundred golden dīnārs, the second seven hundred dīnārs, the third eight hundred and fifty dīnārs, and the best at least a thousand dīnārs each.' 'And would you part with four of them, each of a different grade?' she asked. 'I would part with them all and everything else I have,' he answered. 'Then rise up, my son, rise up, O generous crown upon my head,' said she. 'Seek out the jeweller Ubaid in the goldsmith's market and, when you have met him, do exactly as I tell you.'

She gave him minute instructions, and added: 'Use prudence and patience in all things, my son. And, when you have profited by my advice, do not forget to return with news, bringing a hundred dīnārs for my husband the barber, who is a poor man.' Kamar agreed to this and left the house, repeating the instructions of the scent-seller over and over again, and thanking Allāh Who had set such a powerful talisman upon his way.

At this point Shahrazād saw the approach of morning and discreetly fell silent.

But when the seven-hundred-and-eighty-fourth night had come

SHE SAID:

When he came to the market of the goldsmiths and had been directed to the shop of the sheikh of the jewellers, he hastened forward till he found Ubaid among his apprentices. He wished him peace, carrying his hand with great respect to heart and lips and brow, and the old man returned his greeting and begged him to be seated. Soon Kamar drew from his purse a jewel of miraculous beauty, though chosen from among the lowest grade which he possessed, and handed it, with twenty pieces of gold, to Ubaid, saying: 'Good master, I wish you to mount this stone in a ring; but, though

I require workmanship worthy of your great renown, I do not need any but the simplest and lightest setting. This money is a feeble advance against the completion of the work.' Then he gave a gold piece to each of the many apprentices, as a matter of greeting, and gold to each of the numberless beggars; for they seemed to have sprung up in the street as soon as the richly-dressed young stranger entered the shop. When he retired, he left all who had seen him marvelling at his liberality and beauty and distinguished manners.

Ubaid would not allow a moment's delay in the construction of the ring; as he had unparalleled dexterity, and appliances to his hand such as no other jeweller on earth possessed in that age, he finished the work exquisitely by the time the sun went down. Then, as he did not expect young Kamar until the morning, he took the ring back with him to show it to his wife, for he felt that the flashing quality of the stone would make her mouth water.

The girl found the ring very much to her taste and asked for whom it had been made. 'For a young man far more beautiful than the gem itself, though that is fair enough,' answered her husband. 'He paid me in advance more than I have ever received before for so simple an undertaking; but that is nothing. Believe me, my dear, his eyes wound all the world, his cheeks are petals of anemone fallen upon a terrace strewn with jasmine, his mouth is the seal of Sulaimān, and his lips are dyed with the blood of rubies; he has the neck of a young antelope and it bears up the glory of his head as a lily is carried on its dew-wet stem. He is above all praise, for he has beauty such as a craftsman can appreciate, and is as charming as he is beautiful. These things make him resemble you in everything, my love.'

Thus the jeweller painted Kamar to his wife and did not see that his words lit a flame of passion in her heart, the greater because she had not seen the youth. Though he had a forehead as ripe for horns as a well-dunged field is ripe for cucumbers, he did not know that the most successful pander of all is a husband talking of a stranger's beauty. By this you may see that Allāh blinds His creatures, when He needs them to further the designs of Destiny.

His young wife laid up the glowing description in her heart, but was very careful not to show the agitation which possessed her. Instead, she asked to be shown the ring, in a tone of absolute indifference, and, when she had received it, put it carelessly upon her finger, with an air of utter detachment. 'See how well it fits me,' she said, 'it might have been made for me.' 'The fingers of the hūrīs are all alike,' answered her husband. 'Sweet mistress, the owner is both generous and thoughtful; to-morrow I will ask him to sell me the ring, for any price he cares to name, and then you shall wear it always.'

During that time, Kamar had carried his news to the barber's wife and given her a hundred golden dīnārs for her husband, that poor man. When he asked what more he should do, she answered: 'When you see the jeweller to-morrow, pretend that the ring is too small for your finger and give it to him as a present; then hand him one of those gems which are worth seven hundred dīnārs, and ask him to set it choicely in another ring. Give him sixty dīnārs and present each of his workmen with two. Also do not forget the beggars at the door. All this will turn to your advantage. And when you bring me news, my son, do not forget a little something for the barber, that poor man.'

Next morning Kamar presented himself at Ubaid's shop, and the old man, after greeting him most respectfully and rising in his honour, gave him the ring. Kamar pretended to try it on, and then said: 'It is excellently made, my master, but is a little too narrow for my finger. Keep it, I pray, and give it to one of the numberless slaves in your harīm. In the meantime, I desire you to mount this jewel, which I certainly prefer to the other one.' He handed the second stone to Ubaid with sixty dīnārs for himself and two for each of his apprentices, remarking as he did so: 'Simply to buy sherberts! But I trust that you will all be satisfied with my idea of a payment when the work is over.' Then he departed, throwing gold pieces to left and right among the beggars at the door.

The jeweller was more astonished than ever at such liberality, and that evening he could not help saying to his young wife: 'As Allāh lives, the youth is not contented with being more beautiful than any who have gone before him; he must needs be as open-handed as a king's son.' This speech fanned the flame of love which the woman had in her heart for Kamar; as she slowly put on the ring which his generosity had made her own, she asked if he had not ordered a second. 'He ordered a second and I have already made it,' answered her husband. 'Let me see it,' she commanded and, when he gave it into her hands, exclaimed: 'Oh, I should like to keep it!' 'Who knows?' murmured her foolish husband. 'Perhaps he will leave it with me as he left the other.'

During that time, Kamar had taken his news to the barber's wife, together with four hundred dīnārs for the barber, that poor man. 'Your affair goes excellently, my son,' she said. 'When you see the jeweller to-morrow, pretend that the ring is too big and leave it with him as a gift; but entrust him with one of the eight hundred and fifty dīnār stones. Give him a hundred dīnārs for himself and three for each of his apprentices. And when you bring me news, my son, do not forget a little something for my husband, that poor man, that he may be able to buy a crust of bread. Now Allāh guard you and prolong your days, O child of generosity!'

Kamar followed the scent-seller's instructions to the letter, and the jeweller could find no words to paint the liberality of his young customer to his wife. As she tried on the new ring, she said: 'Son of my uncle, are you not ashamed that you have never asked so generous a buyer to taste the hospitality of your house? You are not a miser, I thank Allāh, nor were any of your ancestors misers; but sometimes you seem to me a little to lack breeding. It is your plain duty to ask this stranger to take bread and salt with you.'

In the meanwhile, Kamar had consulted the barber's wife a third time and given her eight hundred dīnārs to hand to her husband, that poor man, that he might have wherewith to buy a crust of bread. On the following morning he presented himself at the jeweller's shop to try on the third ring; but, after he had slipped it on his finger, he drew it off again and looked at it with disfavour, saying: 'It fits well enough, but the stone does not please me at all. Keep it to give to one of your slaves, and mount this other jewel for me fittingly. Here is an advance of four hundred dīnārs and four for each of your apprentices. I must beg you to pardon me for all the trouble I am causing you.' So saying, he gave Ubaid a white and marvellous stone worth at least a thousand dīnārs, and the jeweller said confusedly: 'Dear master, will you consent to honour my house with your presence and favour me with your company at supper this evening? Your benefits are thick upon me and my heart has gone out to you.' 'Be it upon my head and before my eyes,' replied the youth, and he gave the jeweller the address of the khān at which he lodged.

At this point Shahrazād saw the approach of morning and discreetly fell silent.

But when the seven-hundred-and-eighty-fifth night had come

SHE SAID:

That evening the jeweller fetched his guest from the khān and conducted him to his own house, where the two feasted splendidly together. As soon as the dishes of meat and drink had been removed, a slave served them with sherberts which the jeweller's wife had prepared with her own hands. For, in spite of the desire which burned her, she would not offend the decencies by taking part in the meal; but waited in the harīm for the result of her expedient.

As soon as Kamar and his host had tasted the delicious sherbert, they fell into a profound sleep, for the girl had mingled a soporific powder with their cups; and the slave who had served them retired, as soon as she saw them lying still, to tell her mistress.

The girl had waited, dressed only in her chemise and all prepared as if for a second bridal night; she raised the curtain and walked softly into the feast hall, and if you had seen her eyes languishing among the disorder of her hair you would have felt your heart crack. She came to where Kamar was sleeping and looked down upon him for a long while. Then she sat all against him and began to pass her hands softly across his face; until suddenly, in her hunger, she threw herself greedily upon the boy and bit his lips and cheeks with kisses until the blood came. Finally, excited beyond measure, she sat down upon him in his sleep, and Allāh alone knows what the agitation of her body signified.

She did not weary of this game all night; but when morning came she lifted her hot legs from off him and, taking four knuckle-bones from her breast, placed them in his pocket. As soon as she had returned to the harīm, she sent her faithful slave, the one who guarded her processions with a naked sword, to wake the old jeweller and the boy by making them breathe a powdered antidote. When they sneezed and woke, the slave said to Ubaid: 'My mistress Halīmah commanded me to rouse you and tell you that the muezzin is even now calling Believers to the morning prayer. I have brought you water for ablution.' 'As Allāh lives,' cried the old man in a maze, 'one sleeps soundly in this hall! Each time I lie here, I do not wake until the sun is high.' Kamar did not know what to answer, but, when he felt during his ablution that his lips and cheeks and those parts which did not show were burning as with fire, he said: 'My lips and cheeks feel as if they had been touched with red-hot coals. What can be the meaning of it?' 'That is nothing,' answered the jeweller, 'those are only mosquito bites. It was foolish of us to sleep without a curtain.' 'Why are there no bites upon your face also?' asked Kamar. 'Because mosquitoes love young blood and a fair beardless face, but hate the cheeks of hairy age,' replied Ubaid, as he turned to make his prayer.

The two broke fast together, and then Kamar took leave of his host and went to report to the barber's wife.

She greeted him with a laugh, saying: 'You need not tell me of your night, my son, for I see a thousand tokens of it on your face.' 'Those are mosquito bites and nothing more, good mother,' answered Kamar seriously. The barber's wife laughed more loudly still. 'Mosquito bites?' she scoffed. 'Was that all you bore away from the house of love?' 'No,' said he, 'I bore away four knuckle-bones such as children play with. I found them in my pocket, but I do not know how they got there.' 'Show them to me,' she said and, after examining them, went on in great delight: 'You are very simple, my son, if you cannot distinguish between mosquito bites and the passionate kisses of a desirous woman. She put these bones in your pocket herself, meaning to reproach you for sleeping when you might have been better employed with her. They signify: "You are a child who plays with sleep, because he does not know the other game." You can prove what I say this evening, for I am sure that the jeweller will invite you again. Now, see that you behave to your own satisfaction and to hers, and also to the satisfaction of the mother who loves you, my son. When you come back with news, smile of my eye, remember the wretched state of my husband, that poor man.' 'I shall remember,' answered Kamar, as he took leave before returning to the khān.

'And how did you behave to your young guest?' asked Halīmah when her husband sought her in the harīm. 'With honour and respect,' he answered, 'but I am afraid he must have passed a poor night, for this morning he had been bitten all over his face by mosquitoes.' 'You should have slept under a net,' said Halīmah. 'He will not be troubled in the same way to-night if you take that precaution. . . . I hope you are going to ask him again; it is the least that you can do when he has been so generous.' The jeweller was all the more pleased to agree to this second invitation, as he began himself to feel a great affection for the youth.

When Kamar came to the shop, the old man invited him to a second supper, and, in spite of the mosquito net, the boy had much the same night as before; for Halīmah drugged the two again and, feeling her body hotter than before, spent the dark hours astride her sleeping love, with even more strange contortions. When Kamar came out of his heavy sleep on the following morning, he felt his face burning and all his body wounded with the biting, sucking, and kissing of his ardent hostess; but he said nothing to the jeweller when the old man asked him how he had slept. Instead, he took courteous leave and hurried to the barber's wife. As he arrived at her husband's shop, he plunged his hand into his pocket and found a knife which had not been there before. So, after he had given his wise guide five hundred gold dīnārs as a compliment to her husband, that poor man, he showed her the knife. The old woman kissed his hand and cried: 'Allāh guard you, my child, for your mistress is angry and threatens to kill you if she finds you sleeping a third time.' 'But how can I help sleeping?' asked Kamar. 'I tried to keep awake last night but could not.' 'Let the jeweller drink alone,' urged the barber's wife. 'Throw the sherbert behind you, as you pretend to drink it, and then feign to sleep before the eyes of the slave.' Kamar thanked her for her advice and determined to act upon it.

That night Ubaid invited Kamar to a third supper, according to the usages of hospitality, and, as soon as the slave who brought the sherbert saw the two men lying still before her, she went and told her mistress.

The burning Halīmah raged, because she thought the youth did not understand the signals which she had left upon him, so she entered the hall with a knife in her hand, ready to plunge it into the offender's breast. But Kamar rose with a smile and bowed before her. 'Who taught you that trick?' asked the girl, and Kamar explained that he had been taking lessons from the barber's wife. 'She is clever!' exclaimed Halīmah. 'But now I shall teach you myself. I do not think that you will dislike the lessons.'

At this point Shahrazād saw the approach of morning and discreetly fell silent.

But when the seven-hundred-and-eighty-sixth night had come

SHE SAID:

She drew the virgin flesh of the boy towards her and with skilful fingers taught him how to find all the parts of the verb, to express the active in the passive, and make the two genders agree in number and case. He acquitted himself so valiantly in this battle of legs and thighs, with mighty strokes and strong defence, that it was a night indeed! Glory be to Allāh Who gives wings to the fledged bird and teaches the kid to dance from its first day, Who supples the neck of the young lion, Who jets the river from the rock, and plants in the hearts of His Believers an instinct as strong and beautiful as the cock's desire to crow at dawn!

When the expert Halīmah had appeased something of her flame with this new-wakened valiant, she said between her kisses: 'Fruit of my heart, I cannot live without you. One or two nights, one or two weeks, one or two months, one or two years, will not suffice me. I must leave my old and ugly husband, I must follow you to your own land and live with you for ever. Listen to me now, and if you have loved our night, do as I say: if my husband asks you again, tell him that the nature of man is such that it would be indiscreet of you to keep him for more than three nights away from his harīm. Then beg him to hire a house for you near ours, so that you can pass the evening together without inconvenience to each other. I will advise my husband to do as you request; after that Allāh will provide.' Kamar swore to do her bidding and, to ratify that oath, ran once more through all the gender rules she had taught him, without making a single mistake. The pilgrim's stick tapped many times along the road that night.

At length Kamar laid himself down by the jeweller as if nothing had happened, and in the morning would have taken his leave without a word; but Ubaid constrained him with an invitation to come again that night. So Kamar begged him to hire a house near by, in order that neither might inconvenience the other. The old jeweller readily agreed and immediately went forth to rent the house which lay against his own. While he was furnishing it richly and installing his young friend, the expert Halīmah had an opening made in the wall of partition, and hid it by a cupboard on each side.

Early next morning, to Kamar's joyful surprise, Halīmah came to him in the bedroom of his new house and, after explaining the mystery of the cupboards, bade him imitate a cock with hens. Kamar gave his imitation seven times; when Halīmah was wet with satisfied desire, she drew a dagger from her breast and gave it to her lover, saying: 'This belongs to my husband; he jewelled the hilt of it himself. Take it to his shop to-morrow and ask him how much it is worth. When he wishes to know where you obtained it, tell him that you bought it from a man who boasted that his mistress had stolen it from her old and ugly husband. While he is pondering your words hasten back here and pass the dagger through the wall to me.'

Kamar did as he had been told, and the old jeweller was plunged into a great trouble of spirit by the sight of the dagger. Kamar left him muttering to himself and, hurrying to his own chamber, passed the dagger through the wall to Halīmah.

Ubaid ran home to his wife, hissing like a jealous snake, and rushed into her chamber, crying: 'Where is my dagger?' Halīmah cast wondering eyes at him, and answered innocently: 'It is in the casket, in its usual place; but you look so wild that I will not give it you.' Then, when the jeweller swore that he would do no one a mischief, she opened the casket and handed him the dagger. 'A miracle!' he cried. 'I could have taken any oath that I saw this dagger in my young friend's belt.' 'Unworthy old man!' exclaimed Halīmah. 'Have you dared to suspect me?' So the jeweller humbly begged her pardon and comforted her as best he might.

Next morning, after playing seven games of chess with her lover upon his couch, Halīmah sat down to consider how she might open the eyes of her husband and get him to divorce her. 'I have a better plan this time,' she said at length. 'I will dress myself as a slave, and you must lead me to my husband's shop. Then you must tell him that you bought me at the market, and lift my veil that he may see my face. Surely that will open his eyes!' She rose and, dressing herself as a slave, accompanied her lover to her husband's shop. 'I have bought a slave for a thousand dīnārs,' said Kamar to the old jeweller. 'Does she please you?' So saying, he lifted Halīmah's veil, and poor Ubaid nearly fell to the floor when he recognised his wife, decked with the work of his own hands and wearing the rings which he had made for Kamar. 'What is her name?' he stuttered, and Kamar answered: 'Her name is Halīmah.' At this old Ubaid fell fainting to the floor and the lovers ran from the shop.

As soon as he came to himself, the jeweller hurried to his house and well-nigh perished of surprise when he found his wife sitting demurely in her own chamber, dressed as he had seemed to see her in the shop. 'There is no power or might save in Allāh!' he cried. 'My young friend has just bought a slave, and I could have sworn that you were she.' Feigning great indignation, Halīmah exclaimed: 'Calamitous greybeard, do you dare to suspect me? Go to our neighbour at once and, if what you say is true, you will find the slave sitting beside him.' 'You are right,' answered the unfortunate old man. 'That will be certain proof.' So he climbed painfully downstairs and left the house to visit Kamar.

Halīmah immediately passed through the wall and was sitting with

Kamar when her husband entered. 'Allāh is great!' murmured the jeweller in face of that extraordinary resemblance. 'He forms His creatures in the shapes which please Him best.' In troubled perplexity, he returned to his own house and, finding his wife as he had left her, heaped apologies on her and praises of her virtue, before going back to his shop.

As soon as her husband had retired, Halīmah rejoined Kamar and said to him: 'Nothing will teach these old fools! It only remains for us to leave this city. The camels are ready and the caravan awaits us.' She covered herself with her veil, and the two went out to join themselves to the caravan. Allāh had decreed that they should arrive in Egypt without accident.

Kamar was received at his father's house with tears of jubilation and, when Halīmah entered behind him, the eyes of all were dazzled by her beauty. 'Is she a princess, my son?' asked the merchant; but Kamar answered: 'She is not a princess, yet she was the cause of my departure from among you, the marvellous girl of whom the darwīsh spoke. Now I propose to marry her.' He told his father the whole story of his adventures; but nothing would be gained by repeating it in this place.

When he had heard all, the venerable Abd al-Rahmān cried out in horror: 'I curse you in our world and the next, my son, if you marry a hell-born woman such as this. One day she would treat you as shamefully as she has treated her husband, the jeweller! Put aside all thought of her, and I will choose a well-born wife for you among the daughters of my friends.' He spoke so wisely and at such length that Kamar answered: 'I will act in all things according to your wish, my father.' So the merchant kissed him and ordered Halīmah to be kept prisoner in a pavilion, at some distance from the house, until he could make up his mind concerning her.

After anxious searchings in the city, Abd al-Rahmān married Kamar to the kādī's daughter, who was the fairest maiden in all Cairo. At the end of forty days of feasting and dancing and coloured fires, a special festival was given for the poor, and all the needy of the city gathered round the dishes which were loaded for them.

Kamar, who was overseeing the service of this feast, beheld an old man among the poorest of the poor, dressed in rags and marked both by the sun and heavy grief. Looking at him closely, he recognised the jeweller Ubaid, and ran to tell his father. 'The time has come to undo the wrong you did,' exclaimed the merchant and, going among his guests, he called the old man by name and kissed him tenderly and asked the reason of his sudden poverty. Ubaid told him that he had left Basrah to escape the mockery of his foes, and had fallen into the hands of a troop of marauding Arabs, who spoiled him of everything he carried. Abd al-Rahmān conducted him to the hammām and, after the bath, clothed him in rich garments. Then he said: 'You are my guest and I owe you the truth. Your wife Halīmah is here, prisoned in one of my pavilions. I had thought to send her back with an escort to Basrah, but now that you are here her fate is in your hands. I will lead you to her, and you may either pardon her or treat her as she deserves. I know the whole painful story and can assure you that your wife is alone to blame. A man has nothing with which to reproach himself when he is seduced by a woman, because Allāh has planted in him an instinct to yield; but when a woman is tempted and does not repulse a man, she is most reprehensible. Alas, my brother, a man with a wife needs to be very wise and patient.' 'You are right, my brother,' answered the jeweller. 'She alone is to blame. Where is she?' Kamar's father held out the keys of the pavilion and pointed the way to it. With many expressions of joy, the old man took the keys and, unlocking the door of the pavilion, strode into his wife's presence. He walked towards her without a word and, flinging his two hands about her neck, strangled her, as he cried: 'Thus shall all wantons die!'

At this point Shahrazād saw the approach of morning and discreetly fell silent.

But when the seven-hundred-and-eighty-seventh night had come

SHE SAID:

In order to undo his son's fault, the merchant Abd al-Rahmān considered it meritorious in the sight of Allāh to marry his daughter Morning-Star to Ubaid. But Allāh has more generosity and greater wisdom!

As Shahrazād fell silent, King Shahryār cried: 'May all unfaithful wives suffer the death of Halīmah! A great many of your stories ought to have ended in this way. But I must confess that you have often angered me, Shahrazād, by assigning a quite different Destiny to some of the women in your tales. You ought to have known better, remembering the way I punished my unfaithful wife and all her slaves. The curse of Allāh be upon them!' Not wishing the King to brood further on his wrongs, Shahrazād made no answer, but hastened to begin. . . .

The Tale of the Leg of Mutton

IT is related—but Allāh knows all—that there was once in Cairo a girl of such subtlety that it was as easy for her to pass through the eye of a needle as to drink a cup of water. Allāh had dowered her with so ardent a temperament that, if she had been one of the four wives of a Believer and had received only the nights allowed her by law, she would speedily have died of frustration; but she had arranged her life so well that she was not only a man's single wife, but the single wife of two men, each hardy cocks of Upper Egypt, who could assuage twenty hens one after the other. She had taken such wise precautions that neither man supposed that he was living in a way forbidden by the Faith. In this she was helped by the professions of her two husbands; for the one named Harām was a robber, working by night and returning only for the day, and the other, called Akīl, was a pickpocket who laboured all day and only returned to her for the night.

Weeks and months passed while the two husbands valiantly played the cock indoors and the fox outside, without having the least suspicion that they shared the same hearth. A day came, however, when Harām, after contenting the girl with his inheritance more amply than usual, said to her: 'An affair of great importance calls me from the city. Pray for the success of my enterprise, dear wife, that I may the sooner return to you.' 'May the name of Allāh be upon you and about you, O head of my life!' answered the girl. 'What will happen to this poor wretch while her strong one is away?' She would not let him depart without giving him a thousand ardent proofs of her attachment, so that Harām went forth, swinging a bag of provisions which she had stocked for him and clicking his tongue with delight.

An hour afterwards, Akīl the pickpocket returned and also told the woman that he had to leave the city. The girl gave him an even more remarkable farewell upon her bed, and then packed a bag of food for him, so that Akīl left the house, giving praise to Allāh that he had so warm and thoughtful a wife, and clicking his tongue with happiness.

Destiny waits at the corner of the road, and these two husbands found it when they least expected it. At the end of his day's march, Akīl the pickpocket entered a khān and fell into conversation with the only other guest. 'My friend, you seem weary,' remarked Akīl, and Harām, for it was he, answered with a smile that he had a right to feel weary, since he had walked that day from Cairo. 'I also have walked from Cairo,' said Akīl, 'and I thank Allāh that He has given me a companion for the rest of my journey. For the Prophet (upon whom be prayer and peace!) has said: "A companion is the best provision for the road." Let us seal our friendship by taking bread and salt together. Here is my bag: I think that I can offer you fresh dates and a roast with garlic.' 'Allāh increase you, good comrade!' answered Harām. 'I accept your offer freely; but allow me to add my food to the common stock.'

Both men emptied the contents of their bags upon the mat and, lo! they were exactly the same: loaves of sesame bread, dates, and half a leg of mutton. Though they were surprised at this coincidence, their astonishment was greater still when they found that the two halves of the leg of mutton fitted exactly. 'Allāh akbar!' they cried. 'Surely it was written that this sheep would find its leg whole again, in spite of death and fire and seasoning!' Then the pickpocket said: 'Tell me, in Allāh's name, where you obtained your portion.' 'My wife gave it to me before I started,' answered the robber. 'Now tell me where you found yours.' 'My wife gave it to me,' replied Akīl. 'Will you tell me what part of the city you honour with your dwelling?' 'I live near the Victory Gate,' said Harām. 'And so do I!' cried Akīl. The two rascals went on from question to question until they discovered that they had both shared the same bed and hearth since the first day of their marriage. 'May the devil be far from us!' they cried. 'We have both been fooled by the same woman!' At first they were inclined to violence, but soon, being both wise and cautious, they agreed to return to the city together at once and tax the girl with their equivocal position.

When they came to their common home, the girl opened the door and, seeing her two husbands together, realised that no shift of her imagination could conceal the truth; but she comforted herself with the thought that no man can resist the sight of tears; scattering her hair, she threw herself sobbing bitterly at the feet of the two men, and asked for forgiveness.

As they both loved her and were bound by her beauty, they lifted and pardoned her, after reading her a stiff lecture on the subject of perfidy. She listened in contrite silence, until they said: 'We cannot go on living as before, in the face of all religious teaching; you must choose between us, and at once.'

The girl lowered her head and reflected for a long time; but, in spite of the urgent solicitations of the two men, she could not choose between them; for they were equally strong and valiant, and she loved them equally. When their patience was exhausted and they bade her speak or take the consequences, she lifted her head, saying: 'There is no power or might save in Allāh! You have asked me to choose, but I cannot choose; I can find nothing to weigh the scale in either's favour. You both live by your skill and thus can lie down to rest with an easy conscience; for Allāh judges His creatures according to their use of the talents which He has given, and will surely not repulse you at the last. Akīl picks pockets by day, Harām steals by night; therefore I declare, before Allāh and before you, that I will keep the man who shows the finer address in his next theft.' The two agreed to this test, and, when they cast lots for the first attempt, the choice fell to Akīl.

So Akīl led Harām to the market of the money changers and pointed out an old Jew, who made his way slowly from shop to shop in the exercise of his profession. 'You see that son of a dog?' he said. 'Well, before he has finished his round, I will make him give me the bag of gold which he carries to hold the dīnārs of his exchange.' So saying, he went up light as a feather behind the old man's back and, deftly picking his pocket of the prize, returned to Harām, who marvelled exceedingly and, at the same time, wished to depart in haste, for fear of being arrested as an accomplice. He led Akīl away and congratulated him on his skill, saying: 'As Allāh lives, I know that I could not accomplish so brilliant a feat! I thought that no Believer could ever rob a Jew until he was dead.' But Akīl laughed, and answered: 'That is only a beginning, my poor friend; that is not the way to loot a bag of gold. The law might get upon my track at any time and force me to disgorge. No, I am going to get the kādī himself to decide that the bag and its contents are mine and have never at all belonged to that gold-stuffed Jew.' He took his companion to a retired corner of the market and, after opening the bag, carefully counted the gold pieces. Then he removed ten of them and replaced them by a copper ring. Finally he refastened the bag with great care and, approaching the Jew again, deftly slipped it back into its place in the pocket of the old man's kaftān. O Believers, skill is a gift from God!

The Jew had only taken a few steps when the pickpocket approached him a third time, but, on this occasion, from the front and with ostentatious haste. 'Vile son of Aaron,' he cried, 'you have done it once too often! Give me back my bag or come with me to the kādī!' The Jew, who had never seen his accuser before, confounded himself with excuses in order to avoid being beaten, and swore by Abraham, Isaac and Jacob, that Akīl was making a mistake. But, instead of listening to him, the pickpocket raised the whole market against the Jew and haled him along by his cloak, crying: 'To the kādī, to the kādī!' Then, as the old man resisted, he dragged him by the beard through the hooting crowd, until the two were in the kādī's presence.

'What business is this?' demanded the kādī, and Akīl answered: 'O our master, this Jew is certainly the most audacious thief who has ever appeared before you. He stole a bag of gold from me and then dared to walk about the market, as if he belonged to the Faith and had no sin upon his conscience.' At this point the Jew fumbled at the beard which had been half torn from his chin, and groaned: 'I protest, O master! I had never seen this man before. He came up to me and handled me roughly and raised the whole market against me, so that my credit and my reputation for honesty have gone for ever.' 'Vile son of Israel,' cried Akīl, 'since when has the word of a Jewish dog prevailed against the oath of a Mussulmān? O our master the kādī, this trickster denies his theft with all the cunning of that Indian merchant, of whom you have doubtless heard.' 'I know no story about an Indian merchant,' replied the kādī. 'Tell it to me briefly.' So Akīl said: 'This merchant had succeeded in inspiring such trust among the folk of his market that one day a vast sum of money was confided to him without a receipt. When the owner came to reclaim it, the merchant, knowing that there were no witnesses and no documents, denied that any deposit had been made. He would have enjoyed his ill-gotten gains if the kādī of that city had not made him confess in a most clever fashion and then administered two hundred strokes on the soles of his feet. I am sure that your lordship's known sagacity will easily prove the guilt of this perfidious Jew. May I beg you to have him searched?'

The kādī ordered his guards to search the Jew, and they soon found the bag of gold upon him. Then a great tumult rose, the old man swearing that the bag was his own and Akīl contradicting him in opprobrious phrases. To still the noise the kādī bade each man declare the contents of the bag. The Jew said: 'Good master, it contains five hundred golden dīnārs, neither more nor less.' But Akīl cried: 'You lie, you dog; there are four hundred and ninety gold pieces in the bag and also a copper ring bearing my seal if you have not removed it already.' At once the kādī opened the bag in the presence of witnesses and, naturally, found that its contents agreed with the pickpocket's description; therefore he handed the bag to Akīl and bade his men beat the Jew severely.

When Harām saw Akīl thus come off with flying colours, he first congratulated him and then made an appointment to meet him near the Sultān's palace that night, that he himself might undertake an exploit, with his rival as a witness. They met in the place appointed at the dark of night, and Harām said: 'My friend, you have had the laugh of a Jew and a kādī; I am going to have the laugh of a Sultān. See, here is my rope-ladder. You must come with me as a witness to what I do.' Akīl was terrified at the other's rashness for he was a simple pickpocket, knowing nothing of the higher theft; but, being ashamed to withdraw, he helped him to throw the rope-ladder over the palace wall. The two climbed up and then, descending to the gardens, forced an entrance into the palace under cover of darkness.

They glided along many galleries until they came to the Sultān's sleeping chamber, where Harām lifted a curtain and showed his companion the King sleeping, with a boy who sat beside him and tickled his feet to favour his slumber. The lad himself seemed drowsy and was chewing a morsel of mastic to keep himself awake.

At this point Shahrazād saw the approach of morning and discreetly fell silent.

But when the seven-hundred-and-eighty-eighth night had come

SHE SAID:

Seeing these things, Akīl felt his legs give beneath him for terror, but Harām whispered in his ear: 'There is no need to be afraid. You spoke to the kādī, and I shall speak to the King.' Leaving his companion behind the curtain, he crept up to the boy, with the silence of a moth moving upon velvet, gagged and bound him in one movement, and set him aside by the wall. He sat down in the other's place and began to tickle the soles of the King's feet, increasing the strength of the movement until the Sultān yawned and woke; then Harām imitated the boy's voice, and said: 'O King of time, since you cannot sleep, shall I tell you a tale?' 'Certainly,' answered the Sultān, and Harām began: 'There was once, O King of time, a robber named Harām and a pickpocket named Akīl, who lived in a certain city of the cities of the world and were rivals in audacity and skill. One day each of them undertook . . .' and he told the Sultān of Akīl's stroke in all its details and then most brazenly went on to outline the audacity which was even then taking place, only changing the Sultān's name and the position of the chamber. 'Now tell me, O King of time,' he concluded, 'which of the two companions was more expert?' 'The robber who broke into the King's palace, without a doubt,' answered the Sultān. Having obtained this answer, Harām pretended that he had a pressing need to piss, and went forth to the cabinet. He rejoined his companion, who had been listening in a cold sweat of fear, and the two left the palace by the way they had come.

Next morning the Sultān, who had been drowsily surprised at the long absence of his favourite, was astonished to find him trussed up against the wall, exactly as in the tale which had been told him. He understood at once that he had been the victim of a bold thief; but, instead of growing angry, he announced through heralds that he pardoned the midnight intruder and would reward him generously if he presented himself at the palace. So Harām came and stood before the Sultān, who praised him for his courage, and appointed him chief of police for all his kingdom. When the girl heard this, she chose Harām for her husband and lived with him pleasantly all the days of their life. But Allāh knows all!

Shahrazād did not wish to leave this story to rankle in the King's mind for a whole day, so she at once began the prodigious tale which follows.

She said:

The Keys of Destiny

IT is related, O auspicious King, that the Khalīfah Muhammad ibn Thailūn, Sultān of Egypt, was as wise and good a ruler as his father had been cruel and oppressive. Instead of torturing his subjects to make them pay the same taxes three or four times over, and beating them with sticks to make them dig up the few poor coins which they had hidden in the earth from the collectors, he bent his whole power to bring back tranquillity and justice to his people. He used the treasures which Thailūn had violently amassed, to protect poets and sages, to reward the valiant, and to help the poor. Therefore Allāh blessed his reign; the risings of the Nile had never been so regular and abundant, the crops never so rich and frequent, the fields of lupine and lucern never so green, and the bags of the merchants' gold never so heavy.

One day Muhammad called all the dignitaries of his palace into his presence to interrogate them concerning their duties and wages and past services; for he wished to check their conduct and means of life with his own eyes and ears. 'If I find any who toils wearily for light pay,' said he, 'I will lessen his duties and increase his salary; but if I find any who has easy work and extravagant payment, I will decrease his salary and augment his toil.' First the wazīrs appeared before him, forty venerable old men with long white beards and wise eyes. They wore jewelled turbans and leaned upon long staffs with amber heads, which were the symbols of their power. Next came the walīs of provinces, the captains of the army, and all those whose duty near and far was to render justice and maintain the peace. One after another they knelt before the King and kissed the earth between his hands, while he questioned them closely, blaming some and rewarding others, according to their merits.

The last to present himself was the eunuch who bore the sword of justice, and, though he was a fat and idle man, his face was sad. Instead of stalking into the presence proudly, with his blade borne naked over his shoulder, he entered with his sword in its sheath and a hanging head. He kissed the earth between Muhammad's hands, saying: 'O master and crown upon our heads, surely the day of justice has dawned for your poor executioner! My lord, since the death of your father, the Sultān Thailūn (may Allāh have him in His keeping!). I have seen my duties and my profits dwindling day by day. My life used to be happy, but now it drags a mournful and a useless course. If Egypt remains peaceful and abundant, I shall die of hunger and not leave enough money to buy a winding-sheet. But Allāh prolong our master's life!'

After reflection the Khalīfah Muhammad saw the justice of this complaint; for a sword-bearer's profits do not come from any rich stipend, but are dependent on the gifts and legacies of his victims.

Therefore he cried: 'We come from Allāh and return to Him! Universal good is an illusion, for the happiness of one is bought by the tears of another. Lift up your heart and refresh your eyes, O executioner, for from henceforth you shall receive two hundred dīnārs every year to buy you clothes and victual. I pray to Allāh that, while I live, your sword may lie unused within its sheath and take the rust of peace from the quiet years.' The executioner kissed the hem of the Khalīfah's robe and returned to his place among the rank of officers. This shows the justice and mercy of Muhammad.

As the audience was about to be dismissed, the Sultān saw a wrinkled and bent old man, whom he had not yet questioned; so he signed to him to approach, and asked him of his duties. 'O King of time,' the sheikh replied, 'I have only one duty: to watch over a casket which your dead father put into my charge. I receive ten gold dīnārs from the treasury every month for doing so.' 'But that is high pay for such easy work!' exclaimed the Sultān. 'What is in the casket?' 'As Allāh lives,' answered the old man, 'I have guarded it for forty years and I do not know.' 'Bring it to me quickly!' cried Muhammad.

The old man retired and immediately returned with a chest of solid and wonderfully carved gold; at a sign from his King he opened it for the first time. And lo, it contained only a little red earth, and a manuscript written in bright lettering on the purple-stained skin of a gazelle!

The Sultān took the manuscript and tried to read the brilliant characters in which it was written; but, though he was learned in many tongues, he could make nothing of that lettering; nor were the wazīrs and ulamā who were present at all more successful. The Sultān called all the famous sages of Egypt, Syria, Persia, and India to read the writing; but none of them could read it. What are sages after all but foolish old men in large turbans?

So the Sultān Muhammad caused the news to be published throughout his empire that he would greatly reward any who could point out a man who should be able to read the unknown characters.

A few days after this announcement, an old man in a white turban presented himself before the Sultān, saying: 'Allāh prolong the life of our master! The slave who stands before you used to serve your dead father, the Sultān Thailūn; only to-day has he returned from the exile to which that gracious King condemned him. I come to tell you that the sole man who can read the manuscript written on gazelle skin is its owner, the sheikh Hasan Abdallāh, son of al-Ashar, who was thrown into a dungeon forty years ago by your dead father. Allāh alone knows if he groans there still or if he is dead.' 'Why was he cast into prison?' asked the Sultān. 'Because your dead father wished to force him to read the manuscript, after he had taken it from him by violence,' answered the old man.

Muhammad immediately sent the captain of his guard to visit all the prisons, in the hope that the sheikh Hasan Abdallāh might be still alive. Allāh willed that the captain should find him living, and dress him in a robe of honour, and lead him into the Sultān's presence. Muhammad saw an old man whose face was deeply marked by suffering; so he rose in his honour and begged forgiveness for his father's unjust act. Then he made Hasan Abdallāh sit beside him and gave the manuscript into his hands, saying: 'Oh sheikh, I do not wish to keep a thing which does not belong to me, even though it were the key to all the treasures of the world.'

Hasan Abdallāh shed abundant tears and turned his open palms towards the sky, crying: 'O Lord, the Source of all wisdom, Who makes the poison and the antidote to flower in the same field, I have languished for forty years in a dungeon and now the son of my enemy has stretched out his hand and helped me forth, that I may die in the sunlight! Therefore I praise and adore You, O Lord, Whose secret thoughts are hidden from the sight of man.' Then he turned to the Sultān, saying: 'Dear master, that which I refused to violence, I freely accord to your compassion. Henceforth this manuscript, for which I risked a score of lives, belongs to you for ever. It is the beginning and end of all wisdom; it is the only thing which I brought away with me from the mysterious city of Shaddād ibn Ād where no man may set his feet, from the city of Many-Columned Irām.'

The Khalīfah kissed the old man, as he exclaimed: 'My father, I beg you to tell me all you know about this manuscript and about Many-Columned Irām, the city of Shaddād ibn Ād.' 'O King, the tale of the manuscript is the tale of my life,' answered Abdallāh. 'If it were written with needles in the interior corner of an eye yet would it serve as a lesson to the circumspect.' And he told this story:

My father was one of the richest and most respected merchants in Cairo, and I was his only son. He spared no expense on my education and gave me the best masters in Egypt, so that, by the time I was twenty, I was already renowned among the ulamā for my knowledge of ancient learning. Wishing to rejoice in my marriage, my father and mother wed me to a young virgin, who was light and fair, slim and dainty, and whose eyes were like pools reflecting stars. Magnificent feasts were given for us, and we two lived in great delight, not only for the first few nights but for ten years.

But who may fathom the intent of Destiny? After those ten years had flowed by like a dream, Fate cast all woes at once upon my house. In a few days my father perished of the plague, fire devoured the buildings of my inheritance, and the waters of the sea swallowed the ships which trafficked into far countries for my gain. I was left as poor as a child robbed of its mother's breast, with no resort save a belief in Allāh; so I frequented the courts of the mosques, with the beggars of His bounty, and lived on the noble words of the santons who were my friends. Often I would have to return home without a crust of bread, and famish throughout the night after having fasted all the day. My own misery was much, but I grieved more for the destitution of my mother and my wife and my little children.

One day, when Allāh had sent me no alms, my wife took off her last garment and handed it to me, weeping and saying: 'Try to sell this in the market that our children may have bread.' So I took the garment and went forth with it; but as I walked towards the market, I met a Badawī mounted on a red camel.

At this point Shahrazād saw the approach of morning and discreetly fell silent.

But when the seven-hundred-and-eighty-ninth night had come

SHE SAID:

When the Badawī saw me, he checked his camel and made it kneel. 'Greeting, my brother,' he said, 'can you direct me to the house of the rich merchant named Hasan Abdallāh, son of al-Ashar?' I felt a sudden shame for my poverty, though it comes from Allāh even as riches come from Him; so I hung my head and answered: 'The blessing of Allāh be upon you, O father of Arabs! But I know of no such man in Cairo.' I would have gone on my way, but the Badawī leapt from his camel's back and, taking both my hands in his, said reproachfully: 'Allāh is great and generous, my brother! But are you not yourself the sheikh Hasan Abdallāh, son of al-Ashar? And is it possible that you should hide your name in order to get rid of a guest whom Allāh sends you?' In my confusion I could not check my tears; I begged him to forgive me and would have kissed his hands, but he prevented me and took me in his arms, as if I had been his brother. So I led him towards my house.

The Badawī walked by my side, leading his camel, and, as we went, my heart was tortured by the thought that I had nothing to set before my guest. When we arrived at the house, I hastened to tell my wife of this unexpected meeting, and she said to me: 'A stranger is the guest of Allāh, even the children's bread is due to him. Go out quickly and sell the garment to buy provisions for this Badawī. If anything remains after he has eaten, we will live upon it.' In order to go out, I had to pass the vestibule in which I had left my guest. 'What are you hiding beneath your cloak, my brother?' he asked when he saw me. 'Nothing,' I answered in confusion, but he insisted, saying: 'I beg you in Allāh's name to tell me.' Turning very red in the face, I showed him the garment, saying: 'This belongs to my wife; I am taking it to a neighbour who is skilful at repairing such things.' But the Badawī cried: 'Allāh is generous, my brother! You would sell your wife's robe to fulfil the duties of hospitality towards a stranger! . . . Here are ten gold pieces, O Hasan. Go forth and buy what is necessary for the whole house.' He kissed me so that I could not refuse the offer, and abundance returned to my poor home once more.

Every day the Badawī gave me the same sum which I spent in the same fashion, and for two weeks I glorified the generosity of Allāh.

On the morning of the sixteenth day, my guest said to me: 'Are you willing to sell yourself, O Hasan Abdallāh?' 'I am already your slave, good master,' I answered, 'both I and mine belong to you.' But he continued: 'I do not mean that; I ask you if you are willing to sell yourself in reality. I do not wish to bargain, and will leave you to fix the price.' Not doubting for a moment that he jested, I answered with a smile: 'A free man's price is fixed by the Book at a thousand dīnārs, if he is killed at a single blow. But, if he receives three or four blows or is cut into several parts, the price is one thousand five hundred dīnārs.' 'That does not seem exorbitant,' answered the Badawī. 'If you consent to the sale I will pay you the fifteen hundred.' Realising at last that my guest was quite serious, I murmured to myself: 'Allāh has sent this Badawī to save your children from the bitterness of hunger. If it is your Destiny to be cut in pieces, you cannot escape.' So I answered: 'I agree to the sale, my brother, but I must have time to consult my family about it.' 'Take all the time you need,' said he, and left me to go about his business.

Then, O King of time, I sought my mother, my wife, and my

children. 'Allāh has saved you from adversity!' I cried, and told them of the Badawī's offer; but my mother and my wife beat their breasts, wailing: 'O woeful day! What will he do to you?' and my children ran to me and held me by the garment. They all wept until my wife, who had been dowered with wisdom and a good counsel, exclaimed: 'If you refuse, perhaps this evil Badawī will reclaim the money which he has spent here; therefore you must go at once and try to sell this wretched house, our last possession, so that you may have money with which to satisfy him. Then you will owe him nothing and remain a free man.' But, as she thought of our children in the street, she wept again, and my perplexity was greater than before. 'O Hasan Abdallāh, do not spurn this chance which Allāh sends,' I said to myself. 'If you sell yourself, your children will have bread for many months. But then, but then, why does he want to buy you? For what does he need you? Of what use can you be to him? If you were young and beardless! But your beard is like Hagar's train; you would not tempt a man from Upper Egypt. I fear he means your death to be a slow one, as he is willing to pay the fifteen hundred.'

Yet, by the time the Badawī returned in the evening, I had made up my mind; so I received him with a smiling face, and said: 'I am yours, O guest!' At once he drew one thousand five hundred dīnārs from his belt and counted them over to me. 'Pray for the Prophet, O Hasan Abdallāh!' he cried, and I said: 'The prayer, the peace, and the blessing of Allāh be upon him!' Then said the Badawī: 'Now that you belong to me, O brother, you need have no fear; for you shall retain both life and freedom. I only bought you to be a faithful and agreeable companion to me on a long journey which I am about to undertake. The Prophet has said: "A companion is the best provision for the road."'

I returned joyfully to my mother and wife, and placed the fifteen hundred dīnārs on the mat where they were seated; but, instead of waiting for my explanation, they tore their hair and gave piercing cries of grief, as if they were already about my tomb. 'Woe, woe, it is blood money!' they cried. 'We will never touch the price of your dear life; we would rather die of hunger.' I left them until they were quieter, and then returned to reason with them. By pointing out that the Badawī was a man of excellent intention, only actuated by charity, I succeeded in diminishing their grief; so, taking advantage of the momentary calm, I kissed them goodbye, and kissed my children goodbye, and departed sore at heart.

I accompanied the Badawī to the beast market and, acting under his orders, first bought myself a camel famous for swiftness, and then filled the provision bags with food for a long journey. When all was ready, I helped my master on to the back of his camel and mounted my own. We invoked the name of Allāh and set forth.

Soon we were in the desert, and rode on without a halt through those solitudes in which only Allāh dwelt, and across those moving sands which held no human trace. My master guided himself over these vast waves of sand by some hidden knowledge; and we rode beneath a burning sky for ten days, each as long to me as a night of evil dreams.

At this point Shahrazād saw the approach of morning and discreetly fell silent.

But when the seven-hundred-and-ninetieth night had come

SHE SAID:

On the eleventh morning we came into a mighty plain which seemed to be made of grains of silver. In the middle of this plain there rose a high column of granite, bearing on its top the upright figure of a youth moulded in copper, whose right hand, open and extended, held a heavy key dangling from each of its five fingers. The first key was of gold, the second of silver, the third of Chinese copper, the fourth of iron, the fifth of lead; and all were magical. The man who mastered each had to bear the fate of each, for they were the keys of Destiny: the gold was the key of misery, the silver the key of suffering, the Chinese copper was the key of death, the iron the key of glory, and the lead the key of happiness and wisdom. But I knew nothing of the nature of the keys, and from my ignorance sprang all the misfortunes of my life. Yet good and evil come from Allāh, and His creature must accept them with humility.

When we came to the foot of this column, the Badawī dismounted from his camel and, while I was doing likewise, drew a strangely-formed bow from its case and fitted an arrow to the string. He bent the bow and shot at the copper figure in the air, but, because he either lacked skill or feigned to lack it, the arrow fell far short. Then he turned to me and said: 'Now you can repay me and buy back your liberty, for you are strong and skilful. Take this bow and shoot down the keys.' Happy at the chance to regain my freedom, I took the bow with alacrity and saw that it was of skilful Indian workmanship.

Wishing to cut a good figure in my master's eyes, I shot at the youth's hand with all my strength and skill, and my first arrow caused the gold key to fall to the ground. I picked it up proudly and would have handed it to the Badawī; but he refused it, saying: 'Keep it for yourself, good friend, as a reward for your excellent shooting.' So I placed the gold key in my belt, not knowing that it was the key of misery.

My second shot dislodged the silver key and, as my master refused it also, I put it in my belt with the other, not knowing that it was the key of suffering.

My next two arrows brought down the iron key and the lead key, one of glory and the other of happiness and wisdom, had I but known it. The Badawī pounced on them with a joyful exclamation: 'Blessed be the womb that bore you, O Hasan Abdallāh! Blessed be the man who strengthened your arm and taught your eye! Now you are free!' When I would have kissed his hand, he took me in his arms; but when I would have given him the gold and silver keys, he said: 'Keep them, for they are yours.'

I fitted a fifth arrow and would have shot at the last key, the key of Chinese copper, not knowing that it was the key of death. But my master pulled the bow from my hands, crying: 'What are you about, unhappy man?' I gave a start at his violence and dropped the arrow, which pierced my left foot, leaving a painful wound. That was the beginning of my misfortunes.

My master bound up the hurt as well as he could, and helped me on to my camel.

After three days and nights of riding which caused my foot great agony, we halted in a stretch of meadowland, thickly studded with trees which bore fair and unknown fruits exciting to the eye and hand. As I was driven hard by thirst, I dragged myself to one of the trees and, pulling down a fruit, coloured a gold-red and scented pleasantly, placed it in my mouth and bit upon it. At once my teeth fastened so strongly into it that my jaws would not move; I would have cried out, but the sound which reached beyond the fruit was only a muffled whisper. I felt that I was stifling, and began to limp to and fro, gesticulating like a madman, until I fell to the earth, with my eyes bursting out of my head.

At first the Badawī was frightened at my behaviour, but when he discovered the cause of my torment, he came close and tried to free my jaws. His efforts only hurt me more and made the fruit stick closer, so he left me and began to pick up several fruits of the same kind, which lay under the trees. After a careful consideration of them all, he chose one and threw away the others. 'Look closely at this fruit, Hasan Abdallāh,' he said when he returned. 'You will notice countless insects biting and undermining it. If we have patience, I think we may use these little creatures as a cure for your misfortune. I calculate that, if we place a good number of them upon the fruit which is stopping your mouth, they will free you at the latest in two or three days.' As he was a man of experience, I let him set about the cure; but I could not help thinking: 'Surely death were better than three days and nights of such a torment!'

My master sat beside me in the shade and, after satisfying himself that the insects had begun their work, drew dates and bread from the provision bag and started to eat. But he was good enough to interrupt himself from time to time, to urge patience on me, saying: 'You see, O Hasan Abdallāh, how your greed has interrupted my journey and postponed the execution of my plans. Yet, being a wise man, I do not worry over such a trifling accident. And there is no need for you to worry.' Then he composed himself to sleep, advising me to do the same.

I passed that night and the next day in acute torture, for, over and above the pain of my foot and the pain of my jaws, I was racked by hunger and especially by thirst. To console me, the Badawī would report the progress of the insects from time to time, and in some sort managed to keep me sane until the third day.

Early on the third morning I felt my jaws relax and, blessing the name of Allāh, I hurled the rest of that evil fruit away.

My first care on becoming free was to rummage in the foodbag and shake the waterskin; but, during my three days' fast, my master had emptied both. I wept and accused him sorely, but he answered sweetly and without anger: 'Are you just, Hasan Abdallāh? Would you have had me die of hunger and thirst? Put your trust in Allāh, and search for some water stream.'

I rose and limped about in search of water or some known fruit, but the fruit was all of that one evil kind. At last, however, I found a trickle of bright water flowing from a hollow rock and, going on my knees, drank and drank of it again.

With my thirst allayed, I consented to journey on, and, mounting my beast, followed the Badawī, who was already far ahead on his red camel; but I had not gone a hundred paces before I felt so terrible a colic within me that the fire of hell seemed to be burning in my bowels. 'O Allāh, O my mother!' I cried, as I tried to moderate the speed of my camel, which was taking great swift strides to overtake its fellow. Its bumping and jumping caused me such great agony that I shrieked aloud and cursed the camel, myself, and all the world. At last my master heard me and, riding back, helped me to halt and stagger to the ground. At once I squatted on the sand, if the King of time will excuse the liberty, and gave free course to the impulsion of my bowels. I felt as if my guts were leaving me in thunder; even as I heard the Badawī saying: 'Be patient, O Hasan Abdallāh,' I fell forward in a dead faint.

I do not know how long I was unconscious; when I came to myself, it was evening and I was again mounted on the back of that detestable camel, following my companion across the desert. We halted at the foot of a high mountain behind which the sun was setting, and my master said to me: 'I thank Allāh that we shall not fast to-night. Stay quietly here, for my knowledge of travel will enable me to find safe refreshment, where you, without doubt, would gather us some poisoned thing.' He went up to a cluster of plants, whose broad and fleshy leaves were covered with sharp spines, and, after chopping some of them down with his sword, peeled away their outer covering with his knife, showing a sweet yellow flesh within. He gave me as much as I could eat and I was refreshed by the taste, which was of figs.

I began to forget my sufferings in the hope which I entertained of a night's quiet sleep; for I seemed to have forgotten the savour of it. At moonrise I stretched my camel's-hair mantle on the ground and was making ready to sleep, when the Badawī said to me:

At this point Shahrazād saw the approach of morning and discreetly fell silent.

But when the seven-hundred-and-ninety-first night had come

SHE SAID:

'Now is your chance to show me that you are really grateful; I wish you to climb up that mountain and wait on the summit for the sun's rising. As his rim appears, you must turn to the east and recite the morning prayer; after that you may come down. Be very careful not to let yourself be surprised by sleep, for the exhalations of that peak are deadly beyond belief and would undermine your health for ever.'

In spite of my great weariness and many sufferings, I could not forget that the Badawī had provided my children with bread; so, though thinking the request a strange one and much against my will, I climbed painfully to the top of that mountain, bearing, with what fortitude I might, the agonies which I felt in my foot and belly at the least movement. The peak was white and bare, affording no shelter from a piercing wind which blew violently across it. I had no sooner reached the top than my accumulated weariness took hold of me and cast me to the ground, where I slept, in spite of myself, until morning.

When I woke and saw that the sun was just about to appear, I tried to rise to my feet, but only fell backwards without movement. My limbs had swollen to the size of an elephant's legs and were both painful and flabby, refusing to bear up the enormous weight of my belly, which had grown to the bigness of the largest waterskin. My head was like lead upon my shoulders and I could not move my arms.

Yet I made a superhuman effort, for fear of displeasing the Badawī, and obliged my body to stand upright. Wellnigh swooning from the terrible pain, I turned to the east and recited the morning prayer. As I did so, the sun rose and threw the distended shadow of my unfortunate body away to the west.

As soon as my duty was done, I started to descend the mountain, but I was so feeble and the slope so great that my monstrous legs doubled under me at the first step. I began rolling, like a fast ball, down the sheer slope; the stones and brambles at which I clutched to save myself only tore away strips of flesh and clothing; after watering the whole of that mountain with my blood, I bounded out into the plain and lay groaning at my master's feet.

He leaned over the sand and was so engrossed in certain lines which he was tracing that he saw nothing of the manner in which I had arrived and did not notice my presence until my prolonged moaning drew his attention. He cried over his shoulder without looking at me: 'Let us praise Allāh! You were born under a happy star and all our undertakings shall succeed. Thanks to your shadow, which I measured upon the plain, I have at last been able to discover something for which I have searched for many years.'

'Come and help me to dig,' he said without raising his head, 'just here, where I have planted the point of my lance.' But then, as I only answered with broken sobs, he turned towards me at last and, seeing me lying in a pitiful round mass upon the sand, ran towards me, crying: 'O Hasan Abdallāh, you have been very imprudent! You have slept upon the mountain and the evil vapours, passing into the blood, have poisoned all.' This he said angrily, but afterwards, when he saw that my teeth were chattering with pain and consternation, he spoke more calmly: 'But do not think that I am angry with you. Come, I will cure you.' So saying, he drew a knife with a fine sharp blade from his belt and, before I could oppose the least resistance, stabbed me deeply in many places. Water flowed forth in abundance from the punctures which he had made in my belly and arms, my thighs and legs; I grew to be like an empty waterbag and my skin fluttered upon my bones like a second-hand garment too great for the wearer. Yet I felt a little relieved, and was able to drag myself to my feet and help my master in his digging.

We shovelled away the earth about the lance until we had uncovered a white marble tomb, whose cover the Badawī lifted. Then we saw a flurry of human bones and a manuscript written in bright gold on the purple-stained skin of a gazelle. You hold it in your hands, O King of time.

My master snatched the manuscript with trembling hands and, though it was written in an unknown tongue, began to read it with great attention. As he turned over page after page, his pale brow grew red with pleasure and his eyes began to sparkle joyously. At last he cried aloud: 'Now I know the way to that mysterious city! O Hasan Abdallāh, rejoice with me, for soon we shall enter Many-Columned Irām, where no human has set foot before: soon we shall hold the secret of that red sulphur which is the germ of all precious metals and the principle of all the riches of the world.'

But the thought of further journeying filled me with terror, and I cried: 'Excuse your slave, my lord! Though he rejoices with you, he has found that riches are not profitable to him, and would prefer to live in health and poverty at Cairo than drag all the miseries of his body to Many-Columned Irām.' My master looked at me pitifully, and answered: 'Poor fool, I labour as much for you as for myself.' 'That is true,' I retorted, 'but alas, it is always I who reap the unfortunate results of those labours.'

Without paying any attention to my decision, the Badawī gathered together an ample provision of the fig-tasting flesh of those plants which I have mentioned. Then he mounted his camel and I was obliged to do the same.

We skirted the flanks of the mountain and rode towards the west for three days and three nights until, on the fourth morning, we saw before us on the horizon something which glittered and threw back the sunlight as if it had been a mighty mirror. Drawing closer, we found that our way was barred by a river of mercury, spanned only by a crystal bridge with no handrail and so narrow, steep, and slippery that a man of sense would never have ventured his foot upon it.

But my master, without a moment's hesitation, dismounted and bade me also dismount. After unsaddling the camels that they might graze at ease, he drew two pairs of woollen slippers from his saddlebags and, covering his feet with one pair, told me to put on the other. He commanded me to follow him closely, without looking to right or left, and himself walked firmly on to the crystal bridge. I followed trembling, and we both came, more by Allāh's mercy than by any confidence of mine, safely to the opposite bank.

We walked forward for some hours in silence and arrived at last at the entrance of a black valley, strewn with gigantic black rocks and horribly shaded by black trees. I saw vast serpents covered with black scales slipping to and fro among the black leaves; in my terror I turned to flee from that horrible place, but the black rocks were all about me like the sides of a well.

I fell to the earth weeping, and cried to my master: 'O son of excellence, why have you led me by a road of suffering to a vile death in this place? Alas, alas, I shall never see my children or their mother any more! Why did you lift me from the calm of my poverty? I was only a beggar upon the road of Allāh but I sat at ease in the courts of the mosques and heard the noble words of the saints.' 'Be brave, be a man, Hasan Abdallāh!' answered the Badawī, without a trace of anger in his voice. 'You are not going to die, and when you return to Cairo it will not be as a poor man, but as one richer than the King.'

At this point Shahrazād saw the approach of morning and discreetly fell silent.

But when the seven-hundred-and-ninety-second night had come

SHE SAID:

So saying, my master sat down on the ground and began turning the leaves of the manuscript with a moistened thumb, as calmly as if he were in his own harīm. After reading for an hour, he raised his head and said: 'O Hasan Abdallāh, do you wish to leave this spot as quickly as possible?' 'Most certainly I do!' I cried. 'Tell me what feat I must perform, for pity's sake! Must I recite all the chapters of the Koran? Must I repeat all the names and sacred attributes of Allāh? Must I make a vow to go on pilgrimage to Mecca and Madinah ten years running? Speak, master; I am ready for all and more than all!'

The Badawī gave me a kindly glance, and answered: 'No, Hasan Abdallāh, no, your task is much more easy: take this bow and this arrow, and walk about the valley until you see a vast serpent with black horns. As you are a skilful shot, you should have no difficulty in killing him. When you have done so, you must bring me his head and heart; then you will have done your share.' 'Ay, ay!' I cried. 'Do you call that easy? Why do you not do it yourself? I tell you I would rather lie as I am and perish as I lie.' But the Badawī laid his hand on my shoulder, saying: 'Hasan Abdallāh, have you forgotten your wife's garment and your children's bread?' So I burst into tears and, taking the bow and arrow in my trembling hands, walked towards the black rocks, in and out of which serpents of the same colour writhed in terrifying knots. It was not long before I found my prey; when I beheld a snake vaster than the rest and bearing horns upon its hideous head, I called on the name of Allāh and let fly my arrow. The serpent bounded under the wound, lashing its body like a monstrous whip, until it fell motionless all along the ground. When I was sure that it had died, I cut its head off with my knife and, slitting up the belly, removed its heart.

I carried these things back to my master, who took them from me with an affable smile, saying: 'Now help me to make a fire.' I collected dry grass and small branches, until the pile was large enough; then the Badawī took a diamond from his pocket and, turning it to the sun, darted a reflected ray on to the dry wood, so that it kindled.

Then he drew from beneath his robe a small iron vessel and a tube cut from a single ruby. 'You see this ruby phial, Hasan Abdallāh,' he said, 'but the content is unknown to you. It is the blood of the Phœnix.' He uncorked the tube and, after pouring the liquid into the iron vessel, added the heart and brain of the serpent. Finally he set the iron vessel on the fire and, opening the manuscript which you hold, O King of time, read unintelligible words over the brew.

Suddenly my master rose to his feet, bared his shoulders as do pilgrims when they leave Mecca, and, dipping the corner of his belt in the mixture on the fire, ordered me to rub his back with it. I obeyed him and saw the skin of the shoulders swelling and breaking as I rubbed and a pair of wings grow forth and increase in size until they trailed upon the ground. The Badawī began to beat these wings with greater and greater strength till he shot up into the air; but I, who would have died a thousand deaths rather than be left alone in those sinister places, jumped after him and clung mightily to the skirts of his robe, so that I was carried from that black valley and soared with him above the clouds.

I cannot say how long we flew, my lord, but I know that we found ourselves at length above a mighty plain, bounded at the further end by a wall of blue crystal. The sand of this plain was powdered gold, the pebbles were bright gems, and in its midst rose a city filled with palaces and gardens.

'Behold, Many-Columned Irām!' cried my master and, ceasing the oarage of his wings, let us sink gently to earth beneath the walls of the city of Shaddād, son of Ād. At once the wings grew small and disappeared.

The walls of that city were made of alternate gold and silver blocks, and seven gates opened in them like the gates of Paradise. The first was of ruby, the second of emerald, the third of agate, the fourth of coral, the fifth of jasper, the sixth of silver, and the seventh of gold.

We entered by the gate of gold and, as we advanced, called upon the name of Allāh. We passed through streets bordered by palaces with colonnades of alabaster, and by gardens where the air was milk and the streams ran flower-water. In this way we came to a palace which dominated the city from its centre and was built with a breadth and art which cannot be described. Its terraces were held up on a thousand columns of red gold, and had balustrades of coloured crystal and walls starred with emeralds and sapphires. In the middle of this palace blossomed the glory of an enchanted garden, whose earth was scented with musk and whose flowers were watered by three rivers: one of clear wine, one of rose essence, and one of honey. In the garden's centre stood a pavilion where a throne of gold and ruby was shaded by a vault smoothed from a single emerald. And upon that throne stood the small gold box which you now hold, my lord.

The Badawī took the box and opened it. Finding it full of a red powder, he cried: 'See, see, O Hasan Abdallāh! Here is the red sulphur, the Kīmiyā of the sages and philosophers, which they have given their lives in vain to find!' 'Throw away the dirty stuff, good master,' said I, 'and let us fill the box with those precious stones which lie in heaps about the palace.' 'Poor fool,' he answered with compassion, 'this powder is the very soul of riches. A single grain of it can transmute the vilest metal into gold! O child of ignorance, it is red sulphur, it is the Kīmiyā! With this powder I could build a mightier palace and raise a more magnificent city even than these; I could buy the lives of men and the conscience of the pure; I could seduce virtue herself and make myself a king's son, born of kings.' 'And could you add a day to your life with the powder, master?' I asked. 'Or efface a single hour of the past?' But he answered: 'Allāh alone is great!'

As I had no great faith in this red sulphur, I preferred to pick up great handfuls of pearls and precious stones. I had already filled my belt and pockets and turban, when the Badawī cried: 'What are you doing, O earthy imbecile? If we take a single stone out of this palace, we shall be stricken with instant death.' He strode swiftly forth, carrying the box with him, and I was regretfully compelled to empty my pockets, my belt and my turban, and to follow him, though not without many a backward glance at those winking glittering multitudes. When I caught up with my master, he took me by the hand and led me quickly from the city by the ruby gate, lest I should be tempted to possess myself of some trifle if I walked alone.

Turning our backs on those marvellous walls, we walked straight forward to the horizon of blue crystal, which opened to let us pass. When we reached the other side, we turned for a last look at the Many-Columned city of Irām, but city and plain alike had disappeared, and we found ourselves on the bank of the river of mercury.

We crossed by the crystal bridge and came upon our camels grazing quietly where we had left them. I must confess that I approached mine as eagerly as I would have approached an old friend of my youth. After tightening the girths of our saddles, we mounted. And when my master said: 'Now let us return to Egypt,' I lifted up my arms and gave thanks to Allāh.

Yet, O King of time, the gold and silver keys were still in my belt and I did not know that they were the keys of misery and suffering.

At this point Shahrazād saw the approach of morning and discreetly fell silent.

But when the seven-hundred-and-ninety-third night had come

SHE SAID:

Misery, privation and ill-health dogged our footsteps to Cairo; but, for a reason of which I was still ignorant, these things made head against me only, while my master went his way calmly, blossoming like a flower after the rain and seeming to take on an added prosperity from my griefs. He passed through peril and weariness with a smile and walked in life as upon a silken carpet.

My first care when I came to Cairo was to run to my own house; but I found none to receive me, neither mother, wife, nor children; the door was broken and open, and wandering dogs had made their home within. Hearing my cries of despair, a neighbour opened his door, saying: 'O Hasan Abdallāh, may your span be lengthened by the days which these have lost! All your household is dead.'

I swooned over my threshold and only came to myself to find my master, the Badawī, sprinkling my face with rose-water. I fought down my sobs, and at last gave full rein to my indignation, cursing my companion and accusing him of all my sorrows. He listened in silence and then touched me on the shoulder, saying kindly: 'We come from Allāh and to Allāh we return at last!' Then he took me by the hand and led me from that desolate house.

He brought me to a magnificent palace on the banks of the Nile and constrained me to live there with him. Seeing that nothing would draw me from my misery, he wished to divide all his riches with me and even carried generosity so far as to teach me the hidden sciences and educate me in alchemy and the deciphering of cabalistic books. He would often bring quintals of lead into my presence and transmute them into the purest gold, by means of the red sulphur which we had brought back with us.

But though I lived in the midst of treasures and the luxury of my master's daily feasts, I remained racked in body and soul; a time came when I could not support the weight or contact of the rich garments and precious stuffs which were thrust upon me, and had no taste for the delicate meats and chosen wines which were set before me. Sleep would not come to me on purple couches and beds of scented wood. The gardens of our palace were refreshed by the Nile breezes and planted with rare trees fetched at great cost from India, Persia, China, and the Isles. Cunning machines raised the water of the river and caused it to tumble in refreshing spray among basins of marble and porphyry; but my heart cared for none of these things, since a poison worked in my flesh and upon my soul.

But my master's days passed in the breast of pleasure, and his nights were an anticipation of Paradise. He lived in a pavilion of dark silk branched with gold, where the light was as soft as moonlight. It stood among orange trees and lemons trees, wading fruit-deep among jasmine and roses. Each night he entertained new friends with kingly magnificence and, when their hearts and senses were prepared for lust by exquisite wines and sighing music, caused a procession of girls, bought for their weight in gold in the markets of Egypt, Persia and Syria, to walk in a single file before them. When one of the guests cast the eyes of desire upon a girl, the Badawī would take her by the hand and lead her to him, saying: 'My lord, you will greatly oblige me by taking this slave to your house when you depart.' All who came near him were his friends, and he was known throughout the city as the Magnificent.

He would often visit me in my solitary suffering, and one day he came unexpectedly, bringing a new girl with him. His face was lighted by drunkenness and joy, his eyes gleamed with an extraordinary fire of exaltation. He sat quite close to me, taking the young girl on his knees, and said: 'O Hasan Abdallāh, you have never heard me sing. I am going to sing now.' He took me by the hand and began to sing in an ecstatic voice, wagging his head to and fro the while:

> I am red wise
> For wine is more than roses,
> Water's for prayers;
> Your cheeks run wine,
> My soul reels and runs crimson wisdom.
>
> Here are only the orange trees
> Drinking the wind;
> Drink first, and scent my cup.
>
> Here is only my heart beating
> And the opening of roses;
> Sing wicked and wanton,
> Here are but nightingales.
>
> Though you undress,
> The moon and her lascivious little girls
> Have seen before,

Though I kiss the points of your breasts,
The jasmine is accustomed,
The rose has seen before.

Lie naked,
Veiling your eyes in hair,
O jealousy of God.

When he had made an end of this song, my master gave a great sigh of happiness and, leaning his head upon his breast, seemed to sleep. The girl slipped from his arms, fearing to trouble his repose, and glided from my presence. I went to cover my companion and prop his head with a cushion; but I saw that he had ceased to breathe. I leaned anxiously over him, and discovered that he had died smiling at life, like those who are born under a happy star. Allāh be good to him!

I forgot the misery of all the days since I had met him and remembered only his serene benevolence; I wept and made preparation for a worthy funeral. I washed the body myself in scented water, I closed all the natural openings of the body with perfumed cotton, I depilated the dead and carefully combed his beard, I dyed his brows, blackened his lids, and shaved his head. Then I wound him in a tissue which had been woven for a Persian king and set him in a coffin of aloe wood overlaid with gold.

I called together my master's many friends and bade fifty of the slaves carry the coffin turn by turn. The procession started forth, interspersed with paid weepers uttering plaintive cries and waving their handkerchiefs above their heads, and preceded by readers of the Koran chanting the sacred verses, to which the crowd about our way gave the response: 'There is no God but Allāh and Muhammad is the Prophet of Allāh!' A multitude of the Faithful pressed forward to help in the bearing of the coffin, if only by touching with their fingers, and we buried him among the lamentation of a whole people. I caused a flock of sheep and a herd of young camels to be slaughtered upon his tomb.

When I had finished my last duties to my master by presiding over his funeral feast, I shut myself in the palace and began to put my companion's affairs in order. I opened the gold box and found that only a little of the red sulphur remained (the amount which is now before you, O King of time). The rest had been spent to satisfy the Badawī's unheard-of prodigality. But, as the rest was enough to render its owner more powerful than any king and as I cared nothing for riches, I did not concern myself about the waste of the powder. Instead, being anxious to learn the contents of the mysterious manuscript which my master, while teaching me to decipher written characters, had never let me read, I opened the sheets of gazelle skin and eagerly devoured their contents. I learnt for the first time, among other marvels which I will tell you some day, the powers of the keys of Destiny, and understood that the Badawī had only bought me in order that I should take upon myself the evil influence of the gold and silver keys. I had to call all the noble thoughts of the Prophet to my aid (prayer and peace be upon him!) to prevent myself cursing my master and going forth to spit upon his tomb.

I swore to be rid of the fatal keys for ever; so I snatched them from my belt and set them in a crucible upon the fire, until they should be resolved and fume away. While the vessel was heating I searched everywhere for the other two keys, of wisdom and of happiness; but I could find them nowhere. I therefore returned to my crucible and stood watching the fusion of the silver and gold.

At this point Shahrazād saw the approach of morning and discreetly fell silent.

But when the seven-hundred-and-ninety-fourth night had come

SHE SAID:

While I watched, as I thought, my evil luck melting away before my eyes, the pavilion was suddenly invaded by the Khalīfah's guards, who bound me and carried me into the presence of their master.

The Sultān Thailūn, your father, my lord, told me angrily that he was aware that I had the secret of alchemy and that I must at once reveal it to him; but, fearing that an unjust ruler would use such knowledge for the hurt of his people, I refused to speak. Your father therefore had me loaded with chains and thrown into the darkest of his dungeons. He sacked our palace and destroyed it, after taking away the gold box with its manuscript and the rests of the red sulphur. Also he had me tortured every day, hoping that I would speak. But Allāh gave me fortitude, and I spoke not. Instead I dragged out the long years of my Destiny, hoping for death to strike off my chains and unlock the door of liberty.

But now, my lord, I shall die contented, because my persecutor has gone to render an account to Allāh, and the most just and glorious of Kings reigns in his stead.

Sultān Muhammad rose from his throne and embraced the venerable Hasan Abdallāh, crying: 'Glory be to Allāh Who has allowed his servant to repair an injustice!' He appointed Hasan to be his grand-wazīr and put his own royal mantle upon him; then he placed him in the care of the wisest doctors of his kingdom that they might cure him of his many ills. Also he ordered the most expert of the palace scribes to write down this tale in letters of gold and placed it among the archives of his reign.

As the Sultān Muhammad fully believed in the virtue of the red sulphur, he melted a thousand quintals of lead in vast earthenware crucibles and mingled the remaining powder with them, while crying the magic words which Hasan Abdallāh read to him out of the manuscript.

The lead immediately turned to pure gold, and the Sultān, not wishing to spend it upon things perishable, set it aside for a labour pleasing to Allāh. He dreamed of a mosque which should be without equal in the land of the Faithful and, calling the most famous architects of his empire, bade them trace out the plans of his dream, without thought of cost or difficulty. So the architects drew an immense square, each side facing one chief point of the compass, at the foot of the hill which overlooks that city. In each corner a well-proportioned tower was set, having a gallery and dome of gold; and each side of the mosque was lifted upon a thousand pillars, bearing strong arches of admirable curves which roofed a terrace whose balustrade was of marvellously fretted gold. From the centre of the building rose a mighty cupola, of such airy construction that it seemed to float without support between heaven and earth. It was worked inside with azure enamel and pounced with stars of gold. The floors of the mosque were far fetched marble and the walls were a mosaic of jasper, porphyry and agate. The pillars and arches were deep cut and painted in pure colour with interlacing verses of the Koran. And, that this marvel of time need have no fear of fire, no wood at all was used in the building of it. Seven years, seven thousand men, and seven thousand quintals of golden dīnārs went to the achievement of this mosque, and it is called the Mosque of Sultān Muhammad ibn Thailūn to this day.

The venerable Hasan Abdallāh soon recovered his health and

lived honoured and respected to the age of one hundred and twenty years, which had been marked for him by Destiny. But Allāh knows all! He alone lives, for He dies not!

Shahrazād fell silent and King Shahryār said: 'No man may escape his Destiny. But, O Shahrazād, this tale has made me sad.' 'It is for that very reason,' answered Shahrazād, 'that I am about to tell you the tale of the Everlasting Slippers, taken from the Dīwān of Easy Jests and Laughing Wisdom of the sheikh Majid al-Dīn Abū Tāhir Muhammad. Allāh be good to him!'

And Shahrazād said:

THE DĪWĀN OF EASY JESTS AND LAUGHING WISDOM

The Everlasting Slippers

IT is related that there was once in Cairo a druggist named Abū Kāsim, who was celebrated for his avarice. Though Allāh granted him riches and prosperity in his trade, he lived and dressed like the poorest beggar; his garments were a vast collection of rents and scraps; his turban was so old and dirty that it was impossible to tell its original colour; but, of all he wore, his slippers were the most notorious witnesses to his meanness. They were not only studded with great nails and armoured like a machine of war, and had soles mended a thousand times until they were as thick as the head of a hippopotamus, but their uppers were so patched that for twenty years one of the chief labours of the cleverest cobblers and curriers in Cairo had been to keep their component rubbish from disintegrating. Abū Kāsim's slippers were so heavy that they had become proverbial throughout all Egypt. When a guest stayed too long, they would say of him: 'His manners are as heavy as Abū Kāsim's slippers.' When a pedantic schoolmaster tried to be funny, they would say of him: 'His wit is as heavy as Abū Kāsim's slippers.' Porters would sigh, and say of their load: 'It is as heavy as Abū Kāsim's slippers.' When a nasty old woman in a harīm would stop her master's wives from playing together, they would say: 'She is as heavy as Abū Kāsim's slippers.' When a man ate indigestible food and felt a tempest rising in his belly, he would say: 'Allāh preserve me, that meat was as heavy as

Abū Kāsim's slippers!' In fact, folk would drag in Abū Kāsim's slippers in a thousand connections when heaviness was in question.

One day Abū Kāsim made an unusually good bargain in his business but, instead of giving some little feast as merchants do when Allāh has particularly favoured them, he determined, by way of celebration, to visit the hammām, where he had not set his foot in the memory of man. He shut his shop and set forth, carrying his slippers on his back to save their use; when he arrived at the hammām, he left them on the threshold, with all the other footgear, and entered to take his bath.

Abū Kāsim's skin was so penetrated with filth that the rubbers were a long time in completing their labours upon him, and it was not until sunset that he was ready to depart. When he went forth, he discovered that his slippers were missing and that an exquisite pair in citron yellow leather stood in their place. 'Allāh must have known that I have often thought of buying a pair like this,' said Abū Kāsim to himself, 'or perhaps someone has exchanged with me by accident.' Delighted at this saving of expense, he put on the yellow slippers and departed.

As a matter of fact, the yellow slippers belonged to the kādī, who was still in the hammām. Also, the slipper guard had found Abū Kāsim's monstrosities fuming and stinking on the threshold, and had hidden them in an odd corner. Then, as his duties were over for the day, he had returned home, without thinking of replacing them.

When the kādī had finished his bath, the obsequious attendants searched everywhere for his slippers, but could only find Abū Kāsim's fabulous footwear, which they instantly recognised. They set out in pursuit and brought him back to the hammām, with the missing property hanging about his neck. The kādī exchanged slippers with Abū Kāsim and sent him to prison, where he was obliged to pay the officers an enormous bribe before he could get free.

As soon as he returned to his shop, he cursed his luckless slippers and threw them into the Nile, to get rid of them.

A few days afterwards, certain fishermen with great difficulty pulled their nets to shore and found them laden with Abū Kāsim's slippers, the nails of which had seriously damaged the mesh. They ran to Abū Kāsim's shop and violently threw the slippers inside, with a curse for their unlucky owner. The slippers knocked down a large quantity of flasks, containing rose-water and rare essences, and smashed each into a thousand pieces.

The grief of Abū Kāsim knew no bounds, and he cried: 'Ill-omened slippers, daughters of my arse, you shall do me no more harm!' So he went out into the garden and began to dig a hole in which to bury them; but one of his neighbours, who had a grudge against him, ran to the walī and informed him that Abū Kāsim had dug up a hidden treasure in his garden, without reporting it. The walī believed this, as it chimed with his knowledge of Abū Kāsim; so he sent for the unfortunate druggist and, in spite of the poor man's oath that he was only burying his slippers, made him disgorge a large sum of money.

At this point Shahrazād saw the approach of morning and discreetly fell silent.

But when the seven-hundred-and-ninety-fifth night had come

SHE SAID:

Abū Kāsim tore his beard in despair and walked with his slippers far into the country, meaning to see the last of them at all costs. After walking for many hours, he threw them into a canal and returned home, supposing that he would never hear of them again. But, as ill luck would have it, the current of the water carried the slippers down to a mill, which was served by the canal, and they violently stopped its working by being caught in the wheels. The owners of the mill ran to repair the damage and found two enormous objects caught in the gears, which they instantly recognised as Abū Kāsim's slippers.

At their instigation the druggist was heavily fined, to make good the damage, and again thrown into prison. He came forth after richly bribing the officers, and his slippers were returned to him at the gates.

He walked home in a state bordering upon madness and, placing the slippers behind him on the terrace so that he might not see them, leaned on the balustrade and began to consider deeply what he should do with them. While he was cogitating, a dog belonging to one of the neighbours saw the slippers and, leaping from his own terrace on to that of Abū Kāsim, took one of them in his jaws and began to play with it. In the course of casting it to and fro the wretched animal sent it flying over the balustrade, and it fell upon the head of an old woman who was passing below. Its enormous weight crushed the old woman flat, as if she had been made of paper, and her relations, recognising Abū Kāsim's slipper, appeared before the kādī, demanding either the price of the victim's blood or the death of Abū Kāsim. The poor druggist was obliged to pay the full sum demanded by law, and also to give a monstrous bribe to the police in order to escape being sent to prison for a third time.

This last calamity taught him what to do; he went home, took up the fatal slippers and returned to the kādī. When he was in the presence, he lifted the slippers above his head, and cried so violently that the kādī could not forbear to smile: 'Behold, my lord, the cause of all my tribulations! Because of them I shall henceforward have to beg my bread. Therefore I entreat you to make a formal announcement that Abū Kāsim no longer owns any slippers and is not responsible for anything which any slippers may do in the future.' So saying, he hurled the slippers into the middle of the hall and ran forth bare-footed, leaving all who were in that court fallen upon their backsides and shaking with laughter. But Allāh knows all!

And Shahrazād said again:

Buhlūl the Jester

IT is related that the Khalīfah Hārūn al-Rashīd kept a jester in his palace to divert his moments of dark humour. This jester was called Buhlūl the Wise. One day the Khalīfah asked him: 'O Buhlūl, do you know how many fools there are in Baghdād?' 'It would be a long list, my lord,' answered Buhlūl. 'Yet I bid you make it and make it exactly,' cried Hārūn. Buhlūl gave a long laugh, and then replied: 'As I have no taste for heavy work, I will make you out a list of all the wise men in Baghdād. Those who do not appear upon it will be the fools.'

This same Buhlūl climbed up on to the Khalīfah's throne one day during his absence and received a volley of blows from the officers for his temerity. The Sultān came upon him weeping hot tears and tried to console him. But Buhlūl said: 'O Commander of the Faithful, I do not weep for myself; I grieve because I have calculated how many blows wait you downstairs.'

Buhlūl was wise enough to have a horror of marriage; so Hārūn, being one day angry with him, married him without his consent to a very beautiful slave. But Buhlūl had hardly lain down by his wife's side for a moment on the first night before he leapt to his feet and fled from the room. While he was rushing like a madman about the palace, the Khalīfah came to him, and said severely: 'Vile fellow, why have you offended against the wife I gave you?' 'My lord, there is no remedy for terror,' answered the jester. 'I have no fault to find with the bride of your generosity, for she is beautiful and modest; but as soon as I lay beside her, I distinctly heard voices speaking from the deep of her breast. One asked me for a robe, another for a silk veil, a third for slippers, and a fourth for an embroidered belt. So I took fright and fled, in spite of your orders and the maiden's charms, fearing if I stayed to become more foolish and unhappy even than I am.'

This same Buhlūl refused a present of a thousand dīnārs which the Khalīfah offered twice; so Hārūn asked him the reason of his disinterestedness. For sole answer, Buhlūl stretched out his legs in the Khalīfah's face. Seeing this supreme mark of incivility, the chief eunuch would have taken the jester up and beaten him; but al-Rashīd forbade him, and questioned Buhlūl concerning his great lack of respect. 'My lord,' answered the jester, 'if I had stretched out my hand to receive your present I would have forfeited the right to stretch out my legs.'

One day, as al-Rashīd was returning from a warlike expedition, Buhlūl entered his tent and found the Khalīfah parched with thirst and calling for water. The jester hastened to fetch a cup of water and gave it to him, saying: 'O Commander of the Faithful, before you drink pray tell me how much you would have given for this cup of water if it had been difficult to procure.' 'I would have given half my kingdom,' answered al-Rashīd as he drank. 'And now that you have drunk,' went on Buhlūl, 'supposing this cup of water refused to leave your body, owing to some retention on the part of your honourable bladder, what would you pay to see it safely forth?' 'Surely half of my kingdom,' answered al-Rashīd; then said Buhlūl: 'I suppose, my lord, that an empire which could be bought for a cup of water and a jet of piss is worth these cares and bloody wars? . . .' Al-Rasīd wept.

And Shahrazād said again:

The Invitation to Universal Peace

IT is related that the venerable sheikh of a village had a fair court-yard on his farm, well stocked with poultry who gave him excellent eggs and plump pullets for the table. Among the males in this courtyard there was a certain great and wonderful Cock, with a ringing voice and golden plumage, who possessed, in addition to his fair exterior, the virtues of vigilance, wisdom and knowledge of the world. He was both just and attentive to his wives, fulfilling his duty towards them with zeal and impartiality, so that they did not know the meaning of jealousy or angry looks. Because he was both powerful and benevolent he was cited as a model for husbands among all the dwellers in the courtyard; and his master called him Voice-of-Dawn.

One day, while his wives were looking after their children and arranging their feathers, Voice-of-Dawn went for a visit about the farm. As he walked, he marvelled at all he saw and pecked industriously at any grains of corn, barley, maize or sesame which lay upon the ground. The train of these delicacies led him on, until he found himself beyond the farm and beyond the village, isolated in a savage spot which he had never seen before. He looked to left and right for some familiar face, but could see none; so he became anxious and gave vent to one or two unquiet cries. While he was glancing about to be sure of his way home, he beheld a Fox running towards him with great strides. Trembling for his life, he turned tail and dashed forward with extended wings until he was able to flap to the summit of a ruined wall, where there was just room for him to perch and which the Fox would certainly not be able to climb.

At this point Shahrazād saw the approach of morning and discreetly fell silent.

But when the seven-hundred-and-ninety-sixth night had come

SHE SAID:

Soon the Fox stood yapping and snuffing at the foot of the wall. When he found that he could in no way reach the bird of his desire, he lifted up his head, saying: 'Peace be upon you, O face of good-omen! Peace be upon you, my brother, my charming companion!' Voice-of-Dawn would not look down at him or answer his greeting, so the Fox continued: 'My tender and beautiful friend, why will you not greet or glance at one who brings you great good news?' The Cock made no sign that he had heard this courtesy, and the Fox went on: 'My brother, if you only knew the excellent news which I have been instructed to give you, you would descend in great haste to embrace me and kiss me upon the mouth!' But the Cock feigned to be distracted and fixed round eyes upon something afar off. 'Know then, my brother,' continued the Fox, 'that our lord the Lion, who is Sultān of the beasts, and our lord the Eagle, who is Sultān of the birds, recently met together in a green meadowland, rich in watercourses and wild flowers, and called together representatives of us all. When tigers, hyenas, leopards, lynxes, panthers, jackals, antelopes, wolves, hares, cats, vultures, hawks, crows, pigeons, doves, quails, partridges, and domestic fowl had come together before them, our two monarchs solemnly decreed that henceforth safety, peace, and brotherly love should reign supreme over the whole habitable earth; that a comradeship in sympathy should be the only motive in the lives of savage beasts, domestic animals, and birds; that old enmities and racial hatreds should be forgotten, and that all should bend their efforts to the general and individual good. They also proclaimed that whosoever should prove recalcitrant must be brought before them for summary condemnation. They made me their herald and bade me proclaim their decision about the earth, giving me power to report the names of those who were not instantly obedient. That is why you see me at the foot of this wall, dear brother; for I, I myself and no other, am the representative, the commissioner, the herald, the officer of those great lords. So now you may readily understand why I wished you peace and offered you friendship, sweet acquaintance.'

But the Cock seemed not to hear; he regarded the horizon with round, vague, winking eyes, and wavered his head from time to time. The Fox, who panted to feel his teeth sink in deliciously, went on: 'My brother, why do you not honour me with an answer or one little word? Will you not deign even to cast your charming eye at a representative of our lord the Lion and our lord the Eagle? I must remind you that, if you keep this contumacious silence, I shall be obliged to report you to the council. I have very little hope that you would escape with your life under the new law, for our masters have determined to establish universal peace, even if they have to destroy half the animals and half the birds in doing so. My charming brother, I beg you, for the last time, to tell me why you will not answer.'

The Cock, who until then had remained isled in haughty indifference, stretched out his neck and turned it slightly, so that his right eye looked down upon the Fox. 'In truth, my brother,' he said, 'your words are upon my head and before my eyes. I honour you from the bottom of my heart, as the messenger and representative of our lord the Eagle. Though I did not answer, I assure you I had no thought of rebellion. No, no, I kept silence because I was troubled by a thing which I see far off across the plain.' 'And what do you see far off upon the plain?' exclaimed the Fox. 'I trust that it is nothing serious, nothing calamitous?' The Cock stretched his neck further, as he answered: 'Surely you see it, my brother? Allāh has set piercing eyes upon each side of your nose; though it is true that they are somewhat bleared, if I may say so without giving the least offence.' 'But tell me what you see,' cried the Fox in some alarm. 'My eyes pain me a trifle to-day, though, if I may say so without running the least risk of seeming to contradict you, they are not, and never have been, bleared.' 'If you must know,' replied Voice-of-Dawn, 'I see a cloud of dust and several hunting hawks turning in the air above it.' 'Is that all you see, O visage of good-omen?' asked the anxious Fox. 'Are you sure you see nothing running along the ground?' The Cock looked long before replying: 'I certainly seem to see something running on four legs, high on its feet, long and slim, with a pointed head and drooping ears. Yes, it is coming towards us at some speed.' The Fox trembled, as he asked again: 'Are you sure it is not a greyhound, my brother? Allāh protect us all!' 'I do not know whether it is a greyhound or not,' answered the Cock. 'Allāh alone could tell; I have never seen the kind. But it is a large quick dog of some sort, my handsome brother.'

'I am afraid that I must take leave of you, dear friend,' cried the Fox, as he turned and gave his bushy tail to the wind. 'Wait, wait, brother!' the Cock called after him. 'I am getting down; why do you not wait?' 'Because I have a strange antipathy to greyhounds,' answered the Fox over his shoulder. 'But, O visage of blessing,' cried the Cock, 'did you not tell me just now that you walked as a messenger of universal peace?' The Fox's answer came back from far away: 'You are right, good brother, you are right; but that pimp of a greyhound—God's curse upon him!—never came to the congress, did not send a representative, and is not mentioned in the proclamation. Allāh preserve you in good health, dear Cock, till I return!'

Thus the Cock escaped, thanks to his wit and wisdom. Jumping down from the wall, he returned in good case to the courtyard, glorifying Allāh as he came. He lost no time in telling his wives and neighbours of the excellent trick he had played upon their hereditary foe, and all the cocks in the courtyard crowed joyously to celebrate his triumph.

And Shahrazād said again:

The Tale of the Tied Points

IT is related that a certain King was once sitting on his throne and giving audience to his subjects, when an old farmer entered, carrying a basket on his head, and laid it before the throne. 'What is in your basket, O sheikh?' asked the King, and the farmer answered: 'Fresh fruit and vegetables, my year's first yield, which I have brought as a loyal present to my Sultān.' 'They are accepted!' exclaimed the King, as he lifted the green leaves which protected the contents of the basket from the evil-eye, and found an excellent collection of crisp cucumbers, tender gumboes, bananas, artichokes, lemons, and other early fruits and vegetables. He picked out a crisp cucumber and began to crunch it, calling upon Allāh's name. Then he sent his eunuchs to the harīm with the rest of the gift. The women took their choice, congratulating each other, and saying: 'May the first fruits of next year find us in life and beauty still!' They gave what was left in the basket to the slaves, and sent a hundred dīnārs back by the eunuchs. The King, being delighted by his cucumber, added another two hundred dīnārs. And this was not all which came to that farmer from his fortunate present. For the King questioned him about agriculture and other matters, and the farmer answered with wit and knowledge, in eloquent speech and chosen gesture, so that the King desired to make a companion of him, and asked: 'Do you know how to keep company with kings?' 'I do,' answered the fallāh. 'Very well, then,' commanded the King, 'take the dīnārs to your family and return as quickly as possible.'

The fallāh carried the three hundred dīnārs to his wife and rejoined the King, just as he was sitting down to the evening meal. The Sultān gave him a place beside himself, and made him eat and drink to the limit of his capacity. Delighting in his conversation more and more, he cried: 'Surely you know some charming tales?' 'As Allāh lives, I know many charming tales,' answered the farmer. 'To-morrow night

I will tell you one.' The King rejoiced and, wishing to reward his new-found favourite in advance, made him a present of the youngest and most beautiful girl in the Queen's train. She was an untouched virgin, and the King had set her aside for his own delectation on some special night; but now he gave the two a fair apartment near his own, richly furnished with all the necessaries of love, and bade them a sweet night.

At this point Shahrazād saw the approach of morning and discreetly fell silent.

But when the seven-hundred-and-ninety-seventh night had come

SHE SAID:

The girl undressed and waited on the couch until her lord, who had never tasted the joys of white flesh in his life, gave thanks to the Creator of it and began the thousand foolish games which are usual on such an occasion. But lo! the child would not lift his head; he turned his back and lay there with a lifeless eye. Though the farmer admonished and encouraged him, he remained inert and uninterested, until his father became confused and cried: 'This is a prodigy!' The girl's warm hand played pleasantly with the infant; but neither slaps nor caresses could wake him from his heavy sleep. 'I leave the affair to Allāh,' cried the girl; but still nothing happened. She asked the father why his offspring would not come to life and, when he answered that he did not know, she said: 'I will tell you; some one has tied your points.' 'Is there any way of untying them?' questioned the farmer anxiously. 'Leave it to me,' replied the girl.

She fetched male incense and, burning it in a brazier, fumigated the middle parts of her lord, as mourners fumigate the bodies of the dead. 'Allāh grant His resurrection to this poor sleeper!' she cried. Then she washed the body of the child with rose-water, as the dead are washed, and covered it with a silk napkin by way of a winding-sheet. As soon as the rites of burial were completed, she called in all the slaves, whom the Sultān had told off to wait upon her, and showed them the farmer's luckless heir lying in its shroud among a mist of incense. The women broke into delighted cries and trills of laughter; then they turned tail and ran throughout the palace, telling all they met of this most solemn sight.

Next morning the Sultān, who had risen earlier than his wont, sought out the farmer and asked after his night. The fallāh answered with the whole truth, and the Sultān fell over on his backside in a gust of laughter. 'A clever girl, a fine girl,' he cried, 'I will take her back for my own use.' He called the girl into his presence and made her tell the whole story again. When she had done so, without the omission of a single detail, the King roared with laughter for the second time and, turning to the fallāh, asked: 'Are you sure it is true?' The farmer lowered his eyes and nodded his head; but the King, staggering where he stood, cried out: 'Now you must tell me all over again, from your point of view.' The unfortunate man repeated the tale in all its wealth of incident. 'As Allāh lives, it is a prodigy!' exclaimed the Sultān, as he wept for joy. When the two men had answered the call to prayer, the Sultān said: 'Now, O delightful companion, I pray you begin one of those tales which you promised me, that my pleasure may be complete on this blessed day.' 'Willingly,' replied the farmer, as he sat down cross-legged before the Sultān, and began:

The Tale of the Two Hashīsh-Eaters

THERE was once, my lord and crown upon my head, a man in a certain city, who was a fisherman by trade and a hashīsh-eater by occupation. When he had earned his daily wage, he would spend a little of it on food and the rest on a sufficiency of that hilarious herb. He took his hashīsh three times a day: once in the morning on an empty stomach, once at noon, and once at sundown. Thus he was never lacking in extravagant gaiety. Yet he worked hard enough at his fishing, though sometimes in a very extraordinary fashion. On a certain evening, for instance, when he had taken a larger dose of his favourite drug than usual, he lit a tallow candle and sat in front of it, asking himself eager questions and answering with obliging wit. After some hours of this delight, he became aware of the cool silence of the night about him and the clear light of a full moon above his head, and exclaimed affably to himself: 'Dear friend, the silent streets and the cool of the moon invite us to a walk. Let us go forth, while all the world is in bed and none may mar our solitary exaltation.' Speaking in this way to himself, the fisherman left his house and began to walk towards the river; but, as he went, he saw the light of the full moon lying in the roadway and took it to be the water of the river. 'My dear old friend the fisherman,' he said, 'get your line and take the best of the fishing, while your rivals are indoors.' So he ran back and fetched his hook and line, and cast into the glittering patch of moonlight on the road.

Soon an enormous dog, tempted by the smell of the bait, swallowed the hook greedily and then, feeling the barb, made desperate efforts to get loose. The fisherman struggled for some time against this enormous fish, but at last he was pulled over and rolled into the moonlight. Even then he would not let go his line, but held on grimly, uttering frightened cries. 'Help, help, good Mussulmāns!' he shouted. 'Help me to secure this mighty fish, for he is dragging me into the deeps! Help, help, good friends, for I am drowning!' The guards of that quarter ran up at the noise and began laughing at the fisherman's antics; but when he yelled: 'Allāh curse you, O sons of bitches! Is it a time to laugh when I am drowning?' they grew angry and, after giving him a sound beating, dragged him into the presence of the kādī.

At this point Shahrazād saw the approach of morning and discreetly fell silent.

But when the seven-hundred-and-ninety-eighth night had come

SHE SAID:

Allāh had willed that the kādī should also be addicted to the use of hashīsh; recognising that the prisoner was under that jocund influence, he rated the guards soundly and dismissed them. Then he handed over the fisherman to his slaves that they might give him a bed for calm sleep.

After a pleasant night and a day given up to the consumption of excellent food, the fisherman was called to the kādī in the evening and received by him like a brother. His host supped with him; and then the two sat opposite the lighted candles and each swallowed enough hashīsh to destroy a hundred-year-old elephant. When the drug exalted their natural dispositions, they undressed completely and began to dance about, singing and committing a thousand extravagances.

Now it happened that the Sultān and his wazīr were walking through the city, disguised as merchants, and heard a strange noise rising from the kādī's house. They entered through the unlatched door and found two naked men, who stopped dancing at their entrance and welcomed them without the least embarrassment. The Sultān sat down to watch his venerable kādī dance again; but when he saw that the other man had a dark and lively zabb, so long that the eye might not carry to the end of it, he whispered in his wazīr's startled ear: 'As Allāh lives, our kādī is not as well hung as his guest!' 'What are you whispering about?' cried the fisherman. 'I am the Sultān of this city and I order you to watch my dance respectfully, otherwise I will have your head cut off. I am the Sultān, this is my wazīr; I hold the whole world like a fish in the palm of my right hand.' The Sultān and his wazīr realised that they were in the presence of two hashīsh-eaters, and the wazīr, to amuse his master, addressed the fisherman, saying: 'How long have you been Sultān, dear master, and can you tell me what has happened to your predecessor?' 'I deposed the fellow,' answered the fisherman. 'I said: "Go away!", and he went away.' 'Did he not protest?' asked the wazīr. 'Not at all,' replied the fisherman. 'He was delighted to be released from the burden of kingship. He abdicated with such good grace that I keep him by me as a servant. He is an excellent dancer. When he pines for his throne, I tell him stories. Now I want to piss.' So saying, he lifted up his interminable tool and, walking over to the Sultān, seemed to be about to discharge upon him. 'I also want to piss,' exclaimed the kādī, and took up the same threatening position in front of the wazīr. The two victims shouted with laughter and fled from that house, crying over their shoulders: 'God's curse on all hashīsh-eaters!'

Next morning, that the jest might be complete, the Sultān called the kādī and his guest before him. 'O discreet pillar of our law,' he said, 'I have called you to me because I wish to learn the most convenient manner of pissing. Should one squat and carefully lift the robe, as religion prescribes? Should one stand up, as is the unclean habit of unbelievers? Or should one undress completely and piss against one's friends, as is the custom of two hashīsh-eaters of my acquaintance?'

Knowing that the Sultān used to walk about the city in disguise, the kādī realised in a flash the identity of his last night's visitors, and fell on his knees, crying: 'My lord, my lord, the hashīsh spake in these indelicacies, not I!' But the fisherman, who by his careful daily taking of the drug was always under its effect, called somewhat sharply: 'And what of it? You are in your palace this morning, we were in our palace last night.' 'O sweetest noise in all our kingdom,' answered the delighted King, 'as we are both Sultāns of this city, I think you had better henceforth stay with me in my palace. If you can tell stories, I trust that you will at once sweeten our hearing with a chosen one.' 'I will do so gladly, as soon as you have pardoned my wazīr,' replied the fisherman; so the Sultān bade the kādī rise and sent him back forgiven to his duties. Then he dismissed all save the fisherman, who immediately began to tell him:

The Tale of the Father of Farts

IT is related that there was a kādī in the city of Tarabūlūs in Syria, during the reign of the Khalīfah Hārūn al-Rashīd, who exercised the functions of his office with a notorious severity. His only servant, and the only woman in his harīm, was an old negress like a Nile buffalo; for the man's parsimony equalled the rigour of his judgments. Allāh curse him! Though he was abundantly rich, he lived on stale bread and onions. Also his avarice went hand in hand with an ostentation of generosity. When a neighbour called about meal time, the kādī would cry to the negress: 'Lay the gold-fringed cloth!' No one was ever invited to the repast which followed, and the show of the cloth, instead of being taken as an indication of bounty, passed into a proverb; so that a man who had been ill-served at any feast would say: 'I ate at the kādī's gold-fringed cloth.' It will be seen that this wretched old man, to whom Allāh had given both riches and honour, lived a life which would have sickened a starving dog. May he burn in Hell!

One day, certain folk who wished to influence the kādī to give a favourable judgment, said to him: 'O our master, why do you not take a wife? That old negress is not worthy of you.' 'Who would find me a wife?' asked the kādī, and one of them answered: 'I have a very beautiful daughter. Your slave would be highly honoured if you would take her to your house.' The kādī promptly accepted this offer, and the marriage took place at once. The girl was conducted to her husband's house in the evening and, being most discreet and amiable, refused to show her surprise when no food was produced and no mention made of it. The guests and witnesses stayed on in hope for some time and then, as the kitchen fire was not even lighted, returned to their own homes, cursing the bridegroom's meanness.

The young wife had begun to starve before she heard her husband tell the negress to lay the gold-fringed cloth. As she was accustomed to plenty of excellent food in her father's house, she went forward eagerly as soon as the cloth was laid, but only to discover that the sole dish was a basin containing three bits of brown bread and three onions. As she sat in amaze, the kādī took one of the pieces of bread himself, gave the like to the negress, and invited the girl to devour her share, saying: 'Do not fear to abuse the gifts of Allāh!' He swallowed his portion with great gusto, and the negress made but one mouthful of hers, for it was the first meal of the day; but for all her good will the unfortunate wife could not swallow a mouthful of the horrible stuff. She left the table, fasting and bitterly resenting the darkness of her Destiny. Three days passed and, on each, the gold-fringed cloth was set with brown bread and sorrowful onions. But on the fourth day, the kādī, hearing cries from his harīm, went to investigate and was met by the negress who told him that her mistress had revolted against that house and had sent to fetch her father.

At this point Shahrazād saw the approach of morning and discreetly fell silent.

But when the seven-hundred-and-ninety-ninth night had come

SHE SAID:

The kādī sought his wife with furious flaming eyes, heaped curses upon her, accused her of all debauchery, cut away her hair by force, and repudiated her by the third divorce. Casting her forth into the street, he shut the door violently behind her. May Allāh damn the foul old knave!

A few days afterwards this avaricious son of avarice found another wife in the person of the daughter of certain folk who wished to stand well with him. He married again; but the poor child, after three days of onions, revolted and was divorced. Yet this served as no lesson to others who needed the good graces of that horrible old man, and he married several other daughters on the same terms, casting them forth after a day or so, because they could not abide the onions.

But a time came when the multitude of his divorces was noised abroad and grew to be the general subject of conversation in the harīms; the matrons banded together and decreed that henceforth the miser was to be considered unmarriageable.

Now that no woman would have it, the kādī began to be tormented by his father's inheritance and took long walks to cool its importunity. One evening, he saw a woman approaching him mounted upon a grey mule, and was very much affected by the richness of her clothes and possibility of her figure. He gave a twist to the sad ends of his moustaches and bowed before her respectfully, saying: 'Whence come you, noble lady?' 'Along this road,' she answered. 'I know that, I know that,' answered the kādī with a chuckle, 'but from what city?' 'From Mosul,' she answered. 'Are you married or single?' said he. 'Single,' said she. 'If you would like to be my wife,' said he, 'I will bind the bargain by becoming your husband.' 'Tell me where you live,' said she, 'and I will let you know to-morrow.' The kādī told her where he lived; but she knew already, she knew. She left him with charming glances out of the corners of her eyes.

Next morning she sent a message to the kādī saying that she would marry him if she received a dowry of fifty dīnārs. The miser had a violent struggle with himself, but he sent the fifty dīnārs, bidding the negress to bring back the bride. As soon as the girl arrived at his house, the marriage contract was written out, and the witnesses went away unfed.

Soon the kādī called to the negress, saying: 'Lay the gold-fringed cloth.' When the basin was brought in, holding three dry crusts and three onions, the new bride took her portion and ate it with relish, saying: 'I thank Allāh for an excellent repast.' She smiled gratefully at the kādī, and he cried: 'I also thank Him that He has sent me, out of His generosity, a wife who is all perfection, who takes to-day's little and to-morrow's much with equal mind!' But the blind pig did not know the Destiny which lay in wait for him in the cunning brain of that delightful woman.

Next morning, when her husband was away at the dīwān, the girl inspected all the rooms of the house and came at last to a cabinet whose door was closed with three enormous locks and strengthened by three strong iron bars. She walked about and about this cabinet with the liveliest curiosity, until she found a hole in one of the mouldings which would almost admit the passage of a finger. Setting her eye to it, she was overjoyed to see all the kādī's accumulated treasure of gold and silver set in open copper jars upon the floor inside. Being determined to profit by this discovery, she procured a long palm stalk and, smearing the end of it with a sticky paste, passed it through the hole in the moulding; by twisting it about in the mouth of one of the jars, she caused several gold pieces to adhere to it, and triumphantly withdrew them. Returning to her own apartment, she gave the money to the negress, saying: 'Go out to the market and buy fresh rolls sprinkled with sesame, some saffron rice, some tender lamb, and the finest fruits and pastries which you can find.' The negress went forth in eager astonishment and brought back all these excellent things to her mistress, who made her partake of them in equal shares. 'Light of my head,' the poor old woman cried, 'may this succulent generosity turn to fair white fat upon you! I have never eaten such a meal!' 'You may feed thus every day if you will only keep silence and say nothing to the kādī,' answered the girl; so the negress kissed her hand and promised absolute discretion.

'Lay the gold-fringed cloth!' cried the kādī when he returned at noon; but his wife served him with the remains of her own excellent meal. He ate greedily until he could hold no more, and then asked the source of the provision. 'Dear master,' replied the girl, 'I have many relations in this city; one of them sent these dishes to me. I would have thought nothing of them, had it not been for the joy it gives me to share them with you.' And the kādī rejoiced in his soul that he had married such a wife.

Next morning the palm stalk was no less successful, so that the wife was able to purchase a lamb stuffed with pistachios, and other admirable matters. She invited some of her neighbours to eat with her, and all the women feasted pleasantly until the hour of the kādī's return. Soon after the guests had departed, carrying with them the promise that these joyful mornings should often be repeated, the kādī entered and bade the negress spread the gold-fringed cloth. But when he was served with even more delicate and numerous viands than the day before, he became a little anxious and asked his wife how she had come by such costly things. The girl, who was herself waiting upon him, answered without hesitation: 'Dear master, you must take no more thought for our nourishment. One of my aunts sent me these few trifling dishes. Oh, I am happy if my master is satisfied.' The kādī congratulated himself on having married so thoughtful and well-related a damsel, and set about stuffing himself to the supreme limit of his capacity.

At the end of a year of such living the kādī had become so fat and had developed so notorious a belly that the people used the thing as a proverb, saying: 'As large as the kādī's belly!' 'As stupendous as the kādī's belly!' The poor fool did not know that his wife had sworn to avenge all those unfortunate girls whom he had starved and shorn and cast aside; but you shall now hear how thoroughly she carried out her intention.

Among the neighbours whom she fed daily was a pregnant woman, the wife of a necessitous porter and already the mother of five children. One day her hostess said to her: 'Dear neighbour, as Allāh has given you a numerous family and very little else, would you like to hand over your baby to me when it is born, that I, who am barren, may care for it and rear it as my own? If you agree and promise to keep absolute silence, I will see that you and yours never feel the pinch of poverty again.' The porter's wife accepted this offer and promised absolute secrecy. On the day appointed by Allāh she gave birth to a boy who was twice the size of an ordinary infant, and the kādī's wife received him.

That morning the girl prepared a dish consisting of beans, peas, white haricots, cabbage, lentils, onions, cloves of garlic, various heavy grains and powdered spices. The kādī's enormous belly was quite empty when he returned for the midday meal, so he took helping after helping of this mixture, until all was finished. 'Make me such a dish every day,' he said. 'It slips most pleasantly and easily down the throat.' 'May it be both delicious and digestible!' answered his wife.

The kādī congratulated himself, as he had so often done before, on his excellent choice of a wife; but an hour afterwards his belly began visibly to swell. A noise as of a far-off tempest made itself heard inside him; low grumblings and far thunders shook the walls of his being and brought in their train sharp colics, spasms, and a final agony. He grew yellow in the face and began to roll groaning about the floor, holding his belly in his two hands. 'Allāh, Allāh!' he cried. 'I have a terrible storm within! Who will deliver me?' Soon his paunch became as tight as a gourd and his cries brought his wife running. She made him swallow a powder of anise and fennel, which was soon to have its effect, and, at the same time, to console and encourage him, began rubbing and patting the afflicted part, as if he had been a little sick child. Suddenly she ceased the movement of her hand and uttered a piercing cry: 'Yū, yū, a miracle, a prodigy! O master, my master!' In violent contortions the kādī stammered forth: 'What is the matter, what is the miracle?' But she only answered: 'Yū, yū! O my master, my master!' 'Tell me what the matter is!' he yelled, and she passed her hand afresh over that tempestuous belly, as she replied: 'Exalted be the name of the Highest! He says, and it is done! Who shall discover His secret purposes, my master?' Between two howls, the kādī gasped: 'May Allāh curse you for torturing me so! What is the matter? Tell me at once!' Then said his wife: 'Master, dear master, His will be done! You are with child! And your time is close at hand!'

The kādī rose up at these incredible words, and cried: 'Have you gone mad? How can a man be pregnant?' 'As Allāh lives I do not know,' she answered, 'but the child is moving in your belly; I have felt it kicking and touched its head. Allāh scatters increase where He will, may His name be exalted! Pray for the Prophet, my husband!' So the kādī groaned out in the midst of his convulsion: 'May the blessing of Allāh be upon him!' Then his pains increased and he fell howling to the floor in a crisis of agony. Suddenly came relief. A long and thunderous fart broke from him, shaking the foundations of the house and throwing its utterer violently forward, so that he swooned. Then followed a multitude of other escapes, gradually diminishing in sound but rolling and re-echoing through the troubled air. Last came a single deafening explosion and all was still.

As the kādī came gradually to himself, he saw a little mattress by his side, on which a new-born baby, swaddled in linens, lay squalling and grimacing. His wife bent over him, saying: 'Praise be to Allāh and to His Prophet for this happy deliverance!' Then she went on murmuring the sacred names over her husband and the child, until the kādī did not know whether he dreamed or whether his recent sufferings had turned his head. But when he came to consider the matter calmly, the sight of the child, the cessation of his pains, and the memory of the tempest which had escaped from his belly, forced him to believe in this miraculous birth. Also maternal love caused him to accept the infant. 'Surely Allāh may bring forth His people according to His will!' he said. 'Even a man, if he is fated to do so, may bear a child in due season! Get me a nurse, dear wife, for I cannot feed the child myself.' 'I had already thought of that. I have one waiting in the harīm,' she replied. 'But a mother's milk is best of all. Are you sure that your breasts have not swelled?' The kādī felt anxiously, and answered: 'No, there is nothing there.'

The young wife rejoiced at the success of her strategy and, after telling the kādī that he must keep his bed for forty days and forty nights, gave him such medicines as are usual and petted him till he fell into a doze. Being worn out by his colic, the old man slept for a long time and, when he woke, found his body as well as his mind was ill at ease.

At this point Shahrazād saw the approach of morning and discreetly fell silent.

But when the eight-hundredth night had come

SHE SAID:

His first care was to enjoin secrecy on his wife, saying: 'I am lost for ever if folk get to know that the kādi has given birth to a veritable child.' Instead of reassuring him, his wife answered: 'We are not the only folk who know of the fortunate miracle. All our neighbours have already heard about it from the nurse. And I am afraid that it will be as difficult to prevent the news from spreading through the city, as it would have been to stay the tongue of the nurse in the first place. They are all babblers.'

The kādi spent the forty days upon his bed in deep mortification, not daring to move for fear of complications and internal bleeding, and brooding all the time over his monstrous accident. 'Surely my foes will accuse me of many ridiculous things,' he said to himself. 'They will say that I have let myself be buggered in some extraordinary fashion, and that it is all very well for me to be severe in my judgments when I have given myself up to such strange immoralities that I can bear a child. As Allāh lives, I am sure that they will accuse me of having been buggered, me, their virtuous kādi, and I have almost forgotten what it feels like!'

Thus he reflected, little knowing that his avarice was the cause of all his woes; and the more he thought, the blacker and more pitiable his case appeared to him. When his wife told him at last that he might rise without fear of complications, he bathed in the house, because he did not dare to go to the hammām. Finally he resolved to quit the city of Tarabūlus, rather than run the risk of being recognised in the streets. He informed his wife of his intention and she, while pretending deep grief that he would be obliged to abandon his great office, only made him the more fixed on flight, by saying: 'Evil tongues are certainly wagging about you now; but your adventure will soon be forgotten. Then you can return and devote yourself to rearing your child. . . . I think that we had better call him Miracle.' 'Call him what you like,' answered the kādi. That night he departed from the city by stealth, leaving his wife in charge of the house and child, and journeyed in the direction of Damascus.

He came to Damascus weary, but happy in the thought that no one knew his name or story. Yet, in the next few hours, he heard the tale of his exploit repeated countless times in all the public places of that city. Also, as he had feared, each new gossip added some fresh detail to tickle the laughter of his hearers, attributing extraordinary organs to the kādī and bestowing on him every variety of that name which he dared not formulate even to himself. But happily no one knew his face and he was able to go on his way unrecognised. Towards night he even grew so hardened that he would pause and listen to his own story. In fact, when he heard himself accused not of one child but of a whole family, he could not help laughing a little, and murmuring: 'They may say what they like, as long as they do not recognise me.'

Though he lived in Damascus even more miserly than before, his provision of money at length ran out and he was obliged to sell his clothes for bread. Finally, rather than send a message to his wife in which he would have to tell her where his treasure lay, he hired himself out to a mason as a mortar-carrier.

Years went by, and the old kādī, round whom the curses of the people of Tarabūlus swarmed at night, became as thin as a cat locked in a barn. At last, feeling certain that the years would have effaced the memory of his misfortune, he left Damascus and came, a mere wraith of skin and bone, to his native city. As he went through the gate, he saw a group of children playing together and heard one of them say to another: 'How do you expect to win when you were born in the kādī's year, the year of the Father of Farts?' 'I thank Allāh,' murmured the delighted kādī, 'that He has caused my tale to be forgotten! Behold, some other kādī has become a proverb in the mouths of the children!' He went up to the boy who had spoken, saying: 'What kādī is this whom you call the Father of Farts?' 'He was given that name,' answered the child, 'because once, when he had broken wind enormously, his wife made him think. . . .' But nothing is to be gained by repeating the sorry story here.

Realising for the first time that he had been fooled by his wife, the kādī left the children and ran in all haste to his own house; but the doors were open to the wind, the floor was broken, and the walls had crumbled away. In the remains of the treasure cabinet there was no gold piece or silver piece, nor hint nor smell that such had been. His neighbours, hearing him lament, told him, as well as they could for laughter, how his wife had given him up for dead and departed with all his goods into a far country. Without answering a word, he turned and left that city. Nor was anything ever heard of him again.

Such, O King of time, said the hashīsh-eater, is the tale of the Father of Farts, as I heard it. But Allāh knows all!

In his huge delight at this tale, the Sultān gave the fisherman a robe of honour, saying: 'In Allāh's name, tell me something more, O sugar-mouth!' 'I hear and I obey!' answered the hashīsh-eater, and he told:

The Tale of the Kādī-Mule

IT is related, O auspicious King, that there was a man in one of the cities of Egypt whose profession of tax collector caused him often to be away from home. As he was not dowered with strength, in a woman's interpretation of that word, his wife did not fail to profit by his continued absences. Her lover was as handsome as the moon and always ready to satisfy her. She loved him so, that she not only returned his services in kind, but gave him a plentiful allowance of money in exchange for unlimited coupling. For years they lay together delightfully on every possible occasion, glutting each other with love. Glory be to Allāh, Who has given power to some and impotence to others!

One day the girl's husband harnessed his mule, before setting out to collect taxes. He filled one of the sides of his saddle-bag with papers and garments, and bade his wife stock the other with food. Eager to be rid of him, the woman set about her task and soon discovered that she had no bread. Though the negress had begun to grind corn for a new supply, the tax collector could not wait and set off to the market to buy some loaves, leaving his mule before the manger in the stable.

At this point Shahrazād saw the approach of morning and discreetly fell silent.

But when the eight-hundred-and-first night had come

SHE SAID:

As his wife waited his return in the courtyard, her lover, who thought that the husband had already departed, entered in great haste, crying: 'You must let me have three hundred dirhams!' 'I have not got them to-day, and I do not know where to get them,' she answered. 'But there is the mule, my sister,' the young man urged. 'Give me the mule and I can sell him for three hundred dirhams. I must have the money.' 'You are mad!' cried the girl. 'If my husband comes back and does not find his mule, he will beat me.' But the youth looked so woe-begone and talked so eloquently that she ceded to his prayers at last and let him lead away the mule. She took care, however, to retain the harness.

Soon the husband returned with the bread under his arm, and went into the stable to place it in the bag. When he saw the animal's headpiece hanging on a nail and the saddle lying with the bag on the straw, he cried to his wife to know what had become of the mule. 'He went out just now,' she answered calmly. 'He turned on the threshold and told me that he was going to administer justice at the dīwān.' 'Do you dare to mock at me?' shouted the collector, lifting his fist in a rage. 'Do you not know that I could crush you with one blow of this?' 'The name of Allāh be upon and about us two!' cried the wife without losing countenance. 'Why should I mock you? How could I try to deceive you? If I wanted, how could I succeed when you are so clever? Your wit would tear my clumsy invention into tatters. . . . But I have a thing to tell you which I have not dared to say before, fearing lest I should draw some misfortune upon our heads: the mule is bewitched and sometimes changes into a kādī!' 'Allāh, Allāh,' began the collector, but the girl cut him short and went on: 'The first time I saw a strange man leaving our stable, I was terribly frightened and veiled my face with the corner of my robe. I was about to flee, when he came up to me, and said in a grave and good-natured voice: "Refresh your eyes, calm your dear soul, my girl; I am no stranger, I am your husband's mule. But by nature I am a human being, a kādī; I was turned into a mule by certain foes well versed in sorcery. Being ignorant of these arts, I could not help myself; but I will say this much for my persecutors: they are Believers and allow me from time to time to resume my human form and go to the dīwān on the appointed day. It is my fate to live sometimes as a mule and sometimes as a kādī, until Allāh in His bounty shall break the spell and free me from my foes. Kind mistress, I beg you, in the name of your father and mother, not to say a word of all this to your husband, the tax collector, for he is an upright and religious man and, if he knew that he had a beast in his house under sentence of magic, he might get rid of me. He might sell me to some farmer, who would ill-treat me from dawn till dusk and feed me upon rotten beans. I could not endure that, now that I am accustomed to the rich feeding of your stable. And there is another thing, sweet, kind mistress. I beseech you to request the noble tax collector not to prick me so strongly in the bum when he is in a hurry, for I have an excessive sensibility in that part."

'After he had proffered these two requests, our mule, that is to say the kādī, departed for the dīwān. I am sure you would find him there now, if you were to look for him.

'I cannot keep the mule's secret any longer without incurring your anger; but I beg Allāh to pardon me my lack of faith towards the poor kādī. Now that you know, perhaps you will let me give you a word of advice. I suggest that you do not rashly get rid of the mule, for he is not only a zealous and sober animal, who never farts and seldom shows his tool, but he could, at need, give you excellent advice on delicate questions of jurisprudence.'

'As Allāh lives, this is a strange tale!' cried the astonished tax collector. 'But what am I to do without my mule? I have to go and collect the taxes of such-and-such villages at once. He did not say what time he would be back?' 'He did not mention any hour,' answered his wife. 'He only told me that he was going to the dīwān. But I know what I would do if I were in your place. . . . Yet you are much cleverer than I, and have no need of my suggestions.' 'I never said that you were altogether a fool,' grumbled the man. 'Tell me what you have in your mind.' So the girl continued: 'In your place, I would take a handful of beans and go to the dīwān; when I was in the presence of the poor kādī, I would show him the beans from far off and sign to him that I needed the services of my mule. As he has a sense of duty, and also because he likes beans, he would leave his judge's seat and follow me home.'

'You are a clever woman and I will follow your advice,' exclaimed the tax collector, as he provided himself with a handful of beans and prepared to leave the courtyard. 'One thing more,' cried his wife after him, 'be careful to treat him well, for both kādīs and mules are by nature vindictive.' Armed with patience by this last counsel, the tax collector came to the dīwān and entered the audience chamber, where the kādī sat upon his raised seat.

He stood at the back of the hall, behind the pleaders, and, holding out the beans with one hand, signed to the kādī with the other, as much as to say: 'Come here, I wish to speak to you.' The kādī, recognising him as one of the chief tax collectors, supposed that he carried an important message from the walī, so he suspended the business of the court immediately and followed the man out into the vestibule. But the unhappy tax collector still walked forward, holding out the beans behind him and making a clicking noise with his tongue.

When the two were out of earshot of all, the tax collector bent and whispered in the kādī's ear: 'As Allāh lives, my friend, I was deeply grieved to hear of your misfortune. You must not be annoyed that I have come to fetch you. You will understand that I have several villages to visit, and could not wait until the dīwān was over. Please turn yourself into a mule as quickly as you can, for it is already late.' The kādī recoiled in terror, and the tax collector, seeing this, continued even more kindly: 'I swear by Allāh that I will never prick you in the bum again, for I know how delicate a backside He has given you. Now, good mule, good friend, let us have no more delay; and I promise you a double ration of beans to-night, with a portion of fresh lucerne.'

The kādī was quite sure by now that he had to do with an escaped patient from the madhouse; he turned very yellow and began to edge back towards the hall; but the tax collector dodged behind him and blocked the entrance. Seeing that there was no one in sight to help him, the kādī put his trust in persuasion, and said sweetly: 'It seems, dear master, that you have lost your mule and are anxious to replace it. In my opinion nothing could be more just. Here are three hundred dirhams; you will be able to buy the finest mule in all the city with that money. And Allāh be good to you!' So saying, he gave the collector three hundred dirhams from his belt and retreated to the hall, where he took care to assume an air of grave reflection, that people might think he had received some communication of importance. 'As Allāh lives,' he said to himself, 'it was worth three hundred dirhams to avoid a scandal in front of all these pleaders, and, if I put on the screw a little, I can recoup myself at their expense before the morning is over.' Then he sat down and resumed the business of the court. So much for him.

The tax collector went to the beast market and began leisurely to examine all the mules, one after the other; at length he was attracted by one which seemed to fulfil his requirement, and went up to it, in order to make a final decision. But, when he came nearer, he recognised his own mule and the mule recognised him. It threw back its ears and brayed for joy; but the man was offended at its audacity and recoiled, crying: 'As Allāh lives, I shall not buy you. I need a mule who is always a mule. A mixture of mule and kādī is too uncertain.' He departed in high dudgeon, and bought another and a better mule with the three hundred dirhams. Then he returned to his wife and told her all that had happened.

In this way all the world was satisfied, thanks to the wit of one woman: the lover got his money, the husband obtained a better mule, and the kādī, in a joyful reaction from his danger, took double his usual fees from those who came before him.

That is all I know about the Kādī-Mule, O King. But Allāh knows all!

'O sugar-mouth, delightful friend, I herewith appoint you my grand-chamberlain!' cried the delighted Sultān. He clothed the hashīsh-eater in the insignia of that high office and then sat down again, saying: 'Surely, good grand-chamberlain, you know some more stories?' 'I do,' answered the erstwhile fisherman and, wagging his head from side to side, began:

At this point Shahrazād saw the approach of morning and discreetly fell silent.

But when the eight-hundred-and-second night had come

SHE SAID:

The Kādī and the Ass's Foal

IT is related, O auspicious King, that there were once a poor husband and wife, who gained their food by hawking roasted maize, and had one daughter as fair as any moon. Allāh willed that the kādī of that city should demand the girl's hand in marriage and, though prodigiously ugly, with a beard like hedgehog's spines, and a squint in one eye, gain immediate consent from the father. For the old man was both rich and respected, and the girl's parents only looked to the marriage to bring them an amelioration of their lot, forgetting that, though riches may contribute to happiness, they are not its wellspring: a lesson which the kādī at least was doomed to learn by bitter experience.

To make himself agreeable and to balance the disadvantages of his extreme age and ugliness, the kādī gave daily presents of novelty to his young wife and satisfied all her caprices, without considering that neither indulgence nor presents make up for a young and sturdy love. As time went on, he complained bitterly to himself that he could not rouse in his wife an instinct which she had not yet learnt.

Now this kādī had in his employ a young scribe whom he so cherished that he would, in spite of himself, sometimes speak of him to his wife. He also spoke of his wife to the young man and complained of her coldness, which shows that Allāh blinds those creatures whom He wishes to destroy. His senile idiocy grew so great that he even pointed out the youth to his wife, when he passed before the window. The girl straightway felt the power of love rise in her heart, and very soon passion had found out a way to lull suspicion. As she adored him with her whole soul, the young wife naturally gave the scribe her body, and he paid her back in a hard coin of which the kādī was incapable. The two young people loved each other better as the days went by, and the kādī rejoiced to see his wife grow happier and more beautiful.

In order that their meetings might be safe, the girl used to hang a white handkerchief in a window which looked over the garden, as a sign that the kādī was absent. But if the youth saw a red handkerchief, he knew that the husband was at home and the door closed to him.

One day, the girl heard blows and cries at the door just as she had hung up the white handkerchief, and soon saw her husband, who had been taken ill at the dīwān, carried into her presence on the arms of the eunuchs. He looked so pitiful that his wife sprinkled him with rose-water and cared tenderly for him in spite of her disappointment. She undressed and put him to bed, where he speedily fell asleep; then, in order to make the best of that useless morning, she made a packet of perfumed linen and departed for the hammām, forgetting to replace the white handkerchief by the red danger signal.

Seeing the white handkerchief fluttering in the casement, the lover leapt lightly from the neighbouring terrace and climbed through the window into the chamber, where he was used to find his mistress waiting naked beneath the bedclothes. As the place had been left in obscurity to favour the kādī's sleeping, and as the girl would often receive him in silence, he walked laughing up to the bed and, lifting the clothes, made a dart with his hand as if to tickle his love between the legs. But instead of that which he sought, his hand encountered

—may the Devil avoid us all—something soft and flabby, swimming in a wiry thicket. With an exclamation of horror he snatched back his fingers, but not before the kādī had seized the marauding wrist and furiously fallen upon its owner. Rage gave the old man strength, while shock weakened the younger; so the kādī was able to pick up his adversary, after tripping him, and hurl him into a large chest, where the mattress was kept during the day. He banged down the lid and turned the key in the lock without taking the precaution to see whether or not he recognised the intruder. Then, as the excitement and exercise had quite cured his indisposition, he inquired of the eunuch whither his wife had gone, and hastened to station himself outside the door of the hammām. For he said to himself: 'Before I kill him, I must know whether he is in league with my wife. I will open the box in the presence of witnesses, and thus confound her, if she be guilty. If she knows nothing of the man, I will kill him with my sword; but if they are lovers, I will strangle them both with my own fingers. In either case I must have witnesses; for I am the kādī.'

As each bather entered the hammām, he stopped her, saying: 'In Allāh's name, tell my wife so-and-so to come out at once, as I wish to speak with her.' But he made this request so shortly, with such flashing eyes, such violent gestures, that all the women took him for a madman and ran up the steps with frightened cries. The first called out the news at the top of her voice, when she entered the hall of the hammām, and the kādī's wife suddenly remembered that she had forgotten to change the handkerchiefs. 'Surely I am lost!' she moaned to herself. 'Allāh alone knows what has happened to my lover!' As she hastened the rest of her bath, she heard the doings of the madman outside discussed by all her neighbours; but, since none of them knew her by sight, she was able to behave as if the matter did not concern her and depart without attracting attention. In the entrance hall she saw a poor old woman seated on the floor and endeavouring to sell chick-peas to the bathers; so she went up to her, saying: 'Here is a golden dīnār for you, good aunt, if you will lend me your blue veil and that empty basket.' Delighting in her luck, the old woman gave her the coarse veil and the basket; and the girl disguised herself with these things before venturing forth.

She saw her husband pacing frenziedly up and down in front of the door, with foam on his lips and eyes protruding from his head. When she went up to him and asked him in disguised accents to buy some chick-peas, he was cursing hammāms at the top of his voice, the people who used hammāms, the people who kept hammāms, and the people who built hammāms; but when he heard her request, he broke off to call down all the plagues of the world on chick-peas, those who sold chick-peas, those who planted chick-peas, and those who ate chick-peas. The girl ran off with a laugh and, reaching her home, climbed swiftly to the bedchamber, where she was startled to hear a sound of groaning. She threw back the windows in haste and then, seeing no one, was at first inclined to call for help; but a louder groan than the others led her to the mattress-chest and, turning the key in the lock, she plucked open the lid in the name of Allāh.

At this point Shahrazād saw the approach of morning and discreetly fell silent.

But when the eight-hundred-and-third night had come

SHE SAID:

Though her lover was nearly dead for lack of air, she could not help laughing for a moment at the sight of him doubled up in the chest; but soon her love conquered and she sprinkled his face with rose-water. When he had quite recovered, she briefly told him what had happened and the two sat down together to concoct a plan.

An ass in the stable had dropped a foal the day before. The girl ran forth and, taking the pleasant little animal in her arms, brought it to the bedroom, shut it in the chest, and turned the key in the lock. Then she dismissed her lover, bidding him not come again until she flew the white signal, and returned in the direction of the hammām. She slipped past her husband, but, as she was entering the vestibule, he cried after her: 'O chick-pea seller, tell my wife that if she does not come out at once I will pull the hammām down about her head!' The girl laughed and, gliding through the door, returned her shawl and basket to the old woman; then, taking up her own packet of linen, she left the building again, carelessly swinging her hips.

As soon as the kādī saw her, he bore down on her, crying: 'Where have you been, vile strumpet? I have waited here for two hours; follow me instantly, perverse, unfaithful whore!' The girl checked in her walk, exclaiming: 'In Allāh's name, what is the matter? Have you gone mad, that you make a scandal in the street?' 'Enough!' shouted the kādī. 'You can say what you will at home. Now, follow!' He strode ahead, throwing his arms about and spitting bile, leaving her to follow as best she might.

When they reached the house, the kādī shut his wife in another chamber and went forth to collect the sheikh of the quarter and four witnesses. To these he added a band of neighbours and, after leading them to the bedchamber, freed his wife and led her into their presence.

She ran immediately to a far corner, and sat there in her veils, moaning: 'Woe, woe, for my poor husband! His illness has made him mad. The poor soul has lost his wits, he has cursed me, he has brought strange men into the harīm! Woe, woe, strangers in the harīm! Alas, alas! He is mad, quite mad!'

And indeed the kādī seemed to the witnesses to be in a high fever of delirium; his face was bright yellow, his beard trembled, and his eyes flashed fire. Some of them tried to calm him; but he cried: 'Look, look! Do not listen! This is her last day! This is the day of judgment!' With that he turned the key in the chest and threw back the lid. At once the little ass put forth his head, wagging his ears and regarding the company with round black tender eyes; then, for delight at looking upon the day once more, he threw up his tail and called his mother with a mighty bray.

The kādī was taken with convulsions and spasms; he threw himself upon his wife and tried to strangle her, while she fled round the chamber from him, calling for help.

Seeing foam upon the kādī's lips, the witnesses flung themselves between the two and, taking hold of the old man's arms, forced him to the carpet, where he babbled unintelligible words mingled with threats of strangulation. The sheikh of the quarter, though grieving to see the kādī in such a state, felt obliged to say to those who held him down: 'He must be restrained, alas, until he returns to his senses.' 'Allāh cure him!' cried some. 'He was a most respectable old man.' 'How could one be jealous of a little ass not two days old?' said others. Others again asked: 'How did it get into the chest?' and 'He thought it was a man and locked it in himself,' answered the woman. With words of deep compassion all retired, except those who held the kādī down, and these did not need to stay long: for the old man's struggles and shoutings were so violent, when he caught sight of the mocking grimaces which his wife sent to his address behind the backs of the watchers, that he ruptured the veins of his neck and, spitting a wave of blood, fell back dead. May Allāh have him in compassion, for he was an upright judge and left a sufficiency of riches to enable his young wife to marry the man she loved!

When he had made an end of this tale and saw that the King still listened greedily, the hashīsh-eater said: 'I will now tell you another story,' and straightway began:

The Tale of the Astute Kādī

IT is related that there was once a kādī in Cairo who committed so many prevarications and gave so many interested judgments that he was deprived of his high office and had to live by his wits. One day, when his head was as empty as his pocket, and his pocket as empty as his belly, he called his one remaining slave to him, a rascal as tricky and hungry as himself, and said to him: 'I am ill and cannot leave the house to-day; you must either find us something to eat by going about the streets, or else send some people to me for legal advice.' The slave departed with the intention of molesting some passer-by and then dragging him before his master to be fined. So, as soon as he saw a peaceful citizen coming towards him holding a bundle on his shoulder with both hands, he tripped him up and sent him flat on his back into the mud. The victim rose furiously, with stained garments and torn slippers, and was about to chastise his aggressor when he recognised the kādī's slave and, turning tail, fled away from so dangerous an encounter.

'They all know me, just as they all know my master,' grumbled the slave. 'I must think of some other way.' As he turned a corner, he saw a man carrying on his head a dish which contained a superb stuffed goose, garnished about with tomatoes, artichokes and young marrows in a tempting pattern. The slave followed this man, and saw him enter the public kitchen and deliver the bird to the master of the oven, saying that he would call for it in an hour.

'Here is my chance,' thought the kādī's slave. After a few minutes he entered the kitchen, saying: 'Greeting, O Mustafā!' The master of the oven recognised him, and replied: 'Greeting, O Mubārak! It is a long time since my coals have burnt for your master. Have you brought something for me to cook for him to-day?' 'Nothing except the goose,' answered Mubārak, 'I have come for that.' 'But it does not belong to you, my brother,' objected the cook. 'Say not so, O sheikh,' retorted the slave. 'I watched that goose come out of the egg, I fed it, I killed it, and I stuffed it.' 'If that is so, I am ready to give it to you,' answered the cook. 'But what shall I say to the man who brought it?' 'He was acting under my instructions,' replied Mubārak airily. 'I do not think that he will return; but, if he does, he is fond of a good joke and you had better tell him that the goose gave a sharp cry and flew away as soon as you put the dish in the oven. Now give me the bird, please, for I am sure that it is done.'

At this point Shahrazād saw the approach of morning and discreetly fell silent.

But when the eight-hundred-and-fourth night had come

SHE SAID:

The cook laughed heartily and gave the dish in all confidence to Mubārak, who hastened with it to the kādi's house and helped his master to pick it clean.

Soon the owner of the goose came into the kitchen, saying: 'My bird must be done, good master.' 'Not so,' answered the cook, 'for, as soon as I put her in the oven, she gave a piercing cry and flew away.' The man, who had no humour in all his body, cried angrily: 'O nothing, do you dare to laugh in my beard?' Words led to curses, curses led to blows, and soon the two men were violently fighting in the midst of a crowd which had speedily invaded the kitchen. 'They are fighting over the resurrection of a stuffed goose!' said some of the neighbours, and most of them took sides with the cook, whose honesty had always been unquestioned.

Among the spectators was a pregnant woman, whose curiosity had thrust her into the front rank. As the cook aimed a terrific blow, his adversary stepped aside and the unfortunate woman received the fist in her belly. She fell to the earth, with a scream like that of an outraged hen, and suffered an abortion on that spot.

Her husband, who dwelt in a neighbouring fruit shop, was told of the accident and ran up with an enormous bludgeon, crying: 'I am going to bugger this cook, and his father, and his grandfather! I am going to sweep off all the tribe of cooks from the face of the earth!' The master of the oven, being already weary, would not wait to face him, but fled precipitately. Fearing pursuit, he climbed on to a neigh-bour's terrace, by way of an old wall, and let himself drop over the balustrade. His fate willed that he should fall, with all his consider-able weight, on a Moor who lay sleeping upon the terrace. All the poor man's ribs were broken and he died without waking. Other Moors, who were his kinsmen, ran up and secured the cook, beating him with sticks preparatory to leading him before a judge. The owner of the goose and the husband of the pregnant woman joined themselves to the Moors, and they were all starting off, when the kādī's slave, who had come back to spy the end of that affair, ran before them, crying: 'Follow me, good folk! I will show the way!' Not knowing who he was, the injured parties followed him and were conducted into the presence of his master.

Putting on his gravest air, the kādī first took double deposit from all the pleaders and then pointed his finger at the accused, saying: 'What have you to say in the matter of the goose, O cook?' Thinking that he had better adhere to the story told by the kādī's slave, the cook replied: 'As Allāh lives, O our master the kādī, the bird gave a shrill cry and, stuffed as she was, rose from among the garnishing and flew away.' Hearing this, the owner cried: 'Son of a dog, do you dare to tell such a tale in front of our lord the kādī?' But at this the kādī waxed indignant, saying to the owner: 'And do you dare, O impious unbeliever, to doubt that He, Who shall raise all creatures on the Last Day, collecting their scattered bones from the wide face of the earth, cannot give life to a goose who has all her bones complete and only lacks feathers?' Hearing this, the assembled crowd cried: 'Glory be to Allāh, Who raises the dead!' and hooted the unfortunate owner of the bird until he departed, lamenting his lack of faith.

Then the kādī turned to the husband of the woman who had miscarried, saying: 'What have you to say against this man?' He heard out the complaint, and then gave judgment: 'The matter is clear; the cook certainly caused the abortion. The law of retaliation is strictly applicable here. You, O injured husband, have won your case and I empower you to take your wife and leave her with the guilty party until he makes her with child again. Also, she may live in his house and at his charges for the first six months of pregnancy, as the accident happened in the sixth month.' Hearing this judgment, the husband cried: 'Oh our lord the kādī, I withdraw my complaint. May Allāh pardon my adversary!'

As the husband was leaving the presence, the kādī asked the relations of the dead Moor what charge they brought against the cook. They answered in a spate of words and whirlwind of gestures, showing the dead body and clamouring for the price of blood. 'The evidence is conclusive,' replied the kādī. 'The price of blood is due to you. Will you be paid in money or in kind, that is to say, blood for blood?' 'In kind, O kādī!' shouted the savage Moors. 'Be it so!' proclaimed the kādī. 'Take this cook, wrap him in the coverlet of your dead kinsman and place him underneath the minaret of the mosque of Sultān Hasan. Then the victim's brother may climb up the minaret and fall from the summit on top of the cook, to crush him as the victim was crushed. . . . Which of you is the victim's brother?' A certain Moor stood forth, crying: 'O our lord the kādī, I withdraw my complaint against this man. May Allāh pardon him!' Then he departed, followed by all the folk of his house.

The crowd went out marvelling at the equity, subtlety, and profound legal knowledge of the kādī. When the noise of the affair reached the ears of the Sultān, he took the kādī back into favour and restored him to his high functions, dismissing the honest man who had replaced him. This latter owed his downfall, as far as we may see, to the fact that he had never stolen a goose.

Seeing that the King still hung eagerly upon his words, the hashīsh-eater felt flattered, and also told the tale of:

The Man Who Understood Women

IT is related, O auspicious King, that there were once two young men in Cairo who were close friends; though one, Ahmad, was married, and the other, Mahmūd, was a bachelor. Ahmad, who was the elder by two years, made capital out of this difference to constitute himself his friend's tutor in all things, and especially on the subject of women. He would read him a thousand lessons out of his experience, and ever conclude in this wise: 'You will be able to say that you have known one man in your life who understood the malicious sex. You may indeed count yourself lucky to have a friend who can coach you in the arts of its deceit.' Mahmūd marvelled more and more at his friend's wisdom, and was quite certain that the subtlest woman on earth could never deceive him while he was so guarded. 'You are a great man, Ahmad,' he would often say, and Ahmad would preen himself and tap his friend on the shoulder, as he replied: 'I will teach you to be even as I am.'

One day when Ahmad said: 'I will teach you to be even as I am; for I speak from experience and not by theory,' young Mahmūd ventured to reply: 'Dear friend, if you will be so kind, I would like to learn to enter into relations with a woman, before becoming perfect in the act of guarding against her.'

At this point Shahrazād saw the approach of morning and discreetly fell silent.

But when the eight-hundred-and-fifth night had come

SHE SAID:

'It is the easiest thing in the world,' answered Ahmad in his schoolmaster's voice. 'Go out to-morrow to the Feast of the Prophet, under the tents, and make close observation of all the women. When you have chosen one accompanied by a little child, and have judged, by looking through her veil, that she is worth your trouble, you must buy dates and sugared peas for the child, play with him, caress him, embrace him; but on no account lift your eyes towards the mother. Only when the little boy has become your fast friend, you may ask the woman, without looking at her, the favour of carrying the child home. As you go along, you must keep the flies off his face and tell him a thousand silly pretty things. In the end, the mother will speak to you of her own accord, and the affair will be settled.' With this piece of wise advice he left Mahmūd to marvel by himself and to spend the rest of the day in saying over his lesson.

Early next morning Mahmūd made his way to the Feast and carried out his tutor's prescription to the letter. The result passed his wildest dreams; but Destiny had willed that the woman whose child he carried home should be the wife of his friend Ahmad. As he had never seen the girl, veiled or unveiled, he had not the least idea that he was betraying his friend; and the young wife, though she recognised Mahmūd, was delighted at this proof of her husband's deep knowledge of the sex.

The two took great joy from their first meeting, and the youth, who was a virgin, tasted the full gamut of those joys which may be found between the arms and legs of an experienced Egyptian. They were so pleased with this first attempt that they repeated it several times in the following weeks. The woman rejoiced to play such a trick upon her presumptuous husband, and the husband only wondered why he no longer saw his friend Mahmūd at those hours when they had been used to meet. 'I expect he has profited by my advice,' he said to himself.

One Friday Ahmad went to the mosque and saw his friend near the fountain of ablution. The two men greeted each other, and the elder asked if all had gone well in the matter of the woman. Mahmūd, who was delighted to have a confidant, replied ecstatically: 'She is the most beautiful thing in the world! Butter and milk! Plump and white! Musk and jasmine! And what a brain! And what a cook! But I fear, dear friend, that her husband is a born fool or a complacent cuckold.' 'Most husbands are one or the other,' replied Ahmad with a laugh. 'Well, I am glad to have been of use. Go on with the good work, my friend.' They entered the mosque together and there lost sight of each other.

When Ahmad came out from the prayer, he was at a loss for occupation, as all the shops were shut; so he went to visit a neighbour who lived next door to his own house. As he was talking with the man near a window which overlooked the street, he saw his friend Mahmūd enter the house next door without even knocking, a sure proof that he was expected. At first Ahmad was inclined to rush home and, catching his friend with his wife, severely chastise the two of them; but then he reflected that his wife would be quite clever enough to hide her lover or let him slip from the house, when she heard the knocking on the door. Therefore he determined to enter by a secret way, known only to himself.

The two houses shared a communicating well, one half in each courtyard. 'By Allāh, I have just remembered that I dropped my purse in the well this morning!' remarked Ahmad casually to his host. 'I pray you allow me to go down from your side; then, when I have found it, I will climb out into my own courtyard.' 'Do so, by all means,' replied the neighbour. 'I will bring a light.' But Ahmad refused a light and, after saying goodbye, went down into the well.

Things went comfortably enough on the way down, but, when Ahmad began to climb up the other side and had reached half way, trouble fell upon him in a very singular fashion. The servant came to draw water and, seeing a dark figure in the half light of the well, let the bucket drop from her hand and fled, crying at the top of her voice: 'Help, help! There is an Ifrīt coming out of the well!' But the bucket, going upon the way of its Destiny, hit Ahmad on the head and half stunned him.

Alarmed by the cries of the negress, Ahmad's wife dismissed her lover and, going down into the courtyard, leaned over the margin of the well. 'Who is there?' she cried, and then, as a well-known voice boomed up to her in a thousand curses on wells in general, people who owned wells, folk who went down into wells, and women who let buckets fall from the tops of wells, she cried again: 'O husband, what are you doing in the well?' 'Be quiet, vile wretch!' he answered. 'I have only been looking for a purse. Instead of asking foolish questions, help me out of this accursed place!' His wife laughed to herself as she saw through this excuse, and called certain of the neighbours, who hoisted Ahmad, in a state of collapse, up the well and over the side into safety. He allowed himself to be carried to bed, without making any accusation, but, as he lay recovering, he brooded bitterly over his humiliation and over an insult offered to one who understood women.

He resolved to take greater precaution in future and, as soon as he could rise, selected a suitable ambush at the corner of the street. He had not waited for many days before he saw his friend Mahmūd slip through the half-open door, which was immediately shut behind him. Without a moment's delay he left his hiding-place and began to rain blows upon the panel.

At this point Shahrazād saw the approach of morning and discreetly fell silent.

But when the eight-hundred-and-sixth night had come

SHE SAID:

When she heard this violent knocking, Ahmad's wife bade her lover follow and, leading him forward, hid him behind the very door which was being assaulted. Then she opened to her husband, saying: 'In Allāh's name, my dear, why so much noise?' Ahmad seized her by the wrist and dragged her into the house. He ran up shouting to the bedchamber, while Mahmūd walked calmly forth from behind the door and escaped down the street. Finding himself foiled again, Ahmad in the first throes of his rage resolved to divorce his wife immediately; but, on reflection, he decided to wait for an occasion of surer proof.

Such an occasion was not long delayed. A few days later Ahmad's father-in-law gave a feast to celebrate the circumcision of a son who had been born to him in his old age. Ahmad and his wife were invited, and Ahmad took care to ask Mahmūd to accompany them. Soon all the men were seated before bountiful dishes in the lighted courtyard, which had been carpeted with rugs and made gay with flags for the occasion. The women were massed at the windows of the harīm, so that they might see and hear without offending modesty. During the course of the meal, Ahmad brought the conversation round to those salacious anecdotes which were his father-in-law's chief delight. When several of the guests had contributed examples of that most amusing kind of entertainment, Ahmad pointed to his friend, saying: 'Our brother Mahmūd told me a true tale the other day. It concerns himself and is much too good to be lost.' 'Let us have it at once, dear Mahmūd!' cried their host, and Ahmad prompted his friend, saying: 'You know the one I mean! Butter and milk! Musk and jasmine!' Delighted to be the centre of attention, Mahmūd began to tell the story of his first meeting with his mistress and the ruse by which he had brought it about. He gave so many exact details of the girl and her house, that the giver of the feast soon recognised the heroine as his own daughter. Ahmad was congratulating himself that he would soon have ample proof before witnesses of his wife's misconduct, and his father-in-law was just about to rise in order to create a diversion, when a sudden painful cry rang out, as if a little child had been violently pinched. This cry made Mahmūd aware of the danger which he ran and he had the presence of mind to change the thread of his narrative at the last moment. 'But when I had carried the child into the courtyard of that house,' he concluded, 'and would have climbed up into the harīm, the honest woman suddenly understood my intention and, snatching the infant from my arms, gave me so violent a blow in the face that I carry the marks of it to this day. Then she threatened to call the neighbours, and I departed, cursing her beneath my breath.'

The host and all the guests laughed consumedly at this unexpected termination; only Ahmad seemed a little disappointed. When they rose to go, he asked his friend why he had changed the current of his anecdote, and Mahmūd answered: 'That child's cry from the harīm suddenly put it into my mind that both he and his mother might quite possibly be there. And I considered that, if they were there, the husband was sure to be one of our fellow guests. That is why I made haste to clear the woman's character; but, as you will have noticed, I did not spoil the story.' Ahmad turned a sickly yellow colour and left his friend without a word. Next day he divorced his wife and started on pilgrimage to Mecca.

Thus Mahmūd, who did not understand women, was able to marry the girl of his choice and live happily with her until the day of his death. But Allāh knows all!

When he had made an end of this tale, the chamberlain fell silent. And the delighted Sultān cried: 'O fisherman, O chamberlain, O tongue of honey, henceforth you shall be my grand-wazīr!' At that moment two men entered, seeking satisfaction from the Sultān, and the hashīsh-eater was called upon to settle their difference. Hastily donning the robes of his new office, he cried to the two pleaders: 'Come near, and state the quarrel which has brought you to the justice of our lord the Sultān!'

This is the tale of:

The Hashīsh-Eater in Judgment

WHEN, O auspicious King, the new grand-wazīr had bidden the two pleaders to state their case (continued the farmer who had brought the cucumbers), the first said: 'My lord, I took a cow of mine this morning to pasture in my field of fresh lucerne. Her little calf followed at her heels or played about the road. Before I reached my destination I met this man, riding on a mare which was accompanied by her colt, a little pitiful bandy-legged slip of a thing, almost an abortion.

'As soon as my little calf saw the foal he ran up to make acquaintance with her and jumped round her, caressing her under the belly with his muzzle. He played with her in a thousand ways, sometimes running at her gently and sometimes flinging his little feet in the air until the pebbles flew.

'Quite suddenly this gross and brutal fellow dismounted from the mare and slipped a cord round the neck of my charming little calf, saying: "I think I will have him on a lead. I do not wish him to be perverted by playing with that miserable little foal, or with her mother, your vile cow." Then he called pleasantly to my calf: "Come little son of my mare, we do not wish to be corrupted." In spite of my protestations, he led away my calf and left the horrible foal, threatening to break my head if I tried to take back that which is my own in the sight of Allāh and before all men!'

When he had heard the first in silence, the new grand-wazīr turned to the second man and asked him what he had to urge in his defence. 'My lord,' said the defendant, 'it is a well-known fact that the calf was the offspring of my mare and that the wretched foal was dropped by this man's cow.' 'I suppose it is quite certain that cows can drop foals and mares give birth to calves?' interrupted the wazīr. 'You doubtless have something to bring forward in proof of your assertion?' 'My lord, do you not know that nothing is impossible to Allāh?' retorted the man. 'He creates that which seems good to Him and sows the seed of abundance where He wills. His creatures can only bow to His greater wisdom, giving Him praise and glory.' 'That is a very correct sentiment,' agreed the wazīr. 'Nothing is impossible to the Almighty, at His decree calves can be born of mares and foals from cows. Before you take the calf away, however, I will show both of you another example of Allāh's power.'

He ordered a large sack of flour and a small mouse to be brought into the presence, and said to the two pleaders: 'Watch carefully and do not say a word.' Then he turned to the defendant, bidding him lift the sack of flour and load it on the back of the mouse. 'My lord, it will squash the creature flat!' objected the man. 'O wretch of little faith,' cried the wazīr, 'is not all possible to Allāh Who brings forth calves from mares?' He ordered the guards to seize the defendant and beat him soundly for his ignorance and impiety; but to the plaintiff he delivered all four animals.

Such, O King of time, was the judgment of the hashīsh-eater; his was that higher wisdom which can show forth the truth by reducing the false to an absurdity. The Sultān proved himself a prudent man when he made that fisherman his grand-wazīr and showered honours upon him and took him for a friend. But Allāh knows all!

When the fruit farmer had made an end of these short tales, the Sultān rose to his feet, crying: 'O tongue of honey and sugar, O prince among delightful men, who is more worthy to be my grand-wazīr than a just thinker and charming teller of tales?' He robed the farmer in the garments of a grand-wazīr and kept him ever as a companion, until they were visited by the Separator of friends, by the Destroyer.

'That,' continued Shahrazād, 'is as far as I have read in the Dīwān of Easy Jests and Laughing Wisdom.' 'O sister, your words are sweet and delectable!' cried little Dunyazād; but Shahrazād answered: 'These tales are nothing to the story of Princess Nūr al-Nihār, which I would tell you to-morrow if I were still alive and the King permitted.' 'I must hear that tale, for I do not know it,' said King Shahryār to himself.

But when the eight-hundred-and-seventh night had come

LITTLE DUNYAZĀD cried: 'Dear sister, please begin the tale which you promised us, for our sweet King has given leave.' 'Certainly,' replied Shahrazād, and she told:

The Tale of Princess Nūr al-Nihār and the Lovely Jinnīyah

IT is related, O auspicious King, that there was once, in the antiquity of time and the passage of the age and of the moment, a valorous king, to whom Allāh, in His goodness, had given three handsome sons: the eldest was called Alī, the second Hasan, and the third Husain. These three princes were brought up in their father's palace with their orphan cousin, Princess Nūr al-Nihār, who had no equal among the daughters of men for beauty and intelligence. She had a deer's eyes and her mouth was a rose; the narcissus and the anemone were in her cheeks and she wavered like a branch of the ban tree. She had grown in joy from babyhood with her three cousins, eating and sleeping with them, and the Sultān ever had it in mind to marry her to the son of some neighbouring king.

But when Nūr al-Nihār had put on the veil of puberty, the Sultān saw that all his sons loved her with an equal passion and would give their hearts to conquer and possess her. In his perplexity, he said: 'If I give the child to one of her cousins, the other two will murmur against me, and I could not bear to see them sad and wounded. But if I marry her to some strange prince, all three will be plunged in a black distress and perhaps either kill themselves or depart for some far battle. Indeed I have a difficult problem to resolve.' After long reflection, he called the three princes to him, saying: 'My sons, you are all equal in my sight and I cannot show a preference to one by giving him the hand of our little princess in marriage; also I cannot marry her to all three of you. I only see one way of settling the matter so that there shall be no hard feeling between you: each of you must set out for a different land and bring back the strangest rarity he sees upon his travels. I will give the princess to the one who, in my opinion, returns with the greatest marvel. If you consent to this competition, I am ready to give each of you as much gold as he may need for the enterprise.'

The three princes readily agreed to their father's plan, each feeling certain that he would bring back the greatest marvel and marry Nūr al-Nihār. Seeing them persuaded, the Sultān sent for his treasurer and had each of his sons provided with as many bags of gold as he decided to take. Then, after recommending that they should not stay away too long, he gave them his blessing and bade them farewell. They set out on that same day, disguised as merchant travellers, mounted upon noble horses, and followed by a single slave apiece.

They rode together until they came to a khān at the meeting of three roads. There they took a bountiful repast together and settled the conditions of their search. It was agreed that each should be absent for one year, not a day more or less; that they should meet at this same khān at the end of that time, the first comer to wait for the rest, in order that they might return to their father in company. When their meal was finished, they washed their hands and embraced each other. Then they mounted their horses and each set forth by a different road.

After a journey of three months over mountain and valley, desert and meadowland, the eldest of the three brothers, Prince Alī, came to the kingdom of Bishangarh on the sea coast of India. He hired the largest and cleanest chambers in the chief khān for himself and his slave, and then lay down to rest. As soon as the fatigue of riding had passed away, he rose and went forth to examine the city, which was two parasangs in length and breadth, and girt by a triple wall. He made his way to the market, which he found to be formed of broad elegant streets converging on a central square, which held a marble fountain. All these streets were arched in to keep them cool; but they were pleasantly lighted by fretted openings in the stone. He discovered that each street harboured a different trade with all its merchandise. Thus, in one he saw nothing but fine Indian lawns, painted in bright pure colour with animals, forests, gardens of flowers; Persian brocades and silks from China. In another were fair porcelains and brilliant earthenware, with symmetrical vases, pictured dishes and extravagant shapes of glass. A third street showed every variety of those great Kashmir shawls which are so fine in texture that, when folded, they can be held in the hollow of one hand; with prayer rugs and every design of carpet. One street, further to the left and closed at both ends by massive steel doors, was given over to a prodigious profusion of the goldsmith's work and art of the diamond-setter. Prince Alī noticed with surprise that all the women in the crowd which thronged the market wore jewels about their legs, and on their feet, and through their ears, and even in their noses; also, he perceived that the whiter the woman, the more splendid gems she wore and the greater deference was paid to her, though the blacker women had skins which would have better shown off the precious stones.

But most Prince Alī admired the great quantity of little boys who sold roses and jasmine, the charming air with which they offered these flowers, and the way they seemed to slip through the crowds of people with the ease of quicksilver. He admired the strange liking which all these folk had for flowers, a predilection which caused them to wear blossoms in their hair, and behind their ears, and from their nostrils. Each shop was garnished with vases full of the prevailing rose and jasmine, and the whole market was so balmed with the scent of flowers that he seemed to himself to walk in a hanging garden.

When Prince Alī became weary of wandering among these beauties, he accepted the invitation of a merchant, who smiled at him from the door of his shop and invited him to enter. The man gave him the place of honour and served him with freshments, neither urging him to buy nor plaguing him with idle questions. 'What a delightful country!' thought the prince, 'and what delightful people!' The charm of the merchant so wrought upon him that he was inclined to buy all his stock; but, when he reflected that he would not know what to do with it, he contented himself with friendly talking.

While he was questioning his host concerning the manners and customs of the Indians, he saw a broker passing with a little carpet, not more than six feet square, folded across his arm. Outside the shop the broker halted and turned his head to right and left, crying: 'Folk of the market, O buyers! I offer a bargain! This carpet, this prayer-carpet, for thirty thousand gold dīnārs! I offer a bargain!'

'What a strange land!' thought Alī. 'A prayer-carpet for thirty thousand dīnārs! I wonder if the man is joking?' But when he heard the man offer the carpet again, quite seriously, at the same price, he signed to him to approach and show his goods more nearly. Without a word the broker spread out the carpet; Prince Alī examined it carefully, and then said: 'By Allāh, I cannot see how this carpet can be worth such an exorbitant sum!' The broker smiled, as he answered: 'Yet it is cheap at the price. Indeed I am instructed not to sell it for less than forty thousand dīnārs down, though I have started the sale at thirty thousand.' 'Then,' cried the prince, 'there must be some virtue in the carpet which is not visible to the naked eye.'

At this point Shahrazād saw the approach of morning and discreetly fell silent.

But when the eight-hundred-and-eighth night had come

SHE SAID:

'You are right, my lord,' answered the broker. 'The carpet has this invisible virtue: that he who sits on it is transported in the twinkling of an eye to the place of his desire. Nothing may stay its course; tempests flee before it and storms are dumb; mountains and walls and mighty locks open and give way at its approach.'

Without another word, the broker began to fold up the carpet and move on; but Prince Alī stopped him with a joyful cry: 'O broker of benediction, if what you say is true, I will pay you forty thousand dīnārs and add a further thousand as commission to yourself. But first I must have a demonstration of the miracle.' 'Where are your forty thousand dīnārs, my masters?' asked the broker without showing undue delight, 'and where are the further thousand which your generosity has promised?' 'They are at the chief khān,' answered Prince Alī, 'I will go there with you and pay you, as soon as I have controlled the marvel.' 'Be it upon my head and before my eyes,' replied the broker. 'But the chief khān is far from here; we would go quicker upon the carpet than by walking.' He spread out the carpet at the back of the shop and bade the prince be seated on it. Taking his place by his side, he said: 'Now, my lord, wish to be transported to your own room in the khān.' Prince Alī formulated the wish in his mind and, before he had time to speak a word of parting to the merchant who had so civilly entreated him, found himself transported, without shock or discomfort, to the centre of his own apartment. Nor could he tell whether he had flown through the air or gone beneath the ground. The broker sat beside him, wearing a satisfied smile.

Being thoroughly convinced of the carpet's power, the prince said to his slave: 'Give this excellent fellow forty purses of a thousand dīnārs and, into his other hand, a purse of a thousand.' The slave obeyed, and the broker, after wishing that the purchase might bring luck, went upon his way.

Prince Alī was delighted to think that he had found so extraordinary a marvel in so short a time. 'By the mercy of Allāh I have attained my goal already,' he said to himself. 'Now I know that I shall vanquish my brothers and marry Nūr al-Nihār. My father will be overjoyed when he makes trial of this carpet. Surely my brothers cannot find anything near so wonderful . . . But why should I not return at once, since distance is no object to me?' Then he remembered that he had agreed with his brothers to meet them in a year's time at the khān, so, not wishing to wait for many months in that forsaken place, he preferred to distract himself in the admirable land of India. On the next day he took a second walk throughout the city.

Among other curious wonders of that land, he saw a temple filled with brass idols, having a dome fifty cubits high which bore three levels of pictures in coloured carving. The whole temple was ornamented with shallow-cut designs of cunning chisels, and stood in a mighty rose garden. But its principal wonder was a solid gold statue among those brass idols (may they be damned and broken!). This figure stood at a man's height and had eyes of moving rubies, which rolled incessantly to follow the movements of any who stood before it. The priests celebrated their unbelieving cult morning and evening, and the ceremony was followed by games, music, buffoonery, feasting and the dancing of women. These priests had no stipend and lived entirely on the gifts of pilgrims, who thronged daily to their temple from distant lands.

While he was in Bishangarh, Prince Alī was present at the great annual feast, which is presided over by the walīs of all the provinces, by the captains of the army, and by the Brahmins, for that is the name given to the priests of the idols. The people thronged in their thousands into a vast plain, which was overlooked by a very high tower prepared for the reception of the King and his court. This tower was held up by eighty pillars and painted outside with presentations of birds and animals, flies and gnats. Near it there were three or four broad stands for the common people, and these were so constructed that they could face in any direction and change their decoration every hour. The entertainment began with clever juggling and sleight-of-hand, and dances by fakīrs. Then a thousand elephants advanced in battle order, each bearing a square tower of gold wood, filled with jesters and musicians. The trunks and ears of these elephants were painted with vermilion and cinnabar, their tusks were gilt all over, and their bodies were tinted in bright colours with a grotesque contortion of whirling arms and legs. When the troop had drawn up in a straight line facing the spectators, two much greater elephants, without towers, came forward and stood in the circle formed by the stands.

One of them began dancing to the sound of music, sometimes on his hind and sometimes on his front legs; then he climbed with great agility to the top of a post and, standing with all four legs drawn together, beat his trunk and wagged his ears to the rhythm of the players, while the other elephant swung on the end of a second pole, placed horizontally across a support, and, being balanced by a great stone at the opposite end of the pole, seesawed up and down in time to the music.

With such shows and other delights Prince Alī passed his time, until the torment of his love for Nūr al-Nihār could be combated no longer. Though the year was not over, he took his slave upon the magic carpet and wished himself before the khān at the meeting of the three roads. When he opened his eyes, which he had shut in order to concentrate his mind, he found himself outside the khān. He secured quarters there and set himself to wait for his brothers. So much for him.

The second brother, Prince Hasan, soon met with a caravan going towards Persia. This he joined and, after much weary travel over plain and desert, meadow and mountain, came to the city of Shīrāz. He took lodging at the chief khān and, on the following morning, while his friends the merchants were opening their bales and setting out their merchandise, went forth to view the city. He made his way to the market, which is called the Bazistān, and walked marvelling among the fine display of carpets and brocaded silks. The place was packed with brokers, busily pushing their wares, and among them Hasan saw a venerable man walking slowly and gravely, not thrusting and shouting like the others, but holding an ivory tube in his hand as if it had been a king's sceptre.

At this point Shahrazād saw the approach of morning and discreetly fell silent.

But when the eight-hundred-and-ninth night had come

SHE SAID:

'That broker inspires my confidence,' said Prince Hasan, and he walked towards him, meaning to beg for a closer sight of the tube;

but before he could reach him, the man began proclaiming in a proud magnificent voice: 'A bargain, a bargain, O buyers! Thirty thousand dīnārs for this ivory tube! The maker is dead and there will never be another! Thirty thousand dīnārs for this ivory tube! A bargain, a bargain, O buyers!'

The prince recoiled in astonishment, and said to the owner of a neighbouring shop: 'Can you tell me whether this broker is sane, mad, or jesting, my master?' 'He is the most honest and the most wise of all our brokers,' answered the man. 'We all employ him for important business. I can answer for his sanity, unless he has lost it since this morning. As he is crying that ivory tube for thirty thousand dīnārs it must be worth at least that, though its value is not patent. I will call the man, if you wish, and you can question him. Come into my shop and rest yourself.'

Hasan sat down in the shop and the merchant called to the broker, saying: 'This honourable stranger is surprised that you should ask thirty thousand dīnārs for a little ivory tube, and I, though I know your probity, am surprised too. Can you explain?' The broker turned to the prince, saying: 'I can understand your astonishment, my master, but, when you have seen, you will doubt me no longer. Also, I may tell you that, though I have opened the sale at thirty thousand dīnārs, I am not allowed to sell for less than forty thousand down.' Then said Prince Hasan: 'I am ready to believe that it is worth the money, if you assure me that it has some hidden virtue.' 'You notice that one end is fitted with a crystal,' replied the broker. 'A man who looks through that sees all he wishes to see.' 'If you speak truth,' cried the prince, 'I will not only pay your price, but give you a commission of a thousand dīnārs. Let me look!' The broker handed him the tube and Hasan gazed through the crystal, while he wished fervently to behold the Princess Nūr al-Nihār. Immediately he saw her sitting among her slaves in the bath of the hammām, laughing, playing with the water, and glancing into a mirror. Seeing her so near and fair, the prince uttered a cry and nearly dropped the magic ivory.

Being sure that no greater marvel could be found in a ten years' search, he hastily led the broker to the khān and paid him over the price and commission which he had promised.

To while away the time until he might meet and astonish his brothers, he spent his days with the poets of that city and learnt several of the most beautiful Persian compositions by heart. But when the caravan which had brought him there was about to return, he rejoined it and soon arrived without accident at the khān of meeting. There he stayed with his brother to await the coming of Husain. So much for him.

Prince Husain, the youngest of the three brothers, journeyed without accident to the city of Samarkand al-Ajam, where, O auspicious King, your glorious brother, Shahzamān, reigns to-day. On the morning of his arrival he visited the market, which is there called the bazaar, and, while watching the stream of the people, saw a broker carrying an apple in his hand. This apple, which was as large as a melon, was red on one side and gold on the other. Husain was taken with its beauty, and asked the broker its price. 'I have opened the sale at thirty thousand dīnārs,' the broker said, 'but I am not allowed to sell for less than forty thousand down.' 'It certainly is the finest apple that I have ever seen,' cried Husain, 'but I think that you must be jesting about the price.' 'Not at all, my lord,' replied the man, 'the price falls far short of the value. For this apple's appearance is as nothing to its smell, and its smell as nothing to its virtue for the good of mankind.' 'Let me smell it then,' answered Husain, 'afterwards you can tell me of its virtue.' The broker held the apple under the prince's nose and the youth, having breathed in its suave and penetrating odour, cried aloud: 'As Allāh lives, all the weariness of my journey has departed! It is as if I had been born again!' Then said the broker: 'Now that you have tried a little of its power, you will be more ready to hear the truth about this apple. It is not a natural fruit, but was made by the hand of man; it was born, not of a blind tree, but of the study and vigil of a great philosopher. He passed his long life in learning the curative properties of all plants and minerals, and, as a last triumph, mingled his knowledge and the life-giving simples of the world in this one apple. There is no disease, whether it be plague, purple fever, leprosy, or the awful coming of Death himself, which cannot be cured by smelling at the fruit. As complete proof of what I say, I should like some incurable person to be cured before your eyes. In the meanwhile, the greater part of these merchants will bear witness to what I say and confess that they owe to this apple the fact that they are still alive.'

Many people had paused while the broker was speaking. Now they cried: 'As Allāh lives, all that is true! It is the queen of apples and the universal remedy of time!' As if to confirm what they were saying, a blind and paralytic old man was borne past in a basket on the back of a porter. The broker took a step forward and held the apple beneath the nose of the motionless figure; immediately the old man rose in the basket and, leaping over the porter's head like a young cat, ran swiftly away, turning the eyes of youth to right and left.

Being now convinced that the apple was miraculous, Prince Husain led the broker to his khān and paid him forty thousand dīnārs for the fruit and a thousand as commission for himself. Quite certain of a triumph over his brothers, he waited patiently until a caravan was ready to depart in the direction of his home. When it set forth, he travelled with it and came without accident to the khān at the meeting of the three roads.

The three princes embraced each other tenderly and sat down together to meat.

At this point Shahrazād saw the approach of morning and discreetly fell silent.

But when the eight-hundred-and-tenth night had come

SHE SAID:

When they had eaten, they agreed together to display the marvels which they had found, in order to form some idea of their father's preference.

The eldest displayed his carpet and, after remarking upon its common and lustreless appearance, told them how it had borne him in the twinkling of an eye from Bishangarh to that place. As a proof of his words, he bade them sit upon it and took them to a spot at the other end of the world.

In less than a moment they were back again, and Prince Hasan showed the ivory tube. As a proof of its power, he held the crystal to his eye, saying: 'O magic ivory, I wish to see the Princess Nūr al-Nihār.' Even as he spoke, his face changed colour; when his brothers questioned him concerning his anxiety, he cried: 'There is no power or might save in Allāh! O brothers, we have journeyed in vain, for our sweet cousin lies upon her bed among her weeping women and death is very near. See for yourselves!' Alī looked through the crystal and groaned, but Husain looked and laughed, saying: 'Do not be concerned, my brothers. Though our cousin is very ill this apple will cure her. Nay, were she dead, I believe it would bring her up living from the tomb.' He told the story of the

magic fruit in a few words, and Alī cried: 'Let us make all haste to
the palace upon my carpet; then you can try the saving virtue of your
apple.'

The three princes bade their slaves go forward on horseback and,
seating themselves on the carpet, wished to be transported to the
death chamber of the princess.

In a flash of time they found themselves seated near the bed and
circled by frightened screaming women. The eunuchs did not recognise them at first and were about to fall upon them, when Husain
rose and showed his face. He leaned over the bed where the princess
lay in agony and held the apple to her nostrils. She opened her eyes
and sat up, smiling upon her cousins and congratulating them on
their safe return. She gave them her hand to kiss and, hearing how
Hasan had seen her, Alī had come to her, and Husain had cured her,
thanked Husain most, but all most cordially.

As she was anxious to rise and dress, her cousins left her and presented themselves before their father. The Sultān had already heard
of their strange arrival and of the princess's cure; so, after he had
embraced them with great love, he gave them leave to show him the
rarities which they had brought.

But when he had seen each magic thing and had listened carefully
to an account of its power, he was perplexed, and said: 'My sons, you
have given me a difficult and delicate problem. In the justice of my
mind, I cannot but hold these three rarities of equal value; for the
magic ivory learned of the princess's illness, the magic carpet hastened to her, and the magic apple cured her; yet each would have been
useless without the other. My choice is even more embarrassed now
than it was before you left. There is no other way for it; I must set
you another test. Let each of you join me at once in the polo-ground
beyond the city, and bring a bow and arrow with him. He whose
arrow is found to have gone the furthest shall marry Nūr al-Nihār.'

The three princes went off to fetch their arms, while the Sultān
rode to the polo-ground, accompanied by a troop of officers from
the palace. When his sons arrived, the Sultān bade them shoot in
order of age. Alī bent his bow and his arrow sped far; but when
Hasan shot, his arrow fell further. Husain fired last and watchers,
who had been placed to follow the flight of the arrows, could not
find his shaft, though they searched diligently.

The Sultān then addressed the princes, saying: 'My sons, the matter is decided. Though it would appear that Husain shot furthest,

you will remember that my words were: "He whose arrow is found" . . . therefore I declare that Hasan wins the princess. It is his Destiny.'

On his return to the city the Sultān gave immediate orders for a splendid festival to be prepared, and in a few days Hasan was magnificently married to Nūr al-Nihār. So much for them.

Urged by his hopeless passion for the princess, Alī refused to be present at the marriage and, after publicly renouncing his claim to the succession of the throne, dressed himself as a darwīsh and placed himself under the spiritual direction of a saintly old man, who taught the example of life in a far solitude. So much for him.

Prince Husain, whose arrow had been lost to view . . .

At this point Shahrazād saw the approach of morning and discreetly fell silent.

But when the eight-hundred-and-eleventh night had come

SHE SAID:

Prince Husain, whose arrow had been lost to view, followed his eldest brother's example by abstaining from the feast, but had no thought of giving up the world. Instead, he resolved to prove that he had been cheated out of his prize and, in order to do so, began to search for his arrow. Walking out from the polo-ground, he followed the direction which his shaft had taken and went straight forward for an hour, casting glances to right and left. Though in this time he saw no sign of the arrow, he refused to be discouraged and continued in the same direction until his way was barred by a pile of rocks. Considering that, if the arrow were anywhere, it would be near him, since it could not have passed through the rocks, he began searching in a circle and soon found the shaft, not stuck in the earth, but lying flat with its point forward. 'This is a miracle of Allāh!' he cried. 'No man in the world could shoot so far! And my arrow must have been going bravely, since it had the strength to rebound so far. Surely I have stumbled upon a mystery!'

He picked up his arrow and was examining the broad face of the nearest rock for a trace of its impact, when he perceived the outline of a door masked in the solid stone. He gave it a careless push, hardly expecting it to open, and it swung back as if on new-greased hinges. Without thinking what he did, Husain stepped through the opening and found himself in a gently sloping gallery; also, as soon as he had crossed the threshold, the door shut of its own accord and all his efforts to open it from the inside only resulted in a breaking of his nails.

As he was a brave youth, he strode forward in the gross darkness, following the fall of the gallery, and presently saw light ahead of him. A few more paces brought him out into the open air and he found himself on the border of a grassy plain, in the middle of which stood a palace of strange magnificence. As he looked, a lady came out of the palace followed by a group of damsels, and he was sure, from her queenly carriage and perfect beauty, that she was the mistress and those the slaves. She was dressed in dim fairy silks and her hair fell to her heels in one dark cataract. As she approached, she stretched forth her hand to the youth, and said kindly: 'Be very welcome, O Prince Husain!'

The prince, who had bowed low as the lady approached, straightened himself in astonishment when he heard himself addressed by name; he was about to speak, but she prevented him, saying: 'Do not question me now. I will satisfy your curiosity when we are seated in my palace.' She took his hand with a smile and led him through alleys to a reception hall beyond the garden's marble portico. She sat beside him on a couch, and said, still clasping his hand: 'Charming Prince Husain, I have known you since your birth, I have smiled above your cradle, I am a princess of the Jinn, and my Destiny is twined with yours. I caused the magic apple to be sold in Samarkand, the carpet in Bishangarh, the ivory tube in Shīrāz. I tell you this that you may realise my knowledge of you to be complete. As my fate and yours are mingled, I have judged you worthy of a nobler wife than your cousin. For that reason, I made your arrow invisible and caused it to fall among the rocks, that you might follow it and come to me. Happiness is within your grasp, if you have a mind to clutch it.'

The fair immortal spoke with great tenderness and, when she had finished, lowered her eyelids on her mantling cheeks. Then Husain, who already realised that this girl surpassed Nūr al-Nihār in face and form, intelligence and riches, bowed before her, saying: 'Princess of the Jinn, queen of my captive heart, a human such as I can hardly control his thoughts in your presence. How can so sweet an Ifrītah leave the invisible Kings and love a human? If you have quarrelled with your parents and are receiving me in order to pique them, I pray you let me know, for I would not cause you a moment's discomfort.' Here Prince Husain bowed again and kissed the Jinnīyah's robe; but she raised him, saying: 'I am my own mistress, Husain. I allow no spirit of earth or air to check me in what I do. Do you wish to marry me and love me?' 'Do I wish!' echoed Prince Husain. 'I would give my life for one day in your presence, not as a husband only, but even as a slave!' He threw himself at the girl's feet and she raised him a second time, saying: 'Then I accept your suit, and we are wed. Now let us take our first repast together, for you must be hungry.'

She led him into a second hall, lighted by an infinity of candles perfumed with amber and arranged in patterns of symmetry. To the sound of women's voices singing in the air about them, they sat down before gold dishes and such meat as would snare the hearts of mortal men. The lovely Jinnīyah chose out delicacies and offered them to her husband in her own fingers, and the youth, though still bewildered, gave all his senses to the meat and fruit and wine.

When the repast was over, the princess led Husain into a third hall, which was loftier than the other two: and they sat among cushions worked with large flowers in bright colours. Immortal dancers came to the sound of unseen music and danced before them as light as birds. Then, at a sign from the princess, they drifted, like fluttering scarves, up a staircase of jasper and, leading the way for the married, left them to sleep in a chamber where the bridal bed had been made for them with tinted silks.

At this point Shahrazād saw the approach of morning and discreetly fell silent.

But when the eight-hundred-and-twelfth night had come

SHE SAID:

They lay among the perfumes of that bed, but not to sleep. Husain tasted beauties which no mortal girl could show and, after extreme delight, visited the place again. He found it as close-sealed as it had been before and understood, through the long hours of that night, that the virginity of a daughter of the Jinn is eternally re-newed. As the days passed by, his love grew greater with possession and he found that his bride had ever some new charm to offer him.

But at the end of six months the prince felt a strong desire to see his father again, for he loved him greatly and feared that the old man would be mourning for his absence. At first his wife was afraid that he was making a pretext to abandon her; but he gave her such proofs of his valiant passion and spoke of his father with such eloquent tenderness, that at last she said: 'Dear love, if I only listened to my heart, I could never let you go, even for a day, even for an hour; but my soul tells me that our love is a strong chain. I therefore make no further difficulty.' 'Woman of beauty,' replied Prince Husain, 'I swear by your head, which is the most treasured thing in all the world, that I will only take the time to go and return. Calm your dear spirit and refresh your eyes, for, if I think of you all the time, Allāh will surely allow no evil to befall me.'

The Jinnīyah wept, but said: 'Go then, in Allāh's name, dear love, and be careful not to tell your father or your brothers that you are married to a daughter of the Jinn. Keep secret the place of our abiding and the road which leads to it: tell them you are in all things happy and have only returned to set their minds at rest.'

The Jinnīyah gave Husain twenty well-armed riders as a guard, and had a horse led forth for him of finer mettle than is known in the stables of the world. The prince kissed his wife and, going up to that handsome trembling steed, flattered him with his hand, spoke in his ear, and leaped into the saddle. Then he rode forward with his train, followed by the admiring glances of his wife.

The way was not long, and the prince soon reached the gate of his father's city. The people recognised him and followed him with joyful acclamation to the Sultān's palace. His father wept with joy on beholding him; he embraced him and chid him gently for the long anxiety of his absence. 'I thought I would never see you again,' he said, 'I feared that your disappointment had driven you to some rash act.' 'Indeed, dear father,' answered Husain, 'the loss of the princess was bitter to me, for love is a tree which cannot be uprooted in a moment.' Then he told his father of the search for the arrow; but would reveal nothing beyond the point of his coming to the barrier of rocks. 'I can only say, my father,' he concluded, 'that I have now forgotten Nūr al-Nihār and all my troubles. Life has opened fair and sweet before me; its one shadow has been that you might grieve for me.'

'No father could ask more for his son than happiness,' answered the King. 'I should have liked to have you by me until my death, but it seems that this may not be.' 'I promise to visit you so often, my father, that you will grow wearied of my coming,' cried the prince. 'That is well, my child,' said the Sultān, 'but how may I send to ask news of you?' 'I may not give you a direction for sending,' answered

Husain, 'for that is part of the mystery of an oath which I have sworn. But you may be certain that I am in all things happy, and I swear that I will visit you once a month.' Prince Husain stayed three days with his father in the palace and, on the morning of the fourth day, took leave of him and departed at the head of his escort.

At this point Shahrazād saw the approach of morning and discreetly fell silent.

But when the eight-hundred-and-thirteenth night had come

SHE SAID:

The lovely Jinnīyah, who had not expected him to return so quickly, received him with infinite joy, and they celebrated their reunion with an agreeable diversity of the modes of love.

In the days which followed, the Jinnīyah introduced continual variation into the life of that enchanted place: she found for her husband new fashions of taking the air, of walking, eating, drinking, dancing and singing; of music, poetry, and the perfume of roses; fresh ways of decking themselves with flowers, plucking ripe fruits from the branches, and playing the game of lovers, which is a more subtle game than chess and played with bed for board.

After a month of these delights Prince Husain was obliged, by his oath to his father, to ride forth again at the head of his escort.

Now, during Husain's last absence from his father's court, certain favourite counsellors, dismayed by his rich seeming while he had made his first visit, abused the liberty of free speech and poured poison in the King's ear. 'It seems to us,' they said, 'only prudent that your majesty should find out the place of your son's retreat. Surely the prince only paraded his wealth in the palace to show that he was independent of his father and could still live royally after he had cast off his allegiance. Soon he will be making himself a party among your subjects, to dethrone our Sultān and usurp his empire.'

Though he was disturbed by their words, the Sultān would not admit that his favourite son was capable of such a plot, and he answered his counsellors severely: 'O tongues of venom, do you not know that my son Husain loves me and that I have never tried his fidelity by a single harshness?' Then said the chief of the favourites: 'O King of time, do you think that he has so easily forgotten your decision in regard to our princess? He did not take the matter well; he did not follow his eldest brother in a renunciation of the world.

Also did you not notice that his men were as fresh and untouched by dust when they arrived as if they had but walked out of their own doors, and that their horses were as glossy and unbreathed as if they were returning from a simple canter? Surely it is clear that Prince Husain has some secret abode near your capital, from which he intends to foment trouble among the people. We would have been lacking in our duty if we had not touched upon this delicate affair; we beseech you to have a care for your own preservation and the good of your loyal subjects.'

'I do not know what to believe and what not to believe,' replied the Sultān. 'I am obliged to you for your advice, and will keep my eyes open in the future.' He dismissed these malicious favourites, without showing how far their words had gained upon him, and made up his mind that, when he had regarded his son's words and actions more closely, he would either reward the busybodies or utterly confound them.

When the prince came, the Sultān received him with the same joy as before, and showed no sign of suspicion; but, on the following morning, he called to him a certain old woman who was famous about the palace both for malice and sorcery, and who could have unravelled a spider's web without breaking a single filament. 'Mother of benediction,' he said to her, 'the time has come for you to prove your devotion to the throne. Since my son Husain has returned to me I have not been able to learn from him the place of his present dwelling. As I do not wish to push my authority, I require you to obtain that information for me secretly. My son sets out again to-morrow at dawn, and I suggest that you lie in wait for him near that tumble of rocks which bounds the plain to the east. For he tells me that he found his Destiny where he found his arrow.' The old sorceress bowed low and, going forth to the rocks immediately, hid herself in a place of vantage.

Next morning Prince Husain left the palace at the first show of light in order not to attract undue attention in the streets. Soon he came with his escort to the door in the rock and, greatly to the amazement of the old watcher, passed through it and disappeared.

The hag ran to the place where she had seen horses and riders vanish, but could find no trace of a door; for the entrance was only visible to men who might please the Jinnīyah; from women, and especially from old and horrible women, it was entirely hidden. The sorceress gave vent to her rage in a sounding fart, which raised a storm of dust and lifted the smaller rocks into the air; then she returned to the King and told him what she had seen. 'O Sultān of time, I will do better on the next occasion,' she said. 'I only beg you not to ask what steps I intend to take.' 'Use what means you will,' cried the Sultān. 'Depart under the keeping of Allāh, and I will wait your news impatiently.' He gave her a magnificent diamond, as an earnest of greater rewards to follow, and she departed about her business.

A month later, Prince Husain came out through the door in the rock with his twenty horsemen and, as he picked his way among the boulders, beheld a poor old woman, moaning upon the ground and writhing as if in agony. Her tears and rags appealed to the prince's compassion, so he reined in his horse and asked the woman what he might do for her relief. Without raising her head the sorceress answered in a whisper: 'Lord of my help, Allāh has sent you that I may not die unburied. Alas, alas, I feel my soul slipping away. I left my village this morning to go to the city, but lo! I was taken with a red fever which has cast me down to perish among these rocks.' But Prince Husain cheered her, saying: 'Good aunt, if you will allow two of my men to carry you, I will return with you to my dwelling and have you well looked after.' As the old woman made no difficulty, two of the escort lifted her from the ground and followed their master, who had already returned through the secret door in the rock.

At this point Shahrazād saw the approach of morning and discreetly fell silent.

But when the eight-hundred-and-fourteenth night had come

SHE SAID:

Seeing the riders return, the Jinnīyah hastened forth to meet her husband. He showed her the old woman, who lay back looking very ill in the arms of two of the escort, and said: 'Dear queen, Allāh set this suffering old woman upon our road. I recommend her to your kindness and skill.' The princess gave the sorceress a searching glance and then handed her over to her women, bidding them care for her and show her all respect. Then she turned to her husband, and said in a low voice: 'Allāh will reward you for your good intention. But you need have no fear for this old woman; for she is no more ill than I am. I know why she was sent here and I know by whom; but you may rest assured that none can plot against you in evil without my knowing and flying to your rescue. Now go forth again under the protection of Allāh!' Husain, who had grown used by this time not to question his wife too closely, kissed her again and departed for his father's capital, where he arrived without adventure. The King received him as usual and gave no hint in his greeting that anyone had striven to sow suspicion between them.

The old sorceress was taken to a fair apartment in the palace, laid to rest on a mattress of embroidered satin, and covered first with fine silks and then with heavy cloth of gold. One of the women prepared her a glass of water from the Fountain of Lions and gave it to her, saying: 'This water cures all disease and can give health to the dying.' The old woman drank the draught and, after waiting for a few moments, cried: 'An admirable elixir! I am cured as if my disease had been drawn forth with pincers! Lead me to your mistress quickly that I may thank her for her goodness.' The old deceiver rose up and allowed herself to be led through hall after hall of great magnificence, until she appeared before the throne itself.

This throne was of solid gold, mooned with emeralds, and the lovely Jinnīyah sat upon it, robed in the stuff of dreams. The old woman, dazzled by what she saw, fell babbling thanks before the throne's foot. 'I am delighted to hear of your cure,' said the Jinnīyah kindly. 'I give you leave to stay in the palace for as long as you wish; my women will show you round.' The sorceress kissed the earth and then followed two of the queen's young girls, who displayed all the marvels of the palace to her attentive gaze. When she had seen all, she begged leave to retire, so the women led her outside the door in the rock and wished her well. As soon as they were out of sight, she hurried back to mark the place of the door, but it had disappeared.

When she came to the city, she told the Sultān all that she had seen and assured him that it would be impossible for any human to find the entrance to the palace. The Sultān called his wazīrs and favourite counsellors and, after repeating the tale to them, asked for their advice. Some said that Prince Husain should be put to death, others that he should be imprisoned for life; but the sorceress begged leave to speak, and said: 'O King of time, I think that the best plan of all would be to take advantage of your son's pretence of filial affection to obtain for yourself some of the marvels which I saw in such profusion at his palace. If he consents you will be incalculably richer, if he refuses it will not be too late to take the harsher advice of your counsellors.' 'Be it so,' answered the King, and straightway sent for Husain. 'My son,' said he, 'now that you are richer and more powerful than your poor old father, can you not bring me some little present on your next visit; perhaps a tent which I may use when I am out hunting or go to the wars?' Prince Husain agreed most readily to this suggestion and assured him that he would joyfully make greater gifts than that.

When Husain reached the fairy palace again, he told his wife of his father's wish. 'As Allāh lives, I am sorry that he only asks for such a trifle,' answered the Jinnīyah. Then she called her treasurer, saying: 'Take forth the greatest tent which I have in my treasure, and tell Shaibah to bring it to me.'

A few minutes later the treasurer returned with the treasure's guardian, a Jinnī of unusual and terrifying aspect. He was a foot and a half in height and had a beard thirty feet long; his moustache was twisted up to his ears and his pig's eyes were deeply sunk in a head larger than his body. Over his right shoulder he carried a bar of iron, five times as heavy as himself, and in the palm of his left hand he bore a small folded packet. When this creature appeared, the Jinnīyah addressed him, saying: 'O Shaibah, you will accompany my husband, Prince Husain, to his father's palace. And when you get there you will do your duty.' Shaibah bowed, and asked: 'Shall I take the tent with me, dear mistress?' 'Certainly,' she replied. 'But first set it up here that our lord may see it.' Shaibah went out into the garden and unfolded the little packet which he carried; from it he drew a pavilion which could have shaded a whole army, and whose peculiar property it was to shrink or swell at need. When he had showed off this marvel to the prince, he refolded it and cried: 'Now for the Sultān!'

The people of the city saw Prince Husain enter the city and, at the sight of the immortal dwarf who swaggered in beside him, making play with his iron bar, ran with affrighted cries into their houses. When the two reached the palace, the eunuchs and the guards fled in terror before them, so that they entered the presence unannounced. The Sultān sat talking with the sorceress, in the midst of his favourite counsellors. As soon as Prince Husain had greeted his father, Shaibah advanced to the foot of the throne and cried: 'O King of time, I have brought you the pavilion!' Then, retiring a few paces, he unwrapped the mighty tent from its small covering and set it up, quite little, before him on the floor. From its shelter he suddenly hurled his iron bar at the head of the grand-wazīr, stunning him and bringing him to the ground. Then, with the quickness of an eel, he skipped in and out among the counsellors until he had dealt a blow at each; and only the King, the Prince, and the sorceress remained upright. The dwarf turned next to the old woman, crying: 'I have a better cure than Lion water for such as you!' and brought his weapon down upon her head. After this he shouldered the bar, and spoke to the King: 'I have punished these for their evil counsel; I spare you because you are weak and not wicked. But, as you lent a foolish ear to slander, I deprive you of your throne. If there is anyone in this great city who cares to protest, I shall be glad to answer him with my bar. Indeed, I am quite prepared to convince the whole city, if she does not open her arms to my young master. Now depart quickly, O you who were King, for this iron is heavy and might fall.' At this hint the old King scuttled down from the throne and, fleeing from the palace, joined his son Alī in the far retreat of his holy master.

As Prince Hasan and his wife Nūr al-Nihār had taken no part in the conspiracy, Prince Husain, now King of that city, gave them the finest province of his empire, and lived at cordial peace with them. The lovely Jinnīyah lived for uncounted prosperous years with her sweet lord, and left behind a numerous posterity. But Allāh knows all!

When she had made an end of this tale, Shahrazād fell silent, and little Dunyazād said: 'Dear sister, that was indeed a delectable story!' 'But it is nothing,' answered Shahrazād with a smile, 'to a tale which I have kept in reserve.' 'You have our leave to tell it,' said King Shahryār.